W9-ACE-656

Needlelike Leaves: 60–128

Scalelike Leaves: 129–152

Fan-shaped Leaves: 154

Opposite Leaves: 155–210

Alternate, Compound Leaves: 211–255

Alternate, Simple Leaves: 256–460

Palms, Yuccas, and Cacti: 461–476

Keys

In this guide the trees are divided into sections according to leaf type and arrangement. To find a tree, compare its leaves to those shown in the key above and turn to the pages given. Each section starts with an introduction. Most also include a key that organizes the trees in the section according to features such as leaf shape, fruit type, and the presence of thorns. In many cases the key can help you narrow your tree to just a few possibilities.

The Key to Trees with Alternate, Simple Leaves, a page of which is shown here, divides this large and diverse group of trees into smaller groups, organizing them by features of the leaf margin (lobes, teeth), then by typical leaf shape, and finally by fruit type.

264 · Key to Trees with Alternate, Simple Leaves

LEAVES UNLOBED, TOOTHED

Leaves Obovate

Fruit a capsule
Witch-hazel: p. 330

Fruit a capsule splitting open to reveal white-hairy seeds
Willows: pp. 379–389

Fruit a small drupe
Cascara Buckthorn: p. 326
Bitter Cherry: p. 339
Common Winterberry: p. 356
Possumhaw: p. 358

Fruit a small, wax-covered drupe
Bayberries: pp. 322–323

Fruit a small pome
Hawthorns: pp. 354–355

Fruit an achene
Birchleaf Mountain-mahogany: p. 333

Fruit in a conelike cluster
Alders: pp. 412–413

Fruit an acorn
Oaks, see Key to Oaks: p. 421

LEAVES UNLOBED, TOOTHED

Leaves Ovate to Triangular

Fruit blackberry-like
Mulberries: pp. 271–272

Fruit a capsule splitting open to reveal white-hairy seeds
Poplars and cottonwoods: pp. 390–396
Aspens: pp. 397–398

Fruit a small drupe
Manchineel: p. 321
Cherries: pp. 335–341
Winterberries: pp. 356–357
Hackberries: pp. 364–366
Sugarberry: p. 366
Florida Trema: p. 366

Fruit a burlike drupe
Water-elm: p. 367

Witch-hazel
Common Winterberry
Scentless Bayberry
Chinkapin Oak
Oneseed Hawthorn

Quaking Aspen
Swamp Cottonwood
Northern Hackberry

National Wildlife Federation®

FIELD GUIDE TO
TREES
OF NORTH AMERICA

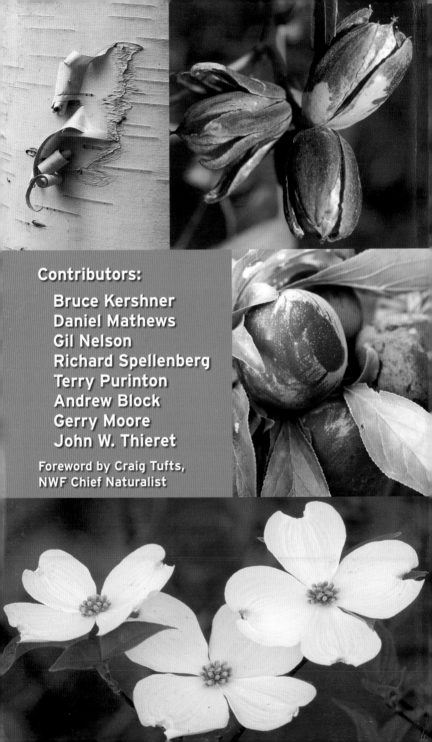

Contributors:

Bruce Kershner
Daniel Mathews
Gil Nelson
Richard Spellenberg
Terry Purinton
Andrew Block
Gerry Moore
John W. Thieret

Foreword by Craig Tufts,
NWF Chief Naturalist

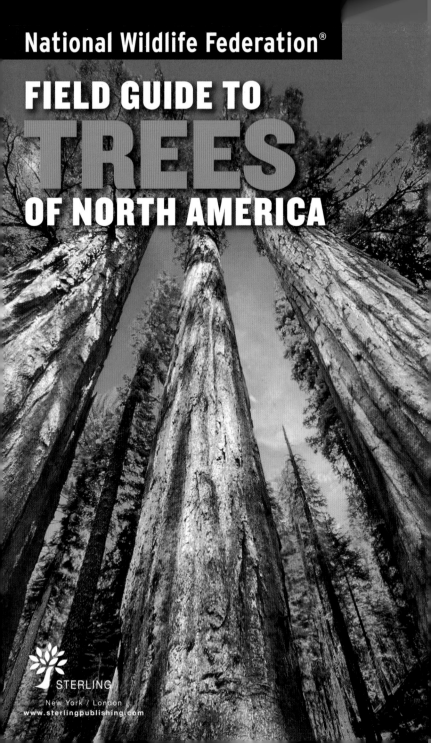

National Wildlife Federation®

FIELD GUIDE TO
TREES
OF NORTH AMERICA

STERLING
New York / London
www.sterlingpublishing.com

This book is dedicated to Bruce S. Kershner, whose passion for finding, identifying, and saving old-growth forests in North America helped protect these natural wonders for generations to come, and to Dr. John Thieret, who is remembered by many as one of the premier botanists of our time.

Published by Sterling Publishing Co., Inc.
387 Park Avenue South, New York, NY 10016

© 2008 by Andrew Stewart Publishing, Inc.

Distributed in Canada by Sterling Publishing
C/o Canadian Manda Group, 165 Dufferin Street,
Toronto, Ontario, Canada M6K 3H6

Distributed in the United Kingdom by GMC Distribution Services
Castle Place, 166 High Street, Lewes, East Sussex, England BN7 1XU

Distributed in Australia by Capricorn Link (Australia) Pty. Ltd.
P.O. Box 704, Windsor, NSW 2756, Australia

Library of Congress Cataloging-in-Publication Data

National Wildlife Federation field guide to trees of North America / Bruce
Kershner ... [et al.] ; foreword by Craig Tufts.
    p. cm.
    ISBN: 978-1-4027-3875-3
    1. Trees—North America—Identification. I. Kershner, Bruce. II. National
Wildlife Federation.

QK110.N38 2008
582.16097—dc22

Printed in Singapore
All rights reserved

4   6   8   10   9   7   5   3

For information about custom editions, special sales, premium and
corporate purchases, please contact Sterling Special Sales
Department at 800-805-5489 or specialsales@sterlingpub.com.

National Wildlife Federation ® name and logo are trademarks of National Wildlife Federation
and are used, under license, by Andrew Stewart Publishing, Inc.

The mission of the National Wildlife Federation is to inspire Americans to protect wildlife for our children's future.

Protecting wildlife through education and action since 1936, the National Wildlife Federation® (NWF) is America's largest conservation organization. NWF works with a nationwide network of state affiliate organizations, scientists, grassroots activists, volunteers, educators, and wildlife enthusiasts—uniting individuals from diverse backgrounds to focus on three goals that will have the biggest impact on the future of America's wildlife.

Connect People with Nature

NWF's legacy for connecting people with nature extends back over 50 years, through its award-winning publications *Ranger Rick, Your Big Backyard, Wild Animal Baby,* and *National Wildlife* to its education and outreach programs encouraging generations of children, youth, and adults to appreciate and nuture nature in their own backyards and the world around them. NWF's *Green Hour* program addresses the growing disconnection that children have from nature and encourages parents and caregivers to commit to having children spend one hour a day outside exploring nature. Extending the connection to nature, NWF's *Certified Wildlife Habitat*™ program teaches homeowners, businesses, schools, and other institutions how to create habitat that supports wildlife in their own backyards and provides people with an easy yet effective way to practice their conservation values at home and work. Building the connection to the larger world and building future generations of conservation leaders are the key focus of NWF's campus and youth programs, demonstrated through direct actions aimed at taking on the largest environmental issue facing the next generation—global warming.

Protect and Restore Wildlife

Loss of habitat due to oil and gas drilling, urban sprawl, and deforestation is a major threat to the future of America's wildlife. NWF works tirelessly to obtain permanent protection for critical habitat areas—areas that are essential to the recovery of species populations such as wolves, salmon, and the Florida panther. NWF's work also includes protecting lands like the pristine Arctic National Wildlife Refuge, the vanishing wild areas of the western United States, and the green forests of the Northeast. Water and wetland protection programs focus on restoring the Great Lakes, the Snake River, the Florida Everglades, Louisiana's coastal wetlands, and the Northwest's Puget Sound. In addition to working to restore these habitats today, NWF fights for expanded Clean Water Act protection and campaigns for smarter water and land management for the future.

For more than 30 years the Endangered Species Act (ESA) has been the primary tool for conserving endangered and threatened species and their habitats. NWF is committed to upholding the full protection of the ESA, despite attempts to weaken it.

Confront Global Warming

Global warming heats up the atmosphere, which causes glaciers to melt, sea levels to rise, water temperatures to creep up, precipitation patterns to change, and droughts and storms to become more extreme. It is the single biggest ecosystem emergency we face today. Scientists predict that unless we act, one-third of wildlife species in some regions could be headed for extinction within the next 50 years.

NWF recognizes this dire situation and is taking action now to help halt global warming. Working with members, state affiliates, and partners, NWF mobilizes grassroots activists to push for state and national policies that reduce carbon emissions that cause heat-trapping pollution. By providing good science and public outreach tools, NWF educates Americans about smart, efficient energy use.

The National Wildlife Federation relies on Americans from all walks of life, of all political and religious beliefs, of all ages to advance our mission: *protecting wildlife for our children's future.* **Visit www.nwf.org or call 800-882-9919 to join us today!**

Contents

NONBROADLEAF TREES

Trees with Needlelike Leaves 60

Trees with Scalelike Leaves 129

BROADLEAF TREES

Trees with Opposite Leaves 155

Foreword

For most of us in North America, trees help to define the landscape as much as the ancient mountains and valleys and flatlands that they embellish. The temperate rainforests of the Pacific Northwest; the blazingly colorful fall woodlands of New England; the southeastern pine savannas; the pinyon-juniper, Saguaro, and Joshua Tree landscapes of the Southwest; and the majestic cottonwoods, tupelos, sycamores, and bald-cypresses of our river bottoms all conjure images of grandeur and great age.

People in the United States have tended to live in areas where these weightiest and grandest of all living organisms dominate and define the natural architecture of our communities. It has been only in the last century, as our numbers have increased and our technology has seemingly freed us from our obvious links to the natural world and the living systems we depend upon, that our trees have declined in their influence on who we are as people.

We are at a critical time in our stewardship of the planet we inhabit. A warming planet will cause many of the woodlands and forests that support so much of our rich biodiversity to change. Indeed, there is no certainty that these carbon-sequestering, oxygen-emitting organisms will be able to keep up with the pace of climate change without significant help from us. We'll be better equipped to take on our new role of assisting our animals and plants in adapting to a warming planet if we learn more about these incredible organisms.

The beautifully illustrated *National Wildlife Federation Field Guide to Trees of North America* is the perfect instructor. Its thorough coverage of the trees growing in North America, compiled by highly respected botanists from America's four corners, can teach us much about our trees and their value in cooling our communities and supporting hundreds of thousands of other species of animals and plants that form the fabric of our natural world.

This new guide can not only inform and teach, it is a handy motivator for getting outside and putting a name to each of the trees that shade and frame our homes, color our views, and support our birds and other wildlife. As we get to know more about our trees we can appreciate them more as symbols of the partnership between humans and the rest of the natural world and how we must work together for a healthy future.

Craig Tufts
CHIEF NATURALIST,
NATIONAL WILDLIFE
FEDERATION

Introduction

Human reverence for trees seems to go back as far as our mutual existence. Is it because trees, like us, stand upright and live longer than 50 years? Because we duck under the arching arms of their branches for shade and shelter? Whatever the source of our deep connectedness, the cliché has a truth to it: if we love nature, trees are the first element of it that we might want to hug. Trees of natural forests, swamps, and fields; of urban parks and streetscapes; of orchards and backyards—all have exalted places in human hearts and eyes.

The Scope of This Guide

For those wishing to know their trees by name and perhaps a little more, we offer this guide to the trees of North America north of Mexico, covering species of the continental United States and Canada. The majority of these are our native trees, which we cover thoroughly, excluding only some very rare or localized, usually shrubby species of remote regions. We also include introduced species known to naturalize (that is, to reproduce and persist without the aid of a gardener's hand), and a few cultivated street and garden trees of special interest or importance.

"Native" is an artificial and sometimes uncertain construct. The term is generally understood to apply to species that were on the continent (or a given region of it) before the arrival of Old World influences in 1492. There are relatively good records, both written and in the form of pollen deposits, of the presence of trees in North America, and with reasonable confidence we can call a tree native.

"Tree" is a little harder to define. Aboveground plant parts that persevere and hold a shape for several years are woody, and woody plants are either trees or shrubs. The distinction between trees and shrubs is murky: trees are generally taller than shrubs and have a single trunk more often than multiple stems. However, this guide does not adhere strictly to a single-trunk requirement, because many incontestable trees can have two or three trunks, and some species are characteristically single-trunked under some conditions and multistemmed under others. We also did not rule out some species that occur most often as shrubs—even some rather low ones like the Common Juniper—if they may sometimes occur in a more typically treelike form.

Names and Classification

Each tree's account in this book begins with a common name, followed by a scientific name in italics. Most accounts cover a single species, the basic taxonomic unit. Taxonomy is the classification of organisms based on the study of their "family relations." Species are part of a taxonomic hierarchy that has many levels, going up to kingdom; trees are in the plant kingdom, Plantae. Species are usually defined as organisms that are so closely related that they are able to breed and produce fertile offspring. (Hybrids, discussed below, are a wrinkle in the definition of "species.")

Every species has a two-part scientific name, called a binomial; the first part is the genus name (plural: genera), and the second designates the species. Species with the same genus name are closely related. Quaking Aspen, for example, has the scientific name *Populus tremuloides*. It belongs to the genus *Populus*, as do poplars and cottonwoods. The taxonomic rank above genus is family. The species of the genus *Populus*, along with those of the genus *Salix*, are all placed in the willow family, Salicaceae. All plant family names end in "-aceae" (pronounced *AY-cee-ee*).

Naturally occurring variations in a species may be classified as subspecies or varieties. Usually there is little real difference between the two categories, and a three-part scientific name is assigned (if a four-part name is used, then subspecies is more inclusive than variety). Both denote geographically distinct populations of a species that differ from other representatives of the species. *Populus balsamifera* ssp. *trichocarpa*, Black Cottonwood, is a subspecies of Balsam Poplar. It has a different range than other populations, and its fruit splits into three parts when mature, rather than two.

A plant variation produced by plant breeders is called a "cultivar," short for "cultivated variety." Cultivar names are often written in single quotation marks; for example, the cultivated Corkscrew Willow is *Salix matsudana* 'Tortuosa'.

Hybrids

Hybrids, plants that result from crossbreeding between two different species, may occur naturally or through human intervention. In several cases, two related tree species that have distinct characteristics over most of their respective ranges also have a zone of intergradation where the range of one meets the range of the other and many or all of the trees are hybrids. In such a situation, geographic distance and environmental differences (sometimes subtle ones) keep the two species distinct except at the zones of intergradation. Within this zone the two species may freely hybridize. True firs include a few such pairs: Fraser and Balsam firs, Grand and White firs, and Noble and California Red firs. They provide an interesting problem in species concepts.

Subspecies and varieties often have common names of their own. Many that people have long regarded as full species have been "demoted" to subspecies ranking as the result of recent taxonomic work; Black Cottonwood (*Populus balsamifera* ssp. *trichocarpa*), left, is an example.

In flowering plants (Horse-chestnut, left) the seeds develop enclosed in an ovary. In the more ancient conifers (Pinyon, right), the seeds do not develop in an ovary; the pine seeds shown here are tucked under the cone's scales.

"Official" Names

Scientific names are often promoted as each species' one-and-only "official" name, universally recognized and used, in contrast to common names, which vary widely. This works in theory, but with ongoing studies of plant species, much of it spurred by advances in genetic analysis, scientists are revising classifications. Species are often "split" (their subspecies or varieties become separate full species) or "lumped" (two or more species merged as one species), and some groups of plants prove difficult to classify. Taxonomists frequently publish new studies proposing changes, but there's never a moment when all pending changes are resolved.

This guide uses the scientific names and taxonomic groupings published as of mid-2007 in *Flora of North America*, a 30-volume reference work that is still in progress. For trees not yet published in *Flora of North America*, we turned to a second authority, the PLANTS Database of the U.S. Department of Agriculture. In some cases, we have consulted regional flora works and other reliable sources. Some names used in this guide differ from those used in other guides.

We have used the same authorities for common names, but any tree may be known by several common names—one region's ironwood may be another's hornbeam; we have included alternate names when possible. We follow the convention of hyphenating names that are associated with a different genus than the tree named. For example, "fir" is the name for genus *Abies*; therefore, Douglas-fir, genus *Pseudotsuga*, is hyphenated. For more on common names see page 331.

Tree Divisions

Trees are traditionally placed in two broad divisions: conifers (gymnosperms, plants with "naked" seeds), which include the cone-bearing trees with needlelike or scalelike leaves, such as pines, firs, cypresses, junipers, and their relatives; and flowering trees (angiosperms, with seeds enclosed in an ovary), which include nearly all of the broadleaf plants in our guide. It is best to avoid thinking of the two groups as "evergreen" versus "deciduous," as there are quite a few deciduous conifers and evergreen broadleaf trees. Ginkgo, once lumped with conifers in the gymnosperms, is the sole remnant of an ancient lineage and now has a division all to itself.

Flowering plants are usually further divided into two classes, monocots (short for monocotyledons: grasses, palms, yuccas, and others with parallel leaf veins and flowers with three or six parts) and dicots (dicotyledons: branched leaf veins; four, five, or more than six flower parts). With new forms of genetic analysis these old classifications are being reconsidered. For more on these divisions see page 153. Note that there is no taxonomic group that corresponds to "tree"; many trees are in families that also include shrubs or herbs.

How Trees Function

Trees are an irreplaceable component of the living earth, our biosphere. They are estimated to account for about two-thirds of all "production" or growth by land plants, and land plants in turn are the source of most oxygen that living things breathe and of most complex carbohydrates that living things burn in their bodies for energy.

Chlorophyll is the green pigment in the green parts of plants. Most chlorophyll is found—and most photosynthesis takes place—in leaves.

Photosynthesis and Transpiration

Oxygen and carbohydrates are products of photosynthesis, which takes place in the green parts of plants. Photosynthesis is a chemical reaction in which plants use energy from sunlight to split molecules of carbon dioxide (from the air) and water and recombine their atoms into complex carbon molecules, giving off oxygen as a byproduct. It can occur only in the presence of chlorophyll, a substance made only in plants, algae, and some bacteria.

Photosynthesis originated in bacteria, which gradually oxygenated the atmosphere, starting around three billion years ago. More than two billion years ago, according to one strong hypothesis, larger one-celled organisms ingested photosynthetic bacteria, which survived inside the larger cells, creating an internally symbiotic organism that eventually, through evolution, gave rise to green algae and plants. The contained bacteria became chloroplasts, the photosynthetic organs in plant cells.

Through photosynthesis, plants make large net contributions of oxygen to the air, and net removals of carbon dioxide, but at the same time they respire as animals do: breathing in oxygen, oxidizing some of their carbohydrates, and breathing out carbon dioxide. Most gas exchange takes place through microscopic pores (stomata) in leaf surfaces, but bark and roots also need to be able to breathe. Short horizontal lines called lenticels, found on the trunks of some smooth-barked kinds of trees, are openings for gas exchange.

Trees pass prodigious quantities of water into the air. Plants convey water from their roots to their stomata, where it evaporates, or transpires, into the air. Trees grow the right number of stomata for conditions, and stomata, which often grow only in the shade of the leaf's underside, close when the tree is water-stressed. But some transpiration is necessary. A tree has to supply all of its parts with materials, such as minerals and nutrients from the soil, as well as the organic molecules that it manufactures through photosynthesis. The tree maintains a continuous column of water throughout all of its parts, with transpiration from the leaves drawing the water upward. When the stomata are shut down to conserve water, photosynthesis quickly slows and stops if carbon dioxide from the air can no longer enter the leaf.

Wood and Bark

The roots, trunk, and branches, in addition to supplying the supportive structure for holding an array of leaves in positions where all can get some light, form a continuous plumbing system that moves water and materials among all parts of the tree. Downward flow containing sugars from the leaves goes on mainly in the phloem, in the spongy inner bark layer. (Year-old phloem gets compressed and converted into bark.) Under the phloem lies the cambium, a thin layer of cells that divide, producing new phloem and wood; under that lies the xylem, the wood proper. Most of the upward flow from the roots takes place—through vessels in broadleaf trees or long thin wood cells in conifers—in the outer portion of the xylem.

The sap-conducting outer portion of the xylem is called sapwood, the inner portion heartwood. From the center outward, as the tree ages it converts sapwood to heartwood, shutting off the flow of water and filling some of the sap-conducting space with compounds that add strength, combat decay, and usually darken the wood distinctly. The process is a little like embalming; the cells are dead by the time they are heartwood, but the wood is stronger than before.

Bark forms a protective barrier against mechanical damage and fire, holds in water, and helps to heal wounds through which sap might bleed out or diseases might enter. It serves as a barrier to some insect pests and, if bitter tasting, discourages some animals from gnawing through to the nutritious cambium.

Though tropical trees may grow more or less continuously, trees in the temperate zone grow only in the growing season. Each year's growth begins with a rapidly grown pale layer of spring wood, followed by a dense, darker layer of summer wood. The two contrasting layers constitute an annual ring; counting the rings on a stump tells you how old the tree was before it was cut. Scientists can also count rings in a slender core section removed with a special drill that doesn't seriously harm the tree. This technique is important in the study of past climates and of fire history, as well as in the study of trees.

Roots

A tree's roots form a branching network roughly equal to the tree's crown. Drought-adapted roots have to be bigger; they might equal the entire aboveground mass of a tree, including the trunk, but in moderate settings the average tree's roots would more nearly equal just the crown of branches, twigs, and leaves. But a root system is not a mirror image of the crown: it is usually much wider and shallower than the crown is wide and tall. For roots to go deep would be inefficient, because essential soil nutrients largely derive from decomposing organic matter in the top several feet of soil. Water is also more abundant near the surface; roots compete to intercept rainwater as it soaks down. Water that gets past a well-developed root zone is water in

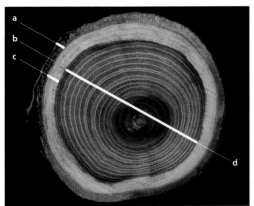

Cross section of a tree trunk showing layers of tissue and annual growth rings in the wood. The dark, outermost layer (a) contains the outer bark and the phloem (spongy inner bark). The cambium (b) is a layer of cells that divide and produce new phloem (toward the outside), and new xylem, or wood (toward the inside). The sapwood (c) is a fairly thin layer here; the darker heartwood (d) fills the center.

excess of what the plants can absorb. The other chief function of roots—keeping the tree from falling over—is also performed effectively by a wide plate of shallow roots enmeshed with roots of other trees.

Roots have two kinds of interfaces for the intake of water and nutrients: root hairs, which form a bottlebrush-shaped fringe on fine roots, and mycorrhizae, structures formed by plant roots in mutualistic symbiosis with fungi. (Some of these are well-known mushrooms; more are underground-fruiting fungi.) Plants can usually control whether or not they form these nutrient loading docks, and in sufficiently moist, fertile conditions they do not form them. But about 90 percent of tree species do have mycorrhizae much of the time. In this symbiosis, they give up some of their carbohydrates, which fungi cannot make for themselves. Their gains start with increased efficiency: a root hair is not nearly as fine as its fungal counterpart, a hypha, which provides perhaps 300 times more surface area from a given investment in tissue mass. These hyphae are already there in the soil—the root tip grows in a universe full of them. If soil moisture is three feet down, a seedling may die before its taproot gets there, but it can latch onto a hyphal hydration tube sooner. A fungus also has unique abilities to derive some types of nutrients from

rocks, animals, and its other plant partners. If the seedling is in shade too deep for it to photosynthesize quite enough to meet its needs in its first several years, the fungus may obtain enough from neighboring plants to keep it going. Finally, these "good fungi" offer some protection from certain fungi and bacteria that can infect and damage trees.

Flowers and Fruits

Flowers and the fruits they become are a flowering tree's reproductive parts; their conifer counterparts are loosely called cones at both the flowering and fruiting stages. Conifers and flowering plants alike are sexual beings, requiring each egg (female) to be fertilized by a pollen grain (male) before it can mature into a seed. In many flowering plant species a single flower produces both eggs and pollen, while in others the male and female flowers are separate; they may be in the same cluster, in different areas on the same tree (the case with most conifers), or on individual all-male and all-female trees.

A flowering plant's eggs are enclosed in an ovary. After they are pollinated, they grow into seeds, while the ovary wall around them grows into a fruit. A conifer's cone, in contrast, only partially surrounds the seed; it does not originate as an ovary wall and is not, strictly speaking, a fruit.

A tree's cones or flowers must be pollinated and its seeds distributed so that they can germinate. The small brown male cones at the tip of this Parry Pinyon branch (left) must deliver their pollen to the female seed cones elsewhere on the tree. The Bigleaf Magnolia flower (right) has both male and female parts; its sweet fragrance attracts insects, which move the pollen from the male stamens to the female pistils so a fruit, containing seeds, can form.

North America's eastern mountains are renowned for the world's most fiery foliage shows, because they most often get the perfect fall weather for them. The brighter the days and the colder the nights, the more the red pigment prevails.

The fruit of a flowering plant may end up as a dry hull or seedpod, or it may become moist, fleshy, and perhaps rich in sugars or oils. No matter what the fruit looks like, it must accomplish dissemination—the spreading of its seeds. Dry hulls and pods protect the seeds within, but also often bear appendages that help it stick to an animal's fur or catch a breeze and fly far. Some trees depend on animals to spread their seeds.

In conifers, adaptations to foster dissemination are similar, if relatively primitive: fleshy, edible seed covers in yews and junipers, fat edible seeds in some pines, winged seeds for air transport in many conifer genera, and the remarkable "fire cones" of cypresses and some pines, which open after a fire has cleared a sunny, nutrient-rich seedbed.

Twigs and Buds

Twigs typically stop growing at some point in the summer. They harden, their bark may darken, and they produce buds, each containing in compact, rudimentary form all the tissues for a shoot, a leaf, or a flower to begin growing the following spring. In most trees the buds are wrapped in one or more modified leaves called bud scales that protect them from the elements. Come spring, flower and leaf buds open and

shoot growth begins. On many trees, such as conifers, a terminal bud at the branch tip produces a main stem, and lateral buds produce side branches.

Autumn Color

Before a deciduous tree drops its leaves in fall, it breaks down some of their nutrient-rich proteins and chlorophyll in order to store key ingredients in its roots over the winter. It converts sugars to either starches or fats. In spring the phloem reverses its normal direction to carry an upward rush of extra-sugary sap, nourishing the rapid growth of new leaves. Evergreen trees don't recycle their leaves to this degree, so their sap is rarely as rich in sugars.

In fall, after leaf breakdown is underway, many leaves produce a bright red pigment called anthocyanin. Its function is not well understood, but a current hypothesis holds that the pigment protects some of the other compounds from being damaged by light as they are broken down and shunted into the branches. Additionally, reduction of the green pigment, chlorophyll, unveils a yellow pigment that was present in the chloroplasts all along. Autumn colors result from different ratios of the red, yellow, and green pigments as nutrient recycling nears completion.

Ecology

Trees in nature exist not in isolation but as parts of living communities whose members powerfully affect each other's survival. Organism A may thrive only where organisms B and C are already established, or only in the absence of organism C. The relatively young science of ecology studies all such relationships; ecologists often feel as if they have just begun to scratch the surface of their field.

Acorn woodpeckers use their strong bills to drill holes in "cache trees" where they store their provisions—acorns—for later use.

Trees and Wildlife

Trees are vitally important to animals as well as to other plants. Birds, mammals, insects, and other wildlife employ trees as nesting sites, for shelter from the weather, for refuge from predators, and as food, both directly and indirectly. Hoofed mammals browse tree twigs and leaves. Porcupines and bark beetles live on the cambium layer of wood, and some woodpeckers, in turn, specialize in bark beetles. Countless insects live on leaves, and countless birds glean those insects. Bats are ubiquitous tree roosters, fruit consumers, and seed disseminators. Conifer leaf chemistry discourages herbivory, but grouse and mountain goats do eat some needles to help tide them through winter, and one mammal, the red tree vole, ekes out a living entirely from Douglas-fir needles.

Some trees have native insect pests that presumably co-evolved with them and yet periodically irrupt in population outbreaks, killing the host tree species in dramatic proportions over entire regions. These epidemics may be entirely "natural," or they may be exacerbated, directly or indirectly, by fire suppression, pesticide use, logging, invasive species, global warming, and other human-induced phenomena. Since birds that prey on the insect pests clearly play a role in turning pest population outbreaks around, bird population declines probably contribute to irruptions of pest insects.

While trees serve wildlife in various ways, many trees are also beholden to wildlife for pollination and seed dispersal. Seeds and fruits rich in sugars or oils evolved to attract eaters. Many seeds with indigestible coats are wrapped in a sweet fruit; such seeds pass intact through an animal's digestive tract and germinate where they are deposited. Oils, which are also attractive to animals, are usually in the seed itself; while many oil-rich seeds are eaten and digested, a certain percentage will be collected and cached but not actually eaten. Thus the seeds are carried farther than gravity and wind can take them. Analogously, pollen and nectar are nutritious plant products that attract many insects (and a few birds and even bats) to a tree's flowers. The plant benefits because when these creatures go from flower to flower, they inevitably deposit some pollen grains, assuring the pollination process.

Many insects and a few vertebrate animals specialize in eating from just one species of tree. Two striking cases are Clark's nutcrackers, which extract seeds from the cones of Whitebark Pine (page 80), and red crossbills. The latter seem to be in the process of evolving from one species into at least five, each with a beak of just the right length to pry open the cones of a particular pine species. All can open cones of various species, but with different levels of efficiency—and efficiency becomes a life-or-death matter in the crossbills' northern environment.

Habitat Succession

When forest land is cleared by logging, or by a fire or a big blowdown, the first trees to appear and grow naturally may not be the same species that dominated the forest before the disturbance. These pioneers are likely to be species whose seedlings grow fast on mineral soil in full sunlight. They'll also be limited to species whose seeds somehow survived the disturbance or had

a good way of getting there afterward; or species that can resprout from stumps or roots. After those "early successional" trees grow big enough to shade most of the ground, additional seedlings of their own species will be far less likely to thrive, since they prefer full sunlight. "Late successional" trees that tolerate shade begin to appear and gradually make their way into gaps in the forest canopy, perhaps where early successional individuals have died. Logically, if no further disturbance fells the forest, the late successional trees should take over completely, creating a stable "climax" community. This does happen occasionally in regions moist and fertile enough to support a dense forest canopy. However, the climax concept no longer receives the emphasis it once did, because it implicitly treats disturbance as abnormal. In fact, the norm on most sites includes frequent creation of canopy gaps due to tree mortality from windthrow, disease, insect attack, or lightning strike, in addition to the more or less regular recurrence of forest fires.

Disturbed Habitats

The habitat note for a species in this guide may list "disturbed habitats." This term does not refer to all land that is not currently supporting natural climax vegetation—that would be most of the United States. It means recently or continually disturbed land: highway embankments, vacant lots, neglected gaps in cropland, and land that has been bulldozed, clear-cut, or plowed and then neither replanted and cultivated nor left alone long enough to reestablish a diverse plant community. Plants of disturbed habitats are generally pioneer species, and quite a few are nonnative invasive species.

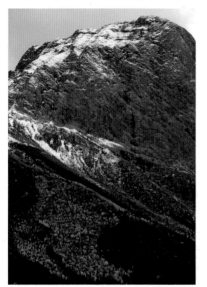

Habitat succession in the northern Rockies: after an avalanche cleared a swath of coniferous forest, a population of Quaking Aspens (the yellow-green patches) sprouted up in the sunny, open ground.

North American Forests

The accompanying map and descriptions cover North America's broad forest categories. The map does not show "disturbed land," which is extensive, nor does it show exactly where forests are currently growing. Instead, it shows broad categories of "potential vegetation": the plant cover that ecologists believe would likely prevail in an area if it were left alone for a few centuries, and if its native soil is intact. Put simply, it describes the naturally occurring forest cover of North America.

Boreal Forests

Boreal forests—vast, northern, and mainly coniferous—cover far more area than any other forest type in North America, or indeed, the world: similar forests cover much of northern Eurasia. In North America they form a swath from Alaska's Yukon River delta to Newfoundland.

As a rule, species diversity is greatest at the equator and gradually diminishes toward the poles. Less than 10,000 years ago, throughout nearly all of boreal North America, huge ice sheets melted, exposing land that was devoid of both soil and viable seeds. The forests appeared only within the past 3,000 to 6,000 years, their development constrained by the various rates at which species could spread northward.

Conditions are harsh in the boreal forest, with bitterly cold winters and a very short growing season. Evergreen leaves have an advantage over deciduous leaves because they are able to photosynthesize at slightly lower temperatures. Beneath the evergreen conifers grow many broadleaf evergreen shrubs, such as Labrador-tea, crowberry, and kinnikinnick. Permafrost, clay layers, and acidic bog waters inhibit nutrient uptake. Plants are generally unable to survive in the boreal environment without a symbiotic relationship with mycorrhizal soil fungi (page 14).

Though boreal soils are not often dry enough for drought to pose a hardship, boreal tree crowns certainly get dry enough

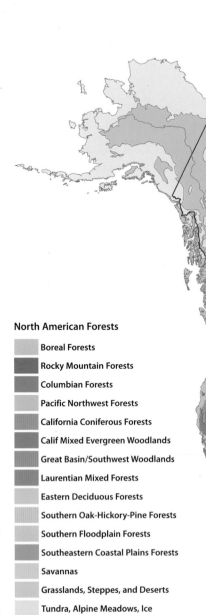

North American Forests

- Boreal Forests
- Rocky Mountain Forests
- Columbian Forests
- Pacific Northwest Forests
- California Coniferous Forests
- Calif Mixed Evergreen Woodlands
- Great Basin/Southwest Woodlands
- Laurentian Mixed Forests
- Eastern Deciduous Forests
- Southern Oak-Hickory-Pine Forests
- Southern Floodplain Forests
- Southeastern Coastal Plains Forests
- Savannas
- Grasslands, Steppes, and Deserts
- Tundra, Alpine Meadows, Ice

to burn. Fire-return intervals (the average time forests grow between forest fires) are generally shorter than 200 years, and fires have rarely been fought or suppressed.

White Spruce dominates the northern two-thirds of America's boreal forests; it is accompanied by Black Spruce and Tamarack, especially on wet ground. Paper Birch, Quaking Aspen, Balsam Poplar, and Black Spruce pioneer after fires. Typically, just one of those species predominates on any one burn, to be gradually joined and perhaps eventually replaced by White Spruce. Toward the northern edge, where boreal forest gives way to treeless tundra, trees are increasingly in scattered clumps. The space in between may be barren, covered with lichens, or filled with low shrub thickets of bog birch, green alder, and various willows. In southwestern Alaska, tall alder thickets make up a sizable portion of the boreal forest region. At the northern extreme, Black Spruce may be the only tree species—and so stunted that it can barely be called a tree.

Trees become a little more diverse in the southern third of the boreal forest. From Manitoba eastward, Balsam Fir is a major component, and Northern White-cedar grows in swamps and bogs. Jack Pine is common from Alberta to Ontario, Subalpine and Rocky Mountain firs from the Yukon to western Alberta, and Engelmann Spruce (or Engelmann–White Spruce hybrids) in British Columbia.

Uplands in the boreal region are dominated by two widespread kinds of forest that are unmistakable at first glance. One is a closed spruce forest carpeted with greenish gold feather mosses. The other is a woodland of scattered spruces, its floor carpeted with brittle whitish lichens, many of them reindeer lichens.

Extensive areas of poorly drained ground are covered with sphagnum species (peat mosses). These hold water like a sponge, creating bogs—acidic, nutrient-poor wetlands that stunt trees (Black

Spruce, Tamarack, Northern White-cedar) and may eventually kill them.

The boreal forest is the land of moose, caribou, lynx, wolf, wolverine, snowshoe hare, raven, lemming, mosquito, and black fly. Brown horsehair lichens drape the tree limbs; woodland caribou turn to these lichens for food in winter when snow covers most of their foods.

Pacific Northwest Forests
The world's tallest trees are found in this forest realm, which begins as a thin coastal strip in northern California and extends northward through eastern Washington, Oregon, and British Columbia (east of the crest of the Cascade Range/Coast Mountains) to southeastern Alaska. Douglas-fir is characteristic almost throughout. Other dominant trees vary with elevation (including several species of true fir), slope aspect, and the stage in forest succession. Western Hemlock

The boreal forest (opposite page), characterized by conifers and peat bogs, is vast, spanning most of Canada. Pacific Northwest forests (this page) support the world's tallest trees, including Redwood and Douglas-fir. An old-growth forest in Washington's Olympic National Park is shown.

can dominate wetter areas as the forest matures. Western Redcedar is widespread, mainly on sites supplied with groundwater near the surface. (The highest mountain forests are discussed under Subalpine Forests, page 26.)

Relatively few broadleaf trees grow in this area, because they are not very shade-tolerant; they occur mainly in gaps or where the habitat has been disturbed. Red Alder, which quickly takes over burned areas and clear-cuts, White Alder, and Bigleaf Maple are the most abundant broadleaf trees. Several broadleaf evergreens (species shared with California mixed evergreen communities, page 27) are common where this forest extends into southwestern Oregon and California.

Despite their moist character, most unlogged stands in the southern half of this region date from fires. Average fire-return intervals seem to have been in the range of a few hundred years. Some fires wiped the slate clean, at least in patches; others spared many of the biggest trees, especially the thick-barked Douglas-firs and Redwoods. Fires are rare toward the north, where summers have more rain and less lightning.

As of 1850, about 70 percent of this area in Washington, Oregon, and northern California was likely covered by old-growth stands containing many trees older than 200 years; the other 30 percent was in younger postfire stages. Today, old growth is virtually gone from private lands and much reduced on public lands, but a few million acres remain in the mountains, which escaped the earliest phases of logging and then came under National Forest management.

Mosses and lichens festoon the trees in old-growth stands. These epiphytes (organisms growing upon a living plant without parasitizing it) grow most prolifically, unseen, in the tree canopy, where they contribute substantially to forest growth by intercepting cloud water and by fixing nitrogen so that it becomes available to the trees. Animals that live up here, such as the red tree vole and the northern flying squirrel, rarely descend to the ground. The larger fallen trees remain conspicuous on the ground for several centuries, providing another set of nutrient pathways and serving as "nurse logs," on which seedlings germinate; as these trees grow to maturity the nurse log eventually disintegrates beneath their root structures.

Though precipitation is ample in this region, summers are quite dry—increasingly so southward into California. Two distinctive forest subtypes are found in a coastal fog belt where the tall trees ameliorate summer drought by intercepting fog. Moss and lichen epiphytes thrive in **coastal temperate rain forests** containing Sitka Spruce, a species limited to the fog belt from northernmost California to southeastern Alaska. Redwood bark, in contrast, resists epiphytes, and **Redwood forests** commonly have only modest vegetation on the forest floor. Nevertheless, older Redwood trees support entire epiphytic communities, and even shrubs and small conifers, in their upper branches. The Redwood is limited to the northern two-thirds of California's fog belt, extending a few miles into Oregon.

The combination of heavy shade and summer drought can reduce forest understories to a bare minimum, especially in forests that are between 30 and 80 years old. More often, shrub and herb layers are well developed, supporting such plants as Oregon-grape, salal, huckleberries, and Vine Maple. Ferns abound, and on some soils mosses carpet the ground.

Characteristic mammals include black-tailed deer, black bear, mountain lion, Douglas' squirrel, and many species of voles and chipmunks. Thanks to the moist environment in and near the soil, salamanders are abundant and reptiles are few. Varied thrush and brown creeper are notable in the forest interior, and bald eagle on rivers and inlets. Pacific salmon (seven species of *Oncorhyncus*) begin and end their lives here, returning from the sea to give the region not only its totem but also a significant portion of the forests' fertility from their decaying remains.

Rocky Mountain Forests

Throughout the Rocky Mountains there is both an upper timberline where subalpine forests (page 26) give way to alpine meadow and tundra, and a lower timberline where aridity forces forests to yield to steppe, grassland, or semidesert. In some areas, Ponderosa or Limber pines are the most drought-tolerant trees and form tall but rather open forests at the lower timberline. In others, especially southward, there are relatively low-stature woodlands downslope from the Ponderosa Pine forests; these woodlands are described under Great Basin/Southwest Woodlands and Forests (page 28). The Rocky Mountain and Great Basin/Southwest forest types are more or less scattered, speckling the map of Arizona, New Mexico, and southern Colorado wherever there is sufficient elevation for forest growth.

A high-elevation belt across Arizona, including the Kaibab Plateau and the Mogollon Rim, forms the southwestern margin of the Rocky Mountain conifer forest. The western margin is at or near the crest of the Cascade Range in Washington, Oregon, and northern California, extending in a long arm up into central British Columbia. The least drought-stressed forests in the Rockies, found in a contiguous section of Idaho, Montana, and especially British Columbia, are discussed separately in Columbian Forests (page 24). They and the Rocky Mountain conifer forests gradually give way to boreal forests at around 54° N latitude, as pines, hemlocks, and Douglas-fir fade from the picture.

The elevational sequence of Rocky Mountain conifer forests begins with Ponderosa Pine, and continues slightly higher with Douglas-fir and White Fir, and often Blue Spruce in the valleys. Higher still, these give way to forests of Rocky Mountain Alpine Fir and Engelmann Spruce, which continue upslope, grading into subalpine forests. Two very widespread species—Lodgepole Pine and Quaking Aspen—that specialize in growing rapidly after fires often form pure stands over large areas; the aspen is the one broadleaf tree that has a major presence here. Numerous thunderstorms strike between May and early August, sometimes bringing heavy rain but also often bringing dry lightning and starting fires. Few forest stands here live as long as 200 years. Aspens seem to be decreasing, for poorly

Rocky Mountain forests contain many types of conifers, including Ponderosa Pine and Douglas-fir, as well as Quaking Aspens, which often form pure stands that blaze golden in autumn.

understood reasons that likely involve both fire-fighting and relations between browsers and predators.

The **Black Hills forests** of western South Dakota and northeastern Wyoming lack Douglas-fir but include White Spruce and Paper Birch as major tree species, and are dominated by Ponderosa Pine, Lodgepole Pine, and groves of Quaking Aspen. White-tailed deer are common in the Black Hills, rather than mule deer, which are more common westward.

A large, relatively arid area of central British Columbia is covered mainly by Lodgepole Pine. Epidemics of mountain pine beetles sweep this area repeatedly; it is unclear to what degree other conifers will replace Lodgepole in the killed stands. Forests in the Alberta Rockies also belong to this type. At low elevations they commonly have little but Lodgepole Pine, White Spruce, or aspens in the canopy. At higher elevations the forests shift, as elsewhere, to Subalpine Fir, Engelmann Spruce, and Lodgepole Pine.

Lodgepole Pine forests can be extremely dense, allowing too few resources for any understory plants to grow. In the more mature and open forests, as well as in aspen groves, abundant shrubs include bitterbrush, sagebrush, buffaloberry, and snowberry. The herb layer includes many bunchgrasses and yellow-flowered members of the aster family.

On broad creek bottoms, "parks" of grassland or low shrubs commonly interrupt these forests. Willows and cottonwoods in the low, wet parts of the parks support beaver, and the parks are home to large populations of elk—too large, according to some critics. Wolves—once extirpated but now locally reintroduced and generally thriving—may help to bring the elk and their preferred food plants back into balance. The ubiquitous ground squirrels and chipmunks total more than a dozen species. An emblematic Rocky Mountain bird, American dipper, inhabits the

Columbian forests are moist in some areas, dry in others. Western Larch, which turns yellow in fall (this page), is a characteristic species. California coniferous forests (opposite page) contain a number of species found only in that state, such as Sugar Pine and Sierra White Fir. A forest in Yosemite National Park is pictured.

mountain streams almost amphibiously, swimming in the torrents in search of its invertebrate prey.

Columbian Forests

Columbian forests occupy an area of the Rockies and surrounding mountains from northern Idaho and Montana into Canada. Here, forests similar to the Rocky Mountain conifer type are interlaced with forests strongly resembling the Pacific Northwest forests, complete with Western Hemlock, Western Redcedar, and a thick drapery of epiphytic lichens and mosses.

This intermingling of forest types reflects the distribution of storm tracks: Rocky Mountain conifer forests receive most of their precipitation in early summer, from thunderstorms bringing moisture from the Gulf of Mexico. Pacific Northwest forests receive precipitation, which peaks in midwinter, from the Pacific. Some of these Pacific winter storms reach as far as the Continental Divide, augmenting the moisture from summer storms that reach the same areas. However, the Pacific storms drop their moisture as they ascend the western slope of any given mountain range; the range's eastern slope receives little aside from those summer thunderstorms. In consequence, individual mountain ranges may have "rain forests" on their western slopes, and rather arid, typical Rocky Mountain conifer forests on their eastern slopes.

Other mountain ranges within the Columbian forest region lie away from Pacific storm tracks and develop no wet forests, but may still abound in tree species that are either absent or little represented in the Rockies farther south: Western

Larch, Grand Fir, White Spruce, Western Redcedar, and Western White Pine. (The latter species has fallen to minor status after a century of selective removal by both loggers and white pine blister rust.) White Fir is absent, but Douglas-fir, Lodgepole Pine, and Ponderosa Pine remain—the common denominators of most of our western forest types. Fire remains a ruling factor in all but the wettest locations.

Broadleaf trees still concentrate near moisture but are more abundant and more diverse in the Columbian than in other western conifer forests. Notable species are Paper Birch, Rocky Mountain Maple, Black Cottonwood, Chokecherry, and Thinleaf Alder. The shrub layer is rich and diverse, with currants, Labrador-tea, wild roses, serviceberries, and fool's-huckleberry in addition to bitterbrush, buffaloberry, and others that abound farther south. The ferociously thorny devil's club, a common species of Pacific Northwest forests, thick mosses, and the evergreen creeper twinflower grow in moist areas, while yellow-flowered arnicas are almost ubiquitous in drier ones.

North America's largest terrestrial carnivore, grizzly bear, perseveres here. Moose, lynx, mule deer, snowshoe hare, marten, and red squirrel are characteristic.

California Coniferous Forests

California's mountains support conifer forests that are part of the greater western conifer forest pattern but have a distinctive set of species. In the typical low- to high-elevation sequence, grassland gives way first to oak woodlands and then to Ponderosa Pine, the lowest part of the conifer forest. These are soon joined (moving upslope) by Douglas-fir, Incense-cedar, Sugar Pine, and Sierra White Fir. Scattered within this elevation zone in the western Sierra Nevada are 75 groves of the world's most massive tree, Giant Sequoia.

Jeffrey Pine is a dominant species in the Cascade Range of northeastern California as well as in the lowest forest zones on the eastern Sierra slope, replacing Ponderosa Pine there. All of these trees are well adapted to survive frequent low fires. California Red Fir takes over increasingly—approaching 100 percent of the tree canopy in many stands—as elevations climb into the zone of long-lasting, deep snowpack. Above the red fir forests are subalpine forests (page 26).

A few southern California mountain ranges are high enough to support areas of California conifer forest, but with fewer species: mainly Ponderosa and Jeffrey pines, and some Bigcone Douglas-fir.

Of the nine conifers named above, only Ponderosa Pine and Douglas-fir are shared with the other western conifer forest types. The other six strongly characterize California conifer forest, phasing out northward between Mount Shasta and central Oregon. Within that stretch of the Cascade Range, the California conifer forest grades into the Pacific Northwest conifer forest, and some of its species grade into their northwestern counterparts: Sierra White Fir into Grand Fir, and California Red Fir into Noble Fir, with Shasta Red Fir as an intermediate variety.

Larches and spruces—the two most northerly genera of conifers—are absent from California conifer forests, except for minor penetration of spruces in northern

California. Hemlocks are also scarce, with Mountain Hemlock mainly in subalpine forests and Western Hemlock in coastal forests. Broadleaf trees are few, except in three situations: streamsides; moist sites in the red fir zone where stands of Quaking Aspen grow; and Ponderosa Pine stands where California Black Oaks infiltrate from the adjacent oak woodlands.

Especially in the red fir zone, herb and shrub layers tend to be sparse. The bright crimson snowplant and other flowering herbs without chlorophyll use the omnipresent soil fungi as intermediaries to parasitize the trees overhead. Thus they thrive where few other small plants can obtain sufficient water and sunlight. In areas with a shrub layer, manzanitas are conspicuous. Characteristic vertebrates, such as mule deer, mountain lion, coyote, golden-mantled ground squirrel, bushy-tailed woodrat, and mountain quail, are found widely in western forests.

Subalpine Forests and Parklands

Throughout the western mountains, from California and the Southwest to the Pacific Northwest and Canadian Rockies, most forests just below the alpine timberline are dominated by two or more of the following species: Subalpine Fir, Rocky Mountain Alpine Fir, Engelmann Spruce, Mountain Hemlock, Whitebark Pine, and Subalpine Larch. These species rarely grow in low-elevation forests south of the boreal.

The spatial pattern of subalpine forests is distinctive. Within the other western conifer forest types, most terrain sustains a closed-canopy forest; where conditions are more arid, the trees are more widely spaced, grading into a woodland or a savanna of scattered individual trees.

Subalpine forests (this page), composed almost entirely of conifers, grow just below the tree line. Some California mixed evergreen woodlands grow on serpentine bedrock (opposite page). Here, Gray Pines, broadleaf evergreens, and patches of chaparral abruptly give way, where the serpentine outcrop ends, to coniferous forest in the distance.

Subalpine forests, instead, shift upslope, as the trees confront more intense cold or wind or shorter snow-free seasons, from a closed canopy to a parkland. There, trees clump together densely, offering mutual protection from the elements, but the clumps are scattered on treeless expanses, often meadows. (This generalization becomes a little less true southward, where aridity becomes more of an issue.)

The stresses of high elevations, especially where combined with aridity, result in very slow tree growth, but with the slow growth may come extreme longevity. Bristlecone pines include the world's oldest tree specimens, well over 4,000 years old. North of their range, Whitebark Pine is among the longest-lived species.

Several tree species adapt to climatic rigors of the highest elevations by growing in a shrub form, called **krummholz**, which spreads mainly by rooting from stems rather than from seeds. Typically a dense mat one to three feet high, krummholz catches and retains snow. The mat directly

reflects the shape of the wind-sculpted snowpack, because any new twigs that grow to stand out from the mat will also stand out from the protective snowpack in winter and be killed by desiccating winds.

Marmots are the mammals most strongly associated with the subalpine zone; their primary habitat is actually the meadows, not the forests, where ground squirrels and chipmunks live. Dusky grouse, gray jay, Clark's nutcracker, and ravens are conspicuous, especially in winter, when other subalpine birds have migrated either southward or downslope.

California Mixed Evergreen Woodlands and Forests

Broadleaf evergreen trees share dominance with evergreen conifers in California's mixed evergreen communities, which cover much of the Coast Ranges and the lower western slopes of the Sierra Nevada; they also extend in interrupted fashion through the Klamath Mountains into southwestern Oregon. These broadleaf evergreens, rather anomalous in North America, are similar to vegetation types found near the world's four other western coasts that have Mediterranean-type climates, in Chile, Australia, South Africa, and the Mediterranean.

In California, hot, dry summers alternate with winters that bring few severe frosts and receive the lion's share of the year's moderate rainfall. Evergreen leaves and needles have an advantage in being able to photosynthesize in winter, when moisture is most available here. Thick and stiff, they are almost wilt-proof, remaining intact through summer and ready to go back to work when the rains return in fall. Many broadleaf evergreen leaves are rich in volatile substances that emit fragrance on hot days.

The chief broadleaf evergreens include Tanoak—rapidly succumbing to a recently arrived invasive pathogen—California Bay, Pacific Madrone, and several species of live oak (a catchall term for oaks with evergreen leaves). Dominant conifers are

Douglas-fir, Incense-cedar, and Ponderosa Pine. Bigleaf Maple and Oregon White Oak are notable deciduous interlopers.

In **California oak woodlands** the droopy, grayish needles of Gray Pine are conspicuous among the mixture of oaks, both evergreen and deciduous. These oak woodlands occupy slightly drier sites within the broader mixed evergreen community category, such as lower elevations or sunnier slope aspects. Tree crowns shade 30 to 80 percent of such sites; grasses (mostly invasive species from Eurasia) predominate beneath. The grasses are green for only a few winter months, becoming excellent fire-carriers the rest of the year. The dominant tree species in all of these related communities are either fire survivors or stump sprouters.

Another major fire-adapted community, bordering mixed evergreen communities on their drier margins, is **chaparral**. This dense community of mostly broadleaf evergreen shrubs cloaks extensive areas in central and southern California, Arizona, and western Mexico. Chaparral rarely exceeds 12 feet in height. It is subject to intense fires that kill virtually all plants, at least their aboveground parts; new shoots from the charred stumps in some species— and fire-adapted seeds in others—quickly regenerate the species that dominated before the fire.

Parts of the Coast Ranges and the Klamath Mountains have an unusual bedrock called serpentine that weathers into soils inhospitable to most plants. Gray Pine, some chaparral species, and several specialists are among the few that can grow in these soils, forming what are called **serpentine communities**.

Lizards, snakes, mice, butterflies, vultures, coyotes, and the secretive bobcat thrive in California mixed evergreen communities. Wolves and populations of grizzly bears (the California emblem) were eliminated by the end of the 19th century. Domestic pigs, escaped long ago, persist as elusive populations of "wild boars."

Great Basin/Southwest Forests and Woodlands

The mountain ranges of the Great Basin (roughly, Nevada, western Utah, and southeastern Oregon) and major portions of Arizona and New Mexico stand as ecological islands, supporting forests that grow above the surrounding desert. The highlands are moist enough to support tree growth for two reasons: there is less evaporation in the cooler air at higher elevations; and the prevailing airflow, which lifts as it passes over the mountain ranges, causes rain or snow to fall locally.

As the ice ages cyclically waxed and waned, biotic communities in many mountain regions migrated downslope and upslope, respectively, tracking the climate change. Extinctions occurred during periods of maximum ice cover, but they were not uniform in the different mountain ranges. Later, as the climate warmed, the inhospitable habitat of the arid valleys prevented ready migration between mountain ranges. The effect of climatic cycles here was to winnow out a great many plant and animal species, leaving fewer species than in other western conifer communities and frequent differences in species composition from one range to the next.

Pinyon-juniper woodland forms the defining plant community of Great Basin/ Southwest conifer woodlands. Singleleaf Pinyon, Pinyon, Mexican Pinyon, Utah Juniper, Oneseed Juniper, and Western Juniper are dominant species, with any given locale featuring one or two of them. Most are between 10 and 25 feet tall, typically spaced so that their crowns do not touch—hence the term woodland rather than forest. These highly flammable trees survive by being sufficiently distant from their neighbors to limit the spread of fire, at least for several decades at a time. This fire avoidance strategy works well enough for pinyon-juniper woodland to cover an impressive 65,000 square miles of North America.

Pinyon-juniper woodlands, such as these in southern Utah, are common in the dry climate of the Great Basin and Southwest. Other conifers grow in the region's higher elevations.

Pinyons and junipers are the most drought-tolerant tree species in this region, so their woodland is the lowest-elevation tree community on each mountain range. From pinyon-juniper upslope to the mountaintops, several forest sequences unfold. These include:

— White Fir forest, giving way upslope to Limber and/or bristlecone pines.
— Mixed forest with Ponderosa and Lodgepole pines, White Fir, and Douglas-fir, changing to subalpine spruce/fir forest, and then to bristlecone pines.
— Shrubland/woodland with Gambel Oak, changing upslope to mixed forest, then to subalpine forest as above, and finally to Limber Pine.
— Sagebrush steppe above the pinyon-juniper woodland, on mountains that high-elevation conifers failed to recolonize after the ice age.

But all such upslope forests together do not add up to as many acres as the pinyon-juniper woodlands do. There are many expanses of pinyon-juniper woodland on mesas or plateaus without higher slopes adjacent.

In southern Arizona and New Mexico and western Texas, the common woodland is an **oak-juniper woodland**, similar to the extensive oak woodlands of northern Mexico. Many of the oak species here retain green leaves through most winters, sometimes becoming nearly or completely leafless in a very dry spring. Their leaves range from spiny-edged to smooth, but are rarely lobed. Arizona, Emory, Gray, and Mexican Blue oaks are abundant. Conifers other than juniper are rather scarce, though Chihuahua and Apache pines grow at high elevations.

Gambel Oak woodland is scattered across Colorado, Utah, and Nevada, often adjacent to pinyon-juniper woodlands. Deciduous oaks and mountain-mahoganies predominate, mixing with such shrubs and small trees as ceanothus, cliffrose, cliffbush, manzanita, Chokecherry, Utah Serviceberry, Apache plume, rabbitbrush, and desert sweet.

Mule deer, mountain lion, bobcat, coyote, and porcupine, as well as many kinds of woodrats, mice, lizards, and squirrels—Uinta chipmunk and Kaibab squirrel among them—are common in Great Basin and Southwest communities. Pinyon jays inhabit their namesake woodland; Steller's jays replace them higher up.

Laurentian Mixed Forests

Laurentian mixed forests stretch from Nova Scotia to the bogs west of Lake of the Woods in Manitoba and Minnesota, encompassing along the way most of northern New England and New York and the northern halves of Michigan and Wisconsin. The very highest elevations in the Appalachians as far south as the Great Smokies support spruce-fir forests whose best fit is with the Laurentian type.

This broad belt is transitional between the continent's two biggest forest types: the coniferous boreal forest and the eastern deciduous forest. It constitutes a grand mosaic, with the pieces determined locally by soils, slope aspect, fire history, and elevation. Some pieces of the mosaic are mostly deciduous, some are mostly coniferous, and some mixed about equally.

Eastern White Pine, Red Pine, and Jack Pine commonly pioneer after fires, gradually giving way to broadleaf trees, or persist indefinitely on sandy soils. Balsam Fir, Eastern Hemlock, and Red and White spruces occur variously in swampy ground, in thin soils over granite, on cold, north-facing slopes and ravines, and at high elevations in New England and New York. These high-elevation forests closely resemble boreal forests. In a small area in New Hampshire's White Mountains they give way to the stunted forest type known as krummholz (see page 26) and then to treeless alpine tundra.

Prominent broadleaf trees in Laurentian forests are Sugar Maple, Red Maple, American Beech, Paper Birch, Yellow Birch, Northern Red Oak, and (in the western half) American Basswood. In general, broadleaf trees prevail on more hospitable sites with fertile, well-drained soils. Forests on these favorable sites resemble the maple-beech stands of the northern part of the eastern deciduous forest, but may include conifers as a long-lasting, albeit minority, component.

Jack, Red, and Eastern White pines dominate **Great Lakes pine forests**, on sandy soils in Michigan, Wisconsin, and Minnesota. Several kinds of oak and both Quaking and Bigtooth aspens are their major associates. This may be the only situation in the region where drought

Laurentian mixed forests (as shown at left, in Michigan's Porcupine Mountains), are transitional between the largely coniferous boreal forests to the north and the eastern deciduous forests to the south. Eastern deciduous forests (opposite page, an example in Ohio) cover a vast area of the East and support about 200 different tree species.

stress is an issue for trees. On at least some of the sites, fires have played a role in forestalling succession to other trees, and in the absence of fire, these pine forests are locally threatened.

At the wet extreme, **conifer bogs**—extensive in northern Minnesota and adjacent Canada, scattered elsewhere—are dominated by Black Spruce, Northern White-cedar, and Tamarack, like bogs in the boreal forest.

Laurentian conifer forests typically have sparse understories. The broadleaf forests accommodate a rich and diverse shrub layer, with several species of viburnum, rhododendron, and laurel (*Kalmia*). The herb layer may feature diverse ferns and clubmosses, Jack-in-the-pulpit, bluebead, Canada mayflower, and trailing arbutus.

Vertebrates of the forest include red squirrel, northern flying squirrel, barred owl, and pileated woodpecker. White-tailed deer, which lack significant wild predators in much of the region, run rampant. Wolves and mountain lions were long ago extirpated from the area south of the Saint Lawrence River; in their absence, coyotes have moved in from the West

but do not prey on deer enough to affect populations, nor do black bears, the only larger carnivore.

Eastern Deciduous Forests

This forest type—North America's second most extensive, after the species-poor boreal forests—is stunningly diverse, with perhaps 200 native tree species, of which at least 30 can be considered dominant. Its area, totaling 9 percent of North America, including fingers reaching into Louisiana, Quebec, Georgia, Minnesota, Maine, and southern Texas, can be divided into narrower forest types, yet experts agree on its essential unity. Common features include a shady broadleaf canopy, rich but not overly dense shrub layers, and a scarcity of conifers.

At least a dozen of the major tree species reach all corners of the region: White, Black, and Northern Red oaks, Red and Silver maples, White and Green ashes, Bitternut and Shagbark hickories, Eastern Hophornbeam, American Hornbeam, Slippery Elm, and formerly American Elm. Trees showing a geographic bias within the region include Sugar Maple and American

Basswood, which increase to the north; Tuliptree, Black Tupelo, Sweetgum, and Blackjack Oak to the south; Burr Oak, Ohio Buckeye, and Black Walnut to the west; American Beech, birches, Scarlet Oak and formerly American Chestnut to the east.

Since the late 19th century, scourges of invasive pests and pathogens have shifted forest composition by decimating or even eliminating a species regionally. American Beech was struck in 1890 but retains a major presence; American Chestnut, hit soon after, is essentially gone, except for sprouts and a newly discovered and apparently healthy population in central-western Georgia. American Elm, Eastern White Pine, Flowering Dogwood, Butternut, and ashes, hemlocks, and firs have been victims of subsequent epidemics.

Natural fires are not an important influence here; deliberately set fires undoubtedly had effects that linger today, but experts debate how pervasively Native Americans ever burned this region. The Massachusetts Bay colonists marveled over magnificent, parklike forests, with no shrubs to impede passage for tens of miles; those were certainly products of management using fire. Westward from western Indiana, forests gave way to tallgrass prairie over a broad belt of savannas and forest/prairie mosaics that were maintained by repeated fires. In central Kentucky and Ohio, Daniel Boone found large prairies that likely resulted from burning by Native Americans. In contrast, extensive openings called cedar glades in central Tennessee, Missouri, and Arkansas were too sparse to carry fire, permitting scattered Eastern Redcedars to persist as the chief tree over a scant ground cover of drought-adapted grasses, ferns, and herbs. The glades occur on uplands with very thin soil over limestone bedrock.

Conifers are generally restricted: Eastern Redcedar to rocky limestone sites; Atlantic White-cedar to the Atlantic and Gulf coastal plains; Eastern White Pine, Northern White-cedar, and Eastern Hemlock to the Appalachians. In the mountains, eastern deciduous forests are found to almost 5,000 feet elevation, above which they give way to spruce and fir.

Sheltered **cove forests** occur on low to mid-level slopes of protected, often north-facing coves (valleys) from about 2,000 feet to 4,500 feet elevation in the southern Appalachians. Cove forests are famous for a typically sparse shrub layer underlain by a rich and diverse herbaceous ground cover of numerous wildflowers, including Jack-in-the-pulpit, blue cohosh, black snakeroot, heartleaf, bloodroot, foamflower, yellow lady's slipper orchid, ginseng, and walking fern. The canopy is mostly deciduous and features American Basswood, Mountain Silverbell, Yellow Buckeye, Northern Red Oak, White Ash, Tuliptree, and Sweet Birch, with a sparse understory of Eastern Hophornbeam, Flowering Dogwood, Mountain Magnolia, silverbells, and other species.

Northern floodplain forests extend the deciduous forest hundreds of miles westward into the otherwise treeless Great Plains. American Elm, Eastern Cottonwood, Black Willow, Black Walnut, American Sycamore, and ashes are common across floodplains that range in width from a few feet to a few miles. Even on small streams in highly arid lands farther west, trees will grow wherever their roots are assured of year-round moisture. Such riparian strips may support just one or two species of willow or cottonwood, sometimes lined up single file along the riverbank.

Numerous wildflowers and shrubs, including spectacularly colorful azaleas, rhododendrons, and Mountain-laurel, adorn the eastern deciduous forest. Characteristic fauna include woodchuck, cardinal, wild turkey, downy woodpecker, white-tailed deer, gray fox, and gray squirrel. Bison, wolves, and mountain lions were widespread here in 1800.

Southern oak-hickory-pine forests vary widely in composition, ranging from pine barrens to oak-dominated forests, to those that resemble eastern deciduous forests. An example in Alabama's Bankhead National Forest is shown.

Southern Oak-Hickory-Pine Forests

These forests occupy a belt roughly congruent with the Piedmont in the southeastern states, extending northeast across southern New Jersey to Cape Cod, and west into Texas and Oklahoma. They are a variant of the eastern deciduous forest, distinguished by the substantial presence (and local dominance) of several pines other than Eastern White Pine.

Pine plantations prevail today, typically grown in 30- to 60-year rotations for paper and framing lumber. Though less valuable per board foot than the native hardwoods, pines are more lucrative because they grow rapidly, even in poor soils. Pines also feature prominently in the earliest written reports on the region, but old-growth pine stands, very rare today, were a product of frequent low fires, most set by Native Americans. From the earliest records on, scientists have debated the relationship between the pines, the deciduous trees, and human influences on the forests; the

complete truth may never be known. Certainly fire history has increased the numbers of pines and oaks.

White Oak is the most abundant tree in unmanaged forests, accompanied in deciduous stands by Southern Red and other oaks, hickories, Tuliptree, Sweetgum, and Sourwood. Chief pines of natural stands are Loblolly and Shortleaf. Diverse shrubs and small trees are common and colorful, including dogwoods, Possumhaw, Eastern Redbud, and Fringetree.

White-tailed deer are the abundant large animal, with red and gray foxes the largest common predators. Fox squirrels inhabit upland forests, and gray squirrels (including an unusual nearly black form) the bottomlands. Box turtle, cottontail, and northern bobwhite also occur here.

The **pine barrens** of New Jersey, Long Island, and Cape Cod are pine and oak of a different stripe: Pitch Pine, Blackjack Oak, Scrub Oak. This distinctive forest developed with frequent fires, including

stand-replacing fires as well as low-intensity ones. Over large portions the pine barren forest is stunted to less than 6 feet tall, though the same three species may produce medium-tall forests not far away.

Southern Floodplain Forests

Southern floodplain forests and southeastern coastal plains forests (page 35) are widely interspersed, and share both their humid climate and their negligible elevation; yet they are remarkably different. The floodplains are rich and moist, with few patches of sandy soil, face fewer nutrient deficiencies, and burn far less frequently. Whereas even the broadleaf trees are commonly evergreen in coastal plains forests, floodplain forests are dominated largely by deciduous trees—Water Tupelo, oaks, and Bald-cypress, with varying presence of Sweetgum, American Sycamore, American Hornbeam, hickories, ashes, and elms. Only Bald-cypress is

a conifer, and it is deciduous. (Atlantic White-cedar and several broadleaf evergreens are locally common in wetlands near the Atlantic.)

Floodplains are flat areas periodically inundated when rivers and streams overflow their banks. Historically, some floodplains were flooded almost every year, others once every 20 to 50 years. Each flood distributed new layers of mud that fertilized the land. Today, levees and dams sharply reduce flood frequency in most of these areas, and many of the remaining forest communities are changing in response. Floodplains make excellent farmland (at least once the swamps are drained), so most were deforested long ago—even thousands of years ago. The Mississippi plain in southern Illinois held some of the densest populations of Native Americans north of Mexico; they cleared patches of forest for crops and towns, and selectively cut the tree species they

Southern floodplain forests are rich and moist; Bald-cypresses and Water Tupelos even grow in standing water (opposite page). Pines are characteristic trees of the southeastern coastal plains forests; Slash Pines are joined by palmettos in Everglades National Park (this page).

is just below the surface, on terraces that are fairly well drained, and on higher (but still rarely dry) "blufflands" with wind-delivered loess soils.

Southeastern Coastal Plains Forests

Fire history, soil type, low elevations, and features of the water table combine to create a mosaic of pine-dominated uplands that are inset with a smattering of moist hammocks (isolated hardwood forests), standing water wetlands, and deciduous hardwood floodplain forests. About 15 percent of the coastal plains region is wetland, half of which is covered in Southern Floodplain Forests (page 34).

Forests of the Atlantic and Gulf coastal plains, from westernmost Texas to Virginia, are best known for a historical expanse of **Longleaf Pine uplands** that once encompassed an estimated 90 million acres before being largely lost to forestry and suburban expansion. Longleaf pinelands are fire-dependent communities that some ecologists have called "fire forests." They have a natural fire-return period of two to five years and in the absence of fire would become hardwood forests. In pre-settlement times, Longleaf pinelands were ignited naturally by lightning and burned for many miles before extinguishing themselves. Later, they were burned regularly by Native Americans and early settlers, and today are burned by forest managers. The Longleaf Pine canopy overtops an understory of Common Persimmon and a variety of oaks, including Southern Red, Post, Turkey, Bluejack, and Sand Live. The ground cover is typically dominated by threeawn grasses or broomsedge, joined by as many as 200 other plant species.

preferred for firewood, structural timber, and canoes. Bald-cypress seems to have been eliminated from the northern edge of its range for use in canoes.

Southern floodplain forests occur along most rivers and estuaries of the coastal plains from eastern Texas to Virginia (areas outside the Mississippi floodplain are too narrow to depict on the forest map, page 18). The Mississippi plain's vast scale derives from a complex geologic history, culminating when the last ice sheet melted away, and rivers rapidly filled the valley with huge volumes of glacial debris. Modern floods spread layers of fine, rich silt on top of the glacial outwash, in patterns typical of river delta formation.

Within the floodplain region, Bald-cypress and Water Tupelo dominate areas with standing water; these swamps are home to alligators, ibises, egrets, and the invasive nutria. Other distinct communities thrive where the water table

In wetter areas Longleaf uplands are replaced by **Slash Pine flatwoods**. From about South Carolina to Mississippi these flatwoods are dominated in the shrub layer chiefly by Saw Palmetto, and in other locations by shrubs of the heath family. All sites support numerous grasses, sedges, and wildflowers. Slash Pine flatwoods often encompass standing-water wetlands variously known as **pocosins** and **bay swamps** that support dense forests of Bald-cypress, Pond-cypress, Pond Pine, Sweetbay, Swamp Bay, Loblolly-bay, and several species of tupelo and titi. Many pocosins and bay swamps have been drained for farming.

Areas with poor drainage, nutrient-deficient soil, and elevations only inches below adjacent pinelands support open expanses that in some places are treeless and in others contain scattered trees. Variously called **savannas**, **wet prairies**, or **bogs**, these meadows are best known for carnivorous plants, such as sundews, butterworts, and pitcherplants, as well as orchids and other wildflowers.

Small areas with slightly lower elevation and other areas that have avoided frequent fire are characterized by hardwood forests with a mix of evergreen and deciduous hardwood trees, including Southern Magnolia, American Beech, Eastern Hophornbeam, and various oaks and hickories. Such forests are referred to as **hammocks**, a Native American name that is often reported to mean "shady place." Ravine slopes along streams and major rivers support hardwood forests that are much like those described above for hammocks, with Tuliptree, Pyramid Magnolia, American Basswood, Loblolly Pine, White Ash, Sourwood, and several hawthorn species.

Barrier islands and coastal dunes from Virginia to Mississippi support prairies of seaoats and dense patches of **maritime forest**. Sea breezes sculpt these patches into smooth, airfoil-like contours, typically tapering from midsized forests bordering the salt marshes to a thicket of low shrubs on the seaward side. Trees are salt-tolerant and most are evergreen; they include Sand Live Oak, Red Bay, Devilwood, Cabbage Palm, and Eastern Redcedar.

Salt-tolerant **mangrove communities** occur along both coasts of Florida, predominantly from about the central peninsula southward. Mangroves are mainly tropical species that independently evolved similar adaptations enabling them to grow in salty, oxygen-poor soil subject to frequent incursions of seawater. Those native to Florida include Red, White, and Black mangroves; Button-mangrove is also often included in the mangrove category.

The Florida panther, a subspecies of mountain lion, hangs on in very small numbers in southern Florida's coastal forests. The red-cockaded woodpecker is dwindling along with its habitat, mature Longleaf Pine forest. More widespread fauna of the coastal plains includes Carolina wren, mourning dove, swamp rabbit, white-tailed deer, raccoon, and eastern diamondback rattlesnake.

Savannas

Savannas are grasslands with scattered trees. Generally, a climate and soil combination that can support trees will grow a forest or, if the moisture is not quite sufficient for a forest, a more open woodland. To keep from filling in with trees, a savanna usually requires an agent, such as frequent grass fires or even heavy populations of herbivores. In the **Everglades**, a unique outlier of tropical wet grassland in the United States, chief obstacles to tree growth are fires in the dry winters, the many flooded months in the wet summers, and the dearth of essential nutrients, particularly phosphorus. Bald-cypresses can grow large in swamps but in marshes are often few and stunted by the lack of nutrients. "Tree islands" have developed in the Everglades where decayed vegetation built up deeply enough to raise the surface above the water; aided

Savannas, grasslands with scattered trees, are kept open by fires or grazing herbivores. Without these agents to clear new tree growth, forests or woodlands might form.

by the birds they attract, these areas became islands of relative fertility as well. Dominant trees include Southern Live Oak, Strangler Fig, and Gumbo Limbo.

Elsewhere in the Southeast, **cypress savannas** feature clumps dominated by Pond-cypresses, in a mosaic with wetland grasses and open water. Fires are surprisingly common and serious in these wetlands, of which Okefenokee and Big Cypress swamps are the largest.

Savannas dominated by broadleaf trees form a broad belt along the northern edge of the Great Plains prairies. In Alberta these are **aspen parklands**; aspens grow in clonal clumps rather than as scattered individuals. The trees typically grow in the swales, or hollows. Southeastward, the aspens are increasingly joined by Balsam Poplar, Boxelder, Green Ash, willows, and Burr Oak—the dominant tree of **Burr Oak savannas** in eastern Minnesota and southern Wisconsin.

The earliest written reports of western Oregon tell of great prairies and **Oregon White Oak savannas**—and of smoky skies from the fires that maintained them. The prairies and savannas occupied lowlands a little drier than the conifer-cloaked mountain slopes nearby. Nevertheless, if fire is excluded conifers do invade the prairies and savannas. We don't know whether burning by Native Americans created the savannas of Oregon, or merely preserved and enlarged grasslands that had already developed under a natural fire regime.

Several types of **oak and mesquite savannas** characterize south-central and western Texas. Honey Mesquite, live oaks, junipers, and (in the southernmost part) acacias grow singly or in groves; most individuals are shrubs, but some reach tree size. Two centuries ago this region was mostly grassland dominated by species of bluestem and grama; shrubs grew in scattered locations, typically those with poor soil. The subsequent broad increase in mesquite is attributed to complex mechanisms involving cattle grazing, fire suppression, and possibly a warming climate.

Threats to Trees and Forests

The United States and Canada have fewer trees today than they did 500 years ago, but more than they did 100 years ago. There are several reasons for the increase. Nearly all of the huge, really old trees have been logged and replaced with smaller, younger trees, allowing more trees per acre. The forested acreage has increased as well, as we have shifted from a culture in which 80 percent of the population farmed any tillable land, to one where just 2 or 3 percent of the population farms the best land very intensively. As part of this shift, marginal farmland has reverted to forest, especially in the East. Over the same century, timber increased in value due to supply and demand, and logged-over land is promptly replanted rather than being left to grow back on its own—a process that sometimes languished in herb or shrub stages. Finally, a century of fire suppression in the West fostered the growth of many small trees in what had been sparse, fire-thinned stands of large trees.

The increase in quantity has been offset by decreases in quality from the standpoint of forest health and wildlife habitat. Many people think wildlife habitat has improved because they see deer and elk numbers increasing, but most ecologists agree that the forests are becoming less diverse. One kind of diversity is structural. Old-growth forests mix trees and shrubs of several heights, forming multiple canopy levels utilized by different sets of animals.

More often we hear about decreasing species diversity. An important species may nearly disappear locally if loggers remove just the highest-cash-value trees, or if they clear-cut and then replant with just one or two species. The resulting plantations support a much shorter list of understory plants and associated animals than the more chaotic natural forests.

Invasive Species

The broad topic of invasive species—those that spread rapidly after humans carry them to a new continent or region—touches on trees in several ways. Most catastrophic diseases of trees are caused by invasive fungi. Invasive insect pests such as gypsy moth, Asian longhorn beetle, emerald ash borer, and woolly adelgids also wreak arboreal havoc; some of these focus on a particular species or genus.

While trees themselves can be invasive species, vines and herbaceous plants are more prominent on the list of plant pests that have altered ecology in parts of North America. Among invasive trees are eucalyptus species in California, tamarisks in the Southwest, punktree in Florida wetlands, and Tree of Heaven continent-wide. Although we don't always use the term "invasive" in the species accounts, any introduced tree that has naturalized may become (or already has become) invasive.

Smaller invasive plants sometimes threaten trees. Kudzu vine in the Southeast

Dutch elm disease is a fungus spread by a type of bark beetle that lays its eggs under the bark of elm trees. The larvae bore away from their hatching site, forming the radiating galleries shown here.

Northern Spotted Owl populations have declined as their habitat, old-growth forest of the Pacific Northwest, has succumbed to logging.

and English ivy in the East and Northwest climb trees, in some cases making them susceptible to windthrow, and occasionally crowd out their foliage. Introduced cheatgrass growing in sagebrush steppe can carry fire to junipers and pinyons that might otherwise be far enough from other flammable plants to avoid a fire.

Pandemic Diseases and Pests
Damage caused by invasive pests and pathogens have repeatedly winnowed our forests, culling out a species over a region or even its entire range. The worst loss may have been American Chestnut, which used to be the quintessential tree of the eastern deciduous forests and an important wildlife resource. The chestnut blight arrived in 1906 and within a few decades erased the tree from the landscape. A few stumps still send up sprouts, but they don't live to maturity, and surviving mature trees are very rare. Ecologists will never know exactly what the oak-chestnut forests were like, since modern plant-community analysis wasn't done in the 19th century. American Elm was the next native tree to go, felled by Dutch elm disease, which deprived many residential streets of the trees for which they had been named. The latest pandemic to sweep eastern deciduous forests is Butternut decline (page 227); its full impact is not yet known.

At the turn of the 20th century Western White Pine was being so rapidly and lucratively logged that foreign nurseries entered the market for replanting stock. In 1910 a shipment of French seedlings brought a fungus known as white pine blister rust, which had previously inflicted great losses on Eastern White Pine and now assailed Western White Pine. Humans fought back. There were massive campaigns to eliminate currants—innocent shrubs that the rust requires as alternate hosts. Such efforts failed, however, and blister rust spread, threatening other five-needled western pine species. One of those most severely affected is Whitebark Pine, a scenic, timberline tree on whose abundance grizzly bear recovery efforts in Yellowstone may depend, as pine nuts are a critical food resource for the bears there.

Port-Orford-cedar has a small natural range, yet as a timber export it ranks among our top species in dollars per board foot—that is, while supplies last. The species is being eliminated from much of its native range by phytophthora root rot, which arrived there in 1952. Fortunately, this beautiful tree appears likely to hang on in roadless, high-elevation areas, since the disease spreads mainly in two ways: downstream (in water) or in mud on tires.

Another species of phytophthora causes a disease that was dubbed Tanoak death when it made its presence known in 1995; it was renamed sudden oak death when live oaks also began to succumb in large numbers. This disease is of particular concern because of the wide variety of plants that it can infect, at least in the lab. Besides oaks, which are gravely threatened, these include camellias, rhododendrons,

This view from Clingmans Dome in Great Smoky Mountains National Park is dominated by conifers killed by invasive insect pests.

heathers, madrones, lilies, roses, maples, magnolias, true firs, Douglas-fir, and Redwood—species worth tens of billions of dollars commercially (and more, when commerce in other species ecologically dependent on them is factored in), not to mention their scenic value and the "ecological service" values they provide, including oxygen production and water purification. We don't know whether sudden oak death could become an epidemic among all those species and more, or if it has always been present in the soil, and some mysterious change suddenly made Tanoak and live oaks mortally susceptible to it. The scale of the sudden oak death catastrophe remains to be seen.

Air Pollution

On high ridges in the Appalachians, from the Great Smokies to the Adirondacks, tree mortality rates have been between 20 and 60 percent in recent decades. Many experts blame air pollution. Fog as acidic as lemon juice has been measured in the Smokies, along with ozone levels typical of Los Angeles freeways. It may be that pollution components are deposited most heavily where the air has to rise over ridges or that the thin, rocky soils offer less buffering, or it may be that something else about high elevation inflicts vulnerability. However, confirming a causal mechanism traceable to particular pollutants has proven elusive.

Climate Change

If global warming proceeds in accord with computer models, many tree species will shift their ranges northward. Those that cannot shift fast enough will decline. Warming temperatures provide the best-guess explanations for some trends that are already measurable, such as the decline in New England maple sugar production and the decrease in Alaska-cedar in southeast Alaska.

Tree species' ranges shift slowly. Current natural ranges are still adjusting to the close of the last ice age. Some of the temperature shifts 10,000 years ago may have been just as fast as anything the 21st century will bring. Unfortunately, in the 21st century the trees simultaneously have to deal with diseases and invasive species from other continents; with shrinkage of old-growth reserves and their associated animal species; and with pollution, rapid deforestation, plantation monocultures, and other factors. Increases in temperature everywhere are relatively easy to model; it's much harder to predict the associated changes in precipitation, cloud cover, evaporation, insect outbreaks, fungus diseases, lightning, and fires. Those factors are likely to affect trees more severely than temperature itself. It's impossible to predict what will happen to North America's native trees in the upcoming decades as the climate warms.

How to Identify a Tree

Tree identification can seem daunting: so many trees, so many leaves, so many possibilities. Our first piece of advice: peruse this guide repeatedly and often. Study the Visual Glossary (pages 43–59), the keys that begin each of the guide's major sections, and the species accounts. The more familiar you become with the flowers, fruits, leaves, and forms of trees, the easier it will be to recognize similarities between the images and descriptions in this guide and the trees you encounter in the landscape. Soon you will find that you recognize many groups of trees at a glance: elms, maples, birches, pines, ashes, junipers. It won't be long before you begin to make species identifications.

Before an outing, review the guide thoroughly. Pay attention to the trees' range maps and note the trees that are distributed in your region. Seek regional tree lists from Cooperative Extension System offices, parks, native plant societies, and other organizations. Visit arboreta and botanical gardens (page 491) and compare the labeled trees to the species accounts.

When you study a tree, record notes about its location, its habitat, and the features of its leaves, fruit, and bark. Take photographs or make sketches. With some species you may need to make multiple visits to the same tree at various times of the year, keeping notes about details of its flowers in spring and fruit in fall, in order to make an accurate identification. Field notebooks are useful not only for reference when you are doing later research (or locating a tree for a second look); they can also provide invaluable data about populations of threatened trees.

Seven Clues to Tree Identification

The following seven clues can help you identify most trees (although there are those that can stump even the experts). In some cases you will need to look at all seven features, in others just one or two.

1. Needlelike, Scalelike, or Broadleaf?

This guide is divided into several categories based on leaf type and arrangement. A first step in field identification is to determine whether the leaves on a particular tree are needlelike (pines, firs), scalelike (junipers, redcedars), or broad (typical leaves, with a flat, expanded blade). Turn to Leaf Shapes (pages 46–47); all but the first two pictured are broad leaves. If your leaf is needlelike,

Maples and sycamores have similar large, long-stalked, palmately lobed leaves. The similarities end there. Maple leaves are opposite; those of sycamores are alternate. A comparison of the fruits (maples' paired samaras, sycamores' fuzzy, spherical clusters) and bark (flaking and colorfully mottled in sycamores, roughly ridged and furrowed in maples) confirms the identification.

turn to the Key to Trees with Needlelike Leaves (page 62); if scalelike, turn to the Key to Trees with Scalelike Leaves (page 131). If broad, continue below.

2. Alternate or Opposite?

With broadleaf trees, the next step is to determine whether the leaves are alternate or opposite; see Leaf Arrangement (page 44). In many trees, leaf arrangement is apparent, with the leaves in obvious opposite pairs or clearly alternating along the branch. In others, the leaves can be very crowded and the leaf arrangement ambiguous. In order to be certain of arrangement, examine leaves from several points along the branch. In winter, look at the leaf scars (page 50) to see whether the fallen leaves were opposite or alternate.

3. Simple or Compound?

Next, determine whether the tree's leaves are simple or compound (pages 44–45). Simple leaves have undivided blades, whereas the blades of compound leaves are divided into two or more leaflets. The easiest way to tell the difference between a leaf and a leaflet is to examine the point of attachment to the supporting stalk. True leaves usually produce buds in the axil (page 43), the angle formed between the stalk and the supporting branch, and may also have stipules (leafy appendages) there; in a few trees a band of tissue, called a stipular ring, encircles the branch. Leaflets typically lack these features.

Once you've determined whether a tree's leaves are opposite or alternate and simple or compound, turn to the guide's keys. For opposite leaves, see the key on page 156; opposite, compound leaves begin on page 158, and opposite, simple leaves on page 178. For alternate, compound leaves, see the key on page 212; the key for alternate, simple leaves begins on page 257.

4. Leaf Features

Once you have found the correct key, examine the tree's leaves more closely.

Note whether they are lobed, their general shape, the shape of the tip and base, and features of the margins (pages 44, 46–48). Flip to the species listed in the key that match your leaves, and scan the accounts to see whether the color and texture of the leaf underside or features of the twigs and buds (pages 49–51) are important.

5. Fruit

Check the tree for fruit, which sometimes provides important clues to identification, especially on leafless trees. Fruit types, defined and illustrated on pages 55–57, are treated as major components in the keys. Fleshy fruits, including berries, drupes, and pomes, can be similar in appearance; some may have to be cut open to ascertain their type. Dry fruits include nuts, capsules, pods, and samaras. Noting if or how a dry fruit splits open is often important. Fruit color, shape, and size, described in the species accounts, can be helpful in distinguishing similar trees.

6. Bark

Take note of bark features. Determine if the bark is smooth, fissured, furrowed, or scaly, or peels off in flakes, sheets, or strips. See the photographs of bark patterns (pages 58–59), as well as the bark photos in the species accounts. Some bark types are associated with a particular genus or family, as with sycamores, cherries, pines, New World cedars, and birches.

7. Flowers

In many trees, flowers are short-lasting or inconspicuous (or both), but in others they can provide clues to identification. If flowers are present, note whether they have conspicuous petals, as well as their general shape and form, their location on the branch, and whether they appear singly or are crowded together into catkins or other types of clusters (pages 52–54).

We end here with our most important advice: enjoy the forest *and* the trees!

Leaf Structure

A typical simple leaf consists of a blade and a leafstalk. The blade is the expanded portion of the leaf. The leafstalk (petiole) attaches the blade to the supporting twig or branch. Leafstalks vary in length; some leaves lack a leafstalk (they are termed "sessile").

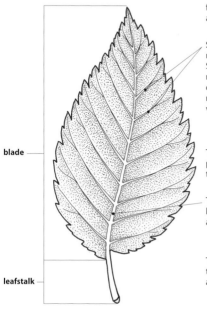

blade

leafstalk

The **leaf tip** (apex) is the end farthest from the point of attachment to the branch.

Side veins angle away from the midvein toward the margin. Side veins may terminate at the margin, fork into smaller branches, or branch repeatedly to form networks of interconnected veinlets.

The **margin** is the edge or perimeter of the blade; it may be toothed or untoothed.

The **midvein**, the extension of the leafstalk, runs along the central axis of the blade from base to tip.

The **base** of the leaf blade is the end nearest the point of attachment to the branch.

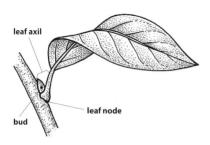

leaf axil

leaf node

bud

The **leaf node** is the point at which a leaf or leafstalk attaches to the twig or branch. The **axil** is the angle formed between the leaf or leafstalk and the twig or branch. Axils often bear **buds** (the beginning of next year's leaves or flowers). Some species, including many willows, also have **stipules**, small, leaflike structures borne at the leaf node or at the base of the leafstalk.

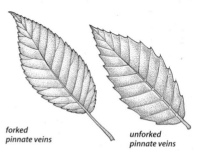

forked pinnate veins

unforked pinnate veins

The patterns formed by leaf veins vary in form, branching, structure, color, and prominence. In a leaf with **pinnate venation**, the main side veins diverge from the midvein in a featherlike pattern. Side veins may be straight or curved, uniformly spaced or arranged asymmetrically. They can be **unforked**, or they may **fork** into smaller veins. In **palmate venation**, seen in maples, the major veins arise from a single point at the base of a leaf.

Leaf Arrangement

The arrangement of leaves along a branch or twig usually takes one of three forms: opposite, alternate, or whorled (a variation on opposite). A few trees have both opposite and alternate leaves or both opposite and whorled leaves.

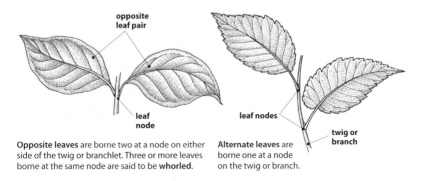

Opposite leaves are borne two at a node on either side of the twig or branchlet. Three or more leaves borne at the same node are said to be **whorled**.

Alternate leaves are borne one at a node on the twig or branch.

Simple Leaves

Simple leaves have a single unbroken margin that runs continuously from one side of the leaf base to the other. The margins of simple leaves may be toothed or untoothed and lobed or unlobed. The margins of lobed leaves are deeply or shallowly cleft with indentations (sinuses) separating the lobes. The tips of lobes may be blunt or rounded, acutely pointed, or bear teeth or bristles.

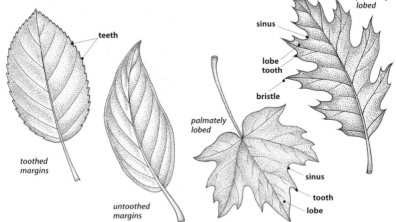

Toothed margins bear few to many bluntly or acutely pointed toothlike projections; teeth may run along the entire leaf perimeter or may occur sporadically or just on the upper or lower portion of the leaf. **Double-toothed** margins bear smaller teeth between larger ones. **Untoothed** leaves have smooth margins that lack teeth. Their margins are sometimes **wavy**, or undulate, when viewed from the side

In **palmately lobed** leaves all lobes emanate from a central point at the leaf base. In **pinnately lobed** leaves lobes spread from a central axis like the barbs of a feather. Indentations between lobes (**sinuses**) can be shallow or deep, and lobes can be toothed or untoothed. Maples and sycamores have palmately lobed leaves. Many oaks have pinnately lobed leaves; in red oaks the teeth are tipped with stiff **bristles** (awns).

Compound Leaves

The blades of compound leaves are divided into segments called leaflets. Leaflets look like leaves but are attached to the tip of the leafstalk (in palmate leaves) or to the leaf axis, rather than directly to a twig, branch, or stem. Compound leaves may be palmate, pinnate, bipinnate, or tripinnate.

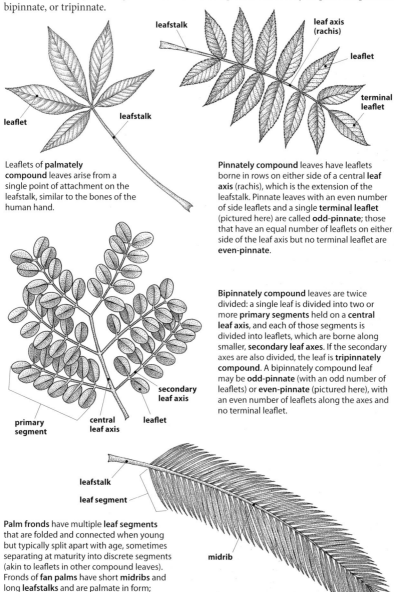

Leaflets of **palmately compound** leaves arise from a single point of attachment on the leafstalk, similar to the bones of the human hand.

Pinnately compound leaves have leaflets borne in rows on either side of a central **leaf axis** (rachis), which is the extension of the leafstalk. Pinnate leaves with an even number of side leaflets and a single **terminal leaflet** (pictured here) are called **odd-pinnate**; those that have an equal number of leaflets on either side of the leaf axis but no terminal leaflet are **even-pinnate**.

Bipinnately compound leaves are twice divided: a single leaf is divided into two or more **primary segments** held on a **central leaf axis**, and each of those segments is divided into leaflets, which are borne along smaller, **secondary leaf axes**. If the secondary axes are also divided, the leaf is **tripinnately compound**. A bipinnately compound leaf may be **odd-pinnate** (with an odd number of leaflets) or **even-pinnate** (pictured here), with an even number of leaflets along the axes and no terminal leaflet.

Palm fronds have multiple **leaf segments** that are folded and connected when young but typically split apart with age, sometimes separating at maturity into discrete segments (akin to leaflets in other compound leaves). Fronds of **fan palms** have short **midribs** and long **leafstalks** and are palmate in form; fronds of **feather palms** (pictured here) have extended midribs and are pinnate in form.

Leaf Shapes

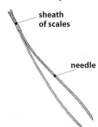

sheath of scales

needle

Needlelike

Needlelike leaves are linear in outline, with straight, parallel sides. Pine needles (left and near right) occur in **bundles** (fascicles) that are held together at the base by a sheath of scales. Needles of spruce, fir, Douglas-fir (far right), hemlock , and yew are borne singly.

leaf

Scalelike

Scalelike leaves are very small, often wrap the stem tightly on all sides, and are usually borne in opposite pairs. Mature leaves of Eastern Redcedar and Western Redcedar are examples.

Elliptic

Elliptic leaves are broadest across the middle and taper gradually to each end, similar to the outline of an American football. Elliptic leaves can vary from narrow to wide, and their bases and tips can vary from pointed to rounded to blunt.

Ovate

Ovate leaves are generally egg-shaped in outline, widest toward the base, tapering toward the tip, and often not much longer than broad.

Lance-shaped

Lance-shaped leaves are broadest toward the base and much longer than wide, similar in form to a lance or spearhead. This term is often used to describe any long, very narrow leaf.

Obovate

Obovate leaves are reverse ovate—that is, they are broadest toward the tip and narrower at the base.

Heart-shaped

Heart-shaped leaves have a wide, indented (cordate) base and a pointed tip, with the general shape of a Valentine heart.

Circular

Circular leaves are more or less round, equal in diameter as measured across any axis.

Triangular

Triangular leaves appear three-sided; the base is flattened to widely wedge-shaped, and the sides are tapered.

Fan-shaped

Fan-shaped leaves are narrow at the point of attachment to the leafstalk and flare toward the leaf tip. Ginkgo is the only broadleaf tree with a true fan-shaped leaf.

Leaf Tips and Bases

The tips of leaves vary from tapered and pointed to rounded to notched. Leaf bases may be pointed or tapered, rounded, nearly straight across, indented, or asymmetrical (with more leaf tissue on one side of the midvein than the other).

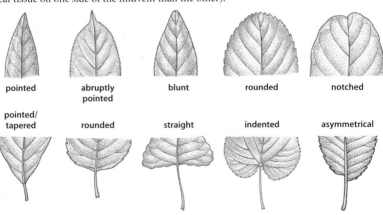

| pointed | abruptly pointed | blunt | rounded | notched |

| pointed/ tapered | rounded | straight | indented | asymmetrical |

Leaf Margins

Leaf margins may be smooth or toothed. The tips of teeth may be rounded, blunt, or pointed and may be vested with bristles, awns, small glands, or prickly outgrowths that are piercing to the touch. Untoothed margins may be lobed or wavy.

On **single-toothed** leaves (left), teeth are uniform in size and shape. **Double-toothed** leaves (right) have teeth of two sizes, with smaller teeth either on or between larger ones.

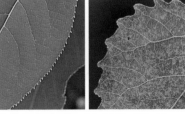

Teeth can be sharply pointed or blunt-tipped, and coarse or fine (left). Teeth that are low and rounded (right) are sometimes described as scalloped.

American Holly

Chinkapin

Teeth can be tipped with piercing **prickles** (left), as in some hollies and golden oaks; or with fine, hairlike **bristles** or awns (right), as in red oaks, Chinkapin, and chestnuts.

Southern Magnolia

Water Tupelo

Leaves with smooth margins (left) lack teeth. Margins can be toothed only partially, such as above or below the middle of the leaf, or teeth can be irregularly spaced, few in number, and/or of different sizes (right).

Leaf Undersides

In some trees, identification details are hidden on the undersides of the leaves. Leaves often have a different color or texture below than above, which may be caused by pigmentation differences or the presence of hairs, glands, or pores.

Canyon Live Oak

Fraser Fir

Clammy Locust

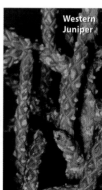

Western Juniper

Color

A whitish waxy coating, called a bloom, on a leaf (or a fruit or twig) can give the leaf a paler, often blue-tinged color. Some Canyon Live Oak leaves (left) are hairless beneath with a pale bloom, while others are covered with—and colored by—golden hairs. Needles of firs have white lines below formed by rows of pores (stomata).

Glands

Tiny glands on leaves, fruits, stems, and other plant parts secrete sticky, shiny, or watery substances. Most glands are very small; they may appear as minuscule dots or depressions (gland dots) on the leaf surface. Stalked glands can look like tiny hairs and make a surface "sticky-hairy" (left). The presence of a visible resin gland on the leaf is an identification feature in cypresses, junipers (right), and similar species.

European Beech

White Poplar

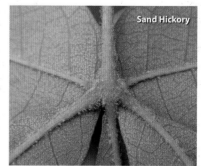

Sand Hickory

Hairs

Leaves, as well as leafstalks, twigs, and other plant parts, may be sparsely to densely hairy. Hairs vary from straight to curly and from stiff to soft. In some species, leaves are hairy when they first emerge (left). In this guide, **velvety** describes surfaces with short, dense hairs that have the texture of velvet. **Downy** describes a covering of soft, fluffy hairs with the feel of feather down. **Woolly** describes a dense covering of hairs that are somewhat coarse to the touch, as in White Poplar.

Scales

Hairlike structures that are wider and flatter than typical hairs, scales sometimes occur on leaf undersides. Sand Hickory leaves are made paler beneath by a thin coating of silvery scales on the leaf surface; additional tufts of rusty scales and hairs gather in vein angles. Hairs and scales described as **rusty** are dull brown to dingy orange to rust red.

Features of Twigs

Twigs represent the current year's growth of a branch, which extends from the termination of the previous year's growth to the branch tip. The previous season's growth is often referred to as a "branchlet"; "branch" refers to older wood, or can mean an entire limb.

Twig Appearance

Twigs have softer tissue than the rest of the branch, are sometimes hairy (even though the branch is not), are usually fresher in appearance, and are often a different color. Hairs may sprout all around the twig, in lines along the twig, or in patches near the leaf base. Differences in twigs can sometimes help distinguish two species. The hairy twigs of Staghorn Sumac are quite different from the smooth twigs with a waxy bloom found on Smooth Sumac.

Smooth Sumac

Staghorn Sumac

Leaf Scars

When a deciduous leaf falls from a twig or branch it leaves a mark where the leafstalk was attached called a **leaf scar**. Within the leaf scar, **bundle scars** mark the sites of vascular connections between the leaf and branch. In winter, leaf scars indicate whether a leafless tree has opposite or alternate leaves. The shape of the leaf scar, the number and position of bundle scars (five on the Horse-chestnut, three on the others pictured), and a leaf scar's position on the branch can help with identification.

Horse-chestnut

Butternut   Black Walnut

Prickles, Spines, Thorns, and Wings

Thorns are modified branches; they sometimes contain active or vestigial leaves or minute leaf scars. **Spines** are modified leaves; they may be borne in the position of a leaf and often have a bud in the axil, similar to a leaf; or they may be borne to the sides of the leafstalk, as in Black Locust. **Prickles** are outgrowths of the epidermis, or "skin." They can form on any part of the trunk, twig, or leaf and are easily broken off by pressing to one side. A **bristle** (or awn) is a slender, hairlike appendage or extension, as in the bristles that tip the lobes of red oaks. **Wings** are extensions of flattened tissue, often on a leafstalk, branch, or fruit. Winged branches have thin, corky extensions.

thorn

wings

spines

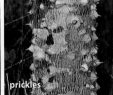
prickles

Buds

Buds, the embryonic beginnings of flowers, leaves, and shoots, occur on several parts of a twig or branchlet. Leaf and flower buds often appear at the end of the summer growing season; in many species they are wrapped in scales that serve as protection against the elements. Bud position and appearance, including scale type, and the number of buds in a leaf axil are all helpful in identifying trees.

Red Maple

Yellow Birch

Longleaf Pine

Types of Buds

Terminal buds grow at the tip of the branch. The terminal buds of each year leave telltale **bud scale scars** on the branch that demarcate the beginning of the current year's growth. **Lateral** or **side buds** grow along the branch. When they grow in leaf axils they are called **axillary buds**. The Red Maple twig pictured has a terminal bud and paired axillary buds (one of which has opened into flowers). The bud scale scars (horizontal rings farther down the branch) show the location of the terminal bud from the previous year; the length of twig from the bud scale scars to the tip is a season's growth.

False terminal buds grow at the tip of the twig and may resemble true terminal buds but are slightly offset from the twig tip. Birches have false terminal buds; in the Yellow Birch pictured the catkins grow from near the branch tip, rather than directly from the branch tip.

Pines and other conifers send out terminal and lateral buds from the **crown leader** (the central growth tip at the treetop) and the tips of branches at the end of each growing season. In some species, such as Longleaf Pine, these **winter buds** are quite large and prominent.

Pecan

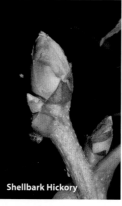

Shellbark Hickory

Bud Scales

Buds may be naked (lacking protective scales) or wrapped in a single caplike scale, as in some willows, in **imbricate scales**, which overlap each other, or in **valvate scales,** two large scales that meet at their edges like the valves of a clamshell. Pecan buds are enclosed in valvate (paired) scales, those of the related Shellbark Hickory in imbricate (overlapping) scales.

Flowers

The majority of the trees in this guide produce **bisexual** or **perfect flowers** that contain functional male and female reproductive organs. **Complete flowers** have an outer whorl of sepals held beneath a series of inner whorls that include the petals, stamens, and pistils successively; generally, there are fewer pistils than stamens. Some broadleaf trees have **imperfect**, **unisexual** male (staminate) and female (pistillate) flowers. These may be borne on the same plant, as in oaks and hickories, or on separate trees, as in hollies. A few trees have both unisexual and bisexual flowers intermixed.

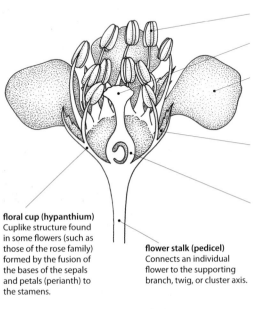

stamen The male reproductive organ of a flower.

pistil The female reproductive organ of a flower.

petal One member of the inner whorl of flower parts in a complete flower; usually colored and showy. All petals collectively called the **corolla**.

sepal One member of the outermost whorl of flower parts in a complete flower. Referred to collectively as the **calyx**.

ovary Seed-bearing portion of the pistil. May be superior, positioned above the sepals and petals (as illustrated), or inferior, positioned below them.

floral cup (hypanthium) Cuplike structure found in some flowers (such as those of the rose family) formed by the fusion of the bases of the sepals and petals (perianth) to the stamens.

flower stalk (pedicel) Connects an individual flower to the supporting branch, twig, or cluster axis.

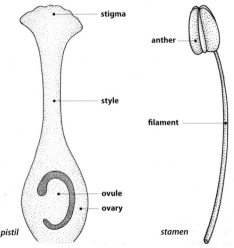

stigma

anther

style

filament

ovule
ovary

pistil

stamen

Pistil The female reproductive organ of a flower, composed of three parts. The **ovary**, at the base, contains one or more ovule-bearing chambers (**carpels**); the **ovules** become seeds. The **style**, a narrow, often elongated, tubelike structure, connects the ovary to the stigma. The **stigma** tips the style and serves as the pollen receptor.

Stamen The male reproductive organ of a flower; composed of a thin, stalklike **filament** and tipped by a pollen-bearing **anther**.

Flowers of the rose family are perfect and complete. They have 4 or 5 sepals and petals, many stamens, and a floral cup that in some plants, such as apples, swells to form part of the fruit.

Magnolias have complete flowers with numerous pistils positioned above numerous stamens, all surrounding an erect, central axis; sepals and petals are similar and are collectively called "tepals."

A unisexual (imperfect), functionally female flower, as found in hollies, is called a pistillate flower.

A unisexual (imperfect), functionally male flower is called a staminate flower.

In some flowers, the petals (and sometimes sepals) are fused from the base, forming a corolla shaped like a tube, trumpet, cup, urn, or bell. Fused corollas may separate into lobes at the tip.

Bracts are modified, often much-reduced leaves. In some dogwoods, they are the four large, spreading, creamy white to pink "petals." The true flowers are tiny and borne in a tight cluster in the center.

Most plants of the pea family bear a typical pea flower, which is bilaterally symmetrical, with the upper petal (the standard or banner) large and outermost, two smaller side petals (wings), and two lower petals joined, forming a boatlike shape (keel).

In conifers, pollen cones serve the function of male flowers, appearing in clusters within the leaves and shedding pollen.

Flower Arrangements

Flowers are borne in various arrangements called **clusters**, or **inflorescences**. A cluster may be drooping or upright, branching or with all flowers attached at a central point, and long and narrow, round and headlike, or loose and diffuse. Clusters may be simple, bearing all flowers on a single axis, or compound, with flowers borne on secondary axes. A cluster's point of attachment to the stem may be **axillary** (in the angle between leaf and stem), **terminal** (at the tip of new twigs), on wood of the previous or current season, or some combination of these.

Sweet Acacia

Chokecherry

Bigberry Manzanita

Flower clusters come in many shapes and forms. Some are dense, compact, and rounded; others are elongated, with flowers borne along a central axis, the individual flowers stalked or unstalked; and many are branched, with flowers borne tightly or loosely on branching stalks.

Black Walnut

Northwest Willow

Catkins are narrow, often hanging inflorescences of tiny male or female flowers, found in oaks, walnuts, willows, birches, cottonwoods, and other species.

Winged Sumac

In a **compound cluster**, the axis branches into secondary axes, which may also branch into smaller axes.

Blackhaw

Terminal clusters are borne at the tip of the branch.

Carolina Laurelcherry

Axillary clusters are borne in the angle between the leafstalk and the branch.

Black Tupelo

In some species, flowers grow at the point of new shoot growth.

Fruit

The fruit of an angiosperm is a matured ovary that usually includes seeds as well as any accessory part that may have become fused to the ovary during maturation. The fundamental unit of the ovary is the **carpel**, which often corresponds to the number of segments, chambers, or rows of seeds in an ovary. A fruit formed from a single carpel is **simple**; one formed from more than one carpel is **compound**. Fruits are divided into two main parts: fruit wall and seed. The **fruit wall** (pericarp) derives from the expanded tissue of the ovary wall and consists of an outer covering (exocarp), middle region (mesocarp), and inner wall (endocarp). Fruits may be dry or pulpy. **Dehiscent** fruits split at maturity to expel the seed; **indehiscent** fruits fall intact and decay to release the seeds. The fruits of some species are not easily classified, even among expert botanists.

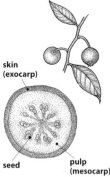

skin (exocarp)

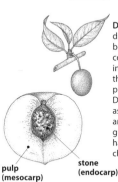

seed **pulp (mesocarp)**

Berry A usually multiseeded fruit consisting of a pulpy (often juicy) fruit wall enclosing seeds. Farkleberries and persimmons are examples. Some berries are one-seeded (called **drupelike berries** in this guide). In Saffron-plum and other bullies the berry derives from an ovary with several incompletely separated compartments, each of which produces a single seed.

Saffron-plum

Farkleberry

Common Persimmon

Drupe An indehiscent, pulpy or dry fruit with usually one hard, bony stone at its center that contains one or more seeds. The inner layer of the pericarp forms the wall of the stone. Peaches, plums, and cherries are examples. Drupes with multiple stones, such as winterberries and other hollies, are called **berrylike drupes** in this guide. Sumacs bear dry, smooth or hairy drupes, often in large, dense clusters.

Chokecherry

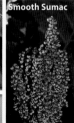

Smooth Sumac

Mountain Winterberry

pulp (mesocarp) **stone (endocarp)**

seed

Pome A fruit in which the ovary is surrounded by a fleshy, expanded **receptacle**, which includes the floral cup (page 52), that is not part of the ovary wall; characteristic fruit of apples, crabapples, pears, mountain-ashes, and some other rose family groups.

Showy Mountain-ash

Southern Crabapple

ovary wall **receptacle**

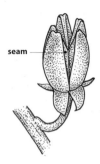

Nut A one-seeded fruit in which the outside of the developed ovary becomes a hard wall (the nutshell). Nuts are often partially or completely enclosed by an **involucre**, such as the cup of an acorn or the husk of a hickory nut. Though lacking a husk, the small, hard fruit of American Basswood is technically a nut; it and similar small nuts are often called **nutlets**.

nut | husk (involucre)

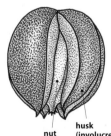
American Basswood

Shagbark Hickory

White Oak

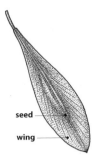

seam

Capsule A hard, usually dry, dehiscent fruit formed from a compound ovary and splitting along two or more seams into two or more parts. Capsules remain tightly closed until maturity, splitting when ripe to release the seeds. Sweetgum capsules are consolidated at their bases into a dense, hard, spiky, ball-like cluster.

Ohio Buckeye

Crapemyrtle

Sweetgum

Samara A dry, indehiscent, winged fruit (often called a **key**) containing a single seed. Maple fruits are composed of two samaras joined at the base. Birch fruits are tiny, two-winged samaras held in a dense, catkinlike cluster. The four-angled, winged samaras of Tuliptree are borne at the base of a primitive, conelike aggregate of numerous ovaries.

seed

wing

Rocky Mountain Maple

American Elm

Tuliptree

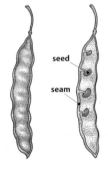

seed

seam

Pod A dry, thin-walled (usually) dehiscent fruit with one or more seeds. In this guide we use "pod" in place of "**legume**," which originates from a single carpel and splits along two seams, with the seeds typically attached along one seam. Some pods (Water Locust, Carob, mesquites) are indehiscent and do not split open.

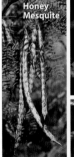
Honey Mesquite

Catclaw Acacia

Black Locust

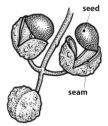

Follicle A dry, often podlike fruit that originates from a single carpel and splits along a single seam. The fruiting "cone" of magnolias, such as Sweetbay, is an aggregate of numerous follicles, each of which splits along one side to release a single, often brightly colored seed with a fleshy coating (**aril**).

Sweetbay

Lime Pricklyash

Osage-orange

Curl-leaf Mountain-mahogany

Pawpaw

White Mulberry

Achene Small, dry, unwinged, one-seeded indehiscent fruit with the seed free from the fruit wall; sometimes tipped with a plume or bristles. The large, round fruit of Osage-orange is composed of many achenes enclosed in fleshy sepals.

Aggregate fruits Some fruits are clusters (aggregates or multiples) of several fruits. The individual drupes that make up a mulberry are evident. The Pawpaw is an aggregate of berries formed from the fusion of multiple pistils.

Conifer "Fruits"

Conifers do not produce flowers or true fruits, and their seeds are "naked," not enclosed within a protective ovary. Most conifers produce cones.

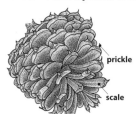

Pine cone Female pine cones, also called seed cones, are composed of a central axis encircled by numerous woody **scales**. Scales are sometimes tipped by a stout, piercing **prickle**. Each scale produces two ovules at its base; fertilized ovules develop into seeds, which in many pines are winged and wind-distributed.

Yew seed Yews produce a single, hard seed surrounded by a red, fleshy, cuplike aril. In the related torreyas, the **aril** is less fleshy and encloses the seed.

Douglas-fir cone Long, conspicuous, three-lobed **bracts** extend from between cone scales in the two Douglas-fir species.

Cypress cone Cones of *Cupressus* trees are typically hard and leathery, with 6–12 rounded scales that are usually tightly closed.

Juniper cone Small, often fleshy, juniper "berries" are cones with fused scales; they produce up to a dozen seeds.

Bark

The color, pattern, and texture of bark provide important clues to identification. For a few species bark alone may be enough for correct identification. For many groups, such as birches, cherries, pines, and several hickories and white oaks, the commonalities of bark features within the group can quickly narrow the field of choices. Noting the age of a tree is important; young bark often differs significantly from mature bark. The bark of plums and cherries, for example, is usually thin and horizontally fissured when young, but becomes scaly or divided into small, blocky plates at maturity.

Plates Relatively large, often thin, distinctly circumscribed portions of bark. Plates can be large and flat, as in a mature Ponderosa Pine, or small and blocky, as in Common Persimmon. Shagbark Hickory takes its name from its conspicuously exfoliating plates.

Ridges Vertical crests, varying in depth and width and divided from each other by intervening furrows. Ridges sometimes interlace, as in Black Locust and several of the hickories.

Furrows Vertical grooves of varying depths that are separated from each other by narrow to broad ridges. Some species, such as Eastern Cottonwood, have very deep furrows. In ashes furrows on the upper trunk seem to form unbroken vertical lines.

Fissures Regular or irregular crevices or cracks, narrower than furrows; may be oriented vertically or horizontally.

Scales Small, thin, often flaking plates, as in some oaks, including Cherrybark and Oregon White Oak, Common Apple, and many pines.

Ponderosa Pine

Common Persimmon

Shagbark Hickory

Mockernut Hickory

Black Locust

Eastern Cottonwood

White Ash

Fringetree

White Alder

Cherrybark Oak

Longleaf Pine

Flaking Separating into thin slivers, chips, scales, or shavings. Sycamores are characterized by flaking bark that falls away to leave the lower trunk mottled with various colors. Eastern Hophornbeam bark has thin, loose, flaking scales.

Peeling Separating into relatively large, thin, and sometimes curling plates or sheets. Birches are well known for their papery, peeling bark, as is Pacific Madrone.

Horizontal lines Partially or completely circumferential raised lines that are often derived from lenticels (small patches of loosely packed, corky cells) in young bark. Cherries and plums often have shiny, horizontally lined bark when young.

Shredding/fibrous Peeling in long, usually vertical, sometimes frayed strips or strings; characteristic of many species of the cypress family.

Smooth With a taut, flat surface lacking in ridges, furrows, and similar features. The smooth, light gray bark of American Beech is the signature feature of one of North America's more widely recognized trees.

Corky Having visible corky or wartlike outgrowths.

Arizona Sycamore

Eastern Hophornbeam

Pacific Madrone

Paper Birch

Pin Cherry

Yaupon

Eastern Redcedar

Alaska-cedar

American Beech

Bigberry Manzanita

Amur Corktree

Netleaf Hackberry

Trees with Needlelike Leaves

The large majority of trees with needlelike leaves are conifers, but conifer leaves can also be scalelike. Trees with scalelike leaves are covered separately on pages 129–152. The difference between "needlelike" and "scalelike" is one of size as well as shape. A species is in the needlelike section if most of the leaves on the plant, assuming it's more than a couple of years old, stick out from the twig by more than a ¼". Needles are many times longer than they are wide, and have straight, parallel sides.

Most conifers with needlelike leaves are in the pine family, Pinaceae. North American members of the family all fall within six genera: *Picea* (spruces,) *Tsuga* (hemlocks), *Larix* (larches), *Abies* (true firs), *Pseudotsuga* (Douglas-firs), and *Pinus* (pines proper). We also include one nonnative genus, *Cedrus* (true cedars). The much smaller yew (Taxaceae, page 122) and araucaria (Araucariaceae, page 128) families are also included in the needlelike section. The cypress family (Cupressaceae) straddles the needle–scale fence; a few trees—including Redwood and Bald-cypress—are included in the needlelike section, but the family is described fully in "Trees with Scalelike Leaves" (page 129).

Needlelike Leaves

Needles, like other leaves on temperate zone trees, emerge and grow in spring, and eventually fall off in fall, though usually not that same year. In most North American species (larches and bald-cypresses are the exceptions) the needles are evergreen, remaining on the tree for three summers or up to (rarely) a few decades before falling. Needles are more or less firm and stiff, are not prone to wilting in drought, and have a thick, waxy skin that helps retain moisture. They exchange oxygen, carbon dioxide, and water with the air through microscopic holes (stomata) that appear as whitish stripes running the length on one or more sides of the needle. The number and location of the stripes is often useful in identification.

Conifers have two kinds of "cones"—small male pollen cones and large female seed cones (the familiar "pine cone"). Pacific Silver Fir pollen cones are pictured here.

The shape of needles in cross section can sometimes help to separate the genera. Needles can be four-angled (mainly spruces); strongly flattened and more or less broad (hemlocks, true firs, yews, bald-cypresses, redwoods); mildly three-angled (pines); or mildly flattened with variable suggestions of three or four angles (Douglas-firs, larches, true cedars). Important variations are noted in the species accounts. The cross section can often be determined by rolling the needle between thumb and forefinger; a clear view of a cross section may require a hand lens and a sharp blade for sectioning.

Resin and Sap

Many conifers, including those of the pine and cypress families, produce resin (often called pitch), a viscous blend of aromatic substances (terpenes) that evolved as a defense against herbivores and fungal diseases. Sticky resin oozes into wood to fill boreholes and block passage of insect larvae. Tiny ducts in leaves produce enough resin to discourage herbivorous creatures. Resin gives scent to crushed foliage as well as wood and bark.

In addition to resin, conifers also produce sap, a water-based, often sugary liquid that serves the circulatory system of conifers and flowering trees alike. Sap travels within the cambium layer in conifers.

The Conifer Tree Shape

Young conifers of most species grow in a conical, "Christmas tree" shape. At the top of the tree, at the end of each year's growth, a set of buds forms—a terminal bud surrounded by smaller lateral buds—that will burst open the following spring and send up a single main stem (the crown leader) and a whorl of branches. Buds also form at the tips of the tree's branches; typically a terminal bud and two side buds. Buds are visible in winter and are often referred to as "winter buds."

The regular growth pattern can maintain a conical shape indefinitely in some species, as long as no neighboring trees impinge. Much more commonly, conifers shift toward a rounded or even a broad top with maturity, and self-prune a great many of their lower branches. If growing in a closed forest, where

the limbs of one tree touch those of the next and collectively they shade most of the forest floor, trees develop a columnar shape, with the lower one- to two-thirds of the trunk bare of limbs. Lower limbs would be shaded, so maintaining leaves on them would be inefficient; they would lose water through their pores, but accomplish too little photosynthesis to "earn" their keep.

Some trees in hot, dry habitats self-prune their lower limbs even when growing in the open, responding to both a greater need to conserve water and the advantages of surviving ground fires by keeping branches out of their reach. Trees that grow under harsh conditions such as constant wind or salt spray can take on forms quite unlike those of their fellows in more benign situations.

Incense-cedar

Slash Pine

Noble Fir

Oneseed Juniper

Whitebark Pines

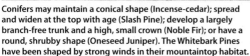
Conifers may maintain a conical shape (Incense-cedar); spread and widen at the top with age (Slash Pine); develop a largely branch-free trunk and a high, small crown (Noble Fir); or have a round, shrubby shape (Oneseed Juniper). The Whitebark Pines have been shaped by strong winds in their mountaintop habitat.

Pitch Pine

Needles in Sheathed Bundles

Needles in bundles of up to 5, each bundle wrapped at its base in a scaly sheath. Cone mostly large, with thick scales, each often tipped with a prickle.

Eastern pines: pp. 66–77
Western pines: pp. 78–93

Tamarack

Needles in Clusters of 10–60

Needles mostly in radiating clusters of 10–60, on short spur twigs; needles at branch tips may be attached singly.

Needles deciduous. Cone small, with thin, persistent scales.

Larches: pp. 94–97

Deodar Cedar

Needles evergreen. Cone sits upright on branch, disintegrates while on tree.

True cedars: pp. 98–99

Sitka Spruce

Needles Single, Attached to Tiny, Woody Pegs

Needles stiff, prickly; radiate from all around branch. Cone hangs from branch, has persistent scales.

Spruces: pp. 101–107

Douglas-fir

Needles Single, Attached Directly to Branch

Cone ovoid to oblong, with protruding, 3-pronged bracts; abundant on the ground.

Douglas-firs: pp. 109–110

Noble Fir

Needles in 2 rows or in a toothbrush or half-round bottlebrush shape. Cone near treetop, sits upright on branch, disintegrates while on tree.

Firs: pp. 110–117

Western Hemlock

Needles soft (not stiff); in 2 flat rows in some species. Cone small (½–3" long), without protruding bracts; may be abundant on the ground.

Hemlocks: pp. 118–121

Pacific Yew

Needles soft; in 2 flat rows. Seed encased in round, fleshy, berrylike covering.

Yews: pp. 122–123

California Torreya

Needles stiff, prickly; in 2 flat rows. Seed encased in oblong, olivelike covering.

Torreyas: p. 123

Redwood

Needles in 2 flat rows; evergreen; entire spray falls intact. Cone ovoid, open.

Redwood: p. 125

Bald-cypress

Needles in 2 flat rows; deciduous; entire spray falls intact. Cone spherical, closed.

Bald-cypress: p. 127

Pines

With 36 native species, pines (genus *Pinus*) are North America's largest, most familiar, most successful group of conifers. They are especially prevalent in the Southeast and in drier parts of western mountains. Their often long needles give them a tufted look that can make a tree recognizable at a glance as a member of genus *Pinus*.

In all pine species but one, the needles are in bundles of two to five, sheathed together at their bases in a little wrapper of scales. The exception, Singleleaf Pinyon, has a "bundle" of just one needle, wrapped in a sheath of scales at its base. Pine needles are evergreen, and remain in their bundles when eventually they fall.

Pine pollen cones are small and encircle the year's new shoot, typically shedding copious amounts of pollen. Pine seed cones run large and have thick, woody scales that are often prickle-tipped. Most cones are stalkless to short-stalked; long stalks are noted in the species accounts. Pine cones usually mature in their second year. In many species, the cones open and release their seeds, which are between the scales, at maturity. Cones may drop from the tree after releasing their seeds. In some species old cones persist on the tree for years.

Some pines have "fire cones." These remain tightly closed on the tree, often for many years, sealed shut by a wax that will melt and drain out in the heat of a forest fire. Over the following weeks, the unsealed cone scales slowly flex open and release the seeds, which then reseed the burn. Pines that have fire cones may also have cones that open upon maturity. Proportions of these cones to fire cones vary by region and habitat, reflecting the likely importance of fire on a site.

Some pine seeds are large, oily, and flavorsome; called "pine nuts," these are adapted for dissemination by birds and mammals. Smaller pine seeds usually have a "wing" to enhance dispersal by wind.

Most pines are fast growers in full sun and often poor growers without it; their seedlings prefer mineral soil and full sun. Pines tend to increase after fire and to decrease in forests that become deeply shady; many species have decreased with fire suppression. Mature Ponderosa, Sugar, and Jeffrey pines commonly survive fires. Several pines are specialists in difficult locations (salty, windy, alkaline) where they may be the only common tree species.

Pine Identification Tips

The first step in narrowing down to a species within *Pinus* is to count needles. Most come two, three, or five to the bundle, though Singleleaf Pinyon has "bundles" of one, and Parry Pinyon of four. Check three or four bundles, since you may find aberrant ones. Refer to the table on the facing page to see which pines within your range match the needle count. Note other features that can help narrow down a species identification, such as cone size and the presence or absence of prickles on cone scales. Old, weathered, open cones on a tree, or the presence of fire cones, can be other important clues.

Left: A newly opened Singleleaf Pinyon cone revealing its seeds, or "pine nuts." Right: These Table Mountain Pine fire cones have weathered and turned gray; they await a fire to unseal their seeds.

NEEDLES PER BUNDLE	NEEDLE LENGTH	CONE FEATURES	REGION	SPECIES
2	¾–2"	asymmetrical; delicate prickle; fire cones	ne US, e Canada to NW Terr.	Jack Pine, p. 68
2	1–3"	small, sharp prickle; old cones persist	e US	Virginia Pine, p. 69
2	1½–3½"	weak prickle	se US	Spruce Pine, p. 70
2 (3)	2–3"	clawlike prickle; fire cones	e US (Appalachians)	Table Mountain Pine, p. 71
2	3–4"	short, stout prickle; old cones persist	FL, AL	Sand Pine, p. 70
2 (3)	2¾–4½"	short prickle; old cones persist	e US to TX	Shortleaf Pine, p. 72
2	4–6½"	lacks prickle	ne US, se Canada	Red Pine, p. 66
2 (3)	8–12"	short, stout prickle	se US	Slash Pine, p. 74
3	3–5"	curved prickle; fire cones	e US (mainly ne)	Pitch Pine, p. 76
3 (2, 4)	5–8"	small prickle; fire cones	se US	Pond Pine, p. 73
3 (2)	6–9"	short, sharp prickle; old cones persist	se US	Loblolly Pine, p. 73
3	8–18"	large (6–10"); stout, sharp prickle	se US	Longleaf Pine, p. 75
5	2½–5"	large (4–8"); lacks prickle	e US, se Canada	Eastern White Pine, p. 77
1 (2)	¾–2"	thick scales; large seeds	sw US	Singleleaf Pinyon, p. 93
2 (1, 3)	¾–2"	thick scales; large seeds	sw US	Pinyon, p. 92
2	1–3"	stiff, curved prickle; some fire cones	w US (ex. desert), w Canada	Lodgepole Pine, p. 91
2	3–6"	clawlike prickle; fire cones	CA	Bishop Pine, p. 90
3 (2, 4)	1–2½"	thick scales; large seeds	sw US, TX, Mexico	Mexican Pinyon, p. 93
3 (2–5)	2–5"	may have prickle; old cones persist	sw US, Mexico	Chihuahua Pine, p. 90
3 (2)	4–6"	asymmetrical; tiny prickle; fire cones	c CA	Monterey Pine, p. 84
3	4–7"	asymmetrical; curved prickle; fire cones	CA, se OR	Knobcone Pine, p. 85
3 (2)	5–10"	large (5–15"); curved prickle	CA, se OR	Jeffrey Pine, p. 88
3 (2, 5)	5–11"	sharp prickle	w US, sw Canada	Ponderosa Pine, p. 89
3	6–12"	very large (10–15"); clawlike prickle; old cones persist	CA	Coulter Pine, p. 86
3	8–12"	large (5–12"); clawlike prickle; old cones persist	CA	Gray Pine, p. 87
4 (3, 5)	1–2¼"	thick scales; large seeds	CA, Mexico	Parry Pinyon, p. 93
5	⅝–1¼"	long (to ¼") prickle	w US (mainly Great Basin)	Intermountain Bristlecone Pine, p. 82
5	1–1½"	long, curved prickle	w US (mainly CO Plateau)	Colorado Bristlecone Pine, p. 83
5	1–2"	scales thick, curved prickle	CA	Foxtail Pine, p. 83
5	1–3"	thick, blunt scale tips; cones closed (opened by animals or decay)	CA, Pacific NW, n Rockies	Whitebark Pine, p. 80
5	1½–4"	thick, blunt scales; lacks prickle	w US, w Can (Rockies)	Limber Pine, p. 81
5	2–3½"	large (5–9"); scales bent back; lacks prickle	sw US, TX, Mexico	Southwestern White Pine, p. 83
5	2–4"	large (5–12") on 1" stalk; lacks prickle	CA, NV, Pacific NW, n Rockies	Western White Pine, p. 78
5	2½–4"	very large (10–26"); on 2–6" stalk; lacks prickle	CA, w NV, OR	Sugar Pine, p. 79
5	7–13"	sharp, downbent scale tips	s CA	Torrey Pine, p. 84

Red Pine

Pinus resinosa
ALSO CALLED Norway Pine
HT 70–80'   **DIA** 1–3'

PINE FAMILY   PINACEAE

Medium-sized evergreen tree. **ID TIP:** Red Pine is the only eastern pine with red-tinged bark from base to crown. (Only the crown bark of mature Scots Pine is orange.) The needles snap easily when bent (compare Austrian Pine).

HABITAT: Primarily in sandy soils, mainly in transition forests just south of the boreal forest of eastern Canada. Elevation 650–4,300'.

NOTES: Red Pine grows quickly and establishes dominance in a postfire setting, but rarely comes up in an established forest. A North American native, it is introduced in Europe. Commonly grown in plantations and parks.

NEEDLES 4–6½" long, 2 to a bundle. Sharp, brittle. Dark green. Winter bud brown, resinous. New twig citrus-scented when broken. **CONE** 1½–2½" long; glossy brown. Broadly ovoid to rounded when open. Scales lack prickle. Opens at maturity.

Scots Pine

Pinus sylvestris
ALSO CALLED Scotch Pine
HT 50–70'   **DIA** 1–2'

Medium-sized evergreen tree. Older trees may have leaning trunk, crown swept to one side. **ID TIP:** Scots Pine has orange, scaly bark on upper trunk and branches.

HABITAT AND RANGE: Introduced in North America; naturalized in northeastern United States, southeastern Canada, and Great Lakes area. Native from northern Europe to China and the Mediterranean.

NOTES: Scots Pine has the largest natural range of any pine in the world, and is a widely planted timber and reforestation tree. One of the first trees introduced to North America (around 1600); planted in cities, landscapes, timber stands, and shelterbelts. Tolerates cold, drought, smoke, even some salt.

PINE FAMILY   **PINACEAE**

NEEDLES 1½–3" long, 2 to a bundle. Stiff, twisted, thick, slightly flattened. Yellow-green to blue-green. Winter bud not resinous (compare Red Pine). **CONE** 1¼–2½" long; yellow-brown to reddish brown. Ovoid when open. Scales thick at tip, usually lacking a prickle. Opens at maturity.

Austrian Pine

Pinus nigra
ALSO CALLED European Black Pine
HT 50–60'   **DIA** 1–2'

ID TIP: The needles are thicker and darker green than those of Red Pine and fold when bent (Red Pine's break). **HABITAT AND RANGE:** Introduced in North America and planted for shelterbelts and landscaping in almost every state and province; naturalized in the Northeast and Great Lakes region but less extensively than Scots Pine. Native to Europe and northern Africa.

PINE FAMILY   **PINACEAE**

NEEDLES 4–7" long, 2 to a bundle. Sharp, glossy, flexible. Dark green. Winter bud silvery (brown in Red Pine). **CONE** 2–4" long; yellow-brown to reddish brown. Ovoid. Scales tipped with tiny prickle (lacking in Red Pine).

Jack Pine

Pinus banksiana

ALSO CALLED Scrub Pine

HT 30–70' **DIA** 9–15"

Small to medium-sized evergreen tree. Crown usually thin, open. Trees may be gnarled, dwarfed at harsh and subarctic sites. **ID TIP:** Jack Pine is North America's only northern, 2-to-a-bundle, short-needled pine. The cones often bulge on one side.

HABITAT: Sandy plains, dry hills, rocky ridges in boreal forest and into tundra. Elevation 0–2,600'.

NOTES: Jack Pine is the most northerly New World *Pinus* species, reaching within 250 miles of the Arctic Ocean, and is often the only tree for vast stretches across northern Canada. It colonizes poor-quality upland soils, including recently burned lands. Young pure Jack Pine stands provide the only nesting site for the endangered Kirtland's warbler; destruction of these stands by fire-suppression practices and development has contributed to the bird's decline.

PINE FAMILY **PINACEAE**

NEEDLES ¾–2" long, 2 to a bundle. Sharp, stiff, thick, slightly twisted, flattened. Yellow-green to gray-green. Winter bud often resinous. **CONE** 1¼–2" long; red-brown. Asymmetrical; often bulging on one side and curved at the tip; in clusters of 2 or 3. Ovoid to narrowly ovoid when open. Scales thick at tip, with delicate prickle (soon shed). Some cones open at maturity; fire cones remain closed on tree for up to 20 years, opening from heat of fire.

Virginia Pine

Pinus virginiana
ALSO CALLED Scrub Pine, Jersey Pine
HT 30–60'   **DIA** 1–1½'

Small to medium-sized evergreen tree, often scrubby, sometimes a shrub. Gnarled and dwarfed on high ridges.
ID TIP: Virginia Pine can be recognized by its short, twisted needles; the purplish to whitish coating on the twigs; and the many old cones persisting on the tree.

HABITAT: Well-drained soils in fields, slopes, and uplands. Often grows with oaks and with other pines. Elevation 0–3,000'.

NOTES: Virginia Pine, a close relative of Jack Pine, is often dismissed as a scrubby tree growing on only the poorest sites, yet that is its greatest value: it stabilizes barren and mined soils, abandoned farmlands, and eroded sites where few other trees will grow.

PINE FAMILY   **PINACEAE**

NEEDLES 1–3" long, 2 to a bundle. Sharp (but not piercing to the touch, as in Table Mountain Pine), stiff, twisted, flattened. Dull gray-green. Twig covered with a purplish to whitish bloom, unlike similar 2-needled pines. Winter bud resinous.

CONE 1½–3" long; red-brown. Ovoid to broadly ovoid when open. Often in clusters. Scales tipped with small, sharp prickle. (Table Mountain Pine has long "claw," Shortleaf Pine a weak prickle.) Opens at maturity; old cones remain on tree for up to 5 years.

Spruce Pine

Pinus glabra

HT 80–100'   DIA 2–2½'

Medium-sized to large evergreen tree. **ID TIP:** Spruce Pine grows in shady, damp places of the South and has distinctively smooth twigs. Bark is smooth and gray, becoming darker, scaly with age. The short needles help distinguish it within its habitat and range.

HABITAT: Hardwood bottomland and swamp forests; upland slope and bluff forests; ravine slopes. Elevation 0–500'.

NOTES: An uncommon tree of the Deep South, Spruce Pine is unusually shade-tolerant for a pine and grows scattered throughout swamp forests, often among magnolias and beeches.

PINE FAMILY   PINACEAE

NEEDLES 1½–3½" long, 2 to a bundle. Slender, flexible. Dark green. Twig smooth. **CONE** 1–2½" long; dull red-brown. Ovoid to cylindrical when open. Scales tipped with weak prickle (soon shed). Cones point away from branch tip or downward. Most open at maturity.

P. glabra

P. clausa

Sand Pine

Pinus clausa

HT 25–70'   DIA 1–1½'

ID TIP: Sand Pine, an uncommon, sometimes scrubby pine, has separate populations on the Florida panhandle's Gulf coast (and into southeastern Alabama), and in central Florida's sandhills. Cones of Gulf coast trees open at maturity; those in central Florida open when heated by fire. Like Spruce Pine, Sand Pine has smooth twigs, but the two species do not overlap in habitat. **HABITAT:** Sandy coastal sites and inland sandy ridges. Elevation 0–200'. (See map above.)

PINE FAMILY   PINACEAE

NEEDLES 3–4" long, 2 to a bundle. Sharp, slender, slightly twisted, flexible. Dark gray-green. Twig smooth. **CONE** 2–3½" long; yellow-brown. Ovoid to broadly ovoid when open. Scales tipped with short, stout prickle. Cones may remain on tree for many years.

Table Mountain Pine

Pinus pungens
ALSO CALLED Mountain Pine
HT 20–40'   **DIA** 1–2'

PINE FAMILY   **PINACEAE**

Small evergreen tree. Dwarfed, contorted on mountaintops and windswept sites. **ID TIP:** Table Mountain Pine has very prickly cones and needles, and can occur with 2-needled bundles, unlike the similar Pitch Pine (p. 76), which is always 3-needled. The two species overlap in range, but Pitch Pine extends beyond the Appalachian Mountains, while Table Mountain Pine does not.

HABITAT: Dry rocky ridges and slopes, cliff rims, and plateaus ("table mountains"). Elevation 400–4,500', usually above 1,000'.

NEEDLES 2–3" long, 2 or 3 to a bundle. Stiff, notably sharp-tipped (piercing to the touch), usually twisted. Yellow-green to dark green. Lemony fragrance when crushed. **CONE** 2–3½" long; light brown. Asymmetrical; heavy; in clusters of 3–5. Cones point toward trunk or downward. Broadly ovoid when open. Scales thick, tipped with long, thick "claw." Some cones open at maturity; fire cones may remain on tree for up to 20 years.

Shortleaf Pine

Pinus echinata

HT 70–100'   DIA 1½–3'

Medium-sized to large evergreen tree. Bark reddish brown, in large, flat plates on mature trees, often containing resin pockets between the layers of bark composing the plates. **ID TIP:** Shortleaf is one of two eastern pines with needles shorter than 5" that are not prickly at the tip. The other, the uncommon Spruce Pine, has shorter needles, and its cones have a less-persistent prickle.

HABITAT: Wide range, from old fields to floodplains to dry, rocky slopes. Elevation 0–3,300'.

NOTES: Shortleaf Pine has the most extensive range of any native pine of the eastern United States and grows in a variety of habitats. As one of the East's most important timber and reforestation conifers, it is widely planted. Old-growth Shortleaf Pine forests have been nearly eliminated, and with them the endangered red-cockaded woodpecker and other species that rely on complex ecosystems that tree plantations cannot emulate. The mainstay of the South's timber industry is "southern yellow pine," a loose term for 4 species often marketed interchangeably: Longleaf, Shortleaf, Slash, and Loblolly.

NEEDLES 2¾–4½" long, 2 (sometimes 3) to a bundle. Slender, flexible. Dark green. Twig pale green, often suffused with purple. Winter bud brown. **CONE** 1½–2½" long; dull brown. Ovoid when open. Often in clusters. Scales tipped with short prickle. Opens at maturity; old cones may remain on tree for many years.

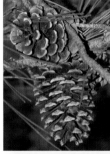

Loblolly Pine

Pinus taeda
ALSO CALLED Bull Pine, Old-field Pine
HT 80–100'   **DIA** 2–3'

Large evergreen tree with tall, straight trunk and large crown. **ID TIP:** Short, sharp, mostly downward-pointing prickles make the cones prickly to the touch.

HABITAT: Wide range, from old fields to old-growth forests, swamps, and floodplains to sandy upland forests. Elevation 0–2,300'.

NOTES: A "loblolly" is a low, boggy or muddy area, and indeed this tree is often found along the margins of swamps. But Loblolly is among the most versatile of eastern pines, growing throughout the Southeast in most habitats. It is also one of the tallest eastern trees (the record height tops 173').

PINE FAMILY   **PINACEAE**

NEEDLES 6–9" long, 3 (rarely 2) to a bundle. Slender, somewhat stiff, often twisted. Yellow-green. Fragrant, especially when crushed. **CONE** 2–6" long; light brown. Ovoid when open. Stalkless or nearly so. Scales tipped with short, sharp prickle. (Cone scales of Pond Pine have weaker prickle.) Cones begin to open at maturity; old cones remain attached for several years.

P. taeda

P. serotina

Pond Pine

Pinus serotina
HT 40–80'   **DIA** 1–2'

ID TIP: Pond Pine is a major component of pocosins, plant- and wildlife-rich southern wetlands. Trees often have many short, needly branches sprouting from the trunk. Cones are top-shaped and grow on a short, thick stalk. Many cones remain closed on the tree until the heat of a fire melts the resin that seals them; long-persisting cones sometimes become embedded in bark. **HABITAT:** Swamps and other wetlands of the southeastern coastal plains. Elevation 0–660'. (See map above.)

PINE FAMILY   **PINACEAE**

NEEDLES 5–8" long, 3 (sometimes 2 or 4) to a bundle. Sharp, twisted, shiny, flexible, 3-sided. Dark yellow-green. Unscented (Loblolly Pine needles are fragrant). **CONE** 2–2½" long; shiny, yellow-brown. Broadly ovoid to rounded when open. Scales tipped with very small prickle (sharp when new, soon shed).

Slash Pine

Pinus elliottii
HT 60–100'   **DIA** 2–2½'

Medium-sized to large evergreen tree. Straight, tall trunk, notably free of branches, and very high, small crown. **ID TIP:** Slash Pine has long needles in bundles of 2 or 3 (often both on same tree). Bark flakes off in thin pieces and is often orange, reddish brown, or purplish.

HABITAT: Moist, coastal plain soils, pond margins, old fields. Elevation 0–500'.

NOTES: Slash Pine is southern Florida's common native pine and the principal pine of Central America and the Caribbean islands. It colonizes burned sites and is a fast-growing ornamental tree. The typical variety of Slash Pine (var. *elliottii*), found from the middle of the Florida peninsula and northward, usually has 3 needles in a bundle. South Florida Slash Pine (var. *densa*) usually has 2 needles per bundle. Seedlings of var. *densa* go through a "grass stage," during which they feature a bunch of needles that looks like a clump of grass.

NEEDLES 8–12" long, 2 or 3 to a bundle. Glossy, stout, stiff. Dark green to blue-green.   **CONE** 3–6" long; shiny, chocolate brown. Ovoid to broadly ovoid when open. Scales tipped with short, stout prickle. Opens at maturity; falls the following year.

Longleaf Pine

Pinus palustris

ALSO CALLED Southern Yellow Pine

HT 60–100'   **DIA** 2–2½'

Medium-sized to large evergreen tree. Straight, tall trunk; high crown of few branches with tufts of needles at their tips. **ID TIP:** Longleaf Pine has the longest needles of the eastern pines, in bundles of 3, and large cones. Ends of branches are thick and stocky (as shown on right side of cone picture); those of Slash Pine are slender.

HABITAT: Wide range; prefers sandy, dry, acid soils of the Atlantic and Gulf coastal plains. Elevation 0–2,300'.

NOTES: Longleaf Pine tolerates many habitats, is fire-adapted, and has a deep taproot (unusual for a conifer). Seedlings start off on the ground as grasslike tufts. When the lumber industry was based on natural stands, Longleaf was the Southeast's most important timber tree, prized worldwide. With plantations taking over, Longleaf Pine is dwindling rapidly, as planters tend to neglect it in favor of faster- and closer-growing species. Natural stands of these pines are scarce and disappearing in many areas; remaining old-growth forests provide habitat for the endangered red-cockaded woodpecker and other vulnerable wildlife.

PINE FAMILY   PINACEAE

winter buds

NEEDLES 8–18" long, 3 to a bundle. Flexible, drooping. Bright green. Clustered at ends of branches in tufts. Winter bud conspicuous, large (1–2"), silvery. **CONE** 6–10" long; brown. Ovoid to cylindrical when open. Usually stalkless. Scales tipped with stout, sharp prickle. Opens at maturity.

Pitch Pine

Pinus rigida
HT 30–60'   **DIA** 1–2'

Small to medium-sized evergreen tree. Ragged and dwarfed in pine barrens and harsh sites on cliffs and high ridges.
ID TIP: Needles are stiff but not prickly; cones bear a small, short-lasting prickle. The only similar tree, Table Mountain Pine (p. 71), has very prickly needles, often 2 to a bundle, and cones with claw-tipped scales, and is restricted to the Appalachians. Tufts of needles may sprout from the trunk of Pitch Pine.

HABITAT: Lowland and upland sandy sites, cliffs, rocky ridges. Elevation 0–4,600'.

NOTES: Pitch Pine is best known as the pine barrens tree of New Jersey. It is fire-adapted; periodic fires clear undergrowth for new seedlings and open resin-sealed cones so they can release seeds. Established trees resprout easily after fire injury. The range of Pitch Pine was once more extensive, but past overcutting for tar and turpentine production has relegated it to only poor sites today.

PINE FAMILY

PINACEAE

NEEDLES 3–5" long, 3 to a bundle. Twisted, stiff. Yellow-green. Twig grayish green when new, becoming orange-brown; older branches brown, flaky, resinous.   **CONE** 1½–3" long; light brown. Broadly ovoid to rounded when open. In clusters of 2 or 3. Scales thick, tipped with curved, ⅛" prickle that is soon shed. Some cones open at maturity; fire cones remain closed on tree for years, opening irregularly or from heat of fire.

Eastern White Pine

Pinus strobus

ALSO CALLED Weymouth Pine, Northern White Pine

HT 80–150' **DIA** 2–5'

PINE FAMILY	PINACEAE

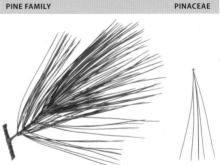

Large evergreen tree with broad crown of distinct tiers of few, widely spaced branches. Develops towering, massive trunk, buttressed at base; old trees can have a small, high crown. **ID TIP:** Eastern White Pine is the only 5-needled native eastern pine, and its long, narrow cone is distinctive in the East.

HABITAT: Cool, upland forests; prefers moist, sandy, acid soils. Elevation 0–4,900'.

NOTES: The East's tallest tree, this pine has been called the "monarch of the eastern forest." A cited "champion" tree had reached a height of about 207' in 1995, when a nearly 25' section of its top was lopped off in a storm. Eastern White Pine was once the world's most important timber tree. Many of the virgin forests were destroyed by the late 1800s, but ancient groves—deep, shady, and evocative of the "forest primeval"—still survive in pockets. The soft, silver-tinted foliage and sturdy, layered branches make this a handsome ornamental in open landscapes.

NEEDLES 2½–5" long, 5 to a bundle. Soft, fine, flexible. Blue-green above; whitish beneath. **CONE** 4–8" long; brown; often whitened at end by resin. Narrowly ovoid to cylindrical when open. Hangs from twig on 1" stalk. Scales thin; lack prickles. Opens at maturity.

Western White Pine

Pinus monticola
ALSO CALLED Mountain White Pine,
Idaho Pine
HT 100–170' **DIA** 2–4'

Very large evergreen tree. Very tall,
straight, often enormous trunk; widely
spaced branches in distinct tiers. **ID TIP:**
In the northern Rockies and much of
the Northwest, this pine has the longest
cones of any native conifer. (From central
Oregon southward, it overlaps the range
of Sugar Pine, which has bigger cones.) In
mature trees the silver-gray bark is broken
into small, squarish plates.

HABITAT: Moist mountain forests; also
grows in wetlands and along coast.
Elevation 0–11,500'.

NOTES: Western White Pine is closely
related to Eastern White Pine and
replaced it as a source for timber after
the East's virgin forests were nearly
all logged. Rampant cutting and the
introduced white pine blister rust have
depleted Western White Pine forests.
Some of the last great stands survive in
Glacier National Park, Montana, and other
protected areas in the northern Rockies.

NEEDLES 2–4" long, 5 to a bundle. Slender, twisted. Pale
green above; blue-green with white lines beneath. **CONE**
5–12" (typically 8") long; reddish brown. Narrowly ovoid to
cylindrical when open. Hangs from 1", curved stalk. Scales
lack prickles. Opens at maturity.

Sugar Pine

Pinus lambertiana
HT 100–200'   DIA 3–6'

Very large evergreen tree. With age, develops huge, notably tall, buttressed trunk, and the crown of massive branches may become flat-topped. **ID TIP:** This very tall-growing pine bears very large and long cones that hang on very long stalks.

HABITAT: Dry to moist mountain forests. Elevation 1,000–10,500'.

NOTES: Sugar Pine is the tallest of the world's pines (one individual reached 268'), and has the largest recorded trunk diameter for a pine (18½'). Trees form magnificent stands in the mountains of Oregon and northern California. The name "Sugar" refers to the sweet resin that exudes from wounded bark. The tree was heavily logged in the late 1800s and early 1900s; today it suffers from a susceptibility to damage from white pine blister rust.

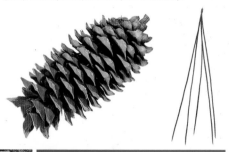

NEEDLES 2½–4" long, 5 to a bundle. Stout, twisted. Deep blue-green above; blue-white with fine white lines beneath. Twig citrus-scented when broken. **CONE** 10–26" (typically 16") long; yellow-brown. Narrowly ovoid to cylindrical when open. Hangs from branch end on 2–6" stalk. Scales thin, glossy, leathery; lack prickles. Opens at maturity.

Whitebark Pine

Pinus albicaulis

ALSO CALLED White Pine, Scrub Pine

HT 20–50' **DIA** 1–2'

Small evergreen tree with a short, twisted trunk. Often dwarfed or multistemmed, especially at windswept sites. **ID TIP:** This high-elevation pine has pale, often silvery bark and very dark, purplish brown cones that remain closed.

HABITAT: Subalpine coniferous forests on high, rocky mountain slopes, to timberline. Elevation 4,300–12,200'.

NOTES: Whitebark Pine grows to the timberline in areas of the northern Rockies and the Northwest, and often has a dramatic, windswept form. The cones do not open on their own; seed-eating wildlife such as Clark's nutcracker pry apart the cone scales to reach the seeds. The disease white pine blister rust has wiped out large numbers of Whitebark Pines, and now the mountain pine beetle is rapidly killing off additional swaths of these trees. Previously restricted by cold to lower elevations, the beetle has moved up to the Whitebark's subalpine habitat as average global temperatures have risen.

PINE FAMILY **PINACEAE**

NEEDLES 1–3" long, 5 to a bundle. Stiff; in tufts near ends of bare branches. Dull yellow-green. Needles have sweet scent and taste. Twig stout, unusually flexible; becomes whitish gray. **CONE** 1–3" long; purple-brown. Ovoid to rounded. Scales thick, with blunt, triangular tip. Cones are opened by animals or decay.

Limber Pine

Pinus flexilis
ALSO CALLED Rocky Mountain
White Pine
HT 40–50'　**DIA** 2–3'

PINE FAMILY	PINACEAE

Small evergreen tree with extremely
flexible branches. Lower branches near
ground level may grow outward farther
than the tree is tall. Dwarfed, gnarled near
timberline. **ID TIP:** Young trees' silvery
gray bark (older trees have darker bark)
resembles that of Whitebark Pine; Limber
Pine has larger, paler brown cones that
open at maturity.

HABITAT: Upper mountain slopes, to
timberline. Elevation 4,900–11,800'.

NOTES: South of Whitebark Pine's
range, in Colorado, the timberline
role is often taken by Limber Pine.
Showing remarkable versatility, Limber
Pine in central Montana becomes the
characteristic tree of the transitional area
between the Rockies and the Great Plains.
Like other northwestern 5-needled pines,
it suffers from white pine blister rust,
especially in Montana. It is named for its
extraordinarily tough and flexible young
branches, which can be bent, looped,
and tied in a knot without breaking. The
"limber" branches enable it to survive the
weight of heavy snow.

NEEDLES 1½–4" long, 5 to a bundle.
Slender, rigid, curved. Glossy, dark
yellow-green above; faintly white-lined
beneath. Tightly clustered toward ends
of very pliable young branches. **CONE**
3–8" long; light brown. Ovoid when
open. Heavy. Scales blunt, very thick;
lack prickle. Opens at maturity.

Intermountain Bristlecone Pine

Pinus longaeva
ALSO CALLED Great Basin Bristlecone Pine
HT 15–40' **DIA** 2–3'

Small evergreen tree that develops a stout, short, often leaning trunk and irregularly shaped crown of hanging, twisted, and gnarled branches; oldest trees have much dead wood. **ID TIP:** Needles are short and packed densely along branches, pointing forward, like a bottlebrush. Cones have long prickles.

HABITAT: Alpine and subalpine zones of desert mountains. Elevation 5,600–11,200'.

NOTES: The uncommon Intermountain Bristlecone Pine is considered earth's longest-living noncloning organism; the oldest known reached 4,844 years. In the oldest groves, fantastically gnarled forms, with strips of living tissue alternating with barren wood, attest to the ages of the trees and the harsh conditions in their timberline habitat. When very large, old trees die, their lifeless trunks may stand for 1,000 years longer. The species is extremely slow-growing; at 700 years a tree may be just 3' tall. The oldest grove is protected in California's Inyo National Forest. The two bristlecone species are very closely related and sometimes have been considered a single species; their ranges do not overlap.

■ *P. aristata*
■ *P. longaeva*

PINE FAMILY **PINACEAE**

NEEDLES ⅝–1¼" long, 5 to a bundle. Stiff, curved, pointed. Deep yellow-green; coated with pale, powdery scales above. Needles remain on tree 10–30 (possibly 40) years. Resin sweet-scented. **CONE** 3–4" long; purple to reddish brown; spotted with shiny, brown resin. Ovoid when open. Nearly stalkless. Scales stiff, thick, tipped with fine, ¹⁄₁₆–¼" long prickle (young cones look bristly). Opens at maturity.

young cone
showing "bristles"

Colorado Bristlecone Pine

Pinus aristata
HT 15–40' **DIA** 1–3'

The maximum known age of this species is 2,435 years. **ID TIP:** Compared to Intermountain Bristlecone, Colorado Bristlecone has slightly longer (1–1½"), sharper needles that are deep blue-green, speckled with tiny resin dots above. Cone is narrower, purple-brown, with stiffer, longer (to ⅜"), curved prickle. Bark is grayer. **HABITAT:** Alpine and subalpine zones in southern Rockies. Elevation 8,200–11,200'. (See map p. 82.)

PINE FAMILY	PINACEAE

Foxtail Pine

Pinus balfouriana
HT 30–50' **DIA** 1–2'

Uncommon, long-lived tree (to about 3,400 years), closely related to the bristlecone pines. Needles may remain on tree for up to 30 years. **ID TIP:** Foxtail Pine, restricted to 2 widely separated areas, has dense, short needles forming bushy, foxtail-like branches. **HABITAT:** Dry, rocky soils in southern Sierra Nevada and Klamath Mountains. Elevation 4,900–11,500'.

PINE FAMILY	PINACEAE

NEEDLES 1–2" long, 5 to a bundle. Densely cover branches. **CONE** 2½–4" long; purplish to red-brown. Narrowly ovoid, with conical base. Scales thick, 4-sided, tipped with tiny, curved prickle. Opens at maturity.

Southwestern White Pine

Pinus strobiformis
HT 50–80' **DIA** 1–3'

A southwestern pine, sometimes considered a subspecies of the more northerly Limber Pine. **ID TIP:** The long, slender cones have scales with slender tips bent back toward the stem. **HABITAT:** Dry mountain slopes. Elevation 6,200–9,800'.

PINE FAMILY	PINACEAE

NEEDLES 2–3½" long, 5 to a bundle. Green, with white lines above. **CONE** 6–9" long; hanging; cylindrical. Scales long, with bent-back tip; lack prickle.

Monterey Pine

Pinus radiata
ALSO CALLED Insignis Pine
HT 40–70' **DIA** 1–3'

Small to medium-sized evergreen tree. Stout, short, usually crooked trunk; crown flat-topped on windswept sites. **ID TIP:** Cones are strongly asymmetrical and often closed; they have thick scales that lack a prominent prickle.

HABITAT AND RANGE: Foggy coastal slopes, with cypress and live oak. Native stands in 3 separate populations on the California coast: in San Mateo–Santa Cruz counties, Monterey County, and San Luis Obispo County; also in Baja California, Mexico. Elevation 100–1,300'.

NOTES: Naturally occurring Monterey Pine is one of the world's rarest pines, restricted to several tiny groves on California's central coast. Thousands of monarch butterflies overwinter in these groves, hanging wings-down from the branches. The tree's cones may remain closed for up to 20 years before opening, usually from very high air temperatures or fire. Groves in protected reserves are maintained by periodic fires. Despite its small natural range, Monterey Pine is an abundantly planted tree. It has reportedly naturalized in other areas along the California coast and north into Oregon.

PINE FAMILY   PINACEAE

NEEDLES 4–6" long, 3 (rarely 2) to a bundle. Slender, flexible. Bright blue-green to dark green. Densely tufted at ends of young branches, pointing outward. **CONE** 3–7" long; yellow-brown to red-brown. Curved, asymmetrical; scales swollen and bulging on one side, flattened on the other, tipped with tiny prickle. Ovoid to broadly ovoid when open. May open at maturity or remain closed and on tree until opened by hot weather or fire.

Torrey Pine

Pinus torreyana
HT 30–50' **DIA** 1–2'

North America's rarest pine, numbering about 3,000 trees. **ID TIP:** The restricted range, long needles in bundles of 5, and large, heavy (up to 1 lb), long-stalked cones characterize this pine. **HABITAT AND RANGE:** Southern California, in 2 coastal cliff sites in San Diego County and 1 site on Santa Rosa Island (Channel Islands). Elevation 0–590'.

PINE FAMILY   PINACEAE

NEEDLES 7–13" long, 5 to a bundle. Dark gray-green with white lines. **CONE** 4–6" long; broadly ovoid to rounded; on long stalk; scales have sharp-pointed, downbent tip.

Knobcone Pine

| PINE FAMILY | PINACEAE |

Pinus attenuata

HT 20–70' **DIA** 1–2½'

Small to medium-sized evergreen tree with a single short, crooked trunk or multiple trunks. **ID TIP:** Asymmetrical, pointed, often closed cones have thick scales with a prominent prickle. Limbs and trunk often ringed with whorls of cones that may become embedded in the bark.

HABITAT: In chaparral on dry, sunny slopes and open woodlands in foothills. Elevation 950–5,900'.

NOTES: Knobcone Pine's cones stay on the tree for so long that bark begins to grow around many of them, and they appear embedded in it. The cones are held closed, often for the life of the tree, by a resin that melts only under very hot temperatures (nearly 400° F). When a fire sweeps through a Knobcone grove, it often kills the standing trees but opens their cones so the seeds are released and a new stand is generated.

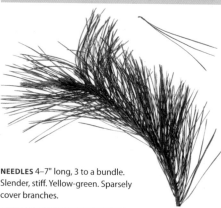

NEEDLES 4–7" long, 3 to a bundle. Slender, stiff. Yellow-green. Sparsely cover branches.

CONE 4–6" long; yellow-brown, becoming gray, weathered. Asymmetrical, knobby, curved, swollen on one side; attached to trunk or encircling stems in tight clusters of usually 3–5 (up to 17). Ovoid when open. Scales tipped with curved prickle. Cones remain closed and on tree until opened by heat of fire.

Coulter Pine

Pinus coulteri
ALSO CALLED Bigcone Pine
HT 40–80' DIA 1–3'

Small to medium-sized evergreen tree.
ID TIP: Coulter Pine bears huge, heavy cones with long, back-curved claws at scale tips.

HABITAT: Hot, dry slopes of the California Coast Ranges, scattered with other conifers and oaks; infrequently in pure stands. Elevation 1,000–6,950'.

NOTES: Coulter Pine has the heaviest cones of any pine. In younger cones the claw-tipped scales point toward the cone tip; in older cones they arch back and point toward the cone base. The large seeds are a substantial wildlife food resource. White-headed woodpeckers forage heavily on Coulter Pines, peeling the bark to reach insects.

NEEDLES 6–12" long, 3 to a bundle. Stiff, sharp, stout. Light gray-green. Grow in tufts at ends of young branches. **CONE** 10–15" long, 6–7" wide; light brown to yellow-brown. Very heavy, to 8 lb (typically 4–6 lb); hangs from stalk to 1" long. Ovoid to cylindrical when open. Scales thick, tipped with 1–1¼", sharp "claw" that becomes back-curved as the cone ages. Cones begin to open at maturity; old cones remain on tree up to 6 years.

Gray Pine

Pinus sabiniana

ALSO CALLED Digger Pine, Ghost Pine, California Foothill Pine

HT 40–75'   **DIA** 1–3'

| PINE FAMILY | PINACEAE |

Small to medium-sized evergreen tree, often with forked or crooked trunk.

ID TIP: Gray Pine has droopy, sparse foliage distinctly grayer than surrounding vegetation, and huge, heavy cones with claw-tipped scales.

HABITAT: Chaparral and coniferous (and sometimes oak) woodlands on dry foothill slopes. Elevation 500–6,200'.

NOTES: Gray Pine has the second-heaviest cones, after Coulter Pine. Its very sparse foliage gives it a "see-through" crown that creates weak shade. Like Coulter Pine, it inhabits hot, dry slopes, but Gray Pine is concentrated farther inland and northward, occupying nearly all slopes surrounding California's Central Valley. It frequently grows with Blue Oak. An oft-used name, Digger Pine, comes from a derogatory term used by settlers to refer to California's native peoples, for whom this was once a major food source.

NEEDLES 8–12" long, 3 to a bundle. Slender, flexible, usually drooping. Gray-green to blue-green. Tufted at ends of stout, young branches. New twig whitish, becoming purple-brown. **CONE** 5–12" long, 5–7" wide; dark brown to light reddish brown. Heavy, ¾–2 lb; hangs from 2" curved stalk. Ovoid to broadly ovoid when open. Scales very thick, woody, tipped with sharp, triangular "claw," up to 1" long, that becomes back-curved as the cone ages. Opens at maturity; old cones remain on tree up to 7 years.

Jeffrey Pine

Pinus jeffreyi

HT 100–150'   **DIA** 4–5'

Very large evergreen tree with tall, straight, stout trunk and narrow crown. Dwarfed (10–20') at highest and harshest sites. **ID TIP:** Jeffrey Pine is similar to Ponderosa Pine, but its cones are larger and less prickly to the touch (because the prickles do not curve strongly outward), its bark is less platelike, and its distribution is confined largely to California.

HABITAT: Dry forests, often on harsh rocky sites or reddish, serpentine soils. Elevation 200–10,200'.

NOTES: The majestic Jeffrey Pine is the typical tree of the Yosemite Valley and Lake Tahoe. It resembles its close relative Ponderosa Pine, but has denser, darker foliage and larger cones. At high elevations, Jeffrey Pines may develop a gnarled, short trunk and a twisted, windswept crown of few, very long branches. **Washoe Pine** (*P. washoensis*), a rare tree of western Nevada and extreme northeastern California, has shorter needles and cones than Jeffrey Pine.

NEEDLES 5–10" long, 3 (sometimes 2) to a bundle. Stout. Blue-green to dark green. Densely cover young branches. Twig fruity- or vanilla-scented when broken. **CONE** 5–15" long; light gray to red-brown. Ovoid when open. Scales tipped with prominent curved prickle. Opens at maturity.

Ponderosa Pine

Pinus ponderosa

ALSO CALLED Western Yellow Pine, Blackjack Pine, Arizona Pine

HT 150–180' **DIA** 4–6'

PINE FAMILY   PINACEAE

Very large evergreen tree. **ID TIP:** Ponderosa Pine often has a straight, tall trunk with bark broken into large, rusty to bright pinkish, orange, or yellow plates outlined in dark gray to black (the black often from charring). Bark is darker in young trees. The cones feel prickly when cupped in the hand.

HABITAT: Wide range, from semiarid to moist mountains, plateaus, valleys; often in extensive forests. Elevation 0–9,800'.

NOTES: Ponderosa Pine is one of the world's tallest pines, sometimes topping 250'. There are several varieties, differing in distribution, needles, cone size, and bark color. **Apache Pine** (*P. engelmannii*), found on dry, rocky slopes and ridges in Mexico and into southern Arizona and New Mexico, strongly resembles Ponderosa Pine, but has longer needles (8–18", the longest among western pines) and mostly larger cones (4–5½" long).

NEEDLES 5–11" long, 3 to a bundle (some populations with 2 or 5). Sharp, stiff. Dark yellow-green to gray-green. Grow in tufts at branch tips. Broken twig has resinous, turpentine-like or orangy aroma, varying by tree. **CONE** 2½–5" long; shiny, reddish brown. Sometimes asymmetrical. Ovoid to broadly ovoid when open. Stalkless or nearly so. Scales tipped with rigid, sharp prickle. Opens at maturity; after cones fall, some scales remain on branches .

Bishop Pine

Pinus muricata

HT 40–80' **DIA** 2–3'

ID TIP: This 2-needled pine has distinctive, spiny, humpbacked cones in clusters of 3–7. Cones remain closed and hanging on the tree for up to 70 years, until opened by heat of fire.

HABITAT: Near the coast on dry ridges and bluffs, sometimes around bogs, often forming wind-shorn forests. Elevation 0–1,000'.

NEEDLES Needles 3–6" long, 2 to a bundle. **CONE** 1½–3½" long, asymmetrical, curved, usually in whorls on branch. Scales tipped with stout "claw."

PINE FAMILY   PINACEAE

Chihuahua Pine

Pinus leiophylla var. *chihuahuana*

HT 30–80' **DIA** 1–3'

ID TIP: Chihuahua Pine, primarily a Mexican species, and Mexican Pinyon (p. 93) are both short-needled pines with 3 needles to a bundle. Chihuahua has ovoid cones, and old cones remain on the tree. Mexican Pinyon has more spherical cones that fall from the tree after they open.

HABITAT: Dry, rocky slopes and ridges. Elevation 4,900–8,200'.

NEEDLES 2–5" long, 3 (rarely 2–5) to a bundle. **CONE** 1½–2" long; broadly ovoid; on ½" stalk. Scales may have prickle. Old cones remain on tree after opening.

PINE FAMILY   PINACEAE

Lodgepole Pine

Pinus contorta
HT 30–100' **DIA** 1–3'

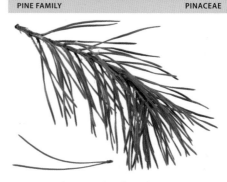

Small to large evergreen tree. Form varies from straight, slender trunk with high, narrow crown to short, crooked trunk with flat-topped crown. **ID TIP:** Over most of its range, Lodgepole Pine has short, yellow-green needles and very flaky bark. The rather asymmetrical, small cones have a prickle at each scale tip.

HABITAT: Forests, mainly in mountains. Elevation 0–11,500'.

NOTES: Over its range *Pinus contorta* is variable in stature and features of bark, needles, and cones. Typical Lodgepole Pine (var. *latifolia*) is a common tree of the West. Sierra Lodgepole Pine (var. *murrayana*), from the Cascades, Sierra Nevada, and southern California mountains, has more symmetrical cones and branches that usually ascend (rather than spread) at the tip. Shore or Beach Pine (var. *contorta*) grows near the coast, to only about 30' tall, and may be wind-sheared and contorted. It has asymmetrical, persistent cones that open from heat of fire.

NEEDLES 1–3" long, 2 to a bundle. Stiff, sharp, twisted. Dark green to yellow-green. **CONE** 1–2½" long; purple-brown. Ovoid to broadly ovoid when open. Some populations asymmetrical. Scales tipped with stiff, curved prickle. Depending on variety, opens at maturity and drops soon after, or remains closed and attached for years; some open from heat of fire.

Pinyon

Pinus edulis

ALSO CALLED Piñón, Two-needle Pinyon, Colorado Pinyon

HT 15–35'   **DIA** 1–2'

Small evergreen tree; sometimes a shrub. **ID TIP:** Pinyon is a 2-needled pine with a short, sometimes twisted trunk; a dense, compact crown; and small, rounded cones with thick scales and very large, nutlike seeds.

HABITAT: Dry plateaus and mountain slopes. Elevation 4,900–8,900'.

NOTES: Four small, shrubby, drought-tolerant pines of the Southwest and Mexico that yield large edible seeds are called "pinyons." The seeds, commonly known as "pine nuts," are harvested for culinary usage (though many pine nuts sold in North America are imported). This pinyon is one of the typical trees of the Grand Canyon rim and is the only pinyon over most of its range.

NEEDLES ¾–2" long, 2 (sometimes 1 or 3) to a bundle. Stiff, sharp. Dark green above, light green beneath. New twig orange or pinkish, becoming bluish brown or gray. **CONE** 1–2¾" wide; shiny, yellow-brown to red-brown. Broadly ovoid to rounded when open. Strongly resinous. Scales thick. Opens at maturity.

Singleleaf Pinyon

Pinus monophylla
HT 16–30' **DIA** 1–1½'

Singleleaf is the pinyon of the Great Basin; its range overlaps with Parry Pinyon in southern California. **ID TIP:** Singleleaf Pinyon is the world's only 1-needled pine. Each needle is wrapped at the base in a translucent sheath (as are the needle "bundles" in other pines). **HABITAT:** Dry mountain slopes, plateaus, and canyons. Elevation 3,300–7,500'.

PINE FAMILY	PINACEAE

NEEDLES ¾–2" long, 1 (sometimes 2) to a bundle. Curved, stiff, sharp. Gray-green to blue-green. **CONE** Small; broadly ovoid to rounded; few thick scales. Large, edible seeds.

Mexican Pinyon

Pinus cembroides
HT 16–20' **DIA** 1'

This small, shrubby pine is the common pinyon (*piñón* in Spanish) of Mexico. **ID TIP:** Unlike other pinyons, it typically has 3 needles to a bundle. **HABITAT:** Hot, dry slopes near the Mexican border from Arizona to Texas and southward. Elevation 5,000–7,500'.

PINE FAMILY	PINACEAE

NEEDLES 1–2½" long, 3 (occasionally 2 or 4) to a bundle. Flexible. Gray-green.

Parry Pinyon

Pinus quadrifolia
HT 16–30' **DIA** 1–1½'

Parry has the most limited distribution of the four pinyons. **ID TIP:** Parry Pinyon is the only pine with typically 4 needles to a bundle. **HABITAT:** Dry slopes, from near San Diego southward into Baja California. Elevation 3,900–5,900'.

PINE FAMILY	PINACEAE

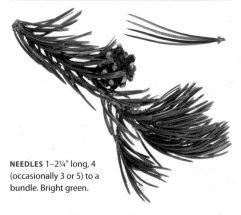

NEEDLES 1–2¼" long, 4 (occasionally 3 or 5) to a bundle. Bright green.

Larches and True Cedars

Larix, the larches, and *Cedrus,* true cedars, are two relatively minor genera of the pine family (Pinaceae) that share a distinctive, easily recognized needle arrangement: tufts of 10–60 needles that grow from spur twigs (very short side branchlets). In larches the needles burst from the spur tip in a single tuft, while in cedars they may sprout from along the spur twig. In both tree types, some needles near the branch ends are borne singly. In cross section the needles are more or less three-edged—flattened on top, keeled beneath—ranging to a four-edged rhomboid shape in some cedars. Apart from needle arrangement, larches and true cedars have little in common. (For more on true cedars, see page 98.)

Tamarack (pictured) and the other larches have deciduous needles that turn yellow and drop off the tree in autumn.

Larches are among the few deciduous conifers: all of their needles turn golden yellow in autumn, and then drop off. The leafless branches are punctuated with peglike spur twigs—a clue that the tree is not a dead evergreen of another genus. When new in spring the needles are tender (and prized as food by grouse) and pale grassy green, contrasting with the usually darker green of neighboring conifers.

Larch cones grow on very short spur twigs on year-old branchlets, and are concentrated in the upper part of the tree. At pollination time the small, ovoid cones are soft (and may be yellow or deep red). They mature and open that same year, and may persist on the tree for several years. Bristlelike bracts protrude from between the scales of the western larch species.

Larix is the conifer genus with the most northerly distribution (larch forests cloak Siberia), which is at odds with the broad trend toward increasing evergreenness in more northerly zones. In mountains where Subalpine Larch grows, it reaches higher elevations than any other tree.

European Larch

Larix decidua
ALSO CALLED Common Larch
HT 40–70'   **DIA** 2'

Small to medium-sized deciduous tree. **ID TIP:** European Larch has longer, more densely clustered needles and larger, more numerous cones than Tamarack. **HABITAT AND RANGE:** Introduced in North America; naturalized, mainly in northeastern United States. Native to Europe. **NOTES:** In Europe, where it is known as Common Larch, this tree can top 150' and attain a trunk diameter of 9'.

PINE FAMILY   **PINACEAE**

NEEDLES 1–1½" long. Bright green; turn golden yellow in autumn before shedding. **CONE** 1–1¼" long. Reddish brown; hairy. Numerous scales; 3-pronged bracts mostly not visible between scales.

Tamarack

Larix laricina

ALSO CALLED Eastern Larch, Hackmatack

HT 40–80'   **DIA** 1–2'

PINE FAMILY   PINACEAE

Small to medium-sized deciduous tree with a sparse, open crown. Dwarfed near timberline. **ID TIP:** Tamarack is the only native eastern conifer with deciduous needles in radiating clusters growing from blunt spurs. Cones are small and often egg-shaped, with no bracts showing. Foliage turns yellow in autumn. The introduced European Larch has larger, hairy cones with more scales.

HABITAT: Bogs, swamps, and lakeshores to upland slopes. Elevation 0–3,900'.

NOTES: Tamarack ranges across the North American continent and is one of the few native deciduous conifers in the East. It thrives even at the Arctic tree line, keeping an erect though tiny tree form in areas where Black and White spruces are reduced to ground-hugging shrubs.

NEEDLES ¾–1¼" long. Dark green; turn yellow in autumn before shedding. Soft, slender, pointed. **CONE** ½–¾" long (smaller than Western Larch); rounded to ovoid. Purplish red (rarely yellow), turning brown. Scales rounded; bracts not visible between scales (compare Western Larch).

Western Larch

Larix occidentalis

ALSO CALLED Western Tamarack

HT 80–150' **DIA** 1½–5'

Large deciduous tree with thin crown of sparse, horizontal branches. **ID TIP:** From a distance, larch trees stand out from the forest by foliage color alone—pale grass green in spring and summer, yellow in fall. Western Larch cones reveal yellowish, bristlelike bracts.

HABITAT: Mountain slopes and valleys, sometimes on swampy ground; often with Douglas-fir and Ponderosa Pine. Elevation 1,600–6,900'.

NOTES: Western Larch's thick bark enables it to survive many fires and live longer than most of its associates. But a larch stand cannot survive lack of fire indefinitely, for in its shade other species will gradually take over. The largest of all larches, Western Larch can reach 200' in height. It is a preferred foraging and cavity species for the pileated woodpecker. The wood is heavy, close-grained, and durable for a conifer.

NEEDLES 1–1¾" long. Bright green; turn yellow in autumn before shedding. Soft, pointed. Twig hairless. **CONE** 1–1½" long. Purplish brown to reddish brown. Rigid. Scales round-tipped, finely hairy. Yellowish, pointed, bristlelike bracts stick straight out from between scales.

Subalpine Larch

Larix lyallii

ALSO CALLED Alpine Tamarack, Mountain Larch, Alpine Larch

HT 30–50' **DIA** 1–2'

PINE FAMILY   PINACEAE

Small deciduous tree with crown of short, sparse, sometimes drooping and crooked branches. Dwarfed near timberline.

ID TIP: The least common of the larches, Subalpine has the largest cones, with purplish, bristlelike bracts.

HABITAT: Open, rocky, subalpine to timberline sites. Elevation 5,900–7,900'.

NOTES: In the harsh environment occupied by Subalpine Larch, in such remote locations as Washington's North Cascades National Park, snow can fall in any month, and the winter's accumulation lingers on much of the ground well into July or August. These larches leaf out typically before the ground under them is bare, displaying perhaps 4 months of summer greenery before decorating the stark subalpine landscape with a brilliant, golden foliage display.

NEEDLES 1–1¼" long. Blue-green; turn yellow in autumn before shedding. Soft, pointed. New twig covered in white hairs. **CONE** 1½–2" long (larger than Western Larch). Purple-brown to brown. Scales round-tipped, densely hairy. Purplish, 3-pronged, recurved bracts protrude from between scales.

True Cedars

Cedrus species

HT 50–100'   **DIA** 3'

PINE FAMILY   PINACEAE

Native to the Mediterranean and Himalayan regions, true cedars are planted in North America but do not commonly naturalize here. (True cedars are not related to the native conifers of the cypress family that we commonly refer to as "cedars"; pp. 133–139.) We describe the typical forms of true cedars here; extreme growth forms and color variants are also cultivated.

Deodar Cedar

NEEDLES ½–2" long; fairly stiff, even prickly. Like larch needles, they grow in tufts from short spur twigs, but unlike larches needles are evergreen. In tufts of as many as 30–40 needles. In cross section, needles are 3-edged—flattened on top, keeled beneath—to 4-edged, in a rhomboid shape.

CONES 2–5" long; ovoid. Closed and green to purplish in first year, light brown to gray in second year; often dripped with resin. Cones stand upright like little barrels on the branches (a characteristic shared with the true firs, p. 108). Scales are thin, dense, and numerous. Scales and seeds fall singly in winter, thickly littering the ground. Cones mature in their second or third year, so a tree may have young, solid cones and older, disintegrating ones at the same time.

Cedar of Lebanon

Cedar of Lebanon

Cedrus libani

Medium-sized evergreen tree. Develops a wide, umbrella- or candelabra-like shape with age. **ID TIP:** Cedar of Lebanon has longer needles (¾–1¼" long) than Atlas Cedar, shorter than Deodar Cedar. They resemble larch needles but are stiff (even prickly) and evergreen. Branch tips are more or less straight. Cones are 3–5" long (larger than cones of Western Larch, p. 96). **HABITAT AND RANGE:** Cultivated ornamental in North America, mainly in Southeast and on West Coast. Native to southwestern Asia (national symbol of Lebanon).

Cedar of Lebanon

Cedar of Lebanon

Cedar of Lebanon

Deodar Cedar
Cedrus deodara

Large evergreen tree, often with drooping branches. **ID TIP:** Deodar has larger cones (3–5" long) than Atlas Cedar and longer needles (2" long) than Atlas or Cedar of Lebanon. **HABITAT AND RANGE:** Introduced in North America; cultivated mainly in Southeast and on West Coast. Native to western Himalayas, at up to 13,000' elevation.

Deodar Cedar

Deodar Cedar

Atlas Cedar
Cedrus atlantica

Medium-sized evergreen tree; often very wide-spreading. **ID TIP:** Needles shorter (½–¾" long) and cones smaller (2–3" long) than in Deodar Cedar and Cedar of Lebanon. **HABITAT AND RANGE:** Cultivated ornamental in North America. Native to the Atlas Mountains of northern Africa.

Atlas Cedar

Atlas Cedar

Atlas Cedar

Spruces

Spruces, trees of the genus *Picea* in the family Pinaceae, can be recognized by their needles, which radiate almost equally in all directions around the branch, like the bristles on a bottlebrush. The name "needles" is appropriate for spruce leaves, as they are stiff and sharp enough (except on Black Spruce) to feel prickly when you grab a branch. The needles grow singly from the ends of short, peglike projections of the twig. These projections make needleless dead twigs rough to the touch. In all spruces except the two Northwest coast species Sitka and Brewer spruces, the needles, as seen under a hand lens, are clearly four-sided, four-angled, and four-striped, with whitish lines of minute pores.

The thin-scaled, lightweight, ovoid to oblong or cylindrical spruce cones tend to be concentrated in the upper branches, hanging downward near the ends of year-old branchlets. (True fir cones also grow near treetops, but they stand upright rather than hang, a difference that can be seen with binoculars.) Spruce cones mature in their first fall, opening and releasing seeds, and generally fall off within a year, except in White Spruce, which can keep cones for two years, and Black Spruce, which may retain cones for more than 30 years.

In addition to seed cones and pollen cones, a third type of "cone," bristling with needlelike points, is often seen at the tips of spruce branches. In fact, these are needles and branch tips that have been attacked by aphidlike parasites called spruce gall adelgids. These insects induce the tree

to form the conelike galls, which protect them while they suck juices from needle bases. The pests rarely kill their hosts, but the tree's growth is somewhat slowed and distorted as these branch tips are aborted. A native spruce gall adelgid infests Blue, Sitka, and Engelmann spruces, while a European species infests Norway Spruce.

Spruces are a northerly genus, centered only a little farther south than larches. Most spruces have no defense against fire except their tolerance or preference for cold sites and wet soils, which helps keep fires away from them. The retained cones on White and Black spruces function like fire cones on pines, releasing seeds onto a fire-prepared seedbed.

woody pegs

Left: Spruce needles radiate from all around the branch, and each needle is mounted on a miniscule, woody, peglike projection. After spruce needles fall, the woody pegs remain, making the branch feel rough to the touch. Above: Sitka Spruce, a characteristic species of the temperate rain forests of the Pacific Northwest, is the tallest and most massive of spruces.

Red Spruce

Picea rubens

ALSO CALLED Eastern Spruce,
Yellow Spruce

HT 50–80'   **DIA** 1–2'

PINE FAMILY   PINACEAE

Medium-sized evergreen tree. Dwarfed
or shrubby at high elevations. **ID TIP:** Red
Spruce has smaller cones, with brittle
scales, than White Spruce. Its yellow-
tinged (rather than blue-tinged) needle
color and more southerly distribution
help distinguish it from both Black and
White spruces.

HABITAT: Mountain forests of the East.
Elevation 0–6,643'.

NOTES: This species has shown extensive
vulnerability to acid rain, and millions
of trees have suffered from its effects,
including an increased susceptibility
to winter damage. It sometimes grows
with fir species at high elevations; firs are
easily recognized by their upright, barrel-
shaped cones. Red Spruce reaches an
elevation of 6,643' at Clingmans Dome on
the Tennessee–North Carolina border, the
highest peak in Great Smoky Mountains
National Park.

NEEDLES ¼–¾" long. Shiny, yellow-green to bright
green with white stripes. Stiff, slender, sharp-pointed.
Applelike and balsam scents when crushed. Twig hairy
or hairless. **CONE** 1¼–1½" long. Glossy, orange-brown to
reddish brown. Ovoid, rigid. Scales stiff; broad, rounded at
tip; edges irregularly finely toothed.

White Spruce

Picea glauca
HT 40–100' **DIA** 1–2'

PINE FAMILY   PINACEAE

Small to large evergreen tree. Dwarfed or shrubby at tree line. **ID TIP:** The odd needle odor—unpleasant and skunky to some, fruitlike to others—identifies White Spruce immediately. The sharp needles and hairless twigs distinguish it from Black Spruce.

HABITAT: Boreal forests, bogs, and uplands. Elevation 0–5,000'.

NOTES: White Spruce is one of North America's hardiest and most northerly trees, its range extending north of the Arctic Circle. The tallest White Spruce trees are in a disjunct population called Black Hills Spruce found in western South Dakota and eastern Wyoming.

NEEDLES ½–¾" long. Blue-green with white stripes. Sharp-tipped. Strong, fruity to malodorous scent when crushed. Twig hairless. **CONE** 1½–2½" long. Shiny, pale brown. Cylindrical. Scales thin, flexible; broad, rounded at tip; edges untoothed. Cones can persist for 2 years.

Black Spruce

Picea mariana
ALSO CALLED Bog Spruce,
Swamp Spruce
HT 20–60'   **DIA** 6–12"

PINE FAMILY   PINACEAE

Small to medium-sized evergreen tree, often with spindly trunk. Dwarfed or shrubby at tree line. **ID TIP:** Black Spruce has hairy twigs and small cones with toothed scale edges. Cones remain on the tree, sometimes for years, after releasing seeds. (In other spruces, cones drop after they open.)

HABITAT: Boreal forests, often in damp soils of swamps and bogs; mountains. Elevation 0–4,900'.

NOTES: Black Spruce is an abundant and widespread conifer. In harsh, northern sites, trees are often dwarfed, and their height may not exceed the average snow depth. The spruce grouse is dependent on the needles of this and other spruces for sustenance.

NEEDLES ¼–¾" long. Pale blue-green with white stripes. Stiff, usually blunt-tipped, not sharp or prickly. Pleasant resinous or menthol scent when crushed. Twig finely hairy. **CONE** ½–1¼" long. Purplish when young (shown on tree below), turning brown to dull gray-brown. Ovoid. Often densely clustered at top of tree. Scales stiff; broad, rounded at tip; edges irregularly finely toothed. Old cones persist several years after maturity.

Engelmann Spruce

Picea engelmannii

HT 80–125'   **DIA** 1½–3'

Large evergreen tree. Dwarfed near timberline. **ID TIP:** The bluish green needles are somewhat flexible and less prickly than those of Blue or Sitka Spruce but still more prickly than nonspruces such as Douglas-fir (p. 109). Cones are smaller than those of Blue Spruce.

HABITAT: Mid- to high elevations of the Cascades and Rockies; often grows with Subalpine Fir and Rocky Mountain Alpine Fir (p. 112). Elevation 2,000–12,000'.

NOTES: Engelmann and White spruces sometimes hybridize where the two species overlap (mainly in British Columbia); the latter has shorter needles, and cones with round-edged, untoothed scales.

NEEDLES ¾–1⅛" long. Steel blue to dark blue-green, with white stripes. Flexible; sharp-pointed. Camphorlike scent when crushed, often regarded as unpleasant. Twig usually finely hairy. **CONE** 1½–2½" long. Glossy, light brown. Cylindrical to ovoid. Scales thin, flexible; narrow, sometimes pointed at tip; edges irregularly toothed.

Blue Spruce

Picea pungens
ALSO CALLED Colorado Blue Spruce,
Silver Spruce
HT 70–100'   **DIA** 1½–3'

Medium-sized to large evergreen tree.
ID TIP: The needles are stiff, prickly, and
variably blue-tinged. Blue Spruce has
a symmetrical, pyramidal shape when
young and growing in the open.

HABITAT: Along streams and on slopes.
Elevation 5,900–9,800'.

NOTES: Blue Spruce is a native species
of the central and southern Rocky
Mountains. The blue tint of its foliage,
caused by waxes on the needle's surface,
and its regular, pyramidal shape (which
can be lost with age) have made it a
desirable ornamental tree; it is now more
common in cultivation than in its natural,
wild state. (There are several dozen
cultivated forms available, bred for various
shape and color characteristics.) Many
wild populations are not notably blue.

PINE FAMILY   PINACEAE

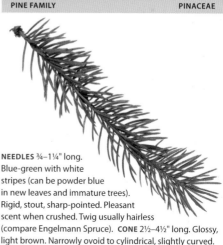

NEEDLES ¾–1¼" long.
Blue-green with white
stripes (can be powder blue
in new leaves and immature trees).
Rigid, stout, sharp-pointed. Pleasant
scent when crushed. Twig usually hairless
(compare Engelmann Spruce). **CONE** 2½–4½" long. Glossy,
light brown. Narrowly ovoid to cylindrical, slightly curved.
Scales thin, flexible; broad to narrow at tip; edges irregularly
toothed.

Sitka Spruce

Picea sitchensis
ALSO CALLED Coast Spruce,
Tideland Spruce
HT 150–200'   **DIA** 4–10'

Very large evergreen tree. Develops
enormous, fluted trunk with huge,
buttressed base. **ID TIP:** The needles of
Sitka Spruce are white-striped above,
sharp, and flat in cross section (needles
are 4-sided in all other common spruces).

HABITAT: Wet forests of the Pacific
Northwest, including temperate rain
forest; rarely more than 50 miles from the
coast. Elevation 0–3,000'.

NOTES: Sitka Spruce is a record-setter:
the world's largest and tallest spruce
(recorded at 317' tall, diameter to 18½');
one of the largest of all trees; and among
the fastest-growers, able to reach 200'
in 100 years. Seedlings of this tree often
sprout on top of fallen trees called nurse
logs; eventually the nurse log rots away,
leaving a hollow beneath the Sitka
Spruce, which perches on stiltlike roots.
Old trees are sometimes topped with
multiple crown leaders if lightning or
wind has shattered the original one. A
primeval Sitka Spruce forest can be seen
in Olympic National Park, Washington.

PINE FAMILY   **PINACEAE**

NEEDLES ½–1" long. Dark green, with white stripe above;
foliage appears blue-gray at a distance. Rigid, very sharp-
pointed; flat in cross section. Twig hairless. **CONE** 2½–4"
long. Light orange-brown (Brewer Spruce cone is purple-
tinged). Narrowly ovoid to cylindrical. Scales thin, stiff;
narrow at tip; edges irregularly toothed or wavy.

trees growing on nurse log

Brewer Spruce

Picea breweriana
ALSO CALLED Weeping Spruce
HT 70–100' **DIA** 1½–3'

PINE FAMILY **PINACEAE**

Medium-sized to large evergreen tree.
ID TIP: Rare spruce with flexible, whiplike, "weeping" branches, an adaptation to the heavy snows of its native range. Cones are purple-tinged, with broad, untoothed scale edges; twigs are hairy; and needles are blunt-tipped and flat or triangular in cross section.

HABITAT: Alpine forests in Siskiyou Mountains. Elevation 3,300–7,500'.

Norway Spruce

Picea abies
HT 80–100' **DIA** 2'

PINE FAMILY **PINACEAE**

Large evergreen tree with broadly conical form, often very wide base. **ID TIP:** The cones are long and narrow and have flexible scales. Needle-clad branchlets often hang like drapery from larger branches.

HABITAT AND RANGE: Introduced in North America; naturalized in areas of the Northeast, the Great Lakes states, and southeastern Canada. Native to Europe.

NEEDLES ½–1" long. Shiny, dark green with white stripes. Stiff, slender, sharp-pointed. Camphorlike scent when crushed. Twig smooth, usually hairless. **CONE** 4–7¼" long. Light brown. Cylindrical, slightly curved. Scales thin, flexible; broad to narrow and sometimes pointed at tip; edges irregularly toothed.

True Firs and Douglas-firs

In true firs (genus *Abies*) and Douglas-firs (*Pseudotsuga*), both in the family Pinaceae, the needles grow singly on the twig, as in spruces, but are arranged, more or less, in two rows, growing outward from the twig and often forming a flattish spray. This arrangement can be highly variable in both genera, and in firs, particularly, even between upper and lower limbs on the same individual tree, frequently ranging from flat to a half-round bottlebrush shape to a seemingly single-row toothbrushlike array. In spite of the variability, there is almost always a notable lack of needles on the twig's underside (in contrast to spruces, which do carry needles on the underside).

Spruce needles are attached to tiny, individual wooden pegs. The needles of true firs and Douglas-firs are attached directly to the twig, but the two differ from each other in needle attachment: in *Abies*, the base of the needle looks like a suction-cup stuck to the twig, and the needle scar is flat; in *Pseudotsuga* the suction-cup base is not nearly as prominent, and the base (away from the twig tip) of the scar is slightly raised. Another easy distinction between the two genera, important when there are no cones (as is often the case with *Abies*), can be seen in the buds at the end of the twig: in *Abies* the buds are blunt and usually covered with a gummy resin; in *Pseudotsuga* the buds are sharply pointed, shiny, and nonresinous.

The two genera are easily distinguished by their cones. The cones of Douglas-firs hang from various points along the outer portions of branches, and are generally abundant on the ground beneath trees. A three-pointed bract sticks out from each cone scale. Douglas-fir needles taper to a slender, but not truly sharp, point.

True fir cones, in contrast to those of Douglas-firs, are rarely seen up close, as they grow on the uppermost branches of the tree. They perch standing upright, often oozing resin. At maturity, fir cones drop their scales and seeds one at a time until only the naked core of the cone is left on the branch. No other conifers except true cedars (page 98) have erect, disintegrating cones. When you do see a fir cone on the ground, completely closed, dense, and heavy, usually with a bit of branch attached, it's because a squirrel has harvested it. The squirrel will come back to pick it apart, leaving heaps of cone scales. The cones of many fir species are colorful when new (in spring); these colors are described in the species texts. All fir cones eventually turn brown when they mature and open in the fall. On young true firs, the bark is smooth except for horizontally elongated blisters full of resin. True fir needles are either rounded or notched at the tip. The leaf pores are crowded, appearing as two white stripes on the underside of each needle, plus another one or two on the upperside in some species.

True fir cones, often colorful when new, then brown, sit erect on branches and disintegrate while on the tree. Douglas-fir cones hang, have 3-pronged bracts, and fall to the ground intact.

Douglas-fir

Pseudotsuga menziesii
ALSO CALLED Douglas-spruce,
Oregon-pine
HT 80–200' DIA 2–5'

PINE FAMILY   PINACEAE

Very large (coast variety) or medium-sized to large (Rocky Mountain variety) evergreen tree. Broadly conical, pointed crown of long branches. ID TIP: Douglas-fir is easily identified by the 3-pronged bracts projecting from between the cone scales.

HABITAT: Forests on coastal and mountain slopes. Elevation 0–11,000'.

NOTES: Douglas-fir is North America's second-tallest tree—recorded at 329' tall and exceeded only by the Redwood—and may once have been the tallest, possibly topping 400' in the past. Coast Douglas-fir (var. *menziesii*), a massive tree (diameter exceeding 15') of moist habitats, has longer, yellow-green needles and larger cones (to 4") with straight bracts pressed against the cone. The drought-tolerant Rocky Mountain Douglas-fir (var. *glauca*) is smaller (rarely exceeding 3' in diameter or 100' in height) and bears shorter, blue-green needles and smaller cones (less than 3") with upward-bent bracts.

NEEDLES ¾–1¼" long. Dark, yellow-green (coast variety) or blue-green (Rocky Mountain variety); white-lined beneath. Flexible, grooved above, not prickly (unlike spruce needles); flat in cross section. Sweet, fruity-resinous scent when crushed (coast variety). CONE 2–4" long. Light brown. Ovoid; short-stalked; hangs from twig (fir cones are erect). Long, 3-pronged bracts, upcurved in inland trees, straight in coastal trees, protrude from between cone scales.

Bigcone Douglas-fir

Pseudotsuga macrocarpa
ALSO CALLED Bigcone-spruce
HT 40–80' **DIA** 2–3'

Limited to southern California, Bigcone does not overlap with the larger, more widespread Douglas-fir in range. It can respond to fire by generating new growth from its trunk and branches. **ID TIP:** Bigcone is a smaller tree than Douglas-fir; it has sharper, grayer needles and longer cones with shorter, rigid bracts.

HABITAT: Chaparral and open woodlands in California's dry southwestern mountains. Elevation 650–7,900'.

PINE FAMILY   **PINACEAE**

NEEDLES 1–1¾" long. Bluish to grayish green. Tip pointed. **CONE** 4–8" long. Brown. Oblong; hangs from twig. Short, stiff, 3-pronged bracts protrude from between cone scales.

Fraser Fir

Abies fraseri
ALSO CALLED Southern Balsam Fir
HT 30–50' **DIA** 1–2'

The Southeast's only native fir, limited in the wild, but widely planted in tree farms. Its numbers have collapsed since the introduction of an insect pest, balsam woolly adelgid. Fraser Fir reaches an elevation of 6,684' at Mount Mitchell, North Carolina, the East's highest peak. **ID TIP:** Shorter than Balsam Fir, Fraser Fir has purplish cone scales obscured by papery, greenish to tan bracts; silvery needles; and reddish, hairy twigs.

HABITAT: Mountain forests, often with Red Spruce, in southern Appalachians. Elevation 4,000–6,684'.

PINE FAMILY   **PINACEAE**

NEEDLES ½–1" long. Lustrous, dark green above; silvery, white-lined beneath. Grooved; tip blunt or notched; flat in cross section. Curving upward on twig. Strong, turpentine-like odor when crushed. Twig reddish, hairy. **CONE** 1½–3" long. Purplish. Conspicuous papery bracts, greenish, turning tan, bent downward over cone scales.

Balsam Fir

Abies balsamea
ALSO CALLED Canada Balsam,
Eastern Fir
HT 40–60'   DIA 1–1½'

Small to medium-sized evergreen tree. Pointed, spirelike crown. Near timberline, dwarfed or shrubby, twisted, multistemmed, flat-topped. ID TIP: Balsam Fir is strongly fragrant and is the only common fir in the East. The rarer, more southerly Fraser Fir has longer-protruding bracts between cone scales.

HABITAT: Moist, acid, organic soils; swamps; also mountains. Elevation 0–5,600'.

NOTES: Balsam Fir is North America's most widely distributed fir and a primary component of northern Canada's vast boreal forest. The redolent foliage makes it a common choice for Christmas trees and wreaths. The tree produces a resin, called Canada balsam, that hardens into a clear cement used for optical and microscope products.

NEEDLES ½–1¼" long. Glossy, dark green above; white-lined beneath. Grooved; tip notched or pointed but not prickly; flat in cross section. Arranged in flat sprays. Strong piney scent, especially when crushed. Twig yellow-green to gray. CONE 2–4" long. Purple, turning bluish brown. Cylindrical, tapering at the end; standing upright on branch. Resinous; papery bracts hidden or only slightly protruding.

Subalpine Fir/Rocky Mountain Alpine Fir

Abies lasiocarpa/bifolia
ALSO CALLED Alpine Fir
HT 50–100' **DIA** 1–2½'

Medium-sized to large evergreen tree. Narrowly conical crown with sharply pointed, spirelike tip. Trees above timberline are bent or dwarfed. **ID TIP:** Needles are flat in cross section and white-lined on both upper and lower surfaces.

HABITAT: Mountain forests. Elevation 2,000–11,800'.

NOTES: Subalpine Fir is a variable tree that is common in western subalpine zones from Yukon to Oregon to New Mexico. Some authorities recognize 2 separate species: Subalpine Fir (*A. lasiocarpa*), in the coastal mountains of Canada south into the Cascades; and Rocky Mountain Alpine Fir (*A. bifolia*), spanning the length of the Rockies. Other experts have not recognized the split but acknowledge that the species may require revision. A southwestern population called Corkbark Fir (sometimes classified as *A. lasiocarpa* var. *arizonica*) has soft, corky, whitish bark.

PINE FAMILY **PINACEAE**

NEEDLES ¾–1½" long. Bluish green; 1 white line above and 2 beneath. Grooved above; tip blunt or slightly notched; flat in cross section. Generally swept forward in a half-round bottlebrush arrangement. Sharp, balsam scent, especially when crushed. **CONE** 2–5" long. Dark purple to grayish purple. Cylindrical, slender; standing upright on branch. Bracts not visible.

■ *A. lasiocarpa*
■ *A. bifolia*

White Fir/ Sierra White Fir

Abies concolor/lowiana
ALSO CALLED Rocky Mountain
White Fir
HT 70–150'   **DIA** 1½–4'

Medium-sized to large evergreen tree with slender, pointed crown. **ID TIP:** At least some of the needles usually exceed 2¼", except in California, where they are distinguished from Grand Fir by relatively uniform length.

HABITAT: Mountain forests, dry uplands. Elevation 3,000–11,200'.

NOTES: White Fir (*A. concolor*) is quite variable, and populations differ from one another in needle length, twig hairiness, and other details. Most authorities recognize Sierra White Fir as a separate species (*A. lowiana*) or a distinct variety. Sierra White Fir grows in moister soils than typical White Fir and has a mainly California range. It is a larger tree (in Yosemite National Park topping 200' tall, trunk diameter to 8'), and its needles are shorter and often notched at the tip.

NEEDLES 1½–2½" long. Bluish green; varies above; 2 white lines beneath. Grooved above; usually rounded at tip; flat in cross section. Arranged in flat sprays on lower branches, grading toward half-round bottlebrush arrangement on upper branches. Strong lemony scent, especially when crushed. **CONE** 3–5" long. Olive, purple, or yellow. Barrel-shaped; standing upright on branch. Bracts not visible.

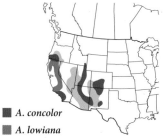

■ *A. concolor*

■ *A. lowiana*

Grand Fir

Abies grandis

ALSO CALLED Lowland White Fir

HT 100–200' **DIA** 1½–3½'

Very large evergreen tree. Crown slender, spirelike; becomes round-topped or open with age; develops several tops if the original breaks off. **ID TIP:** Needles are flat in cross section, unmarked above, white-lined beneath.

HABITAT: Moist, cool valleys and mountain slopes of the Pacific Northwest and northern Rockies. Elevation 0–4,900'.

NOTES: Grand Fir lives up to its name: it is the world's second-tallest fir species. Pacific coast trees can grow substantially taller (to 270' or more) than their inland counterparts, which tend to reach 130–160' tall at maturity.

NEEDLES 1¼–2" long; of mixed lengths. Shiny, dark green above; 2 white lines beneath. Grooved above; usually notched at tip; flat in cross section. Arranged in flat sprays, at least on lower branches. Tangerine-like scent, especially when crushed. **CONE** 2–4" long. Greenish brown or purplish brown. Barrel-shaped; standing upright on branch. Bracts not visible.

Pacific Silver Fir

Abies amabilis
ALSO CALLED Amabilis Fir, Silver Fir,
Cascades Fir
HT 80–150'   **DIA** 2–4'

PINE FAMILY	PINACEAE

Large evergreen tree. Crown conical,
spirelike; becomes flat-topped with
age. **ID TIP:** Needles are dark, glossy green
and hide the twig when viewed from
directly above. They have 2 white stripes
beneath.

HABITAT: Coniferous forests of the Pacific
coastal fog belt and snowy interior
mountains. Elevation 0–6,600'.

NOTES: Pacific Silver Fir is among the
West's most shade-tolerant trees, often
growing beneath the dense canopy of
taller conifers. It commonly retains its
needles for 20 years and may sometimes
hold them for more than 50.

NEEDLES ¾–1½" long. Dark, glossy green above; 2 white
stripes beneath. Grooved; usually notched at tip; flat in
cross section. In deep shade, needles are almost flat-lying,
in 3 rows: 1 out to each side and 1 center row of shorter
needles angled forward, almost lying on top of the twig.
Sprays growing in some sun approach a half-round
bottlebrush arrangement. Tangerine-like scent, especially
when crushed.

CONE 3–6" long. Purple-
green to purple. Barrel-
shaped; standing upright
on branch. Scaly bracts
not visible.

California Red Fir

Abies magnifica

ALSO CALLED Red Fir, Shasta Red Fir

HT 60–130' DIA 1–4'

Medium-sized to large evergreen tree. Conical crown of short branches, rounded at top; may develop several new tops if original crown leader breaks off.

ID TIP: The needles of California Red Fir are ridged, not grooved, on the upper surface, and white-lined on both upper and lower surfaces.

HABITAT: Mixed-conifer forests in mountains with high annual snowfall (to 60'). Elevation 4,600–8,900'.

NOTES: California Red Fir ranks among the tallest and most massive of the true firs; its record height is 252', its diameter 9½'. It is a handsome tree with purple cones and reddish bark (hence its name), common at Crater Lake and Yosemite. **Shasta Red Fir** (classified by some authorities as var. *shastensis*), which grows in the northern part of the species' range from the northern Sierra Nevada into Oregon, may be a hybrid of California Red Fir and Noble Fir, or it may be the progenitor of those two species. The main difference between the two red fir types is the protruding cone bracts in Shasta.

PINE FAMILY   PINACEAE

NEEDLES ¾–1¼" long. Blue-green; white-lined above and beneath. Blunt tip; mostly 4-sided in cross section. Swept forward in a half-round bottlebrush arrangement; needles on underside of twig are bent like hockey sticks. Pungent scent, especially when crushed. CONE 4–8" long. Purple to brown; streaked with clear resin. Barrel-shaped; standing upright on branch. Wide scales. Typical Red Fir usually has no visible scaly bracts. Shasta Red Fir has smaller cones (4–6") with protruding bracts.

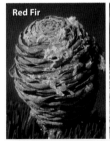

Red Fir

Shasta Red Fir

Noble Fir

Abies procera
ALSO CALLED Red Fir
HT 100–150' **DIA** 2½–4'

Very large evergreen tree. Crown columnar, rounded at top. **ID TIP:** Needles display a combination of features: notchless tip, grooved upperside, and a white stripe on the underside that is more or less divided into 2 lines.

HABITAT: Coniferous forests in windy, high-snowfall, mountain habitats. Elevation 500–8,800'.

NOTES: Noble Fir is the world's tallest true fir and one of North America's tallest trees (recorded at over 290' tall). **Bristlecone Fir** (*A. bracteata*), the world's rarest fir, found only in the Santa Lucia Range south of Monterey Bay, has cones with much longer bristles extending from the bracts; its needles are very wide, sharp-tipped, and white-lined beneath. In firs, needles on underside of branch are sometimes bent like hockey sticks (pictured below).

NEEDLES 1–1⅜" long. Blue-green, with 2 white lines beneath and usually 2 above. Grooved above; tip usually blunt; flat (on lower branches) or 4-sided (upper branches) in cross section; needles on underside of twig are bent like hockey sticks. Swept forward in a half-round bottlebrush arrangement. Pungent scent, especially when crushed. **CONE** 4½–8" long. Green to purple. Nearly cylindrical; standing upright on branch. Scales nearly covered by long, pointed, papery, greenish to tan bracts.

Noble Fir | Bristlecone Fir

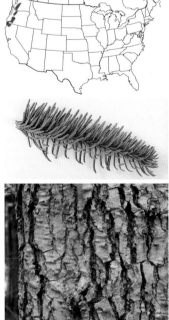

Hemlocks

Hemlocks make up a small genus (*Tsuga*) in the family Pinaceae. As in spruces, firs, and Douglas-firs, the needles grow singly on the twig. In Eastern and Western hemlocks they grow from the branch in two opposite rows, forming a flattened spray. In Carolina and Mountain hemlocks the needles do not form flat sprays, but sprout from all around the branch.

Western Hemlock

Hemlock cones are numerous, often conspicuous at branch tips, and small. (Only Mountain Hemlock's are big enough to confuse with spruce cones.) Hemlock needles have two white stripes beneath. They are pliable and short; most comparably short conifer needles are pointed, whereas hemlock needles are rounded or notch-tipped. They narrow at the base into a short "stalk" portion, which grows from a small projection of the twig that is angled slightly forward. These projections roughen the twigs after the needles are gone (but the twigs are less rough than in spruces).

Needles in Flat Sprays

A number of conifers—firs, Douglas-firs, hemlocks, torreyas, yews, bald-cypresses, and redwoods—can have their needles in a flat spray on each branch. Flat sprays are an adaptation to shady habitats (they maximize light reception on leaf surface area), so they tend to be found on the lower limbs of trees growing close together. Consequently, the flat character may be less clear, or even emphatically lacking, at the top of the same tree, or on entire trees when growing alone, or in entire species that tend not to grow close together. As an identification feature, they serve to rule out pines and spruces.

Carolina Hemlock

PINE FAMILY

PINACEAE

Tsuga caroliniana
HT 40–60' **DIA** 2'

An uncommon southeastern hemlock. **ID TIP:** Carolina Hemlock is very similar to Eastern Hemlock (and like Eastern is threatened by hemlock woolly adelgid), but its cones are longer and its needles grow from all around the branch, not in 2 rows. **HABITAT:** Restricted to rocky ridges and cliffs in high southern Appalachians. Elevation 2,500–4,000'.

NEEDLES ½–¾" long. Dark green above; white-lined beneath. Grow from all sides of the branch; not in flat sprays. **CONE** 1–1½" long. Brown. Ovoid; short-stalked; hangs from end of twig.

Eastern Hemlock

Tsuga canadensis
ALSO CALLED Canada Hemlock
HT 60–70'   **DIA** 1½–3'

Medium-sized evergreen tree with slightly drooping crown leader. **ID TIP:** Very short needles grow in 2 opposite rows; cones are very small. Long branches bear broad, flat sprays; low branches may droop close to the ground.

HABITAT: Moist slopes, rocky areas, and narrow stream valleys. Elevation 0–5,900'.

NOTES: Eastern Hemlock, with its graceful form and flat sprays of lacy, evergreen foliage, creates extensive dark, sheltered forests in the Great Lakes region and the Northeast. Its populations, once ravaged by the tanning industry but then recovered, are now threatened by the hemlock woolly adelgid, an Asian insect pest that infests trees, killing them off in just a few years. Eastern Hemlock provides valuable wildlife food and winter shelter, and the destruction of hemlock forests could have wide-ranging effects on eastern species diversity.

NEEDLES ¼–½" long. Dark green above; white-lined beneath. Flat in cross section. Arranged in 2 rows. **CONE** ½–¾" long. Brown. Ovoid; short-stalked; hangs from end of twig. Scales rounded.

Western Hemlock

Tsuga heterophylla
ALSO CALLED Pacific Hemlock
HT 100–180' **DIA** 3–4'

Very large evergreen tree with fluted trunk and narrow, conical crown. **ID TIP:** The crown has a curved, drooping leader. Needles grow in 2 rows, sometimes a bit raggedly arranged (not as precisely aligned as in Eastern Hemlock); cones are small and ovoid.

HABITAT: Moist forests on coastal and inland slopes. Elevation 0–4,900'.

NOTES: Western Hemlock is the largest of the hemlocks (recorded at 259' tall, with a 9' diameter) and one of North America's tallest tree species, though it is often overlooked as such because it frequently lives among even larger trees. It is extremely shade-tolerant, and therefore tends to take over humid Northwest forests if they remain undisturbed for many decades. The trees thrive while growing close together, and some young Western Hemlock stands may attain record annual increases in biomass per acre.

NEEDLES ¼–¾" long. Dark green; white-lined beneath. Flat in cross section. Arranged in flattish sprays. **CONE** ¾–1" long. Pale brown. Ovoid; stalkless; hangs from end of twig. Scales oval, papery.

Mountain Hemlock

Tsuga mertensiana
ALSO CALLED Black Hemlock,
Alpine Hemlock
HT 30–100'   **DIA** 1–3'

PINE FAMILY   PINACEAE

Small to large evergreen tree with
spirelike, often drooping crown leader.
Dwarfed at timberline. **ID TIP:** Needles
grow from all around branch, not in
2 rows; cones are larger than those of
Western Hemlock.

HABITAT: Coastal and inland mountain
forests, from near sea level to alpine zone.
Elevation 0–11,000'.

NOTES: Mountain Hemlock's blue-green
spires with their nodding tips grace
coastal forests to high mountain country,
especially from southern Alaska to the
Washington Cascades. The drooping
branches are adapted to take heavy snow
loads. Mountain Hemlocks are valuable
to wildlife in some areas, providing food
and cover at high-elevation sites that
sometimes don't support many other tree
species. Hemlock trees are not related to
the deadly European herb called poison
hemlock.

NEEDLES ½–1" long. Blue-green; white-lined above and
beneath. Semicircular to 4-angled in cross section. Grow
from all around branch, curl toward tip. **CONE** 1–3" long.
Purplish, turning brown. Cylindrical; stalkless; hangs from
end of twig. Scales rounded, numerous.

Yews and Torreyas

The very small yew family (Taxaceae) is represented in North America by only a handful of species in two genera (*Taxus* and *Torreya*). These trees have flattened, pointed needles growing in two rows and forming flat sprays. The needles narrow at their bases to a short "stalk" portion, and taper at their tips to a tiny, sharp, drawn-out point. Plants of this family are distinguished by their fully exposed seeds, the outer, fleshy cover (the "aril") actually an outgrowth of the stalk of the seed. To all appearances they are more like berries (in yews) or olives (in torreyas). The fleshy seeds of *Taxus* species are poisonous if ingested. The shrub Canada Yew (*Taxus canadensis*) usually doesn't reach tree size.

California
Torreya

Pacific Yew

Taxus brevifolia
HT 20–50'   **DIA** 1–2'

Small evergreen tree or large shrub. Trunk straight or twisted, often fluted; very long, ascending branches. Peeling outer bark reveals red to purple new bark. **ID TIP:** The colorful bark, soft needles in flat sprays, and fleshy, berrylike seeds distinguish Pacific Yew.

HABITAT: Moist forests, streamsides, ravines. Elevation 0–7,200'.

NOTES: Pacific Yew often grows in the understory of coastal forests, but also thrives in some drier and more open areas. Forest trees may have very long branches growing toward an opening where sunlight shines through. Pacific Yew has been exploited for the substance paclitaxel (Taxol), used in cancer treatment, and for its hard, handsome, reddish wood. The leaves, twigs, and seeds are poisonous to humans if eaten.

YEW FAMILY   **TAXACEAE**

NEEDLES ½–¾" long. Shiny, green above; green with 2 paler bands beneath. Flexible, soft, ridged above; flat in cross section. Arranged in 2 rows in flat sprays. Unscented. **SEED** ⅜" wide, round; fleshy red, cuplike cover (aril) encloses brown, ovoid seed. Borne singly; matures late summer to fall. Red outer flesh edible, but seed poisonous if chewed.

Florida Yew and Torreya

Florida Torreya

Two native eastern trees of the yew family, **Florida Yew** (*Taxus floridana*) and **Florida Torreya** (*Torreya taxifolia*), are restricted in the wild mainly to habitat along the Apalachicola River in northwestern Florida's Torreya State Park. Florida Yew, often cultivated in gardens, is usually single-trunked, attains heights of 20–25', and has the appearance of a small, irregularly branched tree. Its seeds are similar to those of Pacific Yew. Florida Torreya is a victim of fungal disease, and tree-sized or seed-bearing specimens are rare. Like California Torreya, it has an olivelike seed with a green, purple-striped cover. Florida Torreya has laterally spreading branches borne in regularly spaced whorls along the trunk and shiny dark green, 1–1½" needles with sharp-pointed tips that are piercing to the touch. The branches of the superficially similar Florida Yew are borne at irregular intervals, and its leaves are soft and not piercing.

California Torreya

Torreya californica
ALSO CALLED California-nutmeg,
Stinking-cedar
HT 16–70'   **DIA** 8–24"

YEW FAMILY   TAXACEAE

Small to medium-sized evergreen tree.
ID TIP: California Torreya has very sharp, prickly, strongly scented needles and an olivelike, green-skinned seed.

HABITAT: Mainly moist areas, such as streamsides and canyon bottoms, or in chaparral or mountain woodlands. Elevation 0–6,600'.

NOTES: California Torreya is found in scattered locations in both the California Coast Ranges and the Sierra Nevada foothills. It sometimes grows in the understory of Redwood forests but is also found in more open woodlands. The name Stinking-cedar refers to the strong odor emitted by crushed foliage, and California-nutmeg alludes to the aroma and shape of the seed.

NEEDLES 1–3½" long. Glossy, dark green above; green with 2 whitish bands beneath. Stiff; long, sharp, prickly tip; flat in cross section. Arranged in 2 roughly opposite rows. Unpleasant, pungent odor when crushed. **SEED** 1–1½" long, ovoid, olivelike. Green, often streaked with purple. Sheds fleshy cover (aril) to reveal brown seed, ¾–1" long. Borne singly; matures in 2 years. Very aromatic.

Bald-cypresses, Redwoods, and Kin

A group of trees of the cypress family (Cupressaceae)—bald-cypress (*Taxodium*), redwood (*Sequoia*), sequoia (*Sequoiadendron*), Japanese-cedar (*Cryptomeria*), dawn redwood (*Metasequoia*), and several other genera—were traditionally placed in a separate family, Taxodiaceae, which was known as the bald-cypress or redwood family. The groups had been separated mainly on the basis of foliage differences, with trees of the Taxodiaceae group bearing mostly alternate, needlelike leaves and those of the Cupressaceae group bearing scalelike leaves in opposite pairs. However, recent studies have found insufficient reason to keep the two groups separate, and the Taxodiaceae group is now part of Cupressaceae (page 129). In this section we cover those cypress family members that usually feature needlelike leaves. Their small, few-scaled, mostly rather spherical cones are similar to the cones of other cypresses.

The leaves on bald-cypresses and redwoods are usually needles, arranged in two rows in flat sprays (similar to yews). But on some shoots on the same tree, the

Bald-cypress (above), a deciduous conifer of southeastern swamps, and Redwood, an evergreen giant of towering Pacific coast forests, were formerly placed in the family Taxodiaceae. Both are now included in the cypress family.

needles are short and sharp and surround the twig, resembling leaves of the closely related Giant Sequoia (covered in the scalelike leaves section on page 132).

In most genera in the cypress family, needles fall from the tree not singly but as entire sprays. In redwoods and bald-cypresses, the sprays are unbranched and a few inches long. Bald-cypresses and the nonnative Dawn Redwood are deciduous conifers, like larches, and their leaf sprays fall every autumn. The rest of the family retains sprays for several years.

Japanese-cedar

Cryptomeria japonica
HT 50–80'   **DIA** 2'

Medium-sized evergreen tree. **ID TIP:** Branches spiral around the trunk; needles spiral around the branchlets. The rounded cones have prickles at the tips of the scales. **HABITAT AND RANGE:** Introduced in North America. Native to Japan. **NOTES:** This tree grows very large (to 160' tall, with a trunk diameter to 17') in Japan; much smaller in cultivation.

CYPRESS FAMILY   CUPRESSACEAE

NEEDLES ½–¾" long. Blue-green; bronzy sheen in winter. Soft, curved; raised keel above and beneath. **CONE** 1" wide. Brown. Rounded; prickly tips on scales.

Redwood

Sequoia sempervirens

ALSO CALLED Coast Redwood

HT 200–325'   **DIA** 10–15'

CYPRESS FAMILY   CUPRESSACEAE

Very large evergreen tree. Slender, conical shape when young (up to 400 years). Old-growth trees have massive, fluted, strongly buttressed trunks with large fire scars, deep hollows, huge burls. In their upper sections they commonly form "candelabras" of several trunks, each of which would be considered a champion-sized tree of most species. **ID TIP:** Trees have both tiny, scalelike leaves and larger needles arranged in 2 rows in flat sprays; cones are small. Bark is thick, fibrous, reddish brown.

HABITAT: Coniferous forests; virtually restricted to California's 550-mile-long coastal fog belt. Elevation 0–1,000' (occasionally to 3,300').

LEAVES ¼–1" long. Two leaf types: most are flat, pointed needles; dark green above, 2 white bands beneath; arranged in 2 rows in flat sprays. Leaves on new twigs and high branches are slender, scalelike, ¼" long; grow all around branchlet (like those of Giant Sequoia, p. 132). **CONE** ¾–1" long. Brown. Ovoid; hangs from end of green twig. 15–20 flat, short-pointed scales.

NOTES: Redwood is the world's tallest tree and one of the longest-living (up to 2,200 years). The tallest known tree measures just over 379' tall. Some historical Redwoods were probably as massive as the largest Giant Sequoias, but most of the ancient trees were destroyed for their wood. Ninety-five percent of the surviving old-growth Redwoods are in state and national parks. Some old-growth trees on private lands are still subject to logging.

Dawn Redwood

Metasequoia glyptostroboides
HT 60–100' **DIA** 2½–4'

| CYPRESS FAMILY | CUPRESSACEAE |

Medium-sized to large deciduous tree. Symmetrical, conical crown; markedly tapering trunk, deeply fluted with age. **ID TIP:** Dawn Redwood resembles Bald-cypress and also has soft, thin needles that are flat in cross section, but its branchlets and needles are arranged in opposite pairs in featherlike sprays (alternate in Bald-cypress). Young bark is reddish, flaky. Cone has blunt scales.

HABITAT AND RANGE: Cultivated in North America. Native to China.

NOTES: Dawn Redwood was known only from fossils at least 5 million years old until several groves were found by a forestry worker in China in 1947. This "living fossil" is now planted worldwide.

NEEDLES ¾–1½" long. Bright green above; gray-green beneath; turn brick red before shedding in autumn. In opposite pairs. **CONE** ¾–1" long. Dark brown. Blunt scales. Hangs on long stalk.

Pond-cypress

Taxodium distichum var. *imbricarium*
HT 50–90' **DIA** 1–3'

| CYPRESS FAMILY | CUPRESSACEAE |

Pond-cypress is shorter than the typical Bald-cypress. **ID TIP:** Leaves are short (⅛–⅜" long), sharp, scalelike or threadlike, and pressed against the twig. Mature bark has furrows ¾–1" deep (compared to less than ½" deep in Bald-cypress).

HABITAT AND RANGE: Southeastern coastal plains from North Carolina to Louisiana, in peat-rich Carolina bay swamps and other wetlands. Elevation 0–330'.

Bald-cypress

Taxodium distichum var. *distichum*
ALSO CALLED Swamp-cypress
HT 100–150' **DIA** 3–5'

Large deciduous tree. Bark is shallowly furrowed and peels in long, thin, fibrous strips. **ID TIP:** Bald-cypress grows in or near water. The gradually tapering, fluted trunk has a thick, buttressed base often encircled by erect woody pillars ("knees").

HABITAT: Permanent standing water in swamps, creeks, bayous; seasonally flooded sites along lakes and rivers. Elevation 0–1,600' (usually below 500').

NOTES: This species has the largest trunk diameter (to over 17') of all eastern trees and is the longest-living tree (1,622 years) of the East; the oldest trees have a low, wide-spreading crown, up to 100' across. The function of the distinctive "knees" is unknown, but the fact that they occur mainly in trees with submerged root systems suggests they may have to do with aeration or anchorage. A Montezuma Bald-cypress (*T. distichum* var. *mexicanum* or *T. mucronatum*) in Oaxaca, Mexico, the Big Tree of Tule, has the world's largest recorded trunk diameter (35½') of any species.

CYPRESS FAMILY   **CUPRESSACEAE**

NEEDLES ⅜–¾" long. Dark green above; yellow-green beneath; orange-brown in autumn. Soft; tiny, drawn-out, hairlike tip; flat in cross section. Alternate; arranged in flattened, featherlike sprays; branchlets and their needles fall entire in autumn. **CONE** ¾–1" wide. Brown. Round; often in pairs or clusters. Thick, fused, wrinkled scales.

"knees"

Araucarias

Araucarias are conifers native to the Southern Hemisphere; several species are cultivated in North America. Leaves are needlelike to lance-shaped and often arranged spirally. Male and female cones are usually on separate trees.

Norfolk Island–pine

Araucaria heterophylla
HT 40–70'   DIA 1–4'

ARAUCARIA FAMILY   ARAUCARIACEAE

Small to medium-sized evergreen tree. Not a pine, despite its name. Sold as a potted "Christmas tree." ID TIP: The symmetrical, open, conical crown of evenly spaced branches with erect branchlets in rows is distinctive. Trunks of young trees are covered in dead needles.

HABITAT AND RANGE: Cultivated in mild climates in North America. Native to Norfolk Island, east of Australia.

NEEDLES ½" long, curved, sprucelike; spirally arranged. In older trees, leaves are scalelike, ¼" long, curved inward, densely overlapping. Bright green to dark green. CONE 3–5" long. Green, turning brown. Roundish; grows at branch tip. Each scale has a long, curved prickle.

Monkeypuzzle Tree

Araucaria araucana
HT 50–80'

ARAUCARIA FAMILY   ARAUCARIACEAE

Medium-sized evergreen tree. ID TIP: The well-spaced, upcurved, ropelike branches are distinctive. The base of a large trunk can resemble an elephant's foot.

HABITAT AND RANGE: Cultivated in North America, on Pacific coast and in Southeast. Native to southern Andes, in Chile and Argentina.

NEEDLES 1–2" long, leathery, sharp-pointed; in ropelike branches. CONE 6" long. Brown. Rounded to barrel-shaped.

Trees with Scalelike Leaves

Leaves we call "scalelike" are very small and in most cases are pressed flat (appressed) against each other and against the branch, entirely encasing the branch, or at least the current year's growth. In a few species the leaves can be needlelike—prickly, in fact—but these leaves are still less than ½" long, and still entirely encase the branch: there's no branch to be seen between the leaf bases. Some species bear both prickly needles and appressed scales, on different parts or in different growth stages. Redwoods and bald-cypresses can have similar short, prickly leaves, but most of their leaves are needlelike rather than scalelike; they are covered in the "Trees with Needlelike Leaves" section, on pages 124–127.

Most of the trees covered in this section—cypresses, junipers, Giant Sequoia, New World cedars—are in the cypress family, Cupressaceae (as are Redwood, Bald-cypress, and their close relatives). We also include here two genera of introduced flowering trees (not conifers at all) that have tiny, scalelike leaves, *Tamarix* and *Casuarina*.

Trunks of species in the cypress family tend to widen at the base much more than those in the pine family, often developing large flanges or "buttresses." Giant Sequoia is shown here.

The Cypress Family

Recent studies of relationships within the cypress family suggest that revisions to some genus names are necessary, including *Cupressus*, which currently includes both New World and Old World cypresses. Several studies agree that Alaska-cedar (traditionally named *Chamaecyparis nootkatensis*) is more closely related to the *Cupressus* species of North America than to the other *Chamaecyparis* species. Many authorities now call Alaska-cedar *Cupressus nootkatensis*, reflecting this relationship. However, a further study makes the case that no New World species are close enough to the Old World cypresses to belong in genus *Cupressus*; its author uses the genus name *Callitropsis* for the North American cypresses as well as Alaska-cedar. In this guide, we retain the traditional names because no taxonomic consensus has emerged.

Common names, too, can be confusing in this family. European immigrants dubbed many North American native trees of the cypress family "cedars" after the dissimilar true cedars of the Middle East (page 98), apparently because both groups have aromatic wood. To avoid ambiguity, we refer to North American species of *Calocedrus*, *Thuja*, and *Chamaecyparis* as New World cedars. Eastern Redcedar, of the genus *Juniperus*, is not included in the New World cedar group. Several species of the cypress family, mainly of genus *Thuja*, are sometimes called arborvitae, which translates as "tree of life."

New World cedars, as well as the Giant Sequoia, tend to resemble the needle-leaf conifers in shape (see page 61)—conical,

Most trees of the cypress family have thin peeling bark. A stand of Alaska-cedars is pictured.

perhaps maturing into a cylindrical shape, with a straight trunk. Cypresses and junipers are more likely to be irregularly shaped, multistemmed, and rounded or broad-crowned, though they can also be conical (especially some junipers in youth).

Bark is fibrous and shreddy almost throughout the cypress family. In most species it is thin and offers little fire protection; Incense-cedar, Redwood, and Giant Sequoia are thick-barked exceptions.

Aromatic wood characterizes the cypress family. The aromatic phenols in the wood evolved as defenses against boring insects and fungi, and they give the trees greater longevity, on average, than those in other families. These trees also yield wood that is prized for its resistance to decay and insect attack.

Identification Tips

Cones and geography (unless you're looking at cultivated trees) usually provide enough information to narrow an identification of a tree with scalelike leaves down to a genus. Check cone features in the key, opposite, and then check the species' range maps. While there are many fairly similar species in the family, there are typically only one to five native species in any one locale. Once narrowed down by genus and location, many species can be positively identified with close examination of the foliage. A hand lens may be needed to determine whether or not each tiny leaf has a resin gland (which appears as a small central pit) on its surface; this can be an important identifying feature, as noted in many species accounts.

It is difficult to identify New World cedars, junipers, and cypresses by their leaves alone, although there are differences in the arrangement of the scalelike leaves on the branchlet and the presence of minute resin glands. These trees can be distinguished more easily by their cones and their location. Young cones of Incense-cedar are shown here.

Giant Sequoia

Cone Ovoid, 25–45 Scales

Cone 2–3½" long, ovoid, on leafy stalk; persists on tree for years. California mountains, planted elsewhere.

> Giant Sequoia: p. 132
> *see also* Redwood: p. 125

Incense-cedar

Cone Bell-shaped, 5 Scales

Cone ¾–1" long, consisting of 3 main scales and 2 minor. California, Oregon, western Nevada.

> Incense-cedar: p. 133

Northern White-cedar

Cone Oblong, 8–12 Scales

Cone ½" long or less, 8–12 thin scales; upright. Northwest, northern Rockies, Northeast, eastern Canada.

> Western Redcedar: p. 134
> Northern White-cedar: p. 135

Alaska-cedar Atlantic White-cedar

Cone Rounded, 4–9 Scales

Cone to ½" wide, initially spherical, spiky; opening into dry cone of 4–9 scales. Northwest; Atlantic and Gulf coasts

> Atlantic White-cedar: p. 137
> Alaska-cedar: p. 138
> Port-Orford-cedar: p. 139

Monterey Cypress

Cone Rounded, Closed

Cone ⅜–1½" wide, lumpy, spherical, with 6–12 heavy scales; closed or nearly closed; persistent. California, Oregon, Arizona, New Mexico.

> Cypresses: pp. 143–145
> *see also* Pond-cypress: p. 126

Western Juniper

Cone Berrylike

Cone ⅛–⅝" wide, berrylike, often blue. Throughout United States, Canada.

> Junipers: pp. 147–151
> Eastern Redcedar: p. 147

Giant Sequoia

Sequoiadendron giganteum
ALSO CALLED Sierra Redwood, Bigtree
HT 150–250' **DIA** 10–20'

Very large evergreen tree. Conical when young, with a mass of branches down to the base. In older trees, a very tall, mostly branch-free trunk is topped by a high, irregularly shaped crown. **ID TIP:** Thick, reddish brown bark. Trunk becomes buttressed and enlarged. Branchlets are clad in sharp, scalelike leaves.

HABITAT: Granite soils in mixed coniferous forest in a 280-mile-long band on the Sierra Nevada's western slopes. Elevation 3,000–8,900'.

NOTES: Giant Sequoias form sunny, open, scattered groves, unlike the deep, shaded, extensive forests of Redwoods. Giant Sequoia is the most massive single tree known and one of the longest-living (to 3,266 years). The General Sherman tree is the most massive sequoia (275' tall, trunk diameter 36½'); the tallest specimen is just over 311' tall. Many old giants were cut down in the 19th and 20th centuries, wastefully, as the wood of mature trees is often of poor quality, and in many cases the felled trees were simply too large to be transported. About 75 groves survive, nearly all in parks and preserves, including Sequoia and Kings Canyon National Parks. The oldest trees can have bark up to 2' thick and large fire scars, hollow chambers, and buttresses on the trunk. Huge branches, even the crown leader, may become leafless at their ends.

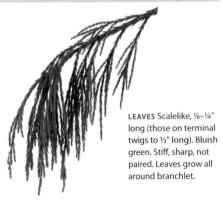

LEAVES Scalelike, ⅛–¼" long (those on terminal twigs to ½" long). Bluish green. Stiff, sharp, not paired. Leaves grow all around branchlet.

CONE 2–3½" long. Rich reddish brown. Ovoid; on leafy stalk. 25–45 scales. Remains on tree for up to 20 years.

Incense-cedar

Calocedrus decurrens
HT 80–150' DIA 3–5'

Large evergreen tree with tall, tapering trunk and large, columnar crown that becomes open and irregular with age. Bark thick, light brown to cinnamon, shredding and fibrous, with deep, irregular furrows. **ID TIP:** The scalelike leaves lack white markings beneath, and their tips are pressed against the twigs. Cones are larger than those of Western Redcedar, with fewer scales.

HABITAT: Lower to mid-elevation mountain slopes, scattered among pines and other conifers. Elevation 950–9,200'.

NOTES: This very tall, slow-growing tree is a major component of the extensive mixed-conifer forests of the Yosemite Valley and other Sierra Nevada locations. The thick bark of large trees protects them against fire damage.

CYPRESS FAMILY CUPRESSACEAE

LEAVES Scalelike, tiny, ⅛" long (½" or longer on terminal shoots). Glossy green; no white marks or resin glands. Leaves in 4 rows along branchlet. Each segment of 4 leaves is about twice as long as wide (longer than in other New World cedars). Leaf tips pressed in toward branchlet. Foliage sprays flattened, fanlike. Very aromatic when crushed. **CONE** ¾–1" long. Light reddish brown. Bell-shaped; hangs at end of slender stalk. 2 basal, short, often inconspicuous scales, 2 middle scales as long as the cone, and 1 end scale (consisting of 2 fused scales) as long as the cone. When the cone opens, the middle scales spread apart and curve outward. Matures in first year.

Western Redcedar

Thuja plicata

ALSO CALLED Giant Arborvitae, Canoe-cedar

HT 100–180' **DIA** 2–8'

Very large evergreen tree. **ID TIP:** The tall, tapering trunk is clad in cinnamon to purplish brown, peeling, fibrous bark. The scalelike leaves are pressed against the twigs and white-marked beneath; the foliage is in hanging, fanlike sprays. Cones are small and elongated.

HABITAT: Coastal and mountain forests. Elevation 0–6,600'.

NOTES: Western Redcedars are abundant in the mountain ranges of the Pacific Northwest, interspersed among Western Hemlocks, Sitka Spruces, and Douglas-firs, and lending their spicy aroma to the overall fragrance of the towering forests. These trees are long-lived and can develop massive trunks; there is a historical record of one with a diameter of about 22½'. The largest Western Redcedars were once carved into canoes capable of carrying as many as 40 people. Old trees sometimes have multiple crown leaders if the original top has been snapped off by lightning or wind.

CYPRESS FAMILY	CUPRESSACEAE

LEAVES Scalelike, tiny, ⅛–¼" long. Dark green; white marks on scalelike leaves on underside of branch spray; resin gland usually inconspicuous. Leaves in 4 rows along branchlet. Leaf tips pressed against branchlet. Foliage sprays flattened, fanlike, hanging, but shorter and less pendent than in Alaska-cedar. May be somewhat bronze-tinged in autumn. Aromatic when crushed. **CONE** ½" long. Brown. Oblong; erect, on curved stalks. 8–12 thin scales, each with pointed tip. Matures in autumn of first year.

Northern White-cedar

Thuja occidentalis

ALSO CALLED Eastern Arborvitae, Eastern White-cedar

HT 40–70'   **DIA** 1–3'

| CYPRESS FAMILY | CUPRESSACEAE |

Small to medium-sized evergreen tree, sometimes with several trunks. On cliffs and steep sites can be dwarfed, contorted. Bark thin, cinnamon red to purple-brown (weathering to gray), soft, shredding, fibrous. **ID TIP:** The foliage is arranged in flattened, fanlike sprays. Cones are very small, narrower than in Atlantic White-cedar.

LEAVES Scalelike, tiny, ⅛–¼" long. Yellow-green above, paler beneath; each leaf has resin gland. Leaves in 4 rows along somewhat flattened branchlet. Foliage sprays flattened, fanlike. Bronze-tinged in autumn. Aromatic when crushed. **CONE** ¼–½" long. Brown. Oblong; erect, on curved stalks. 8–12 thin scales. Matures in autumn of first year.

HABITAT: Swamps, shores, slopes, cliffs, in mixed and pure stands. Elevation 0–3,000'.

NOTES: Northern White-cedar is one of eastern North America's longest-lived tree species. Ancient dwarf cliff-dwellers, estimated at 500–1,000 years of age, have been discovered, and dead specimens have revealed ages of 1,653 years and an estimated 1,890 years. When exposed to harsh conditions these trees can take on fantastic, gnarled shapes, sometimes even hanging from cliffs. This is a very hardy, virtually disease-free tree.

Oriental Arborvitae

Platycladus orientalis
ALSO CALLED Chinese Arborvitae
HT 20–30' **DIA** 6"

Small evergreen tree or shrub, often planted as a hedge. **ID TIP:** This species is easily identified by the hooklike points on the cones. Foliage sprays are flattened, oriented vertically. **HABITAT AND RANGE:** Introduced in North America. Native to northern China, Japan, and Korea.

CYPRESS FAMILY **CUPRESSACEAE**

LEAVES Scalelike, tiny, up to ⅛" long. Glossy, yellow-green; thick, short-pointed. **CONE** ⅝" long. Bright blue-green; becomes dark brown. Rounded; erect. 6 thick scales, each tipped with a strongly curved point. Matures in autumn of first year.

Hiba False-arborvitae

Thujopsis dolabrata
ALSO CALLED Hiba Arborvitae
HT 30–50'

Small evergreen tree. **ID TIP:** The leaves are larger than those of similar trees and slightly succulent and waxy. **HABITAT AND RANGE:** Cultivated in North America as a landscaping evergreen. Native to mountain forests in Japan.

CYPRESS FAMILY **CUPRESSACEAE**

LEAVES Scalelike, ¼" long. Dark green, with broad, white stripes beneath. **CONE** ½–¾" long. Blue-green, becoming blue-brown. Rounded. 6–8 scales.

Sawara False-cypress

Chamaecyparis pisifera
ALSO CALLED Sawara
HT 50–70' **DIA** 1–2'

Medium-sized evergreen tree. Trunk sometimes forked. **ID TIP:** The foliage is bright yellow-green and occurs in flat sprays; branches fall in a loose, open arrangement. **HABITAT AND RANGE:** Cultivated in North America. Native to Japan, where it grows along mountain streams.

CYPRESS FAMILY **CUPRESSACEAE**

LEAVES Scalelike, tiny, ⅛" long. Glossy, yellow-green; sharp-pointed; lower surface often has white marks. Leaves on young plants needlelike. **CONE** ¼" wide. Green, becoming brown. Rounded; wrinkled texture; 10 scales, each with tiny point in center.

Atlantic White-cedar

Chamaecyparis thyoides
ALSO CALLED Southern White-cedar,
Swamp-cedar
HT 50–90'   **DIA** 1½–2'

Medium-sized to large evergreen tree
with narrow, pointed crown. Older trees
have stout, fluted trunk with buttressed
base and irregular, more open crown of
gnarled branches. **ID TIP:** Atlantic White-
cedar overlaps with the similar Northern
White-cedar only along the Maine coast.
Atlantic's foliage sprays are less flattened,
and narrower, than in Northern White-
cedar, and the cones are more rounded.

HABITAT: Peat-filled bogs and swamps
on the Atlantic and Gulf coastal plains.
Elevation 0–1,600'.

NOTES: Atlantic White-cedar is naturally
limited by its habitat requirements
but has been curtailed even more by
the actions of humans over the last 2
centuries. Large trees and old-growth
stands are virtually gone. The tree was
plundered for its wood, which is so decay-
resistant that logs submerged in swamps
for hundreds of years have yielded strong,
usable lumber. The draining of wetlands
and development continue to restrict the
species' habitat.

CYPRESS FAMILY   CUPRESSACEAE

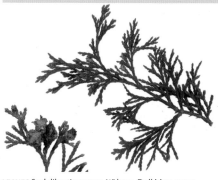

LEAVES Scalelike, tiny, up to ⅛" long. Dull blue-green,
each leaf dotted with a resin gland. Leaves in 4 rows along
branchlet. Leaves on young plants needlelike; grow all
around twig. Exposed foliage turns russet in winter. Gingery
scent when crushed. **CONE** ¼" wide. Dark reddish brown.
Rounded, wrinkled texture; 5–7 thick scales, each often with
small point in center. Matures in first year.

Alaska-cedar

Chamaecyparis nootkatensis

ALSO CALLED Nootka-cypress, Alaska Yellow-cedar, Yellow-cypress

HT 60–100' **DIA** 1–5'

CYPRESS FAMILY   CUPRESSACEAE

Medium-sized to large evergreen tree. Bark peels in thin, silver to brown strips; reddish beneath. Old trees have greatly buttressed, fluted trunks with huge burls. **ID TIP:** Large branches sweep downward, then lift upward at their ends; foliage on branchlets hangs like curtains. Scalelike leaves lack markings and are sharp-tipped; branchlets feel prickly if rubbed against the orientation of the leaves. Cones are rounded.

HABITAT: Moist coastal and inland mountains with very heavy snowfall. Elevation 0–8,000'.

NOTES: In the northern part of the species' limited range, in the Alaska Panhandle, populations of this tree have been experiencing accelerated mortality since the early 20th century. The cause is undetermined, but a likely theory holds that an average warming of the region's climate has resulted in lower snowfalls, leaving the tree's roots, which are accustomed to the insulating snowpack, more exposed to freezing. Also known as *Cupressus nootkatensis* (see p. 129).

LEAVES Scalelike, tiny, ⅛" long. Green above; pale yellow beneath, with no white lines or resin glands. Leaves in 4 rows along branchlet. Leaf tips sharp, not tightly pressed against branchlet. Foliage sprays flattened, long and pendent. Disagreeable, oily scent when crushed. **CONE** ½" wide. Dark reddish brown (green when new). Rounded; wrinkled texture; 4–6 thick scales, each with conspicuous, curved point in center. Matures in second year.

Port-Orford-cedar

Chamaecyparis lawsoniana
ALSO CALLED Lawson-cypress,
Oregon-cedar, Ginger-pine
HT 100–200' **DIA** 2½–5'

CYPRESS FAMILY	CUPRESSACEAE

Very large evergreen tree. Tall trunk with swollen base; crown high, dense, spirelike. With age, develops greatly buttressed, fluted trunk with huge burls. Bark thick, dark reddish brown to purple-brown, shredding in slender, twisted, gray fibers. **ID TIP:** Silvery marks on underside of scalelike leaves form X marks; the leaf tips are pressed against the thin branchlets. Cones are tiny and rounded.

HABITAT: Mixed forest in 220-mile-long Oregon–California coastal fog belt. Elevation 0–4,900'.

NOTES: Port-Orford-cedar has a small native range on the Pacific Northwest coastline and is becoming increasingly rare in the wild. The light, strong, powerfully fragrant, decay-resistant wood is considered highly desirable and commands a high price. The old-growth forests were long ago plundered by loggers, and large specimens (once attaining trunk diameters of 19½') are now rare. Remaining natural stands are fast being destroyed by an introduced fungus that causes root rot and death.

LEAVES Scalelike, tiny, less than ⅛" long. Bright green above; pale green with silvery marks beneath; each leaf dotted with a resin gland. Leaves in 4 rows along branchlet. Leaf tips pressed against branchlet. Foliage sprays flattened, frondlike. Resinous; gingery scent when crushed. **CONE** ¼" wide. Dark reddish brown. Rounded; wrinkled texture; 5–9 thick scales, each often with small point in center. Matures in first year.

Trees and Fire

Fire's influence on North America's forests and other habitats can hardly be overstated. Naturally occurring fires helped shape the continent's flora and fauna over millennia, and for at least 10,000 years Native Americans used fire as a forest-management tool.

In the West, where at least some summers are very dry and feature thunderstorms without significant rain, fires have been a dominating force. In some types of western forests, such as the vast Lodgepole Pine–Engelmann Spruce forests in the northern Rockies, typical fires killed every tree within large patches. At the other extreme, California's Giant Sequoia groves survived for 2,000 years because the typical fire, which came along frequently, was a brush and grass fire that wiped out young trees well before they could grow tall enough to carry a fire up to the lowest sequoia limbs. Today, thanks to fire suppression, young trees have grown to where they can do just that, and many ancient sequoia groves are just one lightning bolt away from incineration.

In the East, certain communities dominated by oaks and pines remain healthy only with regular burns. The Longleaf Pine–wiregrass ecosystem, which once dominated 90 million acres of the southeastern coastal plains, owes its extraordinary biological and ecological diversity to frequent fires. Under natural conditions, Longleaf pinelands probably burned as often as once every three years; this effectively ensured the continuation of a mainly herbaceous groundcover with few additional trees or shrubs. Today, fire is the favored management tool for maintaining and restoring this habitat.

In North America over most of the 20th century, a poorly supported belief that all forest fire is destructive and should be fought brought sweeping and unintended consequences. Forests expanded into former meadows, prairies, and savannas; relatively fire-susceptible

Pines and other conifers send up sprouts after a fire in Yellowstone National Park. The fire creates conditions conducive to seedling gemination: open, sunny ground and nutrient-rich soil fertilized with ash.

trees became more abundant at the expense of fire-resistant trees; and trees grew closer together, to the detriment of understory plants and the animals that depend on them. In many areas the denser forests are now less diverse, less healthy, and more prone to fires. Under such circumstances, fires are expected, especially in a warming world, to become more profoundly damaging than before—and more difficult to extinguish.

How Trees Adapt to Fire

Trees have adapted in diverse ways to their fire-prone world. The small number of species that are good at simply surviving fires tend to share three traits, all of which become effective only as the tree matures: very thick, corky bark, great height, and aggressive self-pruning, in which lower branches die and fall off early. Each of the legendary fire survivors—Giant Sequoia, Redwood, Western Larch, and Ponderosa, Sugar, and Jeffrey pines—is typically the biggest tree species in its community. Mature coastal Douglas-firs have all the right qualities, and some survive some fires, but many die because their forest structure often includes younger trees of all sizes, which act as "ladders" for climbing flames.

Trees that are less resistant to fire and that tend to suffer damage may employ other survival tactics. Redwoods and several chaparral species send up new sprouts from their stumps after other aboveground parts have been destroyed. Aspens sprout new stems from all along their roots. They can produce these suckers in any year, but do so with the greatest success when the ground is sunny after a fire has killed the old aspen stems. In many aspen groves nearly all the stems are exactly the same age, having all come up after one fire.

Some tree species have very low odds of surviving if touched by flame, and depend on scattered surviving individuals to start the next generation. Fires tend to burn patchily, leaving a mosaic of damage of varying severity. Surviving patches or individual trees may appear randomly scattered. If these are tall conifers bearing millions of light, winged seeds in cones mainly near the treetops, they enlist the wind in reseeding most of the severely burned patches within a year or two—a strategy common in spruces, firs, and Douglas-fir.

Perhaps no tree is better adapted to fire than Longleaf Pine. During the early "grass stage," which can last for many years, the tree's growing tip is actually below ground; only needles (which look like a clump of grass) show above ground. In the event of a fire, the needles burn, but not the growing tip. The trunk thickens appreciably below ground, and when conditions are right, such as a gap appearing in the canopy, the young tree grows very rapidly, up to 15' in three growing seasons. The growing tip, now above ground, is surrounded and protected by a large, ball-like cluster of needles. A natural, low-intensity fire will burn only the needles, even in very small trees (those 2–5' tall), leaving the growing tip unburned and healthy. Succeeding fires in well-managed Longleaf pinelands are usually of low intensity due to their frequency and to the lack of woody shrubs in the shrub layer. Hence, fire carries well and quickly and usually does not "crown" (extend into the canopy).

A common fire strategy involves "fire cones," which are found in almost all species of cypress, many pines, and two spruces. These cones remain closed on the tree at normal temperatures, but slowly open and release their seeds after being subjected to the heat of a fire. What we might call "fire seeds" are found in several chaparral species. These fall into the duff and lie dormant for decades, germinating only after being sharply heated. Most of the seeds burn up in the fire, but a few are buried just deeply enough to survive and germinate.

Finally, there are "fire avoiders." If touched by fire, these trees burn to a crisp. Their strategy is to grow where fire will not reach them—in swamps or, at the other extreme, sites so rocky and dry that hardly any other plants grow nearby, and thus fire cannot reach them. On more favorable growing sites, these trees may live a few decades before burning up in a fire, but in barren solitude bristlecone pines and some junipers may live for millennia. The world's oldest trees are extremely slow-growing fire avoiders, closely followed by certain rot- and insect-resistant fire survivors.

Cypresses

Cypresses (genus *Cupressus*) are trees with scalelike leaves in the family Cupressaceae. (Ongoing taxonomic studies may soon result in a genus name change; see page 129.) They live in fire-prone regions of the West and succumb to most fires, but often increase following fires because of fire cones. Most of a cypress's small, dense, woody cones remain completely closed and on the tree for years, until a fire stimulates them to open and release their seeds.

Often two different sizes and colors of cones occur on a cypress tree, as most don't reach full size or turn gray-brown until their second year. The hard, closed, almost spherical but often bumpy cones are quite unlike those of any other American conifer. Within the genus, however, the cones differ too little to be of much help in identification.

Cypress leaves are borne "in fours," in two opposite pairs, a side pair alternating with a front-and-back pair. In several of the species, the back side of each scale has a visible pit, called a resin gland, often bearing a dot of sticky resin.

Monterey Cypress cones are glossy brown and tightly sealed when new. They weather to gray as they age, opening and sowing the ground with seeds when prompted by the heat of a fire.

Most native North American cypresses are found in California. They grow mostly on problematic soils, where small local populations have evolved into distinct species: exactly how many distinct species is a subject of continuing debate. In any case, if you're looking at a wild-grown specimen, the odds are good that your location alone will narrow the possibilities down to one or two species. Cone size and the presence of resin glands are other clues.

Left: Monterey Cypresses often develop a crooked trunk and a flat-topped crown. Right: Italian Cypresses (*Cupressus sempervirens*), a standard feature of formal gardens, grow as tall, slender, evergreen columns.

MacNab Cypress

Cupressus macnabiana
HT 20–30'   **DIA** 1'

Small evergreen tree or shrub with short, sometimes multiple trunks. Crown open, rounded to irregularly shaped. **ID TIP:** MacNab is the only true cypress in the United States with young foliage in flattened, fanlike sprays (not branching out from all around the twig as in other *Cupressus* species). The resin glands appear as white, waxy pits on the leaves.

HABITAT: Chaparral and woodlands in California's northern mountains, Coast Ranges to Sierra Nevada. Elevation 980–2,800'.

NOTES: MacNab Cypress grows over a more extensive range than California's other true cypresses, yet is still rare and restricted to several dozen scattered groves. It is very flammable but fire-dependent, as most of its cones open and release seeds only when fire melts the resin that seals them. In the absence of fire, cones open sporadically as they age.

LEAVES Scalelike, tiny, ⅛" long. Dull green to gray; each leaf bears resin gland. (Monterey and Gowen cypresses lack resin glands.) Foliage sticky, in flattened, fanlike sprays. Pungent, citrusy scent when crushed. **CONE** ¾–1" wide. Brown, weathering to gray. Rounded; 6–8 scales, each with large point in center (smaller, blunter point on cone of Sargent Cypress).

Baker Cypress

Cupressus bakeri
ALSO CALLED Modoc Cypress
HT 30–100'   **DIA** 2'

ID TIP: The only *Cupressus* that ranges as far north as Oregon, Baker Cypress has a small cone and a conspicuous resin gland on each scalelike leaf. It grows at higher elevations than other northern California cypresses. **HABITAT:** Forests and slopes of northern California and southern Oregon, including Siskiyou Mountains. Elevation 3,600–6,600'.

LEAVES Scalelike, tiny, 1/16" long. Dull green; each leaf has conspicuous resin gland, often with dot of resin. Foliage sprays not flattened. **CONE** ⅜–¾" wide. Silvery gray. Rounded. 6–8 thick scales, each with point in center.

Sargent Cypress

Cupressus sargentii

HT 30–50'   **DIA** 2–3'

Small evergreen tree. Crown dense, narrow to broad, and open to flat-topped; branches contorted. **ID TIP:** Each scalelike leaf bears a resin gland beneath (gland is lacking in Monterey and Gowen cypresses).

HABITAT: Scattered forests and chaparral on slopes in the central and northern California Coast Ranges, commonly in reddish, serpentine-rich soils. Elevation 650–3,600'.

NOTES: Sargent Cypress needs the heat of fire to open its cones so they can release seeds. The fires that sweep through the groves often kill mature trees, but the resulting opening of cones fosters a new generation. Sargent Cypresses hold their closed cones for years until the next fire.

CYPRESS FAMILY   **CUPRESSACEAE**

LEAVES Scalelike, tiny, less than ⅛" long. Dusty green; each leaf has resin gland. Foliage sprays not flattened. Pungently aromatic when crushed. **CONE** ¾–1" wide. Glossy brown, weathering to dull brown or gray. Rounded to oblong; on short stalks. 6–8 rounded, hard scales, each often with small, blunt point in center.

Gowen Cypress

Cupressus goveniana

ALSO CALLED Mendocino Cypress, Santa Cruz Cypress

HT 15–100'   **DIA** 6–18"

This variable cypress has distinct populations in Mendocino, Sonoma, Santa Cruz, and Monterey counties. In Mendocino and Sonoma grow both the largest trees (to 150' tall, 7' diameter) and, on seaside terrace soils, "pygmy" stands that rarely exceed 6' tall. Trees in Santa Cruz and Monterey have paler leaves, and are distinguished by cone size.

ID TIP: Gowen Cypresses that grow near the Monterey Cypress groves are usually many-stemmed shrubs or small trees (to 25'), with smaller cones and more pointed, scalelike leaves than Monterey Cypress.

HABITAT: Forests in scattered sites along California's northern coast. Elevation 100–2,600'.

CYPRESS FAMILY   **CUPRESSACEAE**

LEAVES Scalelike, tiny, to ¹⁄₁₆" long. Dark green (Mendocino, Sonoma) or pale yellow-green (Santa Cruz, Monterey); no resin gland. Leaf pointed at tip. Foliage sprays not flattened. **CONE** ½" (Monterey) to 1¼" wide (Santa Cruz and northward). Brownish gray. Rounded. 6–10 scales with central bumps ranging from blunt to (with age) quite flat.

Monterey Cypress

Cupressus macrocarpa
HT 60–80' DIA 2'

Medium-sized evergreen tree. Flat-topped, open, wind-sheared crown and gnarled, leaning trunk in harsh locations. **ID TIP:** The cones are larger than those of other California cypresses; scalelike leaves lack resin gland beneath.

HABITAT AND RANGE: Rocky, exposed coastal promontories at Point Lobos and Cypress Point, in Monterey County, California. Elevation 20–110'.

NOTES: Monterey Cypress is one of North America's rarest trees, growing wild in only 2 fog-bathed groves on the Monterey coast, both in protected reserves. Overhanging the crashing surf, these trees develop dramatic, wind-sculpted forms. Mosslike beards of lichen and fuzzy, orange algae adorn the branches. When grown inland in protected sites, trees take on a bushy, more conical shape.

CYPRESS FAMILY   CUPRESSACEAE

LEAVES Scalelike, tiny, ⅛" long. Bright green; no resin gland. Foliage sprays not flattened. Citrusy scent when crushed. **CONE** 1–1½" wide. Brown, weathering to gray. Rounded; on stout, short stalks. 8–12 thick scales, each with prominent bump in center.

Arizona Cypress

Cupressus arizonica
HT 40–70' DIA 1–2'

ID TIP: Arizona Cypress is the only cypress in much of its range. Its bark can be gray and roughly furrowed or smooth, reddish, and peeling.

HABITAT: Chaparral and woodlands on desert mountains. Elevation 2,500–6,600'.

NOTES: A rare species of southwestern California and Baja California, **Tecate Cypress** (*C. guadalupensis* var. *forbesii* or *C. forbesii*), has colorful, peeling bark. Unlike Arizona Cypress, its leaves lack pits or sticky resin glands.

BARK Large, mature Arizona Cypress trees develop furrowed gray bark (far right). Young trees and some cultivated specimens (center) may have smooth, colorful, peeling bark, similar to that of Tecate Cypress.

CYPRESS FAMILY   CUPRESSACEAE

LEAVES Scalelike, tiny, ⅛" long. Grayish or bluish green; each leaf has a tiny but visible pit with a resin gland. Foliage often sticky; sprays not flattened. **CONE** ⅜–1⅛" wide. Gray to brown. Rounded. 6–8 thick, bumpy scales.

Tecate Cypress   Arizona Cypress   Arizona Cypress

Junipers

Junipers (genus *Juniperus*) are evergreen trees and shrubs in the family Cupressaceae. All 49 continental states are home to at least one of North America's 13 species of juniper. In most of Canada, the only species is the shrubby Common Juniper, though two tree junipers, Eastern Redcedar and Rocky Mountain Juniper, extend into southeastern and southwestern Canada, respectively.

Juniper species are valuable to wildlife, which eat the berrylike cones (and disseminate the seeds), browse the foliage, or seek cover in or under the branches, often in terrain that doesn't offer much other protection. The cones can be fleshy to dry and mealy, contain one to several hard seeds, and have strong resinous flavors and only a touch of sweetness. Humans appreciate the cones as seasonings (of gin, for example) or as breath fresheners rather than as food. When very young, at the time they receive pollen, juniper cones have individual scales. As the cone matures, the scales fuse together, producing the "berry." The mature cone may have a waxy bloom that makes it look pale bluish gray to pale purplish; this bloom may be rubbed off, exposing the darker underlying layer. In some species the cones mature in the first year. Others take two years; first-year and second-year cones may then be present at once, differing in both size and color.

Nearly all junipers have two types of leaves: mature leaves lie flat against the branchlet and are blunt and scalelike, whereas juvenile leaves are sharp and up to ½" long—short, stiff needles, in other words. The latter are found on seedlings, and in some species also on some new shoots on sizable young trees. Common Juniper is the exception, bearing only sharp, needlelike leaves throughout its lifespan. Juniper leaves are commonly borne "in fours," as opposite pairs, a side pair alternating with a front-and-back pair. In a few species leaves are borne mainly in whorls of three, each whorl rotated 60° from the whorls above and below it. In

Junipers, such as this Utah Juniper, often grow on inhospitable sites with little ground vegetation to support large, consuming fires.

most species, each tiny, scalelike leaf has a single, visible resin gland on its underside that looks like a shallow, oval pit.

Most junipers of the arid West are "fire avoiders." Though a few can sprout from a stump, most cannot survive fire, and historically they reached ripe old ages only where fires did not occur—that is, in "rimrock" areas with too little soil over the bedrock to support enough vegetation to sustain and spread a fire. Today, young junipers are spreading rapidly because of a century of fire control. Grazing practices also have opened sites for seedling establishment and have reduced the ability of grasslands to carry a fire that would remove young trees. The resulting new juniper communities may be good for certain wildlife, and perhaps for scenery, but once in place the tenacious trees make it impossible for grass to reestablish beneath them. They are also a problem for rural residents because in dense stands they may carry fire like a fresh oil slick.

Eastern Redcedar

Juniperus virginiana
ALSO CALLED Red Juniper, Pencil-cedar
HT 30–60'   DIA 1–2'

Small to medium-sized evergreen tree with a single, sometimes fluted trunk clad in fibrous, peeling bark, and a dense, often slender, conical crown. On cliffs and other harsh habitats, dwarfed, with open crown of gnarled branches. **ID TIP:** Eastern Redcedars, often recognized by their shape and ubiquity in open habitats, bear both scalelike and sharp, needlelike leaves on the same plant; cones are blue and fleshy.

HABITAT: Dry slopes, harsh rocky sites, sandy areas, limestone soils, open woods, fields, coastal dunes. Elevation 0–4,600'.

NOTES: Eastern Redcedar, the common juniper of the East, is often one of the first tree species to invade abandoned pastures, cleared roadsides, and other open habitats. The trees ring the wildflower-rich cedar glades atop limestone balds in the southern Appalachians. **Southern Redcedar,** the southern coastal plain variety (*silicicola*), has slightly smaller (⅛") cones and more pendulous foliage.

CYPRESS FAMILY   CUPRESSACEAE

LEAVES Mature leaves scalelike, tiny, ¹⁄₁₆–⅛" long; dark green; each leaf has a resin gland. Leaves mostly in 4s, in opposite pairs. Leaves on younger branches of *Juniperus* species (shown below) are needlelike; ½" long; yellow-green to blue-green; sharp. **CONE** ⅛–¼" wide. Rounded, berrylike. Blackish blue, with whitish, waxy coating. Fleshy pulp; 1 or 2 seeds (sometimes 3). Matures in 1 year.

juvenile leaves

Common Juniper

Juniperus communis
HT to 25' DIA 6–8"

Small evergreen shrub, usually about 4' tall, but occasionally a small tree, to 15–25'. Most extensive native range of any conifer, spanning much of the Northern Hemisphere. **ID TIP:** This juniper retains needlelike leaves throughout life, rather than developing mostly scalelike leaves in maturity, as do other junipers.

HABITAT: Poor rocky soils, pastures, coasts, mountains, subarctic sites. Elevation 0–11,300'.

LEAVES Needlelike, ½" long, sharp. Dark green; sometimes bluish from whitish, waxy coating. **CONE** ¼–½" wide. Round to ovoid, berrylike. Blue-black, with whitish, waxy coating. Dry to woody; 2 or 3 seeds. Matures in 2 years.

Junipers of Texas

Juniperus species

Three species of tree junipers have ranges mostly in Texas. All are small evergreen trees or shrubs.

Pinchot Juniper (*J. pinchotii*), also called Redberry Juniper, has red-brown to red cones with little or no waxy coating. Pulp is nonresinous and may be dry or juicy and sweet. A small tree or shrub (to 20' tall), it is found in dry plains, canyons, and foothills, often in open woodlands. Elevation 950–5,600'.

Ashe Juniper (*J. ashei*), of limestone hills from central Texas to the Ozark Mountains, has blue cones, usually with 1 seed; the tiny resin gland on each scalelike leaf is a pronounced, hemispherical bump; forms thickets.

Drooping Juniper (*J. flaccida*), of Mexico and Big Bend National Park, Texas, has dry, red-brown cones with numerous seeds and strongly "weeping" branches.

PINCHOT JUNIPER LEAVES Scalelike, tiny, ¹⁄₁₆–⅛" long. Yellowish green. Each leaf has resin gland. Leaves in 3s or 4s. **CONE** ¼–⅜" wide. Round, berrylike. Red-brown to red. Fleshy or dry pulp; 1 seed (sometimes 2). Matures in 1 year.

J. pinchotii   *J. ashei*

Rocky Mountain Juniper

Juniperus scopulorum
HT 20–50' **DIA** 1–2'

Small evergreen tree or large shrub. Shape varies: straight trunk with narrow, columnar crown to forked trunk with spreading, irregular crown. Bark reddish brown, weathering to gray, fibrous. **ID TIP:** This western juniper has fleshy, blue cones and a resin gland on each scalelike leaf.

HABITAT: Rocky, steep mountains, dry mesas. Elevation 0–8,900'.

NOTES: Rocky Mountain Juniper is the most widely distributed western tree juniper. It is very similar to Eastern

Redcedar, but the two occupy different ranges. It is a very long-lived tree (to 2,000 years or more); the trunk and branches become twisted and weathered with age.

| CYPRESS FAMILY | CUPRESSACEAE |

LEAVES Scalelike, tiny, ¹⁄₁₆–⅛" long; gray-green; each leaf has conspicuous resin gland. Leaves usually in 4s, in opposite pairs, forming 4-sided branchlets. Juvenile leaves needlelike. **CONE** ¼–⅓" wide. Round, berrylike. Bright blue, with whitish, waxy coating. Fleshy to mealy pulp; usually 2 seeds (occasionally 1 or 3). Matures in 2 years.

| CYPRESS FAMILY | CUPRESSACEAE |

Oneseed Juniper

Juniperus monosperma
ALSO CALLED Single-seed Juniper, Cherrystone Juniper
HT 10–40' **DIA** 6–18"

Small evergreen tree or large shrub with 1 to several short trunks; thin, soft, shaggy, ash gray bark; and a spreading, ragged crown. **ID TIP:** Utah Juniper is similar, but its cones are slightly larger, dry and mealy, and may be 2-seeded.

HABITAT: Rocky dry plains, mesas, mountains. Elevation 3,300–7,500'.

NOTES: Oneseed Juniper is a common tree of the Southwest, often a major component of pinyon-juniper woodlands, sagebrush scrub, and other plant associations of dry woodlands,

shrublands, and grasslands. Junipers, pinyons, and broadleaf plants of these habitats often fill the air with fragrance.

LEAVES Scalelike, tiny, ¹⁄₁₆–⅛" long. Pale yellowish green; each leaf has a resin gland. Leaf tip pointed. Leaves usually in 4s, in opposite pairs. **CONE** ¼–⅓" wide. Round, berrylike. Blue, sometimes coppery, with whitish, waxy coating. Fleshy pulp; 1 seed (rarely 2 or 3). Matures in 1 year.

Utah Juniper

Juniperus osteosperma
HT 15–30' **DIA** 6–12"

Small evergreen tree or large shrub with 1 to several short trunks, reddish brown to gray bark shredding in long strips, and a spreading crown of stout branches that become twisted with age. **ID TIP:** Utah Juniper's scalelike leaves lack conspicuous resin glands; the cones are dry, brownish, and 1- or 2-seeded, and can be larger than those of Oneseed Juniper.

HABITAT: Dry slopes and valleys. Elevation 3,000–8,500'.

| CYPRESS FAMILY | CUPRESSACEAE |

LEAVES Scalelike, tiny, 1⁄16" long. Pale yellowish green; the resin gland on each leaf not apparent. Leaves in 4s, usually in opposite pairs. Juvenile leaves needlelike. **CONE** 1⁄4–1⁄2" wide. Round, berrylike. Blue (when young) to red-brown, with whitish, waxy coating. Dry, mealy pulp; 1 seed (occasionally 2). Strongly aromatic. Matures in 1–2 years.

Alligator Juniper

Juniperus deppeana
ALSO CALLED Checkered-bark Juniper
HT 20–50' **DIA** 1½–3'

Small evergreen tree; the Southwest's largest juniper. **ID TIP:** Short, thick trunk becomes massive, with thickened, corrugated bark. Leaves in 3s or 4s.
HABITAT: Pinyon-juniper and other open woodlands on dry mountain slopes. Elevation 6,600–9,500'.

| CYPRESS FAMILY | CUPRESSACEAE |

BARK Broken into squarish plates that make it resemble alligator skin.

LEAVES Scalelike, tiny, 1⁄16–1⁄8" long. Blue-green; each leaf has a resin gland. Leaf tip sharp-pointed.

CONE 1⁄2–5⁄8" wide. Reddish to dark brown, with whitish, waxy coating giving bluish hue. Hard; dry, mealy pulp; 3–6 seeds.

Western Juniper

Juniperus occidentalis
HT 15–40'   DIA 6–12"

Small evergreen tree or large shrub with 1–3 short, thick trunks; cinnamon bark in shaggy, diagonal ridges; a low, spreading crown; and heavy, horizontal branches. **ID TIP:** Western Juniper has a more westerly distribution than Rocky Mountain Juniper; its scalelike leaves are often in 3s (only sometimes in 4s).

HABITAT: Dry mesas, canyons, foothills, and mountain slopes. Elevation 3,300–9,800' (occasionally lower).

CYPRESS FAMILY   CUPRESSACEAE

LEAVES Scalelike, tiny, ⅟16–⅛" long. Gray-green; each leaf has a resin gland. Leaves mostly in 3s (sometimes 4s). Juvenile leaves needlelike. **CONE** ¼–⅜" wide. Round, berrylike. Blue to nearly black, with whitish, waxy coating. Fleshy pulp; usually 2 seeds (sometimes 3). Matures in 2 years.

California Juniper

Juniperus californica
HT 10–30'   DIA 1'

The only juniper in most of California's Coast Ranges (Western Juniper overlaps with it in the north) and the largest Mojave Desert tree. **ID TIP:** It resembles Utah Juniper, but its scalelike leaves are usually in 3s (not 4s), and each has a conspicuous resin gland. **HABITAT:** Desert and mountain slopes, in chaparral, grasslands, and open woodlands, often among oaks and pinyons. Elevation 2,500–5,200'.

CYPRESS FAMILY   CUPRESSACEAE

LEAVES Scalelike, tiny, ⅟16–⅛" long. Light green; each leaf has a conspicuous resin gland. Leaves usually in 3s. Juvenile leaves needlelike. **CONE** ½–⅝" wide. Round, berrylike. Red-brown (sometimes bluish), with whitish, waxy coating. Mealy pulp; 1 seed (occasionally 2). Matures in 1 year.

Tamarisks

Tamarix species
ALSO CALLED Salt-cedar
HT 8–20' **DIA** 4–6"

Small flowering tree or shrub with somewhat juniperlike leaves; not a conifer. **ID TIP:** Appears leafless, with many fine, silvery gray-green branchlets, which are actually enveloped in tiny scalelike leaves. Showy white to pink flowers, followed by fluffy, white seeds.

HABITAT AND RANGE: Introduced in North America. Invasive; naturalized widely in the West (less in the East), in waste places, along waterways, and in salty or alkaline habitats. Old World native.

NOTES: Tamarisks spread from early gardens and erosion-control projects, and can form large, impenetrable thickets along river plains. The trees move salty water from the soil through their roots and branches and out their leaves, increasing soil surface salinity and creating an inhospitable habitat for other plants.

LEAVES Scalelike, tiny, ⅟₁₆–⅛" long. Often overlapping, pressed against slender twigs. Leaf twigs drop in autumn in cooler areas. **FLOWER** Pink or white, in showy, 1–2", wandlike clusters at tips of twigs. In some areas nearly year-round. **FRUIT** ⅛" long; brown, dry, pointed capsule; splits open lengthwise, releasing numerous tiny, cottony seeds.

Australian-pine

Casuarina equisetifolia
ALSO CALLED Beach She-oak, Horsetail Casuarina, Beefwood
HT 50–100' **DIA** 1–1½'

Medium-sized to large deciduous, flowering tree; not a pine or conifer, but looks like one from a distance. **ID TIP:** Shaggy, feathery crown of long, widely spaced branches and drooping bunches of very long, slender, needlelike branchlets.

HABITAT AND RANGE: Introduced in North America; naturalized in Florida along seashores and in young inland forests. Native to Australia.

NOTES: *Casuarina* species are planted in the tropics and warm temperate regions to improve soil fertility and control erosion. Several species are rampant invasives. **River She-oak** (*C. cunninghamiana*), unlike Australian-pine, is not salt-tolerant; it has nearly hairless, needlelike branchlets with 7–10 tiny, scalelike leaves per ring.

LEAVES 4–12" long, flexible, green, needlelike, photosynthetic branchlets are actually wiry, fine-grooved, green twigs encircled with regularly spaced whorls of 6–8 minute, triangular, scalelike leaves; resemble horsetails (*Equisetum*). Branchlets hairy; shed gradually throughout the year. **FRUIT** ¼" samaras in ½–1" long conelike structure.

Broadleaf Trees

Broadleaf trees, in contrast to needle-leaf and scale-leaf trees (most of which are conifers and gymnosperms; see page 13), have expanded, flattened leaf blades that are much broader than thick. With one exception, broadleaf trees are traditionally classified as angiosperms, or flowering plants, one of the two major divisions of the seed plants. Ginkgo, which leads off this section, also has expanded blade tissue but is so distinct that it has been placed in its own division, separate from flowering plants and conifers.

Traditionally, the angiosperms have been called flowering plants to differentiate them from the gymnosperms. However, the word "angiosperm" derives from the combination of the Greek words *angion*, "vessel" or "container," and *sperma*, "seed." Unlike the naked seeds of the gymnosperms, the fruits of broadleaf trees are borne inside an enclosed ovary. It is the presence of both flowers and enclosed fruit that distinguishes the angiosperms.

Flowering plants are further divided into two classes, the monocotyledons (monocots) and dicotyledons (dicots). Palms and yuccas are monocots; all other flowering trees covered in this guide are dicots. Monocot leaves typically have parallel veins, and the flowers usually have three or six parts, but not five. Dicot leaves are typically pinnately or palmately veined, and the flowers often have four or five parts, or more than six. Monocots and dicots also differ significantly in their internal anatomical structure. Only dicots produce true wood. In this guide, truly treelike dicots are presented first. They are divided by leaf arrangement into three sections: opposite leaves (page 155); alternate, compound leaves (page 211); and alternate, simple leaves (page 256). These are followed by three groups that are not typical trees: palms (page 461), yuccas (page 470), and cacti (page 474).

Deciduous and Evergreen Leaves

Most North American broadleaf trees are deciduous, losing their leaves in autumn and remaining leafless until spring. A few species lose their leaves in spring and replace them with new leaves very quickly. Species that do this are often described as semievergreen or as tardily deciduous. A few broadleaf trees are truly evergreen and retain their leaves for several years. The leaves of evergreen broadleaf trees, such as Southern Magnolia and Southern Live Oak, are generally thicker than those of deciduous trees and often have a waxy coating that retards water loss.

Sugar Maple

Ginkgo

Neither a conifer nor a flowering plant, Ginkgo is the most primitive woody tree and the only remaining species of its 280-million-year-old family. Virtually extinct in the wild, it had been preserved as a sacred tree by Buddhists, and was found in a Chinese monastery in 1854. Leaves occur mostly in bundles on spur twigs. Male trees bear pollen sacs in a long, catkinlike cluster; female trees have seed-bearing ovules in stalked, inconspicuous pairs. The naked seed resembles a yellowish plum.

Ginkgo

Ginkgo biloba
ALSO CALLED Maidenhair Tree
HT 50–70' **DIA** 1–3'

| GINKGO FAMILY | GINKGOACEAE |

Medium-sized tree with deciduous, simple leaves. Straight trunk; wide-spreading, irregular crown (upper branches often project outward farther than lower branches). **ID TIP:** The fan-shaped leaf is unique. Leafless trees are recognizable by the many little "pegs" (spur twigs) along the branches.

HABITAT AND RANGE: Introduced in North America; planted in cities. Native to China.

NOTES: Ginkgo is highly tolerant of modern city stresses, succumbs to no diseases, and has become one of the most widely planted city trees. Male trees are most often planted to avoid the problem of the female tree's malodorous fallen fruit. Extracts from the seeds, long used in herbal medicine, are being investigated by researchers as an Alzheimer's cure.

LEAF 1–2" long, 1½–3" wide. Fan-shaped; outer edge wavy, notched in the middle (can be somewhat 2-lobed). Conspicuous veins radiate from leaf base; no midvein. Often leathery. Pale green above and beneath. Leafstalk 1–3" long. Leaves in bundles on spur twigs, or alternate. Autumn color bright yellow to gold. **SEED** 1" wide, plum-shaped; yellowish to orange-brown when ripe; rancid-smelling when rotting. Juicy, soft covering surrounds large, thick-shelled, white seed kernel. Autumn.

spur twigs

Trees with Opposite Leaves

This guide divides the broadleaf trees into two large categories based on whether the leaves are borne in an alternate or an opposite arrangement along the branch. The point on the stem where the leaves attach is called a leaf node. Opposite leaves are borne two at a node on opposite sides of the stem. Alternate leaves are borne one at a node. Sometimes three or more leaves are borne at a single node, an arrangement described as whorled.

The following section of the guide presents trees with opposite (or whorled) leaves, starting with trees with compound, opposite leaves (page 158) and followed by those with simple, opposite leaves (page 178). The Key to Trees with Opposite Leaves (pages 156–157) presents the trees by leaf features and fruit type.

The blades of compound leaves are divided into two or more distinct divisions called leaflets. In palmately compound leaves the leaflets share a common point of attachment, similar to the fingers of the human hand. The horse-chestnut family has trees with palmately compound leaves. The leaflets of pinnately compound leaves are borne oppositely (rarely alternately) along a central axis, similar to the arrangement of barbs on a feather. The ash trees are examples.

Trees with simple, opposite leaves are dominated by members of the maple, olive, honeysuckle, and dogwood families. Simple leaves have an undivided blade with margins that may be lobed, toothed, or untoothed. The leaves of most maples are both lobed and toothed. Unlobed leaves vary in shape from the heart-shaped leaves of Princesstree and catalpas to the generally elliptic outlines of mangroves, dogwoods, and trees of the olive family. The elliptic leaves of Buttonbush are both opposite and whorled, which helps to distinguish the species from the vegetatively similar and closely related Fevertree.

Most opposite-leaf trees are deciduous, and thus more difficult to identify in winter. The fallen foliage, fortunately, leaves telltale leafstalk scars on branches and twigs in pairs at the nodes that signify an opposite arrangement. In early winter it is sometimes possible to make an easy identification of a tree by examining its opposite leaf scars and the fallen leaves. In late winter and early spring the paired buds of the new leaves often swell noticeably and may take on a characteristic appearance (described in species accounts if notable). Close observation may be all that is required to learn the identity of the more common species in winter and early spring.

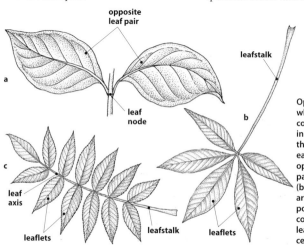

Opposite leaves (a), whether simple or compound, are borne in pairs at a leaf node, the two leaves opposite each other. Compound opposite leaves may be palmately compound (b), with the leaflets arising from a common point; or pinnately compound (c), with the leaflets borne along a central axis.

California Buckeye

California Buckeye

Leaves Palmately Compound

Fruit a capsule
    Horse-chestnut: p. 158
    Buckeyes: pp. 159–163

Fruit a drupe
    Lilac Chastetree: p. 164

Carolina Ash

Carolina Ash

Leaves Pinnately Compound

Fruit a capsule
    American Bladdernut: p. 164
    Texas Lignum-vitae: p. 165
    Catalina Ironwood: p. 165

Fruit a drupe
    Elderberries: p. 166

Fruit a samara
    Ashes: pp. 167–175
    Boxelder: p. 177

Sugar Maple

Leaves Simple, Lobed

Fruit a paired samara
    Maples: pp. 178–191

Northern Catalpa

Leaves Simple, Heart-shaped

Fruit a follicle
    Katsura Tree: p. 191

Fruit a capsule
    Princesstree: p. 192
    Catalpas: pp. 192–193

Black Mangrove

Leaves Simple, Unlobed, Untoothed

Fruit a capsule
Desert-willow: p. 194
Black Mangrove: p. 195
Japanese Tree Lilac: p. 202
Fevertree: p. 203

Fringetree

Redosier Dogwood

Redosier Dogwood

Fruit a drupe
White Mangrove: p. 197
Swampprivets: pp. 197–198
Privets: p. 199
Olive: p. 199
Devilwood: p. 200
Fringetree: p. 201
Dogwoods: pp. 204–207
Viburnums: pp. 208–209

Red Mangrove

Buttonbush

Fruit a berry
Wavyleaf Silktassel: p. 203

Fruit a berry with a hanging seedling
Red Mangrove: p. 196

Fruit a round cluster of nutlets
Buttonbush: p. 202

Fruit a samara
Singleleaf Ash: p. 175

Nannyberry

Nannyberry

Leaves Simple, Unlobed, Toothed

Fruit a drupe
Swampprivets: pp. 197–198
Viburnums: pp. 208–209
European Buckthorn: p. 210

Fruit a pome
Loquat: p. 210

Fruit a samara
Singleleaf Ash: p. 175

Horse-chestnut

Aesculus hippocastanum
HT 60–80' DIA 1–2½'

| HORSE-CHESTNUT FAMILY | HIPPOCASTANACEAE |

Medium-sized tree with deciduous, palmately compound leaves. Straight, often forking trunk; rounded to oblong or pyramidal crown of drooping branches with upturned ends. **ID TIP:** The leaflets are very broad above the middle and have an abruptly pointed tip; the reddish brown leaf buds are protected by sticky gum. The tree's prickly fruit is often confused with the similar-looking fruit of the unrelated true chestnuts (genus *Castanea*, pp. 416–417).

HABITAT AND RANGE: Introduced in North America; occasionally escapes in the Northeast. Native to Europe and Asia.

NOTES: Brought to North America in the 18th century, Horse-chestnut is planted as an ornamental and tolerates urban conditions. The seeds of all *Aesculus* species are poisonous if ingested; seed is glossy, brown, with a pale scar on one side where it attaches to the husk. The edible seeds of *Castanea* species are similar but pointed at one end; the alternate, simple leaves further distinguish true chestnut trees from horse-chestnuts.

LEAF 5–7 leaflets; leafstalk 3–7" long. **Leaflet:** 4–10" long, 2–5" wide; obovate, with abruptly pointed tip; margins unevenly, finely toothed. Dark green above; paler beneath. Autumn color dull yellow to brown. **FLOWER** 1" long; white with red or yellow markings; narrowly bell-shaped, with 4 or 5 unequal-sized, fringed petals. In 6–12" long, showy, upright clusters. Delicate, honeylike fragrance. Late spring. **FRUIT** 2–2½" long, nearly round capsule; thick husk covered with long, sharp prickles (short, blunt prickles in Ohio Buckeye); pale brown. Contains usually 1 (sometimes 2) ovoid seeds, each 1–1½" long, glossy, light to dark brown. Seed poisonous. Early autumn.

Ohio Buckeye

Aesculus glabra

ALSO CALLED Fetid Buckeye, American Horse-chestnut

HT 30–60'   **DIA** 1–2'

Small to medium-sized tree with deciduous, palmately compound leaves. Straight, often forking trunk; broad crown of dense, low, drooping branches with upturned ends. **ID TIP:** This is the only native buckeye with prickly fruit; the prickles are shorter than in the introduced Horse-chestnut.

HABITAT: Stream valleys and moist slopes; variety *arguta* also grows in limestone and sandy soils. Elevation 500–2,000'.

NOTES: The leaves, twigs, and flowers of Ohio Buckeye give off a foul odor. Trees of var. *arguta,* often called **Texas Buckeye,** are smaller (to 20') and have 7–11 lance-shaped leaflets and unequal-sized flower petals. Texas Buckeye occurs in and west of Iowa, Missouri, and Arkansas; some consider it a separate species.

Texas Buckeye

HORSE-CHESTNUT FAMILY   **HIPPOCASTANACEAE**

LEAF 5–11 (usually 5) leaflets; leafstalk 3–6" long. **Leaflet:** 2½–6" long, ¾–2" wide (longer and wider in Yellow Buckeye); elliptic, with pointed tip; margins unevenly, finely toothed. Yellow-green above; paler, often hairy beneath. Autumn color orange or yellow. **FLOWER** ¾–1" long; pale yellow; narrowly bell-shaped, with 4 nearly equal-sized petals. In 4–7" long, showy, upright clusters. Malodorous. Late spring. **FRUIT** 1–2" long, nearly round capsule; thick husk covered with short, blunt prickles (long prickles in Horse-chestnut); pale brown. Contains 1 glossy, dark brown seed, 1–1½" long, ovoid. Seed poisonous. Early autumn.

Yellow Buckeye

Aesculus flava

ALSO CALLED Sweet Buckeye, Big Buckeye

HT 50–90'   **DIA** 2–3'

Medium-sized to large tree with deciduous, palmately compound leaves. Straight, tall trunk; rounded crown of drooping branches with upturned ends. **ID TIP:** Yellow Buckeye has nonprickly fruit capsules (capsules are prickly in Horse-chestnut and Ohio Buckeye). Similar Painted Buckeye and Red Buckeye are smaller trees or shrubs.

HABITAT: Bottomlands and fertile mountain valleys and slopes. Elevation 500–6,300'.

NOTES: Yellow Buckeye occurs in greatest abundance in the mountains of Tennessee and North Carolina. It is often planted as an ornamental shade tree for its shape and showy, yellow flowers. It is one of the first trees to leaf out in spring.

| HORSE-CHESTNUT FAMILY | HIPPOCASTANACEAE |

LEAF 5 (sometimes 7) leaflets; leafstalk 3–7" long. **Leaflet:** 4–8" long, 1½–3" wide (shorter and narrower in Ohio Buckeye); elliptic, with pointed tip; margins evenly, finely toothed. Dark green above; yellow-green, sometimes hairy along veins beneath. Autumn color yellow or pumpkin orange. **FLOWER** 1¼" long; yellow (rarely red, pink, or creamy); bell-shaped, with 4 unequal-sized petals. In 4–7" long, showy, upright clusters. Late spring. **FRUIT** 2–3" long, rounded capsule; thick, leathery husk, not prickly; pale brown. Contains 1–3 glossy, dark brown, ovoid seeds, each 1½–2" long. Seed poisonous. Early autumn.

Painted Buckeye

Aesculus sylvatica
ALSO CALLED Dwarf Buckeye,
Georgia Buckeye
HT 5–30' **DIA** 6–10"

Small tree or shrub with deciduous, palmately compound leaves. Short, narrow trunk and erect branches; sometimes forms thickets. **ID TIP:** This small buckeye is distinguished from all other buckeyes by the leaflet's bright yellow to orange midvein.

HABITAT: Moist woodland slopes. Elevation 100–1,200'.

NOTES: Painted Buckeye is common throughout the Piedmont region in the Southeast.

LEAF 5 (sometimes 7) leaflets; leafstalk 4–6" long. **Leaflet:** 4–6" long, 1½–2½" wide; narrowly elliptic, with pointed tip; margins evenly, finely toothed. Dark green above; lighter green, sometimes hairy beneath; bright yellow to orange midvein. Autumn color yellow or orange. **FLOWER** 1–1¼" long; similar to Yellow Buckeye, but bright yellow with reddish interior (also sometimes pink to red, creamy, or yellow-green). Spring. **FRUIT** 1–2" long, nearly round capsule; similar to Yellow Buckeye. Contains 1 or 2 seeds, each 1–1½" long. Seed poisonous. Early autumn.

Red Buckeye

Aesculus pavia

ALSO CALLED Scarlet Buckeye, Firecracker Plant

HT 5–20' **DIA** 6–10"

| HORSE-CHESTNUT FAMILY | HIPPOCASTANACEAE |

Thicket-forming shrub or small tree with deciduous, palmately compound leaves. Single, short trunk; often multistemmed; rounded crown with erect branches.
ID TIP: The bark is light gray to gray-brown and smooth (not scaly or fissured as in other eastern buckeyes); leaflets are unevenly toothed; flowers are crimson red and tubular.

HABITAT: Stream banks, swamps, floodplains. Elevation to 1,500'.

NOTES: Red Buckeye is native to the South but will grow as far north as Canada. It can begin flowering when only 3' tall. **Red Horse-chestnut**, a hybrid of Red Buckeye and Horse-chestnut, is a common landscaping tree; it is larger than Red Buckeye and has pink flowers and nonprickly fruits.

LEAF 5 (sometimes 7) leaflets; leafstalk 3–6" long. **Leaflet:** 2½–6" long, 1¼–2½" wide; narrowly elliptic, with pointed tip; margins unevenly, finely toothed. Shiny, dark green with recessed veins above; paler green and sometimes thickly covered with short white hairs beneath. Autumn color yellow. Leaves drop early, sometimes by late September. **FLOWER** 1¼" long; crimson red (sometimes yellowish red or yellow); tubular, with 4 unequal-sized petals. In 4–7" long, showy, upright clusters. Late spring. **FRUIT** 1½–2" long, rounded to pear-shaped capsule; thick, leathery husk, not prickly; light brown. Contains usually 1–3 glossy, light brown, ovoid seeds, each 1" long. Seed poisonous. Early autumn.

California Buckeye

Aesculus californica
HT 12–30' DIA 6–10"

HORSE-CHESTNUT FAMILY   **HIPPOCASTANACEAE**

Thicket-forming shrub or small tree with deciduous, palmately compound leaves. Short trunk, enlarged at base, often twisted and multistemmed; crown rounded or flat-topped. **ID TIP:** California Buckeye is the only native western buckeye. It is distinguished from the introduced Horse-chestnut by narrower leaflets and nonprickly fruits.

HABITAT: Chaparral-oak foothills. Elevation to 4,000'.

NOTES: A soil stabilizer, California Buckeye is planted for erosion control along streams and steep slopes. The foliage, seeds, and even the flower nectar are considered poisonous to humans, cattle, bees, and other wildlife; the tree is often eradicated by ranchers and beekeepers where it naturally occurs.

LEAF 4–7 (usually 5) leaflets; leafstalk 3–4" long. **Leaflet:** 3–6" long, 1½–2" wide; narrowly elliptic, with pointed tip; finely toothed margins. Dark green above; paler beneath. Sheds in late summer, with no autumn color. Bud brown, very sticky. **FLOWER** 1–1¼" long; white or pale pink; tubular, with 4 nearly equal-sized petals; stamens protrude beyond petals. In 4–8" long, showy, upright clusters; conspicuous stamens make cluster look fuzzy. Fragrant. Late spring. **FRUIT** 2–3" long, pear-shaped capsule; thick, leathery husk, not prickly; light brown. Contains usually 1 or 2 round seeds, each 1–2" long, glossy, orange-brown. Seed poisonous. Autumn.

American Bladdernut

Staphylea trifolia

HT 15–25'   **DIA** 2–6"

| BLADDERNUT FAMILY | STAPHYLEACEAE |

Small tree or shrub with deciduous, compound leaves. Open crown, usually taller than wide; heavily branched. Shoots spring up freely, often forming a thicket. **ID TIP:** The leaves are composed of 3 leaflets; fruits are unique, 3-lobed, bladderlike capsules, pale green to light brown. The twigs and bark have white, vertical stripes.

HABITAT: Moist soils along waterways, usually in hardwood forests. Elevation to 2,000'.

NOTES: Bladdernut gets its name from its unusual inflated, bladderlike fruit, which persists on the tree into winter.

LEAF 3 leaflets, each 2–4" long; finely toothed margins. Bright green above; hairy beneath. **FLOWER** ⅜" long; white, in showy, drooping, 2–4" long clusters. Spring. **FRUIT** 1–2" long, inflated, papery capsule with 3 lobes; green to brown. Late summer, persists into winter.

Lilac Chastetree

Vitex agnus-castus

ALSO CALLED Monk's-pepper, Hemp Tree, Sage Tree

HT 10–20'

| VERBENA FAMILY | VERBENACEAE |

Small tree or shrub with deciduous, palmately compound leaves. Multi-stemmed; dense, spreading crown is as wide as it is high. **ID TIP:** The leaflets are lance-shaped and untoothed. The leaves and twigs have a spicy scent when crushed; twigs are hairy.

HABITAT AND RANGE: Introduced in North America; tolerant of diverse conditions and widely naturalized. Native to Europe, Asia, and Africa.

NOTES: Lilac Chastetree is hardy as far north as Washington and New York but is more common in the South, where it can top 20' and is spectacular in full bloom.

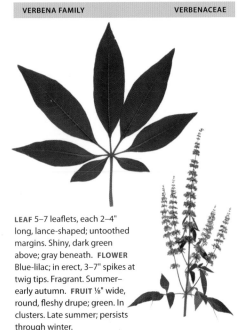

LEAF 5–7 leaflets, each 2–4" long, lance-shaped; untoothed margins. Shiny, dark green above; gray beneath. **FLOWER** Blue-lilac; in erect, 3–7" spikes at twig tips. Fragrant. Summer– early autumn. **FRUIT** ⅛" wide, round, fleshy drupe; green. In clusters. Late summer; persists through winter.

Texas Lignum-vitae

Guaiacum angustifolium
ALSO CALLED Texas Porliera, Soapbush, Guayacan
HT 10–20'   **DIA** 6–8"

CREOSOTE-BUSH FAMILY	ZYGOPHYLLACEAE

Small tree or shrub with evergreen, pinnately compound leaves. Short trunk; clumplike, dense crown. **ID TIP:** In spring, plant shows distinctive, purple-blue, star-shaped flowers set against dark green, feathery leaves. The exposed, large red seeds are conspicuous in autumn.

HABITAT: Open scrub thickets in valleys and canyons. Elevation to 3,000'.

NOTES: The leaves fold up at midday and at night to conserve water. The genus name is sometimes spelled *Guajacum*.

LEAF 1–3" long, with 8–16 paired leaflets. Leaflets ½–¾" long. Shiny, dark green. **FLOWER** ½–¾" wide; purple-blue petals. Each on long stalk; in clusters. Fragrant. Spring. **FRUIT** ½" wide, heart-shaped, fleshy capsule; brown. Seeds red. Summer.

Catalina Ironwood

Lyonothamnus floribundus
ALSO CALLED Lyontree
HT to 50'   **DIA** 10–12"

ROSE FAMILY	ROSACEAE

Small tree or shrub with evergreen, simple or pinnately compound leaves. One or several trunks; narrow crown that broadens at maturity. Often in small groves. **ID TIP:** The bark is red-brown and exfoliates in narrow strips, giving it a shaggy appearance.

HABITAT AND RANGE: Steep slopes of canyons on 4 of the 8 Channel Islands of southern California. Elevation 500–2,000'.

LEAF 4–7" long. Pinnately compound (mostly on Santa Catalina Island); or simple and lance-shaped. Leathery, glossy, dark green. **FLOWER** Small; white; in 4–8" wide, flat-topped clusters. Summer. **FRUIT** Tiny, ovoid capsule. Late summer.

Elderberries

Sambucus species
ALSO CALLED Elders
HT to 25'

Typically shrubs, with deciduous, pinnately compound leaves, but some attain tree size. Several forms of elderberries occur in North America, but authorities disagree on the taxonomy, making identification difficult. Raw fruits and other plant parts may be poisonous if ingested.

HABITAT: Moist woodlands. Elevation to 11,000'.

LEAF 5–10" long. 5–11 (usually 7) leaflets. **Leaflet:** 1½–6" long; elliptic to lance-shaped, with pointed tip; toothed margins. Green above; some have hairy midvein beneath. Twig stout; thin, woody layer encloses thick, spongy pith. **FLOWER** ¼" wide; white; yellow-white, or pink; 5-lobed; in 2–10" wide clusters. Spring–summer; year-round in some subspecies. **FRUIT** ¼–½" wide; berrylike drupe containing 3–5 seeds; in 2–8" wide clusters. Summer–autumn; year-round in some subspecies.

Eastern Common Elderberry

Eastern Common Elderberry

Blue Elderberry

Eastern Common Elderberry
Sambucus nigra ssp. *canadensis*

ID TIP: Flowers are in flat-topped clusters, in spring; fruit is mostly blackish, in autumn. **NOTES:** A western subspecies, **Blue Elderberry** (*S. nigra* ssp. *caerulea*), has sky-blue fruit, summer to autumn. It occurs from southern British Columbia south to Baja California and scattered eastward to Montana and Texas.

Red Elderberry

Red Elderberry
Sambucus racemosa

ID TIP: Flowers are in pyramidal clusters; fruit is red or black, in summer. **NOTES:** The species typically has red fruit in the East and some areas of the West. A western variety, **Black Elderberry** (*S. racemosa* var. *melanocarpa*), has nearly black fruit.

Red Elderberry

Black Elderberry

S. nigra ssp. *canadensis*   *S. racemosa*

Ashes

Ashes (genus *Fraxinus*), the only members of the olive family (Oleaceae) with compound leaves, have opposite, pinnately compound leaves, with the exception of Singleleaf Ash. Most are deciduous; leaves of Gregg's and Goodding's ashes persist through winter, dropping in spring. In most ashes, the flowers are less than ¼" wide, inconspicuous, and wind-pollinated. The western Fragrant Ash and California Ash have showy, insect-pollinated flowers. Male and female flowers usually occur on separate trees and in most species are similar in color. The fruit is a one-seeded

male flowers, White Ash

samara with a generally symmetrical wing; samaras are green, maturing to brown, and occur in hanging clusters. The seed is cylindrical. The location of the wing relative to the seed and the seed's thickness (flat or plump) are important identification clues in ashes.

Black Ash

Fraxinus nigra
ALSO CALLED Swamp Ash, Hoop Ash, Basket Ash
HT 30–70'   **DIA** 1–1½'

Small to medium-sized tree. Slender trunk; notably slim, rounded crown. **ID TIP:** Black Ash is the only eastern ash with stalkless leaflets (except terminal leaflet); The winter leaf buds are blue-black. The dark green foliage emerges late in spring and drops early in autumn.

HABITAT: Cold swamps, bogs. Elevation to 3,500'.

LEAF 10–16" long; 7–11 leaflets. **Leaflet:** 4–5" long; stalkless; narrowly elliptic; margins finely toothed, mostly above the middle. Dark green above; paler, with tufts of rusty hairs beneath. **FLOWER** Purplish. Early spring. **FRUIT** 1–1½" long samara; narrowly obovate; broad wing extends from base of flat seed. Late summer.

OLIVE FAMILY   OLEACEAE

White Ash

Fraxinus americana
HT 70–100' DIA 2–3'

Medium-sized to large tree. Tall, straight trunk; dense, symmetrical crown. Bark fissures make diamond pattern. Older trees have buttressed trunk base, massive branches; in forests, lowest branches may start high on tree. ID TIP: White Ash and Green Ash are easily confused. White Ash has leaves with a grayish white coating beneath and buds that are nested in a U-shaped leaf scar from last year's leaf.

HABITAT: Moist slopes, valleys (Green Ash and Carolina Ash occur in wetter sites). Elevation to 2,000' in the North; 5,000' in the South.

NOTES: White Ash is one of the world's largest and tallest ashes. It is planted as a shade tree and as an ornamental for its spectacular autumn foliage. **Biltmore Ash** (sometimes classified as var. *biltmoreana*) has velvety twigs and velvety leaf undersides; some consider it a hybrid of White and Green ashes.

LEAF 8–12" long; 7 (occasionally 5 or 9) leaflets. **Leaflet:** 3–5" long, 1½–3" wide (much narrower in Green Ash); short-stalked; elliptic, with pointed tip; finely toothed or untoothed margins. Glossy, dark green above; grayish white and hairless, slightly hairy, or velvety (var. *biltmoreana*) beneath. Autumn color purple, bronze, gold, yellow (often all on same leaf). FLOWER Purplish. Early spring. FRUIT 1–2½" long samara; narrowly obovate (broad in Carolina Ash); wing extends from near base of broad, plump seed. Late summer–autumn.

Green Ash

Fraxinus pennsylvanica
ALSO CALLED Red Ash, Swamp Ash
HT 60–70' **DIA** 1½–2'

Medium-sized tree. Tall trunk; compact crown. Bark fissures make diamond pattern. **ID TIP:** This species is very similar to White Ash, making identification difficult. The leaf buds sit above a leaf scar that is nearly straight across (not U-shaped), and the leafstalks of the 2 basal leaflets on each leaf have flattened edges, or "wings" (absent in White Ash).

HABITAT: Seasonally flooded forests along streams, swamps. Elevation to 3,000'.

NOTES: Green Ash has the widest and most northerly range of North America's ashes. Hardy, fast-growing, and resistant to wind and floods, the species is commonly planted as a street and shelterbelt tree, and used to revegetate strip-mine sites.

LEAF 6–10" long; 7 (sometimes 5 or 9) leaflets. **Leaflet:** 3–5" long, 1–1½" wide; short-stalked; elliptic, with pointed tip; margins may be sparsely toothed above the middle. Glossy, bright green above; hairless or covered with fine, pale or reddish hairs beneath. **FLOWER** Purplish. Early spring. **FRUIT** 1¼–2¼" long samara; narrowly obovate; wing extends from middle of narrow, cylindrical seed (much narrower than in White Ash). Late summer–autumn.

Mexican Ash

Fraxinus berlandieriana
ALSO CALLED Berlandier Ash
HT 30' **DIA** 1'

Where the range of Green Ash ends in southern Texas, that of its uncommon southwestern relative, Mexican Ash, begins. **ID TIP:** It is very similar to Green Ash but smaller, and has fewer and smaller leaflets, smaller fruit (1–1½" long). **HABITAT:** Streams and canyons. Elevation to 1,000'.

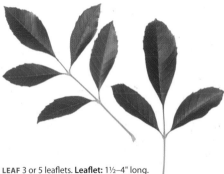

LEAF 3 or 5 leaflets. **Leaflet:** 1½–4" long.

Blue Ash

Fraxinus quadrangulata
HT 60–70' DIA 1½–2½'

OLIVE FAMILY OLEACEAE

Medium-sized tree. Tall trunk; slender crown of S-curved branches; in the open, has short trunk with dense crown. Bark gray to reddish gray; irregularly fissured. ID TIP: The twigs are distinctly 4-sided. The narrow samaras have a rounded and sometimes notched tip.

HABITAT: Limestone outcrops, woodlands. Elevation 400–2,000'.

NOTES: Blue Ash grows largest in the lower Wabash River basin (Illinois) and in the Great Smoky Mountains. The sap, which turns blue when exposed to air, produces a blue dye. The species often occurs with White Ash, but is less common than White Ash within its range. It is planted as a shade tree and an ornamental.

LEAF 8–12" long; 5–11 leaflets. **Leaflet:** 3–5" long; short-stalked; ovate to narrowly elliptic, with pointed tip; margins coarsely toothed. Yellow-green above; paler, with tufts of hair on midvein beneath. Twig 4-sided, slightly winged; dark orange in first year, turning brown or gray. **FLOWER** Purplish. Early spring. **FRUIT** 1–2" long samara; narrowly elliptic to obovate; slightly twisted, with rounded to squared tip that is sometimes notched; wing extends from base of flat seed. Spring–autumn.

4-sided, winged twig

Carolina Ash

Fraxinus caroliniana
ALSO CALLED Florida Ash, Water Ash, Pop Ash
HT 30–40'   **DIA** 7–12"

Small tree. One to several short, often crooked and leaning trunks, swollen at base; slender to rounded crown. **ID TIP:** The large samaras are broad-winged, flat, and widest near the middle; trees occasionally produce triple-winged samaras. Carolina is the only ash found in southern Florida.

HABITAT: Swamp forests, seasonally flooded river floodplains. Elevation to 500'.

LEAF 7–12" long; 5 or 7 (sometimes 9) leaflets. **Leaflet:** 2–6" long; long-stalked; elliptic to broadly elliptic, with pointed tip; margins coarsely toothed, sometimes untoothed. Dark green above; paler or yellow-green, sometimes slightly hairy or velvety beneath. **FLOWER** Male yellowish; female greenish. Early spring. **FRUIT** 1–3" long samara; sometimes 3-winged; thin, broadly elliptic, with pointed tip; flat seed extends more than halfway down length of wing; sometimes violet. Summer–autumn.

Pumpkin Ash

Fraxinus profunda
HT 80–90'   **DIA** 2–3'

Very similar to Green Ash. Tall trunk; elliptic crown. In flooded habitat the trunk base is distinctively swollen. **ID TIP:** Pumpkin Ash has large, drooping leaves, velvety twigs and leaf undersides, and a long samara that is squared at the tip. **HABITAT:** Swamp forests. Elevation to 500'.

LEAF 9–18" long; 5–9 (usually 7 or 9) leaflets. Leaf axis hairy. **Leaflet:** 3–8" long; margins untoothed or sparsely toothed; velvety beneath. **FLOWER** Male yellowish; female greenish. Early spring. **FRUIT** 2–3" long, narrow samara with squared tip; plump seed. Late summer–autumn.

Velvet Ash

Fraxinus velutina

ALSO CALLED Arizona Ash, Desert Ash

HT 25–40'   **DIA** 1–1½'

OLIVE FAMILY   **OLEACEAE**

Small tree. Single trunk; rounded crown. **ID TIP:** The most common ash of the Southwest, Velvet Ash is easily identified by its velvety leaf undersides and twigs.

HABITAT: Diverse; moist sites in canyons, desert, grasslands, and mountains, including streamside woodlands and pine forests. Elevation 2,500–7,000'.

NOTES: Velvet Ash is rapid-growing and drought- and heat-tolerant, but prone to attack by ash borer beetles. **Chihuahuan Ash** (*F. papillosa*) is restricted to canyons along Mexico's border with Arizona, New Mexico, and western Texas, including Coronado National Forest; elevation 5,500–7,000'. The leaf has 7 or 9 leaflets that are whitish beneath.

LEAF 3–6" long; 5 (sometimes 3 or 7) leaflets. **Leaflet:** 1–2" long; short-stalked; usually elliptic, but variable; margins bluntly toothed above the middle, or sometimes untoothed. Shiny green above; paler and usually velvety beneath. Twig velvety or hairy. **FLOWER** Male yellowish; female greenish. Early spring. **FRUIT** ¾–1¼" long samara; narrowly elliptic; wing extends from middle of plump seed. Early summer–early autumn.

Oregon Ash

Fraxinus latifolia
HT 35–80' **DIA** 1–3'

OLIVE FAMILY · OLEACEAE

Small to medium-sized tree. Tall, straight trunk. Dense, narrow crown in forests, broader in open; on poor sites, crown is ragged, with crooked branches. **ID TIP:** Oregon Ash is the West's largest ash and the only native ash of the Northwest.

HABITAT: Wet areas along streams and in canyons. Elevation to 5,500'.

NOTES: Oregon Ash grows largest and most abundantly in southwestern Oregon. Some specimens may live 250 years. It is a good shade tree for moist sites and is planted for erosion control.

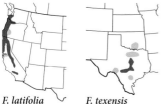

F. latifolia *F. texensis*

LEAF 5–14" long; 5 or 7 (occasionally 9) leaflets. **Leaflet:** 3–7" long; nearly stalkless; elliptic to broadly elliptic, with pointed tip; margins untoothed or finely toothed. Light green with conspicuous veins above; pale and hairy beneath. In southern range, persists through winter and drops in spring. **FLOWER** Male yellowish; female greenish. Early spring. **FRUIT** 1–2" long samara; broad, rounded; wing extends from middle of flat seed. Early autumn.

Texas Ash

Fraxinus texensis
HT 30–40' **DIA** 1–2'

OLIVE FAMILY · OLEACEAE

Some consider Texas Ash to be a smaller, drought-resistant variety of White Ash (p. 168). Broad crown of contorted branches. **ID TIP:** Nine native ash species overlap in Texas, making identification difficult. Texas Ash is distinguished from similar ashes by its whitish leaf undersides, and from White Ash by its smaller leaves. The narrowly obovate samaras mature in late spring; wing extends just past tip of cylindrical seed. **HABITAT:** Dry rocky slopes, canyon bluffs, limestone. Elevation 400–1,600'. (See map above.)

LEAF 5–8" long; 5 (sometimes 3 or 7) leaflets. **Leaflet:** 1–3" long; broadly elliptic; rounded teeth on margins. Dark green above; whitish, sometimes with tufts of white hairs on veins beneath. **FRUIT** ⅝–1¼" long samara; cylindrical seed.

California Ash

Fraxinus dipetala

ALSO CALLED Flowering Ash, Foothill Ash, Two-petal Ash

HT 7–20'   **DIA** 4–8"

Small tree or shrub. Short, erect trunk. **ID TIP:** California Ash and Fragrant Ash are North America's only native ashes with showy flowers. Rare outside of its namesake state, California Ash is distinguished from other compound-leaf western ashes by its 4-sided twigs. (Singleleaf Ash also has 4-sided twigs but usually occurs with simple leaves.)

HABITAT: Dry slopes, chaparral, and foothill woodlands. Elevation to 3,500'.

LEAF 2–6" long; 3–7 (occasionally 9) leaflets. **Leaflet:** ¾–2" long; short-stalked; elliptic to broadly elliptic, with pointed tip; margins coarsely toothed, or sometimes untoothed. Dark green above; pale beneath. Twig usually 4-sided. **FLOWER** White; 2 short (¼") but wide petals. In 4" long, loose, branched clusters. Not fragrant. Spring. **FRUIT** ¾–1" long samara; broadly elliptic; wing extends from near base of flat seed. Early summer.

Fragrant Ash

Fraxinus cuspidata

HT 20'   **DIA** 8"

Uncommon small tree or shrub. **ID TIP:** Fragrant Ash is North America's only ash with fragrant, showy blossoms (California Ash is not fragrant). **HABITAT:** Dry mountain slopes and canyons. Elevation 4,500–7,000'.

LEAF 3–7" long; 5 or 7 leaflets. **Leaflet:** 1½–2½" long; lance-shaped; toothed. **FLOWER** White; 4 long (⅝"), very narrow petals. In loose, hanging clusters. Fragrant. Spring.

Singleleaf Ash

Fraxinus anomala
HT 7–25'   DIA 5–7"

Small tree or shrub with simple, or sometimes compound, leaves. Short, crooked trunk, or multistemmed; rounded crown. **ID TIP:** Singleleaf Ash is one of the world's few ashes that typically occurs with a simple, not compound, leaf; it occasionally has a compound leaf with 2 or 3 small leaflets, more rarely 3–7 leaflets.

HABITAT: Dry canyons, rocky slopes, in higher-elevation deserts and woodlands; var. *lowellii* also occurs along streams. Elevation 2,000–11,000'.

NOTES: Singleleaf Ash is capable of growing at higher elevations than any other North American ash. In the hot desert, it provides vital shelter for mule deer, pronghorn antelope, upland game birds, and small mammals. Common in Zion, Arches, and Grand Canyon national parks. **Lowell Ash** (var. *lowellii*) is a rare, shrubby, compound-leaf variety with 3–7 leaflets; some consider it a separate species. It is restricted to a few sites in central and southern Arizona at 3,200–6,500' elevation.

OLIVE FAMILY   OLEACEAE

LEAF 1–2" long; typically simple; long-stalked. Nearly circular, with rounded or short-pointed tip; margins bluntly toothed or untoothed. Sometimes occurs with 2 or 3 leaflets (rare var. *lowellii* has up to 7). Dark green above; paler beneath. Twig velvety or hairy when young; 4-sided. **FLOWER** Greenish. Spring. **FRUIT** ½–¾" long samara; broadly elliptic; wing extends from middle of flat seed. Summer.

Gregg's Ash

Fraxinus greggii
HT 20'   DIA 5"

Small tree or shrub with pinnately compound leaves. **ID TIP:** The leaflets are the smallest of all ashes and are nearly evergreen, persisting on the tree through winter, dropping in spring. The similar **Goodding's Ash** (*F. gooddingii*), of Arizona's Coronado National Forest and Sonora, Mexico, at 3,600–5,000' elevation, has slightly larger leaves than Gregg's. **HABITAT AND RANGE:** Dry rocky slopes and canyons of the Trans-Pecos region of southwestern Texas. Elevation 1,000–2,000'.

OLIVE FAMILY   OLEACEAE

LEAF 1–2½" long; 3–7 leaflets. **Leaflet:** ½–1¼" long; elliptic to obovate; thick. **FRUIT** ½–¾" long samara, rounded at tip.

Maples

The maple family (Aceraceae) contains two genera: the maple genus, *Acer*, with about 120 species in temperate regions worldwide, and *Dipteronia*, with two species in China. North America has 13 native maple species, several of which are among the world's largest maples. Maples are much admired for their contribution to scenic beauty. They are typically the major element in the extensive, brilliantly colored autumn foliage displays in North America and eastern Asia.

Maples have opposite, deciduous leaves that are usually simple and palmately lobed, with three or five main veins radiating from the leafstalk base. Exceptions with compound leaves are Boxelder, some local variants of Rocky Mountain Maple, and several nonnative ornamentals. Leafstalks are long, generally from three-quarters to the full length of the leaf. Except where noted, the flowers are small and not very showy, with stamens often the most conspicuous part. Most flowers occur in drooping clusters; male and female flowers are usually in separate clusters and may or may not be borne on separate trees. The fruit is a samara, borne in pairs, each samara is strongly asymmetrical. Samaras generally begin green to reddish and dry to brown. The angle formed by the samara pair can be a helpful maple identification clue. The bark varies within the genus.

Sap of some maples is sweet and can be boiled down to make maple syrup; Sugar Maple gives the most copious yields. Climate change is beginning to adversely affect sap collection in New England and other northern regions.

Trees with Maplelike Leaves

While the palmate maple leaf shape is distinctive and recognizable (picture the Canadian flag), several other trees have similar leaves. Unlike maples, all of these are alternate rather than opposite.

Tuliptree, p. 277

White Poplar, p. 396

sycamores and planetrees, pp. 267–269

Sweetgum, p. 270

Boxelder

Acer negundo
ALSO CALLED Ashleaf Maple,
Manitoba Maple
HT 30–70'   **DIA** 1–2½'

Small to medium-sized tree, or large
shrub in the Great Plains, with pinnately
compound leaves. Short trunk, forking
near the ground; uneven, rounded crown.
Sprouts can occur on trunk and branches.
Old trees often lean over, sometimes close
to the ground. **ID TIP:** Boxelder is the only
North American maple with pinnately
compound leaves (Rocky Mountain Maple
and some introduced maples may have 3
leaflets, and introduced maples may have
palmately compound leaves).

HABITAT: Floodplains, stream banks, waste
places. Elevation to 8,000'.

NOTES: Boxelder has the greatest range
of all North American maples, extending
from central Canada south to Central
America, and in the United States is
native in both the East and the West.
Hardy and rapid-growing, it is planted for
shelterbelts and as a street tree, although
it is short-lived and easily storm-damaged.
It has subsequently naturalized in many
areas where it is not native, such as the
Pacific Northwest. It attracts the boxelder
bug, which can become a house pest.

MAPLE FAMILY	ACERACEAE

LEAF 6" long; spring leaves typically have 3 leaflets, summer
leaves have 5 (rarely up to 11). **Leaflet:** 2–4" long; nearly
stalkless, except terminal leaflet; elliptic, with pointed
tip; terminal leaflet sometimes 3-lobed; coarsely toothed
margins. Light green above; gray-green and hairy on veins
beneath. Autumn color pale yellow or red. Twig often has
gray-white bloom; turns amethyst color in winter; velvety
or downy in some populations. **FLOWER** In small clusters
close to twig. Male: tiny, hairy, pink. Female: ¼" long,
yellow-green. Usually on separate trees. Early spring before
leaves. **FRUIT** 1–2" long, paired samaras, making an acute
angle; profusely clustered in 6–8" chains (longer and more
linear than other maple fruit clusters). Late summer–
autumn; chains often persist through winter.

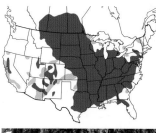

Sugar Maple

Acer saccharum

ALSO CALLED Hard Maple, Rock Maple

HT 70–100'   **DIA** 2–3'

Medium-sized to large tree. Tall, straight trunk; dense, elliptic crown. Bark gray, smooth when young, later splitting into narrow, slightly concave plates. Older maple trees may develop a fluted, buttressed trunk base and massive, crooked or staghorn-shaped branches. **ID TIP:** Sugar Maple leaves have 5 lobes that are drawn out into long-pointed tips; 3 longest lobes often have 2 "shoulder" subpoints, and sometimes a few additional short points.

HABITAT: Moist forests. Elevation to 5,500'.

NOTES: Sugar Maple is the star of eastern North America's autumn foliage show, setting hillsides ablaze with gold, orange, and scarlet. Squirrels gnaw into the bark to reach the sweet sap, which is the principal source for syrup production in the Northeast.

LEAF 4–6" long; usually slightly wider than long. 5 lobes: 3 deeply divided and long-pointed, and 2 smaller, shallower ones toward base. Dull green above; pale green or whitish and often hairy on veins beneath. Autumn color brilliant orange, red, yellow. **FLOWER** Yellowish green. With new leaves in early spring. **FRUIT** 1–1½" long, paired samaras that make an acute angle or are almost parallel to one another. Late summer–autumn.

Southern Sugar Maple

Acer barbatum
ALSO CALLED Florida Sugar Maple,
Hammock Maple
HT 20–60' **DIA** 2'

Small to medium-sized tree. **ID TIP:** Bark
pale gray and smooth (like beech) when
young, furrowing and darkening with age.
The leaf is whitish beneath.

HABITAT: Calcium-rich slopes in coastal
plain valleys. Elevation to 2,000'.

NOTES: Southern Sugar Maple differs in
appearance and habitat preference from
Sugar Maple, but the two intergrade
where their ranges barely overlap. Some
consider it a variety of Sugar Maple,
A. saccharum var. *floridanum*.

MAPLE FAMILY	ACERACEAE

LEAF 1½–3" long (smaller
than Sugar Maple); 3
shallowly divided lobes,
with pointed or, more
often, rounded tips; edges
wavy. Dull green above;
whitish and hairy beneath.
Autumn color scarlet and
yellow. **FRUIT** ½–¾" long,
paired samaras that make
an acute or, more often,
obtuse angle.

Chalk Maple

Acer leucoderme
ALSO CALLED Whitebark Maple
HT 20–25' **DIA** 8–12"

Small tree or crooked shrub. **ID TIP:**
Bark very pale gray and smooth when
young, furrowing and darkening to nearly
black with age. Chalk Maple is similar to
Southern Sugar Maple and occurs within
the same range. Chalk Maple has green,
not whitish, leaf undersides.

HABITAT: Moist woods, stream banks,
ravines. Elevation 200–1,000'.

NOTES: This maple has been considered a
variety of Sugar Maple, *A. saccharum* var.
leucoderme.

MAPLE FAMILY	ACERACEAE

young bark   older bark

LEAF 2–3½" long (larger than Southern Sugar Maple);
3 shallowly divided lobes, with pointed or, more often,
rounded tips. Yellow-green above; yellow-green and soft-
hairy beneath. Autumn color red. **FRUIT** ½–¾" long, paired
samaras that make a right or slightly obtuse angle.

Black Maple

Acer nigrum
HT 70–100'   **DIA** 2–3'

Medium-sized to large tree. Tall, straight trunk; dense, elliptic crown. **ID TIP:** Black Maple so closely resembles Sugar Maple that some consider it to be a Sugar Maple variety. Black Maple has darker, drooping (as if wilting) leaves, orange twigs, and darker bark without smooth plates between the furrows; it occupies a different habitat.

HABITAT: Moist, rich soils in woodlands and along water courses, mainly in low areas. Elevation to 2,500'; to 5,400' in southern Appalachians.

NOTES: Like Chalk and Southern Sugar maples, Black Maple is sometimes considered a variety of Sugar Maple (*A. saccharum* var. *nigrum*), and some reference works list it as such. Black Maple and Sugar Maple hybridize where they meet in some areas, but in others they apparently do not.

MAPLE FAMILY
ACERACEAE

LEAF 4–6" long, usually slightly wider than long. 3 (rarely 5) moderately to shallowly divided, pointed lobes. Dark green above; yellow-green and velvety beneath. Autumn color bright yellow. Leafstalk hairy. Twig green, maturing to orange in first year. **FLOWER** Yellowish. With new leaves in early spring. **FRUIT** 1–1¼" long, paired samaras that make an acute angle or are parallel. Late summer–autumn.

Red Maple

Acer rubrum
ALSO CALLED Swamp Maple,
Scarlet Maple, Soft Maple
HT 60–80' **DIA** 1–2½'

Medium-sized tree. Tall, straight trunk; dense, elliptic crown. **ID TIP:** Red Maple has red or reddish young leaf, leafstalk, twig, flower, and fruit, and even wood and older bark are red-tinged. In autumn, many of its leaves turn deep red. The tree produces a profusion of flowers along its bare branches in late winter and early spring, giving it a conspicuous reddish tinge.

HABITAT: Diverse; low wetlands to moist forests to dry ridges. Elevation to 6,000'.

NOTES: Red Maple spans an impressive range of climates and latitudes and occurs in a variety of habitats. It is planted as an ornamental and shade tree. The seeds germinate and grow as soon as they hit the ground, and can produce several leaves by the following summer (one of the many traits Red Maple shares with its close relative Silver Maple).

LEAF 2½–5" long, usually longer than wide. 3 or 5 shallowly divided, pointed lobes (most often 3 are apparent, as the lower 2 are barely more than teeth); coarsely toothed margins. Dull green above; whitish and slightly hairy beneath. Autumn color brilliant scarlet, orange-red, yellow. Leafstalk reddish green. Twig shiny, reddish.

FLOWER Scarlet to yellow. Late winter–early spring, before leaves emerge. **FRUIT** ¾–1" long, paired samaras that make an acute angle; initially red, then browning somewhat at maturity. Spring–early summer.

Silver Maple

Acer saccharinum
ALSO CALLED White Maple,
Soft Maple, River Maple
HT 50–80'   **DIA** 2–3'

MAPLE FAMILY	ACERACEAE

Medium-sized tree. Short, thick, forking
trunk; open crown of long, curving
branches and brittle, drooping branchlets.
In older trees, bark may become shaggy-
looking. **ID TIP:** Silver Maple samaras are
the largest of all maples. The leaves are
silvery beneath. Twigs are malodorous;

HABITAT: Floodplains, swamps, along
waterways. Elevation to 2,000'.

NOTES: A fast-growing species, Silver
Maple is often planted as a shade tree, but
with a price: the brittle limbs are easily
broken in storms, and the shallow roots
can lift up sidewalks and driveways.

LEAF 5–7" long and nearly as wide. 5 deeply divided,
pointed lobes; coarsely toothed margins. Dull, pale green
above; silver-white, hairless or sometimes hairy on veins
beneath. Autumn color pale yellow-green. Leafstalk red
or reddish green, and drooping. Twig has unpleasant
smell when bruised or broken. **FLOWER** Reddish, turning
greenish yellow. Late winter–very early spring, before leaves
emerge. **FRUIT** 1½–3" long, paired samaras; thin, wrinkled,
broad wings spread at 90° angle; green turning chestnut
brown to red. Late spring–early summer.

leaf underside

Striped Maple

Acer pensylvanicum
ALSO CALLED Moosewood, Whistlewood
HT 20–30' **DIA** 4–8"

Small tree or large shrub. Short, slender, single or forked trunk; columnar crown with upright branches. **ID TIP:** The bark is bright green when young, becoming reddish brown, with distinctive whitish to gray stripes.

HABITAT: Understory of moist, cool, hardwood forests. Elevation to 5,500'.

NOTES: Striped Maple is the largest of the world's group of 21 "snakebark" maples (all with vertical stripes on the bark), and the only one that is not native to China or Japan. It attains its largest size in the southern Appalachians. The fruits provide food for small mammals, and the foliage is browsed by moose and deer.

| MAPLE FAMILY | ACERACEAE |

LEAF 5–9" long and wide. 3 (or 5) shallowly divided, broad lobes with drawn-out tips; finely double-toothed margins. Dull green above; light green beneath; hairless on both surfaces. Autumn color vivid yellow. Leafstalk 1½–2" long. **FLOWER** ½" wide (larger than other maple flowers); petals conspicuous, ⅛" long (longer than the stamens); yellow, sometimes red-tinged. Late spring. **FRUIT** ¾–1" long, paired samaras that make a slightly obtuse angle; in chains (long, linear, hanging clusters). Autumn.

young bark

mature bark

Mountain Maple

Acer spicatum
HT 15–20'   DIA 4–8"

Small tree or large shrub. Short, slender trunk, or multistemmed; bushy crown of upright, often crooked branches.
ID TIP: Mountain Maple is the only North American maple with a tall, upright cluster of flowers; it is the East's smallest maple.

HABITAT: Moist, rocky slopes, ravines, streamsides; in cooler climates. Elevation to 6,000'.

NOTES: Mountain Maple grows best in the North and is increasingly restricted to mountains toward the southern end of its range. Its bright red fruits, colorful autumn foliage, and small size and shape make it an attractive ornamental.

MAPLE FAMILY   ACERACEAE

LEAF 2½–5" long and wide. 3 (or 5) shallowly divided, pointed lobes; coarsely double-toothed margins. Deep yellow-green with recessed veins above; downy beneath. Autumn color yellow, orange, red. **FLOWER** Greenish yellow; in narrow, upright, hairy, branched, 5" long clusters. Early summer, after leaves are grown. **FRUIT** ½–¾" long, paired samaras that make a slightly acute angle; red or yellow, drying brown. Autumn.

flowers

developing samaras

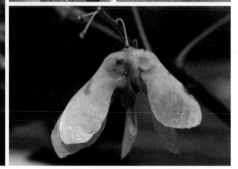

Norway Maple

Acer platanoides
HT 40–70'   **DIA** 1–2½'

Small to medium-sized tree. Straight trunk; dense, rounded to oblong crown that produces deep shade. **ID TIP:** Often confused with Sugar Maple, Norway Maple has larger, paired samaras growing at a very wide angle; the leafstalk oozes milky sap; the bark is darker, with narrower, shallow fissures.

HABITAT AND RANGE: Introduced in North America; naturalized and invasive, found along streams and in moist woods, in and near cities. Native from western Europe to India.

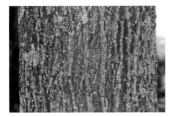

LEAF 5–8" long, slightly wider than long. 5 (or 7) moderately divided lobes, with many small, drawn-out points. Dull green above; pale green and hairless (except in vein angles) beneath. Autumn color yellow-green to bright yellow. Leafstalk pink-yellow; exudes milky sap when broken. **FRUIT** 1½–2" long, paired samaras that make an obtuse angle; spine of wing arches upward; in clusters. Late summer.

Sycamore Maple

Acer pseudoplatanus
ALSO CALLED Planetree Maple
HT 50–80'   **DIA** 1½–2½'

Medium-sized tree. Straight, stout trunk; rounded crown. Bark dark gray, cracking into pinkish to yellowish squares with curling or peeling edges. **ID TIP:** The leaves are 5-lobed, with relatively small, coarse teeth.

HABITAT AND RANGE: Introduced in North America; escapes around cities and is invasive in some woodlands. Native from Europe to western Asia.

LEAF 3–7" long and wide. 5 shallowly divided, pointed lobes; coarsely toothed margins. Very dark green with recessed veins above; paler, with raised, sometimes hairy veins beneath. Autumn color brown. **FRUIT** 1¼–2" long, paired samaras that make an acute angle; in long, hanging clusters. Summer–early autumn.

Bigtooth Maple

Acer grandidentatum

ALSO CALLED Canyon Maple, Western Sugar Maple

HT 20–50' **DIA** 8–12"

Small tree or shrub. Short trunk, or multistemmed; rounded crown. **ID TIP:** Bigtooth Maple twigs are bright red. The only other maple in much of its range is Rocky Mountain Maple, which has coarsely double-toothed leaf margins.

HABITAT: Canyons or stream banks in mountain woodlands. Elevation 4,000–7,000'.

NOTES: Bigtooth Maple is planted as an ornamental for its bright autumn foliage and used to revegetate eroding stream banks and unstable roadsides.

| MAPLE FAMILY | ACERACEAE |

LEAF 2–5" long, slightly longer than wide. 3 or 5 deeply divided, pointed lobes, with relatively blunt tips; few large, blunt teeth along margins. Shiny, dark green above; paler and downy beneath. Autumn color yellow to red. Leafstalk 1–2" long. Twig bright red. **FLOWER** Yellow. With new leaves in early spring. **FRUIT** ¾–1¼" long, paired samaras that make an acute to slightly obtuse angle; often rose-colored initially, maturing to green. Autumn.

Bigleaf Maple

Acer macrophyllum

ALSO CALLED Oregon Maple, Canyon Maple, Broadleaf Maple

HT 30–80' **DIA** 2–3'

| MAPLE FAMILY | ACERACEAE |

Small to medium-sized tree in height, but the most massive of maples. Very variable in form, but usually has short, stout trunk and broad, rounded crown. Bark gray, becoming fissured; often covered with mosses, lichens, and ferns. **ID TIP:** The leaf is the largest of any maple species; with its stalk it can measure 24" long. Bigleaf is the only native maple with fragrant flowers.

HABITAT: Moist mountain and coastal forests, including Redwoods; often under gaps in the coniferous canopy. Stream banks, canyons. Elevation varies with location from 1,000' in northern end of range to 3,000–5,500' in most areas to 7,000' in some southern California mountains.

LEAF 6–12" long and at least as wide; 5 deeply divided, pointed lobes, with relatively blunt tips; margins untoothed or with a few large, blunt teeth. Shiny, dark green above; paler and hairy beneath. Autumn color orange, yellow, yellow-brown. Leafstalk 8–12" long; exudes milky sap when broken. **FLOWER** Yellow; fragrant. With new leaves in early spring. **FRUIT** 1–1½" long, paired samaras that make an acute angle. Autumn.

Vine Maple

Acer circinatum

ALSO CALLED Mountain Maple,
Oregon Vine Maple

HT 25–30' **DIA** 8–12"

Small tree or large, erect or sprawling and contorted shrub. Short trunk or numerous twisted stems; larger limbs often heavily moss-covered. Limbs in contact with moist earth will root. Bark bright green to reddish brown. **ID TIP:** Vine Maple is the only native maple with 7 or 9 lobe points defining a circle. (Cultivated Japanese Maple leaf lobes may also define a circle, but are much more deeply divided.) Winter leaf buds become bright red and very large (1½" long) by spring.

HABITAT: Coastal and mountain forests; prefers stream valleys under towering conifers. Elevation to 5,000'.

NOTES: Vine Maple may dominate, forming tangled thickets, where avalanches or loggers have clear-cut conifers.

| MAPLE FAMILY | ACERACEAE |

LEAF 2–6" long and wide. 7 or 9 shallowly divided, pointed lobes; evenly toothed margins. Bright green above; paler, with tufts of hair on veins beneath. Autumn color brilliant orange and red. Leafstalk 1–2" long. **FLOWER** ½" wide, with red to purple sepals around smaller white petals. With new leaves in spring. **FRUIT** ¾–1½" long, paired samaras, spread at 180° angle; initially rose pink, drying to brown. Autumn.

Rocky Mountain Maple

Acer glabrum

ALSO CALLED Western Mountain Maple, Dwarf Maple, Sierra Maple

HT 10–30' **DIA** 8–12"

MAPLE FAMILY   ACERACEAE

Small tree or large shrub with simple, lobed leaves or pinnately compound leaves. Usually short, numerous stems; narrow, spindly crown (dense and brushy in the open) of upright branches.
ID TIP: This western maple typically has 3-lobed, coarsely double-toothed leaves; sometimes leaves are 5-lobed, or compound with 3 leaflets.

HABITAT: Under conifers in canyons and on stream banks, high ridges, and mountain slopes. Elevation to 11,000'.

NOTES: Rocky Mountain Maple is North America's highest-elevation maple. Heat- and drought-tolerant, it grows well on steep slopes and is planted for watershed protection, to revegetate highway roadcuts and stream banks, and as an ornamental. **Douglas Maple** (var. *douglasii*), which ranges from Montana and Idaho to Alaska, has lobed but never compound leaves and coarser margin teeth; the wings of the fruit are almost touching or parallel. It typically grows with Vine Maple.

LEAF 3–5" long and wide. Variable in form: 3 (sometimes 5) shallowly or deeply divided lobes; or rarely compound, with 3 elliptic leaflets (that can each have 3 shallowly divided lobes); coarsely double-toothed margins. Glossy, dark green above; paler or whitish and hairless beneath. Autumn color yellow or red. Leafstalk reddish. **FLOWER** Greenish yellow. With new leaves in spring. **FRUIT** ¾–1" long, paired samaras that make a slightly acute angle or are almost parallel (var. *douglasii*); rose pink, drying to brown. Late summer–autumn.

By late summer, many leaves may have scarlet splotches—galls caused by either fungi or mites.

Japanese Maple

Acer palmatum
HT 15–20' **DIA** 8–12"

Small tree or large shrub. Short, stout trunk; spreading crown; some cultivated varieties have a low, domed crown of contorted branches. **ID TIP:** Usually seen in parks and gardens, Japanese Maple has leaves with very deeply divided, long-pointed lobes.

HABITAT AND RANGE: Introduced in North America; occasionally escapes cultivation. Native to Japan, China, and Korea.

NOTES: Japanese Maple is a widely planted ornamental in gardens and parks. There are at least 1,000 varieties, in a wide range of leaf shape, color, and overall form (weeping, dwarf, bonsai-like). Many "Japanese Maple" cultivars are actually of **Fullmoon Maple** (*A. japonicum*), a native of Japan distinguished from Japanese Maple by its downy leafstalks and more circular leaf.

| MAPLE FAMILY | ACERACEAE |

LEAF 2–4" long and wide. Highly variable due to selective breeding; 7–11 shallowly to deeply divided, long-pointed lobes (in some, leaflets); double-toothed margins. Pale or bright green, green-gold, or maroon. Intense autumn colors, ranging from scarlet, ruby red, purple to pink, bright gold, orange. **FLOWER** Purple-red; in upright or drooping clusters on long stalks. With new leaves in spring. **FRUIT** 1" long, paired samaras that make an obtuse angle; wings often reddish. Autumn.

Amur Maple

Acer ginnala
HT 20–30' **DIA** 3–10"

Small tree or large shrub. Short, twisted trunk; dense, rounded crown. **ID TIP:** The bark is smooth and grayish, with faint vertical stripes. In spring, the upright clusters of yellow-green flowers are fragrant. Fruit is red most of the summer. **HABITAT AND RANGE:** Introduced in North America; occasionally escapes. Native to China, Manchuria, and Japan. **NOTES:** Amur Maple has shown invasive tendencies in some areas and may encroach upon sensitive native habitats.

| MAPLE FAMILY | ACERACEAE |

LEAF 3" long; 3 shallowly to deeply divided, pointed lobes; coarsely toothed margins. Glossy, dark green above; paler beneath. Autumn color brilliant red. **FRUIT** 1" long, paired samaras that make an acute angle; wings initially rose to red. Summer.

Hedge Maple

Acer campestre
ALSO CALLED English Field Maple,
Field Maple
HT 35–50' **DIA** 2–3'

Small tree. One or more short, often twisted trunks; dense, low, rounded crown. Bark corky, pale brown, cracking into squares and wide, orange fissures; branchlets develop corky ridges. **ID TIP:** The leaf's rounded lobes are distinctive.

HABITAT AND RANGE: Introduced in North America; planted along streets and in landscapes in the East and Northwest. Native to Europe and Asia.

| MAPLE FAMILY | ACERACEAE |

LEAF 3–4" long. 3 or 5 deeply divided, rounded lobes. Leathery. Dark green above; pale and hairy beneath. Autumn color gold, then red or purple. Leafstalk red; exudes milky sap when broken. **FLOWER** Yellow-green. Spring. **FRUIT** 1" long, paired samaras, spread at almost 180° angle; red-tinged. Late summer.

Katsura Tree

Cercidiphyllum japonicum
HT 40–60'

Small to medium-sized tree with deciduous, simple leaves. Straight trunk, sometimes multistemmed; pyramidal or ovoid crown of densely spaced, upright branches spreading 20–30' wide. **ID TIP:** The new leaves are reddish purple; the shaggy brown bark peels and curls in thin strips. In autumn the brilliant amber-colored, heart-shaped leaves have a spicy, burnt-sugar aroma.

HABITAT AND RANGE: Introduced in North America; planted in parks and residential properties. Native to China and Japan.

NOTES: The symmetrical canopy, heart-shaped leaves, and showy, redolent autumn foliage make Katsura Tree an attractive ornamental. The strong, sweet smell given off by dying leaves in autumn and droughts can dominate the tree's surroundings.

| KATSURA-TREE FAMILY | CERCIDIPHYLLACEAE |

LEAF 2–4" long and wide. Heart-shaped; bluntly toothed margins. Dark green above and beneath. New leaves reddish purple. **FLOWER** ½" wide; green; tuftlike; lacks petals. Spring. **FRUIT** ½–¾" long, podlike follicle; green, ripening to brown; in clusters of 2–4. Autumn.

Princesstree

Paulownia tomentosa
ALSO CALLED Empresstree,
Royal Paulownia
HT 30–50'   **DIA** 1–2'

Small tree with deciduous, simple leaves.
Short, sometimes twisted trunk; broad
crown of few stout, heavy branches.
Young bark gray-brown with shallow
fissures and blisters. **ID TIP:** This very
fast-growing nonnative has large, heart-
shaped leaves that are brown-hairy
beneath; large, showy, upright clusters of
fragrant, violet flowers; and woody fruit
capsules.

HABITAT AND RANGE: Introduced in North
America; naturalized in the East from New
York and Connecticut southward. Native
to western China.

NOTES: Princesstree is highly adaptable
and able to survive on disturbed, exposed
habitats; it is planted to reclaim mining
sites. One tree can produce up to 20
million seeds, and this prolific species is
considered invasive.

FIGWORT FAMILY   **SCROPHULARIACEAE**

LEAF 5–14" long. Often heart-shaped; margins untoothed, or
may have 3 small teeth or lobes. Green, slightly hairy above;
paler, with pale brown, soft hairs beneath. Leafstalk 3–8"
long. **FLOWER** 1½–2¼" long; pale violet. In 6–12" long clusters
on hairy stems. Fragrant. Early spring, before leaves. **FRUIT**
1–1½" long, ovoid, pointed, woody capsule. Splits in half to
release thousands of tiny, winged seeds. Autumn.

Southern Catalpa

Catalpa bignonioides
HT 35–50'   **DIA** 2–3'

Small tree with deciduous, simple
leaves. **ID TIP:** Southern Catalpa is similar
to Northern Catalpa, but smaller, with
malodorous leaves, denser flower clusters,
and shorter, slightly wider capsules.

HABITAT: Along
streams, roadsides,
clearings. Elevation
200–500'.

TRUMPET-CREEPER FAMILY   **BIGNONIACEAE**

LEAF 5–10" long. Heart-
shaped, with short-pointed tip.
Malodorous (unlike Northern
Catalpa). **FLOWER** Similar to
Northern Catalpa, but with
stronger colors and in denser
clusters. **FRUIT** 6–15" long
capsule; shorter and slightly
wider than in Northern Catalpa.

Northern Catalpa

Catalpa speciosa
ALSO CALLED Cigar Tree,
Western Catalpa
HT 50–80' DIA 2–3'

| TRUMPET-CREEPER FAMILY | BIGNONIACEAE |

Medium-sized tree with large, deciduous, simple leaves. Short, straight trunk; dense crown. Bark gray brown; ridged and furrowed on older trees. **ID TIP:** Northern Catalpa has heart-shaped leaves; large, dense, upright clusters of white flowers; and long, narrow, cylindrical capsules that are conspicuous in season. Though the 2 North American catalpas do not overlap in range, each is widely planted and naturalized outside its native range.

HABITAT: Riverbanks, bottomlands, clearings, roadsides. Elevation 200–500'.

LEAF 6–12" long. Heart-shaped, with long-pointed tip; untoothed margins; often with 2 lobes near leafstalk. Green above; paler and hairy beneath. **FLOWER** 2" long and wide; white; dotted with 2 yellow lines and purple spots. In showy clusters, 4–8" long and wide, upright. Late spring. **FRUIT** 8–20" long, ½–⅝" wide, cylindrical, podlike capsule; green, turning dark brown. Splits lengthwise to release numerous seeds. Autumn; may persist into winter.

Desert-willow

Chilopsis linearis

ALSO CALLED Flowering-willow, Desert-catalpa

HT 10–30' **DIA** 3–6"

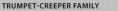

TRUMPET-CREEPER FAMILY · BIGNONIACEAE

Small tree or large shrub with deciduous, simple leaves that can be opposite or alternate. Single trunk, often leaning and twisted, or multistemmed; open, rounded, spreading crown, often as wide as tall. Bark dark brown, scaly; white-spotted on young stems. **ID TIP:** The leaves are very narrow; the showy white to lavender flowers have yellow and purple interior lines, and last from late spring to early autumn; long, sharply pointed, podlike capsules last through winter.

HABITAT: Desert washes, ravines, and arid grasslands of the Southwest. Elevation 1,300–5,300'.

NOTES: This Southwest native is widely planted in parks and along highways in arid areas for its weeping-willow-like appearance and striking, fragrant, long-lasting bloom.

LEAF 3–6" long, ¼–½" wide. Lance-shaped, curved; untoothed margins. Pale green. Alternate, opposite, or in whorls of 3. **FLOWER** 1¼" wide; white, pink, or lavender, with interior yellow and purple lines; trumpet-shaped. In loose, 2–4" clusters. Spring–autumn. **FRUIT** 4–12" long, ¼" wide, podlike capsule; green, ripening to brown. Splits open along length to release seeds. Autumn; persists all winter.

capsule

capsule split open

Black Mangrove

Avicennia germinans

HT 30–40' DIA 8–12"

Small tree or large shrub with evergreen, simple leaves. Short trunk; bushy, rounded crown of dense, upward-spreading branches; often forms thickets. Grows tallest in southernmost coastal waters. Small, exposed roots occasionally hang from mature upper trunks. Bark thick, dark brown; develops narrow furrows in maturity. **ID TIP:** Black Mangrove is readily distinguished from Red and White mangroves by its many conspicuous, erect, unbranched roots that rise out of the water to just above the high-tide mark to take in oxygen.

HABITAT: Mangrove swamp forests; brackish and fresh waters in coastal Florida, Louisiana, and Texas. At sea level.

NOTES: Black Mangrove is hardier than Red Mangrove, tolerating greater tidal fluctuations and extending farther north and inland, where it is smaller and shrubbier. Black Mangrove is found in shallow bays than Red, but does not colonize above the high-tide line. Honey bees produce high-quality honey from the blossoms. Germination occurs on the tree or immediately after the fruit drops from the tree. The capsule can survive floating in water for several months.

LEAF 2–4" long. Lance-shaped or narrowly elliptic; untoothed margins. Leathery. Shiny, yellow-green above; grayish, finely hairy beneath; salt crystals often cover both surfaces. Twig finely hairy when new. **FLOWER** ½" wide, white, bell-shaped, with 4 or 5 lobes; in 2–3" long and wide, upright clusters at twig tips. Fragrant. Late spring–midsummer. **FRUIT** 1" wide, irregular ovoid capsule; fleshy, downy; yellow-green. Late summer–autumn.

erect, unbranched roots

Red Mangrove

Rhizophora mangle

ALSO CALLED American Mangrove

HT 20–40'

Small tree or large shrub with evergreen, simple leaves. Short trunk; dense branches form a bushy crown, wider than tall. Bark smooth, grayish brown, with shallow, reddish furrows when mature. **ID TIP:** Red Mangrove has a unique superstructure of many intertwining, arching roots, exposed above the water and mud. It has a distinctive long, sharp-pointed, green terminal bud at the twig tip; more readily identified by 1–12" long seedlings hanging from the fruits.

HABITAT: Brackish coastal waters and along brackish riverbanks. At sea level.

NOTES: Red Mangrove roots grow downward from branches to anchor the tree in salt marshes and mudflats. It is sometimes called the "walking tree" because it continues to send down new roots toward the water as older roots trap silt and mud to form soil. Red Mangrove more commonly occurs in deeper waters than other mangroves. Germination occurs on the tree or immediately after the fruit drops; the capsule can survive floating in water for several months.

LEAF 2–6" long. Elliptic; untoothed margins. Thick, leathery. Shiny, dark green above; yellow-green beneath. Usually larger, shinier than leaves of other mangroves. Clustered near twig tip. Terminal bud long, with sharp-pointed tip. **FLOWER** ¾" wide, pale yellow, bell-shaped, in forked clusters. Spring–autumn. **FRUIT** 1–1½" long berry; leathery; reddish brown. Distinctive, hanging, spearlike, reddish green seedlings, 1–12" long, protrude from tip. Late summer–autumn; may remain on tree for a year or more.

berries with protruding seedlings

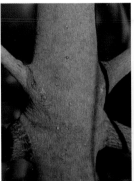

White Mangrove

Laguncularia racemosa

ALSO CALLED White Ironwood

HT 30–60' **DIA** 12–14"

Small to medium-sized tree with evergreen, simple leaves; can grow to 80' in tropics, but smaller, more sprawling in Florida. Short, often crooked trunk, or multistemmed; dense, narrow, rounded or irregular crown; often in thickets. Bark dark gray to reddish brown, marked by long, narrow ridges when mature. **ID TIP:** White Mangrove has fewer erect roots emerging from the water than Black Mangrove (or absent altogether), and often fewer arching roots exposed above the water than Red Mangrove. The leaf is distinguished from other mangrove leaves by two bumps (glands) on the leafstalk just below the base of the leaf blade.

INDIAN ALMOND FAMILY | COMBRETACEAE

leaves and fruits

HABITAT: Shores and bays of southern Florida, especially the Florida Keys. Near sea level (higher than other mangroves).

LEAF 2–3" long. Elliptic to oblong; untoothed margins. Thick, leathery. Yellowish green above and beneath; often covered with salt. Paired glands on leafstalk just below base of leaf. **FLOWER** ¼–½" long; greenish white; bell-shaped. In 1½–2" long spikes. Fragrant. Year-round. **FRUIT** ½–¾" long, vase-shaped drupe; ribbed, dry; greenish white to reddish brown when mature. Late summer–early autumn.

Florida Swampprivet

Forestiera segregata

HT to 15'

Thicket-forming, multistemmed shrub or small tree with evergreen, simple leaves. **ID TIP:** Leaves are narrowly elliptic, with blunt tip and untoothed margins. The leafstalk is much shorter than in Eastern Swampprivet. Walter Viburnum (p. 208) is similar, but occurs in wet habitats.

HABITAT: Coastal pine forests, hammocks, sand dunes; near sea level. Endangered variety of southern Florida (var. *pinetorum*) often occurs on shell middens (ancient seashell mounds).

NOTES: Flowers of *Forestiera* species are tiny, in rounded clusters (unlike *Ligustrum* privets, p. 199), typically arrayed along a branch and appearing before leaves emerge.

OLIVE FAMILY | OLEACEAE

female flowers

male flowers

LEAF ¾–2½" long. Narrowly elliptic, with bluntly pointed tip; untoothed margins. Glossy green or gray-green above; dull light green with tiny gland dots beneath. Leafstalk very short (unlike Eastern Swampprivet). **FLOWER** Tiny; without petals; in short, rounded clusters. Male and female on separate trees. Early spring, before leaves emerge. **FRUIT** ¼–⅜" long; similar to Eastern Swampprivet.

Eastern Swampprivet

Forestiera acuminata
HT to 15'

Thicket-forming, multistemmed shrub or small tree with deciduous, simple leaves. Bark very thin, rough, and slightly furrowed. **ID TIP:** Leaves are elliptic, tapering to a pointed tip, with finely toothed margins above the middle. The leafstalk is about ¼ the length of the blade (longer than in Florida Swampprivet). Fruits are blackish or purplish, pointed drupes.

HABITAT: Along stream banks, lakes, swamps. Elevation to 500'.

NOTES: Five species of *Forestiera* can attain tree size in North America. Eastern Swampprivet is the most widespread, occurring farther north than other swampprivets. It typically has male and female flowers on separate trees, but sometimes has some bisexual flowers. **Godfrey's Swampprivet** (*F. godfreyi*), a rare shrubby tree of northern Florida, is similar to Eastern Swampprivet. The leaves are broadly elliptic, with a blunt tip, and downy beneath.

OLIVE FAMILY · OLEACEAE

male flowers

LEAF 1½–4½" long. Elliptic, with pointed tip; margins finely, sparsely toothed above the middle. Yellow-green above; paler beneath. **FLOWER** Tiny; without petals; in small, rounded clusters. Early spring, before leaves emerge. **FRUIT** ⅜–⅝" long, pointed, fleshy drupe; oblong or round; blackish or purplish; often in dense clusters. Summer.

Desert-olive

Forestiera shrevei

ID TIP: This shrubby privet has evergreen leaves that are finely hairy on both sides. **HABITAT:** Desert canyons and rocky slopes. Elevation 2,000–4,500'. **NOTES:** Another southwestern species, **Texas Swampprivet** (*F. angustifolia*), has ¾–2½" long, evergreen, linear, dark green leaves, and stiff, dense branches that grow at right angles. It occurs on dry, limey slopes, elevation 2,000–4,500'.

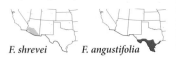

F. shrevei   *F. angustifolia*

OLIVE FAMILY · OLEACEAE

LEAF 1–1½" long. Linear to obovate; erect. Bright green; finely hairy above and beneath. Young branches are black. **FLOWER** In clusters; male and female on separate trees. Late winter. **FRUIT** ¼–⅜" long, ovoid, blackish drupe.

Ornamental Privets

Ligustrum species
HT to 15'

Thicket-forming shrubs or small trees with deciduous or evergreen, simple leaves. Widely planted as ornamentals and often trimmed into landscape hedges. **ID TIP:** The leaves are arranged in flat rows at right angles to the twigs; flowers are in conical clusters.

HABITAT AND RANGE: Introduced in North America; naturalized and invasive, found in cities, fields, moist woods. Native to Asia and Europe.

LEAF 1–4" long (most to 2½"). Elliptic, with pointed tip; untoothed margins; hairless. Glossy or dull green. Arranged in flat rows. Twig generally hairless or finely hairy.

FLOWER Tiny; white; in conical clusters, typically to 2½" long. Musky scent. Late spring.

FRUIT ¼" long, oblong drupe; blackish.

OLIVE FAMILY — OLEACEAE

European Privet

European Privet

Chinese Privet

Olive

Olea europaea
ALSO CALLED Common Olive
HT 20–40'   DIA 1–3'

Small tree with evergreen, simple leaves. Short, twisted trunk; open, spreading crown, often as wide as tall; thick, arching boughs and slender branchlets. **ID TIP:** The foliage has a smoky green hue; leaves are gray-green above, silvery beneath.

HABITAT AND RANGE: Introduced in California; can be weedy and invasive. Native from Africa and Mediterranean region to western Asia.

NOTES: Olive trees are cultivated commercially for their fruits. Inedible when raw, the fruits must be brined and fermented to be made palatable. First cultivated in California in 1769; the state currently produces millions of pounds of olives. The tree is also planted as a drought-tolerant ornamental.

OLIVE FAMILY — OLEACEAE

LEAF 1½–3" long. Lance-shaped or narrowly elliptic; untoothed margins; edges slightly rolled under. Gray-green above; silvery with glossy scales beneath. Leafstalk short. **FLOWER** ¼" long; creamy white; 4 petals. In short, branched clusters at base of leafstalk. Fragrant. Spring. **FRUIT** ¾–1" long drupe; oblong; greenish, maturing to black. Thick, oily pulp surrounds large, ridged stone. Autumn.

Devilwood

Osmanthus americanus
ALSO CALLED Wild Olive
HT to 30' **DIA** 8–10"

Small tree with evergreen, simple leaves; thicket-forming. Long, slender crown; becomes more irregular, with rigid, twisted branches, as it ages. Bark light gray-brown; warty. **ID TIP:** Devilwood is related to Olive, **Sweet Osmanthus** or Tea Olive (*O. fragrans*, native to Asia), and Fringetree, and has features similar to each: the tiny flowers resemble those of Sweet Osmanthus but smell like those of Fringetree, and the fruit resembles that of Olive.

HABITAT: Common in coastal live oak hammocks on barrier islands; occasionally near swamps, streams, sandy uplands, dunes. Elevation to 500'.

LEAF 3½–5" long. Lance-shaped or narrowly elliptic, with pointed tip; untoothed margins, edges rolled under. Leathery. Shiny, bright green above; paler beneath; hairless on both surfaces. Leafstalk ⅝" long, stout. **FLOWER** ⅛" wide; creamy white; bell-shaped, 4-lobed. In short, showy, branched clusters of numerous flowers at leaf axils. Very fragrant. Early spring. **FRUIT** ⅜–¾" long, olivelike drupe; oblong to rounded; green turning dark blue; skin and pulp thin. Autumn; persists through winter.

Fringetree

Chionanthus virginicus
ALSO CALLED Old-man's-beard,
White Fringetree
HT 20–30' **DIA** 4–8"

OLIVE FAMILY   OLEACEAE

Small tree or large shrub with deciduous, simple leaves. Short trunk, often multistemmed; long, slender crown of stout, ascending branches. Bark light gray to brown, with reddish scales. **ID TIP:** Fringetree is one of the last trees to leaf out in spring; leaves are very large, elliptic, and untoothed. The striking, drooping, white flower clusters emerge soon after the leaves. The flowers are very fragrant.

HABITAT: Moist, rich stream valleys, slopes, in hardwood forests. Elevation to 4,500'.

NOTES: A native southeastern species, Fringetree was first cultivated in 1736, and has since been widely planted beyond its natural range.

LEAF 4–8" long. Narrowly elliptic to elliptic, with pointed to rounded tip; margins untoothed, often somewhat wavy; veins prominent. Shiny, dark green above; paler and slightly hairy beneath. Autumn color bright yellow northward; sheds green in South. Leafstalk ¾" long, stout, purplish. **FLOWER** 1" long; creamy-white, dotted with purple inside at petal bases; showy, bell-shaped and fringelike, with 4–6 linear, delicate petals. In clusters of 3; numerous clusters hang loosely from downy, drooping, 4–8" stalks. Fragrant. Late spring. **FRUIT** ½–1" long, oblong to rounded drupe; dark blue or blackish when ripe, often with whitish bloom; thin pulp. Fruits hang in loose, branched clusters, on long stalks. Late summer–autumn.

Japanese Tree Lilac
Syringa reticulata
HT 20–30'

OLIVE FAMILY	OLEACEAE

Small tree or large shrub with deciduous, simple leaves. Single trunk, or multistemmed; pyramidal crown, becoming open and broadly round-topped, with erect branches. **ID TIP:** The bark is red-brown and cherrylike; the showy white flowers and small fruits occur in large, loose clusters.

LEAF 2–5" long. Ovate, with pointed tip; untoothed margins. Dark green.

HABITAT AND RANGE: Cultivated in North America. Native to Asia.

NOTES: Japanese Tree Lilac is one of the hardiest and most versatile of the lilacs (genus *Syringa*) and is planted as an ornamental in North America. The oft-planted purple-flowered Common Lilac (*S. vulgaris*) is a shrub.

FLOWER White; in 6–12" long, loose, branching clusters. Slightly fragrant. Summer. **FRUIT** ¾" long, warty capsule. Late summer; persists through winter.

Buttonbush
Cephalanthus occidentalis
ALSO CALLED Button-willow, Honey-ball, Globe-flower
HT 6–20'   **DIA** 4–6"

MADDER FAMILY	RUBIACEAE

Typically a shrub with deciduous, simple leaves, but can attain tree size. Low, crooked branches spreading to rounded crown; forms thickets. **ID TIP:** The fruits and flowers are distinctive, spherical clusters at the ends of twigs.

HABITAT: Floodplains, swamps; along waterways. Elevation to 3,000'; to 5,000' in California and Arizona.

LEAF 2–6" long. Elliptic to lance-shaped; untoothed margins. Glossy, bright green. Sometimes in whorls of 3 or 4. Persists into winter. **FLOWER** 1" long; white; spherical clusters. Fragrant. Early to late summer. **FRUIT** ¾" wide nutlet, in warty, tightly packed cluster; reddish green. Early autumn–early winter.

Fevertree

Pinckneya bracteata
ALSO CALLED Pinckneya, Georgia-bark
HT 15–20'   **DIA** 6–10"

Small tree or shrub with deciduous, simple leaves. Single trunk, or multistemmed; irregular, narrow, rounded crown; short branches. **ID TIP:** The leaves and twigs are hairy; the unique, conspicuous flowers persist for several weeks in late spring.

HABITAT: Low woodlands, swamps, and streams. Elevation to 300'.

MADDER FAMILY   RUBIACEAE

LEAF 2–8" long. Ovate or elliptic; untoothed margins. Dark green with fine hairs on both surfaces. **FLOWER** 1½" long, tubular; yellowish green with rosy (sometimes white), petal-like lobes, at least one often enlarged and showy; in clusters. Late spring. **FRUIT** ¾" wide, rounded capsules; light brown. Late summer–autumn; persists into winter.

Wavyleaf Silktassel

Garrya elliptica
ALSO CALLED Coastal Silktassel
HT 3–30'   **DIA** 4–7"

Typically a shrub, sometimes a small tree, with evergreen, simple leaves.
ID TIP: Twigs and young branches woolly, branches becoming brown and rough. The showy, silky, dangling flower clusters appear in midwinter. Female clusters are shorter than male; the 2 sexes are found on separate trees. The fruits are round and covered in dense, white wool.

HABITAT: Coastal bluffs, forests, scrub, chaparral. Elevation to 2,000'.

FLOWER In 2–8" long, hanging clusters with silky bracts. Midwinter. **FRUIT** ¼" wide, round berry; purplish black, initially covered in dense, white wool, becoming less woolly; usually contains 2 seeds. In 2–3½" long, hanging clusters. Summer.

SILKTASSEL FAMILY   GARRYACEAE

LEAF 1–4" long. Broadly elliptic, with blunt tip; untoothed, wavy margins, edges often rolled under. Leathery. Dark green and hairless above; woolly beneath.

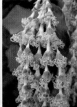

Flowering Dogwood

Cornus florida
ALSO CALLED American Dogwood
HT 15–40'   DIA 6–12"

| DOGWOOD FAMILY | CORNACEAE |

Small tree with deciduous, simple leaves. Short trunk; flat-topped crown of low, spreading or nearly horizontal branches, tiered and candelabra-like. Bark dark reddish brown, checkered, like alligator skin. ID TIP: Dogwood flowers are tiny and inconspicuous, despite the tree's showy springtime display; the true flowers are in a tight cluster surrounded by large, petal-like bracts. In autumn, the distinctive, shiny, red fruits mature and persist through winter. Leaves are similar to those of Alternate-leaf Dogwood (p. 295) but distinguished by opposite arrangement.

LEAF 2½–6" long. Broadly elliptic, with abruptly pointed tip; slightly wavy, untoothed margins. 6 or 7 parallel veins on each side, curve toward leaf tip. Dark green above; paler, finely hairy beneath. Autumn color bright red, purple, orange, yellow. Twig green or reddish, with white pith.

HABITAT: Hardwood forests. Elevation to 4,000'; in Appalachians, to nearly 5,000'.

NOTES: Flowering Dogwood is a common ornamental in parks, gardens, and landscapes, with about a dozen cultivated varieties. Logging and commercial flower harvesting have decreased populations in the wild; the recent spread of anthracnose fungus, which kills tree tissue, is now the greatest threat to the species.

FLOWER Tiny; yellowish green; in tightly packed, ¾" wide cluster surrounded by usually 4 large, notched, white (sometimes pink-tinged or pink), petal-like bracts that form what appears to be a showy flower, 3–5" wide (in some varieties, to 6"). Flower bud clove-shaped. March–April (in South) to June (in North), before leaves emerge.

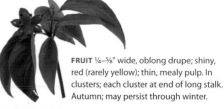

FRUIT ¼–⅝" wide, oblong drupe; shiny, red (rarely yellow); thin, mealy pulp. In clusters; each cluster at end of long stalk. Autumn; may persist through winter.

Roughleaf Dogwood

Cornus drummondii
HT 10–20' **DIA** 4–6"

Thicket-forming shrub (in northern part of range) or small tree (in southern) with deciduous, simple leaves. **ID TIP:** This species and **Toughleaf Dogwood** (*C. asperifolia*), of Florida and into adjoining states, both have leaves covered in stiff, short hairs that are rough to the touch; *C. drummondii* is distinguished by its longer leafstalk (greater than ¼").

HABITAT: Forests, thickets, and forest and prairie borders. Elevation to 2,000'.

NOTES: Birds often use Roughleaf Dogwood as a nesting site.

| DOGWOOD FAMILY | CORNACEAE |

LEAF 2–4" long. Broadly elliptic; abruptly pointed tip. Rough above; finely woolly beneath. 3–5 pairs of side veins (6 or 7 in Flowering Dogwood). Twig hairy; purple- to red-brown or yellow- to green-brown, with brown pith. **FLOWER** White; in 2–3" wide, flat-topped clusters. Late spring. **FRUIT** Tiny drupe; white; in red-stalked clusters. Late summer–autumn.

Shrubby Dogwoods

Cornus species

Typically large shrubs to 15'; can attain tree size.

Redosier Dogwood (*C. sericea*) Thicket-forming. **ID TIP:** Red twigs have white pith; leaves have 5–7 pairs of side veins. The widespread typical Redosier (ssp. *sericea*) has finely silky-hairy leaf undersides. **Western Dogwood** (ssp. *occidentalis*), of California, Nevada, and the Pacific Northwest, has rough-hairy undersides. **HABITAT AND RANGE:** Moist thickets, wetlands. Most of North America; absent from southern Great Plains, Southeast, and far northern Canada. Elevation 1,500–8,900'.

Roundleaf Dogwood (*C. rugosa*) **ID TIP:** Purple-spotted, green twigs have white pith; leaves are very broad and have 6–8 pairs of side veins. **HABITAT AND RANGE:** Woodlands and rocky slopes; Nova Scotia south to Virginia, west to Manitoba and Iowa.

| DOGWOOD FAMILY | CORNACEAE |

Redosier Dogwood

Redosier Dogwood

Roundleaf Dogwood

Pacific Dogwood

Cornus nuttallii

ALSO CALLED Mountain Dogwood, Western Flowering Dogwood
HT 20–50' **DIA** 9–15"

Small tree with deciduous, simple leaves. Straight, single trunk; crown narrow, short (in forest) or dense, rounded (in open).
ID TIP: In spring, and often again in autumn, Pacific Dogwood displays showy white or pink, petal-like bracts just under the inconspicuous flower clusters; in autumn it bears red or orange fruits.

HABITAT: Mountain coniferous forests. Elevation to 6,000'.

NOTES: Like Flowering Dogwood, Pacific Dogwood is critically affected by dogwood anthracnose.

LEAF 3–6" long. Broadly elliptic, often with abruptly pointed tip; margins slightly wavy, occasionally with irregular, fine teeth; 5 or 6 parallel veins on each side, curve toward leaf tip. Shiny, bright green, slightly hairy above; paler, woolly beneath. Autumn color scarlet or orange. Twig dark reddish purple; pith brown. **FLOWER** Tiny; yellowish green; in tightly packed, 1" wide cluster, surrounded by 4–7 bluntly tipped, white or pink, petal-like bracts that form what appears to be a showy flower, 4–6" wide. Spring–early summer; often again late summer–autumn. **FRUIT** ½" wide, oblong drupe; smooth, shiny; red or orange; thin, mealy pulp. In 1½" wide, round, very dense clusters of 30–40; each cluster at end of long stalk. Autumn.

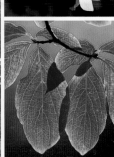

Kousa Dogwood

Cornus kousa

ALSO CALLED Chinese Dogwood, Japanese Flowering Dogwood

HT 15–20' **DIA** 6–8"

DOGWOOD FAMILY | CORNACEAE

Small tree with deciduous, simple leaves. Short trunk, usually multistemmed; broad crown of low, slender, spreading branches. Bark smooth, mottled tan and brown. **ID TIP:** In spring, the trees blossom so profusely that the crowns look like large, white mounds. Unlike North American and European dogwoods, Kousa Dogwood has hanging, raspberry-like fruits; the bark and tree shape are also distinctive.

HABITAT AND RANGE: Introduced in North America. Native to mountain forests of Japan, Korea, and China's Sichuan Province.

NOTES: Kousa Dogwood is planted as an ornamental in North America. Its pinwheel-like white flowers typically blossom 2–3 weeks after Flowering Dogwood.

LEAF 2½–4" long. Broadly elliptic, with pointed tip; slightly wavy margins; 6 or 7 parallel veins on each side, curve toward leaf tip. Dark green above; paler beneath. Autumn color scarlet, purple, bronze. Twig purple to green, turning brown. **FLOWER** Tiny; yellowish green; in tightly packed, ¾" wide cluster, surrounded by 4 large, pale yellow to creamy white (sometimes pink-tinged), pointed, petal-like bracts that form what appears to be a showy flower, 2–3½" wide. Flower bud heart- or clove-shaped. Late spring. **FRUIT** ⅝–¾" wide, raspberry-like, rounded cluster of fused drupes; pink to rose-red. Thin, rough rind contains thick, juicy, orange pulp. Each cluster hangs at end of long stalk. Late summer; persists into autumn.

Cornelian-cherry

Cornus mas

HT 15–25' **DIA** 6–12"

DOGWOOD FAMILY | CORNACEAE

Small, widely planted ornamental dogwood with attractive, early-blooming flower clusters; cultivated varieties show leaves with pink, yellow, or white margins. It is hardy north to southeastern and southwestern Canada. **ID TIP:** The flowers appear before the leaves; the fruit is an oblong, dark red, fleshy, edible drupe. **HABITAT AND RANGE:** Introduced in North America; planted along streets and in parks. Native to Europe.

LEAF 2½–5" long; abruptly pointed tip. Autumn color reddish purple. **FLOWER** Yellow; in 1" wide clusters. Lacks bracts. Early spring. **FRUIT** Oblong, red drupe.

Viburnums

Viburnum species
HT to 30'

Typically multistemmed shrubs, but 5 species can attain tree size in North America. Most have deciduous, simple leaves. To distinguish these species, compare leaf features, especially margins and underside.

HABITAT: Moist woodlands and valleys, near streams and swamps, forest edges.

LEAF 1½–4" long. Elliptic or narrowly elliptic; margins finely toothed or mostly without teeth. Shiny, green above. Leaf bud often shiny brown or red; sometimes hairy; terminal bud frequently longer than lateral buds. **BARK** Gray or brown, with plates and furrows. **FLOWER** ¼–½" wide; creamy white with yellow stamens; 5 rounded lobes. In 1½–6" wide, domed or flat-topped, stalkless or short-stalked clusters. Spring. **FRUIT** ⅜–½" wide drupe; oblong, sometimes round; blue to black, with white, waxy bloom; prunelike pulp surrounding large, flat stone; in clusters. Autumn (summer for Walter Viburnum).

HONEYSUCKLE FAMILY   CAPRIFOLIACEAE

Possumhaw

Possumhaw

Possumhaw

Possumhaw

Viburnum nudum

ID TIP: Distinguished from Walter Viburnum by its longer leaves (2–5") and rusty leaf undersides, and by its larger flower clusters, 2½–5" wide; distinguished from other viburnums by untoothed or slightly wavy leaf margins, with edges rolled under. Leaves are sometimes folded upward. Elevation to 3,000'

Walter Viburnum

Viburnum obovatum
ALSO CALLED Small-leaf Arrowwood

ID TIP: Leaves are smaller than in Possumhaw (1–2½" long), and the undersides are dotted with glands, but not rusty. Flower clusters are 1½–2½" wide. Leaves are similar to those of Chinese Privet and some species of *Forestiera* (pp. 197–198). It is often evergreen in Florida. Elevation to 200'.

Walter Viburnum

V. nudum   *V. obovatum*

Nannyberry
Viburnum lentago

ID TIP: Leaves are 2½–4" long; finely toothed; yellow-green beneath; leafstalk concave, with wavy or warty edges; terminal bud long, pointed. Flower clusters are 3–5" wide. Fruits are on pink stalks; malodorous when overripe; bark and wood also have unpleasant smell. Elevation to 2,500'; to 5,000' in Black Hills of South Dakota and Wyoming.

Nannyberry

Nannyberry

Rusty Blackhaw
Viburnum rufidulum

ID TIP: Leaves are 2–4" long; finely toothed; rusty-hairy beneath and sometimes on midvein above; young leaves, leafstalk, twig, and bud are also rusty-hairy. Flower clusters are 3–6" wide. Fruits are on rusty or red stalks. Bark and wood malodorous (like Nannyberry). It prefers well-drained woodlands and hedge- and fencerows (unlike other tree viburnums). Elevation to 2,500'.

Rusty Blackhaw

Rusty Blackhaw

Blackhaw
Viburnum prunifolium

ID TIP: Similar to Rusty Blackhaw, but lacks rusty-hairy features. Leaves are 1½–3" long. Flower clusters are 2–4" wide. The two species can hybridize where their ranges overlap. Elevation to 3,000'.

Blackhaw

Blackhaw
Blackhaw

V. lentago

V. rufidulum

V. prunifolium

European Buckthorn

Rhamnus cathartica
ALSO CALLED Common Buckthorn
HT 10–30' **DIA** 4–12"

Small tree or large, thicket-forming shrub with deciduous, simple leaves. Usually several slender trunks; rounded, bushy crown of rigid, spreading, crooked branches. Bark thin, smooth, gray-brown to orange-brown, scaly, peeling off in thin, curly strips; may develop deep furrows on oldest specimens. **ID TIP:** European Buckthorn has curly-peeling bark, many twigs terminating in sharp thorns, and fruits that are usually 4-seeded. Leaves are opposite or clustered at twig tips.

HABITAT AND RANGE: Introduced in North America; naturalized in dry, open woods and clearings and along fencerows and roadsides. Native to Europe and Asia.

NOTES: European Buckthorn is considered invasive in North America. Native buckthorns (pp. 324–326) have alternate leaves.

BUCKTHORN FAMILY **RHAMNACEAE**

LEAF 1½–2½" long. Usually obovate (sometimes ovate), with pointed tip; finely toothed margins; 3–5 parallel veins on each side, curve toward leaf tip. Glossy, dark green above; light green, sparsely hairy to hairless beneath. Autumn color green to yellowish green. Leaf bud covered with scales, hairless. Twig often ends in short thorns. **FLOWER** ¼" wide; yellowish green; bell-shaped, with 4 petals, each notched at tip. In small clusters at leaf axils. Late spring. **FRUIT** ⅜–½" wide, round, berrylike drupe, with juicy pulp enclosing 4 (rarely 3) seedlike stones; glossy black. Each fruit on short stalk; in clusters. Late summer–autumn.

Loquat

Eriobotrya japonica
ALSO CALLED Japanese Medlar
HT 15–20' **DIA** 6–8"

Small tree or large shrub with evergreen, simple leaves; trees can sometimes grow to 30' tall. Short trunk; erect branches form a compact, symmetrical crown. **ID TIP:** Loquat is a tropical-looking tree with large, leathery, green foliage and bright yellow-orange fruit.

HABITAT AND RANGE: Introduced in North America; planted in California and the Gulf states; naturalized in Florida. Native to Asia.

NOTES: Loquat is planted as an ornamental and cultivated for its edible fruit. It may be invasive in some areas.

FLOWER ½–¾" wide, in white clusters. Fragrant. Late autumn–winter. **FRUIT** 1–2" long, round pome; yellow-orange; in clusters. Spring.

ROSE FAMILY **ROSACEAE**

LEAF 5–12" long. Narrowly elliptic to lance-shaped; margins toothed. Glossy, dark green above; whitish beneath. Twig woolly when new.

Trees with Alternate, Compound Leaves

The majority of trees bear leaves in an alternate arrangement, with one leaf per leaf node (unlike opposite leaves, borne in pairs at the nodes). Alternate leaves may be compound— divided into separate segments called leaflets—or simple, with a continuous margin. In this section of the guide, we cover compound, alternate leaves. The Key to Trees with Alternate, Compound Leaves (pages 212–213) presents a guide to the species in this section; those with thorns, spines, or prickles are organized by fruit type; thornless trees are organized by leaf features and fruit type.

The trees in this section exhibit several leaf forms. Some have leaves that are pinnately once-compound, meaning that the leaf blade is divided along a single axis with leaflets arranged oppositely (less often alternately) along this axis. The hickories and sumacs are well-known examples of pinnately compound leaves with opposite leaflets. Western Soapberry, West Indian Mahogany, Kentucky Yellowwood, and Paradisetree are examples of trees with pinnately compound leaves with predominantly alternate leaflets. Most once-compound leaves have a terminal leaflet, and thus an odd number of total leaflets. The leaves of a few species, like Inkwood, Western Soapberry, and Carob, lack terminal leaflets and have an even number of leaflets. In Black Walnut, the terminal leaflet is sometimes lacking or is so small that it goes unnoticed, making the leaf appear evenly pinnate, even though it is not. The central leaf axis on most trees is round in cross section, but a few trees have winged or flattened axes, including Lime Pricklyash, Winged Sumac, and Wingleaf Soapberry.

Leaves that are divided along two axes—that is, with a single leaf divided into primary segments, and those segments divided into subleaflets—are called twice compound or bipinnately compound. Some trees in this category, like Silktree and a few of the acacias, have numerous small, closely set leaflets that convey a demonstrably feathery appearance. Others, such as Chinaberry, Kentucky Coffeetree, and Devil's Walkingstick, have twice-compound leaves with larger, more well-spaced leaflets. At least some leaves on Chinaberry and Devil's Walkingstick are divided along three axes (thrice-compound or tripinnate).

A number of alternate-leaf trees have thorns (modified branches), spines (modified leaves), or prickles (growths of the epidermis) along their branches or leafstalks. Thorns or spines may be borne singly in the leaf axils, as in Hardy Orange, Blue Paloverde, and some of the acacias, or in pairs at leaf nodes, as in the locusts, Jerusalem Thorn, and Desert Ironwood. Devil's Walkingstick and the pricklyashes bear sharp, stout prickles along the trunk, branches, and leaf axes.

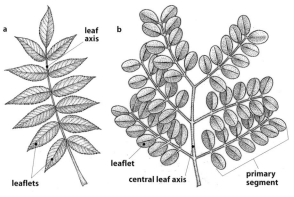

Alternate, compound leaves are largely pinnately compound (a), with each leaf divided into separate leaflets arrayed along a central axis. Some are bipinnately compound (b), or twice divided; the central leaf axis holds two or more primary segments, which in turn bear individual leaflets along a smaller axis.

Common Pricklyash

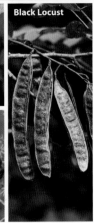
Black Locust

Devil's Walkingstick

Trees Thorny or Prickly

Fruit orangelike, leaf 3-part
Hardy Orange: p. 213

Fruit a small, round berry or follicle
Pricklyashes: pp. 214–215
Devil's Walkingstick: p. 216

Fruit a pod
Honeylocusts: p. 217
Locusts: pp. 218–219
Desert Ironwood: p. 220
Jerusalem Thorn: p. 220
Paloverdes: p. 221
Acacias: pp. 222–223
Mesquites: p. 224

Staghorn Sumac

Paradisetree

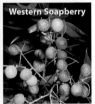
Western Soapberry

West Indian Mahogany

Kentucky Yellowwood

Tree of Heaven

Leaves Once Compound, Untoothed

Fruit a drupe or drupelike
Sumacs and kin: pp. 244–247
Paradisetree: p. 248
Amur Corktree: p. 249
Elephant Tree: p. 250

Fruit a berry
Inkwood: p. 248
Soapberries: pp. 249–250

Fruit a capsule
Gumbo Limbo: p. 247
West Indian Mahogany: p. 251

Fruit a samara
Hoptrees: p. 239
Tree of Heaven: p. 251

Fruit a pod
Japanese Pagoda Tree: p. 252
Carob: p. 252
Kentucky Yellowwood: p. 253

Leaves Once Compound, Toothed

Fruit a nut
Walnuts: pp. 226–229
Hickories: pp. 230–237

Fruit a capsule
Mexican-buckeye: p. 238
Goldenrain Tree: p. 238

Fruit a samara
Hoptrees: p. 239

Fruit a drupe
Sumacs and kin: pp. 242–245

Fruit a pome
Mountain-ashes: pp. 240–241

Leaves Twice Compound

Fruit a capsule
Goldenrain Tree: p. 238

Fruit a pod
Kentucky Coffeetree: p. 254
Silktree: p. 255

Fruit a drupe
Chinaberry: p. 255

Hardy Orange

Poncirus trifoliata
HT 4–20' **DIA** 3–6"

Shrub or small tree with deciduous, simple leaves. Bark green and brown striped. **ID TIP:** No other tree in the eastern coastal plains has the combination of 3-part leaf, winged leafstalk, green branches, and conspicuous flat, sharp thorns. The tree is a sour, inedible, orangelike berry. **HABITAT AND RANGE:** Introduced in North America; naturalized and established in various moist to dry woodlands from Pennsylvania to Texas. Native to China.

RUE FAMILY   **RUTACEAE**

LEAF 1½–2½" long; 3 leaflets. Dark green. Leaf axis winged. Aromatic. **FRUIT** 1½–2" wide, orangelike; yellow. Summer.

Common Pricklyash

Zanthoxylum americanum

ALSO CALLED Toothache Tree

HT to 30'   **DIA** 1–6"

RUE FAMILY	RUTACEAE

Shrub or, rarely, small tree with deciduous, pinnately compound leaves. **ID TIP:** The mostly paired prickles on the stem, smooth (furrowed in older trees) gray to brown bark, strongly aromatic foliage, and stalked fruits distinguish this species.

HABITAT: Moist to dry woodlands or thickets, often in rich soils. Does not tolerate dense shade. Elevation 0–2,000'.

NOTES: This genus—occasionally spelled *Xanthoxylum*—is in the same family as citrus trees, and all parts of these plants have a strong, citrusy aroma when crushed. In all *Zanthoxylum* species, after the fruit follicles open, the ripe, black, shiny seeds often hang from the husks by a threadlike structure known as a funiculus. Male and female flowers are usually on separate plants. Bark contains substances with antibiotic and numbing properties and has been used to treat toothaches. Common Pricklyash individuals sometimes lack prickles.

LEAF 5–8" long; 5–11 leaflets; leaf axis often has a few prickles. **Leaflet:** 1–2¾" long; ovate to elliptic; tip pointed; margins untoothed or with a few small teeth. Leathery. Green to dark green above, paler green and hairy (especially when young) beneath. Autumn color yellow. Prickles often in pairs on stem just below leaves. **FLOWER** ¼" wide; yellow-green (tips sometimes reddish); 5 (rarely 6) petals. In clusters, growing at leaf axils from previous year's growth. Spring, before leaves appear. **FRUIT** ¼" long follicle with 1 (or 2) seeds. Oblong; red-brown; pitted; each fruit on thin stalk to ⅛" long. In clusters in leaf axils. Seeds shiny, black. Summer–autumn.

Hercules' Club

Zanthoxylum clava-herculis
HT to 50'   **DIA** to 20"

Shrub or small tree with spiny branches and trunk, and leathery, deciduous, pinnately compound leaves. Branches are numerous, and the general outline of the tree is often circular. **ID TIP:** This species is readily distinguished by its gray, prickly bark. Leaves have toothed margins; flowers and fruits occur in terminal clusters; flowers have 5 petals.

HABITAT: Dry to moist woods and thickets in nutrient-poor to fertile soils in southern coastal plains. Elevation 0–500'.

NOTES: The closely related species **Texas Hercules' Club** (*Z. hirsutum*), found in Texas and possibly into Oklahoma and Arkansas, rarely reaches tree size. It differs from *Z. clava-herculis* in having shorter leaves (1–5") with fewer (5–11) and shorter (½–1½") leaflets.

LEAF 5–8½" long; 7–19 leaflets; leaf axis often prickly. **Leaflet:** 1–2¾" long; ovate to lance-shaped; tip pointed; base rounded; margins toothed. Shiny, green to dark green above; paler beneath. **FLOWER** ¼" wide; greenish yellow to whitish; 5 petals. In elongated terminal clusters. Spring. **FRUIT** ⅛–¼" long, usually 1-seeded follicle. Ovoid to spherical; turning red; leathery; wrinkled or pitted. In terminal clusters. Seeds shiny, black. Summer–autumn. **BARK** Thin, gray, with numerous scattered, pyramidal, corky, often piercing outgrowths (prickles) that are borne singly, not in pairs as in Common Pricklyash.

Lime Pricklyash

Zanthoxylum fagara
HT to 25'   **DIA** 8"

Shrub or, rarely, small tree with evergreen, pinnately compound leaves. **ID TIP:** The bark has corky protuberances, the leaf axis is winged, flowers have 4 petals, and flowers and fruits appear in small clusters in the leaf axils. **HABITAT:** Moist areas of southern coastal plains. Elevation to 500'.

LEAF 3–4" long; 7 or 9 leaflets; leaf axis winged. **Leaflet:** obovate; tip rounded or notched; margins shallowly toothed or scalloped. **FRUIT** 1-seeded follicle; in leaf axils.

Devil's Walkingstick

Aralia spinosa

HT to 35'   DIA to 6"

Shrub or small tree with deciduous, bipinnately (or tripinnately) compound leaves. Crown rather flat. **ID TIP:** Leaves are very large and usually twice compound. Stem, branches, and leaf axes are armed with piercing, straight or curved prickles. Prickles may shed as plant matures; they are most abundant and conspicuous on younger, smaller stems.

HABITAT: Dry to moist woodlands and thickets, in a wide range of soil types. The species declines in areas that become too shaded. Elevation to 5,000'.

NOTES: A related introduced species, **Japanese Angelica Tree** (*A. elata*), is established in the northeastern United States and becoming invasive. It has smaller fruits and denser flower clusters.

LEAF 15–48" long and nearly as wide; 6–12 primary segments (8–24" long), each with 9–15 leaflets; leaf axis prickly. **Leaflet:** 2–5" long; ovate; tip pointed; margins toothed. Green to dark green above; paler beneath. Autumn color yellow to red.   **FLOWER** Tiny (1⁄16" wide); white; 5 petals. In large, terminal, compound clusters composed of small, spherical clusters. Summer.   **FRUIT** 1⁄4" wide berry containing 3–5 hard seeds. Round; purple; juicy. Autumn.

Honeylocust

Gleditsia triacanthos
HT 70–80'   **DIA** 2–3'

Medium-sized tree with both pinnately and bipinnately compound, deciduous leaves. **ID TIP:** Trees often bear dense clumps of long, branched thorns on trunk and lower branches. Pods twist into a corkscrew shape when dried. Young trees have thin, tight bark; older bark rough.

HABITAT: Variety of well-drained sites, from moist watersides to dry limestone uplands; often in open broadleaf woodlands. Elevation to 2,000'.

NOTES: A naturally occurring thornless variety (*inermis*) of Honeylocust has been used to develop cultivated varieties without thorns or fruit. **Water Locust** (*G. aquatica*), a species with pulpless pods, occupies floodplain forests, swamps, and blackwater bayous, most extensively on the Mississippi River floodplain of Louisiana and Arkansas. A natural hybrid of Honeylocust and Water Locust, **Texas Honeylocust,** lacks thorns on twigs and has rough bark like Honeylocust and a pulpless pod like Water Locust. It is concentrated in floodplains of Brazos River, Texas, and Red River, Louisiana.

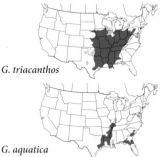

G. triacanthos

G. aquatica

PEA FAMILY   **FABACEAE**

LEAF Once compound (right), 4–6" long; or twice compound (left), 6–14" long, with 4–7 pairs of primary segments, each 6–8" long, with 8–15 pairs of leaflets. **Leaflet:** ½–1½" long; elliptic. Shiny, green above; yellow-green and hairless beneath. Autumn color yellow.

FLOWER ⅜" wide; greenish; bell-shaped, with 5 petals. In narrow, 2" long clusters. Late spring–early summer. **FRUIT** 6–18" long, 1" wide pod. Flattened; red-brown to dark brown. Contains 12–14 shiny, dark brown, ovoid, ⅜" seeds, embedded in sweet-tasting pulp. Pod becomes dry and corkscrew-twisted; drops in late autumn. **THORNS** Glossy, reddish brown to dark brown; those on leafy branches 1–4" long, unbranched or with 2 short prongs; on trunk and lower boughs to 12" long, multibranched, in dense clusters.

Water Locust, a smaller tree than Honeylocust, has smaller leaves with 8–10 pairs of leaflets. It also has thorns on the trunk and stems; its much smaller (1–2" long, ¾" wide), flat, pulpless pods and submerged habitat help differentiate Water Locust from Honeylocust.

Water Locust   Honeylocust

Black Locust

Robinia pseudoacacia
ALSO CALLED Yellow Locust
HT 50–80' **DIA** 1–3'

Medium-sized tree with deciduous, pinnately compound leaves. Trunk often twisted and forking. **ID TIP:** Bark rough, often orangy brown, with braided or ropy-looking ridges and deep furrows. Paired spines on branchlets. Copious, fragrant, white flowers in spring.

HABITAT: Fields, thickets, young woods, roadsides. Elevation 500–5,000'.

NOTES: Black Locust has spread far beyond its original native range, which was centered in the Appalachian Mountains and the Ozark–Ouachita region of Missouri, Arkansas, and Oklahoma. A ready colonizer of open fields and roadsides, it is now considered a weedy invader across the East. It has been widely planted for its wood, its ability to grow in poor soils such as strip mines, its fast growth, and its ornamental foliage and fragrant flowers. On the downside, the branches break easily, pods litter the ground, and trees are easily toppled by wind. Cultivated varieties and mature trees often lack spines. Black Locust leaves droop and fold up at night and in cloudy weather.

PEA FAMILY **FABACEAE**

LEAF 6–14" long; 7–19 leaflets; terminal leaflet present. **Leaflet:** 1–2" long, to ¾" wide; elliptic; often with tiny bristle at rounded tip. Blue-green above; paler beneath. Autumn color yellow. **Spines:** ¼–½" long; stout; often curved; on branches, in pairs at each leaf node. **FLOWER** ¾", white pea flower, with 5 unequal petals, some petals tinged yellow toward base. In showy, dense, drooping, 4–8" long clusters. Very fragrant; honey- or vanilla-like scent. Late spring–early summer. **FRUIT** 2–4" long, ½" wide pod. Flattened; dark brown. Thin, papery walls surround 3–14 smooth, blackish brown, kidney-shaped, ¼" seeds. Autumn; persists into early spring.

Clammy Locust

Robinia viscosa
HT 6–30'   DIA 6–8"

Small tree or shrub, often thicket-forming, with deciduous, pinnately compound leaves. **ID TIP:** Sticky, glandular hairs coat twigs, leaf and flower stalks, and pods.

HABITAT: Dry ridges, open forests, fields, thickets. Elevation 500–4,000'.

NOTES: This species has been planted northward of its native southeastern range and may occur with Black Locust.

LEAF 6–12" long, with 13–21 leaflets. **Leaflet:** ¾–1½" long. Green above; pale and hairy beneath. **Spines:** Small, weak; in pairs at leaf nodes. **FLOWER** ¾", pink pea flower. In showy, 3" long clusters. Unscented. Late spring. **FRUIT** 2–3" long pod. Flattened; covered with sticky hairs.

New Mexico Locust

Robinia neomexicana
HT 6–25'   DIA 6–8"

Shrub or small tree, often thicket-forming, with deciduous, pinnately compound leaves. **ID TIP:** Leaflets tipped with tiny bristle; pods are hairy; flowers are pink and fragrant.

HABITAT: Mountain canyons, arid pine-oak woodlands. Elevation 4,000–8,000'.

NOTES: This is the West's only native locust. It and Black Locust are widely planted and can occur together. Both can be weedy pests.

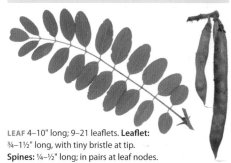

LEAF 4–10" long; 9–21 leaflets. **Leaflet:** ¾–1½" long, with tiny bristle at tip. **Spines:** ¼–½" long; in pairs at leaf nodes.

FLOWER ¾", deep pink pea flower. In showy, 2–4" long clusters. Fragrant. Late spring–early summer. **FRUIT** 2–6" long pod. Flattened; hairy.

Desert Ironwood

Olneya tesota

ALSO CALLED Tesota

HT to 30' **DIA** to 1½'

Small, spiny tree, often multistemmed, with rounded crown of grayish, evergreen, pinnately or bipinnately compound leaves. **ID TIP:** This species can be identified by its very hairy twigs, purple flowers, and thin bark. Fruit is a hairy, glandular pod, 1½–3" long, constricted between seeds.

HABITAT: Mainly in low areas in desert. Elevation to 4,000'.

PEA FAMILY **FABACEAE**

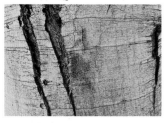

LEAF 1–3" long; usually 2–10 pairs of leaflets. **Leaflet:** ½" long; elliptic to ovate, with rounded tip; margins untoothed. Gray-green and covered with fine hairs above and beneath. Persists for a year, dropping in spring. Leaf axis flattened. **Spines:** ⅛–⅓" long; firm; straight or slightly curved; in pairs, at bases of leafstalks. **FLOWER** ½" long, purple to magenta pea flower. On hairy stalks, in small clusters. Spring–summer.

Jerusalem Thorn

Parkinsonia aculeata

HT to 30' **DIA** to 1'

Small, thorny, often green-barked tree or shrub with deciduous, bipinnately compound leaves. Usually multistemmed, with low, rounded crown of pendulous branches. **ID TIP:** The tree seems leafless much of the year, but the long, narrow green leaf axes persist. The yellow to orange flowers are showy and fragrant.

HABITAT: Variety of moist to extremely dry habitats. Elevation to 4,500'.

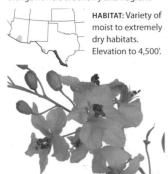

PEA FAMILY **FABACEAE**

pods and leaves

LEAF 8–16" long; 1 or 2 pairs of long, narrow primary segments, each with 20–30 pairs of sparse leaflets that drop early; leaf axis persists. (Above, at left, a long leaf axis lined with tiny leaflets hangs between 2 pods.) **Leaflet:** ¼" long; linear; margins untoothed. **Spines:** ¼–1½" long; firm; straight or slightly curved; paired, along branches at leaf nodes. **FLOWER** ¼–½" long; yellow to orange (can be red-dotted); 5 petals. In clusters. Fragrant. Spring–summer. **FRUIT** 2–4" long, brown to reddish pods with 1 to several gray-brown seeds; constricted between seeds. Pods on stalks ⅓–1" long. Summer; persists year-round.

Blue Paloverde

Parkinsonia florida
HT to 30'   **DIA** to 20"

Small, thorny tree or shrub with deciduous, bipinnately (sometimes pinnately) compound leaves. Trunk usually short; crown irregular. **ID TIP:** This thorny tree, leafless for much of the year, has a blue-green hue to bark, twigs, and leaves; flowers are bright yellow, including uppermost petal; pods are narrow and compressed.

HABITAT: Mostly in desert washes and sandy areas. Elevation usually below 4,000'.

LEAF ¾–1½" long; usually 1 pair of primary segments, each with 1–3 pairs of leaflets. **Leaflet:** ⅟₁₆" long; elliptic, with rounded or slightly notched tip, rounded base; margins untoothed. Blue-green. **Spines:** ⅛–1" long; borne singly along branches at leaf nodes. **FLOWER** ¾" wide; yellow; 5 petals. In clusters of 4 or 5. Spring. **FRUIT** 2–3½" long, narrow (¼" wide), compressed pod, with slight constrictions between the 2–8 brown seeds.

Yellow Paloverde

Parkinsonia microphylla
HT to 30'   **DIA** to 20"

ID TIP: This small, thorny tree or shrub is usually yellow-green overall and smaller than the similar Blue Paloverde. It has more leaflets (4–8 pairs), and the upper petal of its pale yellow flowers is often white at first. **HABITAT:** Desert slopes and hillsides. Elevation to 4,000'.

Acacias

Acacia species

HT 12–30' **DIA** 4–15"

Small trees or large shrubs, often
thicket-forming, multistemmed. They
have small, evergreen or deciduous,
bipinnately compound leaves. Many
acacias occur in tropical and subtropical
regions; in North America, native
species grow mostly in dry or desert
areas. **LEAF** Featherlike, with paired
leaflets (no terminal leaflet); often
grayish green. **Spines:** ⅛–3" long;
straight or curved, along branches,
in pairs at leaf nodes; white in some
species. **FLOWER** Tiny, white to yellow,
densely packed in cylindrical to
spherical clusters; often very fragrant.
FRUIT Woody to papery pod; twisted
in some species and often constricted
around seeds; splits open at maturity.

PEA FAMILY   FABACEAE

Sweet Acacia

Sweet Acacia

Silver Wattle

Sweet Acacia

Acacia farnesiana

ID TIP: Flowers are fragrant and in ½–¾"
spherical clusters. Spines are long,
straight, sometimes white-tipped. Leaf
2–4" long, with 3–8 pairs of primary
segments, each with 10–20 pairs of
leaflets. Pod 1½–3" long, cylindrical,
pithy, thick around seeds (not flat as in
Catclaw), shiny, reddish purple. **HABITAT:**
Sandy, open habitats, roadsides. Planted
and established beyond native range.
Elevation to 5,000'. **NOTES: Whitethorn
Acacia** (*A. constricta*), of the arid
Southwest, also has large, white-tipped
spines, but fewer leaflets (4–7 pairs). The
similar **Viscid Acacia** (*A. neovernicosa*)
commonly grows with it; its leaflets,
in pairs of only 1–3, are shiny, as if
varnished.

Silver Wattle

Silver Wattle

Acacia dealbata

ID TIP: Silver Wattle is large for an acacia,
known to reach 45' tall. Very fragrant,
bright golden yellow flowers are in
small, spherical clusters arranged in
fingerlike compound clusters of 20–25.
Leaf silvery green, feathery, 3–4" long,
with 8–20 pairs of primary segments,

each with 25–40 pairs of leaflets; new growth hairy. Pod 2–4" long, flattened; slightly constricted between seeds. **HABITAT AND RANGE:** Introduced in North America; common street tree from California to Florida. Native to Australia.

Catclaw Acacia

Catclaw Acacia

Catclaw Acacia

Catclaw Acacia

Catclaw Acacia
Acacia greggii

ID TIP: Catclaw Acacia forms dense, spiny thickets; ¼–⅜" long, stout, hooked, brown spines are scattered along branches. Flowers are creamy to bright yellow, in narrow, often upright, 1–3" long, showy clusters. The pod is 2–6" long, compressed, twisted. The leaf is 1–3" long, with 1–3 pairs of primary segments, each with 3–7 pairs of leaflets. The bark is deeply fissured. The variety *wrightii*, often called **Wright's Catclaw**, is the common tree acacia in Texas. **HABITAT:** Along desert streams, slopes, mesas. Elevation to 5,000'.

Roemer Acacia
Acacia roemeriana
ALSO CALLED Roundflower Catclaw

ID TIP: Roemer Acacia has distinctly hooked spines that are weaker than those of Catclaw Acacia. The pod is flat and puckered but not twisted. The flower cluster is spherical. **HABITAT:** Rocky slopes, limestone outcrops, juniper-oak thickets. Elevation 500–4,500'.

Roemer Acacia

Guajillo
Acacia berlandieri

ID TIP: Guajillo has cream-colored flowers in spherical clusters and a long (4–6"), velvety, cylindrical pod. Leaf 4–6" long, with 5–12 pairs of primary segments, each holding 30–50 tiny leaflets. Spines are ⅛–⅜" long. **HABITAT:** Dry limestone hills. Elevation 1,000–3,000'.

Guajillo

A. farnesiana   *A. greggii*   *A. roemeriana*   *A. berlandieri*

Honey Mesquite

Prosopis glandulosa
HT to 30'   DIA to 1'

PEA FAMILY   FABACEAE

Small, usually thorny tree or shrub with deciduous, bipinnately compound leaves, and crooked, sticky branches. **ID TIP:** The leaf is usually divided into a single pair of compound segments. The long, skinny pod is constricted between the seeds. The trunk is often leaning and divided into multiple stems right above the ground.

HABITAT: Wide range, including grasslands, deserts, disturbed areas. Elevation to 2,000'.

NOTES: The sharp spines are the bane of back-road drivers, easily penetrating even stout tires. In New Mexico and western Texas, this is usually a stout shrub; eastward it is a handsome tree. **Velvet Mesquite** (*P. velutina*), from Arizona, adjacent New Mexico, and Mexico, has minutely hairy leaves.

LEAF 5–10" long; 1 pair (rarely 2 or 3) of primary segments, each with 7–20 pairs of leaflets. **Leaflet:** ½–2" long; narrow (up to ¼" wide); linear, with rounded or short-pointed tip; margins untoothed; hairless. **Spines:** ½–2" long; 1 or 2 at leaf nodes; firm, persistent. **FLOWER** Tiny, aggregated into dense, creamy white to pale yellowish, cylindrical clusters 1½–5" long, almost ½" wide. Spring and summer. **FRUIT** 3–10" long pod on short stalk. Rounded to flattened, often constricted between brown, compressed seeds. Summer.

Screwbean Mesquite

Prosopis pubescens
HT to 40'   DIA to 12"

PEA FAMILY   FABACEAE

ID TIP: This species is most readily identified by its screw-shaped seed pods. Twigs are hairy (especially when young) and brown to reddish brown. Leaf 2–3½" long, with 1 or 2 pairs of primary segments and 5–8 pairs of ¼–½" leaflets. **HABITAT:** Floodplains, on gravelly or sandy (often saline) soils, in the arid Southwest. Elevation to 4,000'.

FRUIT 1–2" long, stalkless, spiral- or screw-shaped pod with up to 20 turns. In clusters. Summer.

Walnuts and Hickories

Walnuts and hickories belong to Juglandaceae, a family of aromatic trees and shrubs that are valued for their edible nuts and fine wood.

All species have large, deciduous, pinnately compound leaves. Most have an odd number of leaflets, though Black Walnut leaves sometimes lack a terminal leaflet. In walnuts (genus *Juglans*) the leaflets are largest toward the middle of the leaf axis, while in hickories (*Carya*) the outer leaflets tend to be largest.

The fruit is a nut covered by a fleshy husk. (Some authorities dub it a "drupaceous nut" because it has some of the qualities of a drupe.) In walnuts the husk does not split open along a seam, but either wears away or is opened by animals (including humans). In hickories, the husk splits open at maturity; the number of seams along which it splits and how far open it splits, from the tip to the base, varies from species to species. The nut has a hard shell on most species in the family, but on some, such as Pecan and Water Hickory, the shell is thin and easily cracked. The seed inside is edible, though in some species of hickories it is unpalatable (as evidenced in such names as Bitternut Hickory).

Male and female flowers are borne separately, on the same tree and often on the same branch. The flowers are tiny, and individually inconspicuous. Male flowers occur in slender, dangling catkins. Female flowers are borne singly or in several-flowered spikes at the branch tips.

In the walnut family, the terminal bud is larger than lateral buds. In hickories, features of the terminal bud can offer important identification clues. The buds of most species are covered with overlapping scales, but a few species, such as Water and Bitternut hickories, have valvate scales that resemble the form of a clam shell. In some species the surfaces of the bud scales themselves are flaky or scaly and roughened. In others the scales have a silvery, reddish, or yellowish cast. These features are noted in the species accounts. In walnuts, features of the twig and leaf scar can be important. Walnut branches have a chambered pith; hickories feature a solid pith.

Bark varies in the family. In some species it is very tight, with interlacing ridges, sometimes forming a diamond pattern. In others it has large plates peeling away from the trunk, giving the tree a shaggy appearance.

In both walnuts and hickories the male flowers are clustered into long catkins and are more conspicuous than the female flower clusters.

Black Walnut male flowers are shown (left). The wood of Black Walnut (right) is considered so valuable that large trees are sometimes poached.

Black Walnut

Juglans nigra

ALSO CALLED Eastern Black Walnut

HT 70–90' **DIA** 2–4'

Medium-sized to large tree. Forest-grown trees have a tall, straight trunk topped with a small, rounded crown. In open-grown trees the trunk often forks into 2 stout limbs supporting a symmetrical, domed crown of stout, spreading branches. The bark is thick, dark brown to blackish, scaly, and deeply fissured; very rough in older trees. **ID TIP:** The large, spherical, light green fruits with unseamed husks are distinctive. Unlike most other walnuts and hickories, Black Walnuts are often missing the terminal leaflet. Male catkins are 3–5" long.

HABITAT: Moist forests and other fertile sites. Elevation 0–3,300'.

NOTES: Black Walnut yields very fine wood. Trees give off chemicals that prevent many other plants (including tomatoes) from growing in their vicinity. The fruit husks are sticky and will stain hands; the nut is very difficult to open. The green, ball-shaped fruits often litter the ground, the husk gradually decaying to expose the dark, rough-shelled nut.

LEAF 12–24" long; 9–23 (usually 15–19) leaflets; terminal leaflet often absent. **Leaflet:** 2½–6" long; lance-shaped to ovate, sometimes curved; pointed tip; finely toothed margins. Glossy green above; lighter and downy beneath. Autumn color bright yellow. Aromatic when crushed. Twig shows 3-lobed leaf scar, without fringe of hairs above (see Butternut). Terminal bud whitish, hairy. **FRUIT** 1½–2½" wide, spherical, husk-covered nut, sometimes in pairs or 3s. Husk very thick, light green; surface roughly dotted, sticky-hairy, with no seams or ridges. Nut has irregularly ridged, dark brown, very thick shell; contains edible seed. Autumn.

Butternut

Juglans cinerea
ALSO CALLED White Walnut
HT 40–60'   **DIA** 1–2'

Small to medium-sized tree. Short, straight trunk, often divided into several heavy limbs; broad, irregularly shaped crown of stout, spreading branches with very little forking. Bark is smooth and light gray on young trunks and branches, becoming roughened with age, with dark fissures separated by broad, flattened, light gray ridges. **ID TIP:** Butternut is the only native walnut with oblong, ridged fruits. Leaf scar has hairy fringe along top. (Black Walnut husks are spherical, unridged; leaf scar lacks hairy fringe.)

HABITAT: Moist valleys to dry, rocky slopes. Elevation 0–3,300'.

NOTES: Across the species' range, large numbers of Butternut trees have succumbed to a fungus that causes a disease known as Butternut canker or Butternut decline. The species has been virtually eliminated from some states. Husks stain fingers brown.

WALNUT FAMILY   **JUGLANDACEAE**

LEAF 15–30" long; 11–17 (occasionally 7 or 9) leaflets; leaf and stalk sticky when young. **Leaflet:** 2–5" long; lance-shaped to ovate, with pointed tip; finely toothed margins. Yellow-green and slightly hairy above; paler and soft-hairy beneath. Autumn color yellow to brown; leaf drops early in season. Crushed foliage strongly scented (suggests paint or sweet hay). Twig hairy, becoming smooth with age. **FRUIT** 1½–2½" long, oblong, husk-covered nut, in drooping clusters of 3–5. Husk thick, greenish brown, coated with rusty, sticky hairs; 4–8 obscure ridges. Nut has rough, 8-ridged, light brown, medium-thick shell; contains edible seed. Autumn.

Leaf scar: Both Butternut (left) and Black Walnut (right) have a 3-lobed leaf scar, often likened to a monkey's face, but on Butternut the leaf scar is topped with a fringe of hairs.

Arizona Walnut

Juglans major
ALSO CALLED Nogal
HT 30–50' **DIA** 1–2'

Small tree. Single, straight, stout trunk in moister habitats; numerous spindly trunks in drier sites. Rounded crown of thick, widely spreading branches and slender branchlets with rust-colored hairs. **ID TIP:** Arizona Walnut, primarily found in Mexico, has smaller, narrower leaflets and smaller fruits than Black Walnut. Male catkins are 8–10" long.

HABITAT: Desert and mountain streams, arroyos, and canyons; also grasslands. Elevation 1,000–7,000'.

NOTES: Little Walnut (*J. microcarpa*) and Arizona Walnut can be hard to tell apart. Little Walnut is a smaller tree (10–30' tall), with a smaller nut (½–¾" wide) and catkin (2–4" long) and more numerous (17–25), narrower (¼–½" wide) leaflets, each with a long-pointed tip and untoothed to finely toothed margins. It grows along streams, ravines, and arroyos (elevation 700–6,700').

WALNUT FAMILY   **JUGLANDACEAE**

LEAF 8–14" long; 9–15 leaflets; terminal leaflet sometimes absent. **Leaflet:** 2–4" long, ⅜–1¼" wide; lance-shaped, often slightly curved; long-pointed tip; margins toothed (often more coarsely than other walnuts). Green to yellow-green on both sides; slightly hairy on yellow midvein beneath; scaly-hairy when young. Autumn color yellow. **FRUIT** 1½–2" wide, round, husk-covered nut. Husk thin; green, turning rusty then dark brown; densely covered with hairs. Nut slightly flattened at base; has dark brown or black, deeply vertically grooved, thick shell; contains small, edible seed. Early autumn.

J. major

J. microcarpa

English Walnut

Juglans regia
HT 50–90' **DIA** 2–3'

The commercial walnut, usually grafted onto native stock. Bark silvery-gray, smooth when young; develops narrow, rough ridges, separated by fissures. **ID TIP:** English Walnut differs from native species in having broader, usually fewer leaflets that are hairless beneath and have untoothed margins and a sweet, resinous scent (like shoe polish) when crushed. **HABITAT AND RANGE:** Introduced and cultivated in California. Native to Europe and Asia.

WALNUT FAMILY   **JUGLANDACEAE**

LEAF 8–16" long; 5–11 (usually 7) leaflets. **Leaflet:** 4–6" long; broadly elliptic, with pointed or rounded tip; untoothed margins. Thick, leathery. Dark yellow-green above, with yellow midvein; paler, hairless beneath. **FRUIT** 1½–2" wide. Husk relatively thin, green. Nut has brown, thin shell with gently wrinkled surface, 2 seams.

Southern California Walnut

Juglans californica

ALSO CALLED California Black Walnut

HT 12–40'   **DIA** 1–3'

Small, bushy tree. Short, single, usually leaning trunk, often forking low; or multiple trunks. Open crown of stout, wide-spreading branches that sometimes rest on the ground. **ID TIP:** This walnut has a small nut with a shallowly grooved shell, and wider and fewer leaflets than Northern California Walnut.

HABITAT: Along streams in moist canyons and foothills. Elevation 100–3,000'.

NOTES: Southern California Walnut is planted for landscaping and erosion control far outside its very limited natural range and habitat. Its natural populations are seriously declining, threatened by cattle overgrazing and urban development.

| WALNUT FAMILY | JUGLANDACEAE |

LEAF 6–10" long; 9–17 (usually 11–15) leaflets. **Leaflet:** 1–3½" long; elliptic to lance-shaped, with pointed to rounded tip; finely toothed margins. Glossy green above; paler beneath, lacking hairs in vein angles. Autumn color yellow to brown. **FRUIT** 1¼" wide, round, husk-covered nut. Husk thin, downy; green, turning dark brown. Nut slightly flattened at base; dark brown, thick shell has shallow, vertical grooves; contains small, edible seed. Early autumn.

Northern California Walnut

Juglans hindsii

ALSO CALLED Hinds' Black Walnut

HT 30–70'   **DIA** 1–2'

ID TIP: Sometimes considered a variety of the shrubbier Southern California Walnut, Northern California Walnut has a single, tall trunk, longer leaf with more numerous, narrower leaflets, larger fruit, and a smooth nutshell. **HABITAT AND RANGE:** Widely planted street tree. Used as a root graft for English Walnut. Originally from a few sites in central California, now spread along streams and disturbed slopes. Elevation 0–1,000'.

| WALNUT FAMILY | JUGLANDACEAE |

LEAF 12" long; 13–21 leaflets. **Leaflet:** 2–5" long; narrowly lance-shaped, with pointed tip; toothed margins. Tufts of hair in vein angles beneath, especially near base of leaflet. **FRUIT** 1½–2" wide, round, husk-covered nut. Husk thin, green, turning dark brown. Nut has smooth, brown, thick shell; contains small, edible seed. Early autumn.

Shagbark Hickory

Carya ovata

HT 70–100'   **DIA** 1–2½'

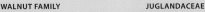

WALNUT FAMILY   JUGLANDACEAE

Medium-sized to large tree. Tall, straight trunk, topped with slender, often irregularly shaped crown that is usually widest toward the top. **ID TIP:** The smoky-gray bark is markedly shaggy in mature trees, with thick, 1–3' strips that are attached to the trunk at the middle and bend outward at each end.

HABITAT: Varies across range; fertile uplands to river bottoms. Elevation 0–4,000', mostly to 2,000'.

NOTES: A smaller, southern, shaggy-barked hickory, variously called **Carolina Hickory** (*C. o.* var. *australis*) or **Southern Shagbark** (*C. carolinae-septentrionalis*), has smaller leaves and nuts than the more widespread Shagbark. It is found inland of the coastal plains, from the Carolinas and Tennessee to Georgia and Mississippi.

LEAF 8–14" long; 5 (occasionally 3 or 7) leaflets. **Leaflet:** 5–7" long, 2–3" wide; broadly ovate, elliptic, or obovate, with pointed tip; margins finely toothed, with dense tufts of hair at tips of teeth. Yellow-green above; paler beneath. Autumn color golden brown, often rusty-spotted. Aromatic when crushed. Twig reddish brown.   **FRUIT** 1–2½" wide, round, husk-covered nut. Husk thick, yellow-green; 4-part, splits open from tip to base. Nut has light tan, 4-angled, thick shell; contains edible seed. Late summer to autumn.

Terminal bud: ½–¾" long, with brown, usually hairy scales.

Shellbark Hickory

Carya laciniosa

ALSO CALLED Big Shellbark, Kingnut
HT 70–100'   **DIA** 1–3'

WALNUT FAMILY	JUGLANDACEAE

Medium-sized to large tree. Tall, straight trunk, topped with slender, cylindrical crown of short branches and stout, orange branchlets that droop at their ends.   **ID TIP:** The light gray bark is smooth with shallow, interlacing ridges when young; it develops long (up to 4' long), narrow, flat plates when mature that eventually separate and bend away from the trunk at each end. (The more common Shagbark Hickory develops shaggy bark when younger; its plates are shorter and wider.)

HABITAT: Bottomlands, floodplains, swamps. Elevation 60–1,000'.

LEAF 12–22" long; 5–11 (usually 7) leaflets. **Leaflet:** 5–8" long, 2–5" wide; ovate, broadly elliptic, or obovate, with pointed tip; toothed margins. Shiny, dark green above; pale and soft-hairy beneath. Autumn color rusty yellow. Aromatic when crushed. Twig stout, hairy; yellowish brown to orange.   **FRUIT** 2–2½" wide, round, husk-covered nut. Husk thick, brown to yellow-brown, downy; 4-part, splits open from tip to base. Nut has tan to light reddish brown, 4-angled, thick shell; contains edible seed. Autumn.

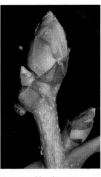

Terminal bud: Large, to 1" long, hairy, with brown scales. Bud larger and scales hairier than in Shagbark.

Mockernut Hickory

Carya tomentosa
ALSO CALLED White Hickory
HT 50–80'   **DIA** 1½–2'

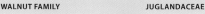

WALNUT FAMILY   JUGLANDACEAE

Medium-sized tree. Tall, straight, slender trunk; slender, open, rounded crown. Bark smooth, with shallow, interlacing ridges; develops rough, prominent ridges with age but is never shaggy or exfoliating as in Shagbark and Shellbark hickories.
ID TIP: Mockernut is the only hickory with thick, velvety twigs and dense hairs on the undersides of the leaves.

HABITAT: Sandy to rocky uplands; occasionally bottomlands. Elevation 0–3,000'.

NOTES: Mockernut is the most difficult of all hickory nuts to crack open, and a partitioned inner structure inhibits removal of the nut flesh. Also known as *C. alba*.

LEAF 8–20" long; 7 or 9 (occasionally 5) leaflets. **Leaflet:** 4–8" long, 2–5" wide; ovate, elliptic, or obovate, with pointed tip; toothed margins. Shiny, dark yellow-green above; pale and velvety beneath. Autumn color bright to tawny yellow. Strongly fragrant when crushed (described as scented like resin, paint, lemon, or mown grass). Twig stout, velvety, red-brown. **FRUIT** 1–2" long, round to oblong, husk-covered nut. Husk thick, dark reddish brown, soft-hairy to nearly smooth; 4-part, splits open from tip to middle (not to base). Nut has light reddish brown, hard, thick shell; often cracks transversely on drying; contains small edible seed. Autumn.

Terminal bud: Stout, to ¾" long, with reddish brown scales that shed in early fall to reveal white, silky inner scales.

Bitternut Hickory

Carya cordiformis

HT 70–100'   **DIA** 1–2½'

WALNUT FAMILY	JUGLANDACEAE

Medium-sized to large tree. Tall, straight trunk; slender, rounded crown of stout, spreading or ascending branches and slender branchlets. Pale gray bark with tight network of smooth, narrow, forking ridges and shallow furrows; never shaggy. **ID TIP:** Bitternut is distinguished by its symmetrical leaflets; large, clear, platelike scales on the leaf underside near the base; the bright yellow terminal bud; the heart-shaped, flattened nut with a prominent point at the tip; and the tight, smooth, light gray bark .

HABITAT: Bottomlands and floodplains to dry uplands. Elevation 0–3,000'.

NOTES: Bitternut is well named. Its nut is so bitter-tasting that both humans and animals avoid it.

LEAF 6–10" long; 5–13 (usually 7–9) leaflets. **Leaflet:** 4–6" long; lance-shaped to narrowly elliptic, with pointed tip; toothed margins. Glossy, dark yellow-green above; lighter and hairy beneath, with large scales, especially at base. Autumn color yellow to rusty yellow. **FRUIT** ¾–1½" long, round, husk-covered nut. Husk thin, coated with yellow, powdery scales; 4-part, splits open from tip to middle (not to base). Nut heart-shaped, with prominent point at tip; smooth, gray to light reddish brown, thin shell; contains bitter, inedible seed. Autumn.

Terminal bud: Bright yellow, powdery; pointed; scales paired, their margins not overlapping.

Pecan

Carya illinoinensis
HT 70–100' **DIA** 2–4'

Medium-sized to large tree. Tall, straight, massive trunk, often with buttressed base. Narrow, symmetrical, rounded crown when forest-grown; broad, domed, open crown when field-grown. Bark is variable and may be ridged or scaly, with scales pressed to the trunk or peeling. **ID TIP:** Pecan can be recognized by its oblong, thin-shelled nut containing a sweet kernel. The combination of scaly bark, low-branching form, vase-shaped outline, and finely branched crown make its winter form unmistakable, especially in groves.

HABITAT: Fertile river valleys and bottomlands. Elevation 0–3,300'; usually below 2,000'.

NOTES: This native of the Mississippi River basin is widely grown commercially for its nuts and is planted to reclaim mined lands.

WALNUT FAMILY	**JUGLANDACEAE**

LEAF 12–20" long; 7–17 (usually 9–13) leaflets. **Leaflet:** 4–8" long; lance-shaped, often curved, with pointed tip; toothed margins. Dark yellow-green above; paler beneath. Autumn color yellow. Foliage aromatic when crushed. **FRUIT** 1–2½" long, oblong, husk-covered nut; round in cross section; in clusters of 3–11 (usually 3–6). Husk thin, dark brown; 4-part, splits from tip to base. Nut has thin, pale reddish brown shell, usually with irregular, dark markings; contains edible seed. Autumn.

Terminal bud: ¼–½" long; pointed; brown-hairy; scales paired, their margins not overlapping.

Water Hickory

Carya aquatica
ALSO CALLED Swamp Hickory,
Bitter Pecan
HT 70–100'   **DIA** 1½–2'

Medium-sized to large tree. Tall, straight trunk; narrow, rounded crown of slender, upright branches. Light brown, thin, scaly bark develops long, platelike scales, with fissures; with age, scales become shaggy. **ID TIP:** The flattened nut is distinctive. Similar Pecan has more leaflets per leaf, and its nut is round in cross section, not flattened.

HABITAT: Bottomlands, flooded swamps, floodplains. Elevation 0–700'.

WALNUT FAMILY   **JUGLANDACEAE**

LEAF 9–15" long; 5–13 (usually 9 or 11) leaflets. **Leaflet:** 3–5" long; lance-shaped, slightly curved, with pointed tip; toothed margins. Dark green above; paler, often hairy, dull brownish (from thin layer of resin glands) beneath. Autumn color yellow. Terminal bud similar to that of Pecan. **FRUIT** 1–1½" long, broadly oblong, husk-covered nut; slightly flattened in cross section; in clusters. Husk thin, dark brown, covered with yellow scales; 4 raised seams, splits open from tip to base. Nut has oblong to round, light brown, thin shell; contains very bitter seed. Autumn.

Black Hickory

Carya texana
ALSO CALLED Texas Hickory,
Buckley's Hickory
HT 20–40'   **DIA** 1–1½'

ID TIP: Bark dark gray to nearly black, with thick, scaly ridges and furrows, rougher and deeper with age. Wavy-margined scales impart a rusty color to buds, lower leaf surface, twigs, and young leaves. **HABITAT:** Dry, sandy to rocky upland areas. Elevation 0–1,700'.

WALNUT FAMILY   **JUGLANDACEAE**

LEAF 6–12" long; 5–9 (usually 7) leaflets. **Leaflet:** 2–6" long. Glossy, dark green above; pale and covered in small clusters of rust-colored scales beneath. **FRUIT** 1¼–1½" long. Husk rusty-downy; 4-part, splits open from tip to base. Autumn.

Pignut Hickory
Carya glabra
HT 60–80'   **DIA** 1–2'

Medium-sized tree. Tall, straight trunk; irregular, oblong crown of small, slender, somewhat drooping branches. Bark light gray, tight, not shaggy, with interlacing ridges and shallow fissures; develops a diamond-shaped pattern. **ID TIP:** Pignut has almost hairless leaflets, tight bark, and smooth, often pear-shaped fruits.

HABITAT: All broadleaf woodlands except swamps. Elevation 0–2,700'; occasionally higher (to 4,800').

NOTES: This is a variable species, with populations differing in bark texture, leaf number, fruit shape and size, and how the husk splits open.

LEAF 8–12" long; 5 or 7 (occasionally 3 or 9) leaflets. **Leaflet:** 3–6" long; ovate, elliptic, or obovate, with pointed tip; toothed margins. Thick. Yellow-green above; paler and almost hairless beneath. Autumn color yellow to rusty yellow. Twig smooth, less stout than in Mockernut. Terminal bud ¼–⅜" long, broadest at base, smooth. **FRUIT** ½–1½" wide, round to pear-shaped, husk-covered nut. Husk thin, brown, smooth; 2-part, splits about halfway from tip to base. Nut has slightly ridged, light brown, hard, thick shell; contains small, sometimes bitter seed. Autumn.

Scrub Hickory
Carya floridana
HT 10–20'

ID TIP: This is the only shrubby hickory. Twigs, terminal buds, and underside of young leaves are coated with rusty-red hairs. May hybridize with Pignut Hickory. **HABITAT AND RANGE:** Scrub woods on sandy ridges of central Florida. Elevation 0–150'.

LEAF 4–8" long, with 3–7 (usually 5) leaflets. **Leaflet:** 2–4" long; margins coarsely toothed. (New leaves, with flowers, pictured.) **FRUIT** ¾–1¼" wide, husk-covered nut; splits open from tip to base; edible seed.

Sand Hickory

Carya pallida
ALSO CALLED Pale Hickory
HT 30–50' **DIA** 1–2'

Small tree. Tall, straight trunk; dense crown of stout branches, upper ones erect, lower ones drooping, and slender branchlets. Bark gray, scaly, with rough ridges and furrows forming diamond-shaped patterns. **ID TIP:** Lower surface of leaflet and leaf axis have silvery scales and tufts of hairs; twig and terminal bud have rusty scales and hairs. Sand Hickory has a smaller terminal bud (less than ¼" long) than other species with 5–9 leaflets.

HABITAT: Dry sandy, rocky sites on plains, valleys, lower slopes. Elevation 0–1,700'.

NOTES: The spottily distributed **Nutmeg Hickory** (*C. myristiciformis*) occurs in swamps and other low-lying, moist areas. It has golden-brown twigs, and bronze-colored scales on leaf undersides, twigs, and leaf buds, giving them a yellowish cast. It has 5–9 leaflets, each 2–5" long. The fruit husk splits open from tip to base, and the nut has a smooth shell.

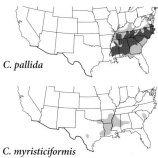

C. pallida

C. myristiciformis

LEAF 8–15" long; 5–9 (usually 7) leaflets. **Leaflet:** 3½–6" long; ovate, elliptic, or obovate, with pointed tip; toothed margins. Glossy green above; covered with silvery scales beneath, with tufts of hairs, especially on veins. Autumn color yellow. Resinous fragrance when crushed. **FRUIT** ½–1½" wide, oblong to round, husk-covered nut. Husk thin, dark brown, coated with yellowish scales when young; opens late in season, splits in 2–4 parts, from tip to middle or to base. Nut has ridged, tan, thin shell; contains small, edible seed. Late autumn.

Twig/terminal bud:
Coated with minute, rusty scales and hairs.

Mexican-buckeye

Ungnadia speciosa

ALSO CALLED Texas-buckeye, Monillo, Spanish-buckeye, False-buckeye

HT 4–30' **DIA** 4–10"

Small tree or shrub, with deciduous, pinnately compound leaves. Multi-stemmed, with spreading, irregular crown of small, upright branches. Mottled, gray-brown bark. **ID TIP:** The brown fruit splits into 3 segments; it remains on the tree through winter. The seeds are marble-sized and shiny jet black.

HABITAT: Along stream banks, in arroyos, and on lower mountain slopes. Elevation 1,000–6,500'.

LEAF 8–12" long; 3–9 leaflets. **Leaflet:** 2–4" long; ovate, with pointed tip; margins toothed. Shiny, dark green above, paler beneath. Autumn color yellow.

FLOWER 1" wide; pinkish purple; 4 or 5 petals; in clusters. Fragrant. Spring. **FRUIT** 1½–2" wide, 3-part capsule. Brown; leathery. Shiny, black, buckeyelike seeds; poisonous. Summer–autumn.

Goldenrain Tree

Koelreuteria paniculata

ALSO CALLED Panicled Goldenrain Tree

HT 20–40' **DIA** 20"

Small tree with deciduous, pinnately (sometimes bipinnately) compound leaves. Single trunk, or multistemmed; rounded to vase-shaped, dense crown of upright, spreading branches. Deciduous leaves. Bark silvery gray, ridged. **ID TIP:** The flowers are showy, yellow, foot-long clusters appearing after most other trees have bloomed and lasting about 2 weeks. The ornamental fruits resemble paper lanterns.

HABITAT AND RANGE: Introduced in North America; planted along streets and as an ornamental. Native to China and Korea.

NOTES: Goldenrain Tree is one of the few trees to flower in midsummer in northern climates. A similar species with the same common name, *K. bipinnata*, has more upright branches, bipinnately compound leaves, and pink fruits.

LEAF 6–15" long; 7–15 leaflets. **Leaflet:** 1–4" long; ovate to elliptic, with pointed tip; margins very coarsely toothed. Dark green above; paler beneath. Autumn color yellow. **FLOWER** ½" wide; yellow with a red center; in 10–15" long, many-branched clusters. Slightly fragrant. Summer. **FRUIT** 1–2" long, triangular, 3-part capsule. Yellow to brown; inflated; papery. Autumn, persists until spring.

Common Hoptree

Ptelea trifoliata

ALSO CALLED Wafer-ash

HT to 25' **DIA** 6–8"

Aromatic shrub or small tree, with a rounded crown; smooth bark; deciduous, 3-part leaves; small, greenish white flowers; and flattened, winged fruits.
ID TIP: The genus *Ptelea* is readily identified by its aromatic, trifoliate leaves and thin, waferlike fruits.

HABITAT: Moist to dry, rich woodlands or thickets, often on rocky slopes. Elevation to 8,500'.

RUE FAMILY · RUTACEAE

LEAF 7–11" long; leafstalk 2½–3" long; 3 leaflets (rarely 5); usually alternate (rarely opposite). **Leaflet:** 3–6" long, 2–3½" wide; ovate to elliptic; tip and base pointed to rounded; margins toothed or untoothed. Side leaflets often stalkless. Green above; paler green beneath. Aromatic. **FLOWER** Small (less than ½" wide), with 4 or 5 greenish white petals, hairless pistil. In small, terminal clusters at ends of branches. Late spring–early summer. **FRUIT** 1" long, thin, circular, waferlike samara, with 2 seeds in the center. In drooping clusters. Persists into winter.

California Hoptree

Ptelea crenulata

HT to 15'

ID TIP: Very similar to Common Hoptree and best distinguished by geographic range, California Hoptree has a hairy pistil in the flower and a thicker seed body in the center of the fruit. (Common Hoptree has a hairless pistil and flat seed body.) **HABITAT:** Valleys, steep slopes, and canyons, with other shrubs or in shade of trees in open woodland. Elevation 80–2,000'.

RUE FAMILY · RUTACEAE

LEAF 3 leaflets, each ¾–3" long, with blunt to rounded tip. **FRUIT** ½–¾" long, nearly circular, waferlike samara, with thickened seed body at center. In clusters.

American Mountain-ash

Sorbus americana
ALSO CALLED American Rowan Tree
HT 15–30'   DIA 6–8"

ROSE FAMILY   **ROSACEAE**

Small tree or large, multistemmed shrub, with a spreading crown and deciduous, pinnately compound leaves. Light gray-brown, often smooth bark, sometimes lustrous in older trees. ID TIP: This eastern species has showy, white flower clusters in spring and bright red, ¼" fruits through winter. Leaflets narrower than in Showy Mountain-ash.

HABITAT: Mountains, cold swamps. Elevation 3,600–8,600'.

NOTES: American Mountain-ash reaches tree size primarily in New England and north of the Great Lakes; it is usually shrubby elsewhere. This is among the most attractive of northern trees, with its abundant white flowers, flame-colored fruits, and brilliant yellow autumn foliage.

LEAF 6–9" long; 11–17 leaflets. **Leaflet:** 1½–4" long, ½–1" wide; lance-shaped, with pointed tip; toothed margins. Yellowish green above; paler beneath. Autumn color bright yellow. Twig stout, reddish brown, hairy. FLOWER ¼" wide; white; 5 rounded petals. In large (3–5" wide), crowded, flat-topped clusters. Late spring. FRUIT ¼" wide pome. Round; orange to red. In large, showy clusters. Bitter pulp; few seeds. Matures late autumn; persists through winter.

Showy Mountain-ash

Sorbus decora
ALSO CALLED Northern Mountain-ash
HT 15–30'   DIA 6–8"

ROSE FAMILY   **ROSACEAE**

ID TIP: Showy Mountain-ash has larger (to ½" wide), redder fruits and smaller leaves (4–6" long) with shorter, wider leaflets than American Mountain-ash. The two overlap, but Showy Mountain-ash does not extend as far south of the Great Lakes. HABITAT AND RANGE: Wide range of habitats, including mountain and valley woodlands. Elevation 500–2,000'. Newfoundland to the Great Lakes, south into New England, New York, and the upper Midwest.

European Mountain-ash

Sorbus aucuparia
ALSO CALLED Rowan Tree
HT 20–40' **DIA** 6–12"

ID TIP: Leaves are smaller than those of the native mountain-ashes, and twig and leaf underside are white-hairy. Leaves are 4–8" long, with 9–17 leaflets, each 1–2" long; margins are toothed except near base. Flowers in 3–6" wide, crowded, flat-topped clusters. Fruit ⅜" wide; orange to red; persists through winter. **HABITAT AND RANGE:** Introduced in North America; naturalized in Canada and northern states, often on roadsides. Native to Europe and Asia.

ROSE FAMILY   **ROSACEAE**

Sitka Mountain-ash

Sorbus sitchensis
HT to 20'

Usually a shrub, occasionally a small tree. **ID TIP:** Sitka Mountain-ash has elliptic, often bluntly tipped leaflets and larger fruit than Greene's Mountain-ash. Leaf 4–8" long, with 7–11 leaflets; margins toothed above the middle. Flowers in 2–4" wide clusters. Fruit to ½" wide; orange to red. **HABITAT AND RANGE:** Mid-elevation to alpine coniferous forests. Elevation 2,800–4,800'. Pacific Northwest north to southeastern Alaska and south in mountains of California.

ROSE FAMILY   **ROSACEAE**

Greene's Mountain-ash

Sorbus scopulina
HT to 20'

Usually a shrub, occasionally a small tree in Alaska. **ID TIP:** This interior species has smaller fruit and flower clusters, and more numerous, longer-pointed leaflets than Sitka Mountain-ash. Leaf 4–9" long, with 11–15 narrow, long-pointed leaflets with toothed margins. Flowers in 1–3" wide clusters. Fruit ¼" wide; red. **HABITAT AND RANGE:** Openings in coniferous forests. Elevation 2,400–6,300'. Primarily interior West, north to Alaska, and south in Rocky Mountains to New Mexico.

ROSE FAMILY   **ROSACEAE**

Smooth Sumac

Rhus glabra

HT 10–30' **DIA** 4–12"

SUMAC FAMILY   ANACARDIACEAE

Large shrub or small tree with deciduous, pinnately compound leaves. Often multi-stemmed, with a broad, flattened crown of few, widely spaced branches. Smooth bark with scattered, horizontal lines.

ID TIP: Tree sumacs can be recognized by their somewhat weedy appearance; proliferation in waste places; smooth bark; sticky sap; crowded, abundant fruit clusters; and large, featherlike, compound leaves that turn a vibrant array of colors in autumn. Smooth Sumac has smooth, hairless twigs; these help distinguish it from the very similar Staghorn Sumac, which has velvety-hairy twigs.

HABITAT: Roadsides, clearings, waste places, forest edges. Elevation 0–7,000'.

NOTES: Birds help spread Smooth Sumac by transporting the seeds away from the parent plant in their droppings; the species thus colonizes open areas and edge habitats. Sumac fruits (with the exception of the white berries of Poison Sumac) are edible; fruits soaked in cool water make a lemonade-like beverage.

LEAF 12–18" long; 11–31 leaflets; leaf axis slender, hairless; leaflets short-stalked. **Leaflet:** 2–4" long; lance-shaped, with pointed tip, rounded base; margins sharply toothed. Shiny green above, whitish beneath; hairless. Autumn color red to orange. **FLOWER** Tiny; white; 5 petals. In large, crowded, 4–8" tall, upright clusters. Early summer. **FRUIT** Tiny, round drupe; dark red, covered with short, sticky, red hairs. In tall (4–8"), densely packed, pointed clusters. Late summer; persists through winter.

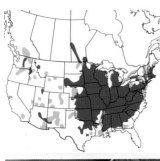

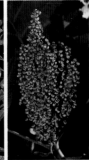

Twig: Hairless; stout; gray, with whitish waxy bloom. White sap.

Staghorn Sumac

Rhus typhina
HT 15–30' DIA 6–8"

Small tree or large shrub with deciduous, pinnately compound leaves. Often thicket-forming, with a broad, flattened crown of few, widely spaced branches. Deciduous, pinnately compound leaves. **ID TIP:** Staghorn Sumac has brown, velvety-hairy branches that form antlerlike, "staghorn" silhouettes. Leaf similar to Smooth Sumac, but longer, with thicker, hairy, reddish leaf axis; the fruits are covered with longer red hairs.

HABITAT: Roadsides and other open and edge habitats. Elevation 0–5,000'.

NOTES: The whitish, sticky sap of this and other sumac species may cause a rash in susceptible people. This species is also known as *R. hirta*.

LEAF 12–24" long; 11–31 leaflets; leaf axis thick, hairy, greenish to reddish or dull red. **Leaflet:** 2–4" long; margins toothed; young leaflets have reddish hairs beneath. Autumn color orange, red, purple. **FLOWER** Tiny; greenish white. In 4–8" clusters on densely hairy stalks. **FRUIT** Tiny, round drupe; dark red, covered with long, red hairs. In dense, 4–8" long clusters. Late summer–autumn; persists through winter.

Twig: Stout; reddish brown; covered with spreading hairs that make the species easily identifiable even in winter.

Winged Sumac

Rhus copallinum
ALSO CALLED Shining Sumac, Dwarf Sumac
HT 15–25' **DIA** 6–8"

Large shrub (uncommonly a small tree). **ID TIP:** The leaves are smaller than those of Smooth Sumac, and the flowers and tiny, hairy fruits are held in looser, smaller clusters. The leaf axis is conspicuously winged between leaflets. Twigs are finely hairy. **HABITAT:** Fields, slopes, roadsides, and other open and edge habitats. Elevation 0–4,500'.

SUMAC FAMILY   ANACARDIACEAE

LEAF 6–12" long; 7–21 leaflets; leaf axis winged, hairy. **Leaflet:** 1–3¼" long; margins mostly untoothed. Thick; shiny, dark green above; pale and finely hairy beneath. Autumn color reddish purple. Twig finely hairy. **FLOWER** Tiny, greenish white. In 4–6" long clusters; often many clusters form a large (1' long) compound cluster. **FRUIT** Tiny drupe, covered with short, red hairs. In dense clusters.

Prairie Sumac

Rhus lanceolata
ALSO CALLED Prairie Flameleaf Sumac, Texan Sumac
HT 15–25' **DIA** 6–8"

ID TIP: Prairie Sumac has shorter leaves and flower clusters (to 6") than Smooth Sumac. The leaf has a very narrow leaf axis that is winged between leaflets. Fruit clusters similar to Smooth, except smaller and more loosely arranged. **HABITAT:** Dry slopes and hillsides, often in limestone soils. Elevation 0–2,500'; sometimes to 4,000'.

SUMAC FAMILY   ANACARDIACEAE

LEAF 5–9" long; 13–19 leaflets. **Leaflet:** 1–2½" long; narrow, lance-shaped; margins usually untoothed; finely hairy beneath. Twig reddish and hairy when new, turning gray and hairless. Terminal bud whitish, hairy.

Peruvian Peppertree

Schinus molle

ALSO CALLED Peruvian Mastic Tree
HT 30–50' **DIA** 10–20"

Small tree with evergreen, pinnately compound leaves. Single trunk, or multi-stemmed; round, dense, spreading crown of drooping foliage. **ID TIP:** Leaves and fruit have a distinctive, peppery scent. Furrowed, peeling, gray-brown bark reveals reddish underbark in cracks. Fruit is resinous, with peppery fragrance.

HABITAT AND RANGE: Introduced in North America; naturalized in California. Native to Peru.

NOTES: Peruvian Peppertree is often planted as a shade tree on lawns and along avenues in warm climates, but it has invasive tendencies and is classified as an exotic pest plant in California. **Brazilian Peppertree** (*S. terebinthifolius*), planted in California, Florida, and Texas, is even more invasive, and considered one of the worst plant pests in Florida in terms of habitat invasion and destruction.

LEAF 6–14" long; 19–41 (or more) leaflets. **Leaflet:** 1–3" long; lance-shaped; margins sparsely toothed. Green to yellow-green above; paler beneath. **FLOWER** Tiny; greenish white. In 3–7" long, branched, drooping clusters. Summer. **FRUIT** ⅛–¼" wide drupe; red; in hanging clusters. Autumn; persists into winter.

American Pistachio

Pistacia mexicana
ALSO CALLED Texas Pistache
HT 10–40' **DIA** 8"

ID TIP: This small tree or shrub (also called *P. texana*) has delicate, feather-shaped, deciduous to semi-evergreen leaves that are dark red when young and shiny, dark green when mature. Bark is reddish when young, turns grayish brown with age. **HABITAT:** Streambeds, canyon cliffs, ravines, and rocky limestone soils of the lower Rio Grande valley. Elevation 600–1,000'.

LEAF 2–5" long; 9–19 leaflets. **Leaflet:** ½" long; elliptic, bluntly tipped; margins untoothed. Red when young, then dark green. **FLOWER** Tiny; red to yellowish red; in 1–3" long, branched clusters. Spring. **FRUIT** ¼" long; round to oblong drupe; red to black. In elongated clusters. Autumn.

Poison Sumac

Toxicodendron vernix
HT 10–25' **DIA** 4–6"

Large shrub or small tree with deciduous, pinnately compound leaves. Often multistemmed. Bark is brownish gray, smooth, with scattered horizontal lines and black splotches from exuded sap.
ID TIP: Poison Sumac's white fruit and soggy habitat separate it from other sumacs.

HABITAT: Wetlands, including creek- and streamsides, bogs. Elevation 0–1,000'.

NOTES: Fruit, flower, leaf, and stems contain irritating oils that cause a skin rash on contact. Humans rarely encounter Poison Sumac because it is uncommon and restricted to wetlands. They more often come into contact with poison ivy and poison-oak, shrubs or woody vines that can cover entire landscapes and invade yards.

| SUMAC FAMILY | ANACARDIACEAE |

LEAF 7–13" long; 7–13 leaflets; leaf axis red. **Leaflet:** 2–4" long, 1½–2" wide; ovate, with pointed tip; margins untoothed. Shiny, green, sometimes with red midvein above; paler and slightly hairy beneath. Autumn color red, orange. Twig hairless; reddish when new, later gray, sometimes with orange speckles. Broken or cut stems exude a dark, irritating sap. **FLOWER** Tiny; yellow-green; with 5 petals. In long (6–8"), loose, branched clusters. Late spring–early summer. **FRUIT** ¼" wide, round, slightly flattened drupe; shiny, white. In long (6–8"), loose, drooping clusters. Poisonous to humans if ingested. Early autumn; often persists until spring.

Poison Ivy and Poison-oak

Poison Sumac and its close relatives, Eastern and Western Poison Ivy (*T. radicans*, pictured, and *T. rydbergii*, respectively) and Pacific and Atlantic Poison-oak (*T. diversilobum* and *T. pubescens*), cause a skin rash on contact in people who are susceptible. About 45 minutes after exposure, the plant's toxic oil bonds with skin proteins and cannot be washed off, even with soap. Prompt use of alcohol wipes or submersion in water (shower, pool, lake) for 10 or more minutes may dilute it to subtoxic levels. Many people report that they successfully prevent the rash by immediately rubbing the exposed skin with crushed jewelweed (*Impatiens* species). The best prevention is to know how to recognize and avoid the toxic plants of your area. Besides Poison Sumac, the only poisonous-to-touch native trees of the United States are Florida Poisontree (page 247) and Manchineel (page 321), both restricted in the United States to southern Florida.

Florida Poisontree

Metopium toxiferum

ALSO CALLED Poisonwood

HT 25–35'   **DIA** 6–18"

Large shrub or small tree with a short trunk; low, wide crown; and evergreen, pinnately compound leaves. **ID TIP:** The bark peels, revealing orange scales; bark and leaves show black splotches from sap.

HABITAT AND RANGE: Lowland, subtropical hardwood hammocks, dunes, and pinelands of Florida and the Caribbean region. Elevation near sea level.

NOTES: All parts of this tree (fruit, flower, leaf, bark) exude poisonous sap that causes a skin rash on contact similar to that caused by exposure to poison ivy. It is said that an oil-dissolving substance such as WD-40 applied to the affected area, before scratching, is effective. The similar, harmless Gumbo Limbo has yellow-green leaflets without black resin glands, and brighter, reddish brown bark.

SUMAC FAMILY · **ANACARDIACEAE**

LEAF 6–10" long; 5 or 7 (occasionally 3) leaflets. **Leaflet:** 3–4" long, 2–3" wide; ovate to elliptic; tip rounded or pointed; slightly curled, untoothed margins. Glossy, dark green, often black-spotted.

FLOWER Tiny, whitish; in long (6–12"), loose, branched clusters.

FRUIT ½–¾" wide drupe. Round; shiny, yellow-orange; resinous. In long (6–8"), open, branched clusters in late autumn.

Gumbo Limbo

Bursera simaruba

ALSO CALLED Turpentine Tree, Tourist Tree, Birch-gum, West Indian–birch

HT 25–65'   **DIA** 2–3'

Small to medium-sized tree with deciduous to semi-evergreen, pinnately compound leaves. Stout trunk; rounded, spreading crown of few, thick, crooked branches. **ID TIP:** The trunk and branches are massive and irregular and clad in coppery-red, smooth, shiny bark, peeling in papery flakes and exposing red, olive green, or gray inner bark. The bark is resinous and has a turpentine-like odor.

HABITAT AND RANGE: Coastal hammocks and mixed forests of southern Florida and Central and South America. Elevation near sea level.

NOTES: This rapid-growing tropical species is often called the Tourist Tree because of its red, peeling "skin." It is planted as a shade tree and as an ornamental for its striking bark color and trunk shape.

FRANKINCENSE FAMILY · **BURSERACEAE**

LEAF 6–12" long; 3–9 leaflets. **Leaflet:** 2–3" long; ovate to elliptic, with pointed tip; margins untoothed. Shiny, dark green above; paler beneath. **FLOWER** Tiny; greenish white; in 2–4" long clusters. Winter to spring. **FRUIT** ½", oblong capsule; dark red; fleshy; splits in 3. In 2–5" long clusters. Summer; persists into winter.

Paradisetree

Simarouba glauca
HT 40–50'   **DIA** 17–20"

Small tree with evergreen, pinnately compound leaves. Straight trunk; rounded, dense crown of slender, upright-spreading branches, often 30' wide at maturity. Bark reddish brown, broken into broad, thick scales. **ID TIP:** Young leaves are reddish and gold; leaflets are round-tipped. The clustered, red to purple fruit occurs in early summer.

HABITAT AND RANGE: Coastal hammocks of southern Florida and the Keys, often with magnolias, live oaks, and bay (*Persea* species). Elevation near sea level.

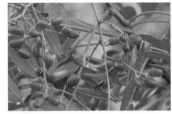

LEAF 6–19" long, 12–16 leaflets; leaflets often both opposite and alternate on the leaf axis. **Leaflet:** 1½–3½" long, obovate; rounded tip; margins untoothed. Leathery; shiny green. **FLOWER** Inconspicuous. **FRUIT** ¾–1" long, ovoid drupe; red to purple; edible. In clusters. Summer.

Inkwood

Exothea paniculata
ALSO CALLED Butterbough
HT 25–45'   **DIA** 6–15"

Small tree with evergreen, pinnately compound leaves. Tall trunk; dense crown of upright branches. Bark mottled reddish brown, separating into large scales. **ID TIP:** The leaf has few, even-numbered leaflets, and the leaflet tip is blunt or notched.

HABITAT AND RANGE: Coastal hammocks and shell mounds of Florida. Elevation near sea level.

LEAF 3–8" long; 1–3 pairs of leaflets. **Leaflet:** 2–5" long; elliptic to lance-shaped; blunt or notched at tip; margins untoothed. Shiny, dark green. **FLOWER** Tiny; white, with orange center; in branched clusters. Fragrant. Spring. **FRUIT** ½" wide berry; orange in summer, ripening to dark purple in autumn.

Amur Corktree

Phellodendron amurense
HT 30–50'   DIA 2'

Small tree with deciduous, pinnately compound leaves. Short trunk; open crown of spreading branches, often wider than it is tall. **ID TIP:** The gray bark is thick, deeply furrowed, and corky; the twigs are covered with corky spots. Buds are almost entirely encircled with leaf scars. Leaves, twigs, and fruit have pungent, turpentine-like odor when crushed.

HABITAT AND RANGE: Introduced in North America; escapes cultivation, especially in woodlands; considered an invasive species. Native to eastern Asia.

FLOWER Tiny; greenish yellow to maroon; in upright, 2–3½" clusters. Late spring. **FRUIT** ⅓–½" long, ovoid drupe; greenish yellow, turning blue-black; in clusters. Autumn; persists into winter, long after leaves have fallen.

RUE FAMILY   RUTACEAE

LEAF 10–15" long; 5–13 leaflets. **Leaflet:** 2–4½" long; ovate to elliptic, with pointed tip; margins untoothed. Shiny, dark green. Autumn color yellow to copper.

Wingleaf Soapberry

Sapindus saponaria var. *saponaria*
ALSO CALLED Florida Soapberry
HT 30–40'   DIA 1'

Small tree with pinnately compound, deciduous to semi-evergreen leaves. Short trunk; crown symmetrical, dense, broad, rounded. Bark gray-brown, scaly, with reddish brown patches. **ID TIP:** Fruits are translucent and in grapelike clusters. The leaf axis usually has narrow wings between the leaflets. Trees in northern part of range may lack wings on leaf axis.

HABITAT AND RANGE: Coastal hammocks and woodlands of Florida and north into southeastern Georgia. Elevation 0–100'.

SOAPBERRY FAMILY   SAPINDACEAE

winged leaf axis

unwinged leaf axis

LEAF 8–13" long; 7–15 leaflets; leaf axis usually winged. Leaflets can be even- or odd-numbered and opposite or alternate. **Leaflet:** 3–7" long; lance-shaped; margins untoothed. Light green; finely hairy beneath. **FLOWER** Tiny; yellowish green to creamy white. In 5–10" long, many-branched cluster. Spring. **FRUIT** ½" wide, drupelike berry (1 seed); round to oblong, sometimes keeled; yellow-orange; in grapelike clusters. Summer–autumn; persists into winter.

Western Soapberry

Sapindus saponaria var. *drummondii*
HT 25–50'   DIA 1–2'

SOAPBERRY FAMILY   **SAPINDACEAE**

Small tree with deciduous, pinnately compound leaves. Broad trunk; rounded or vase-shaped, open crown of erect branches, often nearly as wide as it is tall.   ID TIP: The bark is rough, grayish to reddish brown, flaking, and split by deep cracks into long, narrow plates; the cracks often expose yellowish inner bark. Leaflets are often alternate. The translucent golden fruits can be rubbed with water to produce a lathery soap substitute.

HABITAT: Along wooded stream banks, on canyon slopes, and in desert grasslands. Elevation 2,500–6,200'.

LEAF 6–17" long; 8–20 leaflets. **Leaflet:** 1½–4" long; elliptic to lance-shaped; margins untoothed. Yellowish green above; hairy beneath.   FLOWER Tiny; golden white; 5 petals. In showy, 5–10" long and 5–6" wide clusters at the ends of twigs. Late spring.   FRUIT ½" wide, drupelike berry (1 seed); golden; in clusters of 10–30. Autumn; persists until spring.

Elephant Tree

Bursera microphylla
HT 10–16'   DIA 1–2'

FRANKINCENSE FAMILY   **BURSERACEAE**

Small tree or shrub with deciduous, pinnately compound leaves.   ID TIP: The trunk is short and appears swollen; wide-spreading, sparse crown of thick, crooked, tapered branches that often lie close to ground. The creamy white bark is thin and peels to expose inner layers of gray-green and red; it oozes red gum when cut. Leaves have a strong camphor odor.

HABITAT AND RANGE: Dry, rocky desert mountain slopes. Elevation to 2,000'. Mexico, northward into southern California and Arizona; common in desert regions of Baja California.

NOTES: The trunk and major branches store water and photosynthesize, enabling Elephant Tree to thrive in its arid habitat.

LEAF 1–1½" long, with tiny, ovate, dark green leaflets.   FRUIT ¼" long, round to oblong, fleshy, drupelike capsule; dark red, with waxy bloom. Hangs singly on curved stalk. Summer–early autumn.

West Indian Mahogany

Swietenia mahagoni
ALSO CALLED Florida Mahogany
HT 40–50' **DIA** 1–2'

Small tree with evergreen, pinnately compound leaves. Trunk swollen or buttressed and short, usually dividing into several main limbs; large, dense, rounded crown, often very wide-spreading. **ID TIP:** Scaly, dark gray bark sheds to expose reddish inner bark. Large, thick-walled, woody fruit is held erect on upright branches; splits open to release winged seeds in spring. The off-center midvein makes leaflets appear to curve backward.

HABITAT AND RANGE: Coastal hammocks of southern Florida and the Caribbean. Elevation near sea level.

NOTES: This fast-growing, long-lived Florida native, which is tolerant of salt spray and provides light shade that allows plants to grow beneath it, is planted as a street and landscape tree. It provided the original mahogany for European cabinetry beginning in the 16th century.

| MAHOGANY FAMILY | MELIACEAE |

LEAF 4–7" long; 8–20 leaflets. **Leaflet:** 1–2½" long; ovate to lance-shaped; margins untoothed; midvein off-center. Dark green; leathery. **FLOWER** Tiny; yellow-green; in 3–6", branched clusters. Summer. **FRUIT** 2–4" long, 5-celled, ovoid capsule; brown; held erect. Autumn; persists all winter.

Tree of Heaven

Ailanthus altissima
ALSO CALLED Ailanthus, Paradisetree
HT 40–70' **DIA** 1–3'

Small to medium-sized, thicket-forming tree with deciduous, pinnately compound leaves. Open, irregular crown of stout, upright branches. Bark smooth, gray, turning rougher with age. **ID TIP:** The leaves, flowers, and stems have a rancid or burnt peanut butter odor when crushed or broken. Leaflets have 1 or more blunt teeth near the base that distinguish Tree of Heaven from similar-looking sumacs.

HABITAT AND RANGE: Introduced in North America; widely naturalized. Native to China.

NOTES: The very rapid-growing, thicket-forming Tree of Heaven is extremely invasive in rural and urban areas, and commonly grows along highways. The bark and leaves produce chemicals that inhibit the growth of other plants.

| QUASSIA FAMILY | SIMAROUBACEAE |

LEAF 12–36" long; 11–41 leaflets. **Leaflet:** 2–6" long, ovate to lance-shaped, with pointed tip, and 1 or 2 small, blunt teeth near the base, each bearing a raised, rounded gland beneath. **FLOWER** ¼" wide; yellow-green; papery; in showy 6–12" long clusters. Spring. **FRUIT** 1–1½" long, winged samara; yellow-green to brown; hanging in dense clusters. Summer–autumn.

Japanese Pagoda Tree

Styphnolobium japonicum
ALSO CALLED Chinese Scholartree
HT to 80'   **DIA** 1–2'

PEA FAMILY   **FABACEAE**

Small to medium-sized tree with deciduous, pinnately compound leaves. Rounded crown of spreading branches; young branches green and hairless or nearly so. **ID TIP:** Readily identified by its large, branched flower clusters and seedpods with deep, often stringlike constrictions between the seeds.

HABITAT AND RANGE: Introduced in North America; planted in parks and as a street tree in cities. Native to Asia.

NOTES: The native **Eve's Necklacepod** (*S. affine*) has a blunt or notched leaflet tip and smaller, less-branching clusters of pink-tinged white flowers. Both species were formerly in the genus *Sophora*.

LEAF 5–11" long; 7–17 leaflets. **Leaflet:** 1–2" long, usually ovate, with pointed tip and rounded base; margins untoothed. Dark green above; paler to whitish beneath. Autumn color yellow. **FLOWER** 1–2" long; whitish yellow; 5 petals. In large, branched clusters up to 12" long. Late summer. **FRUIT** 2–3" long, hairless green pod, with distinct constrictions between the 2–8 dark brown seeds. Autumn; persists through winter.

Carob

Ceratonia siliqua
ALSO CALLED St. John's Bread
HT to 55'   **DIA** to 1½'

PEA FAMILY   **FABACEAE**

Small to medium-sized tree with evergreen, pinnately compound leaves. **ID TIP:** The broad, leathery leaflets are even-numbered. Pods are large, thick, flattened; seeds rattle when pod is mature. **HABITAT AND RANGE:** Introduced in North America; escapes cultivation in California. Native to Mediterranean region. **NOTES:** Though the broken pod smells faintly like Limburger cheese, it is milled as a nonallergenic chocolate substitute.

LEAF 4–8" long; 3–5 pairs of leaflets. **Leaflet:** 1–2½" long; broadly elliptic; rounded at tip. Shiny, dark green; leathery. **FLOWER** Tiny; reddish; in 2" clusters. Male and female on separate trees. **FRUIT** 4–12" long, broad pod; dark brown when mature; pulp fleshy. Pods borne on older wood.

Kentucky Yellowwood

Cladrastis kentukea

HT 50–60' **DIA** 1½–2' (rarely larger)

| PEA FAMILY | FABACEAE |

Medium-sized tree with deciduous, pinnately compound leaves. Main trunk usually splits into 2 or 3 trunks 6–8' above the ground; wide crown of often somewhat drooping branches; branchlets hairy and arranged in a zigzag fashion. **ID TIP:** Kentucky Yellowwood is readily identified by its large, alternate leaves, each of which has alternately arranged, hairless leaflets, usually numbering 7 or 9.

HABITAT: Rich woods and open areas; often associated with limestone soils. Elevation 300–3,500'.

NOTES: Native populations of Kentucky Yellowwood are scattered and fairly rare. However, the species is widely planted beyond its native range and occasionally escapes from cultivation.

LEAF 6–13" long; 5–11 (usually 7–9) leaflets. **Leaflet:** 3–4" long; ovate, elliptic, or obovate, with pointed tip and pointed to rounded base; margins untoothed. Green above; paler green beneath. Autumn color bright yellow. **FLOWER** 1" long; white; 5 petals. In large, branched, drooping clusters up to 14" long. Fragrant. Late spring. **FRUIT** 2½–4" long, flat, narrow, hairless pod. Short-stalked; contains 5 or 6 dark brown seeds. Late summer.

Kentucky Coffeetree

Gymnocladus dioicus
HT to 100'   **DIA** to 3'

Large tree with deciduous, usually bipinnately compound leaves. The trunk often splits into multiple stems a few feet above the ground. Bark rough, fissured. **ID TIP:** This species is readily identified by its stout twigs (hairy when young) with pink pith, large bipinnate leaves, clusters of white flowers, and very large, dark pods.

HABITAT: Native populations are usually found in rich woodlands; the species has also escaped from cultivation, particularly in the eastern United States, in various habitats. Elevation 300–2,000'.

NOTES: In the past, the seeds were roasted and used as a coffee substitute. The pulp of the pod is mildly toxic if ingested.

LEAF 12–36" long; 5–9 primary segments, each with 6–15 leaflets (usually an odd number); leafstalk enlarged at base. **Leaflet:** 1–3" long; ovate to elliptic, with pointed tip; base rounded; margins untoothed or toothed. Green above; paler green beneath. Autumn color yellow. **FLOWER** ½" long; greenish to white; 4–5 petals, with narrower sepals between them. In short (male) to long (female) clusters; male and female usually borne on separate trees. **FRUIT** 4–10" long, 1–2" wide, hard, dark brown pod. Contains dark brown, ovoid seeds surrounded by dark pulp. Summer; persists into winter.

Silktree

Albizia julibrissin
HT to 40'   DIA to 20"

Small tree with deciduous, bipinnately compound leaves. Round crown.
ID TIP: Silktree has smooth, brown bark, featherlike leaves, showy pink flowers in round clusters, and flat seedpods.

HABITAT AND RANGE: Introduced in North America; naturalized in the East and the southern tier of western states in thickets and woodland edges, along roadsides, and around abandoned homesteads. Native to Asia and Africa.

NOTES: Planted in North America for its attractive flowers and foliage, Silktree is frequently found escaped from cultivation. It is considered an invasive pest in the East and California, and a threat to native species in certain habitats. In late afternoon and at night the leaves droop and the leaflets fold together.

PEA FAMILY	FABACEAE

LEAF 6–15" long; 3–12 pairs of featherlike, primary segments, each with 15–30 pairs of leaflets. **Leaflet:** ⅓–½" long; asymmetrical in outline; tip pointed; margins untoothed, often rolled inward. Green above; paler green beneath. Autumn color yellow. **FLOWER** 3" wide, round, pink clusters of many tiny (⅟₁₆"), 5-petaled flowers with long (1–1½") protruding stamens. Summer. **FRUIT** 3–8" long, 1" wide, flattened pod; green, turning brown. Contains several oval, flattened, light brown seeds. Summer.

Chinaberry

Melia azedarach
HT to 45'   DIA 1–2'

ID TIP: Chinaberry has large, bipinnately (or tripinnately) compound leaves, pale lilac flowers, and hard, round, yellow fruits that remain on the tree through winter. **HABITAT AND RANGE:** Introduced in North America; naturalized in southern United States, especially in woodland edges and thickets. Native to Asia. **NOTES:** All plant parts are poisonous to humans and livestock if ingested. Chinaberry is considered a noxious or invasive plant in several states.

MAHOGANY FAMILY	MELIACEAE

LEAF 12–24" long. **Leaflet:** 1–2" long; tip tapers to a point; margins untoothed, toothed, or lobed. **FRUIT** ½–¾" wide drupe, the stone containing 3–5 smooth, black seeds.

Trees with Alternate, Simple Leaves

Trees with alternate, simple leaves make up the largest group in this guide (and in nature) and present the greatest challenges for accurate identification. The Key to Trees with Alternate, Simple Leaves (pages 257–266) divides this relatively large collection into several smaller groups based primarily on typical leaf form and secondarily on fruit type.

Simple leaves have a single unbroken margin that runs continuously from one side of the leaf base to the other. Simple leaves may have lobed or toothed margins, but are never divided into the discrete segments that characterize compound leaves. Even deeply lobed leaves, like those of the pin oaks, Post Oak, and Burr Oak, are classified as simple because of their uninterrupted periphery.

Leaf shapes range from narrowly elliptic or nearly linear to almost round. In some species leaf shape and size are relatively consistent from tree to tree. In other species shape and size vary considerably, even among closely adjacent individuals. Oak and hickory saplings, root sprouts, and sun-loving trees growing in shade often produce excessively large, misshapen, or otherwise atypical leaves that do not closely resemble those of mature trees. Leaf size and shape can also vary with position on the tree. Canopy leaves of the White Oak, for example, are often smaller and more deeply lobed than those on lower branches. Although leaf morphology is very important for identifying trees, neither shape nor size is absolute. Allowance for variation is imperative.

In spite of the possible variation, many trees have a typical leaf shape, be it lance-shaped, elliptic, heart-shaped,

ovate, or obovate, that can provide clues for identification. The leaves of Eastern Redbud are heart-shaped: cordate (rounded and indented) at the base and pointed at the tip, with the overall outline of a Valentine heart. Ovate leaves, such as those of Balsam Poplar and Sugarberry, are egg-shaped in outline, widest toward the base of the leaf and not much longer than broad. Obovate leaves are the reverse of ovate leaves and are wider toward the leaf tip than toward the base. Bayberries, Ogeechee Tupelo, Chestnut Oak, and several deciduous native magnolias have obovate leaves. Elliptic leaves are oval, varying from narrow to broad, with the general outline of a football, though both base and tip can vary from pointed to rounded. Lance-shaped leaves are widest at the base, taper to a long narrow tip, and are several times longer than wide. The leaves of the basswoods and elms are often asymmetrical at the base, with a wider expanse of tissue on one side than on the other. This is especially true for the leaves of American Elm and is a helpful identifying feature.

Marginal teeth also vary in form. Witch-hazel, some *Populus* species, and Chestnut Oak have mostly blunt or rounded teeth; leaves of American Holly, chestnuts, Chinkapin, and Sawtooth and a few other oaks have bristly or prickly teeth. The margins of birches and elms are double-toothed, with several smaller marginal teeth between larger ones.

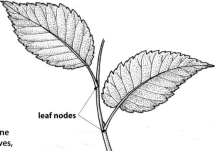

Alternate, simple leaves are attached to the branch in an alternating arrangement, with one leaf per leaf node (in contrast to opposite leaves, which occur in pairs at leaf nodes).

leaf nodes

Leaves Narrow: Lance-shaped to Elliptic

Fruit a capsule
Desert-willow: p. 194
Eucalyptuses: pp. 314–315
Punktree: p. 316

Fruit a capsule splitting open to reveal white-hairy seeds
Willows: pp. 379–389

Fruit a small drupe or drupelike
Russian-olive: p. 292
Camphortree: p. 292
Red Bay: p. 293
California Bay: p. 294
Swamp Titi: p. 298
Sweetleaf: p. 299
Carolina Laurelcherry: p. 338
Hollies: pp. 361–362

Fruit an achene
Curl-leaf Mountain-mahogany: p. 334

Fruit burlike, containing nuts
Giant Golden Chinkapin: p. 418

Fruit an acorn
Oaks, *see* Key to Oaks: p. 421

Bluegum Eucalyptus

Dahoon

Giant Golden Chinkapin

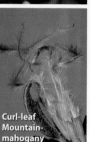
Curl-leaf Mountain-mahogany

Laurel Oak

Leaves Narrow: Obovate

Fruit a capsule
Rusty Staggerbush: p. 310

Fruit a capsule splitting open to reveal white-hairy seeds
Willows: pp. 379–389

Fruit a berry
Bullies: pp. 304–305
Texas Persimmon: p. 306

Fruit a small, wax-covered drupe
Bayberries: pp. 322–323

Fruit an acorn
Oaks, *see* Key to Oaks: p. 421

Scouler's Willow

Tough Bully

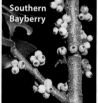
Southern Bayberry

Southern Live Oak

Leaves Elliptic: Narrow to Medium

Fruit a capsule
    Rusty Staggerbush: p. 310
    Mountain-laurel: p. 312
    Rhododendrons: pp. 312–313
    Punktree: p. 316
    Franklin Tree: p. 329

Fruit a capsule splitting open to reveal white-hairy seeds
    Willows: pp. 379–389

Fruit oblong, 4-winged
    Little Silverbell: p. 317

Fruit a berry
    Bullies: pp. 304–305
    Farkleberry: p. 307
    Madrones: pp. 307–308
    Manzanitas: pp. 309–310

Fruit a small drupe
    Camphortree: p. 292
    Red Bay: p. 293
    Black Tupelo: p. 296
    Swamp Titi: p. 298
    Sweetleaf: p. 299
    Sumacs: p. 301
    Buckthorns: pp. 324–325
    Carolina Laurelcherry: p. 338
    Hollies: pp. 361–362

Fruit a large drupe
    Mango: p. 303

Fruit in a spherical cluster
    Osage-orange: p. 288
    Button-mangrove: p. 290

Fruit burlike, containing nuts
    Giant Golden Chinkapin: p. 418

Fruit an acorn
    Tanoak: p. 419
    Oaks, *see* Key to Oaks: p. 421

Mountain-laurel

Rosebay Rhododendron

Little Silverbell

Sitka Willow

Farkleberry

Lemonade Sumac

Mango

Button-mangrove

Giant Golden Chinkapin

Tanoak

LEAVES UNLOBED, UNTOOTHED

Leaves Elliptic: Medium to Broad

Fruit conelike, releasing red seeds at maturity
Magnolias: pp. 278–284

Fruit a capsule
Crapemyrtle: p. 314
Snowbells: p. 318
Greenbark Ceanothus: p. 327

Fruit a berry or berrylike
Strangler Fig: p. 289
Weeping Fig: p. 289
Satinleaf: p. 303
Common Persimmon: p. 306

Fruit a small drupe or drupelike
Sassafras: p. 274
Coco-plum: p. 290
Pigeon-plum: p. 291
Alternate-leaf Dogwood: p. 295
Tupelos: pp. 296–297
American Smoketree: p. 302
Buckthorns: pp. 324–326

Fruit large and round
Pond-apple: p. 286
Cultivated Citrus: p. 287
Osage-orange: p. 288

LEAVES UNLOBED, UNTOOTHED

Leaves Obovate: Medium to Broad

Fruit conelike, releasing red seeds at maturity
Magnolias: pp. 278–284

Fruit a small berry
Bullies: pp. 304–305
Texas Persimmon: p. 306
Farkleberry: p. 307

Fruit a large, oblong berry
Pawpaw: p. 285

Fruit a small drupe or drupelike
Pigeon-plum: p. 291
Ogeechee Tupelo: p. 297

Fruit an acorn
Oaks, *see* Key to Oaks: p. 421

Leaves Ovate to Triangular

Fruit a capsule
American Snowbell: p. 318
Chinese Tallow: p. 320

Fruit a small berry or berrylike
Strangler Fig: p. 289
Farkleberry: p. 307
Texas Madrone: p. 307

Fruit a small drupe or drupelike
Pigeon-plum: p. 291
Sumacs: pp. 300–301
Catalina Cherry: p. 340
Netleaf Hackberry: p. 365
Sugarberry: p. 366

Fruit large and round
Pond-apple: p. 286
Osage-orange: p. 288

Netleaf Hackberry

Farkleberry

Osage-orange

Leaves Heart-shaped to Circular

Coco-plum: p. 290
Seagrape: p. 291
American Smoketree: p. 302
Bigleaf Snowbell: p. 318
Redbuds: pp. 319–320

Leaves with Prickly or Bristly Teeth

Lemonade Sumac: p. 301
Hollyleaf Cherry: p. 340
Hollies: pp. 360–362
Chestnuts: pp. 416–417
Chinkapin: p. 417
Oaks, *see* Key to Oaks: p. 421

LEAVES UNLOBED, TOOTHED

Leaves with Asymmetrical Base

Fruit blackberry-like
Mulberries: pp. 271–272

Fruit a capsule
Witch-hazel: p. 330

Fruit a small drupe
Hackberries: pp. 364–366
Japanese Zelkova: p. 367

Fruit a burlike drupe
Water-elm: p. 367

Fruit a flat, winged samara
Elms: pp. 368–374

Fruit a nutlet with a leafy bract
Basswoods and lindens:
pp. 375–377

Northern Hackberry

American Elm

American Basswood

LEAVES UNLOBED, TOOTHED

Leaves Narrow: Lance-shaped to Elliptic

Fruit a capsule splitting open to reveal white-hairy seeds
Willows: pp. 379–389
Narrowleaf Cottonwood: p. 392

Fruit a small drupe
Sweetleaf: p. 299
Pin Cherry: p. 337

Fruit a large drupe
Peach: p. 346

Fruit in a conelike cluster
Seaside Alder: p. 412

Fruit an acorn
Oaks, *see* Key to Oaks: p. 421

Black Willow

Sweetleaf

Peach

Sawtooth Oak

Leaves Elliptic: Narrow to Medium

Fruit a capsule
Sourwood: p. 311
Blueblossom: p. 327
Loblolly-bay: p. 328

Fruit a capsule splitting open to reveal white-hairy seeds
Willows: pp. 379–389
Narrowleaf Cottonwood: p. 392

Fruit oblong, 4-winged
Little Silverbell: p. 317

Fruit a berry
Farkleberry: p. 307
Madrones: pp. 307–308

Fruit a small drupe
Sweetleaf: p. 299
Lemonade Sumac: p. 301
Buckthorns: pp. 324–326
Cherries: pp. 335–341
Plums: pp. 342–345
Hollies: pp. 356–362
Japanese Zelkova: p. 367

Fruit a large drupe
Peach: p. 346

Fruit a small pome
Southern Crabapple: p. 350

Fruit an achene
Birchleaf Mountain-mahogany: p. 333

Fruit a flat, winged samara
Elms: pp. 368–374

Fruit in a conelike cluster
White Alder: p. 410

Fruit burlike, containing nuts
Chestnuts: pp. 416–417
Chinkapin: p. 417

Fruit an acorn
Tanoak: p. 419
Oaks, *see* Key to Oaks: p. 421

Sourwood

Little Silverbell

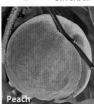

Peach

Black Cherry

Southern Crabapple

Winged Elm

White Alder

American Chestnut

Tanoak

LEAVES UNLOBED, TOOTHED

Leaves Elliptic: Medium to Broad

Fruit blackberry-like
Mulberries: pp. 271–272

Fruit a capsule
Snowbells: p. 318
Greenbark Ceanothus: p. 327
Silky Camellia: p. 329
Witch-hazel: p. 330

Fruit oblong, 4-winged
Two-wing Silverbell: p. 317

Fruit a small drupe
Water Tupelo: p. 297
Buckthorns: pp. 324–326
Cherries: pp. 335–341
Plums: pp. 342–345

Fruit a small pome
Crabapples: pp. 350–351
Serviceberries: pp. 352–353
Hawthorns: pp. 354–355

Fruit a large pome
Common Pear: p. 347
Common Apple: p. 349

Fruit a flat, winged samara
Elms: pp. 368–374

Fruit a nutlet with leafy bracts
Hornbeams: p. 400

Fruit in a cluster of papery husks
Hophornbeams: p. 401

Fruit in a conelike cluster
Birches: pp. 404–408
Alders: pp. 409–412

Fruit burlike, containing nuts
Beeches: pp. 414–415

Silky Camellia

White Mulberry

Water Tupelo

Common Apple

September Elm

American Hornbeam

Eastern Hophornbeam

American Beech

Witch-hazel

Common Winterberry

Scentless Bayberry

Chinkapin Oak

Oneseed Hawthorn

LEAVES UNLOBED, TOOTHED

Leaves Obovate

Fruit a capsule
Witch-hazel: p. 330

Fruit a capsule splitting open to reveal white-hairy seeds
Willows: pp. 379–389

Fruit a small drupe
Cascara Buckthorn: p. 326
Bitter Cherry: p. 339
Common Winterberry: p. 356
Possumhaw: p. 358

Fruit a small, wax-covered drupe
Bayberries: pp. 322–323

Fruit a small pome
Hawthorns: pp. 354–355

Fruit an achene
Birchleaf Mountain-mahogany: p. 333

Fruit in a conelike cluster
Alders: pp. 412–413

Fruit an acorn
Oaks, *see* Key to Oaks: p. 421

LEAVES UNLOBED, TOOTHED

Leaves Ovate to Triangular

Fruit blackberry-like
Mulberries: pp. 271–272

Fruit a capsule splitting open to reveal white-hairy seeds
Poplars and cottonwoods: pp. 390–396
Aspens: pp. 397–398

Fruit a small drupe
Manchineel: p. 321
Cherries: pp. 335–341
Winterberries: pp. 356–357
Hackberries: pp. 364–366
Sugarberry: p. 366
Florida Trema: p. 366

Fruit a burlike drupe
Water-elm: p. 367

Quaking Aspen

Swamp Cottonwood

Northern Hackberry

Slippery Elm

Oregon Crabapple

Gray Birch

Fremont Cottonwood

Hollyleaf Cherry

Largeleaf Linden

Saskatoon Serviceberry

Leaves Ovate to Triangular, continued

Fruit a small pome
Callery Pear: p. 348
Crabapples: pp. 350–351
Hawthorns: pp. 354–355

Fruit a flat, winged samara
Elms: pp. 368–374

Fruit in a cluster of papery husks
Hophornbeams: p. 401

Fruit in a conelike cluster
Birches: pp. 402–408
Alders: pp. 409–412

Fruit an acorn
Western live oaks: pp. 455–457

LEAVES UNLOBED, TOOTHED

Leaves Heart-shaped to Circular

Fruit blackberry-like
Mulberries: pp. 271–272

Fruit a capsule splitting open to reveal white-hairy seeds
Poplars and cottonwoods: pp. 390–396
Aspens: pp. 397–398

Fruit a small drupe
Mahaleb Cherry: p. 337
Hollyleaf Cherry: p. 340

Fruit a small pome
Serviceberries: pp. 352–353

Fruit a nutlet with a leafy bract
Basswoods and lindens: pp. 375–377

Fruit in a conelike cluster
Virginia Roundleaf Birch: p. 404
Black Alder: p. 413

Sweetgum

White Mulberry

Scarlet Oak

Washington Hawthorn

LEAVES LOBED

Leaves Toothed

Fruit in a spherical cluster
Sycamores and planetrees:
pp. 267–269
Sweetgum: p. 270
Paper Mulberry: p. 273

Fruit in an oblong, blackberry-like cluster
Mulberries: pp. 271–272

Fruit in a pear-shaped receptacle
Common Fig: p. 273

Fruit a pome
Crabapples: pp. 350–351
Hawthorns: pp. 354–355

Fruit an acorn
Oaks, *see* Key to Oaks: p. 421

LEAVES LOBED

Leaves Untoothed

Fruit a long-stalked drupe
Sassafras: p. 274

Fruit a capsule or capsulelike
California Flannelbush: p. 275
Chinese Parasoltree: p. 275
White Poplar: p. 396

Fruit a cluster of samaras
Tuliptree: p. 277

Fruit an acorn
Oaks, *see* Key to Oaks: p. 421

Sassafras

Tuliptree

White Oak

California Flannelbush

American Sycamore

Platanus occidentalis

ALSO CALLED American Planetree, Buttonball Tree

HT 60–100'   **DIA** 2–6'

Medium-sized to large tree with deciduous, simple leaves. Straight, stout trunk; broad, open, rounded or irregular crown of heavy, crooked branches spreading 50–80' wide. On lower trunk, bark is gray and flaky; higher up, bark is smooth, creamy white, flaking off and revealing mottled green, yellowish, brown, and whitish inner bark. **ID TIP:** Flaking bark has a distinctive, multicolored, "camouflage" appearance. The leaves resemble large Sugar Maple leaves. The ball-shaped fruit cluster occurs 1 per stalk (compare the paired clusters of London Planetree).

HABITAT: Lowlands, along waterways and floodplains in hardwood forests, abandoned fields. Elevation to 2,800'.

NOTES: This fast-growing North American native can reach a height of 140' and a trunk diameter to 14' and have among the most massive proportions of any hardwood. Its variegated bark, white branches, and wide, shade-casting crown make American Sycamore a favorite for streets and parks.

LEAF 4–10" long and slightly wider. 3 or 5 broad, shallow, pointed lobes; margins wavy, with scattered teeth. Bright green above; paler beneath. Young leaves are hairy beneath. Autumn color yellow-brown. **FLOWER** Tiny, in ⅓–½" wide, dense, round cluster. Male and female flowers on same tree; female, greenish red; male smaller, reddish to yellow. Spring. **FRUIT** Tiny achene, in 1–1½" wide, densely packed, spherical cluster; green ripening to tan; dry; fuzzy. Each cluster hangs on 3–6" long stalk. Autumn; persists into late winter.

California Sycamore

Platanus racemosa
ALSO CALLED Western Sycamore
HT 40–80' **DIA** 2–4'

Small to medium-sized tree with deciduous, simple leaves. Straight or leaning trunk, usually divided into 2 or 3 thick stems near the base; wide-spreading, open, rounded crown; branches stout, irregular. **ID TIP:** Young bark is greenish and sheds to expose white inner bark; older bark is dark, thick, and deeply furrowed. Fruits are in fuzzy, marble-size clusters strung 3–7 in a row on a long stalk. The leaf lobes are deeply divided, each about half the leaf length.

HABITAT: Along waterways and canyon bottoms. Elevation to 4,400'.

NOTES: California Sycamore can live to 200 years and reach 100' tall, with an 11' trunk diameter.

LEAF 5–10" long. 3 or 5 deep lobes; scattered teeth along margin. Light green above; paler, hairy beneath. **FLOWER** Tiny; in ⅓–½" wide, dense, round cluster; reddish green. Spring. **FRUIT** Tiny achene; in 1" wide, densely packed, spherical cluster; green ripening to tan; fuzzy; 3–7 clusters per stalk. Autumn; persists through winter.

Arizona Sycamore

Platanus wrightii
ALSO CALLED Buttonwood, Solar Tree, Alamo Tree
HT 40–80' **DIA** 2–4'

Small to medium-sized tree with deciduous, simple leaves. Stout trunk, usually dividing near the base into 2 or 3 thick stems; open, irregular crown of wide-spreading branches. **ID TIP:** The bark flakes to reveal mottled gray-green, brown, and white inner bark; older bark is not as deeply furrowed as American Sycamore bark. The leaf lobes are deeply divided, each lobe longer than half the length of the entire leaf.

HABITAT: Floodplains and along watercourses in gulches and canyons. Elevation 3,200–6,600'.

NOTES: Arizona Sycamore leaves give off a mildly sweet aroma accentuated by the humid air of its habitat.

LEAF 6–9" long. 3–7 long, deep lobes. Light green; hairy beneath. **FLOWER** Tiny; in ⅓–½" wide, dense, round cluster; reddish green; fuzzy. Spring. **FRUIT** Tiny achene; in 1–1½" wide, densely packed, spherical cluster; tan; 2–4 clusters per stalk. Autumn; persists through winter.

London Planetree

Platanus × acerifolia
HT 70–80'   DIA 2–4'

Medium-sized tree with deciduous, simple leaves. Straight, stout trunk; broad, pyramidal to rounded crown, nearly as wide as tall, of spreading upper branches. (Pruned specimens are pictured below.) Bark smooth, light brown, sheds to expose patches of greenish yellow inner bark. **ID TIP:** The inner bark is more yellowish than that of Oriental Planetree and not as multicolored as American Sycamore bark. The fruit hangs usually 2 per stalk.

HABITAT AND RANGE: Cultivated in North America; planted along streets, in parks.

NOTES: London Planetree, also called *P. hybrida,* is a hybrid of American Sycamore and Oriental Planetree. Tolerant of poor soils and air pollution, it is one of the world's most dependable city trees.

| PLANETREE FAMILY | PLATANACEAE |

LEAF 5–9" long. 3 or 5 shallowly divided, pointed lobes; sparsely toothed margins. Shiny green above; paler beneath. Autumn color brownish yellow. **FLOWER** Similar to American Sycamore; reddish to yellow-green. Early spring. **FRUIT** Similar to American Sycamore, but hanging usually 2 per stalk. Autumn; persists into winter.

Oriental Planetree

Platanus orientalis
HT 60–80'

Medium-sized tree with deciduous, simple leaves. Straight trunk, sometimes dividing near base; symmetrical, wide-spreading, rounded crown of crooked branches. **ID TIP:** The leaf lobes are more deeply divided, sharply pointed, and coarsely toothed than American Sycamore's, and the brown bark sheds to expose white inner bark. **HABITAT AND RANGE:** Cultivated in North America. Native to Asia and Europe.

| PLANETREE FAMILY | PLATANACEAE |

LEAF 4–8" long. Similar to American Sycamore, but with more deeply divided, long-pointed lobes; toothed margins. **FLOWER** Tiny, in ⅓–½" wide, round cluster; greenish. Spring. **FRUIT** In ½–1" wide, densely packed, spherical cluster; brown; fuzzy. Autumn.

Sweetgum

Liquidambar styraciflua
ALSO CALLED Redgum, Sapgum
HT 50–150' **DIA** 2–5'

WITCH-HAZEL FAMILY   **HAMAMELIDACEAE**

Medium-sized to large tree with deciduous, simple leaves. Straight, tall trunk; pyramidal, symmetrical, dense crown, becoming broadly oval or rounded with age. Branches slender and long. Bark grayish brown, furrowed into narrow ridges. **ID TIP:** The leaves are almost star-shaped, with 5 or 7 long-pointed, deeply divided lobes. Leaves have a strong scent when crushed. The fruits are in spiky, brown, ball-like clusters, hanging 1 per stalk, and are prickly to the touch. Branches often have irregular, corky outgrowths.

HABITAT: Floodplains, bottomlands, and swamps; moist to somewhat dry, upland woods; abandoned fields. Elevation 0–2,600'.

NOTES: The long-lived, stately Sweetgum is planted as an ornamental for its broad shade and spectacular autumn color. It grows well in urban conditions, but its shallow roots lift sidewalks, and its winter-falling, spiky fruits can be a hazard underfoot.

LEAF 4–7" long and wide. Nearly star-shaped; deeply divided into 5 or 7 long-pointed lobes; finely toothed margins. Thick. Glossy, dark green above; paler beneath. Autumn color yellow, orange, scarlet, purple. Leafstalk slender, 3–6" long. **FLOWER** Tiny; yellowish green; in 2–3" wide, round cluster; hairy. Spring. **FRUIT** In 1–1½" wide, spherical cluster composed of numerous capsules, each with a stiff, sharp style; green, ripening to brown; woody. Each cluster on a long stalk. Autumn; persists into winter.

branches with corky outgrowths

Red Mulberry

Morus rubra

HT 20–60'   DIA 1–2'

MULBERRY FAMILY   MORACEAE

Small to medium-sized tree with deciduous, simple leaves. Short, stout trunk and dense, broad crown of low branches (sometimes vase-shaped); in forest, an open, rounded, layered crown.   **ID TIP:** Mulberries have distinctive blackberry-like fruit clusters. The coarsely toothed and papery leaves may be unlobed or have 2 or 3 wide lobes; both kinds occur on the same tree. Young branchlets are likeliest to have lobed leaves. The leaves of Red Mulberry are rough above; White Mulberry leaves are typically shiny and smooth above.

HABITAT: Moist forests, along streams, woodland borders. Elevation to 1,000'.

NOTES: Red Mulberry produces huge quantities of sweet fruits each year that are a favorite of many birds; the tree is often planted to attract wildlife. Wild occurrences of Red Mulberry are declining due to disease and its hybridization with White Mulberry, which produces a tree with intermediate leaves that are smooth (not rough) to the touch.

LEAF 4–10" long. Broadly elliptic to almost circular or heart-shaped; may have 2 lobes (mitten-shaped) or 3 wide lobes; tip and lobes end in abrupt point; 3 main veins radiate from often asymmetrical base; margins coarsely toothed. Papery; dull blue-green, typically rough above; paler with soft white hairs on midvein beneath. Autumn color bright yellow. Twig and leafstalk exude white sap when broken.   **FLOWER** 1–2½" long, green, stalked, hanging catkin. Female broader than male. Male and female borne on separate trees. Spring, as leaves emerge.   **FRUIT** 1–1¼" long, red to dark purple, tight, cylindrical or oblong cluster (like a blackberry in shape) of tiny, 1-seeded, drupelike fruits; very juicy and sweet. Early to midsummer.

flowers

fruits

Mountain Mulberry

Morus microphylla
ALSO CALLED Texas Mulberry,
Littleleaf Mulberry
HT 10–20'   **DIA** 1'

ID TIP: Similar to Red Mulberry, but has a smaller leaf and a smaller (½" wide), rounded fruit cluster. Desert-adapted.
HABITAT: Mountain canyons, dry limestone hills, along streams. Elevation 650–7,200'.

MULBERRY FAMILY   **MORACEAE**

LEAF 1½" long. Elliptic or ovate, or 2- or 3-lobed.

White Mulberry

Morus alba
ALSO CALLED Silkworm Mulberry,
Russian Mulberry
HT 30–50'   **DIA** 1–2'

Small tree with deciduous, simple leaves. Short, stout trunk; dense, broad crown of low branches. **ID TIP:** Leaf is shiny and usually smooth (not rough) above. White Mulberry often hybridizes with Red Mulberry, producing an intermediate leaf that makes identification difficult.

HABITAT AND RANGE: Introduced in North America; naturalized along fencerows and woodland edges. Native to China.

NOTES: White Mulberry, a host plant to the silkworm, was introduced in North America in 1603 by the British in order to start a silkworm industry. The cooler climate was not conducive to the silkworm, but the hardy, drought-resistant tree naturalized. It can be weedy or invasive.

MULBERRY FAMILY   **MORACEAE**

LEAF 2½–7" long. Ovate to elliptic to almost circular, or with 3 or 5 lobes; tip and lobes rounded or pointed; margins coarsely toothed. Shiny, light green, and usually smooth (not rough) above; paler and slightly hairy beneath. Autumn color yellow. Leafstalk long. Twig exudes white sap when broken. **FLOWER** 1–2" long catkin; similar to Red Mulberry. Male and female flowers on the same or separate trees. Spring–early summer. **FRUIT** Similar to Red Mulberry but can be white to pink or red to black; not as juicy. Early summer–midsummer.

Paper Mulberry

Broussonetia papyrifera
HT 20–60' DIA 1–2'

MULBERRY FAMILY   MORACEAE

Small to medium-sized tree with deciduous, simple leaves. Single or several trunks; spreading crown; suckers grow from trunk base. **ID TIP:** Similar to Red Mulberry, but leaf is gray-green above and velvety beneath; fruit cluster spherical (not blackberry-like).

HABITAT AND RANGE: Introduced in North America; widely naturalized. Native to China.

NOTES: Paper Mulberry was introduced in North America in 1750, possibly with hopes of cultivating it for paper production. (In its native China, it was one of the earliest sources of paper.) Resistant to pollution, drought, and heat, it has been a popular ornamental, but has invasive tendencies: the tree has naturalized in 29 states in the United States and is considered a serious invasive in Florida.

LEAF Similar to Red Mulberry, but gray-green above, velvety beneath. **FRUIT** ¾" long, spherical cluster of red achenes, each very small, narrow, and protruding from cluster.

Common Fig

Ficus carica
HT 15–30' DIA 3–7"

MULBERRY FAMILY   MORACEAE

Small tree or shrub with deciduous, simple leaves. Single trunk, or multistemmed; broad, spreading crown of thick, irregular branches; crown often wider than it is tall. Bark smooth, silvery gray, flaky.
ID TIP: The upper surface of the leaf has hairs that are rough to the touch, and the leafstalk exudes a sticky, milky sap. The edible fruit is shaped like a small sac.

HABITAT AND RANGE: Introduced in North America; escapes cultivation along roadsides, canyons, and waterways. Native to Asia, Europe, and northern Africa.

LEAF 4–10" long. 3 or 5 narrow, deeply divided lobes. Dark green, with stiff hairs above; paler beneath. **FLOWER** Tiny, green, round, numerous; located inside fleshy, fruitlike receptacle that also bears seeds. **FRUIT** 1–4" long, pear-shaped, leathery receptacle containing tiny fruits; yellowish green to dark purple. Summer.

Sassafras

Sassafras albidum

ALSO CALLED White Sassafras, Ague Tree

HT 30–60' **DIA** 1½–3'

| LAUREL FAMILY | LAURACEAE |

Small to medium-sized tree with deciduous, simple leaves. Can top 90' in the Great Smoky Mountains; usually shrubby in the North. Stout, contorted trunk, or multistemmed; dense, rounded, 25–40' wide crown of short, horizontal branches. Shrubby or pyramidal when young, becoming irregular and often flat-topped with age. Suckers often form thickets. Bark deeply furrowed. **ID TIP:** The unique, mitten- or trident-shaped leaves and deeply furrowed, coarsely ridged, red-brown bark have a spicy fragrance when crushed or cut. The horizontal branches can give the tree a tiered appearance.

HABITAT: Diverse; bottomlands to abandoned fields to open woodlands to dry ridges. Elevation to 4,900'.

NOTES: The native Sassafras yields a distinctive, spicy-sweet oil that is extracted for commercial use. The tree is often planted as an ornamental for its attractive leaf shapes and autumn colors.

LEAF 3–6" long, 2–4" wide. 3 distinct shapes: elliptic (unlobed), mitten-shaped (2 lobes), trident-shaped (3 lobes). Untoothed margins. Bright green. Autumn color yellow, orange, purple, pink, red. Twig green. Leaves and twigs aromatic when crushed or cut. **FLOWER** ¼" wide; bright yellow-green; in 2" long clusters. Mildly fragrant. Male and female flowers similar, occur on separate or the same trees. Spring, before leaves emerge. **FRUIT** ⅜–½" long, round, fleshy drupe; shiny, dark blue; held in bright red cup on 1½" long, upright stalk; in clusters. Late summer; persists into winter.

California Flannelbush

Fremontodendron californicum
HT to 30'   DIA 4–6"

CACAO FAMILY   STERCULIACEAE

Small, single-stemmed tree, or more often a large shrub, with evergreen, simple leaves. Rounded crown of numerous long branches reaching nearly to the ground; twigs velvety. Bark furrowed; inner bark somewhat gelatinous. **ID TIP:** California Flannelbush has soft, velvety, palmately lobed, evergreen leaves. It bears large, yellow flowers from late spring to early summer.

HABITAT: Chaparral; dry, mountain woodland. Elevation 3,000–6,500'.

NOTES: California Flannelbush sprouts from stumps after fire. It belongs to the largely tropical cacao family. Two similar members of its genus are rare and usually shrubs.

LEAF ½–2" long and wide. 3 or 5 rounded main lobes and irregular smaller lobes; thick and soft. Dark green and moderately hairy above; paler and densely velvety beneath. **FLOWER** 1–2" wide; very showy, lemon yellow, stained reddish on outside base; 5 petal-like sepals, 5 thick stamens, no petals. Borne singly on short stalk. Late spring–early summer. **FRUIT** ½–1½" long, dry, spherical capsule coated with stiff hairs. Late summer–autumn.

Chinese Parasoltree

Firmiana simplex
HT 30–50'   DIA 6–18"

CACAO FAMILY   STERCULIACEAE

A small tree with deciduous, simple leaves. **ID TIP:** The leaves are very long and wide; the bark is smooth and greenish, with whitish stripes; showy, lemon yellow flower clusters appear in early summer. The fruit splits to expose reddish brown seeds in summer; persists into autumn. **HABITAT AND RANGE:** Introduced in North America; escapes along roads and in hardwood forests. Native to Asia.

LEAF 8–12" long. 3 or 5 lobes; rounded or like a maple leaf. **FLOWER** ½" long; yellow; in 10–18", upright clusters. **FRUIT** 2–4" long, capsulelike, with 4 or 5 leaflike lobes.

Magnolias and Tuliptree

The magnolia family (Magnoliaceae) is composed of about 220 species worldwide. Nine species are native to the United States and Canada, but many more are used in North American gardening and horticulture. Previous classification schemes recognized as many as 12 genera within the family, but it is now thought to include only the magnolia (*Magnolia*) and tuliptree (*Liriodendron*) genera.

Southern Magnolia

Magnolia flowers have showy petals and sepals; often indistinguishable, they are collectively called "tepals." In the center, an upright cluster of pistils is surrounded by stamens.

Two species of tuliptree are known, one in eastern North America and one in China. Both are large, deciduous trees with alternate, simple leaves that have four triangular lobes. The outline of the leaf resembles the shape of a tulip flower. The flowers are usually borne high in the canopy and are seldom seen; however, fallen flowers may be found on the ground below the tree. The fruit is composed of overlapping, narrow samaras whorled around a central, upright axis. The central axis of the fruit persists into winter and is an excellent field identification character.

The North American native magnolias include two evergreen (or semi-evergreen) and six deciduous species. Magnolia leaves are alternate in arrangement. However, in a few deciduous species the leaves are so closely set near the tips of the branches that they appear whorled. Four of the native magnolias have exceedingly large leaves with a distinctly tropical appearance that has made them popular landscape plants.

Magnolias are an ancient group; they usually bear large, showy, aromatic flowers that have many parts. The petals and sepals, collectively referred to as tepals, often are indistinguishable from each other. The fertile portion of the flower consists of an upright, taller whorl of numerous pistils surrounded by a shorter whorl of numerous stamens. Magnolias are pollinated mostly by beetles.

Magnolia leaves (left) are alternate in arrangement or appear whorled at branched tips. Magnolia fruit (center) is a conelike cluster of follicles, each of which splits open at maturity to release one or two scarlet seeds attached to the follicle by a fine, silky thread. Tuliptree samaras (right) shed sporadically, autumn to spring, the outer samaras dropping last.

Tuliptree

Liriodendron tulipifera
ALSO CALLED Yellow-poplar,
Tulip-poplar
HT 70–120' DIA 3–4'

Medium-sized to large tree with deciduous, simple leaves. Very tall, straight trunk; high, narrow, columnar crown (when forest-grown) or somewhat pyramidal crown (open-grown) of stout branches. Older trees have an extremely large trunk, with a buttressed, often hollowed-out base and thick, deeply furrowed bark.
ID TIP: The leaf, with its unique shape that recalls a tulip flower in profile, and the large, yellow, green, and orange flower are distinctive. The samaras in the center of the fruit cluster shed first, leaving an outer ring of samaras in an upright vase shape, surrounding a central axis.

HABITAT: Moist forests. Elevation to 4,900'.

NOTES: Tuliptree is one of the tallest native broadleaf trees. Its showy flowers, usually hidden in the high crown (but scattered on the ground beneath), produce abundant nectar that attracts bees and hummingbirds. Fossils of the genus *Liriodendron* have been dated to the Miocene era (5 to 24 million years ago).

LEAF 3–7" long and wide. 4 broad, triangular lobes (and occasionally an extra, minor pair of basal lobes); upper pair often shallowly divided; nearly straight base. Shiny, dark green above; paler beneath. Leafstalk 5–6" long. Autumn color golden yellow. FLOWER 1½–3" long and wide; showy, yellow to green (or both), with orange toward base; cup- or tulip-shaped, with 6 rounded petals; upright at end of twig. Spring. FRUIT 2½–3" long, narrow, upright, conelike cluster of overlapping samaras around a central axis. Samara light brown, papery, 1- or 2-seeded. Samaras shed from the inside out, autumn–spring; central axis persists until spring.

Cucumber-tree

Magnolia acuminata
HT 50–80' DIA 2–3'

MAGNOLIA FAMILY   MAGNOLIACEAE

Medium-sized tree with deciduous, simple leaves. Short, straight, stout trunk; narrow, conical crown of upright to spreading branches and slender branchlets; lower branches of open-grown trees tend to swoop low to ground. Older trees have stocky trunk, buttressed base. Bark dark brown, furrowed, and scaly. **ID TIP:** Cucumber-tree's distinctive fruit looks something like a small, lumpy cucumber when immature. The leaves have a pointed tip, and are pale and slightly downy beneath.

HABITAT: Moist forests. Elevation 100–4,000'.

NOTES: Cucumber-tree is North America's northernmost magnolia, and the only magnolia native to Canada. It can live well over 100 years. The flowers of this magnolia are usually hidden by foliage high in the tree and are short-lived, lasting only a few days in bloom. It is planted as an ornamental and shade tree. Due to its resistance to disease, it is often used as rootstock for grafting less vigorous magnolias.

LEAF 6–12" long. Elliptic to broadly elliptic or ovate, with pointed tip; untoothed margins, slightly crinkled edges. Yellowish green above; paler and slightly downy beneath. Bud yellowish green to yellowish brown and covered with silky hairs. Twig has spicy-sweet scent when broken. Autumn color golden yellow or brown. **FLOWER** 2½–3½" wide; yellow-green to bright yellow; bell-shaped, with 9 tepals (3 outer tepals reduced). Upright at end of twig. Slightly fragrant. Spring. **FRUIT** 2½–3" long, conelike cluster of follicles; resembles a small, lumpy cucumber; green at first, turning pinkish red at maturity. Follicle pointed at tip. Autumn.

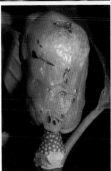

Umbrella Magnolia

Magnolia tripetala
ALSO CALLED Umbrella-tree, Elkwood
HT 15–40'   DIA 6–15"

Small tree with deciduous, simple leaves (they persist into winter in southernmost extent of range). One to several slender, straight or often leaning trunks, often with sprouts at base; broad crown of contorted, stout, spreading branches and brittle branchlets. Bark smooth, light gray. ID TIP: This magnolia is named for the umbrella-shaped clusters of strikingly large leaves near the branch tips. It has white, malodorous flowers. The less widely distributed Bigleaf Magnolia has lobed leaf bases and larger, sweet-smelling flowers.

HABITAT: Moist forests, valleys, and along streams on mountain slopes. Elevation to 3,500'.

NOTES: Umbrella Magnolia's large leaves and contorted shape impart a subtropical look to forest and garden alike.

MAGNOLIA FAMILY   MAGNOLIACEAE

LEAF 10–24" long. Elliptic to obovate, with blunt or short-pointed tip; pointed at base (Bigleaf Magnolia has 2 rounded lobes at base); untoothed margins. Glossy, green, with thick midvein above; gray-green beneath. Bud purplish, hairless. Autumn color greenish yellow, brown. FLOWER 2–4½" wide, showy; creamy white; cup-shaped, with 9–12 spatulate tepals (outer 3 reduced and downcurved). Stamens bright purple. Malodorous. Spring. FRUIT 2½–4" long, conelike cluster of follicles; ovoid; green at first, turning rose-red at maturity. Follicle has long point at tip. Late summer–autumn.

Sweetbay

Magnolia virginiana

ALSO CALLED Swamp Magnolia,
Swampbay

HT 10–60' **DIA** 9–30"

MAGNOLIA FAMILY   MAGNOLIACEAE

Small to medium-sized tree or large shrub
with deciduous to evergreen, simple
leaves. More often treelike, 30–60' tall,
in the South; shrubbier, usually only
10–30' tall northward. One to several
slender trunks; narrow, rounded crown
of erect to spreading branches and
slender branchlets. Bark light brown or
gray, smooth to scaly. **ID TIP:** The crushed
leaves and twigs of Sweetbay have a
spicy scent; flowers have a strong, lemony
scent; fruit and bark are also aromatic.

HABITAT: Coastal swamps; borders of
streams and ponds. Elevation to 1,800'.

NOTES: Sweetbay is planted as an
ornamental for its long season of fragrant
flowers, striking dark and light foliage, and
tolerance of wet soils. It does not blossom
as abundantly as other magnolias. In the
South, leaves persist through winter.

LEAF 4–6" long. Elliptic to broadly elliptic or obovate, with
bluntly pointed tip; untoothed margins. Thick. Glossy, bright
green above; silvery gray, with downy hairs beneath. Leaf
and twig have spicy scent when crushed. Bud covered with
white, velvety hairs. **FLOWER** 2–3½" wide, showy; creamy
white; cup-shaped, with 9–15 spatulate tepals, rounded at
the tips; green pistils and yellow stamens. Lemony, strongly
fragrant. Late spring–early summer. **FRUIT** 1½–2" long,
conelike cluster of follicles; ovoid; green at first, turning
pinkish red to reddish brown at maturity. Follicle pointed at
tip. Aromatic. Early autumn.

Southern Magnolia

Magnolia grandiflora

ALSO CALLED Evergreen Magnolia, Bull-bay

HT 60–80' **DIA** 2–3'

| MAGNOLIA FAMILY | MAGNOLIACEAE |

Medium-sized tree with evergreen, simple leaves. Tall, straight, stout trunk; dense, broadly conical to rounded crown of spreading branches; open-grown trees have short trunks and lower branches that swoop low to ground. **ID TIP:** Southern Magnolia has huge, very fragrant white flowers and dark, leathery foliage. The leaves are rusty-hairy beneath.

HABITAT: Moist lowland forests, especially on the southeastern coastal plains. Elevation to 400'.

NOTES: Southern Magnolia is native to the South, but can be successfully cultivated as far north as the southern Hudson Valley of New York; it is planted as an ornamental in warm regions worldwide.

LEAF 5–10" long. Elliptic to broadly elliptic, with typically blunt or rounded tip; margins untoothed; edges slightly rolled under. Leathery. Waxy, shiny, bright green above; pale and variously rusty-hairy beneath. Leafstalk, twig, and bud rusty-hairy. Twig and branchlets have citrusy odor when broken. **FLOWER** 6–12" wide, very showy; white, often with pale yellow tint; cup-shaped, with 9–15 elliptic tepals, rounded at the tips; sepals shed soon after flower opens. Wonderfully fragrant. Late spring–summer. **FRUIT** 3–4" long, conelike cluster of follicles; ovoid; green at first, turning pinkish red and rusty-hairy at maturity. Follicle has long point at tip. Autumn.

Bigleaf Magnolia

Magnolia macrophylla
ALSO CALLED Silverleaf Magnolia,
Umbrella-tree
HT 30–40' **DIA** 1½'

Small tree with deciduous, simple leaves.
Straight trunk; narrow and conical to
wide-spreading and rounded crown.
ID TIP: This species has the largest leaf
blade of the native magnolias. The flowers
have an intense, sweet fragrance; the
leaves are whorled near the end of the
twig, forming an umbrella-shaped cluster.
The leaf is lobed at the base.

HABITAT: Moist, forested valleys, ravines.
Elevation 500–1,000'.

NOTES: Bigleaf Magnolia is a rare tree
in its native range. It is planted as an
ornamental, though the size of its foliage
limits its use in smaller gardens, and
the leaves are easily wind-torn. The rare
Ashe's Magnolia (*M. ashei*) is sometimes
considered a variety of Bigleaf. It is smaller
(15–30' tall) and often shrubby, and has a
shorter leaf (14–24" long), often smaller
flower (6–15" wide), and narrower fruit
cluster. Ashe's occurs only in northwestern
Florida, on upland bluffs to 160' elevation.

LEAF 20–35" long. Broadly elliptic to obovate, with blunt
to pointed tip; leaf base has 2 rounded lobes; margins
untoothed. Bright green, with thick midvein above;
paler and silvery, with downy midvein beneath. Autumn
color dull yellow-green to brown. Leafstalk, twig, and
bud hairy. **FLOWER** 10–16" wide, showy; creamy white,
sometimes rose- or purple-speckled inside; cup-shaped,
with 9 elliptic tepals. Intensely and sweetly fragrant. Late
spring–early summer. **FRUIT** 2½–3" long, conelike cluster of
follicles; ovoid to nearly round; green at first, turning rose-
red and downy at maturity. Follicle pointed at tip. Autumn.

Ashe's
Magnolia

Mountain Magnolia

Magnolia fraseri
ALSO CALLED Earleaf Umbrella-tree,
Fraser Magnolia
HT 30–40'   DIA 1–1½'

Small tree with deciduous, simple leaves.
Straight or leaning trunk, often branched
near the base; crown of stout, contorted
branches and thick, brittle branchlets.
ID TIP: Fraser Magnolia's leaves are obovate
and deeply indented at the base, forming
2 lobes, and appear whorled near branch
tips. The flowers are sweet-smelling.

HABITAT: Moist mountain valley forests.
Elevation 1,000–5,000'.

NOTES: Mountain Magnolia occurs in
greatest abundance in Great Smoky
Mountains National Park and along the
Blue Ridge Parkway in Virginia and North
Carolina. The rare **Pyramid Magnolia** (*M.
pyramidata*) may be a smaller, geographic
variety of Mountain Magnolia. It has a
distinctive, pyramid-shaped crown, 5–9"
long leaves with shallower lobes, and
white flowers that are 4–7" wide. It occurs
in lowland, coastal plain forests close to
the Gulf coast; elevation to 400'. Although
very similar in appearance, Mountain
and Pyramid magnolias do not overlap in
range and elevation and are not likely to
be confused in the wild.

MAGNOLIA FAMILY   MAGNOLIACEAE

LEAF 8–18" long. Obovate, with blunt tip; deeply indented
base that forms 2 lobes; untoothed margins. Shiny, bright
green above; paler and whitish beneath. Autumn color
unchanged or reddish brown. Twig and leaf bud purplish
brown.   **FLOWER** 6–9" wide, showy; yellow to creamy white;
cup-shaped, with 3 sepals and 9–12 spatulate tepals; green
pistils. Sweetly fragrant. Spring.   **FRUIT** 4–5" long, conelike
cluster of follicles; ovoid; green at first, turning rose-red at
maturity. Follicle has long point at tip. Early autumn.

M. fraseri

M. pyramidata

Pyramid
Magnolia

Chinese Magnolia

Magnolia × soulangeana
ALSO CALLED Saucer Magnolia
HT 20–30' **DIA** 6"

MAGNOLIA FAMILY	MAGNOLIACEAE

Small tree with deciduous, simple leaves. Shrubby; typically has several stems and a very broad, rounded crown of low branches; can be as broad as it is tall.
ID TIP: This cultivated tree produces an abundance of white to deep purple, large and showy flowers in the spring.

HABITAT AND RANGE: Introduced in North America. Hybrid of *M. denudata* and *M. liliiflora*, both native to China.

NOTES: This hybrid magnolia was first noted in a nurseryman's Paris garden in 1820. It is planted as an ornamental around the world for its gorgeous flowers, although its fragile limbs tend to break in ice storms and under heavy snow. It blooms a week earlier than many other magnolias and when only 2–3' tall.

LEAF 5–8" long. Elliptic to obovate, with abruptly pointed tip; untoothed margins. Dark green above; paler and fuzzy beneath. Terminal leaf bud very fuzzy. Autumn color yellow-brown. **FLOWER** 5–10" wide, very showy; white to pink to deep purple-pink; shallow or deep, cup- to saucer-shaped, with usually 9 elliptic tepals. Sometimes fragrant. Spring–early summer. **FRUIT** 2¼–4" long, conelike cluster of follicles; narrowly ovoid, knobby; green at first, turning pink at maturity. Late summer–early autumn; usually few fruits are produced.

Star Magnolia

Magnolia stellata
HT 10–20'

This is one of the hardiest of the Asiatic ornamental magnolias. Some consider it a variety of the **Kobus Magnolia** (*M. kobus*). **ID TIP:** Star Magnolia has silvery-gray bark and showy flowers with long, narrow petals. It is the earliest-blooming magnolia. **HABITAT AND RANGE:** Introduced in North America. Native to Japan.

MAGNOLIA FAMILY	MAGNOLIACEAE

LEAF 2–4" long. Elliptic; green; young leaf and autumn color bronze. **FLOWER** 4" wide, showy; pink or white; resembling a starburst in shape, with up to 20 narrow petals, rounded at tips. Very fragrant. Spring, before new leaves.

Pawpaw

Asimina triloba

ALSO CALLED Indian-banana, Dog-banana

HT 15–40' **DIA** 4–12"

Small tree or large shrub with deciduous, simple leaves. Straight trunk, sometimes multistemmed; often thicket-forming in forests. Rounded, symmetrical crown, as wide as it is tall. Bark thin, smooth, dark brown with gray blotches; wartlike bumps on bark of older trees. **ID TIP:** The large, downward-pointing leaves have a distinctive drooping appearance and have a strong odor when crushed; terminal buds are dark brown, flat, and feathery.

HABITAT: Understory of deciduous forests; ravine slopes; deep, rich soils of floodplains and along streams. Elevation to 2,600' in the South, lower northward.

NOTES: Pawpaw is one of the few hardy species of the large tropical and subtropical custard-apple family. The flesh of the fruit resembles—and some say tastes like—a banana. Handling fruits can cause skin irritation in some people. The fruit is often eaten by animals.

| CUSTARD-APPLE FAMILY | ANNONACEAE |

LEAF 6–12" long. Obovate, with pointed tip; untoothed margins. Light green above; paler green beneath. Young leaf finely hairy. Autumn color brilliant yellow. **FLOWER** 1½–2" wide; purplish maroon; broad, bell-shaped, with 6 petals. Malodorous. Early to late spring, with leaves. **FRUIT** 3–6" long, oblong to cylindrical berry; fleshy; green at first, ripening to yellow, then turning black. Aromatic.

Pond-apple

Annona glabra

HT 10–30' **DIA** 4–10"

Small tree with evergreen, simple leaves. Short trunk, swollen at base; rounded to spreading crown. Bark rough. **ID TIP:** The shiny, dark green leaves are bluntly pointed and often folded upward along the midvein, forming a V-shaped profile. The leaves might be confused with those of figs, but Pond-apple and fig species are easily distinguished by their fruits and flowers.

HABITAT: Swamps, sloughs, wetland edges, at sea level.

NOTES: Trees in the genus *Annona* bear a fruit that appears to be a single fruit but is composed of many fruits fused together. **Sweetsop** or Sugar-apple (*A. squamosa*) is a small, introduced tree or shrub planted in southern Florida and the Florida Keys. The round, yellowish green, 2–4" wide fruit has a knobby surface; seeds are oblong. The leaves are 4–6½" long, narrower and longer than those of Pond-apple.

LEAF 3–5" long. Elliptic to ovate, with bluntly pointed tip and somewhat rounded base; margins untoothed. Leathery; folds upward from midvein (V-shaped in profile). Shiny, dark green, with yellowish veins. **FLOWER** 1" wide; creamy white to yellowish; 6 triangular petals and 3 sepals; typically nods from branch. Spring. **FRUIT** 3–5" wide, apple-shaped aggregate of fused berries; matures to pale yellow with brown spots. Fleshy, with flat seeds. Summer–autumn.

Pond-apple flower

Sweetsop fruit

Pond-apple fruit

Cultivated Citrus

Citrus hybrids

HT 6–18'   **DIA** 3–8"

Small trees or large shrubs with evergreen, simple leaves. Short trunk; densely rounded to somewhat spreading crown. **ID TIP:** Sweet Orange, Sour Orange, and Grapefruit represent three groups of plants that are part of a hybrid complex resulting from many years of cultivation. These trees bear large fruits and green twigs that often have sharp thorns at the leaf axils. The dark green leaves with a winged leafstalk help distinguish these hybrids. Wings on the leafstalks of the Grapefruit and Sour Orange groups are widest near the leaf base and narrow rapidly toward the branch; those of Sweet Orange are more uniform in width from blade to branch.

LEAF 1–6" long. Elliptic, with pointed tip. Dark green. Leafstalk broadly to narrowly winged; sometimes has a thorn. **FLOWER** 1½" wide; white; 4–6 spreading petals; borne singly or in small clusters at leaf axils. Fragrant. Spring. **FRUIT** A large berry, about 3½" wide for Sweet Orange; 5–6" for Grapefruit; 2–4" for Sour Orange. Thick rind, orange to reddish orange to yellowish. Autumn.

HABITAT AND RANGE: Cultivated in North America; seen mostly in peninsular Florida; occasionally escape.

Osage-orange

Maclura pomifera

ALSO CALLED Hedge-apple, Bois-d'arc, Bow Wood, Horse-apple

HT 20–40' **DIA** 1½–3'

Small tree with deciduous, simple leaves. Short, straight trunk; rounded or irregular crown of densely spaced, stiff, stout, intertwining branches; nearly as wide as it is tall. Thicket-forming. Bark orange-tinged brown; deeply furrowed. **ID TIP:** The branches have stout, ½–1" spines; milky-white sap appears when leaves, fruits, or spines are crushed or broken. The distinctive large, spherical, bumpy green fruit has a citrusy smell.

HABITAT: Rich bottomland forests and sandy terraces. Elevation to 4,900'.

NOTES: This fast-growing native of Arkansas and Texas has become naturalized throughout much of the United States. Commonly planted as farm fencing before the advent of barbed wire, it is still planted to provide windbreaks and hedges with its dense, spiny, impenetrable canopy. It is cultivated as an ornamental for its unusual fruit, which vaguely resembles an orange.

MULBERRY FAMILY — **MORACEAE**

LEAF 3–5" long, 2–3" wide. Ovate to elliptic, with long-pointed tip; untoothed margins. Bright green above, paler beneath. Leafstalk finely hairy. Autumn color yellow-green. Twig has spines. **FLOWER** Tiny; white; in dense, 1–1½" long, round to oblong, hanging clusters (females slightly larger). Male and female flowers on separate trees. Late spring–early summer. **FRUIT** 3–6" wide, spherical; brainlike, bumpy surface; composed of hundreds of tightly packed achenes; fleshy; green to yellow-green. Autumn.

female flowers

Strangler Fig

Ficus aurea
ALSO CALLED Florida Strangler Fig,
Golden Fig
HT 20–60'   **DIA** 1–3'

MULBERRY FAMILY   **MORACEAE**

Small to medium-sized tree with
evergreen, simple leaves. Rounded crown.
Bark whitish gray when young, turning
darker with age. **ID TIP:** Branchlets and
leafstalks ooze a milky sap when cut or
broken. The aerial roots of this tree are
often seen wrapped around the trunk of
a host tree (often Cabbage Palm, p. 467).
Strangler Fig is distinguished from **Wild
Banyantree** (*F. citrifolia*) by its stalkless or
very short-stalked fruits; fruit stalks of Wild
Banyantree are up to 1" long.

HABITAT: Tropical hammocks and the
edges of mangrove swamps, near sea
level. Wild Banyantree typically occurs
naturally only in tropical hammocks.

NOTES: Seeds of Strangler Fig often
germinate on the trunks of other trees
and form aerial roots that extend to the
ground and eventually become part
of the trunk. As the fig tree grows, it
smothers and kills the host tree.

LEAF 2–5" long. Ovate to elliptic; leathery; margins
untoothed. Shiny, dark green above; paler beneath.
FLOWER Tiny, borne inside a fleshy, fruitlike receptacle with
a tiny pore to allow for pollination. Spring–summer. **FRUIT**
½" wide; berrylike; yellow to red; develops from the
softening tissue of the flower receptacle following
pollination. Summer–autumn.

Weeping Fig

Ficus benjamina
ALSO CALLED Benjamin Fig
HT 20–50'   **DIA** 1–3'

MULBERRY FAMILY   **MORACEAE**

Small tree with evergreen, simple leaves.
Straight trunk; symmetrical crown of
weeping branches and dense foliage.
ID TIP: The narrowly elliptic leaves have
up to 15 or more pairs of closely set side
veins. **HABITAT AND RANGE:** Introduced in
North America; escaped from cultivation
in southern Florida and the Florida
Keys. **NOTES:** Weeping Fig is a very
common potted tree.

LEAF 2–4" long. Elliptic, with abruptly long-pointed tip;
8–15 or more side veins angle away from the midvein at
regular intervals and angles. Shiny, dark green. **FRUIT** ½"
wide; nearly round; yellowish or reddish.

Coco-plum

Chrysobalanus icaco

ALSO CALLED Icaco Coco-plum

HT 6–15' **DIA** 3–6"

| COCOA-PLUM FAMILY | CHRYSOBALANACEAE |

Large, dense shrub or small tree with evergreen, simple leaves. Short, upright or leaning trunk. **ID TIP:** The leaves of Coco-plum are notched at the tip, and the leafstalks are twisted, so that the leaves appear to point in a single direction and often look as if they are borne on the same side of the branch.

HABITAT AND RANGE: Hammocks, edges of beaches and freshwater wetlands; central and southern Florida and the Florida Keys, at sea level.

LEAF 1–3" long. Elliptic to nearly circular, notched at tip; stiff, leathery. **FLOWER** ¼" long; creamy white; 5 petals. Year-round. **FRUIT** 1" long drupe; purple, white, reddish, or pinkish. Year-round.

Button-mangrove

Conocarpus erectus

HT 15–40' **DIA** 8–20"

| INDIAN ALMOND FAMILY | COMBRETACEAE |

flowers

Small tree or large shrub with evergreen, simple leaves. Short, straight trunk; narrow to rounded crown. Bark brownish, rough, somewhat scaly. **ID TIP:** The leaf has a pair of small glands near the leafstalk and tiny depressions in the vein angles beneath (best seen with magnification). The buttonlike, tightly packed fruit clusters distinguish this species from other mangroves (pp. 195–197) in southern Florida.

HABITAT AND RANGE: Tidal wetlands and the landward edges of mangrove swamps in extreme southern Florida, at sea level.

NOTES: Some trees of this species have distinctive, hairy, silvery foliage; they are recognized by some authorities as var. *sericeus* (which means "silky" and refers to the texture of the hairs) and commonly called **Silver Buttonwood**. Others consider the silvery leaves (shown in fruit picture) a minor genetic difference that does not warrant a varietal distinction.

LEAF 1–4" long. Elliptic; often with a tiny, toothlike point at tip; 2 small glands near base of leaf blade. Green; hairless to densely covered with silky, silvery hairs (appearing grayish green or silvery). **FLOWER** ⅛" long; greenish; 5 triangular sepals and no petals; in ¼" spherical clusters, several clusters on 1–2" long, branched stalks. Year-round. **FRUIT** ⅛", scalelike drupe; in ½", tightly packed, round clusters; several clusters branch off central stalk. Year-round.

fruits

Seagrape

Coccoloba uvifera
ALSO CALLED Shore-grape
HT 10–30' **DIA** 6–12"

Shrub or small tree with evergreen, simple leaves. Sprawling, broad crown with lower branches that sometimes reach the ground. Bark smooth, brown. **ID TIP:** Seagrape is easily distinguished by its large, wide, nearly circular, grayish green leaves with conspicuous reddish to yellowish veins and by its elongated, dangling clusters of fruits that resemble grapes.

HABITAT AND RANGE: Dunes, beaches, hammocks; mostly coastal; central to southern Florida and the Florida Keys, at sea level.

NOTES: The fruits of *Coccoloba* species appear drupelike but are technically achenes held inside fleshy petals and sepals. Seagrape is widely used in landscaping, often along roadsides, in parking lots, and around commercial buildings. The fruits are used to make jelly.

LEAF 4–8" wide. Nearly circular. Grayish green above; conspicuous yellowish to reddish veins. Twig stout. **FLOWER** ¼" long; white; in 5" long clusters. Spring–autumn. **FRUIT** ½" wide, drupelike; reddish purple when ripe; in elongated clusters. Year-round.

Pigeon-plum

Coccoloba diversifolia
ALSO CALLED Tietongue, Doveplum
HT 20–60' **DIA** 6–15"

Small to medium-sized tree with evergreen, simple leaves. Straight trunk; dense, compact, rounded crown. **ID TIP:** The bark is smooth, grayish, mottled with brown. The leaves vary widely in shape and size on the same tree (but are never as distinctly circular as in Seagrape) and the leaf nodes are surrounded by a membranous sheath that extends a short way up the branch above the leafstalk.

HABITAT AND RANGE: Tropical and coastal hammocks of central and southern Florida and the Florida Keys, at sea level.

NOTES: The canopy leaves of Pigeon-plum vary in size and shape: those in shade are typically larger than those in direct sunlight.

LEAF 2–12" long. Ovate to elliptic to obovate. Dark green above, with recessed veins. **FLOWER** ⅛" long; white; in upright clusters. Spring–autumn. **FRUIT** ½" wide, drupelike; reddish to blackish when ripe. In elongated clusters; less densely clustered than in Seagrape. Year-round.

immature fruits

Russian-olive

Elaeagnus angustifolia
ALSO CALLED Oleaster
HT 15–40'   **DIA** 4–20"

Small tree or large shrub with deciduous, simple leaves. Short, crooked trunk, or multistemmed; suckers grow freely and often form thickets. Dense, wide-spreading, oval crown; young branches may have thorns. Bark smooth, gray; peels in long strips; turns blackish on old trunks.   **ID TIP:** The bark, flowers, fruit, and undersides of the leaves are all somewhat silvery; small brown scales dot the leaf beneath.

HABITAT AND RANGE: Introduced in North America; widely naturalized along waterways, drainages, and roadsides and in open fields, to 5,000'. Native to eastern Europe, western and central Asia.

NOTES: The fast-growing, hardy Russian-olive can be invasive in the West. Its fruit, which resembles an olive, is an achene surrounded by a fleshy, dryish coating.

LEAF 1–4" long. Lance-shaped to ovate; margins untoothed. Dull gray-green above; silvery beneath; silver scales on both sides, brown scales beneath.   **FLOWER** ⅜–⅝" long; silvery white and yellow; bell-shaped; 4 petal-like lobes. Abundant on tree. Very fragrant. Late spring.   **FRUIT** ⅜–½" long, ovoid, drupelike; yellowish brown, with silvery scales. In clusters. Late summer; turns red in autumn; persists into winter.

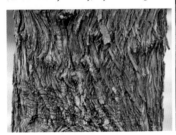

Camphortree

Cinnamomum camphora
HT 25–60'   **DIA** 10–25"

Small to medium-sized tree with evergreen, simple leaves. Short, straight trunk and dense, vase-shaped or rounded crown.   **ID TIP:** Crushed leaves emit strong odor of camphor.   **HABITAT AND RANGE:** Introduced in North America; naturalized from South Carolina to Texas. Native to Asia.   **NOTES:** Camphortree is considered an invasive species in North America.

LEAF 2–5" long. Elliptic to lance-shaped, with long-pointed tip. Shiny, medium to dark green above.   **FRUIT** ½" wide; shiny black drupe. Summer–autumn.

Red Bay

Persea borbonia

HT 20–50'   **DIA** 6–20"

Small tree or large shrub with evergreen, simple leaves; often shrubby and less than 6' tall on sandy sites. Straight trunk. Bark dark gray, fissured. **ID TIP:** The leaves are long, elliptic or lance-shaped, dark green and shiny above, paler and often whitish beneath; twigs are greenish and typically hairless. Crushed leaves have a fragrance similar to that of the culinary bay leaf.

HABITAT: Dry, sandy woodlands, dunes, and maritime forests; often near the coast; sometimes in rich, moist, hardwood forests. Elevation to 400'.

NOTES: Red Bay grows largest in rich, moist, hardwood forests. Leaves on this and other species of *Persea* may bear conspicuous, yellowish green insect galls. **Silk Bay** (*P. humilis* or *P. borbonia* var. *humilis*), usually a shrub, is restricted to central peninsular Florida; Silk Bay's trunk, twigs, and branches often have a blackish cast. **Swamp Bay** (*P. palustris*) shares a range with Red Bay but is smaller, with reddish brown twigs and brownish hairs on the midvein of the leaf beneath.

| LAUREL FAMILY | LAURACEAE |

LEAF 1–6" long. Narrowly elliptic to lance-shaped; untoothed margins. Shiny, dark green, hairless above; paler, often silvery or whitish beneath, partly the effect of flattened hairs (seen best under magnification). **FLOWER** ⅛" long; greenish white; 6 petal-like lobes. In stalked clusters on new branches. Spring. **FRUIT** ⅜" wide; rounded or oblong drupe; dark blue to nearly black. Borne singly or in clusters, each at the tip of a long stalk; individual drupes borne on short stalks. Summer–autumn.

California Bay

Umbellularia californica

ALSO CALLED Oregon-myrtle, Pepperwood, California Laurel

HT 30–80' **DIA** 1–3'

LAUREL FAMILY **LAURACEAE**

Small to medium-sized tree with evergreen, simple leaves. Sometimes multistemmed; may be shrubby on serpentine soils. Dense, rounded crown; when open-grown, initially oblong and reaching to the ground; can become very broad. Bark brown, thin; with age, breaks up into plates that shed. **ID TIP:** The leaf resembles the culinary bay leaf and is spicy-aromatic, though more suggestive of a liniment than a seasoning.

HABITAT: Understory of Redwoods; mountain forests; chaparral. Elevation to 4,900'.

NOTES: California Bay is susceptible to the disease sudden oak death. The tree responds to fire that kills its aboveground parts by sprouting and rapidly regrowing.

LEAF 2–5" long. Lance-shaped or narrowly elliptic, with pointed tip; untoothed margins. Stiff and leathery. Shiny, dark yellow-green above; somewhat paler beneath. Pungently aromatic when crushed. **FLOWER** ½" wide; yellowish green; 6 sepals, 9 broad stamens (6 outer and 3 inner), no petals. In dense clusters. **FRUIT** ¾–1" long, round, hard, olivelike drupe; green ripening to dark purplish brown; contains 1 seed. Borne singly on a thick, flaring base (like a short golf tee). Autumn.

Alternate-leaf Dogwood

Cornus alternifolia

ALSO CALLED Pagoda Dogwood

HT 15–25' **DIA** 4–8"

DOGWOOD FAMILY   **CORNACEAE**

Small tree or large shrub with deciduous, simple leaves. Short, very narrow trunk, sometimes multistemmed, forking relatively low to form flat-topped crown of long, slender, horizontal branches and short, upright branchlets. **ID TIP:** This is the only native dogwood with alternate leaves and blue fruits; most dogwoods have an opposite leaf arrangement (pp. 204–207) and red or white fruits. It has a distinctive, layered, pagoda-shaped crown. Leaves appear clustered (whorled) at branch tips.

HABITAT: Moist forests and stream banks; also dry, rocky forests, forest margins, old fields. Elevation to 6,500'.

NOTES: Alternate-leaf Dogwood has a unique shape, bright autumn color, and red-stalked blue fruits. It is often planted as an ornamental for these showy features; however, if cultivated in a well-lit site, the tree tends to lose its layered structure, becoming shrubbier.

LEAF 2½–5" long. Elliptic to broadly elliptic, with pointed tip; slightly wavy margins; 5 or 6 parallel veins on each side, curve toward tip. Green, with orange midvein above; pale or whitish and finely hairy beneath. Autumn color scarlet, maroon, yellow. Twig usually greenish yellow. **FLOWER** ¼" long; white; 4-lobed. In 1½–2½" wide, upright, branched, flat-topped clusters. Late spring. **FRUIT** ¼–⅜" wide, round drupe; shiny, deep blue to bluish black. Thin pulp; contains 1- or 2-seeded stone. Each fruit on long, bright red stalk; in loose clusters. Early autumn.

Black Tupelo

Nyssa sylvatica

ALSO CALLED Blackgum, Sourgum, Pepperidge

HT 50–80' **DIA** 1–3'

| DOGWOOD FAMILY | CORNACEAE |

Medium-sized tree with deciduous, simple leaves. Tall, straight trunk; dense crown of slender, spreading branches; very slender side branchlets are set at right angles to the branches. Bark is light brown to reddish brown, with narrow, scaly ridges and shallow furrows. Older trees have a wide trunk with a buttressed, often hollow base; bark becomes deeply fissured, and can develop a checkerboard pattern or resemble alligator skin.

ID TIP: Black Tupelo has smaller fruits than other tupelos; fruits occur in clusters. It often has "knees" (upright roots) when in standing water.

HABITAT: Swamp margins, moist forests. Elevation to 4,000'.

NOTES: Black Tupelo usually has several cavities in the trunk, making it a choice nesting site for many birds. It is often planted as an ornamental for its brilliant autumn foliage. **Swamp Tupelo** (*N. biflora*) has an enlarged, swollen trunk base.

LEAF 2–5" long. Narrowly elliptic to broadly elliptic, with blunt or pointed tip; untoothed margins (rarely a few teeth). Shiny, green above; paler and often hairy beneath. Often clustered at ends of short twigs. Autumn color bright scarlet, gold, orange, purple. Bud multicolored, including purple and green. **FLOWER** Male: ⅛" wide; greenish yellow; 5 petals; in ½" tightly packed cluster, at end of long stalk. Female: tiny, greenish; 2–6 flowers clustered at end of loose, long stalk, at base of new leaves. Male and female flowers on same tree. Early spring. **FRUIT** ⅜–⅝" long drupe; ovoid; purplish blue to blue-black or black. Thick skin and thin, dry pulp; contains large, oblong stone with 10–12 winglike ridges. In clusters of 2 or 3, at end of long stalk. Late autumn.

male flowers

female flowers

mature bark

older bark

Water Tupelo

Nyssa aquatica
ALSO CALLED Swamp Tupelo, Cottongum
HT 50–80' **DIA** 2½–4'

DOGWOOD FAMILY   CORNACEAE

Medium-sized tree with deciduous, simple leaves. Tall, straight trunk, swollen at base in flooded habitats; narrow, conical or rounded crown of short, stout, spreading branches. **ID TIP:** Water Tupelo has larger leaves than Black Tupelo and longer fruit stalks and leafstalks than Black and Ogeechee tupelos. Its fruits grow in groups; each fruit is attached directly and separately to the twig.

HABITAT: Swamps and flooded areas. Elevation to 500'.

NOTES: This species' swollen trunk base is a feature adapted for growing in flooded

habitats. New leaves produce a cottony down that drifts from treetops in spring.

LEAF 4–12" long. Elliptic to broadly elliptic, with blunt or pointed tip; margins mostly untoothed, except for a few large teeth. Shiny, dark green above; paler and hairy beneath. New leaves downy. Leafstalk 1–2½" long, stout, grooved, and hairy. Autumn color bright scarlet, gold, orange, purple. **FLOWER** Similar to Black Tupelo. Male: ¼" wide; greenish white; in ⅝" cluster, drooping from long, hairy stalk. Female: ⅜" long; borne singly. Early spring. **FRUIT** Similar to Black Tupelo; 1–1½" long; dark blue to purple. Each fruit on drooping, 3–4" stalk. Early autumn.

immature fruits

Ogeechee Tupelo

Nyssa ogeche
ALSO CALLED Ogeechee-lime
HT 10–40' **DIA** 1'

DOGWOOD FAMILY   CORNACEAE

ID TIP: Ogeechee is usually smaller than Water Tupelo, and often has multiple stems and a leaning stature; leaves are typically rounder at the tip, with shorter leafstalks; the twig is velvety-hairy; and the fruits are reddish, on short stalks. **HABITAT AND RANGE:** Swamps, riversides, and stream banks of the coastal plains in southeastern South Carolina, Georgia (grows in abundance along the Ogeechee River), and northern Florida. Elevation to 250'.

LEAF 4–5½" long. Usually obovate; rounded at tip. Leafstalk ½–1" long. Twig velvety-hairy. **FRUIT** 1–1½" long, reddish drupe; each fruit on ¼–½" stalk.

Swamp Titi

Cyrilla racemiflora

ALSO CALLED Swamp Cyrilla, Leatherwood

HT 10–20' **DIA** 3–6"

CYRILLA FAMILY   **CYRILLACEAE**

Small tree or large shrub, sometimes to about 30' tall, with deciduous, simple leaves; leaves sometimes persist until spring in peninsular Florida. Dense crown; young trees have short trunk, grayish bark; mature trees often have twisted, gnarly trunk, darker gray bark. **ID TIP:** Swamp Titi is distinguished from **Black Titi** or Buckwheat Tree (*Cliftonia monophylla*), with which it is often associated, by leaves having visible midvein and side veins, and by the midvein of the leaf beneath being slightly raised or ridged to the touch. The fruit of Black Titi is winged.

HABITAT: Depressions in wetlands and flatwoods, acid swamps and bogs. Elevation to about 500'.

NOTES: Swamp Titi typically reproduces vegetatively (asexually) and forms extensive, dense thickets in swamps and wetland depressions. Some authorities recognize 2 species, the other being **Littleleaf Titi** (*C. parvifolia*), which has leaves less than 1½" long and flower clusters less than 3½" long. Intermediate leaf and flower cluster sizes are common, even on a single plant, which leads other authorities to classify Swamp Titi as a single, highly variable species.

LEAF ½–4" long. Elliptic to narrowly elliptic, or sometimes obovate, with bluntly pointed tip; untoothed margins. Midvein and side veins visible above; midvein raised beneath. Shiny, dark green above; paler beneath. Leaves turn reddish to rusty in late winter. **FLOWER** Tiny; borne in elongated, 1–6" clusters; several flower clusters occur together, sometimes whorled, at tips of previous year's twigs. Spring–summer. **FRUIT** ⅛" long, ovoid drupe; dry, brownish. In elongated clusters. Summer–autumn.

flowers

flowers

fruits

Sweetleaf

Symplocos tinctoria
HT 6–25' DIA 3–6"

Small tree or large shrub with deciduous to evergreen, simple leaves. Slender trunk; irregularly branched crown. Bark smooth or slightly fissured. ID TIP: Sweetleaf is similar at a glance to several trees in the laurel family (including *Persea* species, p. 293); it is distinguished most easily by the rounded clusters of yellow flowers and the greenish, oblong drupe with tiny teeth surrounding the tip.

HABITAT: Upland and lowland woods, floodplains; often in moist areas but also sandy soils. Elevation to about 3,000'.

NOTE: The midvein on the lower side of the leaf (especially on older leaves) has a slightly sweet taste (hence the common name), making the leaves a favorite browse for deer and other wildlife. In the northern parts of its range, Sweetleaf loses its leaves in autumn; leaves of plants in the extreme southern part of the range tend to persist through the winter, falling just before flowering and as the new leaves appear.

LEAF 3–6" long. Elliptic to lance-shaped, with a short stalk; margins untoothed or with inconspicuous, blunt to rounded teeth. Moderately hairy beneath. **FLOWER** ⅜" long; creamy yellow to yellow. In ½" wide, rounded clusters on previous year's branchlets. Fragrant. Spring. **FRUIT** ½" long, oblong to ovoid drupe; green; tips of sepals form series of short teeth at tip of drupe. Summer.

flowers

flowers

fruits

Sugar Sumac

Rhus ovata

ALSO CALLED Chaparral Sumac, Sugarbush

HT to 15'   **DIA** 5"

| SUMAC FAMILY | ANACARDIACEAE |

Small tree with evergreen, simple leaves. **ID TIP:** Sugar Sumac is similar to Lemonade Sumac, but the leaves are longer and tend to fold; twigs are hairless; and fruits are ¼" long, flattened, and covered with red, resinous hairs.

HABITAT AND RANGE: Dry rocky ridges and hillsides; restricted to southern California, Baja California, and central Arizona. Elevation to 5,000'.

NOTES: Sugar Sumac and Lemonade hybridize in nature. **Kearney's Sumac** (*R. kearneyi*) is similar, but the leaf edges tend to roll under. It occurs in southwestern Arizona and Baja California.

LEAF 1½–3¼" long, 1–2" wide. Ovate, with pointed tip; untoothed margins; tends to fold upward lengthwise. Shiny, light green above and beneath. Twig hairless. **FLOWER** ¼" wide; white; 5 round petals. In 2" long clusters. Buds pink or reddish. Early spring. **FRUIT** ¼" long, flattened drupe; red, covered with red, resinous hairs. In 2" long, dense clusters extended like fingers. Summer.

Kearney's Sumac

Lemonade Sumac

Rhus integrifolia
ALSO CALLED Lemonadeberry, Mahogany Sumac
HT to 20'   **DIA** 8"

| SUMAC FAMILY | ANACARDIACEAE |

Small tree with evergreen, simple leaves. Thicket-forming; rounded crown of wide-spreading branches. **ID TIP:** The bark on older trees splits to reveal reddish inner bark between gray flakes. The reddish, resinous fruits are produced in dense clusters, often extended like fingers in all directions.

HABITAT AND RANGE: Beaches and dry slopes; restricted to southwestern California and Baja California. Elevation to 2,500'.

NOTES: Native Americans made a tart beverage from the bitter, lemon-flavored fruits of this sumac. Where the two species grow in proximity, Lemonade Sumac tends to grow on north-facing slopes, Sugar Sumac on south-facing slopes.

LEAF 1–2" long, ¾–1½" wide. Elliptic, with blunt tip; margins untoothed or with short, prickly teeth. Sometimes has 1 or 2 lobes at base, or rarely is compound, with 3 leaflets. Shiny, dark green above; paler beneath. Twig reddish, finely hairy. **FLOWER** ¼" wide; white to pinkish; 5 round petals. In 2" long clusters. Buds pink or reddish. Early spring. **FRUIT** ½" long, ovoid drupe; red, often completely covered with white resin. In 2" long, dense clusters, extended like fingers. Summer.

Laurel Sumac

Malosma laurina
HT to 16'   **DIA** 6"

| SUMAC FAMILY | ANACARDIACEAE |

Small tree or shrub with evergreen, simple leaves. Short trunk; round crown of reddish branches. **ID TIP:** Laurel Sumac, formerly placed in the genus *Rhus*, is distinguished from similar *Rhus* sumacs by the applelike aroma of its leaves (*Malosma* means "with the odor of apples") and its white fruits. The flowers occur in conical clusters.

HABITAT AND RANGE: Dry slopes of woodlands and scrub forests. Restricted to southwestern California and Baja California. Elevation to 3,000'.

LEAF 2–4" long, ¾–2" wide. Elliptic to ovate; untoothed margins; edges rolled or folded upward. Shiny green, with reddish veins above; paler beneath. Applelike aroma. Twig reddish, hairless. **FLOWER** ⅛" wide; white; 5 petals. In 2–6" long, conical clusters. Late spring–early summer. **FRUIT** Tiny, round drupe; white; waxy. In 2–6" long clusters. Late summer.

American Smoketree

Cotinus obovatus
ALSO CALLED Chittamwood
HT 20–30'   **DIA** 12–14"

Small tree or large shrub with deciduous, simple leaves. Straight trunk, or multistemmed; open, rounded crown of upright, spreading branches, often as wide as it is tall. Bark gray-brown; flakes off and becomes scaly with age. **ID TIP:** The leaves and twigs have a strong odor when crushed. Young twigs are covered in purplish wax. The dense flower clusters remain on the tree and look like puffs of smoke at a distance. Autumn leaves are vibrantly colored.

HABITAT: Rocky woods and bluffs; high, dry hills and mountain canyons in Texas. Elevation to 3,200'.

NOTES: American Smoketree most commonly occurs in Texas; it is scattered in mountainous locations in the South. The similar **European Smoketree** (*C. coggygria*), native to Europe and Asia, is introduced in North America. It is usually multistemmed and shrubby. The leaves are smaller (1½–3½" long), with blunt tips. The hairy flowers are in 6–8" long clusters. The fruits are ⅛" long.

LEAF 3–6" long, ½–3½" wide. Elliptic to nearly circular; untoothed margins. Blue-green. Autumn color yellow, orange, red, purple. Twig orangish. **FLOWER** ½–¾" long; greenish yellow to pinkish; on hairy stalks in 6–10" long, finely branched clusters. Spring. **FRUIT** ¼" long, hard, kidney-shaped to circular, flattened drupe; tan; on ½–2" long, slender stalks. Late summer–early autumn.

European Smoketree

Mango

Mangifera indica
HT 20–50'   **DIA** 10–20"

Small tree with evergreen, simple leaves. Short, stout trunk; broadly rounded crown of dense foliage. Bark thick, light to dark gray or brownish, becoming fissured and roughened at maturity. **ID TIP:** The leaves are long and narrow, with a pointed tip, and are borne in closely set, crowded clusters at the tips of the branches; the base of the leafstalk is swollen. The large, ovoid, pinkish to reddish fruit (the commercial mango) is distinctive.

HABITAT AND RANGE: Introduced in North America; naturalized and established in southern and central peninsular Florida, at sea level. Native to India.

NOTES: Mango is in the same family as Poison Sumac and the poison-oaks and poison ivies (p. 246). Handling the fruit causes a skin irritation in some people.

SUMAC FAMILY   ANACARDIACEAE

LEAF 4–10" long. Narrowly elliptic, with pointed tip and base. Shiny, dark green above. Leafstalk 1¼" long, swollen at base. New leaves often pinkish red. **FLOWER** ¼–⅜" long; 5 petals; greenish to creamy white with a yellowish or orange spot and reddish streaking. In large upright, loose, branching, terminal clusters. Spring. **FRUIT** 2–6" long, ovoid drupe; fleshy; green or yellow, tinged pink or red at maturity. Summer.

Satinleaf

Chrysophyllum oliviforme
HT 6–25'   **DIA** 3–6"

Shrub or small tree with evergreen, simple leaves. Straight trunk; open, rounded crown. Bark reddish brown. **ID TIP:** The elliptic leaves are dark, shiny green above and coppery below from a dense covering of matted hairs. The contrasting colors of the upper and lower leaf surfaces give the tree a 2-toned appearance in a breeze.

HABITAT AND RANGE: Tropical and coastal hammocks of central and southern Florida and the Florida Keys, at sea level.

NOTES: The lower surfaces of the leaves have a smooth, satiny feel, which explains the common name. Satinleaf is listed as an endangered species in Florida, but is widely cultivated and regularly used in landscaping for its attractive foliage. In southern Florida, the tree is similar only to **Star-apple** (*C. cainito*), a strictly cultivated species that has much larger, 2" fruit.

SAPODILLA FAMILY   SAPOTACEAE

leaf underside

LEAF 2–3" long. Elliptic. Shiny, dark green above; coppery brownish and densely hairy beneath. **FLOWER** ⅛" wide; white; 5 spreading lobes. Borne in leaf axils. Year-round. **FRUIT** ½–¾" long, 1-seeded berry; oblong to ovoid; fleshy; purple when ripe. Year-round.

Gum Bully

Sideroxylon lanuginosum
ALSO CALLED Gum Bumelia, Chittamwood, Woolly-buckthorn
HT 10–40' **DIA** 1'

Small tree or thicket-forming shrub with deciduous, simple leaves; grows largest in Texas (to 50'), but occurs as a smaller tree toward the Atlantic coast (to 20'). Straight trunk, sometimes multistemmed; narrow crown of short, thick, rigid branches that emerge close to the ground, and slender, zigzagging, thorny branchlets. Bark has gray to brown, narrow ridges with reddish brown scales; turns dark with age.

ID TIP: The leaves are obovate, and the leaf undersides are densely covered with matted hairs and feltlike to the touch. The twigs are often armed with straight thorns.

HABITAT: Forested rocky slopes and valleys; in southwestern parts of range, along watercourses. Elevation to 2,500'; 5,000' in the Southwest.

NOTES: The sap of Gum Bully is milky and sticky and can be used to make a crude chewing gum. The bullies formerly were in the genus *Bumelia* and were commonly known as bumelias.

SAPODILLA FAMILY   **SAPOTACEAE**

LEAF 1–3" long. Obovate, with rounded, sometimes bluntly pointed tip; untoothed margins. Glossy, dark green above; densely copper- or gray-hairy beneath. Clustered at ends of side twigs, appearing whorled. Twig has gray or rusty hairs when young, and straight thorns (to ¾") between leaves or at tip. Autumn color yellow. **FLOWER** ⅛" long; white; bell-shaped, 5-lobed. In small clusters at bases of leaves, each on 1", slender stalk. Strong, sweet fragrance. Summer. **FRUIT** ⅜–½" wide, round berry; black. Thick, mealy pulp encloses a large, thin-walled stone containing many flattened, pale brown seeds. Each fruit on a slender, drooping stalk. Borne singly or in clusters of 2 or 3. Late summer–autumn.

flowers (unopened)   immature fruit

Tough Bully

Sideroxylon tenax
ALSO CALLED Tough Bumelia, Ironwood
HT 10–20' **DIA** 3–6"

ID TIP: The tough, flexible branches are armed with 1" long thorns. Leaves are 1–2½" long, with yellow, white, or rusty, silky hairs beneath; evergreen in southern Florida. Flowers are greenish. **HABITAT AND RANGE:** Sandy pine forests of outer coastal plains, from South Carolina to southern Florida. Elevation to 100'.

SAPODILLA FAMILY   **SAPOTACEAE**

Buckthorn Bully

Sideroxylon lycioides
ALSO CALLED Buckthorn Bumelia
HT 10–25' **DIA** 4–6"

Small tree with deciduous, simple leaves. Bark smooth, light red-brown; becomes scaly and sheds. **ID TIP:** Buckthorn has larger leaves than other bullies; twigs have slightly curved thorns. Flowers are rusty-hairy. Fruits are ¾" wide and have thin pulp.

HABITAT: Swamp and stream borders, rocky bluffs, dunes. Elevation to 1,000'.

SAPODILLA FAMILY   SAPOTACEAE

LEAF 3–6" long. Elliptic, with pointed tip; untoothed margins. Bright green above; pale green and only sometimes downy beneath. Twig reddish brown, with slightly curved thorns. **FRUIT** ¾" long, ovoid berry; black. Each fruit on a slender, drooping stalk. Borne singly or in clusters. Autumn.

Saffron-plum

Sideroxylon celastrinum
ALSO CALLED Silver-buckthorn
HT 10–20' **DIA** 4–6"

ID TIP: This species has the largest fruit (½–1" wide) of the tree bullies. Leaves are 1–1½" long, hairless beneath; twigs are armed with ½" thorns; otherwise similar to Gum Bully. **HABITAT AND RANGE:** Coastal hammocks and ridges in southern Florida and southern Texas, near sea level.

SAPODILLA FAMILY   SAPOTACEAE

Common Persimmon

Diospyros virginiana
ALSO CALLED Possumwood
HT 20–60' **DIA** 1–2'

Small to medium-sized tree with deciduous, simple leaves; sometimes a thicket-forming shrub. Short, straight, slender trunk; dense, low-branching, rounded crown of stout branches and slender branchlets. Bark brown or blackish, in thick, scaly plates; develops into small squares separated by deep furrows, resembling charcoal briquettes. **ID TIP:** This tree, common in the Deep South, is distinguished in winter by the distinctive bark and conspicuous fruit on the bare branches.

LEAF 2½–6" long. Elliptic to broadly elliptic, with pointed tip; untoothed margins. Shiny, dark green above; paler and hairless to slightly hairy beneath. Autumn color yellow. **FRUIT** ¾–2" wide, plum-shaped berry; pale brown to golden orange when ripe, turning to purplish brown or black after repeated freezes. Thick, sweet, juicy pulp contains up to 8 large, flat seeds. Autumn; persists into winter.

HABITAT: River valleys, dry uplands, roadsides, clearings. Elevation to 3,500'.

FLOWER ½" wide; white to greenish white; 4-lobed; on short stalk at leaf base. Female flower bell-shaped, occurs singly; male tubular, in clusters of 2 or 3. Male and female flowers on separate trees. Fragrant. Spring.

female flowers

Texas Persimmon

Diospyros texana
ALSO CALLED Black Persimmon
HT 40' **DIA** 20"

ID TIP: Texas Persimmon is similar to Common Persimmon, but has smaller, round-tipped leaves and black fruits, which yield juicy, sweet, dark pulp that can leave hands stained. **HABITAT:** Dry rocky uplands, canyons, limestone soils of central and Trans-Pecos Texas, south into Mexico. Elevation to 4,000'.

LEAF ¾–1½" long; smaller and thicker than in Common Persimmon, with rounded tip; hairy beneath. Sometimes leaves persist late into the year. **FRUIT** ¾–1" wide, round, black berry.

Farkleberry

Vaccinium arboreum

ALSO CALLED Tree Huckleberry, Tree Sparkleberry, Gooseberry

HT 7–30'

Small tree or large shrub with deciduous, simple leaves. Single trunk; irregular or rounded crown. **ID TIP:** The leaves turn red in late autumn, and the distinctive black berries persist into winter. The thin, reddish-brown bark shreds or flakes.

HABITAT: Rocky slopes and woodlands, wet bottomlands, and along creek banks. Elevation to 2,500'.

NOTES: Farkleberry is the tallest member of the blueberry genus, but its fruit is palatable only to birds and other wildlife, not humans.

LEAF 1–3" long, 1" wide. Ovate to elliptic to obovate; margins untoothed or sometimes with tiny teeth. Leathery. Shiny green above; paler beneath. Autumn color red. **FLOWER** ¼" wide; white; urn-shaped. In small, loose clusters. Spring. **FRUIT** ¼" wide, round berry; shiny, black. In clusters. Summer; persists into winter.

Texas Madrone

Arbutus xalapensis

HT 5–20'   **DIA** 6–8"

Small tree or shrub with evergreen, simple leaves. **ID TIP:** Texas Madrone has an ovate to elliptic leaf that is pale and hairy beneath, and young bark that tends toward pinkish or whitish. **HABITAT:** Dry hills of western Texas, New Mexico, and adjacent Mexico. Elevation 2,000–6,000'.

LEAF 1½–3" long. Ovate to elliptic, rounded or pointed at tip; margins untoothed or finely toothed. Shiny green above; paler and hairy beneath. **FRUIT** ⅜" wide, round berry; orange-red, red, or yellow; granular surface. In clusters. Summer.

Pacific Madrone

Arbutus menziesii

ALSO CALLED Madrona, Madroño
HT 20–80' **DIA** to 2'

HEATH FAMILY   ERICACEAE

Pacific Madrone   **Arizona Madrone**

Small to medium-sized tree with evergreen, simple leaves. One to several arching, leaning trunks; broad rounded crown (or straggly when grown in partial shade) of stout, reddish branches. Bark peels in smooth sheets, revealing smooth, newer bark that is initially chartreuse, sometimes becoming grayish, pink, or lilac, but aging to orange or red. Old trees have rough, dark, nonpeeling bark near their bases. **ID TIP:** This is one of the most distinctive broadleaf trees of the Northwest, if only for its gorgeous exfoliated bark. It has white or pink-tinged flowers, and clustered orange-red and yellow fruits. Two other madrones occur in North America; all occur in separate ranges.

HABITAT: Well-drained rocky slopes; woodlands and forests, among oaks, firs, and Redwoods. Elevation usually to 5,000' (to 6,000' in California).

LEAF 3–6" long. Elliptic, with bluntly pointed tip; margins untoothed or minutely toothed. Leathery; veins conspicuous. Glossy, dark green above; grayish beneath. Turns scarlet or orange before dropping, in second summer. Twig pea green, maturing to red-orange. **FLOWER** ¼" long; white or pink-tinged; urn-shaped, nodding. In 3–6" long, drooping, branched clusters. Fragrant. Early spring. **FRUIT** ⅜" wide, round berry; orange-red or yellow; granular surface. Thin, mealy pulp encloses a few, large, thin-walled, stony seeds tightly grouped together. In dense, drooping, branched clusters. Late summer–autumn.

NOTES: Pacific Madrone grows well in the shade of other trees. **Arizona Madrone** (*A. arizonica*) is similar to Pacific Madrone, but it has 1½–3" long, narrower, paler leaves and shorter (2½") flower clusters. It occurs to the west of Texas Madrone, in oak and evergreen woodlands of Arizona and Mexico, at 4,000–8,000' elevation.

Bigberry Manzanita

Arctostaphylos glauca
HT 12–25' **DIA** 5–8"

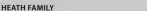

| HEATH FAMILY | ERICACEAE |

Small tree or large shrub with evergreen, simple leaves. Usually multistemmed and contorted, with a broad, rounded crown of largely bare limbs. **ID TIP:** The leaves are pale grayish green, covered with a whitish wax that may be easily rubbed off, exposing green underneath; the bark is dark red. The fruit seeds are fused.

HABITAT AND RANGE: California, from Contra Costa County (East Bay area) southward in the Coast Ranges and most other southern mountains, except Sierra Nevada. Elevation to 4,500'.

LEAF 1–2" long. Elliptic; leaf base straight to slightly indented; margins may or may not have slight teeth. Dull green, with whitish, waxy coating. **FLOWER** ⅜" long; white; urn-shaped, with 5 minute lobes; in hanging, terminal clusters. Winter–early spring. **FRUIT** ½" wide, ovoid to round berry that consists of a sticky, leathery skin over a ⅜" wide, spherical mass of fused seeds.

NOTES: Manzanitas, quintessential California plants, are represented in the state by 56 species ranging in form from a prostrate, ground-hugging shrub to a 30' tree. They are a major component of a highly flammable vegetation type called chaparral (p. 30). Some manzanitas resprout after fire from bulbous burls at their bases. Others, including Bigberry and Common, are killed by fire but regenerate from seeds that lie dormant in the ground until stimulated by the heat of a fire. The ground beneath manzanitas is usually bare due to toxic secretions from the leaves, which the plant has evolved to suppress competition. "Manzanita" means "little apple," referring to the shape and color of the fruit.

Common Manzanita

Arctostaphylos manzanita
ALSO CALLED Parry Manzanita, Whiteleaf Manzanita
HT 12–30' **DIA** 5–8"

HEATH FAMILY — **ERICACEAE**

Small tree or large shrub with evergreen, simple leaves. Usually multistemmed and almost always contorted, with a broad, rounded crown of largely bare limbs. Bark orange to deep red-brown, peeling in sheets to reveal paler bark. Bark is rough and gray where it no longer peels. **ID TIP:** The leaves are usually held upright and mainly in the outer shell of the plant's shape. In most of California, a species with smooth, reddish bark that exfoliates in thin sheets can be only a manzanita or a Pacific Madrone; the latter is rarely shrublike and has leaves longer than 3".

HABITAT AND RANGE: Grassy slopes, chaparral, woodlands, coniferous forests. Northern California, from San Francisco Bay area to northern Coast Ranges and foothills of Cascade Range, and Sierra Nevada. Elevation to 5,000'.

LEAF 1–2" long. Elliptic, with pointed tip and pointed to broadly rounded base; untoothed margins. Thick and leathery. Bright green (may be gray-green in northern Coast Ranges); hairless on both sides. **FLOWER** Similar to Bigberry Manzanita. **FRUIT** ⅜–½" wide, round, dry berry; red; contains 8–10 separable seeds. Spring; persists through summer.

Rusty Staggerbush

Lyonia ferruginea
ALSO CALLED Tree Lyonia
HT 3–20' **DIA** 1–3"

HEATH FAMILY — **ERICACEAE**

Small tree or shrub with evergreen, simple leaves. Bark brownish, somewhat scaly and peeling. **ID TIP:** Young leaf is typically rust-colored; becomes shiny green above, but some rusty color remains beneath. Leaf ½–3" long; margins often rolled under. Flower ¼" long, white; fruit ¼" long, ovoid, 5-angled capsule. **HABITAT AND RANGE:** Sandy soils of poorly drained to well-drained pine flatwoods; coastal plains, southeastern South Carolina to central Florida. Elevation to 300'.

Sourwood

Oxydendrum arboreum

ALSO CALLED Lily-of-the-valley Tree, Sorreltree

HT 40–60' **DIA** 1'

Small to medium-sized tree with deciduous, simple leaves. Slender, often leaning trunk; narrow, pyramidal crown of crooked, upright, spreading branches. Trunk sometimes divides into stout stems with drooping branches. **ID TIP:** The bark is blocky, resembling alligator skin; the hairless twigs are red and green; the flowers are urn-shaped, similar to other members of the heath family. In autumn, the leaves turn a brilliant crimson and last up to 6 weeks before falling.

HABITAT: Forest understory in moist, well-drained soils above waterways, on bluffs, and in ravines of the Southeast. Elevation to 5,000'.

NOTES: The leaves of this tree taste sour, like sorrel. It is planted as an ornamental for its attractive, heavy, midsummer bloom of creamy-white flowers and its flaming red, long-lasting autumn color.

HEATH FAMILY **ERICACEAE**

LEAF 4–7" long. Elliptic to lance-shaped; finely toothed margins. Leathery. Shiny, dark green above; paler beneath. Twig red and green, hairless. Autumn color red, maroon, purple. **FLOWER** ¼" long; white; urn-shaped; in 7–8" long, drooping clusters. Fragrant. Midsummer. **FRUIT** ¼–½" long, ovoid, 5-part capsule; greenish yellow, maturing to silvery gray. Contains very small, 2-winged seeds. Erect, in 4–8" elongated clusters. Autumn; persists into winter.

fruits

fruits

flowers

Mountain-laurel

Kalmia latifolia

ALSO CALLED Calico-bush, Ivybush, Spoonwood

HT 6–30'

Small tree or large shrub with evergreen, simple leaves; typically to 12', taller in the South. Short, crooked trunk, or multistemmed; rounded crown of twisted branches; thicket-forming, especially in the Appalachian Mountains. Bark thin, red-brown; shreds and forms ridges with age. **ID TIP:** Showy white to pale pink flower clusters appear at the tips of leafy branchlets in spring and last for 2 weeks or more. Characteristic of the genus, the flower stamens are curved outward, with the anthers lodged in tiny "pockets" in the petals.

HABITAT: Rocky woods, mountain slopes, along streams, in the shade of deciduous forests. Elevation to 4,000'.

NOTES: When a pollinator, often a bee, lands in the center of the flower, the stamens, under tension with the anthers, spring forward, catapulting pollen onto the bee's back.

LEAF 2–5" long. Elliptic; untoothed margins. Leathery. Shiny, dark green above; paler beneath. **FLOWER** ¾–1" wide; shallowly bell-shaped; white to pale pink. In 3–6" wide clusters. Spring. **FRUIT** ¼" wide, round capsule; reddish brown. In upright clusters. Summer; persists into winter.

Pacific Rhododendron

Rhododendron macrophyllum

HT 3–25'   **DIA** 4–7"

The only tree-sized rhododendron in the West. **ID TIP:** Pacific Rhododendron has long, contorted, mostly bare limbs. Bark is brown, with thin, loose flakes. Leaves are 3–6" long, stiff, with edges rolled under; evergreen. Flowers are pink, upper petals usually spotted; in 4" wide clusters. **HABITAT AND RANGE:** Coniferous forests, mainly on coastal mountain slopes. In California, often found at the bases of Redwoods. Southern British Columbia to Monterey, California. Elevation to 4,000'.

Rosebay Rhododendron

Rhododendron maximum
ALSO CALLED Great-laurel
HT 10–40'

HEATH FAMILY　　　　**ERICACEAE**

Small tree or large shrub, with evergreen, simple leaves. Multistemmed and often thicket-forming; broad, rounded crown. **ID TIP:** Rosebay flowers are less crinkled than other rhododendrons and more symmetrical, with rounded petal tips. The leaves of this genus are elliptic and straplike, and often crowded near branch tips, appearing whorled.

HABITAT: Moist, shady mountain slopes; along streams, bogs, and ponds. Elevation to 6,000'.

LEAF 4–12" long. Elliptic, with pointed tip; margins untoothed, edges often rolled under. Dark green; hairy beneath. In whorls, near branch tips. Bud pointed, ovoid, large. **FLOWER** 1–2" wide; bell-shaped; 5 petals fused at base, 5 sepals, 5 stamens; pink or white upper petals usually spotted. In 5–8" wide, very showy, rounded clusters. Spring. **FRUIT** ½" long; 5-celled capsule; woody; reddish brown. In clusters, each capsule on long stalk. Autumn.

fruits

Catawba Rhododendron

Rhododendron catawbiense
ALSO CALLED Catawba Rosebay
HT 10–20'　　**DIA** 4"

HEATH FAMILY　　　　**ERICACEAE**

A spectacularly flowering small tree or shrub with evergreen, simple leaves. **ID TIP:** Often shrubbier than Rosebay, Catawba Rhododendron has showier, deep pink-purple flowers and smaller (3–8" long), less pointed, hairless leaves. **HABITAT AND RANGE:** Mountain ridges and bluffs and along stream banks in woods, from West Virginia to northern Alabama. Elevation 600–4,000', usually above 1,500'.

Crapemyrtle

Lagerstroemia indica
HT 10–30'

Small tree or shrub with deciduous, simple leaves; can be as small as 6' or as tall as 40', depending on cultivated variety. Sometimes multistemmed; symmetrical, often vase-shaped crown of upright, spreading branches. **ID TIP:** The showy flowers are somewhat crinkled (like crepe paper) and bloom for up to 4 months. The bark peels into thin strips, exposing distinctive, multicolored inner bark. In autumn, Crapemyrtle's foliage turns attractive red, orange, and yellow hues.

HABITAT AND RANGE: Introduced in North America; widely naturalized; planted along streets in the South. Native to Asia.

NOTES: One of the longest-blooming trees on the continent, Crapemyrtle is called the "lilac of the South" for its popular ornamental use in southern states.

LEAF 1½–3" long. Elliptic; untoothed margins. Dark green above; paler beneath. Leaves sometimes opposite in arrangement. Autumn color red, orange, yellow. **FLOWER** ½" wide; pink, red, purple, or white. In 8" long clusters. Summer–autumn. **FRUIT** 1–1½" wide, ovoid capsule; green, ripening to brown; splits into 6 parts; in upright, branched cluster. Autumn; persists into winter.

immature capsules

open capsules

Red-ironbark Eucalyptus

Eucalyptus sideroxylon
HT 40–100'

This medium-sized to large eucalyptus is extensively planted along highways, especially in southern California. Bark dark red to black, with rugged ridges, deep furrows; infused with oil. **ID TIP:** Red-ironbark is distinguished from Bluegum Eucalyptus by its red leafstalk and dark red bark that does not peel; flowers are cream, pink, or red, in clusters of 3 or more. **HABITAT AND RANGE:** Introduced, and naturalized, in California. Native to Australia.

Bluegum Eucalyptus

Eucalyptus globulus
ALSO CALLED Tasmanian Bluegum
HT 100–180'   **DIA** 2–4'

MYRTLE FAMILY   MYRTACEAE

Very large tree with evergreen, simple leaves. Very tall, straight trunk; narrow, rounded or conical crown of stout branches; leaves and twigs hang.
ID TIP: This introduced species is the tallest broadleaf tree in North America. The sickle-shaped, hanging leaves and showy, brushy flowers are distinctive. The bark is smooth, mottled blue-gray to gray-brown, peeling in long strips (which pile up at the base) to reveal streaked and blotched inner bark.

HABITAT AND RANGE: Introduced in North America; can be invasive, escapes along streets and rural roads and in fields. Native to Australia.

NOTES: Some 500 species of *Eucalyptus* are native to Australia. Many are cultivated in California, and 9 or 10 have escaped to greater or lesser extent. Worldwide, 3.2 million acres of Bluegum Eucalyptus have been planted, mostly for use as fuel and for eucalyptus oil, which is extracted from the leaves and twigs. The fast-growing and water-hungry plantations can dry up soils in low-rainfall regions. This high oil-content tree responds to fire by burning like a torch and then resprouting from the roots—an excellent fire adaptation in nature, but one that is sometimes catastrophic for California communities.

LEAF 4–12" long. Lance-shaped, sometimes curved to 1 side; pointed tip; untoothed margins. Thick, leathery. Dull green above; bluish or whitish waxy coating beneath. Strong, camphorlike smell when crushed. Young leaves are blue-gray and may occur in opposite arrangement. Leafstalk greenish to reddish. Twig 4-sided. Leaf and twig hang.   **FLOWER** 2" wide, showy; white; round, fuzzy, dense clusters of very long stamens; like a bottlebrush; borne at leafstalk base. Camphorlike scent. Winter and spring.   **FRUIT** ½–1" wide capsule; top-shaped; woody; bluish white, maturing brown, warty, and dry; splits along 4 or 5 slits at top, releasing tiny, black seeds. Spring.

Punktree

Melaleuca quinquenervia
ALSO CALLED Cajeput-tree
HT 20–45' **DIA** 8–20"

Small tree with evergreen, simple leaves. Straight trunk and slender crown. **ID TIP:** Abundant in disturbed wetlands, Punktree is easily recognized by its spongy, whitish bark, which peels in successive and seemingly endless layers, and its narrow, grayish green leaves, which give off the smell of camphor when crushed.

HABITAT AND RANGE: Introduced in North America; established and ubiquitous in central and southern peninsular Florida, in swamps, wet flatwoods, marshes, and disturbed wetlands. Native to Australia.

NOTES: Punktree was introduced to Florida as an ornamental tree in 1906 and was widely recommended for landscaping until the 1970s. It is now one of Florida's most troublesome invasives and is well known as a major threat to the ecology of the Florida Everglades. It flowers and fruits continuously and can gain as much as 6' per year in height; a single tree can produce several million seeds per year.

LEAF 1½–5" long. Lance-shaped to elliptic; margins untoothed; 5–7 parallel veins run lengthwise from the base of the blade to the tip. Grayish green. **FLOWER** Showy; petals less than ¼" long; stamens up to ⅝" long, numerous, borne in creamy white whorls along 6" clusters, often said to resemble a bottlebrush. Year-round. **FRUIT** ⅜" round capsule; woody; brown. Each capsule contains up to 300 seeds. Borne in clusters around stem. Year-round.

fruits and flowers

fruits

Little Silverbell

Halesia carolina

ALSO CALLED Carolina Silverbell

HT 10–30'   **DIA** 2–6"

STORAX FAMILY   STYRACACEAE

Small tree or multistemmed shrub with deciduous, simple leaves and low, spreading branches. **ID TIP:** Little Silverbell is distinguished from Two-wing Silverbell by its dry, hard, ovoid fruit with 4 narrow, equal-sized wings and by flower petals that are fused together from the base to about half their length.

HABITAT AND RANGE: Well-drained floodplains, lowlands, moist woods; usually in sandy soils. Piedmont and southeastern coastal plains, from South Carolina to northern Florida, west to Mississippi. Elevation to about 450'.

NOTES: The name *H. carolina* has been misapplied to what is now *H. tetraptera*. As used here, *H. carolina* refers to what was formerly called *H. parviflora*. **Mountain Silverbell** (*H. tetraptera*) is very similar but has ¾" flowers and oblong fruit and occurs at elevations to 5,000'.

LEAF 3–5" long. Elliptic, narrower than in Two-wing, with pointed tip; untoothed or finely toothed margins. Green above; paler and sparsely hairy beneath. Autumn color yellow. **FLOWER** ½" long; white; bell-shaped; 4 petals fused from the base to half their length. In clusters. Spring. **FRUIT** ¾–1¾" long; dry, ovoid or elliptic, 1-seeded; 4 narrow, marginal wings extend from stalk to tip. Spring–summer.

Two-wing Silverbell

Halesia diptera

HT 15–30'   **DIA** 6–15"

STORAX FAMILY   STYRACACEAE

Small tree with deciduous, simple leaves. Crown low-branched, rounded. **ID TIP:** Two-wing Silverbell is distinguished from Little and Mountain silverbells by its broadly elliptic to nearly circular, toothed leaves, flattened fruit with 2 wide wings and 2 small, ridgelike wings, and flower petals fused only at the base.

HABITAT: Moist soils; floodplains and rich woods. Elevation to about 450'.

LEAF 4–7" long. Similar to Little Silverbell; broadly elliptic to nearly circular; irregularly toothed margins. **FRUIT** 1–2" long; flattened, with 2 wide and 2 narrow wings. Summer–autumn.

Bigleaf Snowbell

Styrax grandifolius
HT 10–18' DIA 2–4"

Shrub or small tree with simple, deciduous leaves. Straight trunk; rounded crown. **ID TIP:** Bigleaf is distinguished from American Snowbell by its mostly longer, broader leaves (over 1½" wide) and by flowers that lack conspicuously recurved petals. It is difficult to distinguish from Two-wing Silverbell in the absence of flowers or fruit; flowers of silverbells typically have 4 petals, whereas those of snowbells typically have 5.

HABITAT: Moist to somewhat dry, well-drained woodlands; drier areas of bottomland woods. Elevation to 1,000'.

LEAF 3–5" long. Broadly elliptic to nearly circular; margins occasionally toothed near tip. Thick. Dark green above; grayish and hairy beneath. Autumn color yellow. **FRUIT** ⅜" long; nearly round to oblong capsule; brown to orange-brown. In elongated, drooping clusters. Spring–summer.

FLOWER ¾" long; white; 5 petals; in drooping, 6" clusters. Spring.

American Snowbell

Styrax americanus
HT 8–15' DIA 1–3"

Shrub or small tree with deciduous, simple leaves. Open, spreading crown of slender branches. Bark smooth, grayish. **ID TIP:** Fully open flowers have distinctly recurved petals, with petal tips often extending backward beyond the base of the flower, leaving the stamens and pistils completely exposed and visible.

HABITAT: Swamps, wet woods, marsh edges; typically in standing water. Elevation to 600'.

LEAF 1–3" long. Elliptic, ovate, or lance-shaped; margins untoothed, or sometimes irregularly toothed. Dark green or grayish green above; paler green beneath. **FLOWER** ⅜" long; white; 5 narrow, recurved petals. Borne singly in leaf axils or in few-flowered, terminal clusters. Spring. **FRUIT** ⅜" long, round capsule; grayish, hairy, with scaly surface. Borne mostly singly in leaf axils. Spring–summer.

Eastern Redbud

Cercis canadensis
ALSO CALLED Judas Tree
HT 20–40' **DIA** 8–12"

Small tree or large shrub with deciduous, simple leaves. One to several short trunks, branching within 12' of the ground; broad, rounded to flat-topped crown of stout branches and slender branchlets; crown becomes irregular with age.
ID TIP: The leaves are heart-shaped, papery, with untoothed margins; the fruit is a pod. In early spring before leaves emerge, the trees are profusely covered with conspicuous purplish-pink flowers.

HABITAT: Moist forested valleys and slopes. Elevation to 2,200'.

NOTES: Eastern Redbud is planted as an ornamental for its showy, early-spring flowers. It is drought-tolerant and not prone to disease, but short-lived.

PEA FAMILY **FABACEAE**

LEAF 5–8" long, nearly as wide. Broadly heart-shaped, with pointed tip; untoothed margins. Thin and papery. Dull blue-green above; paler and sometimes hairy beneath. Autumn color yellow. Leafstalk 2–5" long, swollen just below base of leaf. **FLOWER** ½" wide, very showy, light pink to purplish pink (rarely white) pea flower, with 5 slightly unequal petals. In slender, short-stalked clusters of 4–8, on older branches or sometimes from trunk. Early spring, before leaves. **FRUIT** 2–4" long, flattened, elliptic pod; dry, thin-walled; pink to dark red-purple, turning brown. Splits open along 1 edge; contains 6–12 flat, brown seeds. Each pod hangs on a stalk; often in clusters. Summer; persists until late autumn or winter.

California Redbud

Cercis orbiculata
ALSO CALLED Western Redbud
HT to 20'

ID TIP: Very similar to Eastern Redbud; has a slightly smaller, somewhat leathery, more circular leaf and a smaller pod; the bright, purplish pink blossoms are just as large and profuse. **HABITAT:** Slopes, foothills, and canyons. Elevation 500–6,000'.

Chinese Tallow

Triadica sebifera
ALSO CALLED Popcorn Tree, Tallowtree
HT 15–40'   **DIA** 5–15"

Small tree with deciduous, simple leaves. Short, straight trunk; open crown of spreading or ascending branches. Bark light brown. **ID TIP:** No other native or naturalized tree of the Southeast has similar, untoothed leaves.

HABITAT AND RANGE: Introduced in North America; naturalized in lawns, wetlands, and maritime forests and along roadsides, from North Carolina to Florida, west to Texas, at about sea level. Native to China.

NOTES: The fruit splits at maturity to reveal 3 white, popcornlike seeds, hence the name Popcorn Tree. Planted as a landscape tree, Chinese Tallow is a serious invasive species in the Southeast, especially near the coast. It was once recommended for planting by the U.S. Department of Agriculture and is now considered a major threat to natural ecosystems; it is known to displace native vegetation and alter soil conditions.

LEAF 1¼–2½" long; often as wide as long. Broadly ovate to triangular (like a poplar), with long-pointed tip; untoothed margins. Medium to dark green above; paler beneath. Autumn color yellow to bright red. Leafstalk 1" long. **FLOWER** Tiny, yellow; in showy, cylindrical, 3–8" clusters; borne at branch tip, may be in whorls. Spring. **FRUIT** ⅜" long; 3-lobed capsule; green at first, black at maturity. Splits to reveal 3 white seeds. In branched, terminal clusters. Summer–autumn.

Manchineel

Hippomane mancinella
HT 10–20' DIA 2–6"

SPURGE FAMILY   EUPHORBIACEAE

Small tree or large shrub with evergreen, simple leaves. Bark silvery gray. **ID TIP:** The long-stalked leaves are light green and shiny above, with a yellowish green midvein, and finely and evenly toothed margins.

HABITAT AND RANGE: Coastal hammocks, at sea level; southernmost Florida and Florida Keys, as well as the Caribbean, Mexico, and Central and South America.

NOTES: Manchineel sap is capable of causing serious skin irritation. The fruit, if ingested, can be fatal. This toxicity previously led to significant eradication attempts, and this species is now considered threatened in Florida due primarily to human interference.

LEAF 2–4" long. Broadly ovate; finely and evenly toothed margins. Shiny, light green above and beneath; yellowish green midvein. Leafstalk long. **FLOWER** Tiny, greenish; borne in upright clusters. Year-round. **FRUIT** 1" wide, round drupe; green. Year-round.

Manchineel Toxicity

Manchineel (from "manzanilla," meaning "little apple" in Spanish), the only species in its genus, is one of the most toxic trees in the world. The most likely toxins are tigliane phorbol esters. The sap may cause painful blistering of the skin upon contact. The fruit, which is sweet and pleasant to the taste, will cause painful ulceration and swelling of the mucus membranes, and can be fatal if ingested. Burning the plant produces toxic smoke, irritating the eyes, even causing blindness. The Carib used the sap to poison their darts, and used leaves to poison the water supply of enemies. This is a tree to learn well, and leave strictly alone, when on Caribbean vacations.

Southern Bayberry

Morella cerifera

ALSO CALLED Southern Wax-myrtle, Candleberry

HT to 30'   **DIA** 6–10"

Small tree or shrub with evergreen, simple leaves. Often multistemmed and thicket-forming, especially in Florida; narrow, rounded crown and upright branches. Bark light to dark gray, thin, smooth. **ID TIP:** Crushed leaves and fruits have distinctive aroma. Both leaf surfaces have gland dots; twigs are hairless (though young twigs are rusty-woolly and dotted with glands). Fruits are hairless under a wax coating.

HABITAT: Southern coastal sandy swamps and pond margins; moist upland forests. Elevation to 1,500'.

NOTES: Seven species of bayberries are native to North America, but only 3 regularly attain tree size. They are sometimes placed in genus *Myrica*. **Northern Bayberry** (*M. pensylvanica*) and **Evergreen Bayberry** (*M. caroliniensis*) are similar to Southern Bayberry, but nearly always shrubs. Northern Bayberry occurs on the northeastern coast; the leaves are deciduous and do not have gland dots above, twigs are gray-hairy, and fruits are usually hairy under wax coating. Evergreen Bayberry occurs in the same habitat and range as Southern, but has larger, evergreen leaves and black-hairy twigs. The fruits of these bayberries, when boiled, yield fragrant wax used to make scented candles.

LEAF 1½–3½" long. Narrowly obovate, with pointed tip; margins untoothed, or toothed above the middle; edges rolled under. Thick, leathery. Shiny, yellow-green above; paler, often hairy beneath; gland dots on both surfaces. Twig hairless (rusty-woolly and gland-dotted when young). **FLOWER** Tiny; yellowish green or reddish green; in ¼–1" long, cylindrical, catkinlike cluster at base of leaf. Male and female flowers usually occur on separate trees. Early spring. **FRUIT** ⅛–½" wide, round drupe; coated with granular white to pale blue wax. Green maturing to purplish or black; hairless under wax coating. In small clusters along twigs. Aromatic scent. Early autumn.

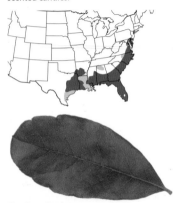

Northern Bayberry

Scentless Bayberry

Morella inodora
ALSO CALLED Odorless Wax-myrtle
HT to 18'   **DIA** 2–8"

Small tree or shrub with evergreen, simple leaves. Often multistemmed and thicket-forming. **ID TIP:** The leaves and fruits are not aromatic as in other bayberries. The leaves are obovate, bluntly pointed, and only slightly hairy beneath; they are typically strongly angled upward near the branch tips. Fruits are densely hairy under a wax coating; they are sometimes borne on a long stalk.

HABITAT: Coastal sand dunes, swamps, pinelands. Elevation to 30'.

BAYBERRY FAMILY   **MYRICACEAE**

LEAF 1½–3½" long. Narrowly obovate, with bluntly pointed tip; margins untoothed, or toothed above the middle; edges rolled under. Thick; leathery. Shiny, dark green above; green, sometimes slightly hairy beneath; inconspicuous gland dots on both surfaces. Twig usually hairy when new, becoming hairless. **FRUIT** ⅛–½" wide drupe; similar to Southern Bayberry but densely hairy under wax coating. In small clusters along twigs. Not aromatic. Early autumn.

Pacific Bayberry

Morella californica
ALSO CALLED California Wax-myrtle
HT to 30'   **DIA** 6–10"

Small tree or shrub with evergreen, simple leaves. **ID TIP:** Crushed leaves and fruits have distinctive aroma. Leaves are obovate and have tiny, black gland dots beneath. Fruits are similar to other bayberry fruit; hairless to sparsely hairy under wax coating.

HABITAT: Coastal sand dunes, along streams; ravines. Elevation to 3,300'.

BAYBERRY FAMILY   **MYRICACEAE**

male flowers

male flowers

LEAF 2–4½" long. Narrowly obovate, with blunt or pointed tip; margins untoothed or toothed above the middle. Thick; leathery. Shiny, dark green above; yellow-green, hairless or slightly hairy, with tiny, black gland dots beneath. Twig usually hairy when young, becoming hairless. **FLOWER** In small clusters; male and female on same plant.

Carolina Buckthorn

Frangula caroliniana
ALSO CALLED Indian-cherry
HT 10–40' **DIA** 6–12"

Small tree or large shrub with deciduous, simple leaves. Slender, straight trunk and rounded crown, or multistemmed and shrubby. Bark smooth, ash gray to gray-brown, often with dark blotches; becomes slightly furrowed. **ID TIP:** The flowers, leaves, and twigs of this tree are all pungent when crushed.

HABITAT: Stream valleys, limestone ridges, rich, sheltered slopes. Elevation to 2,000'.

NOTES: As with other buckthorns, the bark and fruit are strong purgatives and have been used medicinally for centuries. **Birchleaf Buckthorn** or Beechleaf Frangula (*F. betulifolia*) closely resembles Cascara and Carolina buckthorns, but occurs from Texas west of the Pecos River to Nevada and Arizona, in moist canyons and along streams, typically with oaks and Ponderosa Pine, to 7,700' elevation. The leaf is 2–6" long, elliptic, with a rounded to long-pointed tip and 7–11 veins on each side; margins are usually toothed, at least near the tip; it is usually hairy beneath.

LEAF 2–5" long. Elliptic, with pointed tip; margins have very small, rather sparse teeth, or less often are untoothed; 8–11 straight, parallel veins on each side. Shiny, dark green, and nearly hairless above; pale green and sometimes hairy beneath; side veins and midvein often yellow. Leafstalk usually finely hairy. Autumn color yellow to red. Young leaf, new twig, and bud rusty-woolly. **FLOWER** ¼" wide; greenish yellow; bell-shaped; 5 petals, each notched at tip. In clusters at leaf axils. Malodorous. Late spring. **FRUIT** ⅜–½" wide, round, berrylike drupe, with juicy pulp enclosing 2–4, usually 3, stones; red, turning shiny black. Each fruit on short stalk; in clusters. Late summer or autumn.

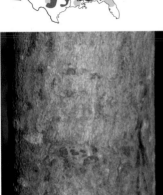

California Buckthorn

Frangula californica
ALSO CALLED California Coffeeberry
HT to 20'   **DIA** 6"

Small tree or large shrub with evergreen, simple leaves. Short trunk; rounded crown. Bark reddish brown. **ID TIP:** The leaves are similar to those of Cascara Buckthorn but are evergreen and hairless. The smooth seeds resemble coffee beans.

HABITAT: Canyons, ravines, hillsides, and coastal habitats. Elevation to 7,500'.

BUCKTHORN FAMILY   RHAMNACEAE

LEAF 1–3¼" long. Elliptic, with pointed or rounded tip; margins finely toothed or untoothed; 7–11 straight, parallel veins on each side. Shiny, dark green, and hairless above; pale green and sometimes hairy beneath. **FLOWER** ¼" wide; greenish; bell-shaped; 4 or 5 petals. In clusters at leaf axils. Late spring. **FRUIT** ¼–⅜" wide, round, berrylike drupe, with juicy pulp enclosing 2 or 3 stones. Glossy black, red, and green drupes all may be present at once due to staggered ripening. Each fruit on short stalk; in clusters. Late summer to early autumn.

Glossy Buckthorn

Frangula alnus
ALSO CALLED European Buckthorn
HT 10–20'   **DIA** 4–8"

Small tree or large shrub with deciduous, simple leaves. Usually several slender trunks and an elliptic, gangly crown of spreading and arching branches. Bark thin, smooth, gray-brown, with horizontal lines; may develop shallow fissures. **ID TIP:** Glossy Buckthorn leaves have more side veins than those of European Buckthorn (p. 210), which has opposite leaves. Glossy Buckthorn's leaves are alternate but can be clustered at twig tips.

HABITAT AND RANGE: Introduced in North America; naturalized in swamps, damp open woods, and old fields, and along fencerows. Native to Europe, northern Africa, and western Asia.

NOTES: The fruits attract birds and other wildlife, and the species has become widely naturalized by animal dispersal and is considered an invasive species. The bark is a purgative.

BUCKTHORN FAMILY   RHAMNACEAE

LEAF 1–4" long. Broadly elliptic, with bluntly pointed tip; margins untoothed or sparsely, minutely toothed; 5–8 nearly parallel veins on each side. Somewhat glossy, dark green above; paler and sometimes slightly hairy beneath. Leafstalk hairless (or almost so). Autumn color yellow to greenish yellow. Bud rusty-woolly. **FLOWER** ⅛" wide; creamy yellow; bell-shaped; in 5 parts. In clusters at leaf axils. Early spring–early summer. **FRUIT** ¼–⅜" wide, round, berrylike drupe, with juicy pulp enclosing 2 stones; green, turning red, then black. Each fruit on short stalk; in clusters. Midsummer–autumn.

Cascara Buckthorn

Frangula purshiana
ALSO CALLED Pursh's Buckthorn
HT 15–40' **DIA** 6–12"

BUCKTHORN FAMILY   **RHAMNACEAE**

Small tree or large shrub with deciduous, simple leaves; young plants may retain green leaves through the winter in warm regions. Slender, straight trunk, dividing 10–15' above the ground into several, stout branches, forming a narrow, rounded crown; shrubby in southern part of range. Bark smooth, silver-gray to gray-brown, often with pale, creamy yellow vertical stripes; often mottled with white patches of lichens; with age, becomes darker, scaly. **ID TIP:** Cascara Buckthorn has elliptic leaves with straight side veins that are parallel to each other and distinctly recessed above.

HABITAT: Variable, from alder bottomlands and conifer understories to chaparral and roadsides. Elevation to 5,000'.

NOTES: Cascara bark yields the purgative cascara sagrada; overcollection of the bark for this herbal remedy has decreased wild populations.

LEAF 2–6" long. Elliptic to obovate, with blunt tip; margins minutely but regularly toothed, or less often untoothed; 10–15 conspicuous, straight, parallel veins on each side. Slightly shiny, green, and nearly hairless above; paler and slightly hairy beneath. Leaves can be clustered at or near twig tips. Late autumn color pale yellow to orange, red, or purple. Bud rusty-woolly. **FLOWER** ⅛" wide; greenish yellow; bell-shaped, with 5 sepals and 5 barely visible petals. In clusters at leaf axils. Spring–early summer. **FRUIT** ⅜" wide, round, berrylike drupe, with juicy pulp enclosing 2–4 stones; red, becoming shiny, purplish black or black. Each fruit on short stalk; in clusters. Late summer or autumn.

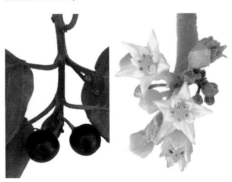

Cascara Sagrada

The aged bark of Cascara has long been used by Native Americans and other groups—including pharmaceutical companies—as a natural purgative and laxative called cascara sagrada (Spanish for "sacred bark"). Freshly cut and dried bark can cause violent vomiting and diarrhea; bark aged for three years is considered safe for use in the preparation of health remedies. In 2002, the U.S. Food and Drug Administration issued a ban on the use of cascara sagrada in over-the-counter medicines. If you find cascara sagrada in herbal remedies, check with your physician about using it safely.

Blueblossom

Ceanothus thyrsiflorus

ALSO CALLED Blue-myrtle, Bluebrush

HT to 20' **DIA** 6–12"

Small tree or shrub with simple, evergreen leaves. **ID TIP:** Blueblossom can be distinguished from Greenbark Ceanothus, where their ranges overlap near Santa Barbara, California, by Blueblossom's sparsely and finely toothed leaves with 3 prominent veins radiating from the base. Blueblossom's bark is greenish, turning red-brown, scaly.

HABITAT AND RANGE: Coniferous forests, woodlands, chaparral; coastal southwestern Oregon to Santa Barbara, California. Elevation to 2,000'.

NOTES: There are more than 5 dozen species of *Ceanothus*, nearly all restricted to California. Three species found near the California coast can attain tree size; Blueblossom is the most common of these. The flowers of all *Ceanothus* yield a green dye, and all tree parts contain lather-producing saponins.

BUCKTHORN FAMILY **RHAMNACEAE**

LEAF ¾–2" long. Elliptic, or sometimes ovate, with rounded to pointed tip; sparsely and finely toothed margins. 3 prominent veins radiate from the base. Glossy, green above, paler and minutely hairy on veins beneath. Twig has fine, lengthwise ridges, later stripes. **FLOWER** ⅛" long; deep blue to lavender (rarely white); 5 petals; in 2–3", upright clusters. Fragrant. Spring. **FRUIT** ⅛–¼" long, round, 3-part capsule; black; in small, open clusters. Summer.

Greenbark Ceanothus

Ceanothus spinosus

ALSO CALLED California-lilac, Redheart

HT to 20' **DIA** 6–12"

Small tree or shrub with simple, evergreen leaves. **ID TIP:** This *Ceanothus* has green bark and thorny branchlets. The leaf margins are untoothed. The flowers and fruits are similar to those of Blueblossom; flowers are pale blue to whitish, in clusters up to 6" long.

HABITAT AND RANGE: Dry slopes from Santa Barbara, California, into Baja California. Elevation to 3,000'.

NOTES: This species, like all *Ceanothus*, fixes nitrogen in the soil, thereby fertilizing and rehabilitating poor sites. **Feltleaf Ceanothus** (*C. arboreus*) also attains tree size, but is restricted to the Channel Islands. It has broadly elliptic, leaves to 3½" long that are finely toothed and hairy on both surfaces. Flowers and fruits are similar to those of Blueblossom; flowers are pale blue, in 2–6" long clusters.

BUCKTHORN FAMILY **RHAMNACEAE**

LEAF To 1" long. Elliptic to broadly elliptic, with rounded to notched tip; usually untoothed margins. Glossy on both surfaces; midvein prominent. Twig has ridges; branchlets are thorny.

Greenbark Ceanothus Feltleaf Ceanothus

Loblolly-bay

Gordonia lasianthus
HT 30–65' DIA 1–3'

Small to medium-sized tree with evergreen, simple leaves. Tall, straight trunk; slender, conical crown. Bark dark gray; on older trees deeply divided into furrows and thick ridges. **ID TIP:** Loblolly-bay is distinguished from Sweetbay (p. 280), a magnolia with which it shares a similar habitat, by its leaves, which have toothed margins and are pale green beneath (not silvery gray and downy), and by its flowers, which have fewer petals and a loose mass of yellow stamens (held in a central whorl in Sweetbay).

LEAF 3–7" long. Narrowly elliptic; coarsely toothed margins. Leathery. Dark green above; paler green beneath. **FLOWER** 3" wide; 5 white petals surround a mass of yellow stamens. Borne on stout, 2–3" stalk. Summer. **FRUIT** ⅝–¾" long, hard, woody capsule; silky hairy; grayish green. Splits into 5 parts. Borne singly in leaf axils but sometimes appears to be in clusters due to closely set leaves. Autumn.

HABITAT: Acid soils of swamps, pocosins, Carolina bays, and flatwood depressions. Elevation to 500'.

NOTES: Loblolly-bay is the only species of the genus *Gordonia* that is native to North America.

Silky Camellia

Stewartia malacodendron

ALSO CALLED Virginia Stewartia
HT 12–20' **DIA** 1–3"

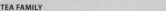

TEA FAMILY   **THEACEAE**

Small tree with deciduous, simple leaves. Side branchlets spread so that each branch appears to be in a single plane that is oriented parallel to the ground. **ID TIP:** The 5 white flower petals have crinkled, wavy margins; they surround a mass of numerous stamens with purple filaments.

HABITAT: Understory of rich, moist to dry woods, bluffs, and ravine slopes, in the southeastern coastal plains and extending into the Piedmont. Elevation to 500'.

NOTES: Mountain Camellia (*S. ovata*) is similar, but is chiefly an understory tree in rich soils of the southern Appalachians, at 1,000–2,500' elevation. The flowers of Mountain Camellia typically have yellow to creamy white (rarely purple) stamens.

LEAF 2–4" long. Elliptic; margins very finely toothed. Side veins conspicuously recessed. Dark green above; grayish green beneath. Autumn color purple. **FLOWER** 2–3" wide; 5 petals; bright white, aging to creamy white. Numerous stamens have purple filaments. Spring–early summer. **FRUIT** ½" long; hard, woody, ovoid capsule; green, turning brown. Borne singly at leaf nodes. Autumn

Franklin Tree

Franklinia alatamaha

HT 4–15' **DIA** 1–5"

TEA FAMILY   **THEACEAE**

Franklin Tree was first recorded by the early American naturalists John and William Bartram on the Altamaha River in southern Georgia in 1765, but has not been seen in the wild since 1790. All cultivated specimens originate from Bartram's Philadelphia garden. **ID TIP:** Franklin Tree is distinguished from the similar, evergreen Loblolly-bay by its untoothed, deciduous leaves. **HABITAT AND RANGE:** Extinct in the wild. Cultivated in North America.

LEAF 2½–7½" long. Narrowly elliptic to slightly wider above the middle; untoothed margins. Dark green above; paler below. Autumn color orange to reddish. **FLOWER** 3" wide; 5 white petals; stamens yellow. Summer–early autumn.

Witch-hazel

Hamamelis virginiana
HT 15–30' **DIA** 4–11"

Small tree or shrub with deciduous, simple leaves. Multistemmed, or single short trunk; irregular, broad, rounded crown of numerous crooked, spreading branches, nearly as wide as it is tall; usually shrubby, sometimes vase-shaped; can form thickets. Bark gray-brown, thin, smooth to slightly scaly, warty. Hairy young branches become smooth with age. **ID TIP:** The lemon yellow, spidery flowers bloom in autumn, after the leaves drop. The leaves are asymmetrical at the base, and new leaves are reddish. The twigs have a zigzagging shape. Buds and twigs are finely hairy.

HABITAT: Woodland understories; shady bottomlands, along waterways and swamps. Elevation to 4,000'.

NOTES: Witch-hazel's seeds audibly explode from their capsules, flying up to 30' from the plant. The bright yellow, spidery flowers bloom when the leaves fall, have a mildly spicy fragrance, and last into late autumn. **Ozark Witch-hazel** (*H. vernalis*) is a shrub with red to orange flowers found in the Ozark region of Missouri, Arkansas, and Oklahoma.

LEAF 3–6" long, 2–3½" wide. Elliptic to obovate, with an asymmetrical base; irregularly scalloped margins. Bright green, turning to dark green above in summer; paler beneath. Twig hairy. Autumn color yellow. **FLOWER** ¾–1" long; bright yellow; 4 thin, straplike, curled petals per flower, in spidery splay; in clusters of 3. Fragrant. Autumn; persists, sometimes into winter. **FRUIT** ½" long, partially rounded capsule; green ripening to brown; woody. Splits open, ejecting seeds. Autumn; persists for 1 year.

immature capsules

open capsules

What's in a Tree Name?

The common and scientific names of plants derive from differing sources and largely serve different purposes. The two-part scientific names that are created by systematic taxonomists attempt to express evolutionary lineages and to divide the plant kingdom into genetically similar and scientifically defensible groupings. Scientific names are meticulously constructed from latinized adjectives, nouns, and adverbs, adhering to a rigid set of internationally agreed-upon rules.

Many scientific names suggest a distinguishing morphological attribute. The epithet *quadrangulata* in the scientific name for Blue Ash refers to its four-winged twigs. *Glabra* (or *glabrum*) means "without hairs"; *angustifolia* means "long narrow leaves"; and *attenuata*, "narrowing to a long point." Scientific names sometimes commemorate influential botanists: The genus name *Torreya* honors 19th-century Harvard botanist John Torrey; *Quercus douglasii* recognizes the contributions of Scottish botanist David Douglas (1799–1834), for whom Douglas-fir is named. Other names reflect geographic origin, such as *occidentale*, "western"; *australis*, "southern"; or *caroliniana* and *virginiana*—both usually meant to encompass a much larger area than the present states of similar names.

Common or vernacular names utilize a more colorful language than scientific names and are not subject to rigorous conventions. Some modern botanists have proposed standardizing the selection and spelling of vernacular names, but common names that arise from everyday language and reflect colloquial biases and cultural traditions will likely always remain in use.

Common names may offer clues about a tree's historical use by humans or its habitat preferences, morphological features, or perceived medicinal properties. The straight-grained Lodgepole Pine was used by Native Americans in the construction of tepees and other structures. The sap of the well-known Sugar Maple formed the basis for Vermont's early superiority in the syrup and sugar trade. Table Mountain Pine is differentiated from many other eastern pines by its typically high-elevation home, and Water Tupelo by its preference for periodically inundated floodplains. The upper branches and large leaves of Umbrella Magnolia create the appearance of a spreading, umbrella-like canopy. The bark of Fevertree was used during the American Civil War as a replacement for quinine in the treatment of malarial fevers. Devilwood has a hard, fine-grained wood that is devilishly difficult to work.

Witch-hazel (facing page) is assumed to have been named for its resemblance to European Hazel, which was believed to be used by witches to find water and gold—and by nonwitches to find the witches themselves. Early American colonists used forked branches of Witch-hazel as divining rods for finding water and mineral deposits, a process often called dowsing or water witching.

Hornbeams are so named for their hard, whitish wood. The sinewy, muscular appearance of the trunk and limbs of this American Hornbeam makes it easy to see why this tree is also often called Musclewood.

Rose Family

The very large rose family, Rosaceae, contains a wide array of herbs, vines, shrubs, and trees, many with showy flowers and edible fruits. Flowers are bisexual. This section of the guide covers trees of the family with alternate, simple leaves. Catalina Ironwood (p. 165) and Loquat (p. 210) are covered in the opposite leaf section, mountain-ashes (pp. 240–241) in the alternate, compound leaf section.

Cherries, Plums, and Peach

Cherries, plums, and peaches belong to the genus *Prunus*. The fruits are sweet, fleshy drupes with a central stone containing a single seed (which can be poisonous if ingested). The Peach is an introduced species, mainly seen in cultivation. Plums and cherries are larger groups, with both native and introduced species. Plums have larger fruits, borne singly or in clusters. Many plums have spur branches (short side twigs) that in some species end in a sharp point. Plums do not have true terminal buds; the bud is found near but slightly offset from the tip of the twig. Without fruits present, cherries can be distinguished from plums by the absence of spur branches and the position of the leaf bud: cherries have true terminal buds (occurring at the twig tip). Cherry leaves generally have two glands on the leafstalk near the base of the leaf; Hollyleaf Cherry has glands on the leaf blade near the base of the leaf (not on the leafstalk), and Bitter Cherry may show only one gland. The bark of plums and cherries is smooth and often displays horizontal pores, called lenticels, especially on young trees. The bark of older American Plums is usually flaking and peeling, and that of mature Black Cherry is blocky, divided into cubelike plates. Peach bark is smooth when young, becoming shallowly furrowed with age.

Crabapples, Apples, and Pears

Apples and crabapples belong to the genus *Malus*; pears to *Pyrus*. The fruits are pomes, with a fleshy exterior and several seeds in the center, enclosed in often papery or leathery partitions. The fruits range from sweet to inedibly sour. Several crabapples are native to North America; Common Apple and Pear are widely planted for their edible fruits; other apple and pear varieties are planted as ornamentals. *Malus* leaves are toothed or lobed; *Pyrus* leaves are toothed and leathery. Like plums, crabapples have sharp spur branches. The bark of apples and crabapples is typically scaly and flaking on mature trees; bark of pears is smooth when young, but becomes shallowly and irregularly ridged.

Serviceberries and Hawthorns

Serviceberries (*Amelanchier*) and hawthorns (*Crataegus*) are mostly shrubs and small trees that bear small pomes. Serviceberry leaves are unlobed, toothed, and elliptic to rounded. The fruits are applelike, but smaller than crabapples. The flowers have narrow, rather than round, petals and are in drooping terminal clusters. Serviceberry bark is mostly

Pin Cherry

Allegheny Plum

The bark of *Prunus* species is thin and horizontally peeling when young (left). It becomes rougher and develops vertical ridges and fissures as it ages (right).

Flatwoods Plum

Plums and crabapples have short, often sharp-pointed side twigs called spur branches; hawthorns have more typical, smooth thorns.

smooth, often becoming furrowed. Hawthorn leaves are variable in shape, and many have toothed or lobed margins. The fruit is a small orange or red pome, similar to serviceberry fruit in shape and size. The flowers have round petals and are in flat-topped clusters. Hawthorn bark is variable; in some species it is grayish, flaking, and peeling; in others the inner bark is smooth and deep brown. The hawthorns

compose a large, variable group and are notoriously difficult to identify, varying mostly in leaf shape, fruit, and twigs. They have blunt buds with overlapping scales, but are virtually impossible to identify in the winter season. Some authors recognize several hundred species in this genus, many of them shrubs; we include 13 tree-sized species in this guide.

Mountain-mahoganies

Mountain-mahoganies (*Cercocarpus*) are small trees and shrubs of the West that are most easily identified by their distinctive fruit, an achene with a long, featherlike style. Flowers lack petals, and leaves are narrowly elliptic to obovate, and can be toothed or untoothed along the margins.

Birchleaf Mountain-mahogany

Cercocarpus montanus var. *glaber*
ALSO CALLED Hardtack
HT to 25'   **DIA** 6–18"

Of the many varieties of *C. montanus,* only this variety regularly attains tree size. It is sometimes classified as *C. betuloides*.
ID TIP: The long, silky style on the fruit is up to 3½" long, and the fruits and flowers are in clusters. The leaves are often obovate, are toothed above the middle, and have prominent veins. Leaves are aromatic when crushed.

HABITAT: Mountain chaparral; open oak and pine woodlands. Southwestern Oregon to Baja California; central Arizona. Elevation 3,500–6,500'.

| ROSE FAMILY | ROSACEAE |

leaves and immature achenes

LEAF ½–1½" long. Elliptic to obovate; usually toothed above the middle; veins prominent. Leafstalk short; pair of stipules at base. **FRUIT** ¼–½" long achene with white-silky, 2–3½" long, featherlike style. Achene reddish brown; contains 1 seed. In clusters. Summer.

Curl-leaf Mountain-mahogany

Cercocarpus ledifolius
HT to 25'   **DIA** 6–18"

Small tree or shrub with simple, evergreen leaves. Rounded or open crown; stiff, spreading branches. Bark gray to brown, becoming scaly. **ID TIP:** The fruit is distinctive of the genus, with a long, featherlike style; in season, it is quite showy on the tree. The leaf margins of this species are often strongly rolled under.

HABITAT: Mountain chaparral; open oak and pine woodlands. Elevation 4,000–10,500'.

NOTES: Only 2 species of *Cercocarpus* regularly attain tree size in North America. This species forms pure thickets on south-facing slopes near the sagebrush-conifer forest boundary. It rarely survives fires, but can be long-lived if undisturbed, reportedly to 1,350 years on some sites. Mountain-mahoganies propagate by wind dispersal; the featherlike style carries the seeds long distances in the wind. The roots of *Cercocarpus* host nitrogen-fixing bacteria. **Catalina Island Mountain-mahogany** (*C. traskiae*) rarely attains tree size; it is an endangered species, restricted to a single canyon on California's Santa Catalina Island.

LEAF ½–1½" long. Narrowly elliptic; untoothed margins, usually strongly rolled under; veins not strongly marked. Leathery. Often shiny above and resinous. Pair of small, leaflike stipules at base. Aromatic when crushed. Leafstalk short. Twig reddish brown, hairy. **FLOWER** ⅜–½" long; yellowish; hairy; funnel-shaped, 5-lobed cup of fused sepals with numerous protruding stamens; no petals. Spring. **FRUIT** ¼–½" long achene; 1½–3" long, featherlike style, often curling, has white to tan silky hairs. In clusters. Summer.

achenes   flowers

Black Cherry

Prunus serotina
ALSO CALLED Wild Cherry,
Rum Cherry
HT 30–100' **DIA** 1–4'

Small to large tree with deciduous, simple leaves; smaller in the West. Tall, straight, stout trunk; crown narrow and elliptic (when forest-grown) or broad (open-grown). Older trees develop buttressed trunk base, large burls. **ID TIP:** Black Cherry is distinguished from Pin Cherry by its pointed leaf base and elongated flower and fruit clusters at the ends of leafy twigs. The leaves have more pairs of side veins than Chokecherry. Bark is smooth and shiny, with transverse markings (lenticels) when young; becomes dark, very blocky, and breaks up into little cubes at maturity.

HABITAT: Wide variety of habitats, except wet or very dry. Elevation usually to 5,000' (to 7,500' in the Southwest).

NOTES: Black Cherry is the tallest North American member of the rose family, but few old, large trees remain, most having been harvested for the commercially valuable wood.

ROSE FAMILY

ROSACEAE

LEAF 2–5" long. Narrowly elliptic, pointed at tip and base; finely toothed margins, teeth often incurved or blunt; 12–16 pairs of side veins. Shiny, dark green above; paler, with cinnamon to whitish hairs on midvein beneath. Autumn color yellow to reddish-yellow. **FLOWER** ⅜–½" wide; showy; white; 5 rounded petals. In 4–6" long, cylindrical, often drooping clusters, at ends of leafy twigs. Late spring. **FRUIT** ⅜–½" wide, round drupe; red to dark purple to nearly black. In 4–6" long, hanging clusters. Late summer.

mature bark

Chokecherry

Prunus virginiana
HT 10–30' **DIA** 4–12"

Small tree or large shrub with deciduous, simple leaves; smaller in western and northern parts of its range. Several short, often crooked trunks bear a narrow crown of slender branches, many of which start from or near trunk bases; often forms thickets. **ID TIP:** Chokecherry has broader leaves than Pin and Black cherries, with fewer side veins than either species.

HABITAT: Forest borders, clearings, thickets. Elevation to 8,000'.

NOTES: The wide-ranging Chokecherry is an important revegetation tree for wildlife habitats and cutover lands, and is planted for windbreaks and reclamation of mine spoils.

ROSE FAMILY **ROSACEAE**

LEAF 2–4" long. Broadly elliptic or ovate, with abruptly pointed tip; pointed to rounded base; finely toothed margins; 8–11 pairs of side veins. Shiny, dark green above; light green and hairless beneath. Autumn color yellow. Twig malodorous when broken (unlike Black Cherry). **FLOWER** ½" wide; creamy white; 5 rounded petals. In 4–6" long, dense, cylindrical clusters, at ends of leafy twigs. Spring. **FRUIT** ¼–⅜" wide, round drupe; shiny, crimson to dark red to almost black. In 4–6" long, hanging clusters. Summer.

Pin Cherry

Prunus pensylvanica

ALSO CALLED Fire Cherry, Bird Cherry, Wild Red Cherry

HT 10–30'   **DIA** 4–12"

Small tree or large shrub with deciduous, simple leaves; smaller in western and northern parts of its range. Short, straight trunk; narrow, rounded crown; sometimes forms thickets. **ID TIP:** The leaves are narrow and yellow-green, and have a rounded base and finely toothed margins. Flower clusters are shorter than the elongated clusters of Black Cherry and Chokecherry. Fruits are long-stalked.

HABITAT: Moist woodlands, clearings, and roadsides. Elevation to 6,000'.

NOTES: Pin Cherry establishes quickly and stabilizes soil; it plays an important role in revegetating eroded, cutover, or fire-ravaged land. It is used as grafting stock for cultivated cherries.

LEAF 2–4½" long. Lance-shaped or narrowly elliptic, with long-pointed tip; sometimes curved to one side; rounded base; finely toothed margins; 10–20 pairs of side veins; fragile, easily torn. Shiny, yellow-green above; paler beneath. Autumn color bright yellow mixed with orange or red. **FLOWER** ½" wide; creamy white; 5 rounded petals. Each flower on long stalk; in small, short-stalked clusters of 3–7. Spring. **FRUIT** ¼" wide, round drupe; bright red. Each fruit on long stalk; in clusters. Late summer.

Mahaleb Cherry

Prunus mahaleb

HT 20'   **DIA** 8"

Small tree with deciduous, simple leaves. **ID TIP:** This is the only cherry with nearly circular leaves. The foliage, seeds, bark, and wood are all aromatic. **HABITAT AND RANGE:** Introduced in North America; escapes near farms and habitations in the Pacific Northwest and in the northeastern United States and southeastern Canada. Native to Europe and western Asia.

LEAF 2–4" long. Nearly circular, with pointed tip; fine, blunt teeth along margins. **FLOWER** White; 5 rounded petals; in clusters of 6–10. **FRUIT** ⅜" wide, blackish drupe.

Carolina Laurelcherry

Prunus caroliniana

ALSO CALLED Cherry-laurel, Carolina Cherry

HT 30–40' **DIA** 6–10"

Small tree or large shrub with evergreen, simple leaves. Short trunk, or multistemmed; usually dense, narrow crown (sometimes broad). **ID TIP:** This southeastern cherry has glossy, evergreen leaves. In spring, elongated clusters of small, white, fuzzy-looking flowers (due to protruding stamens) appear at leaf bases.

HABITAT: Lowland forests, stream banks, thickets; upland woods; disturbed sites. Elevation to 500'.

NOTES: The flowers and fruits of Carolina Laurelcherry are often present (even both in profusion) on a single tree at the same time. It is planted as an ornamental or in hedges throughout its native range and in California. It escapes from gardens and occurs along fence lines, where its fruits are consumed and dispersed by birds.

LEAF 2–5" long. Lance-shaped to narrowly elliptic, with pointed tip and base; margins untoothed, somewhat wavy or with a few teeth; edges slightly rolled under. Leathery. Glossy, waxy, dark green above; distinctly paler beneath. **FLOWER** ⅛" wide; creamy white; 5 rounded petals; orange interior and long stamens are more conspicuous than petals. In dense, 1–2" long, elongated clusters, at leaf axils. Very fragrant. Late winter–early spring. **FRUIT** ½" wide, ovoid drupe; shiny, black or blue-black. Each fruit on short stalk. Late fall; persists until spring.

Bitter Cherry

Prunus emarginata
HT 20–30'   DIA 4–12"

Small tree or large, thicket-forming shrub with deciduous, simple leaves. Short, straight trunk; narrow, rounded crown of slender branches. **ID TIP:** Bitter Cherry has leaves with a rounded or blunt tip, a pointed base, and margins with fine, blunt, gland-tipped teeth. Flowers and fruits are in clusters, each on a long stalk.

HABITAT: Valleys, mountain slopes, chaparral, coniferous forests; burned and cutover lands. Elevation to 9,000'.

NOTES: Bitter Cherry is the most common western cherry and can grow at the highest altitude of any cherry. With roots that spread up to 50' from the tree, it is planted to rehabilitate acid mine spoils and control erosion.

LEAF 1–3" long. Elliptic to obovate, with rounded or blunt tip; pointed at base; fine, blunt, gland-tipped teeth along margins. Dull, dark green above; paler, sometimes slightly hairy beneath. 1 or 2 glands near leaf base. **FLOWER** ½" wide; white, tinged with green; 5 rounded petals. In 1½" long, loose, flat-topped clusters of 6–12. Spring. **FRUIT** ¼–½" wide, round drupe; bright red to nearly black. Each fruit on long stalk; in small clusters. Summer.

Hollyleaf Cherry

Prunus ilicifolia
ALSO CALLED Evergreen Cherry,
Islay Cherry
HT 8–30'   **DIA** 4–12"

Small tree or large shrub with simple,
evergreen leaves. Short trunk, often
multistemmed; dense crown of long,
stout branches. Bark reddish brown.
ID TIP: This is the only North American
cherry with a prickly, hollylike leaf.

HABITAT: Dry chaparral slopes, canyon
bottoms; along coast of California and
Baja California. Elevation to 5,000'.

NOTES: Hollyleaf Cherry
is abundant in scrub oak
chaparral. It is planted to
stabilize steep, eroding
slopes. As an ornamental,
it requires little care and
has been widely planted
in North America.

LEAF ¾–2" long. Broadly ovate to nearly circular, with
pointed, rounded, or straight base; coarse, prickly teeth
along margins; large, dark glands on teeth near leaf base.
Leathery. Shiny, dark green above; paler beneath. **FLOWER**
¼" wide; creamy white; 5 rounded petals. In 1½–3" long,
cylindrical, upright clusters, at leaf bases. Early spring,
before leaves. **FRUIT** ½–⅝" wide, round drupe; dark red,
becoming purple (sometimes yellow) to nearly black. Each
fruit on long stalk; in clusters of 3–5. Late autumn; persists
into winter.

Catalina Cherry

Prunus ilicifolia ssp. *lyonii*
HT to 30'   **DIA** 1–3'

Small tree with deciduous, simple
leaves. **ID TIP:** Catalina Cherry is a variety
of Hollyleaf Cherry with larger, nonprickly
leaves, larger and more abundant flower
clusters, and larger fruit than the typical
variety. It is sometimes classified as a
distinct species, *P. lyonii*. **HABITAT AND
RANGE:** Fertile valleys, canyons, and dry
ridges. Restricted to California's Channel
Islands and southern Baja California.
Elevation to 3,000'.

LEAF 2–4" long. Pointed to rounded base; mostly untoothed
margins. **FLOWER** In 2–4" long clusters. **FRUIT** ½–1" wide
drupe; dark purple.

Cultivated Cherries
Prunus species

Sweet Cherry

Sweet Cherry (*P. avium*) and **Sour Cherry** (*P. cerasus*) are cultivated in North America for their edible fruit and are used as grafting stock in the cultivation of other varieties. Both species are native to western Asia but are known to escape in North America; they have naturalized in the East and some areas of the West.

Sour Cherry is multistemmed and thicket-forming and is typically smaller than Sweet Cherry, which can grow to 60' tall. Both trees have deciduous, simple leaves. Sour Cherry leaves have fewer side veins than those of Sweet Cherry and similar native cherries, and have finely double-toothed margins; Sweet Cherry leaf margins have coarse, blunt teeth. There are more fruits per cluster in Sweet Cherry than in Sour Cherry.

SWEET CHERRY LEAF 2½–6" long. Broadly elliptic, with pointed tip; rounded base; coarse, blunt teeth along margins; 10–14 pairs of side veins. Dull green above; paler and hairy (sometimes only on veins) beneath. Usually drooping. Autumn color yellow. **FRUIT** ¾–1" wide, round drupe; red to dark red, sometimes yellow. Each fruit on long stalk; in clusters of 10–12. Summer.

Sour Cherry

SOUR CHERRY LEAF 2–4" long. Finely double-toothed margins; 6–8 pairs of side veins. Glossy, bright green above; paler beneath. Little or no autumn color. **FLOWER** 1–1¼" wide; showy, white; 5 rounded petals. Each flower on long stalk; in clusters. Spring. **FRUIT** ⅝–¾" wide; red to dark red; in clusters of 2–4. Early summer.

Ornamental Asiatic Cherries
Prunus species and hybrids

Asiatic ornamental flowering cherries—some 20 species and many hybrids—are among the most widely planted flowering trees in cities and landscapes of temperate climates. Japanese (and Chinese, to a lesser degree) growers have been breeding them for 1,500 years. Their glorious blossom displays draw crowds to botanical gardens and cherry blossom festivals each spring. Strictly ornamental, these cherries yield inedible fruit or no fruit at all.

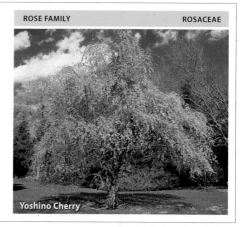

Yoshino Cherry

Thorny Plums
Prunus species

American Plum

Four native plum species regularly bear thorny, sharp-tipped spur twigs. (Bullace Plum is also thorny; p. 345.) The native thorny plums bear red to yellow fruits. They are small, often thicket-forming trees or large shrubs with deciduous, simple leaves. Bark is usually brown or reddish brown, sometimes scaly. **ID TIP:** Plums are very similar to cherries, but plum flowers and fruits are usually in rounded or flat clusters; the fruits are larger than cherries; the seeds are large and flat; and trees usually produce sharp-pointed spur branches. Plums do not have true terminal buds; the bud near the tip of the twig is slightly offset from the tip and not directly in line with the twig.

LEAF Usually elliptic, narrow; margins toothed. Usually dark green above; pale green and somewhat hairy beneath. **FLOWER** White; 5 rounded petals. Each flower on slender stalk; mostly in clusters of 2–5. Spring. **FRUIT** Round drupe; juicy pulp. Late summer.

American Plum

American Plum
Prunus americana
HT 30' **DIA** 1'

ID TIP: American Plum has larger leaves than the other thorny plums (2–5" long). Leaf pointed at the tip; double-toothed margins, with pointed teeth. Leafstalk lacks glands (compare Canada Plum). Twig reddish brown, hairy or hairless. Flower ¾–1" wide, white, sometimes pinkish before opening and with age; malodorous. Fruit ¾–1" wide, red. Bark breaks into curling plates with age. **HABITAT:** Rocky or sandy soils in woodlands, along streams, and in fields. Common in the East and Midwest. Elevation to 6,000'.

American Plum

P. americana

P. nigra

P. angustifolia

Canada Plum
Prunus nigra
HT 20' **DIA** 8"

ID TIP: Leaf 1–2½" long; abruptly pointed tip; margins coarsely double-toothed, often with rounded teeth. Leafstalk has glands (compare American Plum). Flower ¾–1" wide; white, aging to pink. Fruit 1–1½" wide, red or yellow-red. **HABITAT:** Limestone hillsides and river valleys. Elevation to 1,500'.

Canada Plum

Chickasaw Plum
Prunus angustifolia
HT 5–20' **DIA** 4"

ID TIP: The leaves fold upward along the midvein, especially when young; the thornless Flatwoods Plum (p. 344), with which it is often confused, has leaves that lie flat. Chickasaw leaf 1–3" long, with pointed tip; finely toothed margins; shiny above. Twig red, hairless. Flower ⅜" wide, white. Fruit ½–¾" wide, red or yellow. Chickasaw Plum often forms thickets; Flatwoods usually occurs as a single tree. **HABITAT:** Margins of fields and nearby habitats in the South; widely naturalized in the Southeast. Elevation to 3,000'.

Chickasaw Plum

Chickasaw Plum

Klamath Plum
Prunus subcordata
HT 20' **DIA** 8"

ID TIP: The only native plum in its range. Distinguished from the introduced Garden Plum by its thorny twigs and smaller, lighter-colored fruit. Leaf 1–2¾" long, with pointed to rounded tip; margins double-toothed, with pointed teeth. Twig bright red. Flower ⅝" wide; white, aging to pink. Fruit ⅝–1" wide, dark red or yellow. **HABITAT:** Dry rocky hillsides and woodlands. Elevation to 6,000'.

Chickasaw Plum

Klamath Plum

P. subcordata

Thornless Plums

Prunus species
HT 5–20' DIA 6"

There are 5 native plums in North America that regularly lack thorns (Allegheny Plum occasionally has thorny twigs). The introduced Garden Plum usually lacks thorns, but its variety Bullace Plum is thorn-bearing.

ROSE FAMILY   ROSACEAE

Allegheny Plum

Allegheny Plum

Prunus alleghaniensis

ID TIP: Leaf 2–3½" long; long-pointed tip; finely toothed margins. Twig occasionally has thorns. Bark becomes fissured with age. Flower ½" wide; white, aging to pink; abundant. Fruit ½" wide; dark reddish purple, with whitish bloom. HABITAT: Uncommon in moist woodlands. Elevation 1,200–2,000'.

Allegheny Plum

Allegheny Plum

Mexican Plum

Prunus mexicana

A common soil stabilizer on forest-prairie borders. ID TIP: Leaf 2–4½" long, with pointed tip; finely double-toothed margins; yellow-green above; paler, with prominent veins and soft hairs beneath. Flower ¾" wide, white. Fruit ⅝–1½" wide; purplish red, with bloom. HABITAT: Open woodlands and hillsides. Elevation to 1,500'.

Flatwoods Plum

Prunus umbellata
ALSO CALLED Hog Plum

ID TIP: Side twigs are sharp-pointed and can appear thorny. Flatwoods can be confused with Chickasaw Plum, but the leaves lie flat (not folded upward), and it usually occurs as a single tree (not in thickets). Leaf 1½–3" long; pointed tip; finely toothed margins. Flower ⅝–¾" wide, white. Fruit ½–¾" wide; nearly black, or dark red, with whitish bloom. HABITAT: River swamps and hammocks; open pine forests, pine flatwoods, coastal scrub. Elevation to 1,000'.

Mexican Plum

Flatwoods Plum

Flatwoods Plum

Wild Goose Plum
Prunus munsoniana

ID TIP: Leaf 2½–4" long, with long-pointed tip; light green (Hortulan Plum leaf darker and to 6" long). Flower ½" wide, white. Fruit ½–¾" wide, bright red; in summer. Wild Goose and Hortulan plums overlap in range. Wild Goose has spur branches; Hortulan does not. Under magnification, Wild Goose has leaf glands at the base of the teeth; Hortulan near the tooth tip. **HABITAT:** Stream banks, moist woodlands, and roadsides. Elevation 100–1,000'.

Hortulan Plum
Prunus hortulana

ID TIP: Leaf to 6" long, with long-pointed tip; dark green. Flower ⅝–1" wide. Fruit ¾–1¼" wide, dark red to yellow; in autumn. **HABITAT:** Along stream banks. Elevation 400–1,200'.

Garden Plum
Prunus domestica
ALSO CALLED Damson Plum

The domesticated plum. **ID TIP:** Leaf 2–4" long; pointed tip; coarsely toothed margins; hairy, with prominent veins beneath. Flower ¾–1" wide, white, in clusters on hairy stalks. Fruit 1–2" long, blue-black. **Bullace Plum** (var. *institia*) has hairy, thorny twigs; leaves 1½–3" long. **HABITAT AND RANGE:** Introduced in North America; escapes in northern United States, southern Canada. Native to Asia.

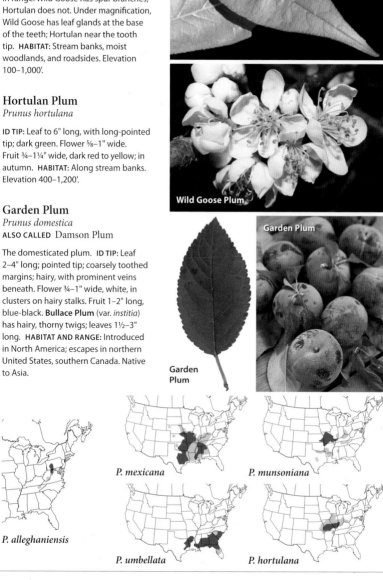

Wild Goose Plum

Wild Goose Plum

Garden Plum

Garden Plum

P. mexicana

P. munsoniana

P. alleghaniensis

P. umbellata

P. hortulana

Peach

Prunus persica
HT 10–25'   DIA 8–12"

Small tree or shrub with deciduous, simple leaves. Straight trunk; dense or open, rounded crown of upwardly spreading branches; can be as wide as it is tall. Young bark smooth, reddish brown, and peeling; older trees have gray bark that splits and becomes scaly. **ID TIP:** Peach bark has many long, horizontal bumps. In spring, the showy pink blossoms often fill the crown. In summer, trees produce distinctive, fuzzy, succulent fruit.

HABITAT AND RANGE: Introduced in North America; occasionally escapes along roadsides and abandoned fields from Canada to Florida. Native to China.

NOTES: Related to almonds, apricots, cherries, nectarines, and plums, the Peach is widely planted, for both its fruits and its showy flowers. It has been cultivated since ancient times, and many commercially important varieties have been developed to produce peaches of different colors and tastes. Varieties have also been bred to produce flowers that are showier, with more petals.

LEAF 3–6" long. Elliptic to narrowly lance-shaped, with long-pointed tip; slightly folded along midvein; finely toothed margins. Shiny dark green above; paler beneath. Autumn color bright yellow. Bud hairy.   **FLOWER** ½–1½" wide; white to pink; 5 petals; in clusters. Early spring.   **FRUIT** 2–6" wide, round drupe; fuzzy, yellow and red; fleshy. Sweet, juicy pulp when ripe; seed ovoid, ridged and pitted. Summer.

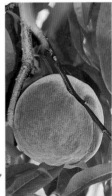

Common Pear

Pyrus communis

HT 20–60' DIA 6–12"

ROSE FAMILY   ROSACEAE

Small to medium-sized tree, typically to 40', with deciduous, simple leaves. Straight trunk; short, thick, narrow or conical crown of upright branches. Bark smooth, thick, scaly gray-brown, with shallow furrows. **ID TIP:** The fruit is the familiar large, fleshy pear. The showy, white flower clusters appear very early in spring. Pear trees have a shorter, narrower crown than apple trees; branchlets are sometimes thorny; the twigs are often hairy.

HABITAT AND RANGE: Introduced in North America; planted near houses, roadsides; grows wild in clearings, at forest borders. Native to Europe and western Asia.

NOTES: Many varieties of orchard pear have been developed from this commercially important fruit tree. Pear trees are not found in the wild as commonly as apple trees.

LEAF 1–4" long. Elliptic, with pointed tip; finely toothed margins. Thick, leathery. Shiny dark green above; duller beneath. Autumn color red-maroon. **FLOWER** ½–¾" wide; white or sometimes pinkish; 5 petals; in clusters on ½–2" long stalks. Early spring. **FRUIT** 3–4" long pome; green, yellow, or brown; flesh grainy. Autumn.

Callery Pear

Pyrus calleryana
HT 30–50'   DIA 10–14"

Small tree with deciduous, simple leaves. Single trunk, tends to split with age; rounded, dense crown (pyramidal in youth) of upright branches. **ID TIP:** In spring the tree is covered in showy, white, malodorous flowers. The autumn foliage is bright and multicolored.

HABITAT AND RANGE: Introduced in North America; planted along streets, in parks; may be invasive. Native to Asia.

ROSE FAMILY   ROSACEAE

LEAF 2–3" long. Ovate; finely toothed margins. Shiny, dark green above; paler, dull below. **FLOWER** ½–¾" wide; white; in 3" wide clusters. Spring. **FRUIT** ½" wide, round pome; brown; in clusters. Autumn; persists into winter.

Ornamental Flowering Crabapples

Malus hybrids and cultivars

There are perhaps 800 *Malus* cultivars. Breeding of crabapples for flowers, rather than fruits, began in the 18th century in England. Today they are a hybrid complex originating from primarily 20 species, dominated by European (*M. sylvestris*), Siberian (*M. baccata*), and Japanese Flowering (*M. floribunda*) crabapples, and Asiatic (*M. spectabilis*) and Common apples. Many "wild" crabapples are invasives derived from *M. floribunda*.

LEAF Variable: elliptic, toothed to lobed (resembles a hawthorn or Amur Maple); some varieties have purple leaves when blooming. **FLOWER** White, pink, crimson, rose, or purplish red; most have 5 rounded petals (number varies depending on cultivated variety; some hybrids have more than 30 petals). **FRUIT** ⅛–2" wide, round pome; yellow, red, or purplish.

ROSE FAMILY   ROSACEAE

Redjade Crabapple

Sundog Crabapple

Common Apple

Malus pumila

HT 10–35' **DIA** 1–1½'

Small tree or large shrub with deciduous, simple leaves. Short trunk; broad, rounded crown of rigid branches. Bark gray-brown to pale purple-brown, scaly; with age, develops thin, peeling flakes. Older trees have gnarled, hollow, fluted, stocky trunk. **ID TIP:** Escaped Common Apple produces a smaller, greener, tarter fruit than cultivated varieties and can be easily confused with a crabapple. The fruits are generally larger (over 2" wide) than crabapples and red. Without fruit, the Common Apple can be distinguished from a crabapple by its gray-hairy leaf underside.

LEAF 2–4" long. Elliptic to broadly elliptic, with pointed tip; bluntly pointed teeth along margins. Green above; densely gray-hairy beneath. Leafstalk hairy. Autumn color golden and orange. Twigs and branchlets without thorns. **FLOWER** 1–1½" wide, showy; white tinged with pink; 5 rounded petals. Each flower on long stalk; in small clusters. Fragrant. Late spring. **FRUIT** 2–4" wide, round pome; depressed at both ends; green, red, or yellow, or a combination. Thick pulp. Late summer–early autumn.

HABITAT AND RANGE: Introduced in North America. Escapes in abandoned fields and orchards, and along forest edges.

NOTES: Common Apple (sometimes called *M. × domestica*) is considered a descendant of European Crabapple (*M. sylvestris*) and Asian apple species. It has hybridized with other European and Asian species to create nearly 8,000 varieties. Fruits are not as bitter or unpleasantly sour as crabapples.

American Crabapples

Malus species
HT 10–30' DIA 6–18"

ROSE FAMILY   ROSACEAE

Small trees with deciduous, simple leaves; sometimes thicket-forming shrubs. Trees have a short trunk and broad crown of rigid branches. Of the world's 25 *Malus* species, 4 trees are native to North America: 1 on the Pacific coast, 3 in the East. These crabapples are uncommon or rare in most areas, but can be confused with escaped Common Apple or escaped Eurasian flowering crabapples. Native crabapples are occasionally planted as ornamentals. Apple varieties often gain greater hardiness when grafted onto the rootstock of one of these species. The fruits have a more bitter or sour taste than the cultivated apple.

Crabapples are distinguished from Common Apple by smaller fruit that is usually green rather than red. Eurasian flowering crabapples usually have smaller fruits (⅛–1" wide), that are more brightly colored yellow, orange, or red, than native crabapples. Distinguishing between native crabapples is less confusing, as the species do not overlap in range, but authorities disagree on their taxonomy.

LEAF Dark green; autumn color brilliant yellow, orange, red (except Southern Crabapple). Twig sharp, or often with sharp thorns. **FLOWER** ¾–2" wide, showy; deep pink in bud, pink to white when open; 5 rounded petals; each flower on long stalk; in clusters, usually of 3–6; fragrant. Spring. **FRUIT** ½–2" wide pome; rounded to oblong; yellow, green, or reddish. **BARK** Reddish brown or gray, scaly and fissured.

Southern Crabapple

Southern Crabapple

Southern Crabapple

Malus angustifolia

ID TIP: Usually occurs without thorns. Leaf narrowly to broadly elliptic or ovate; blunt teeth along margins down to pointed base; somewhat thick and shiny; hairless beneath. Fragrant. Fruit ¾–1" wide, very slightly pointed, yellowish green. Late summer. **HABITAT:**

Southern Crabapple

Moist forest borders and openings, fencerows, stream valleys of the Southeast. Elevation to 2,000'.

Sweet Crabapple
Malus coronaria

ID TIP: Leaf broadly elliptic, with indented base; small lobes near base, or margins coarsely toothed above the middle; hairless beneath. Fruit 1–2" wide, round, ribbed at top; greenish, with thick, juicy pulp; late summer. **HABITAT:** Moist forest borders and openings, thickets, fencerows, stream valleys. Elevation to 3,300'.

Prairie Crabapple
Malus ioensis

ID TIP: Leaf elliptic; margins bluntly toothed, often slightly lobed, sometimes indented at base; woolly beneath (denser than in Common Apple). Fruit 1–1¼" wide, yellowish green; late summer. **HABITAT:** Prairies; calcium-rich soils. Elevation 500–1,500'.

Oregon Crabapple
Malus fusca
ALSO CALLED Pacific Crabapple

ID TIP: This is the West's only native crabapple. Leaf ovate, toothed or slightly lobed; slightly hairy beneath. Flower to 1" wide, not fragrant, produced in clusters of 8–12. Fruit ½–¾" wide, oblong, yellow-green to reddish purple; late summer. **HABITAT:** Moist forests, along streams; swamps and bogs. Elevation to 1,000'.

Sweet Crabapple

Sweet Crabapple

Prairie Crabapple

Prairie Crabapple

Prairie Crabapple

Oregon Crabapple

Oregon Crabapple

M. angustifolia

M. coronaria

M. ioensis

M. fusca

Serviceberries

Amelanchier species
ALSO CALLED Juneberries

ROSE FAMILY   ROSACEAE

Saskatoon
Serviceberry

Six species of serviceberries native to
North America regularly attain tree
size; some can be multistemmed and
thicket-forming. All have deciduous,
simple leaves. Though these 6 are
usually distinguishable from one
another, hybrids can make identification
difficult. Fruits are rich in copper and
iron and are eaten by many animals.

LEAF Dull green or often dark blue-
green above; paler beneath. Buds
reddish. Autumn color orange-red
(except Utah Serviceberry). **FLOWER**
White; 5 narrow petals; in drooping,
terminal clusters. Early spring. **FRUIT** ¼–
½" wide, round pome; red turning dark
blue to purple or blackish; in clusters.
Soft, juicy pulp (Downy Serviceberry's
fruit is dry). Summer. **BARK** Grayish with
thin, vertical ridges.

Saskatoon Serviceberry

Amelanchier alnifolia
ALSO CALLED Western Serviceberry,
Alderleaf Serviceberry
HT 30–40' **DIA** 8–12"

ID TIP: Leaf ¾–2" long; broadly elliptic
to nearly circular, usually blunt-tipped;
coarsely toothed above the middle;
7–9 pairs of side veins; hairless (except
when young); leafstalk hairless (unlike
Roundleaf). Twig reddish brown. Flower
¾–1" wide. **HABITAT:** Temperate to
boreal forests, coastline, rocky slopes,
thickets, stream banks. Elevation to
6,000'.

Saskatoon
Serviceberry

Saskatoon
Serviceberry

Saskatoon
Serviceberry

Utah Serviceberry

Amelanchier utahensis
HT to 26' **DIA** 4–6"

ID TIP: Similar to Saskatoon Serviceberry.
Leaf ½–1¼" long, with a layer of soft
hairs and a green-gray cast; no autumn
color. Twig gray, hairy. **HABITAT:** Dry,
rocky slopes, gullies, and canyons
in deserts; mountains, pine forests.
Elevation 3,900–7,900'.

Utah Serviceberry

Downy Serviceberry
Amelanchier arborea
ALSO CALLED Shadbush, Shadblow
HT 20–50' **DIA** 6–12"

ID TIP: Leaf 2–4½" long; slightly downy beneath; elliptic, with somewhat pointed tip and rounded or slightly indented base. Flower 1¼" wide. Fruit pulp dry. **HABITAT:** Upland hardwood forests, thickets. Elevation to 6,000' in southern Appalachians.

Allegheny Serviceberry
Amelanchier laevis
ALSO CALLED Sarvis Tree
HT 20–50' **DIA** 6–12"

ID TIP: Leaf similar to Downy; 1½–2½" long, usually hairless and bluntly pointed at tip; new leaves are purplish. Flower ½–¾" wide. Fruit juicy. **Canadian Serviceberry** (*A. canadensis*) is similar; occurs in swamps in the East, only as far west as Pennsylvania and Mississippi. **HABITAT AND RANGE:** Swamp edges; upland forests; thickets. Range similar to Downy Serviceberry. Elevation to 6,000'.

Roundleaf Serviceberry
Amelanchier sanguinea
HT 5–20' **DIA** 4–6"

ID TIP: Leaf 1¼–2¾" long; nearly circular; toothed nearly to base; 12–15 pairs of veins; hairless; leafstalk finely hairy. Flower 1" wide. **HABITAT:** Rocky, open woods, especially on steep slopes and stream banks. Elevation to 2,000'.

Downy Serviceberry

Downy Serviceberry

Downy Serviceberry

Allegheny Serviceberry

Roundleaf Serviceberry

A. alnifolia

A. utahensis

A. arborea

A. sanguinea

Hawthorns

Crataegus species
ALSO CALLED Thorn-apple
HT 8–40' **DIA** 4–12"

Small trees or large shrubs with deciduous, simple leaves. Short trunk, or multistemmed and thicket-forming; rounded crown; dense, spreading branches and zigzagging, thorny branchlets. **ID TIP:** There are dozens, perhaps hundreds of species of hawthorns in North America, only a few of which are featured here. Similarities between species, disagreement about classification, and frequent hybridization make this a challenging group to identify to species level. Flowers, fruits, and bark do not vary significantly among species, and leaves can vary among lobed, obovate, elliptic, and ovate, sometimes within a single species. **HABITAT:** Moist meadows, open woodlands, and river bottoms.

LEAF Size varies but usually 1–3" long. Margins single-toothed or jaggedly double-toothed. Mostly shiny green above; paler, mostly hairless beneath, although some species are fuzzy or have hairy veins beneath. Autumn color usually brilliant red, orange, or gold. Twig and branchlets bear ¾–4" long, stout thorns.

FLOWER ¼–1" wide, showy; white, pink, or red; 5 petals. In flat-topped clusters of usually 3–20. Most are malodorous; some have a sweet fragrance. Spring.

FRUIT ¼–¾" wide, round pome; similar to a small crabapple; mostly red, sometimes orange, dotted in some species. Dry, mealy, or occasionally juicy pulp; contains 3–20 seeds. Most ripen in autumn.

ROSE FAMILY ROSACEAE

Downy Hawthorn (*C. mollis*)
LEAF 1½–5" long; ovate and lobed. **FLOWER** White. **FRUIT** Red and dotted; 4 or 5 seeds. Nova Scotia and southern Quebec to Louisiana, Texas, and North Dakota.

Dotted Hawthorn (*C. punctata*)
LEAF 2–3" long; ovate to obovate and often lobed. **FLOWER** White. **FRUIT** Red or yellow and dotted; 2–5 seeds. Newfoundland to northern Georgia; west to Wisconsin and Oklahoma.

Washington Hawthorn (*C. phaenopyrum*)
LEAF ¾–2½" long; ovate to triangular and lobed. **FLOWER** White. **FRUIT** Bright red; 2 or 3 seeds. Western Virginia to northern Florida, west to Missouri.

Kansas Hawthorn (*C. coccinioides*)
LEAF 1½–3" long; ovate and lobed. **FLOWER** White. **FRUIT** Bright red and dotted; 5 seeds. Southern Illinois to Arkansas, west to southeastern Kansas and northeastern Oklahoma.

Downy Hawthorn

Parsley Hawthorn (*C. marshallii*)
LEAF ¾–2" long; ovate and lobed, parsleylike. **FLOWER** White. **FRUIT** Red; 1–3 seeds. Southeast and Midwest.

Fanleaf Hawthorn (*C. flabellata*)
LEAF ¾–4" long; ovate to triangular and lobed. **FLOWER** White. **FRUIT** Bright red; 3 or 4 seeds. Nova Scotia to South Carolina, west to Wisconsin and Louisiana.

Oneseed Hawthorn (*C. monogyna*)
LEAF ⅝–1½" long; ovate or obovate and sometimes lobed. **FLOWER** White. **FRUIT** Red; 1 seed. Introduced to North America; native to Europe and western Asia.

Biltmore Hawthorn (*C. intricata*)
LEAF 1¼–2½" long; ovate to elliptic and lobed. **FLOWER** White. **FRUIT** Green, yellow, orange, or red; 3–5 seeds. New Hampshire to northern Georgia, west to Oklahoma.

Green Hawthorn (*C. viridis*)
LEAF 1¼–2⅜" long; usually obovate. **FLOWER** White. **FRUIT** Red to orange to yellow; 5 seeds. Southeastern coastal plains; lower Ohio and Mississippi river valleys.

Fireberry Hawthorn (*C. chrysocarpa*)
LEAF ¾–4" long; elliptic to circular and lobed. **FLOWER** White. **FRUIT** Bright red or yellow; 3 or 4 seeds. Newfoundland to Kentucky and west to Rocky Mountains.

Cockspur Hawthorn (*C. crus-galli*)
LEAF ¾–4" long; elliptic to obovate. **FLOWER** White to red. **FRUIT** Red or green; 2 or 3 seeds. Throughout the East.

Pear Hawthorn (*C. calpodendron*)
LEAF 2–4½" long; elliptic to ovate and lobed. **FLOWER** White. **FRUIT** Orange-red to red; 2 or 3 seeds. Southern Ontario and New York to Georgia, west to Minnesota and Texas.

Fleshy Hawthorn (*C. succulenta*)
LEAF 1¼–2⅜" long; ovate to obovate and lobed. **FLOWER** White. **FRUIT** Bright red; 2–4 seeds. Nova Scotia south to North Carolina; west to Manitoba, Utah, and Missouri.

Fanleaf Hawthorn

Parsley Hawthorn

Oneseed Hawthorn

Oneseed Hawthorn

Biltmore Hawthorn

Biltmore Hawthorn

Green Hawthorn

Green Hawthorn

Cockspur Hawthorn

Fireberry Hawthorn

Fleshy Hawthorn

Pear Hawthorn

Hollies

The genus *Ilex* is the only native representative of the holly family (Aquifoliaceae) in North America. Most hollies are native to the Southeast. Many species are shrubs, but several can attain tree size. The leaves are alternate, simple, and can be evergreen or deciduous.

The leaf texture can be useful in identification: evergreen leaves tend to be leathery and somewhat thicker and stiffer than deciduous leaves. The flowers of *Ilex* species are tiny, white or greenish white, with usually four rounded petals. Male and female flowers look similar, but are usually borne on separate trees. Only trees with female flowers will produce fruits. The fruit is a berrylike drupe, usually containing four small, hard stones; each is on a short stalk and borne singly or in clusters along branchlets. Fruits are mostly red but can be black or yellow in some species. The bark is usually smooth.

American Holly

Common Winterberry

Native hollies have either evergreen leaves (left), which are usually thick and leathery, or deciduous leaves (right), which are thinner and may turn yellow before dropping.

Common Winterberry

Ilex verticillata
HT to 15'

HOLLY FAMILY   AQUIFOLIACEAE

Typically a shrub, Common Winterberry only rarely attains tree size, to 25'. It is the only holly occurring in Canada and the northern Midwest. **ID TIP:** Winterberry is distinguished from other deciduous hollies by its dull, slightly thick leaves and fringed flower-petal margins.

HABITAT AND RANGE: Wet woodlands and swamps. Newfoundland and southern Quebec south to Florida, west to Minnesota and Louisiana. Elevation 300–4,000'.

LEAF 2–4" long. Pointed at tip. Dull above, somewhat hairy beneath. **FLOWER** ¼" wide; petals fringed; borne in leaf axils. **FRUIT** ¼" wide; round; shiny, bright red. Autumn; persists through winter.

Mountain Winterberry

Ilex montana

ALSO CALLED Largeleaf Holly,
Mountain Holly

HT 6–20' **DIA** 2–10"

Small tree or large shrub with deciduous,
simple leaves. Short, slender trunk;
narrow, pyramidal crown. **ID TIP:** This
deciduous holly has thin, papery leaves
and flower petals that are fringed along
the margins; the fruit stones are grooved.

HABITAT: Moist soils of mixed broadleaf
forests. Elevation to 5,500'.

NOTES: The term "winterberry" is often
applied to the deciduous species of the
genus *Ilex* for their showy displays of
abundant, brilliant red fruits through the
winter; all are planted as ornamentals.
Carolina Holly (*I. ambigua*) is an upland,
shrubby holly of the Southeast, the only
deciduous holly ranging into central to
southern Florida. It has much smaller
(⅜–1" long), narrower leaves and smaller
fruits than Mountain Winterberry. It
occurs from South Carolina to Florida,
west to Oklahoma and Texas.

LEAF 4–6½" long. Elliptic or ovate, with pointed tip; finely
toothed. Dull green above; paler green, hairy on veins
beneath. Autumn color yellow. Twig brown-gray, hairless
when young. **FLOWER** ¼" wide; white; 4 rounded petals
with fringed margins. In clusters on slender stalks, in leaf
axils. Spring. **FRUIT** ⅜–½" wide; bright reddish orange,
red, or yellow. Borne singly or in clusters along branchlets.
Autumn; persists through winter.

**Carolina
Holly**

Possumhaw

Ilex decidua

ALSO CALLED Deciduous Holly

HT 5–25'   **DIA** 2–6"

Small tree or large shrub with deciduous, simple leaves. Short, slender trunk; spreading crown of stout branches.
ID TIP: This holly is distinguished from other deciduous hollies—all of which have thin, papery leaves—by its silvery-gray twigs and flowers with smooth (not fringed) petal margins and 4 or 5 petals.

HABITAT: Lowland forests, along streams, swamps, floodplains. Elevation to 1,200'.

NOTES: The similar **Smooth Winterberry** (*I. laevigata*) is the only deciduous holly with shiny leaves (½–1½" long); its flowers have smooth (not fringed) petal margins and usually 6–8 petals. It usually occurs as a shrub but can attain tree size; it ranges from the northeastern United States to South Carolina. Some consider **Georgia Holly** (*I. longipes*) to be a variety of *I. decidua*. It occurs in moist soils of mixed broadleaf forests from West Virginia to Florida, west to Tennessee and Louisiana. It has ½–4" long leaves and fruit stalks up to 1" long.

HOLLY FAMILY   **AQUIFOLIACEAE**

LEAF 1–3" long. Variable shape, from obovate to narrowly elliptic; blunt-tipped; blunt, rounded teeth along margins, mostly above the middle. Dull green above; paler green, hairy on veins beneath. Twig light or silvery gray, hairless. **FLOWER** ¼" wide; white; 4 or 5 rounded petals; on slender stalk. In clusters at ends of side twigs. Spring. **FRUIT** ¼" wide; round; shiny, bright reddish orange (or red or yellow). In clusters, along branchlets. Autumn; persists through winter.

Georgia Holly

Yaupon

Ilex vomitoria
ALSO CALLED Cassine
HT 6–20' **DIA** 6"

Small tree or large shrub with evergreen, simple leaves. Short, slender trunk, or several tall, thicket-forming stems; rounded, open crown; dense branchlets at right angles to the stems. **ID TIP:** This is a wetland holly, with a narrowly elliptic, blunt-tipped leaf, rounded at base, with blunt teeth along margins (unlike Dahoon), and red fruits.

HABITAT: Edges of coastal marshes, sandhills, pine flatwoods, and maritime forests. Elevation to 500'.

NOTES: Yaupon is North America's only native plant that contains caffeine. Tea made from the leaves, when drunk in excess, can be emetic, hence the plant's species name *vomitoria*. It is often planted in landscapes, especially for hedges and topiary, and there are many cultivated varieties, their forms varying from weeping to columnar to short and compact.

HOLLY FAMILY   AQUIFOLIACEAE

LEAF ¾–1¼" long. Narrowly elliptic, with blunt tip; rounded base; bluntly toothed margins, edges often rolled under. Thick, stiff, leathery. Shiny green above; paler green beneath; both surfaces hairless (young leaves densely hairy). Twig purplish and hairy when young, turning whitish gray and nearly hairless. **FLOWER** Less than ¼" wide; similar to American Holly; white. Spring. **FRUIT** ¼" wide; shiny, bright red (sometimes yellow or orange). Borne singly or in clusters along branchlets. Produced in abundance. Autumn; persists through winter.

American Holly

Ilex opaca

ALSO CALLED Christmas Holly
HT 15–50' **DIA** 9–18"

| HOLLY FAMILY | AQUIFOLIACEAE |

Small tree with evergreen, simple leaves; a shrub on coastal beaches. Short, narrow trunk; narrow, dense pyramidal crown of spreading, short, slender branches. Bark light gray, thin, smooth; old trunks develop wartlike bumps. **ID TIP:** This holly has leathery, elliptic, toothed leaves, with prickly points at tips.

HABITAT: Rich soils, mixed forests, swamp borders, coastal sand dunes. Elevation to 3,000'; lower elevations in the North than the South.

NOTES: American Holly is a hardy, evergreen broadleaf tree capable of surviving at temperatures as low as –20° F. Its leathery, prickly leaves and red fruits once made it such a popular Christmas decoration that it was legally preserved in the wild. In the holly family, male and female flowers are usually borne on separate plants; the attractive, berrylike fruits are produced only on females. Trees in Florida with smaller (⅜– 1" long), lighter green leaves with edges rolled under are sometimes classified as var. *arenicola.* There are more than 1,000 cultivated types of American Holly.

LEAF 2–4" long. Elliptic, with pointed tip; coarsely prickly toothed margins. Thick, stiff, and leathery. Green above; yellow-green beneath. Twig hairy at first, becoming hairless, with whitish, waxy bloom. **FLOWER** ¼" wide; greenish white. In clusters on short stalks; borne along twigs and at leaf axils. Spring–summer. **FRUIT** ¼–½" wide; red (rarely orange or yellow). Borne singly along branchlets. Autumn; persists through winter.

English Holly

Ilex aquifolium
ALSO CALLED European Holly
HT to 50'

English Holly is often planted in gardens; it has numerous cultivated varieties, including some grown specifically for Christmas decorations, that have larger berries and leaves. **ID TIP:** Leaves are 1¼–2¾" long; waxy and glossy, with or without prickly teeth. **HABITAT AND RANGE:** Introduced in North America; naturalized and invasive from British Columbia to California. Native to southern Europe, northern Africa, and western Asia.

HOLLY FAMILY | AQUIFOLIACEAE

Myrtle Dahoon

Ilex myrtifolia
HT to 20'

A close relative of Dahoon; sometimes considered to be a smaller variety of it. **ID TIP:** Myrtle Dahoon has small, narrow (½–1¼" long and less than ⅜" wide), evergreen leaves, each tipped with a prickle, and whitish gray bark. **HABITAT AND RANGE:** Bald-cypress and pine swamps in the Southeast. Ranges farther north than Dahoon, to North Carolina, but not as far south into Florida. Elevation to 200'.

HOLLY FAMILY | AQUIFOLIACEAE

Tawnyberry Holly

Ilex krugiana
HT to 20'

Rare shrub or small tree. **ID TIP:** The leaf is evergreen, leathery, 2½–5" long, and wavy-edged; the fruit is black. Dahoon, which also occurs within its range, has red fruit. **HABITAT AND RANGE:** Restricted in the United States to hammocks of the southern Florida Everglades; also known from Puerto Rico. Elevation near sea level.

HOLLY FAMILY | AQUIFOLIACEAE

Dahoon

Ilex cassine
ALSO CALLED Christmas-berry
HT 20–30'   **DIA** 12–15"

Small tree or large shrub with evergreen, simple leaves. Short, narrow trunk; dense, low, broad, rounded crown of slender branches. **ID TIP:** Dahoon leaves are narrowly elliptic, pointed at the base and mostly untoothed along the margins (sometimes with a few teeth above the middle). The red fruits are produced in abundance.

HABITAT: Near swamps and streams; sandy banks. Elevation to 200'.

NOTES: Trees in Texas have larger leaves (up to 5½" long) and are known as var. *latifolia*.

HOLLY FAMILY   **AQUIFOLIACEAE**

LEAF 1½–3½" (5½" in Texas) long. Narrowly elliptic, with usually pointed tip and base; margins mostly untoothed; edges often rolled under. Slightly thick, leathery. Shiny, dark green above; paler green beneath; densely hairy when young. Twig brown, densely silky-hairy when young. **FLOWER** To ¼" wide; white. In clusters on short stalks; along twigs and in leaf axils. Spring. **FRUIT** ¼" wide; shiny, bright red (or yellow or orange). Borne singly or in clusters along branchlets. Autumn; persists through winter.

Large Gallberry

Ilex coriacea
ALSO CALLED Sweet Gallberry
HT to 20'

Small tree or large shrub with evergreen, simple leaves. **ID TIP:** Though usually a shrub, this is the only black-fruited holly in its range that attains tree size. The leaf has very short, prickly teeth along the margins, but most prominent toward the tip, and minute black gland dots on the underside; young twigs are often sticky. **Inkberry** (*I. glabra*) is also a black-fruited, evergreen holly, but it almost never reaches tree size, and its leaves have a few blunt teeth, usually at the tip or only along the upper third of the blade, and lack minute black dots beneath.

HABITAT: Swamps and sandy soils. Elevation to 500'.

HOLLY FAMILY   **AQUIFOLIACEAE**

LEAF 2–3" long. Similar to Dahoon, but with small, slightly prickly teeth (prominent toward tip) and black dots beneath. Twig can be sticky. **FRUIT** ¼" wide; shiny, black. Autumn; persists through winter.

Elms, Hackberries, and Kin

The elm family, Ulmaceae, has four native genera in North America that are grouped into two subfamilies. In the family, leaves are often asymmetrical at the base, with more leaf tissue on one side of the midvein than the other. Tiny, leaflike appendages (stipules) are borne at the leaf axils.

Celtis and *Trema*

The genera *Celtis* and *Trema* make up the subfamily Celtidoideae (or Celtoideae). Their leaves have three arching veins that radiate from the base; the outer two typically produce secondary veins that run to the leaf margin. The fruit is a pulpy drupe with round seeds.

Celtis species, called hackberries, are small to medium-sized trees with deciduous leaves. Flowers are functionally either male or female (with only vestigial stamens or pistils, respectively). Bark is usually smooth and gray, but the bark of some species produces distinctive corky or warty outgrowths. These can be a sign of injury from woodpeckers, which excavate small holes in the bark to release the sticky, watery sap. The birds feed on both the sap and the insects the sap attracts.

Tremas are small, fast-growing trees or shrubs with smooth to slightly furrowed bark and toothed, evergreen leaves. The base of the leaf is indented or squared.

Flowers are male or female. This is one of the few genera of the elm family with species restricted mostly to the tropics. Only two species occur in North America.

Planera and *Ulmus*

The genera *Ulmus* and *Planera* compose the subfamily Ulmoideae, characterized by dry fruits and flat seeds. The leaf veins are pinnately arranged (like a feather), with the secondary (side) veins running parallel to each other and terminating at the leaf margin. *Planera* is a monotypic genus, containing only a single species worldwide, Water-elm, a small, deciduous, wetland tree of the southeastern United States. The flowers are mostly either male or female; the fruit is a dry, nutlike drupe.

Elms (*Ulmus*) are small to large trees with deciduous leaves that turn usually yellow to yellow-brown in autumn. The tiny (⅛"), bisexual flowers lack petals. Fruits are samaras, with flat papery wings. Bark is rough and reddish brown, brown, or gray. Elms can be difficult to identify; useful features include the presence of "wings" on branches, the texture of the leaf surface, whether the flowers and fruits are in branched clusters (racemes) or bundled clusters (fascicles), the shape of the leaf base, the samara shape, and the presence of hairs on the samara.

Slippery Elm

Netleaf Hackberry

Slippery Elm

Elms have pinnately veined leaves with straight side veins; their fruits are flat, papery samaras. Hackberries have three arching central leaf veins; their fruits are drupes.

Northern Hackberry

Celtis occidentalis

ALSO CALLED Common Hackberry, American Hackberry, Nettletree

HT 50–80' **DIA** 1–3'

Medium-sized tree; can be shrubby on very poor, dry sites. Straight trunk; broadly columnar to rounded crown of stout, spreading, and arching branches. Branches are sometimes deformed by mites and fungi into bushy clusters called witches'-brooms. **ID TIP:** Northern Hackberry leaves are glossy, dark green, and papery, with mostly toothed margins; the bark is gray and warty; the dark fruit is plentiful in autumn.

HABITAT: River valleys, slopes, bluffs, woodlands. Elevation to 5,900'.

NOTES: This widely distributed eastern hackberry is an important winter food source for birds and a larval host plant for many butterflies, including American snout, question mark, and hackberry emperor. **Dwarf** or **Georgia Hackberry** (*C. tenuifolia*) is similar, with rough, shorter-pointed leaves that are toothed above the middle. Usually a shrub, it occurs along streams and on rocky, exposed forested uplands, especially on limestone bluffs, to 1,600'; it is irregularly and spottily distributed from southern Michigan, southeastern Kansas, and eastern Texas eastward.

ELM FAMILY   ULMACEAE

LEAF 2–5" long. Narrowly ovate to ovate, with long-pointed, curved tip; asymmetrical base; margins coarsely toothed, but untoothed near base. Papery. Glossy, green, and often rough above; paler, sometimes hairy on veins beneath. Autumn color yellow. **FLOWER** ⅛" wide; greenish; 4 or 5 lobes. In very small clusters at base of young leaves, each flower on hanging stalk. Early spring, with new leaves. **FRUIT** ⅜–⅝" long, round drupe; orange-red, ripening to dark purple. Tough skin; pulp thin, slightly dry (occasionally juicy). Contains large, round stone. Each fruit on slender ⅜–¾" stalk, at leaf base. Autumn.

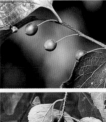

Georgia Hackberry

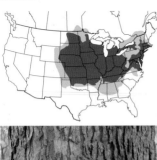

Netleaf Hackberry

Celtis reticulata

ALSO CALLED Western Hackberry, Palo Blanco

HT 20–30' **DIA** 1–1½'

ELM FAMILY   **ULMACEAE**

Small tree. Short, low-branching, often crooked and spindly trunk; contorted branches sometimes deformed into bushy clusters called witches'-brooms. The bark is smooth and gray; may develop corky or warty outgrowths. **ID TIP:** This hackberry has thick, yellow-green leaves that have raised, slightly hairy veins beneath.

HABITAT: Desert hills, grasslands, streams, canyons. Elevation 950–7,500'.

NOTES: In winter this tree provides important bird food in Utah's Wasatch Range. **Lindheimer Hackberry** (*C. lindheimeri*) has narrower, gray-green leaves with soft hairs beneath, ¼–½" long leafstalks, and reddish brown fruits. It is restricted to the limestone hills and ravines of the Edwards Plateau, Texas, and south to northern Mexico, at 300–650'.

LEAF 1–3" long. Similar to Sugarberry, but more broadly ovate. Thick. Dark green and rough above; yellow-green, with raised, slightly hairy veins beneath. Autumn color yellow. Leafstalk ⅛–¼" long. Twig hairy. **FLOWER** ⅛" wide; greenish. Late winter–early spring. **FRUIT** ¼–⅜" long, round drupe; glossy, orange-red, yellow, or reddish black. Each fruit on ⅜–½" long, hairy stalk, at leaf base. Autumn.

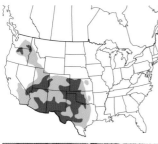

bark with corky outgrowths

Sugarberry

Celtis laevigata

ALSO CALLED Southern Hackberry

HT 60–80' **DIA** 1½–3'

ELM FAMILY   ULMACEAE

Medium-sized tree. Short, straight trunk; broadly columnar to rounded crown of spreading or arching branches. **ID TIP:** The leaves are narrow, mostly untoothed; the bark is smooth and light-colored, with corky warts.

HABITAT: Forested stream banks, rocky slopes, floodplains. Elevation to 1,000'.

LEAF 2½–5" long. Narrowly ovate, with long-pointed, curved tip; asymmetrical base; margins untoothed or sometimes with a few teeth. Light green above; paler beneath; smooth (not rough) on both surfaces. Autumn color yellow. **FLOWER** ⅛" wide; greenish white. Late spring–early autumn. **FRUIT** ¼–⅜" long, round drupe; orange-red to purple or black. Each fruit on slender, ⅛–¼" stalk, at leaf base. Autumn.

Florida Trema

Trema micrantha

HT 10–20' **DIA** 1–2'

ELM FAMILY   ULMACEAE

This small tree flowers and fruits year-round. **ID TIP:** The leaves are 2–2½" long, ovate with an indented base, finely toothed, rough above, and white-woolly beneath. The fruit is a ⅜" long, round, orange, fleshy drupe; each fruit on short stalk, in clusters at leaf base. **West Indian Trema** (*T. lamarckiana*) of the Florida Keys and West Indies has smaller leaves (½–1" long) and pink fruits. **HABITAT AND RANGE:** Roadsides, clearings, and edges of hammocks in southern Florida. Elevation to 350'.

Water-elm

Planera aquatica
ALSO CALLED Planertree
HT 30–40'   **DIA** 10–15"

Small tree or large shrub. Short, slender trunk; low, broad crown of slender, spreading, arching branches; sometimes vase-shaped. Bark gray to light brown, with large, patchy scales that peel to expose reddish brown inner bark. **ID TIP:** Water-elm has distinctive, burlike fruit.

HABITAT: Riverbanks, swamps, floodplains. Elevation to 650'.

NOTES: Water-elm is an uncommon wetland elm that grows in association with Water Oak, Water Tupelo, Water Hickory, and large Bald-cypresses. It grows largest in western Louisiana and southern Arkansas.

LEAF 2–2½" long. Ovate; may have asymmetrical base; blunt teeth along margins. Slightly thick. Dull, dark green, rough above; paler beneath, straight side veins conspicuous. Leafstalk short, hairy. **FLOWER** Similar to hackberries; each flower on short stalk. **FRUIT** ⅜–½" long, dry, soft, burlike drupe; light chestnut brown; surface covered with warty or fleshy projections. Early spring.

Japanese Zelkova

Zelkova serrata
ALSO CALLED Keaki
HT 40–70'   **DIA** 1–2½'

Small to medium-sized tree. Short, straight trunk with domed or broad, rounded crown of wide-spreading, slender branches, starting low on the trunk. **ID TIP:** The bark is smooth, with pink, brown, and orange horizontal stripes (most apparent in young bark); peels to reveal orange inner bark.

HABITAT AND RANGE: Introduced in North America. Native to Asia.

NOTES: This elm relative is an exquisite ornamental planted for its colorful autumn foliage and unique bark. It is resistant to Dutch elm disease.

LEAF 2–3¾" long. Narrowly elliptic, with long-pointed tip; asymmetrical base; coarsely toothed margins; straight side veins. Dark green, slightly rough above; paler, slightly hairy on veins beneath. Twig brown, hairy when new, becoming smooth. **FLOWER** ⅛" wide; yellow-green; in small clusters on very short stalks. Early spring. **FRUIT** ⅛–¼" long, ovoid drupe; brownish. Borne singly, at leaf base. Autumn.

Cedar Elm

Ulmus crassifolia
ALSO CALLED Southern Rock Elm,
Basket Elm
HT 50–60'   **DIA** 1–2'

ELM FAMILY   **ULMACEAE**

Medium-sized tree. Straight trunk; open, rounded crown of spreading, drooping branches. Bark light brown to reddish brown; ridges and broad plates separated by shallow furrows. **ID TIP:** Cedar Elm has slender, corky-winged branchlets. It has the smallest leaf of native elms, and it flowers and fruits later in the growing season than most other species. The leaf base is less asymmetrical than that of American Elm (and usually of Slippery Elm).

HABITAT: Along streams, on limestone slopes. Elevation to 1,600'.

NOTES: Cedar Elm, the most common elm in Texas, occurs with Ashe Juniper (locally called "cedar") in limestone hills of central Texas. Cedar Elm is susceptible to Dutch elm disease but less so than American Elm. It is hardy and drought-tolerant and planted as a shade tree.

LEAF 1–2" long, ¾–1" wide. Ovate to elliptic; tip blunt or pointed; margins finely, single- or double-toothed. Thick. Dark green, rough above; paler, soft-hairy beneath. **FLOWER** Greenish or brownish; in small, bundled clusters. Late summer. **FRUIT** ⅜–½" long, elliptic samara, deeply notched at tip; broad wings. Light brown, with soft, white hairs, especially along margin. In small clusters; each fruit on short stalk. Autumn.

September Elm

Ulmus serotina
ALSO CALLED Red Elm
HT 30–65'   **DIA** 1½–2'

ELM FAMILY   **ULMACEAE**

Small to medium-sized tree. **ID TIP:** Like Cedar Elm, September Elm flowers in late summer and early autumn, but its flowers are in branched (not bundled) clusters, and it has larger, smooth (not rough) leaves. The branchlets sometimes have small, corky wings, but the leaves are longer than in Winged Elm.

HABITAT: Bottomlands, especially in limestone. Elevation to 1,300'.

LEAF 3–4" long, 1–2" wide. Similar to Cedar Elm; smooth on both surfaces. **FRUIT** ⅜–½" long, elliptic samara, deeply notched at tip; wings narrower than in Cedar Elm; margin fringed with white hairs. In branched clusters. Autumn.

Winged Elm

Ulmus alata

ALSO CALLED Cork Elm, Wahoo

HT 40–50' **DIA** 1–2'

| ELM FAMILY | ULMACEAE |

Small tree. Short, straight trunk; rounded or narrowly elliptic crown of short, stout branches. Bark light reddish brown to ash gray; broad, flat, scaly ridges and uneven fissures; becomes thicker and rougher with age. **ID TIP:** Slender branchlets have 2 broad, corky wings. Of the 4 elms with winged branchlets, Winged Elm has the broadest wings, up to ½" wide. It is distinguished from similar Rock Elm by its nearly hairless twigs.

HABITAT: Dry, gravelly uplands; river flats. Elevation to 2,000'.

NOTES: Winged Elm is the most common of the southern elms. Branches and twigs of some individuals may lack the corky wings, making identification more difficult. It occurs on drier sites than most other southeastern elms, but is also found in moist hammocks and floodplains that are subjected to only occasional flooding. Winged Elm seems to be more resistant to Dutch elm disease than some other elms, especially within the confines of its natural distribution. It is relatively pest-free and planted as a street tree, mostly in the southern United States.

LEAF 1–3" long, ¼–1½" wide. Narrowly elliptic, slightly curved; tip pointed; base pointed or slightly indented; coarsely double-toothed margins; yellow midvein. Leathery. Dark green and smooth above; pale and soft-hairy beneath. Leafstalk hairy. Twig nearly hairless. **FLOWER** Reddish; in branched clusters, less than 1" long. Early spring, before leaves. **FRUIT** ⅜–½" long, narrowly elliptic samara, with distinctive, notched, 2-pronged tip; narrow wings. Gray-tan, with orange-red on margins and fringe of white hairs. In branched clusters; each fruit on long stalk. Early spring.

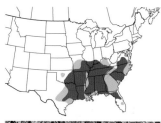

branchlets with corky wings

Rock Elm

Ulmus thomasii

ALSO CALLED Cork Elm

HT 50–80' **DIA** 1–3'

ELM FAMILY	ULMACEAE

Medium-sized tree. Tall, straight trunk; narrow, cylindrical or elliptic crown of stout branches. Bark rough, reddish brown to grayish brown; broad, flat, scaly ridges and deep fissures. **ID TIP:** Slender, rigid branchlets usually have 3 or 4 corky wings, but Rock Elm can occur with both corky-winged and wingless branchlets. It is distinguished from Winged Elm by its hairy twig and usually larger leaf and fruit; from American Elm by its hairy twig, smaller leaf, and often dry habitat; and from Slippery Elm by the glossy, smooth (not rough) upper surface of its leaf.

HABITAT: Rocky ridges and slopes, dry woodlands, flatlands. Elevation 100–3,000'.

NOTES: Rock Elm takes its common name from its very hard wood. It is typically slow-growing in its natural habitat; this feature, coupled with the early harvesting of trees for shipbuilding and other uses, reduced the number of large specimens to be found today. Rock Elm has also been affected by the spread of Dutch elm disease. Typical trees produce good fruit crops about every 3 or 4 years. The samaras are light in weight, but are dispersed only short distances by wind; birds, small mammals, and water may also be agents of seed distribution.

LEAF 2–4" long, ¾–2" wide. Elliptic to obovate; pointed tip; rounded, often asymmetrical base; coarsely double-toothed margins. Thick. Glossy, dark green above; paler, soft-hairy beneath. Leafstalk hairy. Twig somewhat hairy. **FLOWER** Reddish; in 2" long, drooping, branched clusters. Early spring, before leaves. **FRUIT** ½" long, broadly elliptic to rounded samara, notched at tip; flat, papery wings. Greenish; hairy overall; margins have short fringe. In drooping, branched clusters; each fruit on long stalk. Late spring.

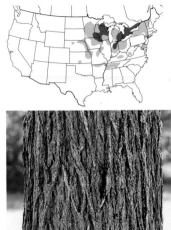

American Elm

Ulmus americana

ALSO CALLED White Elm, Soft Elm

HT 60–100'   **DIA** 2–3½'

Medium-sized to large tree. Tall, very stout, straight trunk, often with buttressed base; in the open, usually forks 25–40' above the ground into massive, upright limbs that form a very broad, rounded crown (can be as broad as the tree is tall), vase-shaped overall. In forests, forms narrowly elliptic crown of stout branches. Bark dark gray; ridges covered with reddish gray flakes, separated by deep furrows. **ID TIP:** The leaf base is significantly asymmetrical on most leaves. The leaves are not as rough as those of Slippery Elm. In early spring, flowers give tree a conspicuous rusty cast.

HABITAT: Deciduous woodlands, bottomlands, along rivers, and in fields; planted along streets. Elevation to 4,600'.

NOTES: Once reliably large and long-lived, American Elm was a common street tree, its arching branches framing avenues throughout the East. After the introduction of Dutch elm disease in 1930, American Elm largely disappeared from the urban landscape. However, many planted trees survive, and in the wild, younger trees are still found in floodplain and bottomland forests.

ELM FAMILY	ULMACEAE

LEAF 3–6" long, 1–3" wide. Elliptic to broadly elliptic, with abruptly pointed tip; strongly asymmetrical base; coarsely double-toothed margins; side veins fork less than in Slippery Elm. Dark green, usually smooth above (sometimes rough, especially if rubbed from tip toward base); paler, usually soft-hairy beneath. Twig reddish brown, shiny, slender; hairy when emerging, becoming hairless. **FLOWER** Reddish; in 1" long, drooping, bundled clusters; each flower on long stalk. Early spring, before leaves. **FRUIT** ⅜–½" long, broadly elliptic samara, deeply notched at tip; flat, papery wings. Green, turning creamy yellow; wing margin fringed with tiny yellow to white hairs. In drooping, bundled clusters; each fruit on long stalk. Early spring.

Slippery Elm

Ulmus rubra

ALSO CALLED Red Elm

HT 50–80' **DIA** 1–2½'

ELM FAMILY   **ULMACEAE**

Medium-sized tree. Tall, straight trunk; in the open, main limbs form a broad crown of spreading branches, vase-shaped overall; in forests, forms narrowly elliptic crown of short branches. Bark rough, gray to reddish brown; plates separated by irregular furrows. **ID TIP:** The leaves have a very rough upper surface; side veins fork more than in American Elm, and the leaf base is less asymmetrical. The small flowers are conspicuous on leafless trees in early spring.

HABITAT: Moist, low slopes, floodplains; dry uplands. Elevation to 3,000'.

NOTES: The inner bark of Slippery Elm exudes a slick gel or mucilage (hence the name) that is used to treat coughs and other ailments. This species is less seriously affected by Dutch elm disease than American Elm. The introduced **Wych Elm** (*U. glabra*) has leaves similar to Slippery Elm, with stiff, white hairs beneath; the bark of young trees is smooth (rough in Slippery Elm), and the fruit is elliptic and large (1" long), with broad wings. Native to Europe and western Asia, Wych Elm is established in Canada, California, possibly elsewhere.

LEAF 5–7" long, 2–3" wide. Elliptic, ovate, or obovate, with abruptly pointed tip; rounded, asymmetrical base; coarsely double-toothed margins; many side veins fork. Dark green, very rough above; paler, densely hairy, and sometimes rough beneath. Buds purple-black to black, covered by rusty hairs. Twig gray to brownish gray, with rough, sandy hairs when young; becomes hairless. **FLOWER** Dark reddish; in 1–1½" long, dense, bundled clusters; each flower on a short stalk. Early spring, before leaves. Bud large, copper-colored, hairy. **FRUIT** ½–¾" long, rounded samara, slightly notched at tip; flat, papery wings. Yellowish; hairy in center, hairless along margin. In bundled clusters; each fruit on short stalk. Late spring.

English Elm

Ulmus procera
HT 40–100'   DIA 1–3'

Small to large tree. Tall, straight, very stout trunk; dense, broad, rounded crown. Bark dark brown; thick, rugged, small, squarish plates and deep furrows. **ID TIP:** The leaves are very rough above, and have soft hairs in vein angles beneath and on the leafstalk. Twigs are densely hairy. Slender branchlets sometimes have corky wings. The trunk base is often encircled by twiggy branches and root suckers.

HABITAT AND RANGE: Introduced in North America; escapes along roadsides and forest borders in the Northeast and California. Native to Europe.

NOTES: Once a distinctive part of the English landscape, English Elm was brought to North America by colonists and has since been widely planted. Though the spread of Dutch elm disease nearly wiped out the species in Europe, it had less of an effect on the trees in North America.

ELM FAMILY	ULMACEAE

LEAF 2–3½" long, 1¼–2½" wide. Broadly elliptic, with abruptly pointed tip; rounded, asymmetrical base; coarsely double-toothed margins. Dark green, very rough above; paler, with tufts of soft hairs in vein angles beneath. Leafstalk ⅛–½" long, finely hairy. Twig densely hairy. **FLOWER** Dark reddish; in small, dense, branched clusters; each flower on a short stalk. Abundant in early spring, before leaves. **FRUIT** ½" long, rounded samara, narrowly notched at tip; flat, papery wings; greenish; hairless. In clusters; each fruit on short stalk. Spring.

Chinese Elm

Ulmus parvifolia
ALSO CALLED Lacebark Elm
HT 50'   DIA 1½'

Medium-sized tree. Tall trunk; rounded crown of drooping branches. **ID TIP:** Chinese Elm is similar to Siberian Elm, but its keys are elliptic and produced in abundance with the flowers in autumn. The bark is mottled gray and brown, flaking and peeling when young into irregular patches, exposing lighter inner bark.

HABITAT AND RANGE: Introduced in North America; naturalized in many areas, can be invasive. Native to Asia.

NOTES: Chinese Elm is planted as an ornamental in North America. It is less hardy than Siberian Elm, but resistant to Dutch elm disease.

ELM FAMILY	ULMACEAE

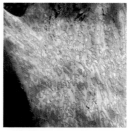

LEAF ¾–2" long. Asymmetrical base; single-toothed margins. Smooth above and beneath. **FLOWER** Reddish; in small, bundled clusters. Late summer–autumn. **FRUIT** ⅜–½" long; elliptic, flat.

Siberian Elm

Ulmus pumila

ALSO CALLED Asiatic Elm, Dwarf Elm

HT 50–70' **DIA** 1–1½'

Medium-sized tree. Tall, straight trunk; rounded or broadly columnar crown of slender, twisted branches; often sprouts at trunk. Bark brown to grayish brown; broad, flat ridges and deep fissures.

ID TIP: Siberian Elm has the largest leaves of the 3 single-toothed elms. Often confused with Chinese Elm, it has a more symmetrical leaf base, rounded fruit, bark that does not peel and flake, and flowers that bloom in spring. It is distinguished from Cedar Elm by the leaf's nearly symmetrical base, more pointed tip, and smooth (not rough) surface.

HABITAT AND RANGE: Introduced in North America; naturalized in dry regions, poor soils, and moist soils. Native to China and northern and eastern Asia.

NOTES: Siberian Elm is the world's hardiest elm species. The bark is sometimes streaked with lighter stains caused by a bacterial growth common to this tree. In North America it is susceptible to some insect pests, but there are varieties that are very tolerant of cold, heat, pollution, drought, and sterile soil, and some are even resistant to Dutch elm disease. It is invasive in some regions.

ELM FAMILY   **ULMACEAE**

LEAF 1–3" long, ¾–1" wide. Narrowly elliptic, with pointed tip; nearly symmetrical base; finely single-toothed margins. Glossy, dark green above; paler and nearly hairless beneath; smooth on both surfaces. Leafstalk red-tinged.   **TWIG** slender, grayish to grayish brown.   **FLOWER** Reddish; stalkless; in tiny, bundled clusters. Early spring, before leaves.   **FRUIT** ½–⅝" long, round samara, notched at tip; flat, papery, very broad wings; greenish to light brown; hairless. In small, bundled clusters; each fruit on short stalk. Early spring.

American Basswood

Tilia americana

ALSO CALLED American Linden

HT 60–80' **DIA** 2–3'

Medium-sized tree with deciduous, simple leaves. A tall, straight trunk or, often, 2 or more trunks; dense, broad, rounded crown (columnar in forests) of often drooping branches. Several suckers may sprout from lower trunk. Bark gray or brown, furrowed on older trees. **ID TIP:** American Basswood is the only *Tilia* native to North America, and has the largest leaves of any species. Fruits are attached to a large, leaflike bract and are larger than those of similar nonnatives.

HABITAT: Moist forests, lowlands. Elevation to 3,200'.

NOTES: This large tree provides cavity nesting sites for woodpeckers, wood duck, and other wildlife, and its flowers produce an abundance of nectar. There are 2 varieties in addition to the typical (var. *americana*, which occupies the northern part of the species' range); they are sometimes treated as 3 distinct species. **White Basswood** (var. *heterophylla*) occurs in rich, mountainous woodlands and ravines from Missouri and Arkansas to New York, and south to Georgia and just into Florida, at 200–5,000'. **Carolina Basswood** (var. *caroliniana*) is found in moist valleys, hammocks, and uplands, to 2,000', from Texas and Oklahoma east to North Carolina and Florida.

LEAF 5–8" long, nearly as wide. Asymmetrically heart-shaped, with abruptly pointed tip; coarsely toothed margins. Shiny, dark green above; light green and rusty-hairy in vein angles beneath (white- to rusty-woolly beneath in White Basswood; soft, rusty hairs beneath in Carolina Basswood). Autumn color pale yellow. Leafstalk long, slender. **FLOWER** ½–⅝" wide; yellowish white; 5 petals. In hanging, branched clusters of usually 5–15. Fragrant. Cluster stalk attached to middle of 4–5" long, narrow, leaflike bract. Summer. **FRUIT** ⅜" wide, ovoid or spherical nutlet; gray-brown; hard, dry, and covered with fine, reddish brown hairs. Contains 1 or 2 seeds. Fruit in cluster, on wiry stalk attached to middle of leaflike bract that carries the seeds in the wind. Autumn, often persists

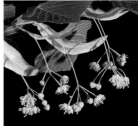

Littleleaf Linden

Tilia cordata

ALSO CALLED Small-leaf Lime

HT 30–100' **DIA** 1–3'

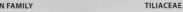

Small to large tree with deciduous, simple leaves. Straight, short, thick trunk; dense, broad, rounded or sometimes columnar crown of stout branches. Older trees have a buttressed trunk base with many sprouts around it and a dome-shaped crown. Bark brown to dark gray, with narrow, flat fibrous ridges and long, thin, shallow fissures. **ID TIP:** The leaves can be more rounded than in other lindens. This tree often has many suckers at the base of the trunk; branch tips touch the ground.

HABITAT AND RANGE: Introduced in North America; planted in parks and along streets. Native to Europe and Siberia.

LEAF 1½–3" long. Circular to asymmetrically heart-shaped, with abruptly pointed tip; finely toothed margins. Shiny, dark green above; pale, sometimes whitish, with whitish or rusty hairs in vein angles beneath. Autumn color yellow. Leafstalk long, slender, hairless. **FLOWER** ½" wide; pale yellow to cream; 5 petals. In cluster of 5–12, attached to leaflike bract. Fragrant. Early summer. **FRUIT** ¼" wide, spherical nutlet; hard, dry, 4-ribbed, with fine gray-brown hairs; leaflike bract. Autumn; often persists into winter.

European Linden

Tilia × europaea

HT 70' **DIA** 2'

This hybrid of Largeleaf and Littleleaf lindens occurs naturally where the trees' European ranges overlap. Unlike Largeleaf Linden, European Linden is susceptible to aphid attacks, which makes the tree exude its sticky sap, eventually causing mold. **ID TIP:** The fruit is faintly 5-ribbed. The tree often has a ring of suckers around the trunk base; burls form on the trunk. **HABITAT:** Introduced in North America; planted along roadsides.

LEAF 4" long (smaller than Largeleaf Linden, larger than Littleleaf Linden).

Largeleaf Linden

LINDEN FAMILY
TILIACEAE

Tilia platyphyllos
ALSO CALLED Largeleaf Lime,
Bigleaf Linden
HT 50–75' **DIA** 2–3'

Medium-sized tree with deciduous,
simple leaves. Tall, straight, slender trunk;
high, dense, rounded to broadly columnar
crown of stout branches ascending at
narrow angles. Bark light to dark gray, in
ribbed pattern or in flat-topped ridges
with long, narrow, shallow fissures. **ID TIP:**
Largeleaf Linden is the earliest linden to
flower. The leaves are the largest among
European lindens, but in North America,
the leaves of American Linden are larger.

HABITAT AND RANGE: Introduced in North
America; planted along streets. Native to
Europe and western Turkey.

NOTES: Species of the genus *Tilia* are
called "limes" in Europe; in North America
they are called "lindens" and "basswoods,"
the former term used in horticulture, the
latter in forestry. Unlike European Linden,
Largeleaf is not susceptible to aphid
attack. It is the first linden to blossom in
the summer and is planted as a street tree.
Cultivated varieties include trees with
red twigs, yellow branches, and twisted,
sharply lobed leaves.

LEAF 3½–6" long, nearly as wide. Asymmetrically heart-
shaped to circular, with abruptly pointed tip; coarsely
toothed margins. Shiny, dark green, slightly hairy above;
paler and densely hairy in vein angles beneath. Autumn
color yellow. Leafstalk long, slender, white-hairy. **FLOWER**
¾" wide; pale yellow; 5 petals. In hanging, branched clusters
of usually 3 flowers; clusters at end of long stalk that is
attached to middle of 4–5" long, narrow, leaflike bract. Very
fragrant. Summer. **FRUIT** ½" wide, ovoid or spherical nutlet;
gray-green; hard, dry, and 5-ribbed. Contains 1 or 2 seeds.
Fruit on wiry stalk attached to middle of leaflike bract.
Autumn; often persists into winter.

Willows

Willows (genus *Salix*) and poplars, aspens, and cottonwoods (*Populus*) are generally considered to comprise the willow family, Salicaceae. In both genera, the flowers are tiny, lack petals and sepals, and are packed into long clusters called catkins. Male and female catkins occur on separate trees. The fruits are capsules that split at maturity and release hairy seeds. Capsules are numerous, in elongated clusters. The genus *Salix* is covered below; *Populus* is described on page 390.

In willows, each tiny, individual flower within a catkin is borne in the axil of a small scale. Male flowers usually have two protruding stamens (exceptions noted in species accounts). The stamens have yellow tips (anthers), which may be red or purple before turning yellow. Female catkins produce nectar and are largely insect-pollinated. Male and female catkins are about the same length, unless otherwise noted. Catkins are generally erect at flowering time in early spring. Female catkins usually droop as they mature, the capsule clusters hanging. Seeds have cottony fluff to aid dissemination by wind.

Willow leaves are alternate, deciduous, and hairy at least in early developmental stages and often through the summer. Leaves commonly persist late in autumn, and are green or yellow when they drop. Leaves on young, fast-growing shoots are often quite different from typical leaves—larger, especially. (Species accounts give measurements for typical, mature leaves.) In many willow species, the leafstalk is flanked at its base by a pair of tiny, leaflike structures called stipules. Some willows have a pair of glands, which appear as tiny, round, raised bumps, on the leafstalk just below the base of the leaf blade. Both these minute features of the leafstalk, which are noted in the species accounts, can be useful clues in willow identification.

Willow twigs are generally pliable, yet in many species they are also brittle, snapping off easily and cleanly, as a means of propagation; new trees can sprout from

Willows generally grow in wet soils, such as streamsides and lakeshores. Twigs, buds, and young bark are the staple food of moose, and also important to grouse, beaver, and deer.

the fallen twigs. Buds in winter are pressed closely to the twig; each is enveloped in a single scale. In most willows, the scale forms a complete cap, with no edges, and a more or less blunt tip. In a few species, as noted in species accounts, the two edges of the scale overlap (a bud must be pried off to see this). The bud at the twig tip is not a true terminal bud and is not larger or otherwise different from the side buds. In individual trees, twig tips may have conelike growths; these are actually galls—deformities—caused by midges, sawflies, and other insects.

Willows hybridize freely, and their leaf features (shape, teeth, hairiness) are too variable to rely on for identification. Nevertheless, we often have to use those features as clues. Positive identification is often simply impossible without a magnifying lens, a very detailed key, and observations of both flowers and fruits—requiring visits in two different seasons to both male and female trees.

Scouler's Willow

Salix scouleriana

ALSO CALLED Fire Willow

HT 15–45' **DIA** 10–15"

Small tree or large shrub. Short trunk; compact, rounded crown of slender, drooping branches and stout branchlets. Bark gray to gray-brown, thin and smooth, with diamond-shaped markings; becomes dark brown and fissured with age. **ID TIP:** Scouler's Willow has broad leaves and late-winter "pussy willow" catkins. This is the willow most likely to be found in western mountains on slopes well away from streams.

HABITAT: Upland coniferous forests, especially on burned sites and clear-cuts; sometimes near streams. Elevation to 10,000'.

NOTES: With a north-to-south range of 2,700 miles, Scouler's Willow survives in a wide range of climates and temperatures. It can grow in shade, unlike most willows, and colonizes burned sites. Individuals grow largest around Puget Sound, Washington.

LEAF 1½–4½" long. Obovate to lance-shaped; blunt or slightly pointed tip; margins usually untoothed, edges often rolled under. Shiny, dark green above; paler, with waxy coating (and usually hairy) beneath. Leafstalk velvety; lacks paired glands; often flanked by pair of small stipules at base. Winter bud large, pointed; red or orange. Twig skunky smelling when crushed. **FLOWER** In ½–2" long catkin. Male catkin initially white, silky-furry (similar to Pussy Willow). Each male flower has 2 protruding stamens. Late winter, before leaves. **FRUIT** ⅛–⅜" long capsule; seeds white-hairy.

male catkin

fruit clusters

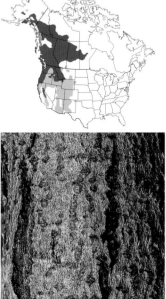

Pacific Willow

Salix lucida ssp. *lasiandra*
ALSO CALLED Western Shining Willow, Whiplash Willow
HT 15–45'   **DIA** 1–2'

Small tree or thicket-forming shrub. Slender trunk and open, irregular crown with straight branches. **ID TIP:** There are 3–5 stamens per flower in catkins on male trees. At least 2 warty glands are present on the leafstalk near the base of the leaf blade.

HABITAT: Streamsides and lakesides; roadside ditches. Elevation to 8,500'.

NOTES: The eastern **Shining Willow** (*S. lucida* ssp. *lucida*) is similar to but smaller than Pacific Willow. Shining Willow occurs along streamsides and in swamps, to 1,700' elevation. Some authorities consider the two to be separate species rather than subspecies.

WILLOW FAMILY   SALICACEAE

LEAF 2–6" long. Lance-shaped, with long-pointed tip; often slightly twisted; finely toothed margins. Glossy, dark green above. In Rockies and Great Plains, green with raised yellow midvein beneath; in Southwest and near coasts, a heavy, whitish, waxy coating beneath and raised yellow midvein on both sides. Two or more small, warty glands on leafstalk near base of leaf blade. Twig brittle; shiny, becoming hairless. **FLOWER** In 1½–4" long catkin. Each male flower has 3–5 protruding stamens. Early spring, with new leaves.

S. lucida ssp. *lasiandra*

S. lucida ssp. *lucida*

Bonpland Willow

Salix bonplandiana
ALSO CALLED Polished Willow
HT 15–45'   **DIA** 12–15"

ID TIP: The leaves are thick, with silvery undersides. There are 3 stamens per flower in catkins on male trees. Bark dark brown to charcoal black. Twig not brittle. **HABITAT:** Desert canyons and mountain streams, often with oaks and junipers. Elevation to 5,000'.

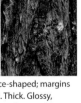

LEAF 4–6" long. Narrowly elliptic to lance-shaped; margins untoothed, scalloped, or finely toothed. Thick. Glossy, yellow-green, with yellow midvein above; silvery-white beneath; both surfaces generally hairless at maturity. Winter bud scale is split in back, the 2 sides overlapping.

Red Willow

Salix laevigata
HT 20–50'   DIA 12–15"

WILLOW FAMILY   **SALICACEAE**

Small tree. Broad, rounded crown of slender, upright branches and often drooping branchlets. Bark dark gray; rough, ridged, and fissured. **ID TIP:** Red

Willow has thick leaves with silvery undersides. There are typically 5 stamens per flower in male catkins.

HABITAT: Stream banks. Elevation to 7,200'.

LEAF 3–7" long. Lance-shaped to elliptic, with pointed tip; margins untoothed, slightly scalloped, or occasionally finely toothed. Thick. Glossy above; whitish, waxy coating beneath; generally hairless at maturity. Leafstalk often flanked by a pair of sizable stipules; 2 or more minute, round glands on leafstalk near base of leaf blade. Winter bud scale is split in back, the 2 sides overlapping. Twig often brittle. **FLOWER** In 2–4½" long catkin. Each male flower has 3–7 (typically 5) protruding stamens. Spring, as leaves emerge.

Arroyo Willow

Salix lasiolepis
ALSO CALLED White Willow
HT to 40'   DIA to 6"

WILLOW FAMILY   **SALICACEAE**

Small tree or shrub; multistemmed, thicket-forming. **ID TIP:** The leaves are rather thick and firm, with edges rolled under.

HABITAT: Understory of Redwoods; gravel, sandbars, dry-country wetlands, desert gullies (arroyos). Elevation 3,900–9,200'.

NOTES: Yewleaf Willow (*S. taxifolia*) has small, linear, gray-hairy leaves densely crowded on twigs; mountain and canyon streams, oak woodlands, desert grasslands, 1,200–6,400' elevation.

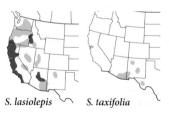

S. lasiolepis   *S. taxifolia*

LEAF 1½–4½" long. Narrowly elliptic to obovate, with bluntly pointed tip; finely toothed or untoothed margins; edges slightly to strongly rolled under. Thick, firm, leathery. Shiny, dark green above; paler beneath; either surface hairy or hairless. **FLOWER** In 1–2½" long catkin; densely white-woolly. Each male flower has 2 protruding stamens. Early spring, before new leaves.

Sitka Willow

Salix sitchensis

ALSO CALLED Silky Willow, Coulter Willow

HT 10–30'   **DIA** 4–12"

Small tree or shrub. **ID TIP:** Sitka Willow has brittle twigs; fine, silky hairs on leaf underside; and 1 stamen per flower in male catkins. **HABITAT:** Beaches, stream edges, openings in coastal coniferous forests. Elevation to 6,000'.

WILLOW FAMILY   SALICACEAE

male catkins

fruit clusters

LEAF 2–5" or longer. Elliptic to obovate, with blunt or pointed tip; margins untoothed, or with a few shallow teeth, edges often strongly rolled under. Shiny, dark green above; usually silvery (or red-tinged), silky hairs beneath. Leafstalk velvety. Twig brittle; hairy through at least the first summer. **FLOWER** In 1½–4" long catkin; hairy. Each male flower has 1 protruding stamen. Spring, with new leaves.

Hooker Willow

Salix hookeriana

ALSO CALLED Bigleaf Willow, Coast Willow, Dune Willow

HT 10–30'   **DIA** 6–12"

Small tree or shrub. **ID TIP:** The male catkins are stout and white-hairy; each flower has 2 protruding stamens.

HABITAT: Sand dunes and bluffs, edges of coastal marshes, streams, coniferous forests. Elevation to 160'.

WILLOW FAMILY   SALICACEAE

male catkins

LEAF 2–5" long, about half as wide. Elliptic to obovate, and rounded at tip or with a small point; untoothed margins. Shiny, yellow-green, nearly hairless above; usually woolly, mostly on veins, beneath. Leafstalk hairy. Twig brittle; often woolly. **FLOWER** In densely hairy catkin. Female: unusually long, 3–4". Male: stout, 1½" long, ¾–1" wide. Each male flower has 2 protruding stamens. Spring, before or with new leaves.

Northwest Willow

Salix sessilifolia
ALSO CALLED Velvet Willow, Silverleaf
Willow, Northwest Sandbar Willow
HT 7–27'   DIA to 4"

Small tree or shrub. ID TIP: This is the only
native, tree-sized willow retaining a silver,
silky-woolly coating on both sides of its
leaf through summer. Flowering catkins
are white-woolly, showy, and abundant
after trees leaf out—unusual for a willow.

WILLOW FAMILY   SALICACEAE

HABITAT: Stream banks.
Elevation to 650'.

NOTES: In the
population **River
Willow** (sometimes
called *S. fluviatilis*),
found in Oregon and
Washington near the
Columbia River, the
leaves usually lose
most of their hair by
midsummer, and are
longer (2–6") and
narrower.

LEAF 1–4" long. Narrowly elliptic, with pointed tip; margins
untoothed (or sometimes a few teeth). Silky-woolly on
both sides of leaf (woolly only beneath in Feltleaf Willow),
suggestive of Olive leaf. Nearly stalkless. Twig not brittle;
densely woolly first year, retaining some hair in second and
third years. **FLOWER** In 1–2½" long catkin; densely white-
woolly. Each male flower has 2 protruding stamens. Spring
and into summer, after leaves unfold.

Feltleaf Willow

Salix alaxensis
HT 20–30'   DIA 4–7"

Small tree or shrub. ID TIP: This willow is
named for the feltlike white coating on its
leaf undersides and twigs.

HABITAT: Stream banks, lakeshores, alpine
slopes and meadows, forest openings.
Elevation to 3,200'.

NOTES: This is the most northerly North
American tree willow. It becomes a shrub
past the tree line. **Littletree Willow** (*S.
arbusculoides*), with a similar range, has
smaller, shiny, finely toothed leaves and a
shiny, mostly hairless, red-brown twig.

WILLOW FAMILY   SALICACEAE

LEAF 2–4" long. Obovate to lance-shaped, with a bluntly
pointed tip; margins usually untoothed, edges often
strongly rolled under. Dull green above; densely white-
woolly beneath. Leaves may persist through 1 or 2 winters.
Leafstalk base flanked by pair of green stipules. Twig usually
densely white-woolly through second year. **FLOWER** In 2–4"
long catkin. Each male flower has 2 protruding stamens.
Spring, emerging before new leaves.

Sandbar Willow

Salix exigua
ALSO CALLED Coyote Willow,
Narrowleaf Willow
HT 3–20' DIA 3–6"

Small tree or shrub east of the Rockies;
thicket-forming, multistemmed shrub in
the West. ID TIP: Leaves are very narrow
and have a grayish cast. *S. interior* (east
of Rockies) and *S. hindsiana* (California to
Oregon) are similar.

HABITAT: Sandbars, stream banks, silt flats.
Elevation 550–5,800'.

WILLOW FAMILY   **SALICACEAE**

LEAF 2–6" long, ⅜" wide (occasionally to ¾" wide). Lance-
shaped, with very long-pointed tip and pointed base;
often curved to one side; margins untoothed or with
widely spaced, small teeth. Both surfaces yellow-green to
gray-green, varying from hairless to silky-hairy. Leafstalk
short, usually less than ⅜" long. Twig not brittle. **FLOWER**
In ½–2½" long catkins. Each male flower has 2 protruding
stamens. Spring, as leaves unfold or (more typically) later.

Peachleaf Willow

Salix amygdaloides
ALSO CALLED Peach Willow,
Almond Willow
HT 10–60' DIA 12–15"

Small to medium-sized tree or large shrub.
One to several straight trunks; spreading
crown of straight branches. ID TIP: There
are typically 5 stamens per flower in
catkins on male trees. Leaf undersides
have a distinctive whitish coating.

HABITAT: Forests with wet soil;
streamsides; very common along prairie
streams and rivers. Elevation 200–7,700'.

WILLOW FAMILY   **SALICACEAE**

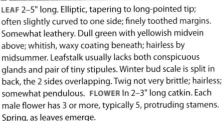

LEAF 2–5" long. Elliptic, tapering to long-pointed tip;
often slightly curved to one side; finely toothed margins.
Somewhat leathery. Dull green with yellowish midvein
above; whitish, waxy coating beneath; hairless by
midsummer. Leafstalk usually lacks both conspicuous
glands and pair of tiny stipules. Winter bud scale is split in
back, the 2 sides overlapping. Twig not very brittle; hairless;
somewhat pendulous. **FLOWER** In 2–3" long catkin. Each
male flower has 3 or more, typically 5, protruding stamens.
Spring, as leaves emerge.

Bebb Willow

Salix bebbiana
ALSO CALLED Beaked Willow
HT 10–25' **DIA** 6–8"

Large shrub, or sometimes a small tree; often multistemmed; forms vast, impenetrable shrub thickets. Bark gray, with reddish, horizontal lines. **ID TIP:** The mature seed clusters are looser than those of most willows, and individual seed capsules are larger and on longer stalks.

HABITAT: Moist soils; common in mountains. Elevation to 11,000'.

LEAF 1–3½" long. Elliptic, with pointed tip; margins untoothed or, less often, toothed or scalloped. Dull green above; gray or pale bluish and conspicuously net-veined beneath. Typical western form hairless on both sides; east of the Rockies usually densely fuzzy beneath. **FLOWER** Female: in ¾–2½" long catkin. Male: in ½–1¼" long catkin. Each male flower has 2 protruding stamens. Spring, as new leaves emerge. **FRUIT** ¼–⅜" long capsule (larger than in other willows); on ¼–⅜" long stalk; in loose cluster.

WILLOW FAMILY SALICACEAE

Pussy Willow

Salix discolor
HT 20–30' **DIA** 4–12"

Small tree or large shrub. **ID TIP:** Pussy Willow has "furry" male flower catkins, which open fully in later winter. It is one of the earliest-flowering willows.

HABITAT: Stream banks, lakeshores, and wet meadows near coniferous forests. Elevation to 8,000'.

NOTES: **Balsam Willow** (*S. pyrifolia*), of cold swamps and bogs in Canada, has aromatic twigs and leaves.

WILLOW FAMILY SALICACEAE

male catkins

LEAF 2–5" long. Elliptic to lance-shaped, with pointed tip; margins untoothed or with a few shallow teeth. Shiny, bright green above; whitish coating and raised, yellowish veins beneath. Leafstalk lacks paired glands. **FLOWER** In ¾–1½" long catkin. Each male flower has 2 protruding stamens. Male catkin initially silvery and silky-furry, before golden stamens emerge. Late winter, before leaves.

Black Willow

Salix nigra

ALSO CALLED Swamp Willow

HT 40–80' **DIA** 1½–2½'

Small to medium-sized tree; often shrubby on Atlantic coast. One to several straight, stout trunks; broad crown of thick branches and slender, orange-brown branchlets. **ID TIP:** One of the largest willows, Black Willow has a large trunk, with rough, dark brown to blackish, scaly, and furrowed bark. There are 4–6 stamens per flower in catkins on male trees.

HABITAT: Streamsides, floodplains, lakeshores. Elevation 40–4,500'.

NOTES: Goodding's Willow or Western Black Willow (*S. gooddingii*) is very similar to Black Willow (some consider it a variety), but its twigs are yellow to brown to greenish, not reddish, and may or may not be brittle; the leaves are a little shorter and nearly elliptic in shape. It occurs along streams, desert gullies (arroyos), and marshes, often with Fremont Cottonwood, to 8,200' elevation. It is not likely to be confused with Black Willow, as the ranges overlap only spottily in Texas.

LEAF 3–6" long. Lance-shaped, with long-pointed tip, often slightly curved; fine reddish teeth on margins. Shiny, dark green above; slightly paler green beneath; hairless or nearly so. Two small, round glands on leafstalk near base of leaf blade; 2 tiny, green stipules at base of leafstalk. **FLOWER** In 1–3" long catkin. Each male flower has 4–6 protruding stamens. Early spring, as leaves emerge. **FRUIT** ⅛" long, ovoid capsule, in elongated cluster; seeds white-hairy.

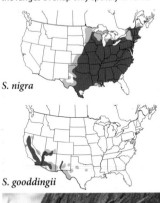

S. nigra

S. gooddingii

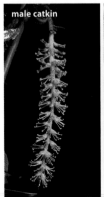

male catkin

fruit cluster

Coastal Plain Willow

Salix caroliniana
ALSO CALLED Carolina Willow
HT 10–30'   **DIA** to 6"

Small tree or shrub. **ID TIP:** Very similar to Black Willow, but with whiter leaf undersides and paler bark. There are 4–8 stamens per flower in catkins on male trees.

HABITAT: Stream banks, lakeshores, coastal areas. Elevation to 1,700'.

LEAF 2–7" long. Glossy, green above; whitish, waxy coating beneath; either surface hairy or hairless; margins toothed or untoothed. Twig somewhat brittle. **FLOWER** In 2–3½" long catkin; hairy. Each male flower has 4–8 protruding stamens. Spring, as leaves emerge.

WILLOW FAMILY   **SALICACEAE**

Purple-osier Willow

Salix purpurea
ALSO CALLED Basket Willow
HT 10–20'   **DIA** 4–10"

Small tree or large shrub; often thicket-forming. **ID TIP:** Purple-osier Willow has nearly opposite, narrowly elliptic leaves and 1 stamen per flower in male catkin. First-year twigs are sometimes purplish.

HABITAT AND RANGE: Introduced in North America; naturalized in the East and the Pacific coast states. Native to Europe, Mongolia, and northern Africa.

NOTES: Purple-osier Willow was introduced in North America probably for the use of the twigs and branches in basketry. **Osier Willow** (*S. viminalis*), native to Europe and Asia and planted for similar purposes, has naturalized in the Northeast. It has very long (4–8"), narrow, woolly, untoothed leaves and long, flexible twigs.

WILLOW FAMILY   **SALICACEAE**

LEAF 1½–3" long. Linear to lance-shaped; untoothed or toothed margins; edges rolled under. Hairless. Twig sometimes purplish. **FLOWER** In ¾–1¼" long catkin; hairy. Each male flower has 1 protruding stamen. Early spring, before leaves emerge.

Crack Willow

Salix fragilis
ALSO CALLED Brittle Willow,
Snap Willow
HT 50–80'   **DIA** 2–4'

Medium-sized tree. One to several stout, often leaning trunks; rounded crown. Bark paler than Black Willow. **ID TIP:** Crack Willow is named for its especially brittle twigs and branchlets, which "crack" when snapped, breaking off easily and cleanly almost anywhere along their length. **HABITAT AND RANGE:** Introduced in North America; escapes along roadsides and streams. Native to Europe, western Asia.

WILLOW FAMILY   **SALICACEAE**

LEAF 4–6" long. Lance-shaped, with long-pointed tip, usually curved to one side; finely toothed margins. Glossy, dark green above; bluish white beneath. Two small, round glands on leafstalk at base of leaf blade; stipules at base of leafstalk are very small or absent. Winter bud sticky. Twig very brittle; remains glossy, bright golden or orange-brown into winter. **FLOWER** In 1–2¼" long catkin. Each male flower has 2 protruding stamens. Spring, as new leaves emerge.

White Willow

Salix alba
ALSO CALLED European White Willow
HT 50–80'   **DIA** 1½–3'

Medium-sized tree. One to several stout, sometimes leaning trunks; narrow, open crown of stout branches and drooping branchlets. Bark brown when young, becoming grayish brown; rough; with narrow ridges and fissures. **ID TIP:** The foliage is dense and looks blue-gray from a distance.

HABITAT AND RANGE: Introduced in North America; naturalized along stream banks. Native to Europe, Asia, and northern Africa.

NOTES: White Willow is planted as an ornamental, shade, and shelterbelt tree. Plants sold as White Willow are most often hybrids between *S. alba* and *S. fragilis*, with intermediate characteristics; such hybrids also abound in the wild and are sometimes called White-crack Willow.

WILLOW FAMILY   **SALICACEAE**

LEAF 2–4" long. Usually narrowly elliptic, with pointed tip; finely toothed margins. Glossy, pale green above; usually silky, white hairs beneath (typically retains more hair in summer than Black Willow). Young leaf densely silvery-hairy on both sides. Twig not brittle; silky, white in first few weeks, turning olive-brown. **FLOWER** In 1¼–2¼" long catkin. Each male flower has 2 protruding stamens. Spring, before new leaves, or as new leaves emerge.

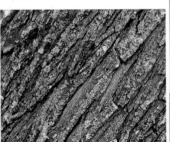

Weeping Willows

Salix hybrids

Trees sold as weeping willows (often as *S. babylonica*) in North America are usually hybrids. Golden and Wisconsin weeping willows are hybrids of *S. babylonica* and White Willow and Crack Willow, respectively. A true *S. babylonica* would probably be found only in the South, as the species is not hardy. Weeping willows were likely bred in China about 2,000 years ago and may have reached the Middle East via the Silk Road trade route about 1,000 years ago. They were brought to North America in colonial times. The original, natural species probably was not "weeping," or pendulous, in its growth habit. It may have been the same species as the Peking Willow (*S. matsudana*), from which Corkscrew Willow was bred. Weeping willows are planted as ornamentals throughout the world, but the roots may damage drain pipes, and the easily broken branches and twigs are messy.

WILLOW FAMILY   SALICACEAE

Corkscrew Willow

Salix matsudana 'Tortuosa'
ALSO CALLED Hankow Willow, Dragon's Claw Willow
HT 25–35'   **DIA** 12–15"

Small tree or shrub. Short trunk; broad, rounded crown of contorted branches (may be upright or pendulous). Bark thin; pale gray-brown; somewhat shiny ridges and deep furrows in a lattice pattern.
ID TIP: The branchlets are extremely crooked, most often in a chaotic fashion, but sometimes in corkscrew twists.

HABITAT AND RANGE: Cultivated in North America.

NOTES: Corkscrew Willow is a variety of the rare Peking Willow, native to China and Korea. Planted as an ornamental (and grown for bonsai), it is short-lived, requires pruning, and is susceptible to storm breakage and disease.

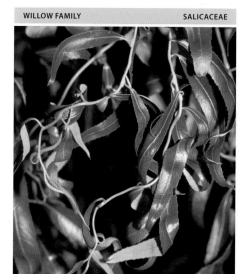

WILLOW FAMILY   SALICACEAE

LEAF 2–4" long. Lance-shaped, tapering to a long-pointed tip; curled, forming a long, deep cuplike depression; finely toothed margins. Pale yellow-green, with a few long, silky hairs above; silvery gray beneath. Leafstalk twisted. **FLOWER** In 1–1½" long catkin. Spring, as leaves unfold.

Poplars, Cottonwoods, and Aspens

The genus *Populus* includes poplars, cottonwoods, and aspens. All have flowers clustered in long, dangling catkins that first appear before the leaves in spring. About ¼" long and wide, the tiny flowers have no sepals or petals. At the base of the flower is a cuplike structure, sometimes fringed; in males the cup may hold 15 or more stamens, in females two to four pistils. Male and female flowers occur on separate trees. Female catkins elongate as the flowers mature into small, two- to four-part capsules; these split open in spring, releasing tiny seeds covered in long, white hairs. The cluster of hairy seeds forms a cottony mass that is dispersed by wind.

The deciduous leaves are alternate, their margins toothed and mostly unlobed. Leaves of saplings, or even early leaves of spring, may strongly differ from the typical leaf shape. Buds are resinous and often fragrant. On species with flattened leafstalks, the leaves flutter dramatically in a breeze; as the wind picks up they will rustle (aspens) or chitter noisily (cottonwoods). Quaking Aspen, with the lightest leaves and flattest leafstalks, trembles in even the slightest breeze.

Swamp Cottonwood

Populus heterophylla
ALSO CALLED Swamp Poplar
HT 30–80'   **DIA** 1½–2'

Small to medium-sized tree. Tall, straight trunk; narrow, rounded crown of slender branches and stout branchlets. Bark brown, in long, narrow plates. **ID TIP:** This cottonwood has ovate or heart-shaped leaves that are hairless above even when newly emerged, but that become pale woolly beneath for at least part of the season.

HABITAT: Wet soil in swamps, floodplains. Elevation to 800'.

NOTES: Swamp Cottonwood is uncommon in its range, occurring in a few widely scattered locations, mainly in the Mississippi and Ohio river lowlands and the coastal plains. It grows in wetter areas than Eastern Cottonwood, and its seeds require wet soil to germinate.

LEAF 4–8" long. Heart-shaped to ovate, with bluntly pointed tip; fine or coarse, blunt teeth. Thin. Dark green, not shiny above; paler and sometimes downy (especially on veins) beneath. Young leaf densely white-woolly beneath. Autumn color dull yellow or brown. Leafstalk shorter than blade; rounded in cross section. Terminal bud ⅜" long, rather broad, only slightly resinous, not fragrant. Twig dark brown to gray under a heavy, white-woolly coat that rubs or falls off early. **FLOWER** In 1½–2½" long, drooping catkin; brownish. Early spring. **FRUIT** ½" long, oblong capsule; brown. In 2–4" long, hanging clusters. Seeds tiny, white-hairy, in cottony mass. Early spring.

fruit clusters

Eastern Cottonwood

Populus deltoides

ALSO CALLED Carolina Poplar, Southern Cottonwood

HT 75–100'   **DIA** 2–4'

Medium-sized to large tree. Tall, massive trunk forks into stout limbs; broad, open crown of branches. Older trees have a huge trunk, buttressed base, massive branches; very thick (2–5") bark with deep furrows. **ID TIP:** Leaves are triangular to heart-shaped, with curved, blunt teeth. (Quaking Aspen leaves have fine teeth.) The leaf margins of Eastern Cottonwood are thin, translucent.

HABITAT: Stream banks, floodplains; mostly lowlands. Elevation to 1,000' in the East, 5,000' in the West.

NOTES: Eastern Cottonwood is one of North America's most massive broadleaf trees. The leaves flutter in a breeze; in wind they make a noisy, chittering sound. **Plains Cottonwood** (var. *monilifera* or *occidentalis*) is a smaller variety with a smaller leaf (3–3½" long), usually wider than it is long, with larger teeth. It is common in the Great Plains, occurring along creeks and roadsides. The common poplar used in eastern landscaping is a hybrid of Eastern Cottonwood and European Black Poplar (*P. nigra*, a Eurasian species), known as **Carolina Poplar**.

WILLOW FAMILY   SALICACEAE

capsules

LEAF 4–6" long and wide; 6–8" in the South. Nearly triangular to heart-shaped, with long-pointed tip; margins have coarse, curved, blunt teeth. Thick. Shiny, green above; paler beneath. Autumn color yellow. Leafstalk nearly as long as blade; flattened. Terminal bud up to 1" long, pointed; chestnut-brown; sticky, not fragrant. Twig yellowish brown and ridged. **FLOWER** In 2–4" long, drooping catkin; reddish brown. Early spring. **FRUIT** ⅜" long, oblong capsule; light brown. In 3–5" long, hanging clusters. Seeds tiny, white-hairy. Late spring.

male catkins

fruit clusters

Narrowleaf Cottonwood

Populus angustifolia

ALSO CALLED Mountain Cottonwood

HT 30–50'   **DIA** 1–1½'

Small tree, sometimes thicket-forming. Slender trunk; compact, narrow, conical or rounded crown of upright, slender branches and yellowish branchlets. Bark light gray when young, becoming darker, thick, and rough. **ID TIP:** With its long, narrow leaves, Narrowleaf Cottonwood can be mistaken for a willow, but it is easily identified as a cottonwood by the distinctive balsam fragrance of its winter bud.

HABITAT: Lower-elevation stream banks. Elevation 3,000–8,000'.

NOTES: This species is a common cottonwood of the Rocky Mountains. Narrowleaf Cottonwood colonizes flood-disturbed land, and is sometimes planted for erosion control.

LEAF 2–5" long. Lance-shaped, with pointed tip; finely toothed margins (teeth pointed, not blunt). Thick. Glossy, yellow-green above; paler beneath. Leafstalk less than one-third length of leaf blade; slightly flattened. Autumn color dull yellow. Terminal bud ¼–¾" long; sticky; with balsam fragrance. Twig yellow to orange. **FLOWER** In 1½–3" long, drooping catkin; reddish. Early spring. **FRUIT** ¼" long, oblong capsule; light brown. In 2–4" long, hanging clusters. Seeds tiny, white-hairy. Late spring.

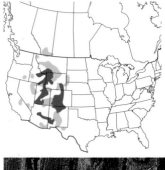

Fremont Cottonwood

WILLOW FAMILY   SALICACEAE

Populus fremontii

ALSO CALLED Rio Grande Cottonwood, Meseta Cottonwood

HT 40–80' **DIA** 2–4'

Small to medium-sized tree. Short single trunk, or multistemmed; broad, flattened crown of stout, widely spreading branches that may curve downward at their tips. **ID TIP:** Fremont Cottonwood is the only western poplar that has a triangular to heart-shaped leaf with a long-pointed tip and bluntly toothed margins.

HABITAT: Stream banks. Elevation to 6,500'.

NOTES: Fremont Cottonwood is a common cottonwood of Arizona and New Mexico. It is an important nesting site for many birds, including Swainson's hawk, red-tailed hawk, and golden eagle; it also provides valuable cover and forage to many other animals. The leaves flutter in the slightest breeze; in wind, they make a noisy, chittering sound. It is sometimes planted as an ornamental or shade tree, as a windbreak, or for erosion control.

LEAF 2–3" long and wide. Nearly triangular to heart-shaped, with long-pointed tip; coarse, curved, blunt teeth along margins. Thick. Shiny, yellow-green above; paler beneath. Autumn color bright yellow. Leafstalk yellow, flattened. Winter bud sticky and fragrant. Twig yellow. **FLOWER** In 1½–3¼" long, drooping catkin; reddish. Early spring. **FRUIT** ⅜–½" long, round to oblong capsule; light brown. In 4" long, hanging clusters. Seeds tiny, white-hairy. Late spring.

fruit capsules

fruit clusters

Balsam Poplar

Populus balsamifera
ALSO CALLED Tacamahac
HT 60–80'   **DIA** 1–3'

Medium-sized tree. Tall, straight trunk; open, narrow, elliptic crown of stout, erect branches. Bark dark gray-brown, with broad, flat, scaly, vertical ridges and furrows. **ID TIP:** The sticky winter buds have a mild honeylike or spicy-balsam fragrance. The seed capsule splits open in 2 parts (compare Black Cottonwood).

HABITAT: Stream valleys and lower slopes. Elevation to 5,500'.

NOTES: This poplar is one of the most northerly deciduous trees in North America. A female cultivar of Balsam Poplar, **Balm-of-Gilead** (*Populus × jackii*), possibly hybridizes with Eastern Cottonwood; it has escaped from gardens, establishing itself on riverbanks in the East. Balm-of-Gilead has downy, triangular to heart-shaped leaves that are dark green above, white beneath; it produces no male catkins. As in Balsam Poplar, its winter buds are sticky, resinous, and fragrant.

LEAF 3–5" long. Ovate, with pointed tip; fine, blunt teeth along margins. Rather thick. Glossy, resinous, dark green above; whitish, often with rusty veins beneath. Autumn color bright yellow. Leafstalk 3–4" long; rounded in cross section. Winter buds chestnut brown, very sticky, oozing yellow resin, and fragrant; terminal bud large, to 1" long. Twig reddish brown. **FLOWER** In 2–4" long, drooping catkin; reddish brown. Early spring. **FRUIT** ⅜" long, oblong capsule; light brown; in 4–5" long, hanging clusters. Capsule splits in 2 parts at maturity, releasing tiny, white-hairy seeds. Late spring.

fruit clusters

Balm-of-Gilead

Black Cottonwood

Populus balsamifera ssp. *trichocarpa*
ALSO CALLED Western Balsam Poplar, California Poplar
HT 60–120'   **DIA** 1–4'

WILLOW FAMILY   **SALICACEAE**

Medium-sized to large tree. Very tall, straight trunk; open, narrow, elliptic crown of stout, erect branches. Older trees have large trunk, massive boughs beginning high on tree; gray bark with corky ridges, deep furrows. **ID TIP:** The sticky winter buds have a mild honeylike or spicy-balsam fragrance. The seed capsule splits open in 3 parts (2 parts in similar Balsam Poplar).

HABITAT: Stream banks, floodplains, and upland slopes. Elevation to 2,000' in northern parts of range, to 9,000' in southern.

NOTES: Black Cottonwood is the West's tallest native broadleaf tree. The winter bud's resin makes a strong adhesive, and bees use it in hives as an anti-infectant and sealant. Ospreys and bald eagles often choose streamside Black Cottonwoods as nesting sites, returning to them for many years. Large plantations of identical hybrid poplar clones are grown in the Pacific Northwest. Silviculturists try new hybrids every year, typically crossing Black Cottonwood with Eastern Cottonwood and European Black Poplar, in an attempt to create the fastest-growing tree possible, which after harvesting (for pulp or biofuel) will resprout from the stump and grow even faster, taking advantage of large root systems in place.

LEAF 3–6" long. Ovate, with pointed tip; fine, blunt teeth along margins. Thick, leathery. Glossy, resinous, dark green above; whitish, often with rusty veins beneath. Autumn color lemon yellow to yellowish brown. Leafstalk almost as long as blade; rounded in cross section. Winter buds golden brown, very sticky, resinous, and fragrant; terminal bud up to ¾" long. **FLOWER** In 1½–3¼" long, drooping catkin; reddish purple. Early spring. **FRUIT** ¼" long, round capsule; light brown. In 4–6" long, hanging clusters. Capsules split in 3 at maturity to release tiny, white-hairy seeds. Late spring.

fruit clusters

White Poplar

Populus alba
HT 50–80'   DIA 2–3'

WILLOW FAMILY   **SALICACEAE**

Medium-sized tree. One to several stout trunks, usually leaning; open crown, broadest near top, of greenish white or grayish white branches. **ID TIP:** White Poplar is easily recognized by its lobed leaves with white undersides; they flash light and dark in the wind.

HABITAT AND RANGE: Introduced in North America; planted in parks and gardens and along streets; invasive, naturalized along sandy coasts and roadsides. Native to Europe, Asia, and northern Africa.

LEAF 3–4" long. 3 or 5 pointed or rounded lobes (similar to a maple leaf when pointed); young leaves are ovate, with merely wavy margins. Thick. Dull dark green above; white-woolly beneath. Autumn color yellow to pale reddish. Leafstalk somewhat shorter than leaf blade; rounded in cross section. Winter bud and twig coated with white wool that rubs off. **FLOWER** In 2–3" long, drooping catkin; densely covered with white fuzz. Early spring, before new leaves. **FRUIT** ¼" long, oblong capsule; green. In 1½–4" long, hanging clusters. Seeds tiny, white-hairy. Late spring.

Lombardy Poplar

Populus nigra 'Italica'
HT 40–60'   DIA 1–3'

WILLOW FAMILY   **SALICACEAE**

Small to medium-sized tree. **ID TIP:** Lombardy Poplar is distinguished by its unusual columnar shape.

HABITAT AND RANGE: Cultivated in North America.

NOTES: This poplar is a male cultivar propagated by cuttings, and so produces no female flowers or fruit. Though its form of short, dense, upright branches makes it ideal for use as a street tree, it also cracks pavements and is prone to storm damage and diseases.

LEAF 2–3½" long. Triangular to distinctly widest at middle, with pointed tip; fine, blunt teeth along margins. Shiny, green above; light green beneath. Winter bud red-brown, sticky, resinous. Autumn color rich golden yellow. **FLOWER** Male only; in 2–3" long, drooping catkin; reddish or yellow-green. Early spring.

Quaking Aspen

Populus tremuloides

ALSO CALLED Trembling Aspen, Golden Aspen, Popple

HT 30–70' **DIA** 1–1½'

WILLOW FAMILY · SALICACEAE

Small to medium-sized tree. Slender trunk; pyramidal to round crown of spreading branches with sparse foliage. Grows in clonal groves. Bark whitish to yellowish white to light green, with blackish, warty patches. **ID TIP:** The leaves have pointed teeth along the margins and a long, flattened leafstalk that lets them flutter and rustle in a breeze.

HABITAT: Diverse; mixed-conifer forests, hardwood forests, and rocky to clay to sandy soils. Many stands originate after fires. Elevation to 10,000' in northern parts of range, to 3,000' in southern.

NOTES: Quaking Aspen is the most widely distributed tree in North America. Most stems originate as root suckers that form extensive clones; one male clone in the Wasatch Range in Utah covers about 107 acres, has 47,000 trunks, and is often considered the world's most massive organism. Though the tree is emblematic of the Rocky Mountains, its populations there have dropped sharply over the last century. This may be because of fire suppression practices, as aspens benefit when fires clear away conifers, giving the aspens sunny ground to shoot up in. Another hypothesis is that the drop is the result of the decline in wolf populations; wolves keep elk, moose, and deer vigilant and on the move, preventing them from settling in one place and eating all of the aspen shoots.

LEAF 1–3" long. Nearly circular to heart-shaped, with pointed or abruptly pointed tip; somewhat straight base; finely toothed margins. Thin. Green above; pale silvery-green beneath. Autumn color golden yellow. Leafstalk as long as blade or slightly longer; flattened. Terminal bud ¼" long; pointed, shiny, but scarcely sticky, not fragrant. Twig reddish brown. **FLOWER** In 1–3" long, drooping catkin; brownish. Early spring. **FRUIT** ¼" long, pointed, oblong capsule; light green. In 2–4" long, hanging clusters (denser than in cottonwoods). Capsules split open at maturity to release tiny, white-hairy seeds. Late spring.

fruit clusters

Bigtooth Aspen

Populus grandidentata
ALSO CALLED Large-tooth Aspen
HT 30–60' **DIA** 1–2'

Small to medium-sized tree. Straight, slender trunk; narrow, open, rounded crown of spreading, rigid, stout branches and slender branchlets. Bark pale green to gray; becoming dark gray, furrowed.
ID TIP: The bark is darker than that of Quaking Aspen. The leafstalk is often shorter than the length of the leaf blade.

HABITAT: Sandy soils of stream valleys and slopes. Elevation to 600' in northern parts of range, to 3,000' in southern.

NOTES: Though less widespread than Quaking Aspen, with which it often grows, Bigtooth Aspen is important in reclaiming burned, logged, and eroded lands, old fields, and mine sites. Leaves flutter in a slight breeze and rustle loudly in wind.

LEAF 2½–4" long. Ovate to nearly circular, with blunt or pointed tip; margins coarsely scalloped or with teeth that curve toward the leaf tip. Thin. Dark green, not glossy above; paler beneath. Autumn color pale to bright yellow. Leafstalk often shorter than blade; flattened. Terminal bud ¼–⅜" long, blunt and rather broad; minutely hairy; not resinous, not fragrant. **FLOWER** In 1½–2½" long, drooping catkin; brownish. Early spring. **FRUIT** ¼" long, narrowly ovoid capsule; light green; similar to Quaking Aspen. In 3–5" long, hanging clusters (denser than in cottonwoods). Seeds tiny, white-hairy. Late spring.

Birches, Alders, and Kin

Trees of the birch family, Betulaceae, include birches (genus *Betula*), hornbeams (*Carpinus*), hophornbeams (*Ostrya*), and alders (*Alnus*). All have alternate, simple, deciduous leaves with toothed margins. Male and female catkins occur on the same tree. The one-seeded fruit is a nut or nutlet or a two-winged samara. Hazelnuts (*Corylus*) are shrubs in North America, rarely tree-sized.

Hornbeams and Hophornbeams

Hornbeams and hophornbeams have leaves with double-toothed margins and unusual fruits, both of which occur in clusters. In hornbeams, the seed is attached to leaflike bracts. In hophornbeams, it is enclosed within a papery, inflated husk.

Birches

Birch leaves have double-toothed margins and typically turn yellow in autumn. Bark (except on the lower trunk of old trees) is smooth, marked with horizontal lines, and may curl and peel; twigs are marked with similar horizontal lines. Winter buds at branch tips are the same size as side buds. Birches regenerate readily from stump sprouts after fire, often in clumps.

Male catkins first appear in late summer or fall; they are borne, often several together, at or near the tips of long shoots. They are erect at emergence, and remain so through winter. In spring, as the leaves emerge, the male catkins double to quadruple in length, moving from an erect to a drooping position as they flower. Female birch catkins flower in early spring before leaves emerge, borne singly or in pairs along year-old growth. They are conelike in shape, but not woody. The catkins are made up of tiny, individual, three-lobed scales that hold the flower parts. Birch fruit is a small, two-winged samara that is borne in the scales of a conelike structure (called a strobilus) that develops from the female catkin. The scales and seeds fall when ripe, leaving a thin, central stem on the tree.

Birches hybridize easily in nature, causing much taxonomic uncertainty. The sweet sap can be reduced to syrup, once used in birch beer. The twigs, buds, and bark are preferred browse for deer, hares, grouse, and other animals. The wood is an important hardwood lumber.

Alders

In alders, the leaves can be single- or double-toothed. Male catkins are soft and flexible, and drop after the tiny flowers release their pollen. The female catkins are at first hard, green, and somewhat fleshy; after their tiny flowers are pollinated, female catkins become dry, brown, and woody. At maturity, these woody, conelike structures (strobili) open to release tiny, seedlike nuts. Catkin stalk length and the seasons in which catkins form and mature are useful identification features in alders. Alder bark is mostly smooth.

Red Alder strobilus

Red Alder male catkins

Red Alder female catkins

In birches and alders the female flower catkin, after pollination, develops into a conelike fruit structure, called a strobilus, composed of scales holding tiny seeds.

American Hornbeam

Carpinus caroliniana

ALSO CALLED Ironwood, Blue-beech, Musclewood

HT 15–30' **DIA** 6–12"

Small tree or large shrub. Short, slender trunk with twisted, sinewy appearance (pictured on p. 331); loose, broad, rounded, finely branched crown of long, slender, spreading, slightly zigzagging branches that droop at their ends. **ID TIP:** The beechlike bark is smooth and gray to blue-gray. The fruits are in distinctive clusters of long, leaflike bracts.

HABITAT: Lowland forests; along streams, ravines. Elevation to 1,000'.

BIRCH FAMILY   BETULACEAE

LEAF 2–4" long. Elliptic, with rounded to pointed base and abruptly pointed tip; double-toothed margins; prominent, straight side veins (not forking). Dull, dark blue-green above; paler and white-hairy in vein angles beneath. Autumn color orange to deep scarlet. Leafstalk short, hairy. Twig green, turning orange or reddish brown, flexible, shiny; finely silky when young.

FLOWER Male and female on same tree in early spring. Female: in very slender, ½–¾" catkin; reddish green. Male: in slender, 1¼–1½" long, hanging catkin; greenish. **FRUIT** ¼" long, oblong nutlet; ribbed, hairy; greenish. In pairs, within cluster of several leaflike bracts; each bract 1–1½" long, 3-lobed, and toothed. Cluster hangs at end of 2–4" long stalk. Late summer–autumn.

fruit cluster

European Hornbeam

Carpinus betulus

HT 40–60'

This nonnative tree is much larger than American Hornbeam. It is pyramidal to rounded in shape and often planted in tall hedges. **ID TIP:** The bark is steel gray. Leaves similar to American; leaflike bracts attached to fruits are narrower. The long leaf buds hug the twig (they do this less so in American Hornbeam). **HABITAT AND RANGE:** Introduced in North America; planted in hedgerows. Native from Europe to southwestern Asia.

BIRCH FAMILY   BETULACEAE

fruit cluster

Eastern Hophornbeam

Ostrya virginiana

ALSO CALLED American Hophornbeam, Ironwood

HT 30–50' **DIA** 9–15"

| BIRCH FAMILY | BETULACEAE |

Small tree. Trunk sometimes divided 2–3' above ground into several stout, upright limbs; narrow, rounded crown. In older trees, trunks become sinewy, gnarled, knobby, twisted, and buttressed. Bark light brown, slightly tinged with red; thin; covered by fine, loose, rectangular, flaky scales. **ID TIP:** The bladderlike seed husks are distinctive (resembling hops, the fruit of hop-vine). The bark is rough and scaly.

HABITAT: Limestone woods, dry gravelly slopes, ridges; understory of upland forests. Elevation to 1,000'.

NOTES: This is a slow-growing tree, very wind-firm, and fairly pest-free (unusual for a tree with a deep taproot). Two western species, **Knowlton's Hophornbeam** (*O. knowltonii*) and **Chisos Hophornbeam** (*O. chisosensis*), occur in moist canyons of the Southwest and have smaller leaves (1–2½" long) than Eastern Hophornbeam. In Knowlton's, the leaves are yellow-green and less pointed at the tip; in Chisos, dark green and long-pointed. Knowlton's occurs in southeastern Utah, northern Arizona (especially Grand Canyon), southeastern New Mexico and south into Texas, at 3,900–7,900'. Chisos is confined to Big Bend National Park, Texas, at 4,900–7,500'.

LEAF 2–5" long. Ovate or elliptic, with usually abruptly pointed tip; rounded at base; double-toothed margins; prominent straight side veins, some forking at ends. Dull yellow-green above; lighter with tufts of hairs in vein angles beneath. Autumn color yellow. Leafstalk short, hairy. Twig green, turning orange or reddish brown, flexible, shiny; finely silky when young. **FLOWER** Female: in ½–¾" long, hanging catkin; reddish green; early spring. Male: in 1½–2½" long, slender, hairy, hanging catkin; greenish to reddish brown; in clusters of 1–3. Early spring. **FRUIT** ¼" long nutlet; flat, ribbed; brown. Each nutlet is contained in an ovoid, papery, cream-colored, inflated husk. Husks hang in 1½–2" long cluster. Late summer.

male catkins

fruit cluster

Knowlton's Hophornbeam

Paper Birch

Betula papyrifera

ALSO CALLED White Birch, Canoe Birch, Silver Birch

HT 50–70' **DIA** 1–2'

| BIRCH FAMILY | BETULACEAE |

Medium-sized tree. One to several slender, straight trunks; narrow to broad crown; branches upraised in youth, often becoming horizontal or drooping in age. Bark white, papery; older trees have rough black bark near base, large burls, and sometimes stilt roots. **ID TIP:** Paper Birch is named for its white, papery bark, which peels and sheds in narrow bands to reveal orange or pink inner bark; blackish, chevron-shaped branch scars mark the trunk.

HABITAT: Young forests; cutover and burned lands; rocky slopes at the base of cliffs. Elevation 1,000–3,000'.

NOTES: Paper Birch is one of the most widely distributed trees of North America, ranging from the Atlantic Ocean to the Pacific and north to the tree line. Both Paper Birch and European White Birch are cultivated for their attractive bark and foliage.

LEAF 2–5" long. Ovate, with pointed tip; coarsely double-toothed margins; 5–9 pairs of side veins. Dull, dark green above; light yellow-green and finely hairy on veins beneath. Autumn color bright yellow. Twig reddish brown. **FLOWER** Male: in 1½–4" long, drooping catkin; yellowish; in clusters of 2 or 3; early spring, before leaves. Female: in 1–1½" long, upright catkin; pale green; often in pairs; early spring. **FRUIT** In 1–2" long, cylindrical, drooping, conelike cluster; brownish; composed of numerous scales, each containing a tiny seed. Late autumn.

male catkins

developing fruit clusters

Gray Birch

Betula populifolia

ALSO CALLED Old-field Birch, Poplar Birch

HT 20–30' **DIA** 6–12"

Small tree; sometimes shrubby. One to several slender trunks; narrow, conical crown. **ID TIP:** Gray Birch bark is dull white, but not papery or peeling; it becomes rough and gray with age, especially near the base. Male flower catkins are borne singly. As in aspens, the leafstalks are flattened, letting leaves droop and flutter in the wind.

HABITAT: Dry forests, slopes, old fields. Elevation 300–2,000'.

NOTES: Gray Birch grows well on disturbed, barren, or polluted sites where many other trees would not survive. It has been planted to revegetate mine spoils (sites where waste materials have been brought up from excavation dredging) and other disturbed areas. A soil stabilizer, it allows other trees to become established. The species name, *populifolia*, refers to the resemblance of its leaves to those of the poplars.

BIRCH FAMILY   BETULACEAE

LEAF 2–3" long. Triangular, with very long-pointed tip; coarsely double-toothed margins; 5–19 pairs of side veins. Glossy, dark green above; paler beneath. Autumn color pale yellow. Leaf, leafstalk, and twig all rough from tiny gland dots. Leafstalk reddish. Twig reddish brown or gray. **FLOWER** Male: in 2–3½" long, drooping catkin; yellowish; usually single; early spring, before leaves. Female: in ½" long, more or less upright catkin; greenish; often in pairs; early spring. **FRUIT** In ¾–1" long, cylindrical, more or less drooping, conelike cluster; brownish; densely hairy (sparsely hairy in European White Birch). Early autumn.

developing fruit clusters

European White Birch

Betula pendula
ALSO CALLED Weeping Birch,
European Silver Birch
HT 40–80'   DIA 1½–2'

Small to medium-sized tree. Straight
trunk; elliptic, rounded, or pyramidal
crown. Bark chalky white, peeling and
curling (but less strongly than in Paper
Birch); on older trees, blackens near base
and develops deep, vertical fissures.
ID TIP: Pendulous branchlets and
triangular leaf, combined with chalky
white, somewhat peeling bark, distinguish
this birch. Autumn color arrives later
and lasts longer than in native species.
Paper Birch has a longer leaf with a more
rounded base.

HABITAT AND RANGE: Introduced in North
America; naturalized in the Northeast and
Northwest, to 1,100'. Native to Europe,
Asia, and northern Africa.

NOTES: European White Birch has one of
the widest natural distributions of any
broadleaf tree in the world, extending
from the Atlantic coast of Europe to the
Pacific coast of Asia and north to the
tundra line.

BIRCH FAMILY   BETULACEAE

LEAF 1–3" long. Ovate to triangular, with long-pointed
tip; base pointed to almost straight; margins coarsely
double-toothed. Autumn color yellow or yellow-green.
Twig reddish. FLOWER Male: in 1–4" long, drooping catkin;
yellowish; usually in clusters of 2–4; early spring, before
leaves. Female: in 1" long, upright catkin; green; often in
pairs; early spring. FRUIT ¾–1¼" long, cylindrical, upright
to drooping, conelike cluster; brown; sparsely hairy (densely
hairy in Gray Birch). Late summer–early autumn.

fruit cluster

Virginia Roundleaf Birch

Betula uber
HT to 30'   DIA to 4"

This small, extremely rare birch was first
recorded in 1914, in a single grove in
southwestern Virginia. The grove could
not be relocated, and the species was
presumed extinct. In 1975, a dozen or so
trees were found, only to be vandalized
later. Conservationists created 10 secret
new groves apart from the original, and
the species survives today. It is classified
as threatened.   ID TIP: The usually round
or oval leaf has a rounder tip and fewer
veins than most other birches.

BIRCH FAMILY   BETULACEAE

LEAF 1½–2½" long; oval to circular, with coarsely toothed
margins; 3–6 veins on each side. BARK Glossy, gray, with
horizontal lines. Twig has wintergreen aroma when broken.

River Birch

Betula nigra

ALSO CALLED Red Birch

HT 40–80'   **DIA** 1–2½'

BIRCH FAMILY	BETULACEAE

Small to medium-sized tree. One to several trunks; low-forking limbs form a broad, rounded crown; can be thicket-forming. Bark papery, scaly, rust- to salmon-colored, peeling in horizontal strips, revealing creamy or pinkish inner bark. On older trees, bark is thick, brown to black, very shaggy, platy, or furrowed. **ID TIP:** River Birch has rust- to salmon-colored bark. It is the only birch that fruits in the spring.

HABITAT: Stream banks, swamps, floodplains. Elevation to 1,000'.

NOTES: River Birch is the most wetland-adapted birch; it is also somewhat drought-tolerant, and more heat- and disease-resistant than other birches, though not especially resistant to floods. Planted for erosion control, to revegetate strip-mining sites, and as a landscaping tree in the South.

LEAF 1½–3" long. Ovate to elliptic, with pointed tip; broad, pointed base; margins coarsely double-toothed, except near base; 5–12 pairs of veins. Glossy, dark green above; whitish and more or less hairy beneath, especially on veins. Autumn color dull yellow; short-lasting. Leafstalk hairy. Twig hairy in first spring, becoming hairless, shiny; reddish brown by second year; begins to peel in third year; lacks wintergreen scent. **FLOWER** Male: in 2–3" long, drooping catkin; yellowish; in clusters of 2 or 3; early spring, before leaves. Female: in ¼–½" long, upright catkin; pale green; often in pairs; early spring. **FRUIT** In 1–1½" long, stout, cylindrical, upright, conelike cluster; brownish; hairy. Late spring–late summer.

fruit cluster

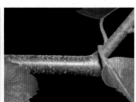

mature bark

exposed inner bark

older bark

Sweet Birch

Betula lenta
ALSO CALLED Cherry Birch,
Black Birch
HT 50–80' **DIA** 1–2½'

Medium-sized tree. Straight trunk; broad, dense, rounded crown (narrower and less dense in forest-grown trees). Bark smooth, glossy, red-brown, and papery or peeling when young; closely resembles young bark of Black Cherry; matures to dull gray to nearly black; in older trees, forms small, square, scaly plates. **ID TIP:** Sweet Birch has strongly aromatic twigs and branchlets, and in summer has hairless twigs. The leaves are very similar to those of Yellow Birch, which usually occurs at higher elevations on wetter sites.

HABITAT: Moist, often rocky forests. Elevation 300–5,000', usually 2,000–4,000' in Appalachians.

NOTES: Sweet Birch twigs and bark have a strong wintergreen aroma and taste.

BIRCH FAMILY   BETULACEAE

LEAF 3–5" long. Ovate to elliptic, with pointed tip; indented at base; finely double-toothed margins; 12–18 pairs of veins. Shiny, dark green above; light yellow-green and finely hairy on veins beneath. Autumn color bright yellow. Winter bud covered with distinct green and brown scales. Twig hairless by summer; strongly wintergreen-scented when cut. **FLOWER** Male: in 2–3" long, drooping catkin; bright reddish brown; in clusters of 3–8; early spring, before leaves. Female: in ½–1" long, upright catkin; pale green; often in pairs; early spring. **FRUIT** In ¾–1½" long, ovoid, upright, conelike cluster; brown; hairless. Autumn.

developing fruit clusters

mature fruit clusters

young bark

mature bark

Yellow Birch

Betula alleghaniensis
ALSO CALLED Swamp Birch
HT 70–100'   **DIA** 1½–2½'

Medium-sized to large tree. Straight or leaning trunk; narrow, rounded crown. Bark golden and peeling; older trees have duller bark and less peeling, and crack into large, dull gray, soft, often loose plates, with few horizontal lines. **ID TIP:** This birch has distinctive, golden or silvery-gray young bark that peels horizontally into thin, filmy strips.

HABITAT: Cool, moist forests, mountain streams, ravines. Elevation to 2,500' in North, 3,000–6,600' southward.

NOTES: Yellow Birch can attain the greatest age and size of North American birches, assuming bizarre shapes in its old-growth stage, with stilt roots, corkscrew trunks, and giant burls. Stilt roots result from germinating and growing on a nurse log or stump, which eventually rots away. Commercial wintergreen flavoring is extracted from the bark and twigs of this birch and Sweet Birch. (True oil of wintergreen comes from a small shrub called wintergreen or teaberry.)

LEAF 3–5" long. Ovate to elliptic, with pointed tip; rounded to indented at base; finely double-toothed margins; 12–18 pairs of veins. Shiny, green above; light yellow-green and finely hairy on veins beneath. Young leaf bronze-green, with long hairs beneath. Autumn color bright yellow. Twig hairy and green in spring, reddish and less hairy in summer through first winter; mildly wintergreen-scented when cut. **FLOWER** Male: in 1–4" long, drooping catkin; yellowish; in clusters of 5–8; early spring, before leaves. Female: in ⅝–¾" long, upright catkin; red-tinged green; hairy; often in pairs; early spring. **FRUIT** In ¾–1¼" long, ovoid, upright, conelike cluster; brown; hairy. Late autumn.

male catkins in spring

male catkins in winter

older bark

mature bark

fruit clusters

Water Birch

Betula occidentalis

ALSO CALLED Rocky Mountain Birch, Western Birch

HT 10–25' **DIA** 4–12"

Small tree or, more often, large shrub. Trunks often multistemmed; narrow, rounded crown; often forms large thickets. Bark shiny, reddish or purplish brown (nearly black when young); may begin to curl, but does not peel. **ID TIP:** The bark remains glossy into maturity. This is the only tree-sized birch in most of the western United States. It has small leaves, with fewer pairs of side veins than other birches. As in aspens, the leaves flutter in the wind.

HABITAT: Streamsides, mountain canyons, open woods. Elevation 300–9,800'.

BIRCH FAMILY　　　　　　**BETULACEAE**

fruit clusters

LEAF ¾–2" long. Ovate, with blunt or pointed tip; single- or more often, double-toothed margins; 4 or 5 pairs of veins. Shiny, dark green above; paler beneath. Leaf, leafstalk, and twig are all rough, with tiny gland dots. Twig often hairy, especially in spring; lacks wintergreen scent. **FLOWER** Male: in 2–2½" long, drooping catkin; yellowish; in clusters of 2–4; early spring, before leaves. Female: in ¾" long, upright catkin; pale green; often in pairs; early spring. **FRUIT** In 1–1¼" long, cylindrical, drooping, conelike cluster; brownish; hairy. Late summer.

mature and developing fruit clusters

Red Alder

Alnus rubra

ALSO CALLED Oregon Alder, Western Alder

HT 30–80' **DIA** 1–2½'

BIRCH FAMILY

BETULACEAE

fruit clusters

Small to medium-sized tree. Straight or leaning trunk; narrow, pyramidal crown of slender branches. Bark thin, smooth, patchy light gray to whitish; becoming somewhat scaly and warty on older trunks. **ID TIP:** The leaf undersides are gray-green with a rusty tinge. Unlike other alders, Red Alder may have leaf edges slightly rolled under. The twigs, even when young, are hairless or only sparsely hairy.

HABITAT: Lowlands, streamsides; often takes over clear-cuts. Elevation to 1,000'.

NOTES: Red Alder is a fast-growing, short-lived tree. Patches of variable white to gray on bark are crust lichens, which typically envelop the tree. Once considered a forest weed, Red Alder now is understood to be an important part of the ecosystem. An association of bacteria and the roots of this species fixes atmospheric nitrogen, making it available to other plants in the soil.

LEAF 3–6" long. Ovate to elliptic; coarsely double-toothed margins; edges minutely rolled under; main veins recessed on upper surface. Dull dark green above; gray-green and rusty-hairy beneath. Twig and leafstalk mostly hairless. **FLOWER** Male: in 4–6" long catkin; orange-yellow; drooping on red stem; early spring, before leaves. Female: in scaly, ⅜–½" long catkin; dark red; early spring. **FRUIT** In ½–1" long, ovoid, woody, conelike cluster; brown; composed of hard, blackish scales, each with 2 tiny, winged seeds. On short stalk. Late summer; often persists through winter.

White Alder

Alnus rhombifolia

ALSO CALLED California Alder, Sierra Alder

HT 50–80' **DIA** 1–2½'

Medium-sized tree. Tall, straight trunk; rounded crown of slender branches. Bark thin, smooth, light gray; developing flat, scaly ridges and fissures; on oldest trees, trunks develop reddish plates. **ID TIP:** Fuzzy twigs and leafstalks combined with a tall, single-stemmed form distinguish this western alder. The main veins of the leaf are not recessed, as in Red Alder. (Red Alder's twigs and leafstalks are hairless or only sparsely hairy in all stages of growth.) White Alder is southern California's only native alder species.

HABITAT: Stream banks and valleys in coniferous woodlands or chaparral. Elevation 300–7,900'.

NOTES: The southwestern **Arizona Alder** (*A. oblongifolia*) is a small alder (to 30') found in desert canyons and along mountain streams, at 3,300–7,500'. The leaves are 1½–3¼" long, narrowly elliptic, with double-toothed margins; the bark is red-tinged; the fruit cluster is ½–¾" long.

BIRCH FAMILY · BETULACEAE

fruit clusters

LEAF 2–4" long. Narrowly to broadly elliptic, with somewhat rounded tip; margins usually finely toothed (not double-toothed); main veins not recessed. Dark green, not shiny above; light yellow-green beneath. Twig and leafstalk minutely and finely gray-hairy when young, becoming hairless. **FLOWER** Male: in 1½–5" long, drooping catkin; golden; winter to early spring, before leaves. Female: in ½" long catkin; dark red; early spring. **FRUIT** In ½" long, ovoid, woody, conelike cluster; brown; composed of hard, blackish scales, each with 2 tiny, flat, winged seeds. On short stalk. Late summer, remains attached through winter.

male catkins

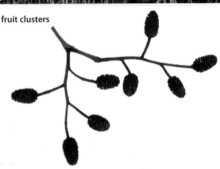

fruit clusters

Thinleaf Alder

Alnus incana ssp. *tenuifolia*
ALSO CALLED Mountain Alder
HT to 35' **DIA** 6–8"

Large shrub or small, bushy tree. **ID TIP:** The leaves are thicker, with rounder teeth, than in Sitka Alder. Thinleaf Alder's eastern relative, Speckled Alder (p. 412), lacks rusty-hairy leaf undersides.

HABITAT: Wet sites; common on Rocky Mountain streamsides. Elevation 300–9,800'.

developing fruit clusters

BIRCH FAMILY   **BETULACEAE**

LEAF 2–4" long. Ovate to elliptic; margins double-toothed, teeth rounded. Dull (not shiny) above; rusty-hairy beneath and on young twig. **FRUIT** In ⅓–½" long, conelike cluster (smaller than in Sitka Alder), on short stalk.

fruit clusters

Sitka Alder

Alnus viridis ssp. *sinuata*
ALSO CALLED Wavyleaf Alder
HT 16–30' **DIA** 8"

A shrub or, occasionally, a small tree. Sitka Alder forms impenetrable thickets that help stabilize and fertilize soils. **ID TIP:** Leaves are thin, yellow-green, double-toothed, with pointed teeth.

HABITAT: Stream banks and moist slopes. Elevation to 8,000'.

BIRCH FAMILY   **BETULACEAE**

mature and developing fruit clusters

LEAF 1½–5" long. Ovate; thin, almost translucent; margins coarsely double-toothed, teeth pointed. Shiny, speckled yellow-green on both sides (unlike other alders). Twig orange-brown. **FRUIT** In ½–1" long conelike cluster, on stalk that is often longer than cluster.

Eastern Alders
Alnus species

Three species of alder are native to eastern North America. All are small trees or shrubs, sometimes thicket-forming.

Smooth Alder
Alnus serrulata
ALSO CALLED Hazel Alder
HT 5–20' **DIA** to 4"

Small tree or large shrub, often multistemmed. **ID TIP:** Smooth Alder is similar to Speckled Alder but occurs farther south; it has obovate leaves and fruits that are held erect, not hanging as in Speckled. **HABITAT:** Along streams and swamps. Elevation to 2,600'.

Speckled Alder
Alnus incana ssp. *rugosa*
HT 5–20' **DIA** to 4"

Shrub, or sometimes a small tree; thicket-forming. **ID TIP:** Speckled Alder is an eastern relative of Thinleaf Alder. Leaves are broader near the base than those of Smooth Alder, which are broader toward the tip. Fruit clusters hang downward. **HABITAT:** Stream banks and swamp edges. Elevation to 2,600'.

Seaside Alder
Alnus maritima
HT to 30'

Small tree or shrub limited to 2 widely separated localities (probably relicts of wider, pre–Ice Age distribution). **ID TIP:** The narrow leaves are shallowly toothed and hairless. Seaside Alder flowers in autumn (unlike all other alders). **HABITAT AND RANGE:** Stream and pond banks; occasionally near the coast. Southern Delaware and eastern Maryland, near sea level; Red River, Oklahoma, to 300' elevation.

BIRCH FAMILY | BETULACEAE

Smooth Alder

SMOOTH ALDER LEAF 2–5" long. Usually obovate; single- or double-toothed margins, teeth fine; hairless or hairy beneath. Young leaves are resinous; young twig and bud purplish, finely gray-hairy. **FRUIT** In ⅓–½" long, erect, conelike clusters.

Smooth Alder fruit clusters

SPECKLED ALDER LEAF 2–5" long, ovate to elliptic; margins coarsely single- or double-toothed; whitish green and hairless to slightly hairy on veins beneath. **FRUIT** In ⅓–½" long, hanging, conelike clusters.

SEASIDE ALDER LEAF 1¾–3½" long. Narrowly elliptic to obovate; widely spaced teeth along margins.

A. serrulata | *A. incana* ssp. *rugosa*

Black Alder

Alnus glutinosa
ALSO CALLED European Alder
HT 50–70'   **DIA** 1–2'

Medium-sized tree. Single trunk or multistemmed; crown narrow. Bark dark brown, smooth, with horizontal lines, becoming fissured with age. **ID TIP:** The leaves are circular to obovate, unlike those of other alders.

HABITAT AND RANGE: Introduced in North America; planted in public gardens and parks, along streams and swampy areas; escaping and naturalizing in the Northeast. Native to Europe, Asia, and northern Africa.

LEAF 1–3" long. Circular to obovate; coarsely double-toothed margins. Slightly shiny, dark green above; paler, with hairy veins beneath. **FRUIT** ½–1" long; ovoid to round, conelike cluster, on long stalk.

BIRCH FAMILY   BETULACEAE

fruit cluster

Beech Family

The beech family (Fagaceae) includes beeches (*Fagus*), chestnuts and chinkapins (*Castanea* and *Chrysolepis*), tanoaks (*Lithocarpus*), and oaks (*Quercus*). The oak genus is covered in depth on page 420.

Species in this family can be shrubs or trees, with deciduous or evergreen leaves. Flowers are tiny and lack petals; male and female flowers are borne in separate structures on the same tree.

In beeches, female flowers are reddish green, borne singly or in pairs on a short, stout, hairy stalk; male flowers are in a yellowish, rounded cluster, hanging on a slender stalk. One to three angular, oily nuts are enclosed in a bristly, egg-shaped, short-stalked husk that splits along four seams when ripe.

In chinkapins and chestnuts, the long male catkins are at leaf axils near twig tips; they often have a fishy odor. Female flowers are much smaller and usually borne at the base of the male catkins. One to three glossy brown, rounded nuts are enclosed in a round, burlike husk that is covered with long, sharp prickles.

Tanoak is the only North American species of the mostly Asian genus *Lithocarpus*. The flowers are similar to those of the chestnuts, but the fruit is an acorn, an oblong, pointed nut that sits in a shallow, bristly, cuplike structure.

Species in the beech family produce nuts that are partially or wholly enclosed in a cupule: either a burlike husk, as in beeches, chinkapins, and chestnuts (left), or an acorn cup, as in Tanoak and oaks (right).

American Beech

Fagus grandifolia

HT 50–80'   **DIA** 1½–2½'

Medium-sized tree with deciduous, simple leaves. Tall trunk (stout when open-grown); dense, narrow, rounded crown. Stems may encircle tree, forming thicket. **ID TIP:** The bark is smooth and light gray. The leaves are dark green, ovate or elliptic, with a pointed tip; the side veins are parallel to each other and each ends at the margin with a distinctly pointed tooth.

HABITAT: Forests, moist slopes, ravines, and moist hammocks, mostly in loamy or clay soils. Elevation to 3,300'.

NOTES: American Beech is a common forest tree in eastern North America. It produces large crops of fruits every 2 to 8 years, though less often in southern parts of its range. This beech is susceptible to early frost that may retard development, which partly explains poor fruit production in some years. In the years it produces a good fruit crop, it is a major source of food for birds and small mammals, but animals cannot rely solely on this species. It was once a major food source for the now-extinct passenger pigeon.

LEAF 3–6" long. Elliptic to broadly elliptic; pointed (often abrupt) tip; coarse, widely spaced, pointed teeth along margins; 9–14 pairs of side veins. Glossy, dark green above; paler, often with silky tufts of hairs on veins beneath. Autumn color gold to brown. Leaves may persist into winter. Leafstalk short, hairy. Twig glossy, reddish. Winter bud glossy, slender, sharp-pointed. **FLOWER** Female: ¼" long, hairy, reddish green. Male: in ¾–1" long, rounded, hanging cluster, on 1½–2" long stalk. Early spring. **FRUIT** ½–¾" long, ovoid, pointed, burlike husk, covered with short, stiff bristles; dark orange-green to brown; short-stalked. Splits along 4 seams when ripe; contains 1–3 nuts. Nut ⅜–½" long, unevenly angular, with slightly winged margins; oily; yellowish to reddish brown. Autumn.

male flower cluster

European Beech

Fagus sylvatica

ALSO CALLED Common Beech

HT 50–70' **DIA** 2–4'

| BEECH FAMILY | FAGACEAE |

Medium-sized tree with deciduous, simple leaves. Short, stocky trunk; dense, broad, rounded or pyramidal crown; low-hanging branches. Older trees have knots and burls on trunk, and a domed crown with heavy, twisted boughs descending to the ground. Bark silver-gray to dark gray-blue (usually darker than in American Beech). **ID TIP:** The leaves are similar to those of American Beech, but the margin teeth are bluntly rounded rather than pointed.

HABITAT AND RANGE: Introduced in North America; planted in parks and landscapes. Native to Europe.

NOTES: European Beech was introduced to North America in the late 1600s. Massive specimens may be seen in parks and estates. There are about 20 horticultural varieties of European Beech, some of which developed naturally. The striking **Copper Beech** has reddish purple foliage that turns blackish purple by summer. **Weeping Beech** has a graceful form at maturity, with pendant branches that reach from the crown to the ground.

LEAF 2–4" long. Broadly elliptic, with pointed tip; margins bear short, blunt, widely spaced teeth, and sometimes appear wavy; 5–9 pairs of side veins. Glossy, dark green above; paler, often with long hairs beneath (silky-hairy when young). Autumn color golden yellow, reddish bronze, rich orange-brown. Leaves persist through winter. Leafstalk short, hairy. Twig light brown, turning darker. Winter bud very slender, glossy, very sharp-pointed. **FLOWER** Female cluster very small; male cluster hangs on shorter stalk than in American Beech. **FRUIT** 1" long, ovoid, burlike husk, covered with short, soft bristles; similar to American Beech. Each nut ⅝" long, angular, often with concave sides; oily; deep brown. Autumn.

Weeping Beech

Copper Beech

European Beech

American Chestnut

Castanea dentata

HT 10–30' **DIA** 4–12"

Small tree or large shrub with deciduous, simple leaves. Slender trunk, or multistemmed; dense, narrow, rounded crown. Once occurred as a large tree with a massive trunk and a broad, rounded or domed crown. **ID TIP:** The leaves are generally longer than 6", coarsely toothed, and bristle-tipped.

HABITAT: Rich, mixed deciduous forests and well-drained mountain slopes. Elevation to 3,900'.

NOTES: American Chestnut was North America's largest broadleaf tree and occurred throughout eastern forests—until chestnut blight arrived in 1904 and killed nearly every tree. The species is now rare. Blight-infested trees have split bark showing orange fungus. Original old-growth root stock still survives, sending up sprouts from stumps but producing only small trunks that rarely exceed 15'. Mature chestnuts have been found in Roosevelt State Park, Georgia, that are seemingly resistant to the blight. The American Chestnut Foundation is exploring the viability of using genetic material from these trees to reestablish the grand American Chestnut and save the species from extinction.

BEECH FAMILY	FAGACEAE

LEAF 5–9" long. Narrowly elliptic, with pointed tip ending in a bristle; 12–20 pairs of straight side veins, parallel to each other and each ending in a curved, bristle-tipped tooth at margin. Glossy, yellow-green above; pale green, slightly hairy along midvein beneath. Autumn color yellow. Leafstalk short. **FLOWER** Male: in 6–8" long, upright, creamy white catkin; on stout stalk at leaf base; fishy odor. Female: in ⅜" long catkin, at base of male catkin. Early summer. **FRUIT** 2–2½" long, round, burlike husk, with very sharp, stout, ½" prickles; contains 2 or 3 nuts. Nut ½–1" long, broadly rounded, flattened on one side; glossy, dark brown. Autumn. Fruits are rarely seen; nuts are almost always shriveled or sterile.

male catkins

Chinkapin

Castanea pumila

ALSO CALLED Allegheny Chinkapin, Chinquapin

HT 10–30'   **DIA** 6–18"

BEECH FAMILY   FAGACEAE

Small tree or multistemmed, thicket-forming shrub with deciduous, simple leaves. Short trunk and rounded crown. **ID TIP:** Leaves are smaller than in American Chestnut, longer than in Ozark Chinkapin, and white-downy beneath.

HABITAT: Sand ridges and other dry, well-drained sites; sometimes in dry to moist, mixed hardwood forests. Elevation to 3,300'.

NOTES: Ozark Chinkapin (*C. ozarkensis*) occurs in the deciduous forests of the Ozarks, at 500–2,000'. It has a shorter leaf than Chinkapin, with a distinctly woolly underside. It can reach 20–50' in height, though the largest trees were destroyed by chestnut blight.

LEAF 3–6" long. Narrowly elliptic, with pointed tip; 13–18 straight side veins, parallel to each other and each ending in a large, curved, bristle-tipped tooth at margin. Yellow-green above; white-downy beneath. Autumn color yellow. Leafstalk short, thick, hairy, flat. Twig white- or grayish-woolly when young, becoming orange-brown and hairless. **FLOWER** Male: similar to American Chestnut, in 4–6" long catkin. Female: ⅛" long, often at base of male catkin, sometimes in inconspicuous catkins in axils of developing leaves at branch tips. Late spring–early summer. **FRUIT** ¾–1¼" long, round, burlike husk, with sharp, hairy prickles; contains 1 nut. Nut ¾" long, rounded, glossy, dark brown, with silky hairs near tip. Autumn.

Chinese Chestnut

Castanea mollissima

HT to 30'

BEECH FAMILY   **FAGACEAE**

Small tree with deciduous, simple leaves. Straight trunk; rounded crown of broad, spreading branches; nearly as wide as tall. Bark dark grayish brown, furrowed. **ID TIP:** Similar to American Chestnut; leaves have less strongly curved teeth than in American Chestnut. **HABITAT AND RANGE:** Introduced in North America; occasionally naturalizes. Native to Asia.

LEAF 4–8" long. Elliptic; many side veins, each ending in tooth at margin. **FRUIT** 2–3" wide; prickly husk; contains 2 or 3 nuts, each 1" wide, brown. Autumn.

Giant Golden Chinkapin

Chrysolepis chrysophylla
ALSO CALLED Giant Chinquapin,
Goldenleaf Chestnut
HT 50–100' **DIA** 1–3½'

BEECH FAMILY   FAGACEAE

Medium-sized to large tree with
evergreen, simple leaves. Tall, stout, often
fluted or grooved trunk; dense, conical
or broad, rounded crown; sometimes
shrubby at high elevations or on arid
sites. **ID TIP:** The leaf underside, leafstalk,
new twig, twig pith, female flower, and
fruit are all golden in color. Leaves are
lance-shaped or narrowly elliptic and
have untoothed margins.

leaf underside

HABITAT: Mountains,
canyons, in evergreen
forests, often under
Redwoods. Elevation
to 6,600'.

NOTES: Though
closely related to
the chestnuts, Giant
Golden Chinkapin
was not affected
by chestnut blight; it occurs scattered
throughout forests of the Pacific coast.
The seeds are eaten by chipmunks
and squirrels, but are not produced in
abundance and therefore are not a major
wildlife food. The tree sprouts vigorously
after fire and is drought-tolerant. It is
planted to stabilize soils after fire or
erosion. The catkins have an unpleasant,
fishy odor that attracts midges for
pollination.

LEAF 2–6" long. Lance-shaped to narrowly elliptic, with
pointed tip; margins untoothed, slightly wavy; generally
flat (usually folded upward along midvein in shrub form).
Leathery. Shiny, dark green above; covered with golden,
scalelike hairs beneath. Leafstalk golden-hairy, grooved.
Twig has golden scales when young, turns reddish brown;
pith yellow, star-shaped in cross section. **FLOWER** Male:
in 1–3" long, nearly erect, creamy white catkin; at base of
leaves near end of twig. Female: tiny; dull yellow; at base
of male catkin. Fishy odor. Early summer. **FRUIT** 1–1½"
long, burlike, with ½" long, slender, stiff prickles; golden;
contains 1–3 nuts. Nut ½" long, 3-sided or rounded in cross
section; glossy, brown (sometimes purplish red); resembles
a hazelnut. Single or in clusters. Autumn; ripens in 2 years.

male catkins

fruit

Tanoak

Lithocarpus densiflorus
ALSO CALLED Tanbark Oak
HT 60–80'   **DIA** 1–3'

Medium-sized tree with evergreen, simple leaves. Forest-grown: tall, stout trunk; narrow, pyramidal crown. Open-grown: short trunk or sometimes multistemmed; dense, broad, symmetrical, rounded crown. Shrubby under deep shade, in chaparral, or on harsh sites. **ID TIP:** Tanoak has rock-hard, oaklike acorns with bristly cups; chestnutlike flowers; and glossy leaves with whitish, waxy-coated, woolly undersides.

BEECH FAMILY	FAGACEAE

LEAF 2–5" long. Elliptic; margins untoothed or with 1 tooth per side vein; edges often curled under. Stiff and leathery. Shiny, dark green, with thin coat of wool above; whitish, waxy-coated, with dense coat of wool beneath; wool may eventually rub off. Twig and winter bud stout, yellowish-hairy. **FLOWER** Male: ⅛" long, with numerous protruding stamens; in 2–4" long, narrow, upright catkin. Female: in larger, green catkin, single or in pairs near the base of some male catkins. Early spring; sometimes again in autumn. **FRUIT** Acorn ¾–1" long, ½–1" wide. Nut ovoid, usually pointed; glossy, maturing to yellow-brown; in a shallow cup densely covered with bristles; densely rusty-hairy inside of cup. Borne singly or in pairs. Autumn.

HABITAT: Understory of Redwoods; mountain forests; chaparral. Elevation to 7,200'.

NOTES: Tanoak was the first-detected host of sudden oak death in 1995, and remains one of the main hosts, along with several species of live oaks. The pathogen, *Phytophthora ramorum*, may prove to be either a fungus or an alga. There is no known way of killing this pathogen without killing the host. It infects an ever-increasing range of hosts, from ferns to conifers, and threatens to become one of the most disastrous plant pathogens in history. Tanoak resembles chestnuts and chinkapins in flower characteristics, but has acorns like the oaks. A prolific acorn producer, it provides vital food for flying squirrels, redwood chickarees (Douglas' squirrels), band-tailed pigeons, black bear, deer, woodpeckers, and other wildlife.

male catkins

Oaks

Ninety species of oaks (genus *Quercus,* family Fagaceae) are native or naturalized in North America; most achieve tree stature at maturity. The majority of oaks are placed in two groups: white oaks and red oaks. Red and white oaks differ in microscopic structures of the wood, characteristics of leaves and acorns, and in how long it takes the acorns to reach maturity. In general, the heartwood and interior of the bark are reddish or orange in red oaks, tan or cream in white oaks (hence their names). A third group, golden oaks, includes four western species (one a shrub); all have prickly, unlobed, evergreen leaves, and their acorns have cups with woolly scales and mature in two years. "Golden" refers to the color of the hairs on the acorn cups of some species.

Oaks are predominantly wind-pollinated. Chinkapin Oak male catkins are pictured at left, Water Oak female flowers at right.

Oaks produce male and female flowers on the same tree. Individual flowers are tiny and inconspicuous. Female flowers are borne singly or in compact, few-flowered, elongated clusters, mostly in the axils of developing leaves. Male flowers are borne in conspicuous, dangling catkins, usually near the tips of developing twigs. They mature before or with expansion of the new leaves, releasing large quantities of pollen in early spring. Hybrids within the red oak group and within the white oak group are common, resulting in individual trees with intermediate features.

The fruit of an oak tree is an acorn, composed of a rounded or oblong nut nested inside a scaly cup (cupule). Acorns of the white oak group typically mature in a single growing season. The scales of the cup of white oaks usually are prominently thickened at the base, the cup appearing rough. The inside wall of the acorn is smooth, lacking hairs, or minutely hairy near the base and tip. White oak nuts are sweet to the taste. Red oak nuts usually require two years to mature and have a bitter taste. The scales of the cup of red oaks usually are thin, the cup appearing smooth. The inside wall of the acorn is hairy, sometimes velvety. Trees that have

all acorns at a similar stage of growth and borne on new wood are probably white oaks. Trees with acorns at two growth stages borne on new and old wood are probably red oaks.

The leaf also offers clues to whether an oak tree is a red or a white oak. Most red oaks have slender bristles (awns) at the tips of the leaves and the main lobes. These bristles are often conspicuous, although in some species, such as Laurel, Darlington, and Shingle oaks, they are stubby and can be difficult to discern. The lobes and tips of white oak leaves are typically smooth and lack awns (but can be prickly). Leaf form and size in most oak species is quite variable even on the same tree, especially in young or heavily shaded trees. Relying solely on leaf form can lead to misidentification.

The wood of hardwood trees is composed of water-conducting tissues (vessels) that are essentially the remains of empty dead cells strung together end to end forming narrow pipelines. The vessels in the wood of red oaks are free of clogging structures (tyloses), allowing for the absorption of water and other liquids—hence the ability of red oak lumber to absorb stains and finishes easily. In white oaks, the vessels are clogged and impermeable when they no longer function in water conduction; this makes the wood good for watertight wine and liquor barrels.

EASTERN OAKS

Red Oaks: Leaves mostly unlobed
Arkansas Oak, *Quercus arkansana*, p. 432
Darlington Oak, *Quercus hemisphaerica*, p. 426
Shingle Oak, *Quercus imbricaria*, p. 428
Bluejack Oak, *Quercus incana*, p. 427
Florida Oak, *Quercus inopina*, p. 429
Laurel Oak, *Quercus laurifolia*, p. 426
Myrtle Oak, *Quercus myrtifolia*, p. 429
Water Oak, *Quercus nigra*, p. 425
Willow Oak, *Quercus phellos*, p. 427

Red Oaks: Leaves lobed
Scarlet Oak, *Quercus coccinea*, p. 437
Northern Pin Oak, *Quercus ellipsoidalis*, p. 436
Southern Red Oak, *Quercus falcata* , p. 439
Georgia Oak, *Quercus georgiana*, p. 438
Bear Oak, *Quercus ilicifolia*, p. 440
Turkey Oak, *Quercus laevis*, p. 440
Blackjack Oak, *Quercus marilandica*, p. 432
Cherrybark Oak, *Quercus pagoda*, p. 439
Pin Oak, *Quercus palustris*, p. 435
Northern Red Oak, *Quercus rubra*, p. 433
Shumard Oak, *Quercus shumardii*, p. 438
Texas Red Oak, *Quercus texana*, p. 436
Black Oak, *Quercus velutina*, p. 434

White Oaks: Leaves mostly unlobed
Chapman Oak, *Quercus chapmanii*, p. 429
Sand Live Oak, *Quercus geminata*, p. 431
Swamp Chestnut Oak, *Quercus michauxii*, p. 425
Chestnut Oak, *Quercus montana*, p. 424
Chinkapin Oak, *Quercus muehlenbergii*, p. 423
Oglethorpe Oak, *Quercus oglethorpensis*, p. 431
Dwarf Chinkapin Oak, *Quercus prinoides*, p. 422
Bastard Oak, *Quercus sinuata*, p. 441
Southern Live Oak, *Quercus virginiana*, p. 430

White Oaks: Leaves lobed
White Oak, *Quercus alba*, p. 443
Bastard White Oak, *Quercus austrina*, p. 442
Swamp White Oak, *Quercus bicolor*, p. 442
Overcup Oak, *Quercus lyrata*, p. 441
Burr Oak, *Quercus macrocarpa*, p. 444
Sand Post Oak, *Quercus margaretta*, p. 446
Bastard Oak, *Quercus sinuata*, p. 441
Post Oak, *Quercus stellata*, p. 445

WESTERN OAKS

Golden Oaks: Leaves unlobed, prickly
Canyon Live Oak, *Quercus chrysolepis*, p. 454
Palmer Oak, *Quercus palmeri*, p. 452
Channel Island Oak, *Quercus tomentella*, p. 457

Red Oaks: Leaves mostly unlobed
Coast Live Oak, *Quercus agrifolia*, p. 456
Emory Oak, *Quercus emoryi*, p. 452
Chisos Oak, *Quercus graciliformis*, p. 448
Silverleaf Oak, *Quercus hypoleucoides*, p. 453
Interior Live Oak, *Quercus wislizenii*, p. 455

Red Oaks: Leaves lobed
Graves Oak, *Quercus gravesii*, p. 448
California Black Oak, *Quercus kelloggii*, p. 457
Robust Oak, *Quercus robusta*, p. 448
Lateleaf Oak, *Quercus tardifolia*, p. 448

White Oaks: Leaves mostly unlobed
Arizona Oak, *Quercus arizonica*, p. 450
Engelmann Oak, *Quercus engelmannii*, p. 455
Gray Oak, *Quercus grisea*, p. 451
Mohr Oak, *Quercus mohriana*, p. 449
Mexican Blue Oak, *Quercus oblongifolia*, p. 449
Netleaf Oak, *Quercus rugosa*, p. 450
Toumey Oak, *Quercus toumeyi*, p. 451
Turbinella Oak, *Quercus turbinella*, p. 451

White Oaks: Leaves lobed
Blue Oak, *Quercus douglasii*, p. 460
Gambel Oak, *Quercus gambelii*, p. 447
Oregon White Oak, *Quercus garryana*, p. 459
Lacey Oak, *Quercus laceyi*, p. 448
Valley Oak, *Quercus lobata*, p. 458
Pungent Oak, *Quercus pungens*, p. 449

	RED OAKS	WHITE OAKS	GOLDEN OAKS
LEAF	Leaf unlobed or lobed; leaf tip and often lobes or teeth tipped with bristle (awn).	Leaf unlobed or lobed; margins may have prickly teeth but no awns.	Leaf never lobed; margins have prickly teeth (no awns); leaf pale beneath; evergreen.
ACORN	1st- and 2nd-year acorns on tree; cup looks smooth, scales thin, inner wall hairy.	All acorns 1st year; cup looks rough, scales thick at base, inner walls usually hairless.	1st- and 2nd-year acorns on tree; cup scales partly hidden by woolly, often golden hairs.
BARK	Bark smooth to deeply furrowed, not flaky or scaly; usually dark gray to blackish.	Bark smooth, flaky, or scaly (rarely furrowed); usually pale gray, may be whitish.	Bark smooth to scaly to furrowed; may be dark or pale gray.

Sawtooth Oak

Quercus acutissima

HT to 60'

| BEECH FAMILY | FAGACEAE |

Small to medium-sized tree with deciduous, simple leaves. Crown pyramidal when young, becoming broader and more rounded with maturity. **ID TIP:** A red oak. The general outline of the leaf is similar to that of American Chestnut and Chinkapin (pp. 416–417), but acorns distinguish the tree as an oak.

HABITAT AND RANGE: Introduced in North America; becoming invasive. Native to Asia.

LEAF 3–7½" long. Lance-shaped to narrowly ovate, with 12–16 pairs of straight side veins, parallel to each other and each terminating in a more or less blunt, bristle-tipped tooth. Shiny, dark green above; paler beneath. **ACORN** 1" long; nut about ⅔ enclosed by a cup of spreading, back-bent scales that give acorn a shaggy appearance. Autumn; ripens in 2 years.

Dwarf Chinkapin Oak

Quercus prinoides

ALSO CALLED Scrub Chestnut Oak

HT to 15'

| BEECH FAMILY | FAGACEAE |

This small tree or large shrub is sometimes considered a subspecies of Chinkapin Oak that is adapted to grow on sterile, acidic, sandy barrens. It attains tree size mostly in Missouri and Kansas. It produces an abundance of acorns. **ID TIP:** A white oak. Chinkapin Oak has larger, more pointed leaves that are rounded at the base; leaves of Dwarf Chinkapin Oak are pointed at the base.

HABITAT: Sterile, acidic, dry, sandy barrens. Elevation to about 1,600'.

LEAF 2½–5" long. Similar to Chinkapin Oak; 5–9 large, blunt teeth along each margin; fewer than 10 pairs of side veins (Chestnut Oak has more than 10). Green above; gray-downy beneath. **ACORN** ½–¾" long. Nut oblong to ovoid; brown; ¼–⅓ enclosed within a shallow to deep cup of hairy, gray scales. Autumn; ripens in 1 year.

Chinkapin Oak

Quercus muehlenbergii
ALSO CALLED Yellow Chestnut Oak,
Rock Oak
HT 20–80' **DIA** 1–2½'

BEECH FAMILY	FAGACEAE

Small to medium-sized tree with
deciduous, simple leaves. Tall trunk;
dense, small, narrow crown; short trunk
and broad crown on open sites; dwarfed
or shrubby on harsh sites. Bark thin, with
loose, light gray or silvery white flakes
or scales; resembles bark of White Oak
(p. 443). Bark of older trees develops
distinctive, checkered pattern of light
gray "knobs." **ID TIP:** A white oak. Leaves
resemble those of genus *Castanea* (pp.
416–417) and Chestnut Oak (p. 424) but
are pointed at the tip (Chestnut Oak
leaves are rounded) and lack bristles
(*Castanea* leaves have larger, pointed,
bristle-tipped teeth).

HABITAT: Calcium-rich and limestone
soils, fertile valleys; also harsh, rocky sites,
bluffs, canyons. Elevation to 7,500'.

NOTES: This wide-ranging species spans
2,300 miles in latitude, from Canada to
Mexico. The hard, strong, durable, very
heavy wood is used to make cabinets,
furniture, and railroad ties; once
commercially important, the species has
been overlogged. Some sources spell the
species' scientific name *muhlenbergii*.

LEAF 4–7" long. Obovate, with pointed tip; straight side
veins, parallel to each other; 8–16 curved, blunt or often
pointed teeth along each margin. Shiny, yellow-green,
with stout, yellow midvein above; pale or silvery white,
downy beneath. Autumn color deep yellow, orange, brown,
red. **ACORN** ½–1" long. Nut oblong; light chestnut brown;
⅓–½ enclosed within thin, deep cup of hairy, gray-brown
scales that form fringe at cup rim. Borne singly or in pairs,
stalkless or on short stalk. Autumn; ripens in 1 year.

Chestnut Oak

Quercus montana

ALSO CALLED Rock Chestnut Oak, Rock Oak, Mountain Chestnut Oak

HT 60–80'   **DIA** 1½–2½'

| BEECH FAMILY | FAGACEAE |

Medium-sized tree with deciduous, simple leaves. Tall (on fertile sites) or short, stout trunk; in mountains and on rocky sites, forks into large limbs not far above the ground. Compact, broad crown; dwarfed on exposed ridges, cliffs, summits. Bark reddish brown to nearly black, with distinctive, thick, chunky ridges that resemble corrugated cardboard; bark has deep grooves in northern part of its range; flaky, less prominent ridges in south. **ID TIP:** A white oak. The leaves resemble those of Chinkapin Oak and Dwarf Chinkapin Oak but are broader, and the teeth are more rounded. The thick, dark bark distinguishes it from Swamp Chestnut Oak and Chinkapin Oak.

HABITAT: Primarily in mountains and dry, rocky uplands. Elevation to 4,600'.

NOTES: Chestnut Oak sprouts easily and is planted to reclaim land disturbed by mines. The species is sometimes listed under the name *Q. prinus*, a name that has been applied to at least 2 species.

LEAF 4–9" long. Obovate; 8–16 large, rounded teeth along each margin; more than 10 pairs of side veins (Dwarf Chinkapin Oak has fewer than 10). Slightly shiny, yellow-green with stout, yellow midvein above; pale green and slightly hairy beneath. Autumn color dull yellow, orange, rusty brown. **ACORN** 1–1½" long. Nut round to ovoid; glossy, chestnut brown; ⅓–½ enclosed within deep, thin cup of warty, hairy, reddish brown scales. Cup is ¾–1" wide (1–1⅓" wide in Swamp Chestnut Oak). 1–3 acorns, on short stalk. Autumn; ripens in 1 year.

Swamp Chestnut Oak

Quercus michauxii

ALSO CALLED Cow Oak, Basket Oak

HT 60–80'   **DIA** 2–4'

BEECH FAMILY   **FAGACEAE**

Medium-sized tree with deciduous, simple leaves. **ID TIP:** A white oak. The leaves are similar to those of Chestnut Oak but are moderately to densely covered with evenly distributed hairs beneath and are typically somewhat velvety or feltlike to the touch. The bark is light gray, thick, and scaly, similar in appearance to that of White Oak (p. 443).

HABITAT: Swamps; well-drained floodplains; moist, mixed hardwood forests; rich woods (not rocky uplands as in Chestnut Oak). Elevation to 2,000'.

LEAF 3–11" long; obovate; similar to Chestnut Oak; 9–14 large, rounded teeth along each margin; hairy beneath. Autumn color dark red. **ACORN** ½–1" long. Nut ovoid to oblong; light brown; ½ enclosed within deep, thin cup of warty, hairy, gray to light brown scales. Cup 1–1⅓" wide. 1–3 acorns, on short stalk. Autumn; ripens in 1 year.

Water Oak

Quercus nigra

ALSO CALLED Spotted Oak, Possum Oak

HT 50–70'   **DIA** 2–3'

BEECH FAMILY   **FAGACEAE**

Medium-sized tree with deciduous to semi-evergreen, simple leaves. Tall trunk; symmetrical crown. **ID TIP:** A red oak. The leaves are variable, with as many as 5 distinct shapes on a single tree, but with at least some leaves obovate in outline.

HABITAT: Diverse: pine flatwoods to old fields, mixed upland woods, and roadsides. Elevation to 1,500'.

NOTES: Probably once confined to bottomlands and floodplains, Water Oak now inhabits a variety of habitats and colonizes disturbed sites.

LEAF 2–5" long. Variable in shape; obovate; sometimes with 3 broad, shallowly divided, bristle-tipped lobes. Stiff. Dull blue-green above; paler, with tufts of hairs on veins beneath. Autumn color yellow. **ACORN** ⅜–⅝" long. Nut nearly round; light yellow-brown; ¼–⅓ enclosed within shallow, thin cup of red-brown scales. Borne singly or in pairs, on short stalk. Autumn; ripens in 2 years.

Laurel Oak

Quercus laurifolia

ALSO CALLED Diamond-leaf Oak, Swamp Laurel Oak

HT 60–80' **DIA** 1–3'

Medium-sized tree with nearly evergreen, simple leaves (persisting until early spring). Tall trunk; dense, broad crown. **ID TIP:** A red oak. The tall trunk has a conspicuous. narrow buttress that may be 3–6' tall on large trees. At least some of the leaves are widest near the middle.

HABITAT: Floodplains, near rivers, swamps. Elevation to 500'.

NOTES: Laurel Oak leaves resemble the leaf of the Old World Bay Laurel (*Laurus nobilis*). It is widely planted as a shade tree throughout the Southeast. Some experts recognize **Darlington Oak** (*Q. hemisphaerica*) as a variety of Laurel Oak. It occurs in nearly the same range, but on dry sites. Darlington was more limited in habitat during presettlement times, but is opportunistic and weedy, and has now become established on lawns, in second-growth woods, and in other suitable dry uplands. It is distinguished from Laurel Oak by its lance-shaped leaf shape.

LEAF 2–6" long. Lance-shaped to elliptic, very variable, but at least some leaves are widest near middle; bristle at tip. Shiny, dark green above; paler beneath; usually hairless on both surfaces. Twig dark reddish brown. **ACORN** ½" long. Nut nearly round; dark brown; ¼ enclosed within shallow, reddish brown, hairy-scaly cup. Usually borne singly, on short stalk or nearly stalkless. Autumn; ripens in 2 years.

Darlington Oak

Willow Oak

Quercus phellos
HT 60–80' **DIA** 2–3'

BEECH FAMILY	FAGACEAE

Medium-sized tree with deciduous, simple leaves. Tall, slender trunk; dense, conical to rounded crown, with straight, very slender spur branchlets. **ID TIP:** A red oak. Willow Oak leaves are very narrow, closely resembling willow leaves, and are narrower than Laurel Oak or Darlington Oak leaves. There are tufts of hairs in at least some of the vein angles of at least some leaves, and the leaves are bristle-tipped; similar Southern and Sand Live Oak (pp. 430–431) leaves lack bristle.

HABITAT: Floodplains, stream banks, and bottomland woodlands. Elevation to 1,300'.

LEAF 2–5" long. Linear to narrowly elliptic, widest near middle, with tiny bristle at tip. Slightly shiny, light green above; pale green, sometimes with tufts of hairs in vein angles beneath. Autumn color pale yellow. **ACORN** ½–¾" long. Similar to Laurel Oak; downy and yellow-brown. Borne singly or in pairs, on short, stout stalk. Autumn; ripens in 2 years.

Bluejack Oak

Quercus incana
ALSO CALLED Upland Willow Oak, Sandjack
HT to 20' **DIA** 5–20"

BEECH FAMILY	FAGACEAE

Thicket-forming shrub or small tree with deciduous, simple leaves (may persist into spring during mild winters) and drooping branches. **ID TIP:** A red oak. Bluejack Oak has distinctive, shiny, blue-green or ashy green foliage and black bark with thick, square plates.

HABITAT: Sandhills and dry, sandy, oak-pine uplands of the coastal plains. Elevation to 800'.

LEAF 2–4" long. Narrowly elliptic to obovate, with bristle at tip; untoothed margins. Shiny, blue-green or ashy green, with prominent veins above; grayish-hairy beneath. Autumn color red. **ACORN** ½–⅝" long. Nut ovoid; brown; about ¼ enclosed within shallow cup. Borne singly or in pairs, on very short stalk. Autumn; ripens in 2 years.

Shingle Oak

Quercus imbricaria
HT 50–60' **DIA** 1–2'

Medium-sized tree with deciduous, simple leaves. Tall trunk; symmetrical crown. **ID TIP:** A red oak. The usually elliptic, unlobed leaves are dark green above and velvety to the touch beneath, with a dense covering of brownish hairs.

HABITAT: Stream valleys, fertile hillsides, moist to dry slopes. Elevation 350–2,300'.

NOTES: The eastern Shingle Oak has the largest leaves of all untoothed and unlobed oaks in North America. The tree grows largest and occurs in greatest abundance in the lower Ohio River basin. Its wood was once heavily harvested for shingles.

| BEECH FAMILY | FAGACEAE |

LEAF 4–7" long. Ovate, elliptic, or obovate, usually widest at middle; with bristle at pointed tip; edges rolled under. Glossy, dark green above; brown-hairy beneath; yellow midvein. Autumn color yellow, red, reddish brown. **ACORN** ½–¾" long. Nut nearly round; brown; ⅓–½ enclosed within thin, bowl-shaped cup of hairy scales. Borne singly or in pairs, on stout stalk. Autumn; ripens in 2 years.

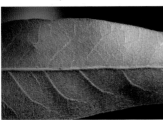

Myrtle Oak

Quercus myrtifolia
HT 15–30'   **DIA** 4–8"

Small tree or shrub with nearly evergreen leaves (persisting until new growth in spring). Short trunk; dense crown; trunk often coated with lichens at maturity. **ID TIP:** A red oak. Myrtle Oak is similar to Chapman Oak and **Florida** or **Sandhill Oak** (*Q. inopina*), a small evergreen tree or shrub of the sandhills and scrub of central peninsular Florida (to 160' elevation). Chapman Oak leaf edges are not rolled under, and the acorns are stalkless. Florida Oak leaves are more severely curved under; the underside typically has golden to yellow specks (scales, best seen under magnification). Myrtle only seldom has golden specks.

HABITAT: Dunes, sandhills and ridges, hammocks. Near sea level to 350'.

NOTES: Myrtle Oak grows in secondary dunes along Florida's coastal strip and is a major component of inland Sand Pine–oak scrub. It is typically shrubby in habit and forms extensive thickets inland.

BEECH FAMILY — **FAGACEAE**

LEAF 1–3" long. Obovate, with bristle at rounded tip; untoothed margins; edges rolled under. Leathery. Shiny, dark green above; pale green, yellow-green, or orange-brown, with tufts of hairs in vein angles beneath. Young leaf rusty-woolly. Leafstalk very short, sometimes winged. Twig dark red-brown, downy. **ACORN** ½" long. Nut ovoid, sometimes spherical; dark brown; ¼–⅓ enclosed within shallow, downy-scaly cup. Borne singly or in pairs, on short stalk. Autumn; ripens in 2 years.

Florida Oak

Chapman Oak

Quercus chapmanii
HT to 30'   **DIA** 6–8"

Small, shrubby tree with deciduous to semi-evergreen, simple leaves. **ID TIP:** A white oak. Chapman Oak, Myrtle Oak, and Florida Oak (restricted to central peninsular Florida) occur together and in similar habitats. The leaf of Chapman Oak is darker green above than that of Myrtle Oak, and has a flat or wavy edge or 3 shallow lobes at tip; Florida Oak leaf edges are rolled under. **HABITAT AND RANGE:** Sandhills, coastal dunes; southern South Carolina, southeastern Georgia, and Florida. Elevation 0–350'.

BEECH FAMILY — **FAGACEAE**

LEAF 1½–3½" long. Obovate; margins untoothed, wavy, or shallowly 3-lobed at tip. Shiny, dark green above; paler, with hairy midvein beneath. **ACORN** ⅝–¾" long. Nut ovoid; dark brown; ½ enclosed within deep cup of hairy, gray scales. Borne singly or in pairs, stalkless. Autumn; ripens in 1 year.

Southern Live Oak

Quercus virginiana
ALSO CALLED Coastal Live Oak,
Live Oak, Virginia Live Oak
HT 40–50' **DIA** 2–4'

Short but massive tree with evergreen or
semi-evergreen, simple leaves. Thick trunk
with buttressed base. Short trunk and
very broad crown in open; in forest, tall,
often straight or slightly leaning trunk.
ID TIP: A white oak. Open-grown Southern
Live Oaks are identified by the massive
trunk and large branches that originate
low on the trunk and extend upward into
the crown.

HABITAT: Diverse, from wet to well-drained
sites, fertile to poor soils, in hammocks,
flatwoods, mixed uplands, parks, yards,
pastures, roadsides. Elevation to 650'.

NOTES: Southern Live Oak is a common
oak of the South, where it is often
heavily draped with Spanish moss.
Its range extends south to Cuba and
Central America. The wood was once so
important in shipbuilding that the United
States created the first publicly protected
forest to insure a continuing supply of live
oak timber for naval use.

BEECH FAMILY **FAGACEAE**

LEAF 2–5" long. Narrowly elliptic to obovate; tip rounded
to pointed, sometimes with tooth; margins untoothed,
or occasionally toothed or lobed, especially on leaves of
summer shoots (above right); edges flat or slightly rolled
under. Leathery. Glossy, dark green above; densely gray-
hairy beneath. Twig gray-woolly into first winter. **ACORN**
⅝–1" long. Nut narrowly oblong; dark chestnut brown; ¼–½
enclosed within deep cup of reddish brown, downy scales.
1–3 acorns, near tip of long stalk. Autumn; ripens in 1 year.

Sand Live Oak

Quercus geminata
HT to 15'   **DIA** 1–2'

Small evergreen tree or shrub. Closely related to Southern Live Oak, but less massive. **ID TIP:** A white oak. The leaves are convex, their edges strongly rolled under, and they have recessed veins above. Acorns are similar to those of Southern Live Oak, with a cup composed of grayish white, hairy scales. **HABITAT AND RANGE:** Deep coastal plain sands, often with pines. North Carolina to Mississippi and south to southern Florida. Elevation to 650'.

Oglethorpe Oak

Quercus oglethorpensis
HT 60–80'   **DIA** 1–2½'

Medium-sized tree with deciduous, simple leaves and crooked branches. **ID TIP:** A white oak. The bark is whitish gray and scaly. The leaves are blunt at the base and tip, and have velvety, yellowish branched hairs beneath (star-shaped under magnification).

HABITAT: Well-drained terraces along rivers and streams, and on adjacent forested slopes. Elevation to 650'.

NOTES: This rare oak is somewhat susceptible to the same blight that destroyed the American Chestnut.

LEAF 2–5" long. Narrowly elliptic, with blunt base and tip; velvety, yellowish, branched hairs beneath. Autumn color scarlet. Twig purple-tinged when young, becoming grayish with age. **ACORN** ⅜" long. Nut ovoid; grayish brown; ⅓ enclosed within shallow cup of tan-hairy scales. Borne singly or in pairs; on very short stalk or stalkless. Autumn; ripens in 1 year.

Blackjack Oak

Quercus marilandica
ALSO CALLED Blackjack
HT 20–50' **DIA** 6–12"

Small tree with deciduous, simple leaves. Stout trunk; open crown on fertile sites, or narrow, compact crown on poor sites; often pendulous branches; dead branches remain on tree for years. On poorest sites, shrubby, multistemmed, or dwarfed. **ID TIP:** A red oak. The leaves are very broad near the tip, have a short terminal lobe, and are densely covered with rusty brown hairs beneath.

HABITAT: Poor, dry sandy soils where clay is present; rock outcrops and ridges. Elevation to 3,000'.

NOTES: Blackjack Oak is one of the major oaks of the New Jersey pine barrens. It is a soil stabilizer on eroding, poor, or burned lands and is an excellent indicator of clay subsoils.

LEAF 3–8" long. Obovate (almost triangular); usually 3 (rarely 5) very broad, squarish, bristle-tipped lobes, shallowly divided. Shiny, dark yellow-green above; paler, with rusty brown hairs beneath; orange midvein and raised veins on both surfaces. Autumn color yellow or brown. Leaves persist through winter. Leafstalk downy. Twig gray-downy, 5-sided in cross section, becoming hairless and dark gray or brown at maturity. **ACORN** ⅝–¾" long and wide. Nut ovoid with stout point; light yellow-brown; about ½ enclosed within deep cup of loose, glossy, rusty brown scales. Borne singly or in pairs, on short stalk. Autumn; ripens in 2 years.

Arkansas Oak

Quercus arkansana
ALSO CALLED Water Oak
HT 40–60' **DIA** 1'

Uncommon, small to medium-sized oak of the Southeast with deciduous, simple leaves. **ID TIP:** A red oak. Arkansas Oak has a very wide, obovate leaf with a rounded tip. **HABITAT AND RANGE:** Sandy upland hardwood forests. Separate ranges in southwestern Arkansas and northwestern Louisiana; Alabama and southwestern Georgia; the panhandle of Florida; and eastern Texas. Elevation 150–500'.

LEAF 2–6" long, often as wide. Obovate; rounded tip; 3 bristles along margin or sometimes at tips of 3 very shallow lobes. Yellow-green above; paler with tufts of hairs in vein angles beneath. **ACORN** ¼–½" long. Nut ovoid to round; ¼ enclosed within shallow, scaly, hairy cup. Ripens in 2 years.

Northern Red Oak

Quercus rubra
ALSO CALLED Red Oak
HT 60–90' **DIA** 2–3'

BEECH FAMILY   **FAGACEAE**

Medium-sized to large tree with deciduous, simple leaves. Tall trunk; narrow to broad crown. Bark smooth, light gray, with furrows running length of trunk, between dark gray-brown, rough ridges (Black Oak lacks long furrows). Older trees have very rough, black bark with long plates and deep fissures. **ID TIP:** A red oak. The leaf is symmetrical, and the depth of the leaf sinus at the middle of the leaf is consistently less than halfway to the midvein (leaves are asymmetrical and variable in shape in Black Oak). The terminal bud is mostly hairless, with at most only tufts of reddish hairs at the tip; the terminal bud is hairy in Black Oak.

HABITAT: Moist woods, slopes, valleys. Elevation to 5,900'.

NOTES: Northern Red Oak is a widely distributed eastern oak, often found in association with other oaks, and sometimes a dominant tree. Fast-growing, it is planted to revegetate disturbed sites. It is hardy in cities and planted as a street tree and ornamental.

LEAF 4–9" long. Symmetrical, widest at middle; 7–11 lobes; depth of middle sinus is usually less than halfway to midvein; each lobe ends in bristle-tipped teeth. Dull, dark green above; dull, light green, with tufts of hairs in vein angles beneath. Autumn color deep red, orange, brown. Terminal bud mostly hairless (sometimes with tufts of reddish hairs at tip). **ACORN** ¾–1¼" long. Nut broadly ovoid; pale brown; ¼ enclosed within shallow cup of thin, reddish brown scales. Borne singly or in pairs, on short stalk or stalkless. Autumn; ripens in 2 years.

Black Oak

Quercus velutina

ALSO CALLED Quercitron Oak, Yellow Oak

HT 50–80'   **DIA** 1–3'

Medium-sized tree with deciduous, simple leaves. Tall trunk; narrow crown. Bark very rough; dark brown to nearly black.

ID TIP: A red oak. This species has the most variable leaf in the red oak group. The leaves are easily confused with those of Northern Red Oak, but are asymmetrical in shape (symmetrical in Northern Red Oak). The terminal buds of Black Oak are covered with hairs; terminal buds of Northern Red Oak are not hairy or have at most a tuft of reddish hairs near the tip.

HABITAT: Dry rocky ridges and slopes; tolerates drier, less fertile sites than Northern Red Oak. Elevation to 4,900'.

NOTES: Black Oak shares a range with Northern Red Oak but skews slightly more southerly, only just reaching into Canada. It is an important wildlife food (unusual for a red oak).

BEECH FAMILY   **FAGACEAE**

LEAF 4–10" long. Variable in shape; asymmetrical; 5–9 lobes, shallowly divided in leaves growing in shade, more deeply divided (halfway to midvein) in leaves in sun; each lobe ends in bristle-tipped teeth. Leathery. Shiny, green above; yellow-green, with tufts of brown hairs in vein angles beneath (appears coppery at a distance). Autumn color dull red-orange, brown. Terminal bud gray- or tan-hairy.   **ACORN** ⅝–¾" long. Nut ovoid; light chestnut brown; about ½ enclosed within deep cup of thick, shaggy, rusty-woolly scales. Borne singly or in pairs, on short stalk. Autumn; ripens in 2 years.

Pin Oak

Quercus palustris
HT 50–90'   **DIA** 1–2½'

Medium-sized to large tree with deciduous, simple leaves. Broadly conical crown of upturned upper branches and spreading side branches; pendulous, often dead, retained lower branches can form a "skirt" around lower trunk. Bark dark gray; smooth, eventually developing ridges and furrows. **ID TIP:** A red oak. Pin Oak has numerous, very slender, tough, pinlike twigs and branchlets. Similar Scarlet Oak is generally smaller and prefers drier habitats.

HABITAT: Moist soils and wet woods of stream edges, river bottoms, and swamps. Elevation to 1,100'.

NOTES: Pin Oak is a hardy, wind-firm oak. It is most abundant in New Jersey and Delaware and along the lower Ohio River. It is planted as a street tree for its bright red autumn foliage and handsome shape.

LEAF 3–6" long. Widest at middle; 5 or 7 lobes, divided nearly to midvein; each lobe ends in bristle-tipped teeth. Glossy, dark green above; slightly shiny, light green, with tufts of hairs along midvein beneath. Autumn color scarlet, brown. **ACORN** ½" long. Nut nearly round; brown; ¼ enclosed within thin, shallow cup of finely hairy, reddish brown scales; cup tapers to base of short stalk. Borne singly or in clusters. Autumn; ripens in 2 years.

Northern Pin Oak

Quercus ellipsoidalis
ALSO CALLED Jack Oak, Hill's Oak
HT 40–65'   **DIA** 1–2½'

BEECH FAMILY   FAGACEAE

Small to medium-sized tree with deciduous, simple leaves. Short trunk; crown of forked branches; can be straggly. Bark gray-brown, with shallow fissures. **ID TIP:** A red oak. Northern Pin Oak is similar to Pin Oak and Scarlet Oak. On some leaves, the uppermost leaf sinuses are much deeper than the lower sinuses, giving a narrow aspect to the upper third of the leaf. The acorns are not as distinctly round as Pin Oak acorns.

HABITAT: Dry, sandy soils. Elevation 500–1,600'.

Q. ellipsoidalis

Q. texana

LEAF 3–6¾" long. Widest at middle; 5 or 7 deeply divided lobes; each lobe pointed and bristle-tipped; sinuses rounded. Bright green above; pale, with tufts of hairs in vein angles beneath. Autumn color red. **ACORN** ½–¾" long. Nut ovoid to nearly round, light brown; ¼–⅓ enclosed within shallow or deep cup of light brown, hairy scales. Borne singly or in pairs; stalkless or on short stalk. Autumn; ripens in 2 years.

Texas Red Oak

Quercus texana
ALSO CALLED Nuttall's Oak
HT 60–100'   **DIA** 1–3'

BEECH FAMILY   FAGACEAE

Medium-sized to large tree with deciduous, simple leaves. **ID TIP:** A red oak. The only wetland oaks in its range that have similar leaves are Pin Oak and Shumard Oak. Pin Oak's leaf is symmetrical and usually has fewer lobes; Texas Red Oak's trunk is swollen at the base and lacks "pinlike" branches. Texas Red Oak has a shorter terminal bud than Shumard, and a deep acorn cup. **HABITAT:** Wetlands. Elevation to 650'. (See map above.)

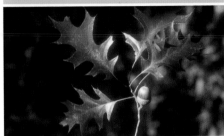

LEAF 3–7¾" long. 6–11 deeply divided, bristle-tipped lobes; asymmetrical. Dull green above; pale, with tufts of hairs in vein angles beneath. Terminal bud less than ¼" long. **ACORN** ¾–1¼" long. Nut ovoid to oblong; dark-striped; ⅓–½ enclosed within deep cup that tapers at the base.

Scarlet Oak

Quercus coccinea
HT 60–80'   **DIA** 1–2½'

| BEECH FAMILY | FAGACEAE |

Medium-sized tree with deciduous, simple leaves. Narrow crown of glossy foliage. Bark gray; smooth, vertical stripes alternating with dark gray to dark brown, rough ridges; older bark becomes entirely rough, with dark gray-brown ridges and furrows. **ID TIP:** A red oak. Scarlet Oak has brilliant red autumn foliage and red new leaves in early spring. The leaves have deeply divided lobes (more than halfway to the midvein) that are rounded at the base of the sinus; both sides of the leaf are shiny and hairless except for small tufts of hairs in the vein angles beneath. Scarlet Oak is similar to Shumard Oak but has a slightly hairy terminal leaf bud and a deep acorn cup, and prefers dry habitats.

HABITAT: Uplands, dry slopes, ridges, sandy barrens. Elevation to 4,900' in Appalachian Mountains.

LEAF 3–7" long. Widest at middle; 7 (rarely 9) lobes divided at least halfway to yellow midvein; each lobe has bristle-tipped teeth. Glossy, green above; pale yellow-green, with tufts of hairs in vein angles beneath. Autumn color scarlet. Leafstalk long. Terminal bud slightly hairy. **ACORN** ½–1" long, ⅝" wide. Nut ovoid; brown; ⅓–½ enclosed within deep, light brown cup of thick, slightly hairy scales; cup tapers to base of very short stalk. Borne singly or in pairs. Autumn; ripens in 2 years.

Shumard Oak

Quercus shumardii
ALSO CALLED Swamp Red Oak
HT 60–90' **DIA** 1–2½'

Medium-sized to large tree with deciduous, simple leaves. Tall trunk; broad crown. Bark has whitish ridges and dark furrows. **ID TIP:** A red oak. Shumard Oak is similar to Scarlet Oak, but has a longer leaf, hairless terminal bud, and shallow acorn cup, and it prefers a moist habitat. Shumard has a longer terminal bud than Texas Red Oak.

HABITAT: Moist, well-drained mixed woodlands, riverbanks, and bluffs, often in soils with a limestone influence. Elevation to 1,600'.

NOTES: Shumard Oak is uncommon in its range. It is occasionally planted as a street tree, and is increasingly used in commercial and residential landscapes.

BEECH FAMILY   **FAGACEAE**

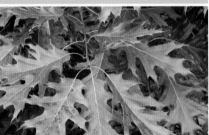

LEAF 6–8" long and very wide (to 5" across). Broadest toward tip; 5–9 lobes, deeply divided (nearly to midvein), each lobe ending in bristle-tipped teeth. Slightly shiny, dark green, and hairy above; paler green, with tufts of hairs in vein angles beneath. Leafstalk long (2½"). Autumn color red or brown. Terminal bud longer than ¼", straw-colored, hairless. **ACORN** ¾–1⅛" long. Nut ovoid; gray; ¼–⅓ enclosed within shallow cup of blunt, sometimes hairy scales. Borne singly or in pairs on short, stocky stalk. Autumn; ripens in 2 years.

Georgia Oak

Quercus georgiana
HT to 30' **DIA** 4–12"

Rare small tree or, more typically, a bushy shrub; often with a stunted form, especially on rock outcrops. **ID TIP:** A red oak. Leaves have 3 or 5 lobes, each lobe tipped by a conspicuous bristle; bark is rough; acorn is ⅜–½" long, with brown, scaly cup and very short stalk (similar to Pin Oak acorn). **HABITAT AND RANGE:** Rock outcrops and dry slopes. Stone Mountain, Georgia, and in some parts of Alabama and South Carolina. Elevation 150–1,600'.

BEECH FAMILY   **FAGACEAE**

LEAF 2–4" long. Widest at middle; 3 or 5 deeply divided lobes, each pointed and bristle-tipped. Glossy, green above; pale, with tufts of hairs in vein angles beneath. Autumn color red or yellow; sometimes remains green.

Southern Red Oak

Quercus falcata
ALSO CALLED Spanish Oak
HT 50–80' **DIA** 1–3'

Medium-sized tree with deciduous, simple leaves. Tall trunk; high crown. **ID TIP:** A red oak. The leaves have narrow, pointed, bristle-tipped lobes, a U-shaped base, and a relatively long (¾–1⅜") leafstalk.

HABITAT: Upland forests; dry, sandy sites; ridgetops with sandy or clay soils. Elevation to 2,600'.

NOTES: Southern Red Oak is primarily an upland forest tree, but it grows largest in fertile stream valleys.

BEECH FAMILY **FAGACEAE**

LEAF 4–9" long. Widest at middle; 3 or 5 lobes; terminal lobe long and narrow; side lobes narrow, pointed, and deeply divided; each lobe bristle-tipped. Shiny, green above; rusty or gray-woolly beneath. Autumn color yellow or yellow-brown. **ACORN** ½–⅝" long. Nut round; brown; ⅓–½ enclosed within shallow cup of reddish, sparsely hairy scales; cup tapers to a blunt point; short stalk. Borne singly or in pairs. Autumn; ripens in 2 years.

Cherrybark Oak

Quercus pagoda
ALSO CALLED Swamp Red Oak, Swamp Spanish Oak, Pagoda Oak
HT 70–100' **DIA** 2–4'

Medium-sized to large tree with deciduous, simple leaves. Tall, largely branch-free trunk; high crown. Bark scaly, red-tinged as in Black Cherry. **ID TIP:** A red oak. Some consider Cherrybark Oak to be a variety of Southern Red Oak, but Cherrybark occurs in lowlands and lacks U-shaped leaf base. It is distinguished from Northern Red Oak by its densely hairy leaf underside. The leaf shape (upside down) resembles the outline of a pagoda.

HABITAT: Floodplains and poorly drained bottomlands and lowlands. Elevation to 1,000'.

BEECH FAMILY **FAGACEAE**

LEAF Similar to Northern Red Oak, but has 5–11 broad, shallow, usually single-toothed lobes; whitish-hairy (not rusty) beneath. **ACORN** ½–1" long. Nut nearly round; about ⅓–½ enclosed within deep cup of brown, hairy scales. Autumn; ripens in 2 years.

Turkey Oak

Quercus laevis
ALSO CALLED Catesby Oak
HT 20–40' **DIA** 1–1½'

Small, fire-adapted tree or shrub with crooked branches and deciduous, simple leaves. **ID TIP:** A red oak. This tree is distinguished by the orientation of the leaf, which is typically twisted on the branch so that the plane of the leaf is perpendicular to the ground (the tops and bottoms of the leaves are seen when looking at the tree from the side).

HABITAT: Coastal dunes, sandy ridges, sandhills. Elevation to 500'.

| BEECH FAMILY | FAGACEAE |

LEAF 4–12" long. 3 or 5 (rarely 7) long, narrow lobes (shape suggests a turkey's footprint); each ends in bristle-tipped teeth. Stiff. Glossy, yellow-green above; rusty hairs on veins beneath. Autumn color red. **ACORN** ¾–1" long. Nut ovoid; brown; ½ enclosed within deep cup of hairy, brown scales that taper to the base of a short, stout stalk. Borne singly or in pairs. Autumn; ripens in 2 years.

Bear Oak

Quercus ilicifolia
ALSO CALLED Scrub Oak
HT to 18' **DIA** 3–6"

Large, thicket-forming shrub with deciduous, simple leaves; rarely attains tree size. **ID TIP:** A red oak. The leaves are less than 5" long; they typically have 5 lobes and are covered with feltlike hairs beneath.

HABITAT: Ridges, sandy barrens, fire-adapted pine-oak woods; often burned or cutover sites. Elevation to 4,900'.

| BEECH FAMILY | FAGACEAE |

LEAF 2–5" long. Variable in shape; 3–7 (typically 5) lobes, shallowly divided and pointed, with bristle at each lobe tip. Dull, dark green above; densely gray-hairy beneath. Autumn color dull red or yellow. **ACORN** ½" long. Nut ovoid; light brown; ¼–½ enclosed within shallow or deep cup with fringelike scales. In pairs, stalkless or on short stalk. Autumn; ripens in 2 years.

Overcup Oak

Quercus lyrata
ALSO CALLED Swamp Post Oak,
Water White Oak
HT 60–80'   **DIA** 2–3'

Medium-sized tree with deciduous,
simple leaves. Single trunk; often has
asymmetrical, dense, broad crown with
drooping branchlets. Bark light gray
or gray-brown; large scales or slightly
shaggy; can resemble White Oak bark.
ID TIP: A white oak. Overcup Oak is named
for its acorn: the nut is almost entirely
enclosed in a very deep, burlike cup.

HABITAT: Swamp and floodplain forests,
fringes of bayous. Elevation to 650'.

NOTES: Overcup
Oak is a common
tree of southern
wetlands. The
heavy, strong
wood is used for
lumber, but most
older trees have
been logged.

LEAF 5–9" long. Widest at middle, often narrower toward
the base than the tip; very variable margin with 7–11
irregular, rounded, moderately to deeply divided lobes.
Slightly shiny, dark green above; gray-green and white-
hairy or hairless beneath. Autumn color yellow, bright
orange, red, brown. **ACORN** ½–1" long. Nut round; brown;
almost entirely enclosed within deep, round, gray cup of
thin, warty, downy scales. Borne singly or in pairs; stalkless.
Autumn; ripens in 1 year.

Bastard Oak

Quercus sinuata
ALSO CALLED Bastard White Oak,
Durand Oak, Bluff Oak
HT to 70'   **DIA** 1–2'

Small to medium-sized tree or shrub
with deciduous, simple leaves. Two
varieties are recognized: var. *sinuata* is
typically over 45' tall; the short-leaved var.
breviloba is a large, thicket-forming shrub
or a small, multistemmed tree (4–18'
tall). **ID TIP:** A white oak. The leaves are
unlobed or have 3–9 rounded, shallowly
divided lobes. They are dark green above
and gray-green beneath.

HABITAT: Variable; wooded wetlands,
river edges, dry limestone bluffs, and
prairies. Elevation to 1,300' in var. *sinuata*;
600–2,000' in var. *breviloba*.

■ *Q. s. sinuata*   ■ *Q. s. breviloba*

LEAF 1–2½" long in var. *breviloba*, 2–5"
in var. *sinuata*. Obovate; no lobes or 3–9
rounded, shallowly divided lobes. Shiny,
dark green above; gray-green with mat of
tiny, flattened, branched hairs (star-shaped
under magnification) beneath. Autumn color
bronze or rusty red. **ACORN** ½–⅝" long.
Nut ovoid; brown; ¼ enclosed within very
shallow cup of thin or slightly thick, silvery,
hairy scales. Borne singly or in pairs, stalkless
or on short stalk. Autumn; ripens in 1 year.

Swamp White Oak

Quercus bicolor
ALSO CALLED Swamp Oak, Kellogg Oak
HT 50–70' **DIA** 2–3'

Medium-sized tree with deciduous, simple leaves. Single trunk and narrow crown; lower branches are short and drooping, and grow directly out from trunk; higher branches are stout and ascending.
ID TIP: A white oak. Swamp White Oak is a northern oak with round-lobed leaves that is largely restricted to swamp habitat. The name *bicolor* refers to the leaf color: dark green above, silvery beneath.

HABITAT: Poorly drained bottomlands and swamp edges; often in association with clay or mineral-rich soils. Elevation to 3,300'.

LEAF 4–7" long. Obovate; 5–10 rounded, shallowly divided, wavy or toothlike lobes of varying sizes along each margin. Shiny, dark green above; pale green, often with silvery white hairs beneath. Autumn color dull yellow-bronze, sometimes orange or red. Young leaf unfolds bronze-green. **ACORN** ¾–1½" long. Nut broadly ovoid; glossy, light brown; ⅓ enclosed within shallow cup covered by woolly scales, often with fringe of mossy hairs along cup rim. Often in pairs on 2–4" long stalk. Autumn; ripens in 1 year.

Q. bicolor

Q. austrina

Bastard White Oak

Quercus austrina
ALSO CALLED Bluff Oak
HT 30–80'

Small to medium-sized tree with deciduous, simple leaves. Bark whitish, shaggy. **ID TIP:** A white oak. The leaves typically have fewer, less pointed, and more shallowly divided lobes than Swamp White Oak and White Oak. Young leaves soft-hairy. **HABITAT:** Calcium-rich bluffs, often in association with limestone; along streams and river bottoms. Elevation to 650'. (See map above.)

LEAF 4–8" long. 5 or 7 shallowly divided lobes. **ACORN** ⅜" long; cup deep, enclosing ⅓–½ of nut.

White Oak

Quercus alba

ALSO CALLED Eastern White Oak

HT 60–80'   **DIA** 2–3'

Medium-sized tree with deciduous, simple leaves. Tall trunk (when forest-grown) or short and stocky trunk (open-grown); broad, rugged crown. **ID TIP:** A white oak. White Oak is most easily distinguished by its loose, shaggy, scaly, gray to whitish bark and deeply divided, lobed leaves that are pale grayish beneath.

HABITAT: Moist, fertile valleys to dry, sterile mountains. Elevation to 5,200'.

NOTES: White Oak can occur in a wide range of habitats. Trees can produce abundant seeds in good crop years, which occur irregularly, every 4 to 10 years. White Oak is one of the most important North American timber oaks. The wood is important commercially and was widely used to make barrels and in shipbuilding. It is planted as a street tree.

LEAF 5–9" long. Broad, widest at middle; 7 or 9 rounded lobes, deeply divided almost to midvein (leaves growing in shade have shallower lobes). Dull to somewhat shiny, bright green above; pale green or whitish beneath. Autumn color light pink, deep red, violet-purple. Young leaf unfolds pink. **ACORN** ¾–1" long. Nut ovoid; light brown; ¼–⅓ enclosed within shallow, light gray cup of warty, finely hairy scales. Borne singly or in pairs, stalkless or on short stalk. Autumn; ripens in 1 year.

Burr Oak

Quercus macrocarpa

ALSO CALLED Mossycup Oak, Blue Oak
HT 60–80'   **DIA** 2–4'

BEECH FAMILY   **FAGACEAE**

Medium-sized tree with deciduous, simple leaves. Tall, stout trunk; very broad crown; shrubby in dry, western edge of its range.   **ID TIP:** A white oak. The large acorn has a fuzzy, burlike cup that resembles the prickly fruits of the chestnuts. The middle leaf sinus on some leaves is so deep it nearly divides the leaf into 2 parts.

HABITAT: Bottomlands and poorly drained woods, often in association with clay or limestone, but adapts to a variety of habitats and soil types, including dry upland soils. Elevation to 3,300'.

NOTES: Few oaks range as far north as Burr Oak; it is the only native oak of Montana, Wyoming, North Dakota, South Dakota, and Saskatchewan. The species once formed great savannas throughout its range. It is planted as a shade tree and ornamental, for shelterbelts, and to reclaim land disturbed by coal mining.

LEAF 6–12" long. Obovate, with a narrow "waist" (lobes in the middle are divided almost to midvein); 5–9 rounded lobes along each margin; lower half deeply lobed, upper half shallowly lobed, becoming blunt-toothed toward tip. Shiny, dark green above; gray-green and finely hairy beneath. Autumn color yellow or yellow-brown. Twig stout, sometimes with corky wings that persist on branchlets.   **ACORN** ¾–2" long. Nut broadly ovoid; light brown; ½–¾ enclosed within very deep cup of gray scales; mosslike fringe along cup rim. Usually borne singly, on short to very long (2–4") stalk. Autumn; ripens in 1 year.

Post Oak

Quercus stellata

ALSO CALLED Iron Oak

HT 30–60' **DIA** 1–2'

BEECH FAMILY **FAGACEAE**

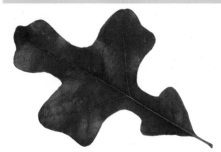

Small to medium-sized tree with deciduous, simple leaves. Short trunk; broad, dense crown of gnarled branches; shrubby on poor sites. Bark light gray to reddish brown, scaly, finely fissured and checkered (like alligator skin). **ID TIP:** A white oak. The 3 terminal leaf lobes are more or less square or rectangular in outline; the uppermost side lobes are of nearly equal size, opposite one another, forming a cross.

HABITAT: Dry sites in oak-pine forests and in prairie-forest borders in Texas and Oklahoma. Elevation to 2,500'.

NOTES: Known for its heavy, durable, decay-resistant wood, Post Oak is used to make fence posts, railroad ties, construction and mine timbers. The tree is planted to stabilize sterile slopes.

LEAF 3½–6" long. Very variable in shape, often with an outline suggesting a Greek cross; 5 or 7 broad, rounded lobes, with center lobes largest and typically square or rectangular. Leathery. Shiny, dark green, and rough-textured above; gray or yellowish hairs beneath. Autumn color dull yellow or brown. Twig has yellowish hairs when young; hairs turn darker and shed with age. **ACORN** ½–1" long. Nut broadly ovoid; brown with dark, lengthwise stripes; ⅓–½ enclosed within deep cup of warty, reddish brown scales. Borne singly or in pairs, stalkless or on short stalk. Autumn; ripens in 1 year.

Sand Post Oak

Quercus margaretta
ALSO CALLED Dwarf Post Oak
HT to 20' **DIA** 6–12"

BEECH FAMILY   **FAGACEAE**

Small tree or shrub with deciduous, simple leaves; sometimes considered a variety of Post Oak. **ID TIP:** A white oak. The leaf lobes are rounded (not squared or as evidently cross-shaped as in Post Oak) and point toward the leaf tip, and the acorn cup is downy. Hairs on twig are star-shaped under magnification. **HABITAT AND RANGE:** Sandhills, forests, scrublands. Southeastern Virginia to central Florida; Alabama west to Oklahoma. Elevation to 2,000'.

LEAF 2½–6" long. 3 or 5 small, rounded lobes, angled toward tip. Twig sparsely covered with branched hairs; hairless with age. **ACORN** ½" long. Nut ovoid; ½ enclosed within deep cup of downy scales. Borne singly or in pairs, stalkless or on short stalk. Autumn; ripens in 1 year.

English Oak

Quercus robur
ALSO CALLED Common Oak, Pedunculate Oak, Irish Dair
HT 60–100' **DIA** 2–3'

BEECH FAMILY   **FAGACEAE**

Medium-sized to large tree with deciduous, simple leaves. Short, stout trunk; broad, domed crown of massive branches. **ID TIP:** A white oak. The leaves are similar to those of White Oak but have a very short leafstalk and 2 small lobes at the base that nearly clasp the stem.

HABITAT AND RANGE: Introduced in North America; naturalized locally in the Northeast, southeastern Canada, and the Pacific Northwest. Native to Europe, western Asia.

NOTES: English Oak is one of the most common and most massive trees of northern Europe. It is planted in North America; ornamental varieties have colorful autumn foliage.

LEAF 2–5" long. Obovate; 6–14 rounded lobes, divided halfway to midvein; 2 small lobes at leaf base. Glossy, dark green above; pale blue-green beneath. Autumn color coffee brown, orange-brown. Leafstalk very short (longer in White Oak). **ACORN** ⅝–1" long. Nut oblong; chestnut brown; ¼–⅓ enclosed within shallow cup of grayish, hairy scales. 1–3 acorns on long, slender stalk. Autumn; ripens in 1 year.

Gambel Oak

Quercus gambelii

ALSO CALLED Rocky Mountain White Oak, Utah White Oak

HT 15–30' **DIA** 1–2½'

Small tree or thicket-forming shrub with deciduous, simple leaves. Short trunk; narrow crown. **ID TIP:** A white oak. Leaves are glossy, dark green, with 7–11 rounded lobes.

HABITAT: Hills and plateaus, often in association with Ponderosa Pine. Elevation 3,300–9,900'.

NOTES: Gambel Oak is the most common oak of the Rocky Mountains and the primary oak of Arizona's Oak Creek Canyon. It is often found as a shrub and in clumps. It provides valuable food and shelter to deer, elk, spotted owls, peccaries, and other wildlife. The red autumn foliage is rare among western oaks.

| BEECH FAMILY | FAGACEAE |

LEAF 2½–7" long. Widest at middle or toward tip; 7–11 rounded lobes, divided about halfway to midvein. Glossy, dark green above; pale green and soft-hairy beneath. Autumn color yellow, orange, red-brown, red. **ACORN** ½–¾" long. Nut ovoid; light brown; ⅓ enclosed within deep, thick, rounded cup of downy scales. Borne singly or in pairs, on very short stalk. Autumn; ripens in 1 year.

Lacey Oak

Quercus laceyi

ALSO CALLED Rock Oak, Smoky Oak

HT to 35' **DIA** 10–20"

Small tree or sometimes a shrub with leathery, deciduous, simple leaves. **ID TIP:** A white oak. The new spring leaves are a striking pinkish color, becoming smoky gray-green at maturity, with branched hairs (star-shaped under magnification) beneath. **HABITAT AND RANGE:** Limestone bluffs and canyons of Edwards Plateau, Texas; separate population in Mexico near Big Bend. Elevation 1,100–7,200'.

LEAF 2–4½" long. Rounded at tip; margins untoothed, may have shallow lobes. Smoky gray-green above; paler, with branched hairs beneath. New twig gray, hairy; turns reddish brown, hairless. **ACORN** ½–¾" long. Nut oblong; ¼–⅓ enclosed within shallow cup of hairy scales. Borne singly or in pairs, stalkless or on short stalk. Autumn; ripens in 1 year.

Graves Oak

Quercus gravesii

ALSO CALLED Chisos Red Oak

HT to 40' **DIA** 1–2'

Small, local tree with deciduous, simple leaves. Best seen at Big Bend National Park. **ID TIP:** A red oak. The narrow leaves have a few broad, triangular lobes, each tipped with a prickly bristle; they are sparsely hairy or hairless and are on a slender stalk at least ½" long.

HABITAT AND RANGE: Woodlands of Chisos, Davis, and Glass mountain ranges of Texas. Elevation to 3,900'.

NOTES: Chisos Oak (*Q. graciliformis*), a red oak restricted to the Chisos Mountains of southwestern Texas, has narrow, 3–4" long leaves (3 times longer than wide) that are unlobed or have 8–10 shallow, bristle-tipped lobes. Shiny, green above; dull coppery and hairless or nearly so beneath. Chisos Oak and 2 others of the same region, **Robust Oak** (*Q. robusta*) and **Lateleaf Oak** (*Q. tardifolia*), are all of conservation concern. Robust Oak leaf has 6–8 small lobes (or large teeth), Lateleaf Oak leaf has 3–4 lobes.

LEAF 2–4" long. 3–7 triangular, pointed or blunt lobes; each lobe bristle-tipped. Shiny, dark green above; light green with tufts of hairs on raised veins beneath. Autumn color red. Leafstalk longer than ½". **ACORN** ½–⅝" long. Nut ovoid; ¼–½ enclosed within deep, light brown, scaly cup. Borne singly or in clusters, on short stalk. Autumn; ripens in 1 year.

Mohr Oak

Quercus mohriana
ALSO CALLED Shin Oak, Scrub Oak
HT to 20' **DIA** 6–8"

Small tree or large shrub with simple, usually evergreen leaves. **ID TIP:** A white oak. The dark green leaves are hairy, with raised veins beneath; and usually lack teeth. The acorn cup is deep.

HABITAT: Limestone soils, plains, and hillsides. Elevation 2,000–8,200'.

NOTES: Pungent Oak (*Q. pungens*) has narrow, ¾–2" long leaves; 7 or 9 shallow, pointed or blunt lobes, each with short, thickened, "callus" at tip. The leaf is sandpaper-rough above; gray-hairy with conspicuous veins beneath. The acorn cup is shallow.

BEECH FAMILY **FAGACEAE**

Q. mohriana **Q. pungens**

LEAF 1–3" long. Elliptic to narrowly elliptic; margins untoothed and wavy, or sometimes sparsely toothed. Shiny, dark green above; densely gray-hairy, with conspicuous raised veins beneath. Twig yellowish or white-woolly. **ACORN** ⅜–⅝" long. Nut ovoid; brown; ½ enclosed within deep cup of gray-hairy scales. Borne singly or in pairs, stalkless or on short stalk. Autumn; ripens in 1 year.

Mexican Blue Oak

Quercus oblongifolia
ALSO CALLED Sonoran Blue Oak
HT to 30' **DIA** 15–20"

Small tree or shrub with evergreen, simple leaves. Spreading branches form a rounded, dense crown. Bark is gray and breaks up into small, squarish plates. **ID TIP:** A white oak. The blue-green foliage is distinctive. Leaves lack both hairs and teeth.

HABITAT: Open, dry woodlands, canyons, mountains. Elevation 4,300–5,400'.

NOTES: Mexican Blue Oak is a common tree of high grasslands and mesas and a key component of foothill and mountain oak woodlands of the Arizona–Mexico border region.

BEECH FAMILY **FAGACEAE**

LEAF 1–2" long. Narrowly elliptic to ovate; untoothed margins. Shiny, blue-green above; paler beneath. **ACORN** ½–¾" long. Nut ovoid; ⅓ enclosed within scaly cup. Usually borne singly and stalkless. Autumn; ripens in 1 year.

Arizona Oak

Quercus arizonica
ALSO CALLED Arizona White Oak
HT 30–50' **DIA** 1–3½'

Small tree with nearly evergreen, simple leaves (persisting until early spring). Short trunk and symmetrical, domed crown (irregular in harsh habitats); shrubby at high elevations; largest in moist canyons. Bark gray to whitish, with deep fissures. **ID TIP:** A white oak. Leaves are blue-green, with a broad, yellow midvein.

HABITAT: Evergreen oak-pinyon woodlands, chaparral edges, arroyos, moist canyons. Elevation 4,300–8,200'.

LEAF 1½–3" long. Elliptic, with blunt tip; usually slightly wavy margins that are untoothed or coarsely toothed toward tip. Leathery, usually stiff. Dull, blue-green, with recessed veins above; pale green, densely hairy, with raised veins beneath; broad, yellow, nearly hairless midvein. Twig yellowish, woolly, turning reddish brown, glossy. **ACORN** ¾–1" long, ½" wide. Nut ovoid; chestnut brown; ⅓ enclosed within shallow cup of finely hairy, cream to brown scales. Borne singly or in pairs, on short stalk or stalkless. Autumn; ripens in 1 year.

Netleaf Oak

Quercus rugosa
HT to 40' **DIA** 1'

Small tree with nearly evergreen, simple leaves (persisting until early spring). **ID TIP:** A white oak. The leathery, stiff leaves are obovate, often concave or cupped, with prickly teeth toward the tip; twigs are woolly. Acorns are borne singly or in clusters of 2 or 3, at end of long stalk. **HABITAT:** Mountain oak woodlands and canyons. Elevation 6,600–8,200'.

LEAF 1–4" long. Obovate; several small, prickly teeth toward tip. Dark green, with recessed veins above; yellow-hairy, with raised veins beneath. **ACORN** ½–¾" long. Nut ovoid; ¼ enclosed within shallow, scaly cup. Autumn; ripens in 1 year.

Turbinella Oak

Quercus turbinella
ALSO CALLED Sonoran Scrub Oak
HT 6–16'   **DIA** 4"

BEECH FAMILY   FAGACEAE

Small tree or, more typically, a shrub with evergreen, simple leaves. **ID TIP:** A white oak. Blue-green leaves have a white bloom; underside is downy. Acorns occur singly or in clusters on long stalk.

HABITAT: Arizona chaparral (where it's a shrub); juniper-pinyon mountain woodlands. Elevation 2,600–6,600'.

NOTES: Toumey Oak (*Q. toumeyi*) is a small tree or shrub with ½–1" long, shiny, dark green, deciduous or semi-evergreen leaves. The margins have prickly teeth toward the tip or are untoothed, and the underside is usually densely covered with golden glands but not at all velvety. Bark is usually scaly and flaking on twigs ½" wide. Acorns are smaller than in Turbinella and stalkless. Toumey occurs in evergreen-oak woodlands on mountain slopes, at 4,900–5,900'.

LEAF ⅝–1½" long. Elliptic, with prickly-toothed margins. Blue-green with pale white bloom above; yellowish or grayish green and downy beneath. Leathery. Bark usually intact (not peeling) on twigs ½" wide (unlike Toumey Oak). **ACORN** ⅝–1" long. Nut narrowly ovoid; light brown; ¼–⅓ enclosed within scaly cup. Borne singly or in clusters, on long stalk. Autumn; ripens in 1 year.

Q. turbinella

Q. toumeyi

Gray Oak

Quercus grisea
ALSO CALLED Scrub Oak, Shin Oak
HT 16–20'   **DIA** 1'

BEECH FAMILY   FAGACEAE

Small tree with deciduous to semi-evergreen, simple leaves. Occasionally to 60' tall. **ID TIP:** A white oak. Leaves are elliptic to ovate, more or less dull gray green and only sparsely hairy above, duller and hairier beneath. Veins

less prominent than in Arizona Oak. **HABITAT:** Rocky, mountain slopes; moist canyons. Elevation to 8,500'.

LEAF 1–2" long. Narrowly elliptic to ovate; margins with a few teeth toward tip or untoothed. Dull gray-green. **ACORN** ½" long. Nut elliptic; ⅓–½ enclosed within deep cup of hairy, flat scales. Autumn; ripens in 1 year.

Emory Oak

Quercus emoryi

ALSO CALLED Desert Live Oak, Blackjack Oak

HT 30–60'　**DIA** 2–3'

Small to medium-sized tree with nearly evergreen, simple leaves (persisting until early spring). Short trunk; symmetrical crown; shrubby on exposed slopes or at high elevations. Branches are glossy, red-brown or black. Bark dark brown to blackish, with deep fissures. **ID TIP:** A red oak. The shiny, stiff leaves have wavy margins with bristly teeth and tip.

HABITAT: Canyons, slopes, oak-pine woodlands, desert grasslands. Elevation 3,300–7,200'.

NOTES: Emory Oak is a dominant tree of oak woodlands in Southwest mountains, growing largest in sheltered canyons.

LEAF 1–2½" long. Narrowly elliptic to broadly lance-shaped, with bristly tip; margin slightly wavy, with several large, bristle-tipped teeth. Leathery, stiff. Shiny, yellow-green; paler, nearly hairless beneath. Twig dark reddish brown, finely hairy when young, becoming hairless. **ACORN** ½–¾" long. Nut ovoid; dark chestnut brown, turning light brown; ¼–½ enclosed within deep cup of flat, thin, downy, light brown scales. Borne singly or in pairs, nearly stalkless. Autumn; ripens in 1 year (rare for a red oak).

Palmer Oak

Quercus palmeri

ALSO CALLED Dunn Oak

HT to 20'　**DIA** 4"

Small, multistemmed tree or thicket-forming shrub with evergreen, simple leaves. **ID TIP:** A golden oak. Leaves are very small and nearly circular in outline,

with prickly teeth. **HABITAT:** Dry slopes, canyons, chaparral, pinyon-juniper woodlands. Elevation 2,300–5,900'.

LEAF ½–1¼" long. Elliptic to nearly circular; prickly teeth along margins. Gray-green above; fine, white hairs beneath. **ACORN** ¾–1¼" long. Nut ovoid; enclosed within shallow cup of flat, hairy scales. On very short stalk.

Silverleaf Oak

Quercus hypoleucoides
HT to 60'   **DIA** 1–2½'

Small to medium-sized tree or large shrub with evergreen, simple leaves. Tall, slender trunk; conical or narrowly rounded crown; frequently a shrub growing in thick clumps. Bark blackish, with deep furrows. **ID TIP:** A red oak. Leaves are glossy green above and silvery white beneath, unlike other evergreen oaks.

HABITAT: Moist, shaded canyons, and mountain slopes, in association with other evergreen oaks. Elevation 4,900–8,900'.

LEAF 2–4" long. Lance-shaped, with rounded base; tiny, bristle-tipped teeth along margins; edges rolled under. Very thick, leathery. Glossy, green above; silvery white, densely white-woolly beneath. **ACORN** ½–¾" long. Nut ovoid; light chestnut brown; ⅓ enclosed within thick, deep, bowl-shaped cup of silvery downy scales. Borne singly or in pairs; stalkless or on short stalk. Autumn; ripens in 2 years.

Canyon Live Oak

Quercus chrysolepis
ALSO CALLED Maul Oak
HT .15–70' **DIA** 1–5'

BEECH FAMILY **FAGACEAE**

Small to medium-sized tree with evergreen, simple leaves. Short, thick, crooked trunk, or multistemmed; very broad, dense crown; tall trunk in deep canyons; shrubby on harsh sites. **ID TIP:** A golden oak. Dark green foliage and golden-woolly twigs and acorn cups distinguish this species.

HABITAT: Canyon cliffs, woodlands, chaparral. Elevation 650–8,500'.

NOTES: Canyon Live Oak is widely distributed through-out the Pacific coast region. Its old-growth form is often seen on canyon cliffs.

LEAF 1–4" long. Elliptic; margins untoothed or, on young twigs, wavy with several large, prickly teeth; edges rolled under. Leathery. Bright green above; golden-hairy or bluish white and hairless beneath. Twig golden-woolly. **ACORN** ⅝–1¼" long. Nut variable in shape and size: ovoid to oblong; light chestnut brown; ¼ enclosed within flat-bottomed cup of golden-woolly, warty scales. Usually borne singly and on very short stalk. Autumn; ripens in 2 years.

Interior Live Oak

Quercus wislizenii

ALSO CALLED Sierra Live Oak, Highland Live Oak

HT 30–75' **DIA** 2–3'

BEECH FAMILY **FAGACEAE**

Small to medium-sized tree with evergreen, simple leaves. Short, thick trunk; very broad crown; shrubby on arid or fire-prone sites. **ID TIP:** A red oak. Interior Live Oak is very similar to Coast Live Oak; their ranges overlap along the California coast. Interior is distinguished by its hairless leaf (tufts of hairs beneath in Coast Live Oak), which typically has more than 5 pairs of side veins.

HABITAT: Inland foothill woodlands, Sierra Nevada mountain slopes; sandy

chaparral. Elevation 1,000–6,200'.

NOTES: Interior Live Oak is often found in fire-prone chaparral. It sprouts readily from the trunk and stumps after fires.

LEAF 1–2" long. Variable in shape (as pictured); usually has short, bristle-tipped teeth along margins. Thick, leathery. Shiny, dark green above; glossy, yellow-green, with prominent veins beneath; hairless on both sides. Twig woolly. **ACORN** ¾–1½" long. Nut ovoid; light chestnut brown with darker, lengthwise streaks; ½ enclosed within deep cup of thin, flat scales. Borne singly or in pairs, stalkless or on short stalk. Autumn; ripens in 2 years.

Engelmann Oak

Quercus engelmannii

ALSO CALLED Evergreen White Oak, Mesa Live Oak

HT 20–60' **DIA** 1–2½'

BEECH FAMILY **FAGACEAE**

Small to medium-sized tree with nearly evergreen, simple leaves; crown of few branches. **ID TIP:** A white oak. The twigs are densely hairy; the leaves are blue-green, their margins toothed or untoothed and sometimes wavy. **HABITAT AND RANGE:** Restricted to woodland belt in foothills of southwestern California, west of the Coast Ranges, from San Gabriel Mountains south into Baja California. Elevation 200–3,900'.

LEAF 1–2" long. Broadly to narrowly elliptic; margins untoothed or toothed, often wavy. Blue-green above, yellow-green below. **ACORN** ¾–1" long. Nut oblong; light brown; ⅓ enclosed within cup of warty, gray-hairy scales. Stalkless or on short stalk. Autumn; ripens in 1 year.

Coast Live Oak

Quercus agrifolia
ALSO CALLED California Live Oak
HT 30–80'   **DIA** 3–4'

BEECH FAMILY   FAGACEAE

Small to medium-sized tree with evergreen, simple leaves. Short, thick, crooked trunk, or multistemmed; low, dense, very broad crown; shrubby in chaparral.   **ID TIP:** A red oak. The leaf underside has tufts of hairs in the angles of the veins. The leaves are somewhat convex and have 5 pairs of side veins or fewer (Interior Live Oak has more than 5 pairs).

HABITAT: Dry valleys and slopes. Elevation to 4,600'.

NOTES: Old-growth Coast Live Oaks have long been a familiar feature of the California coastal landscape; they once occurred in open groves in valleys and on slopes. Despite conservation efforts, populations are now at risk of decline due to development, overcutting, overbrowsing, and disease. The species has been hit hard by sudden oak death.

LEAF 1–3" long. Broadly elliptic to broadly ovate; wavy, with large, bristle-tipped teeth along margins (some leaves lack bristles); edges rolled under. Thick, leathery, upper surface somewhat convex. 5 pairs of side veins, or fewer. Shiny, dark green above; yellow-green, often with tufts of hairs in vein angles beneath. Young leaf woolly on both sides.   **ACORN** ¾–1½" long. Nut narrowly ovoid; light chestnut brown; ⅓ enclosed within deep, rounded cup of finely hairy, flat, thin scales. Borne singly or in clusters, stalkless. Autumn; ripens in 1 year.

Channel Island Oak

Quercus tomentella
ALSO CALLED Island Live Oak
HT 20–40'   **DIA** 1–2'

BEECH FAMILY	FAGACEAE

Small, local tree with evergreen, simple leaves; grows in association with Canyon Live Oak. **ID TIP:** A golden oak. Channel Island Oak has conspicuous veins beneath. The acorn nut is more rounded than in Canyon Live Oak, and has a shallow, flat-bottomed cup covered with thick wool. **HABITAT AND RANGE:** Along canyons of Channel Islands off southern California and Guadalupe Island off Baja California. Elevation 300–2,100'.

LEAF 1–2" long. Ovate to lance-shaped; margins untoothed or with very short, prickly teeth. Shiny, dark green; pale and hairy beneath. **ACORN** 1½–2" long. Nut ovoid; light brown; shallow, flat-bottomed cup of thick, woolly scales. Borne singly or in pairs, on short stalk. Autumn; ripens in 2 years.

California Black Oak

Quercus kelloggii
ALSO CALLED Black Oak, Kellogg Oak
HT 30–80'   **DIA** 1–4'

BEECH FAMILY	FAGACEAE

Small to medium-sized tree with deciduous, simple leaves. Stout trunk, often forked partway up; broad crown; in open areas, lower branches can nearly touch the ground; shrubby on poor sites. **ID TIP:** A red oak. California Black Oak has deeply divided, bristle-tipped lobes.

HABITAT: Slopes, valleys, woodlands, coniferous forests. Elevation 1,000–7,900'.

NOTES: California Black Oak can be an abundant producer of acorns and an important food source for wildlife, but acorn yields vary from year to year. The tree is fire-adapted, able to resprout after aboveground parts have been destroyed. Natural stands of California Black Oak have declined due to overcutting, habitat destruction, excessive wildlife browsing, and drought, and it is one of the species affected by sudden oak death. The tree is planted for erosion control and as an ornamental.

LEAF 3½–8" long. Widest toward tip; 7 or 9 lobes divided about halfway to midvein; each lobe ends in bristle-tipped teeth. Shiny, dark green above; light yellow-green and often hairy beneath. Autumn color yellow, orange, brown. **ACORN** 1–1½" long. Nut ovoid; light chestnut brown; about ½ enclosed within deep cup of thin, flat, glossy, light brown scales. Borne singly or in clusters, on short stalk. Autumn; ripens in 2 years.

Valley Oak

Quercus lobata

ALSO CALLED California White Oak

HT 30–90'   **DIA** 2–4'

Small to large tree with deciduous, simple leaves. Short, massive trunk; dense, very broad crown of ascending branches that spread at wide angles. Older trees develop a sort of "weeping" form: branchlets become very long and vinelike, sometimes sweeping the ground.

ID TIP: A white oak. Valley Oak is a massive lowland tree; leaves have 7–11 rounded lobes and are hairy on both surfaces.

HABITAT: Savannas, on slopes and in valleys. Elevation to 5,600'.

NOTES: Closely related to the eastern White Oak, Valley Oak is one of the most massive native broadleaf trees of the West. Near the coast, trees are scrubby and stunted by ocean salt. Populations are steadily declining due to urban sprawl invading the species' habitat.

LEAF 2–4" long. Widest toward tip; 7–11 rounded lobes, deeply divided more than halfway to midvein; tips of larger lobes notched. Dark green and often downy above; pale green, finely hairy, with yellow veins beneath.   **ACORN** 1¼–2" long. Nut narrowly ovoid (bullet-shaped), gradually tapered toward tip; bright chestnut brown; ⅓ enclosed within deep, rounded cup of hairy scales. Borne singly or in pairs, on very short stalk. Autumn; ripens in 1 year.

Oregon White Oak

Quercus garryana
ALSO CALLED Garry Oak, Oregon Oak
HT 25–90' **DIA** 1–3'

Small to large tree with deciduous, simple leaves. Short trunk; dense, compact, broad crown; gnarled, drooping branchlets, with foliage sometimes reaching the ground. **ID TIP:** A white oak. Leathery, waxy leaves have stout, yellow midvein and 5–9 rounded lobes.

HABITAT: Slopes, woodlands, mixed evergreen or coniferous forests; chaparral. Elevation to 6,200'.

NOTES: Oregon White Oak has one of the most northerly ranges of North American oaks and is the Northwest's only native oak. In areas of heavy rain or fog, moss coats its branches. The wood is prized as fuelwood for its high heat output. The species is now in grave decline due to overcutting and land clearing. A shrubby form (var. *breweri*) occurs at high elevations (2,000–6,000') and windswept sites.

BEECH FAMILY **FAGACEAE**

LEAF 3–6" long. Widest toward tip; 5–9 irregular, rounded lobes, divided about halfway to stout, yellow midvein; edges rolled under. Leathery, waxy. Glossy, dark green above; pale green and usually hairy beneath. May turn scarlet in autumn. Leafstalk downy. Young twig and bud densely hairy. **ACORN** ½–1" long. Nut oblong; light brown; ¼–⅓ enclosed within a shallow, rounded cup of downy, loose scales. Nearly stalkless. Borne singly or in pairs. Autumn; ripens in 1 year.

Blue Oak

Quercus douglasii
ALSO CALLED Mountain White Oak, Iron Oak
HT 20–60' **DIA** 1–3'

Small to medium-sized tree with deciduous, simple leaves. Short or leaning trunk, occasionally forked; dense, usually symmetrical, broad crown; stout, brittle, hairy branchlets; foliage sometimes reaches the ground. Sometimes shrubby in the southern part of its range. **ID TIP:** A white oak. The distinctly bluish or grayish green leaves usually have 3, 4, or 5 shallow lobes.

HABITAT: Dry woodland on slopes; grasslands. Elevation to 4,000'.

NOTES: Drought-resistant, with roots reaching 100' deep, Blue Oak is an important stabilizer for eroding soils. It provides vital habitat and food for deer and small mammals, rodents, lizards, and dozens of bird species, including bald eagle and golden eagle. The wood is very brittle, but has been used for goldmine supports, fences, and fuel. The species is rapidly declining in the wild due to cutting and development. It is planted as an ornamental for its attractive, smoky blue foliage.

BEECH FAMILY   **FAGACEAE**

LEAF 2–5" long. Elliptic to obovate, with 3–5 shallow lobes or with margins toothed or untoothed; sometimes wavy. Waxy, stiff. Bluish or grayish green and hairless to slightly downy above; pale green and slightly downy beneath. Leafstalk stout, downy. **ACORN** ¾–1½" long. Nut ovoid; light chestnut brown; only base enclosed within shallow, flat-bottomed cup of warty scales. Borne singly or in pairs; very short stalk. Autumn; ripens in 1 year.

Palms

Palms, family Arecaceae, are monocots, plants that have one seed leaf (all trees that precede palms in the guide are dicots, which have two). Palm leaves are compound, and the individual leaf segments usually have parallel veins. The flower parts occur in threes. Palm trunks are composed of interconnected vascular bundles and fibers, and are not divided into wood and bark like those of conifers and hardwoods. Also unlike conifers and hardwoods, palms typically add height from a single point of apical growth (from one growing tip) and seldom develop branches.

The large, compound leaves of palms are often referred to as fronds. Palms are typically divided into those with palmately compound leaves, with the leaf segments radiating from a central point (something like fingers from the palm of a hand), and those with pinnately compound leaves, with all leaf segments aligned along opposite sides of a central axis, like a feather. Leaf segments in most palms are straplike and pointed at the tip (with the exception of Fishtail Palm, which has obovate leaf segments). Some palms with leaves that appear palmate, such as Cabbage Palm, are technically costapalmate: the leaf segments are borne along the sides of a short, riblike extension of the leafstalk, called a costa. The leaves of some palms, notably Cuban Royal Palm, arise from a conspicuous crownshaft composed of the tightly overlapping bases of developing leaves.

The fruits of palm trees have been described as both drupes and berries; however, the fruits of many species do not seem to fit clearly into either of these fruit types. Some experts call the fruit of at least some species drupelike; others describe the fruit's appearance without reference to a type. The fruits of Coconut Palm and the date palms, for example, may technically be berries, whereas those of thatch palms are more clearly drupes. Here we have chosen to use "drupe" for the fruit type of the palms.

Palms can be recognized and often identified to genus or species by their overall shape. The *Washingtonia* palms, for example, have a shaggy "skirt" of dead leaves just below the crown in their natural state. The shiny green crownshaft below the arching leaves and its majestic form help identify the Cuban Royal Palm. Even at a distance the curving, leaning trunk of Coconut Palm is unmistakable.

Left: Palm trunks are composed of interconnected vascular bundles and fibers. Right: Fruits of the palm family include the coconut and the date. California Fan Palm (pictured) bears tiny drupes in large, grapelike clusters.

Coconut Palm

Cocos nucifera

HT 50–80'   **DIA** 12–20"

Medium-sized tree. Trunk light gray-brown, smooth, with horizontal rings of old leaf scars up the entire trunk; becomes smoother with age. **ID TIP:** This palm has a tall, slender, branch-free, usually curved and leaning trunk that is swollen at the base and only slightly tapering, with a crown of 12–20 huge, pinnately compound leaves. The coconut fruit distinguishes this species.

HABITAT AND RANGE: Introduced in North America; planted worldwide along warm coasts; naturalized in the United States on beaches and disturbed sites only at southernmost tip of Florida and in Florida Keys. Near sea level. Native to southeastern Asia.

NOTES: Coconut Palm is cultivated for its coconuts. A tree typically produces about 25 fruits per year. Coconut lethal yellowing disease, caused by a funguslike parasite spread by insects, has obliterated plantations throughout the tropics. Resistant trees are being sought.

LEAF 6–20' long, 4–6' wide; massive; arches and hangs; lacks spines. 25–40 pairs of leaf segments per leaf; leaf lies flat. **Leaf segment:** 2–3' long. Dark green, turns yellow before shedding. Leafstalk 4–6' long; fibrous matting wrapped around leaf base. **FLOWER** Small; creamy white or pale yellow; in dense, large, 3–5' long, branched, upright clusters at leaf bases. Spring, or throughout year. **FRUIT** 8–15" wide, 3-sided to round, dry drupe; shiny, green, and smooth, maturing to dull brown and ridged; hard, thick, fibrous layer surrounds 5–10" wide, round seed. Seed has thick shell containing white, moist flesh (coconut "meat"); 3 soft spots near base for sprouting roots and stems. In hanging clusters.

flower clusters
at leaf bases

Date Palm

Phoenix dactylifera

HT 25–60'   **DIA** 1–2'

| PALM FAMILY | ARECACEAE |

Small to medium-sized tree. Trunk brown to gray, rough, covered by leaf bases, some of which form jagged "boots"; these persist for years, gradually falling off and leaving large leafstalk scars; trunk becomes smoother with age. **ID TIP:** Date Palm has a stout, straight trunk with a crown of very large, upright and arching, pinnately compound leaves. It produces the familiar cultivated date. Species of this genus are difficult to distinguish from one another.

HABITAT AND RANGE: Introduced in North America. Native to western Asia and northern Africa.

NOTES: Date Palm is among the world's earliest cultivated food trees. More than 1,500 varieties have been developed over thousands of years. In North America, these palms are grown mostly for their fruit, principally in California and Arizona, but they are also planted as ornamentals in both those states and in Florida. A single Date Palm may yield up to 175 lbs of dates annually; some varieties can yield more than 220 lbs per year. **Senegal Date Palm** (*P. reclinata*) is planted in Florida and California. It has several slender trunks.

LEAF 9–20' long; massive. 120–240 pairs of leaf segments; leaf lies flat. **Leaf segment:** 2–3½' long. Gray-green, covered with a powdery, waxy bloom. Spines at base of leafstalk and along stalk in place of first few leaf segments. Leafstalk 3–4' long. **FLOWER** Tiny; white; produced in dense clusters inside a hard sheath, or bract, that falls as the orange stalk of the inflorescence grows. Fragrant. Spring. **FRUIT** 1–3" long, oblong, fleshy drupe; waxy, amber-colored; tender skin and thick, fibrous flesh; in large clusters, hanging on orange-yellow stalks. Autumn–early winter. Produced in abundance in California and Arizona; less abundant in southern Florida.

Senegal Date Palm

Canary Island Date Palm

Phoenix canariensis

HT 50–60' **DIA** 2'

Medium-sized tree. **ID TIP:** Massive trunk; crown composed of numerous ascending to arching, 8–15' long, pinnately compound leaves with sharp spines at their bases. 1" wide fruit is bright orange and datelike. Growing tip or terminal bud yields tasty "palm honey." Hybridizes with Date Palm. **HABITAT AND RANGE:** Introduced in North America; familiar ornamental palm, planted as a street and landscape tree in Florida, on the Gulf coast, and in California; naturalized in California. Native to the Canary Islands.

Cuban Royal Palm

Roystonea regia

ALSO CALLED Florida Royal Palm

HT 70–100' **DIA** 1½'

Medium-sized to large tree. **ID TIP:** The tall trunk is pale gray, smooth, sometimes tinged with powdery white, resembling concrete, with distinctive horizontal rings and often lichen growth. The trunk is swollen at the base and sometimes just below the crownshaft, where flowers and fruit hang in a dense, conspicuous cluster. The thick, green crownshaft continues vertically, for 8–10', opening into an impressive cluster of huge, pinnately compound leaves that arch downward from the tip of the crown.

HABITAT AND RANGE: Swamps, moist hammocks, cypress sloughs. Occurs naturally only at southern tip of Florida, near sea level; often planted.

NOTES: The Florida form of the Cuban Royal Palm and the very similar, introduced Cuban form are two of the most planted street and landscape palms in southern Florida. In the past, thousands of Florida's royal palms were cut for their fruits (to feed hogs), and the species is now endangered in the wild. Natural stands are best seen in Fakahatchee Strand Preserve. The Cuban form has a more cylindrical trunk with swollen trunk sections. The Florida form is considered a separate species (*R. elata*) by some authorities.

LEAF 9–20' long. 20–70 pairs of leaf segments; leaf does not lie flat; lacks spines. **Leaf segment:** 2½–3' long. Deep green, with prominent parallel veins above; densely covered by tiny, pale gland dots beneath. Leafstalk 8–9' long, scaly, with peeling threadlike fibers, enlarged, clasping base. **FLOWER** ¼" long; white; in 2' long, hanging clusters. **FRUIT** ½" long, round drupe; dark blue to purple-black; olivelike.

Queen Palm

Syagrus romanzoffiana
HT 25–50'   **DIA** 1'

Small tree. Trunk gray, smooth, ringed with widely spaced old leaf scars. **ID TIP:** Queen Palm has a tall, slender, straight trunk with an 8–10' tall crownshaft and a crown of huge, loosely spread, upright, and arching leaves. Leaves are pinnately compound, their segments glossy, bright green, and flexible; they do not lie flat. Just below the leaves, the trunk is surrounded by dead leafstalks and persistent leafstalk bases that form a conspicuous, cuplike structure called a "boot."

HABITAT AND RANGE: Introduced in North America. Native to Brazil. Naturalized in central and southern Florida.

NOTES: Queen Palm is planted as a street and landscape tree in central Florida and southern California. It is also grown as an indoor houseplant.

| PALM FAMILY | ARECACEAE |

LEAF 12–16' long. 150–250 pairs of leaf segments per leaf; lacks spines. **Leaf segment:** 1½–3' long. Soft, fine, textured, flexible. Glossy, bright green. **FLOWER** Small; yellow or creamy white; in dense, large, 3–6' long, brushlike clusters at leaf bases. Summer. **FRUIT** 1" long, round drupe; yellow to bright orange; datelike. Winter.

Saw Palmetto

Serenoa repens
HT to 20'

Large shrub or occasionally a small tree; thicket-forming. It is the dominant ground cover of pine flatwoods throughout Florida. **ID TIP:** Saw Palmetto and rare **Paurotis Palm** (*Acoelorraphe wrightii*, restricted to Everglades National Park) are the only native palms with palmately compound leaves that have prickly leafstalks.

HABITAT: Pine forests, especially pine flatwoods, and sandy prairies along the coast. Elevation to 160'. Widely planted in parks, gardens, and landscapes.

| PALM FAMILY | ARECACEAE |

LEAF 2–3' wide. Palmately compound. Leafstalk flat and lined along the margins with numerous prickles that are very sharp to the touch and give it the appearance of a saw blade. **FLOWER** Tiny; ivory white, fragrant; in 1–3' long cluster. **FRUIT** ½–1" long, oblong drupe that turns from orange to black.

California Fan Palm

Washingtonia filifera
ALSO CALLED California Washingtonia,
Desert Palm, Petticoat Palm
HT 30–50' **DIA** 1–3'

Small tree. Trunk thick, smooth, with
gray-brown or dull, red-brown rings,
intersected by vertical chinks and
fissures. **ID TIP:** California Fan Palm has
a tall, stout, straight trunk with a tufted
crown of very large, fan-shaped leaves.
Dead leaves persist and, if not removed,
droop from the trunk, sometimes forming
a wide, shaggy "skirt" or "petticoat" that
may extend down the trunk nearly to
ground level.

HABITAT: Along alkaline streams; in desert
canyons. Elevation 300–3,900'.

NOTES: California Fan Palm is the only
native palm in the West. It is widely
planted as a street tree throughout the
South. In its natural habitat, the thatch
on the trunk extends to the base and
provides habitat for wildlife nests and
shelter; the thatch is usually removed
from cultivated specimens for pest and
fire control.

PALM FAMILY   ARECACEAE

LEAF 3–6' wide. Palmately compound; divided into roughly
50 segments. **Leaf segment:** Leathery; gray-green, with
frayed fibers along margins. Leafstalk 3–5' long; stout, with
hooked spines. **FLOWER** Small; white; in enormous, 8–10'
long, branched, hanging clusters at leaf bases. Somewhat
fragrant. Spring. **FRUIT** ⅜–½" wide, oblong drupe; black;
datelike (pictured on p. 461). Abundantly produced, in
hanging clusters. September; persists into winter.

Mexican Fan Palm

Washingtonia robusta
ALSO CALLED Mexican Washingtonia,
Petticoat Palm, Washington Palm
HT to 100' **DIA** 10–18"

A large, common, ornamental palm.
Salt-tolerant, it grows better along coasts
(as far north as San Francisco) than
California Fan Palm. **ID TIP:** Tall, with
disproportionately slender trunk; tuft of
palmately compound leaves forms crown.
Produces a shaggy "skirt" of persistent
dead leaves around at least the upper
fifth of the trunk. **HABITAT AND RANGE:**
Introduced in United States; naturalized in
Florida and California. Native to Mexico.

PALM FAMILY   ARECACEAE

Cabbage Palm

Sabal palmetto
ALSO CALLED Swamp Cabbage,
Sabal Palmetto, Cabbage Palmetto
HT 30–50' **DIA** 12–22"

Small tree. Trunk brown to gray, thick, rough, covered by criss-cross pattern of leaf bases or jagged "boots" that persist for years; trunk weathers with age, becoming smoother. **ID TIP:** This palm has a tall, straight, stout trunk, with a rounded crown of very large, fan-shaped leaves. The combination of fan-shaped, folded leaves and the whitish fibers along the margins of the leaf segments help distinguish Cabbage Palm.

HABITAT: Sandy shores, hammocks. Elevation to 130'.

NOTES: Cabbage Palm is a frost-tolerant palm occurring along the southeastern coastline; also planted along roads and in gardens and parks throughout Florida. The terminal bud of Cabbage Palm was formerly cut from the tree and eaten, a process that killed the tree.

PALM FAMILY   **ARECACEAE**

LEAF 6' long, 8' wide. Appearing palmately compound; lacks spines. Leaf folded upward along midrib, often appearing V-shaped; divided into 40–90 or more drooping segments. **Leaf segment:** Coarse, leathery; shiny, dark green; creamy white, threadlike fibers along margins. Leafstalk 6–7' long; very stout, stiff, arching, with pointed base; often persists on tree after leaf sheds. **FLOWER** ¼" long; whitish; in large, 4–6' long, branched, hanging clusters at leaf bases. Fragrant. Spring–early summer. **FRUIT** ⅛–¼" wide, nearly round, dry drupe; shiny black. Abundant, in hanging clusters. Autumn; persists into winter.

Mexican Palmetto

Sabal mexicana
ALSO CALLED Rio Grande Palmetto
HT 30–45' **DIA** 8–14"

Small tree. **ID TIP:** Mexican Palmetto is similar to Cabbage Palm but is a smaller tree, with larger fruit (½–¾" wide); it flowers from spring through summer, or year-round in warmest regions, and prefers a wetter habitat. The two species' ranges do not overlap in the United States. **HABITAT AND RANGE:** Riverbanks, swamps, floodplains. Coastal Texas into Mexico and south to Nicaragua. Elevation to 160'.

PALM FAMILY   **ARECACEAE**

Florida Thatch Palm

Thrinax radiata

HT 20–28' DIA 4–6"

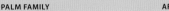

Small tree. Trunk gray, smooth, with horizontal rings created by old leaf scars. **ID TIP:** Florida Thatch Palm has a slender, branch-free trunk, only slightly tapering; the leaf-scar rings ascend the trunk to the thatch layer of dead leafstalk bases just below the compact cluster of fan-shaped leaves.

HABITAT AND RANGE: Coastal hammocks, pinelands, and limestone scrub, at southernmost tip of Florida, near sea level.

NOTES: Florida Thatch Palm is planted as a very salt-hardy landscaping tree in southern Florida, but is endangered in its native range. It is similar to **Brittle Thatch Palm** (*Thrinax morrisii*), but leaves of Florida Thatch Palm are dull green beneath, while those of Brittle Thatch Palm are silvery white. The fruits of Brittle Thatch are smaller, ⅛" wide, and the flower clusters are larger, 4–7' long. Brittle Thatch Palm occurs in coastal hammocks at the extreme southern tip of Florida and the Florida Keys.

LEAF 2–3' wide. Palmately compound; lacks spines; divided into roughly 30 segments. **Leaf segment:** Thick. Shiny green above; paler beneath, with conspicuous, raised midvein. Leafstalk 4' long; stiff, flat; split at leaf base. **FLOWER** Small; white; in dense, 3–4' long, branched clusters at leaf bases. Fragrant. Spring. **FRUIT** ¼–½" wide, round drupe; ivory white; borne in elongated clusters. Autumn.

Florida Thatch Palm

Brittle Thatch Palm

Brittle Thatch Palm

Fishtail Palm

Caryota mitis

ALSO CALLED Burmese Fishtail Palm, Clustering Fishtail Palm

HT 15–25'   **DIA** to 6"

PALM FAMILY   ARECACEAE

Small, clump-forming, multistemmed tree with a crown of arching leaves. Trunk light brown, smooth, with horizontal rings. **ID TIP:** *Caryota* is the only palm genus with double-compound leaves. The fruits and flowers hang from the leaf nodes in long, flowing clusters.

HABITAT AND RANGE: Introduced in North America; naturalized in disturbed hammocks in southern Florida. Native from India to the Philippines.

NOTES: Fishtail Palm is planted outdoors in Florida, and can be planted in atriums indoors. The tree parts contain oxalic acid and can cause severe skin irritation; the fruits are poisonous. The first flower cluster of a mature stem emerges from the base of the uppermost leaves. Succeeding flower clusters emerge from successively lower leaf nodes until the lowest node is reached. When the fruit of the lowest node matures, the individual stem dies, leaving the remaining stems unaffected. The regular production of new stems allows a single clump of Fishtail Palms to remain vital for many years.

LEAF 6–10' long. Bipinnately compound; lacks spines; slender, erect central axis. **Leaf segment:** 4–8" long; obovate (inversely triangular), with coarsely veined, ragged margins on the outer end, resembling the tail of a fish. **FLOWER** White; in dense, branched, hanging clusters. Year-round. **FRUIT** ½" wide, nearly round drupe; dark red, purplish, or black. Abundant, in hanging clusters. Year-round.

Yuccas

Yuccas are large shrubs or small trees with stiff, evergreen leaves that radiate from the tops of branches or the trunk base. The main stem is densely fibrous and spongy, and is either unbranched or has two or more stout, clublike branches. The stems of most western species are surrounded by a thick thatch of hanging, persistent, dead leaves, at least around the upper trunk.

In yuccas, the similar petals and sepals are known collectively as "tepals."

The densely clustered leaves are dagger-shaped, spine-tipped, and leathery, and lined with parallel veins. The showy, waxy, creamy white flowers are bell-shaped, with six petal-like tepals (undifferentiated petals and sepals). They blossom in tall, branched clusters from among the uppermost leaves. The fruit is a six-sided, six-celled, oblong capsule with a short, stout terminal appendage, or "beak." The capsule contains numerous smooth, flat, black seeds.

Yuccas have a mutualistic relationship with small, white moths known as yucca moths that deliberately deposit pollen into the stigma tube of flowers they visit. Yucca plants depend upon these moths for pollination, and the moth larvae in turn feed on developing yucca seeds to complete their life cycle. The relationship between yucca plants and yucca moths is an often-cited example of coevolution and plant–pollinator interdependency.

Moundlily Yucca

Yucca gloriosa
HT to 16'   **DIA** 4–6"

Small tree or shrub. **ID TIP:** Moundlily Yucca is a smaller and less common yucca than Aloe Yucca. It is distinguished by its bluish green, 16–24" long, and mostly untoothed leaves (can have very fine teeth at leaf base). It has a longer flower cluster (2–5' long) that is elevated above the tips of the encircling leaves and blossoms in the spring. The fruits are black and dry.

HABITAT: Coastal dunes and edges of salt marshes. Elevation to 300'.

AGAVE FAMILY   **AGAVACEAE**

Aloe Yucca

Yucca aloifolia
ALSO CALLED Spanish-bayonet,
Spanish-dagger, Dagger Plant
HT to 22' **DIA** 4"

Small tree. **ID TIP:** Aloe Yucca can be
distinguished from Moundlily Yucca by its
very finely toothed, dark green leaf (18–
32" long), its shorter flower cluster (1½–2'
long) seated within and partially covered
by the uppermost leaves, and its purple-
black, fleshy fruit. It usually flowers from
late spring to autumn, whereas Moundlily
Yucca usually flowers in midspring.

HABITAT: Coastal dunes. Elevation to 500'.

NOTE: Aloe Yucca is the only species of
Yucca for which seed production has
been documented in the absence of
pollination by yucca moths. The origin of
this species is in doubt. Not all authorities

agree that it is
native to the
southeastern
United States.

Soaptree Yucca

Yucca elata
ALSO CALLED Soapweed, Palmilla
HT 4–15' **DIA** 6–10"

Small tree or shrub. **ID TIP:** Soaptree
Yucca is the only tree-sized yucca with
yellow-green, slender, grasslike leaves
(Mojave Yucca's leaves are yellow-green
but sword-shaped). Leaf is 12–18"
long, leathery and flexible, with curling
fibers along margins. Soaptree is also
distinguished by its long-stalked flowers
and very long (3–6') flower clusters, which
bloom in spring. Fruit is dry, pointed, light
brown; matures in early summer.

HABITAT: Southwestern desert plains,
mesas, grasslands. Elevation 1,000–6,200'.

Mojave Yucca

Yucca schidigera
ALSO CALLED Spanish-dagger,
Mohave Yucca
HT to 16' **DIA** 6–12"

AGAVE FAMILY AGAVACEAE

Small tree or shrub. **ID TIP:** Mojave Yucca
is the only southwestern tree-sized
yucca outside of Texas that has yellow-
green, sword-shaped leaves, and white,
purple-tinged flowers on drooping stalks,
blossoming in spring. Leaf is 18–48"
long; grooved; broadest at middle;
coarse fibers along margins; thick, stiff.

Fruit blunt, fleshy; in late
summer. **HABITAT:** Deserts
and mountain slopes; often
grows with Joshua Tree.
Elevation 1,000–3,900'.

Sierra Madre Yucca

Yucca madrensis
ALSO CALLED Spanish-bayonet,
Spanish-dagger
HT 6–23'

AGAVE FAMILY AGAVACEAE

Small tree or shrub. **ID TIP:** Sierra Madre
Yucca is the only tree-sized yucca with
blue-green, sword-shaped leaves with
reddish margins and a reddish spine
at the tip, and a short-stalked flower
that blossoms in summer. It is also the
only western, tree-sized yucca with fruit
maturing in autumn. Leaf is 16–32" long;
no filaments along margin; leathery,
flexible. Fruit blunt, fleshy; green, turning
black.

HABITAT AND RANGE: Oak woodland
slopes and canyons. Elevation 4,000–
7,000'. In Mexico's Sierra Madre Occidental
and related mountains immediately to the
north in Arizona and New Mexico.

NOTES: Plants in the United States have
long been known as *Y. schottii*, Schott's
Yucca, which is now proposed to
represent a hybrid complex.

Faxon Yucca

Yucca faxoniana
ALSO CALLED Eve's Needle
HT 8–22' **DIA** 1'

Small tree or shrub. **ID TIP:** Faxon Yucca has yellow-green, sword-shaped leaves with brown, curling margins. The flowers are greenish white to white, blossoming late winter–spring. Leaf is 17–45" long, stiff, with filaments along margin. Fruit fleshy. **HABITAT AND RANGE:** Slopes and plains of southwestern Texas and Mexico. Elevation 2,600–6,900'.

AGAVE FAMILY · AGAVACEAE

Joshua Tree

Yucca brevifolia
HT 15–30' **DIA** 1–3'

Small tree. Short, stout trunk; broad, open crown. Bark gray or reddish brown, rough, with corky plates and deep furrows; trunks and branches often covered by thatch of dead, hanging leaves. **ID TIP:** Joshua Tree is easily recognized by its unique growth form of multiple, stout, forking, sometimes drooping, clublike branches, tipped with bunches of spiny, daggerlike leaves.

HABITAT: Deserts. Elevation 1,300–5,900'.

NOTES: Joshua Tree is the largest yucca; it is most abundant in Joshua Tree National Park, California, and along Joshua Forest Parkway, Arizona.

Its trunk cavities and dead leaves provide homes for numerous birds, reptiles, and mammals.

FLOWER 1½–2½" long; greenish yellow or creamy white; bell-shaped, with 6 leathery tepals; in 1–1½' long, dense upright, branched clusters. Unpleasant odor of mushrooms. Blossoms irregularly, mostly in early spring. **FRUIT** 2½–4" long, narrowly ovoid capsule; 6-celled; reddish brown or yellow-brown; slightly fleshy to dry. Late spring.

AGAVE FAMILY · AGAVACEAE

LEAF 8–14" long, ¼–½" wide; stiff, daggerlike; flat, with exception of a ridge along outer surface; margins yellow, with numerous tiny, sharp teeth; leaf tipped with short spine. Blue-green. In dense clusters from branch tips.

Cacti

Cacti (family Cactaceae) are natives of the Americas, except for one epiphytic species that occurs naturally in the Old World tropics. After European settlement, humans transported cacti to the Old World, where many are now weeds. The familiar, succulent, leafless, arid-land forms of cacti evolved from a shrubby primitive cactus with deciduous leaves, similar to *Pereskia*, which grows in the dry tropical scrub of Central and South America.

Cacti range from massive giants 70 feet tall to thimble-sized midgets. The Saguaro, with its humanoid shapes, is the most well known of the tree-sized cacti. Cacti are succulent (moist and fleshy), and their stems store great quantities of water. Compact stems and the absence of "normal" leaves minimize surface area, thus reducing heat exposure and water loss. The waxy epidermis (the "skin") retards water loss and, when pale, reflects light and heat. Ribs and small knobby tubercles allow expansion as water is absorbed after rains and later contraction as it is lost during drought.

The clusters of spines arise from areoles, which are modified branches that usually do not develop further; the spines are modified leaves. Spines inhibit herbivores and also shade the plant surface and reflect heat. In the absence of leaves, the pores (stomata) are in the stems. In cacti and other succulents the pores open in the cool of the night and close in the day, the reverse of other plants, another water-conserving adaptation. Carbon dioxide taken in at night is chemically stored within the plant until sunlight provides the energy for photosynthesis.

Cactus flowers last a few hours to many days. Their often numerous sepals and petals may intergrade with each other; stamens are numerous. The ovary is beneath the other flower parts (inferior), and is usually fleshy, in some species producing edible fruits (usually berries). Nectar may be held in a "cup" at the top of the ovary.

Species of *Cylindropuntia* (chollas) and *Opuntia* (pricklypears and beavertails), often shrubs, can be large and treelike. These cacti and their smaller relatives are common on North American deserts. In addition to spines, they have glochids, irritating, bristly hairs at the bases of their spine clusters. Glochids are reversely barbed—like little harpoons; they easily penetrate skin and can be annoying to painfully irritating. New stems grow from an areole near the tip of a stem segment, forming an obvious joint, and ceasing to grow after a season. This unit of growth is the stem joint, many of which are detachable and will root and form new plants when in contact with soil. The stem joints are cylindrical in chollas and flat and padlike in pricklypears and their kin. Chollas and pricklypears also have short, cylindrical vestigial leaves that grow on new stems, soon to be shed as the stem matures.

The numerous stamens in a cactus flower (Saguaro pictured) may produce copious pollen for pollinators—bees, flies, beetles, birds, or bats, depending on the species.

Chain-fruit Cholla

Cylindropuntia fulgida
ALSO CALLED Jumping Cholla
HT 3–10' **DIA** 4–8"

Densely branched shrub or small tree, sometimes with several stems. **ID TIP:** Stem joints are 3–8" long, 1–1½" in diameter, and easily dislodged; spines are yellowish, aging brown. This is the only cholla (pronounced CHOY-yah) that has fruits hanging in chains.

HABITAT: Sandy flats and rocky slopes in shrubby desert. Elevation 1,000–3,600'.

NOTES: The name "Jumping Cholla" alludes to the easily detached joints, which when even lightly touched detach and stick in the skin. The easiest way to remove the joint is to slide a comb under it and quickly flip it away. New plants mostly come from fallen joints that grow new stems and roots; thus plants commonly occur in colonies. In chollas, the stem joints are cylindrical.

SPINES 1–1½" long; covered by a loose golden sheath when young; up to 12 or 18 per cluster; sometimes a cluster contains only glochids. **FLOWER** 1" wide; 5–8 pink to magenta petals and greenish sepals. Stamens many, white to cream. Flowers open in late afternoon. **FRUIT** ¾–2" long. Grayish green, fleshy, inversely ovoid. In hanging chains of 2–12; fruits persist for years; new fruits are added to chain at 1 per year.

fruits

flowers and fruits

Saguaro

Carnegiea gigantea

ALSO CALLED Giant Cactus

HT 4–50' **DIA** 1–2½'

Tall, densely spiny, columnar cactus with a few erect branches as stout as the main stem; sometimes the branches bend and curve. About 12–30 ridges on the stem, bearing stout, sharp spines. **ID TIP:** There is no other cactus so tall and massive north of the Mexican border.

HABITAT: Sonoran Desert in southern Arizona, southeastern California, and Mexico. Elevation 600–4,000'.

NOTES: The photogenic pillars or candelabra of the Saguaro (pronounced sah-WAH-ro) dominate some desert flats and hills in southern Arizona. A cactus may produce its first "arms" at between 50 and 100 years of age; plants live perhaps 200 years. In the first years of its life a Saguaro grows very slowly and is vulnerable to heat, frost, rabbits, rodents, and birds; successful plants usually have been protected by a dense shrub, a "nurse plant." Bees, birds, and bats visit the cuplike flowers, which produce copious nectar. This cactus is also one of the most popular for landscaping in warm desert climates (with permits, plants may be transplanted), but the survival rate beyond 5 years of large transplanted individuals is only about 10 percent.

SPINES To 1¾" long; grayish or pinkish gray. 15–30 per cluster, spreading in all directions, the longer ones pointing downward. **FLOWER** 2–2½" wide, with numerous greenish white, sepal-like parts intergrading into numerous white, petal-like parts; nearly 3,500 stamens in some flowers. Flowers arranged in a "crown" near the top of the stem. Open at night, remain open the following day. **FRUIT** 2–3" long; ovoid; smooth but scaly. Greenish red and juicy at maturity, splitting into 3 or 4 segments, exposing bright red lining and black seeds.

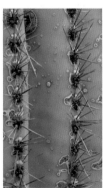

fruits

Tree Families

Aceraceae — Maple Family

Trees and shrubs, mainly of the Northern Hemisphere, valued for colorful autumn foliage, good lumber, and sweet syrup. Some species, especially Red Maple and Silver Maple, planted to reclaim disturbed sites, including strip mines. Members provide food and cover for wildlife. Leaves mostly deciduous, usually simple (sometimes pinnately or palmately compound), opposite, often palmately lobed and toothed. Flowers in small clusters, inconspicuous, greenish, usually unisexual; sexes may or may not be on separate trees. Pollination by insects or wind. Fruits paired samaras. The family contains 2 genera and about 113 species worldwide. For more on the family, see p. 176. *Acer* (maples, including Boxelder), pp. 177–191.

Agavaceae — Agave Family

Trees, shrubs, or low, stemless plants native to tropical and arid regions of the world. In North America they are known for striking foliage and bloom in deserts. Members provide small mammals, birds, and reptiles with food, nesting sites, and habitat. Leaves small to very large, simple, alternate, usually in rosettes, often succulent, leathery, some with prickly edges. Flowers mostly bisexual, usually showy, in large spikes or clusters, some clusters reaching heights of more than 20'. Pollination by bats, birds, or insects. Fruit a capsule, sometimes winged or lobed. The family contains 13–18 genera and 200–550 species worldwide (authorities disagree). Also known as the century-plant family. *Yucca* (yuccas, Joshua Tree), pp. 470–473.

Anacardiaceae — Sumac Family

Trees, shrubs, and woody vines, mostly of tropical and subtropical regions of the world, important for edible fruits and nuts, including cashew, pistachio, and mango. Some species reach colder regions of North America. Seeds, fruits, and leaves provide food for birds and mammals. Leaves deciduous or evergreen, usually alternate, simple or pinnately compound. Leaves, wood, and fruits of some species contain aromatic, often skin-irritating substances. Flowers in clusters, minute, usually bisexual, often white; petals 3–5 or none. Pollination by insects or wind. Fruit a resinous drupe. The family contains 70 genera and some 875 species worldwide. Sometimes called the cashew family. *Rhus* (sumacs), pp. 242–244, 300–301; *Schinus* (peppertrees), p. 245; *Pistacia* (American Pistachio), p. 245; *Toxicodendron* (Poison Sumac, poison ivy, poison-oak), p. 246; *Metopium* (Florida Poisontree), p. 247; *Malosma* (Laurel Sumac), p. 301; *Cotinus* (smoketrees), p. 302; *Mangifera* (Mango), p. 303.

Annonaceae — Custard-apple Family

Aromatic trees, shrubs, and, rarely, woody vines, predominantly of tropical climates, notable for ornamental merit. Fruits provide food for birds and mammals. Leaves deciduous or evergreen, simple, alternate, often arranged in flat sprays. Flowers typically large, solitary, fragrant, bisexual, often with 6 brown to yellow petals arranged in whorls. Pollination by beetles. Large, pulpy fruit usually an aggregate of many berries, sometimes a single berry. The family contains about 120 genera and more than 2,100 species worldwide. *Asimina* (Pawpaw), p. 285; *Annona* (Pond-apple), p. 286.

Aquifoliaceae — Holly Family

Shrubs and trees, occurring in tropical and temperate climates, valued for their often decorative evergreen leaves and handsome fruits. Fruits an important source of food for birds. Some species, especially American Holly and Yaupon, planted to rehabilitate beach and dune areas damaged by salt spray. Leaves deciduous or evergreen, usually simple, alternate, sometimes leathery. Flowers single or in small clusters, small, white or greenish, usually unisexual, on separate plants, though sometimes bisexual; petals 4–6. Pollination by insects. Fruit a small red, black, orange, or yellow drupe, usually with multiple stones. The family contains 2 genera, with more than 400 species worldwide. *Ilex* (hollies), pp. 356–362.

Araliaceae — Ginseng Family

Trees, shrubs, vines, and herbaceous plants, widely distributed in tropical and temperate regions of the world, important for ornament and timber. Some species exploited for the medicinal properties of their roots. Fruits a source of food for birds and mammals, including black bear. Leaves deciduous or evergreen, often very large, typically compound, usually alternate, aromatic when crushed. Flowers small, borne in small to very large, branched, flat-topped clusters, usually bisexual, often greenish white or white, usually with 5 petals. Pollination of *Aralia* is by insects. Fruit a small berry or drupe. The family contains about 47 genera and more than 1,300 species worldwide. *Aralia* (Devil's Walkingstick), p. 216.

Araucariaceae — Araucaria Family

Resinous, coniferous trees, primarily of the Southern Hemisphere, valued for timber, resins, amber, and attractive, hardy ornamentals. Leaves evergreen, opposite or alternate, scalelike or needlelike to broad, sometimes sharply pointed. Branches in distinct, large whorls. Cones unisexual, sexes usually on separate trees. Male cones catkinlike, large. Female cones large, somewhat woody, usually borne erect, with a single large seed in each cone scale. Pollination by wind. The family contains 3 genera and about 40 species worldwide; there are no species native to North America. *Araucaria* (Norfolk Island–pine, Monkeypuzzle Tree), p. 128.

Arecaceae — Palm Family

Trees, shrubs, and vines, mostly of tropical and subtropical climates, important as sources of coconuts, dates, oils, and wax. The family has many species of fine ornamental palms and palmettos. Members provide cover for wildlife; fruits are eaten by birds and bats and other mammals. Leaves evergreen, generally palmately or pinnately compound, alternate; leafstalks large, conspicuous, with tubular sheaths at base in most genera. Flowers in branched clusters that are sometimes large; individual flowers small, often fragrant, bisexual or unisexual, with 2–4 petals. Pollination usually by insects. Fruit small to very large, usually considered a drupe. The family contains between 200 and 1,900 genera (authorities disagree) and more than 2,500 species worldwide. For more on the family, see p. 461. *Cocos* (Coconut Palm), p. 462; *Phoenix* (date palms), pp. 463–464; *Roystonea*

(royal palms), p. 464; *Syagrus* (Queen Palm), p. 465; *Serenoa* (Saw Palmetto), p. 465; *Washingtonia* (fan palms), p. 466; *Sabal* (palmettos), p. 467; *Thrinax* (thatch palms), p. 468; *Caryota* (Fishtail Palm), p. 469.

Betulaceae — Birch Family

Trees and shrubs, mainly of the Northern Hemisphere, but also native to mountainous regions of South America; known for thriving in cold climates. Members esteemed for lumber, edible nuts (hazelnuts and filberts), and ornamental value. Important source of cover, nesting sites, and food for wildlife. Some species planted for rehabilitating soil, strip-mine reclamation, and erosion control. Leaves deciduous, simple, alternate, toothed. Flowers tiny, unisexual, sexes on same tree, borne in pendulous or erect, slender catkins, pollinated by wind. Fruit a small nut or a 2-winged samara, in some genera in a conelike structure (strobilus). The family contains 6 genera and 110–125 species worldwide. For more on the family, see p. 399. *Carpinus* (hornbeams), p. 400; *Ostrya* (hophornbeams), p. 401; *Betula* (birches), pp. 402–408; *Alnus* (alders), pp. 409–413.

Bignoniaceae — Trumpet-creeper Family

Trees, shrubs, vines, and herbaceous plants, especially common in the tropics of South America, important for lumber and showy ornamentals. Leaves deciduous or evergreen, often large, usually compound, often opposite, sometimes whorled. Flowers solitary or in large, showy, branched clusters, tubular or bell-shaped; corolla 5-lobed; bisexual. Pollination by birds, bats, or insects. Fruit a 2-valved capsule, some very long and narrow, others large, fleshy, and gourdlike. The family contains more than 100 genera and some 750 species worldwide. *Catalpa* (catalpas), pp. 192–193; *Chilopsis* (Desert-willow), p. 194.

Burseraceae — Frankincense Family

Resinous trees and shrubs, predominantly of the tropics and subtropics, important for balsam, lumber, perfume resins, oils, and incense. Leaves deciduous, aromatic, usually alternate, generally pinnately compound with small leaflets. Flowers solitary or in branched clusters, small, usually unisexual, sexes on same or separate trees; petals usually 3–5. Pollination usually by insects. Fruit a fleshy drupe or a capsule that dries and splits to release seeds. The family contains 17 genera and some 540 species worldwide. *Bursera* (Gumbo Limbo, Elephant Tree), pp. 247, 250.

Cactaceae — Cactus Family

Mostly succulent trees, shrubs, and small plants, primarily distributed in hot, dry regions, valued for their ornamental interest and ecological importance in arid zones. Members provide food and shelter for a wide variety of animals, especially during dry spells. Originally almost entirely restricted to the Americas; some "weedy" species have become established in the Old World and are now considered pests. Leaves small and vestigial or completely lacking in most species. Stems usually spiny, segmented in some species. Flowers solitary or in clusters, often colorful, showy, mostly bisexual, often of short duration. Pollination by bats, hummingbirds, and insects. Fruit usually a fleshy berry, small to pear-sized, sometimes spiny. The family contains 97–130 genera and some 1,400–1,800 species worldwide (authorities disagree). For more on the family, see p. 474. *Cylindropuntia* (chollas), p. 475; *Carnegiea* (Saguaro), p. 476.

Caprifoliaceae — Honeysuckle Family

Trees, shrubs, vines, and herbaceous plants, mostly of the Northern Hemisphere, important for edible fruits and fragrant, flowering ornamentals. Provide food for deer, elk, and birds. Leaves deciduous or evergreen, small to medium-sized; opposite or whorled, simple or compound. Flowers in branched, often flat-topped clusters, usually showy, bisexual, tubular or bell-shaped. Fruit a berry, capsule, or drupe. The family contains 15 genera and some 420 species worldwide. *Sambucus* (elderberries), p. 166; *Viburnum* (viburnums), pp. 208–209.

Casuarinaceae — She-oak Family

Trees and shrubs, native to the Malaysian region and Australia, important for tannins and lumber, commonly grown as ornamentals, now widespread and often invasive in dry, tropical and subtropical regions. Members planted for windbreaks; can be invasive. The plants usually have slender, drooping branchlets that are green and jointed. Leaves evergreen, small, scalelike, simple, typically in whorls of 6–17 at each branch joint. Flowers unisexual, sexes on same or separate trees, inconspicuous, without petals; male flowers in elongated clusters; female flowers in larger, rounded clusters that become conelike and dry. Pollination by wind. Fruit a samara. The family contains 4 genera and some 90 species worldwide; there are no species native to North Americ. *Casuarina* (Australian-pine), p. 152.

Cercidiphyllaceae — Katsura-tree Family

Family native only to China and Japan, with a single genus, *Cercidiphyllum*, esteemed for its distinctive foliage, graceful branching, and fine lumber. Widely introduced elsewhere as an ornamental. Leaves have a spicy fragrance in autumn. Leaves deciduous, simple, opposite or alternate, with heart-shaped bases. Flowers in clusters, unisexual, sexes on separate trees, small, without petals, pollinated by wind. Fruit a nonfleshy, podlike follicle, usually 2–4 in a cluster. The family contains 2 species worldwide; not native to North America. *Cercidiphyllum* (Katsura Tree), p. 191.

Chrysobalanaceae — Cocoa-plum Family

Trees, shrubs, and woody vines, mainly of the tropics and subtropics, cultivated for ornamental value and edible fruits. Leaves mostly evergreen, simple, alternate, untoothed. Flowers solitary or in clusters, bisexual or unisexual, small and asymmetrical, with 4 or 5 petals or none. Pollination usually by insects. Fruit a fleshy drupe, usually oval. The family contains 17 genera and some 460 species worldwide. *Chrysobalanus* (Coco-plum), p. 290.

Combretaceae — Indian Almond Family

Trees, shrubs, and woody vines, mainly of the tropics and subtropics, valued for timber, resins, gums, and decorative ornamentals. Leaves evergreen, simple, alternate or, rarely, opposite, untoothed. Flowers in showy clusters of various shapes, usually bisexual, small, symmetrical. Fruit a drupe or samara, frequently leathery. The family contains 20 genera and about 500 species worldwide. *Laguncularia* (White Mangrove), p. 197; *Conocarpus* (Button-mangrove), p. 290.

Cornaceae   Dogwood Family
Trees, shrubs, and herbaceous plants, primarily of the Northern Hemisphere, commonly planted as ornamentals for their abundant spring blooms and graceful branching. Fruits and leaves are sources of food for songbirds, game birds, and mammals. Leaves deciduous or evergreen, simple, usually opposite, occasionally alternate. Flowers small, usually bisexual, with 4 or 5 petals, or no petals, borne in showy, branched clusters; in some species dense flower clusters are surrounded by large showy bracts. Pollination chiefly by insects. Fruit a drupe or berry. The family contains 14 genera and 120 species worldwide. *Cornus* (dogwoods), pp. 204–207, 295; *Nyssa* (tupelos), pp. 296–297.

Cupressaceae   Cypress Family
Aromatic, resinous, coniferous trees and shrubs from temperate regions throughout the world, valued for ornamental beauty, good lumber, resins, and oils. The family provides essential food and cover for wildlife. Leaves mostly evergreen, opposite or whorled, scalelike or needlelike, often persisting for 3–5 years. Leaves and branchlets often arranged in flattened sprays. Cones unisexual, on same or different plants. Pollen-producing (male) cones occur singly or in clusters, shed annually. Seed-bearing (female) cones usually woody, maturing in 1 or 2 seasons; in junipers the cone scales fuse early in development, the mature cone resembling, and often called, a berry. Pollination by wind. The family contains 20–30 genera and 110–130 species worldwide (authorities disagree). For more on the family, see pp. 124, 129–130. *Taxodium* (bald-cypresses), pp. 124, 126–127; *Cryptomeria* (Japanese-cedar), p. 124; *Sequoia* (Redwood), pp. 124, 125; *Metasequoia* (Dawn Redwood), p. 126; *Sequoiadendron* (Giant Sequoia), p. 132; *Calocedrus* (Incense-cedar), p. 133; *Thuja* (Western Redcedar, Northern White-cedar), pp. 134–135; *Platycladus*

(Oriental Arborvitae), p. 136; *Thujopsis* (false-arborvitae), p. 136; *Chamaecyparis*, (Sawara False-cypress, Atlantic White-cedar, Alaska-cedar, Port-Orford-cedar), pp. 136–139; *Cupressus* (cypresses), pp. 142–145; *Juniperus* (junipers, including Eastern Redcedar), pp. 146–151.

Cyrillaceae   Cyrilla Family
Trees and shrubs, primarily of the Americas, cultivated as landscape plants for their fragrant flowers. *Cyrilla* provides cover for birds, mammals, and aquatic wildlife. Leaves deciduous or evergreen, simple, alternate, untoothed, leathery, with short stalks. Flowers in elongated, fragrant clusters, bisexual; petals 5–8. Fruit a capsule, drupe, or samara. The family contains 4 genera and some 78 species worldwide. *Cyrilla* (titis), p. 298.

Ebenaceae   Ebony Family
Trees and shrubs, primarily of the tropics, prized for edible fruits and very hard, dark-colored wood (ebony). Persimmons and date plums are the family's most familiar fruits. The fruit provides food for wildlife. Leaves deciduous or evergreen, simple, usually alternate, typically untoothed, often leathery. Flowers solitary or in small clusters, usually unisexual, sexes on separate plants; lobes 3–7. Fruit a berry. The family contains 2 genera and some 485 species worldwide. *Diospyros* (persimmons), p. 306.

Elaeagnaceae   Oleaster Family
Trees and shrubs, principally of coastal and steppe regions of the Northern Hemisphere and Australia, important for timber, fruits, and ornamental beauty. Members planted for windbreaks and erosion control; Russian-olive can be invasive. Plants commonly thorny. Leaves deciduous or evergreen, simple, usually alternate, with distinctive silvery or yellow scales underneath. Flowers solitary or in clusters, small, bisexual or unisexual, bell-shaped, without petals. Pollination by insects or wind. Fruit an achene or fleshy and drupelike. The family contains 3 genera and 45 species worldwide. *Elaeagnus* (Russian-olive), p. 292.

Ericaceae — Heath Family

Trees, shrubs, vines, and herbaceous plants, widely distributed throughout the world, important for ornamental merit (azaleas, rhododendrons) and edible fruits (blueberries, cranberries). The fruits provide food for wildlife. Leaves deciduous or evergreen, simple, usually alternate, sometimes opposite or in whorls, often leathery. Flowers solitary or in clusters, bisexual, typically urn-shaped; corolla lobes 4–7. Pollination by birds and bees and other insects. Fruit a capsule, berry, or drupe. The family contains 107 genera and some 3,400 species worldwide. *Vaccinium* (Farkleberry), p. 307; *Arbutus* (madrones), pp. 307–308; *Arctostaphylos* (manzanitas), pp. 309–310; *Lyonia* (Rusty Staggerbush), p. 310; *Oxydendrum* (Sourwood), p. 311; *Kalmia* (Mountain-laurel), p. 312; *Rhododendron* (rhododendrons), pp. 312–313.

Euphorbiaceae — Spurge Family

Trees, shrubs, woody vines, and herbaceous plants, primarily of the tropics, but found in temperate regions, important as ornamentals (poinsettia) and for many commercial products, including rubber, waxes, oils, cassava, and medicinal extracts. Some are noxious weeds. Plants often have a milky sap and often are poisonous. Leaves deciduous, mostly simple, usually alternate, sometimes vestigial in cactuslike species. Flowers bisexual or unisexual, usually with 5 petals, or sometimes none. Bracts surrounding the flowers often very showy, the entire structure of bracts and small flowers resembling a single flower. Pollination by bats or insects. Fruit usually a 3-lobed capsule, rarely a drupe. The family contains some 313 genera and 8,100 species worldwide. *Triadica* (Chinese Tallow), p. 320; *Hippomane* (Manchineel), p. 321.

Fabaceae — Pea Family

One of the largest families of plants, consisting of trees, shrubs, woody vines, and herbaceous plants, distributed worldwide, important as sources of food, fodder, timber, and ornamentals. The family is mainly made up of herbaceous plants. Some trees and shrubs are used for erosion control and soil enrichment. Members provide important food and cover for birds and mammals. Leaves deciduous or evergreen, usually alternate, often pinnately compound, sometimes aromatic. Flowers usually borne in clusters, tiny to large, usually bisexual, usually with 5 petals. The family has 3 general flower types: those with small petals and conspicuous stamens (example, Catclaw Acacia), those that are nearly radially symmetrical with the upper petal innermost (Blue Paloverde), and those that are bilaterally symmetrical, with the upper petal (standard) large and outermost, 2 side petals (wings), and 2 lower petals usually joined to form a boatlike structure (keel), forming the typical "pea flower" (Black Locust). Pollination by birds or insects. Fruit usually a legume, a long, 2-valved pod with 1 chamber (technically, 1 carpel, the basic unit of the ovary) and the seeds attached to 1 seam. The family contains 642 genera and about 18,000 species worldwide. *Gleditsia* (honeylocusts), p. 217; *Robinia* (locusts), pp. 218–219; *Olneya* (Desert Ironwood), p. 220; *Parkinsonia* (Jerusalem Thorn, paloverdes), pp. 220–221; *Acacia* (acacias), pp. 222–223; *Prosopis* (mesquites), p. 224; *Styphnolobium* (Japanese Pagoda Tree), p. 252; *Ceratonia* (Carob), p. 252; *Cladrastis* (Kentucky Yellowwood), p. 253; *Gymnocladus* (Kentucky Coffeetree), p. 254; *Albizia* (Silktree), p. 255; *Cercis* (redbuds), pp. 319–320.

Fagaceae — Beech Family

Widespread family of trees and shrubs, primarily of the Northern Hemisphere, valued for excellent hardwood lumber and horticultural uses, especially oaks, beeches, and chestnuts. Members provide important food, nesting sites, and cover for wildlife. Leaves deciduous or evergreen, simple, often deeply lobed, alternate. Flowers small, unisexual, sexes on same tree, without petals, borne singly or in catkins, pollinated by insects or wind. Fruit a relatively large nut, borne singly or clustered, often with a bristly or scaly cap (as in the acorns of oaks and Tanoak) or a burlike husk (chestnuts, chinkapins). The family contains 8 or 9 genera and about 600–800 species worldwide (authorities disagree). For more on the family, see p. 413. *Fagus* (beeches), pp. 414–415;

Castanea (chestnuts, Chinkapin), pp. 416–417; *Chrysolepis* (Giant Golden Chinkapin), p. 418; *Lithocarpus* (Tanoak), p. 419; *Quercus* (oaks), pp. 420–460.

Garryaceae   Silktassel Family

Trees and shrubs found predominantly in North and Central America. Several species cultivated as ornamentals. Leaves evergreen, simple, opposite, untoothed, leathery. Flowers small, unisexual, without petals, sexes borne on separate plants in conspicuous, pendulous, catkinlike clusters, pollinated by wind. Fruit a fleshy or nonfleshy berry. The family contains 1 genus and 13 species worldwide. *Garrya* (Wavyleaf Silktassel), p. 203.

Ginkgoaceae   Ginkgo Family

Family native to China (and introduced primarily in the Northern Hemisphere), with only 1 species, *Ginkgo biloba*, esteemed for its edible and medicinal seeds and, particularly, as a hardy ornamental with unique, fan-shaped foliage. Millions of years old, the family was once widely distributed throughout the world. Leaves deciduous, simple, alternate, in bundles on spur twigs, leathery. Reproductive structures small, unisexual, with sexes on separate trees. Pollen cones borne in catkinlike clusters. Pollination by wind. Plum-shaped, flesh-covered seed becomes malodorous when ripe. The family contains 1 species worldwide; it is introduced in North America. *Ginkgo* (Ginkgo), p. 154.

Hamamelidaceae   Witch-hazel Family

Trees and shrubs, found in tropical and warm-temperate regions, valued for lumber, medicinal extracts, and ornamental merit. Sweetgum is planted for stream-bank protection and strip-mine reclamation. Witch-hazel fruit provides food for game birds and deer. Leaves deciduous, alternate, simple, deeply lobed or unlobed. Flowers solitary or in clusters, unisexual or bisexual, sexes on same or different plants; petals 4 or 5 or none. Pollination by insects or wind. Fruit a woody or leathery capsule. The family contains some 30 genera and about 100 species worldwide. *Liquidambar* (Sweetgum), p. 270; *Hamamelis* (Witch-hazel), p. 330.

Hippocastanaceae   Horse-chestnut Family

Trees and shrubs, widespread in the Northern Hemisphere, with species important to horticulture and the lumber industry. Leaves deciduous, opposite, palmately compound, with 3–11 leaflets. Flowers usually in large, showy, conical clusters, usually bisexual, conspicuous, bilaterally symmetrical; petals 4 or 5. Pollination usually by insects. Fruit a capsule, usually leathery, sometimes prickly, containing 1–3 large seeds. Seeds are poisonous if ingested. The family contains 2 genera and 15 species worldwide. *Aesculus* (Horse-chestnut, buckeyes), pp. 158–163.

Juglandaceae   Walnut Family

Aromatic trees and shrubs, primarily of the Northern Hemisphere, prized for their edible nuts and fine lumber. Nuts provide important food for birds and mammals, especially squirrels. Leaves deciduous, large, pinnately compound. Flowers tiny, yellowish green, without petals, unisexual, both sexes on same plant; male flowers in narrow, pendulous clusters; female flowers very inconspicuous, single or few in a tight, short cluster, pollinated by wind. Fruit a hard-shelled nut covered by a thin to thick husk, which may or may not split and fall from the nut. The family contains 7 or 8 genera and some 59 species worldwide. For more on the family, see p. 225. *Juglans* (walnuts), pp. 226–229; *Carya* (hickories, Pecan), pp. 230–237.

Lauraceae   Laurel Family

Trees and shrubs, usually aromatic, found mainly in the tropics and subtropics. The best-known members produce cinnamon, avocados, fragrant oils, camphor, and good lumber. Fruits and seeds provide food for wildlife. Leaves evergreen or deciduous, simple, usually alternate, sometimes opposite or whorled. Flowers in clusters, bisexual or unisexual, small, usually greenish yellow to white; petals in whorls of 3, or no petals. Pollination by insects. Fruit a fleshy drupe or berry. The family contains some 50 genera and 2,000–3,000 species worldwide. *Sassafras* (Sassafras), p. 274; *Cinnamomum* (Camphortree), p. 292; *Persea* (bays), p. 293; *Umbellularia* (California Bay), p. 294.

Lythraceae   **Loosestrife Family**
Trees, shrubs, and herbaceous plants found mostly in the tropics, valued as sources for dyes, and cultivated as ornamentals for their showy flowers. Most members herbaceous. Leaves deciduous, simple, usually opposite or whorled, occasionally alternate. Flowers solitary or in clusters, bisexual, tubular to bell-shaped, commonly with 4 or 6 petals, or sometimes none. Pollination by insects. Fruit usually a dry capsule, though family also includes tree that produces the edible pomegranate. The family contains 27 genera and about 600 species worldwide. *Lagerstroemia* (Crapemyrtle), p. 314.

Magnoliaceae   **Magnolia Family**
Trees, shrubs, and woody vines, primarily of Asia, the Pacific Islands, and the Americas, esteemed for good lumber and often striking, fragrant blooms. Members provide food and cover for birds and small mammals. Leaves evergreen or deciduous, usually large, alternate (sometimes appearing whorled), simple, untoothed. Flowers large, showy, predominantly bisexual, pollinated by beetles. Fruit a cone- or headlike cluster of follicles or samaras. Seeds often hang by threads from fruit. The family contains 6–12 genera and 165–200 species worldwide (authorities disagree). For more on the family, see p. 276. *Liriodendron* (Tuliptree), p. 277; *Magnolia* (magnolias, including Cucumber-tree, Sweetbay), pp. 278–284.

Meliaceae   **Mahogany Family**
Trees and shrubs, usually aromatic, chiefly of tropical and subtropical regions, valued for hardwood lumber and medicinal extracts. Leaves deciduous or evergreen, often large, alternate, usually pinnately compound. Flowers mostly branched clusters, small, usually bisexual; petals 3–5. Pollination by insects. Fruit a capsule, berry, drupe, rarely a nut; some fruits edible. The family contains 5 genera and some 565 species worldwide. *Swietenia* (West Indian Mahogany), p. 251; *Melia* (Chinaberry), p. 255.

Moraceae   **Mulberry Family**
Trees, shrubs, vines, and herbaceous plants, commonly of tropical and subtropical climates. Family members yield many economically important products, including figs, hops, food for silkworms, and ornamental plants. Fruits and leaves are important sources of food for wildlife. Plants usually contain a milky, latexlike sap. Leaves evergreen or deciduous, simple, usually alternate, sometimes toothed, sometimes lobed. Flowers inconspicuous, unisexual, with sexes on same or different plants, borne in small, tight clusters or, as in figs, within a fleshy receptacle. Pollination by insects or wind. Fruits achenes or drupelets, some, as in mulberries, encased in juicy flesh and tightly clustered; some edible. The family contains some 40 genera and 1,100 species worldwide. *Morus* (mulberries), pp. 271–272; *Broussonetia* (Paper Mulberry), p. 273; *Ficus* (figs), pp. 273, 289; *Maclura* (Osage-orange), p. 288.

Myricaceae   **Bayberry Family**
Trees and shrubs, usually aromatic and resinous, native throughout temperate and subtropical regions, important for resins, waxes, and oils. Members planted to enrich soil and control erosion. Leaves and fruits provide food for wildlife. Leaves evergreen or deciduous, fragrant, alternate, simple; often with tiny glandular dots. Flowers in small, tight clusters, inconspicuous, greenish to purplish, usually unisexual, sexes on same or separate trees. Pollination by wind. Fruit a drupe or nutlet, smooth or warty, often with a waxy coating. The family contains 2–4 genera (authorities disagree) and some 50 species worldwide. *Morella* (bayberries), pp. 322–323.

Myrtaceae   **Myrtle Family**
Trees and shrubs, primarily of the Southern Hemisphere, valued for lumber, gums, oils, spices, edible fruits, and ornamentals. Eucalyptuses are sometimes planted as windbreaks. Leaves mostly evergreen, generally simple, opposite, untoothed, often leathery; typically with conspicuous glandular dots that emit an aromatic scent. Flowers solitary or in clusters, usually bisexual, with 4 or 5 petals or none. Pollination by hummingbirds or insects. Fruit a berry, drupe, capsule, or nut. The family contains some 129 genera and 4,600 species

worldwide. *Eucalyptus* (eucalyptus), pp. 314–315; *Melaleuca* (Punktree), p. 316.

Oleaceae · Olive Family

Trees, shrubs, and woody vines, widely dispersed throughout the world, important for hardwood lumber, flowering ornamentals, and olives. Leaves evergreen or deciduous, mostly simple (pinnately compound in most ashes), usually opposite, rarely alternate or whorled. Flowers in clusters, small, often fragrant, usually bisexual, often with 4 petals joined at the base. Pollination mostly by wind. Fruit a berry, drupe, capsule, or samara. The family contains 24 genera and about 615 species worldwide. *Fraxinus* (ashes), pp. 167–175; *Forestiera* (swampprivets, Desert-olive), pp. 197–198; *Ligustrum* (privets), p. 199; *Olea* (Olive), p. 199; *Osmanthus* (Devilwood), p. 200; *Chionanthus* (Fringetree), p. 201; *Syringa* (lilacs), p. 202.

Pinaceae · Pine Family

Aromatic, resinous, coniferous trees and shrubs, mostly of the Northern Hemisphere, important for lumber, pitch, turpentine, oils, seeds, and use as ornamentals. Members commonly planted for reforestation; many species provide important food and cover for wildlife. Leaves mostly evergreen, needlelike, solitary or clustered. Cones unisexual, sexes on same tree. Pollen (male) cones small, either solitary or clustered, shed annually. Seed-bearing (female) cones have overlapping scales; when mature, often large, woody, persisting for 1–3 years or more. Pollination by wind. The family contains 10–12 genera and some 200 species worldwide. *Pinus* (pines, including pinyons), pp. 64–93; *Larix* (larches), pp. 94–97; *Cedrus* (true cedars), pp. 98–99; *Picea* (spruces), pp. 100–107; *Pseudotsuga* (Douglas-firs), pp. 108, 109–110; *Abies* (true firs), pp. 108, 110–117; *Tsuga* (hemlocks), pp. 118–121.

Platanaceae · Planetree Family

Large trees, primarily of the Northern Hemisphere, valued for their size, shade, and timber. The family includes sycamores, familiar favorites in urban landscapes because of their hardiness, commanding height, and distinctive, colorful, scaling bark. Sycamores are sometimes planted for strip-mine reclamation, and they provide important shelter for wildlife in bottomland forests. Leaves deciduous, alternate, simple, usually palmately lobed. Flowers tiny, unisexual, sexes on same tree, in dense, spherical clusters on pendulous stalks, pollinated by wind. Fruit an achene, in a dense, round cluster, often with a fuzzy coating. The family contains 1 genus and about 8 species worldwide. *Platanus* (sycamores, planetrees), pp. 267–269.

Polygonaceae · Buckwheat Family

Trees, shrubs, vines, and, mostly, herbaceous plants, primarily of the Northern Hemisphere, important for food, medicinal extracts, and lumber. Leaves deciduous, simple, usually alternate. In some genera the stem above the attachment of a leaf is surrounded by a sheath (ocrea), which represents modified stipules. Flowers in clusters, mostly bisexual, small, usually white, yellowish, or greenish, without petals (but sepals may resemble petals). Pollination by insects or wind. Fruit an achene, sometimes winged, occasionally fleshy; some edible. The family contains about 48 genera and more than 1,100 species worldwide. *Coccoloba* (Seagrape, Pigeon-plum), p. 291.

Rhamnaceae · Buckthorn Family

Trees, shrubs, woody vines, and, rarely, herbaceous plants, widespread throughout much of the world, members important as ornamentals and sources for dyes and shellac. Some bear thorns. The fruit is an important source of food for wildlife. Leaves deciduous or evergreen, simple, usually alternate, occasionally opposite. Flowers solitary or in clusters that are sometimes showy, usually small, bisexual; petals 4 or 5 or none. Pollination by insects. Fruit a drupe or nut, sometimes a capsule. The family contains 49 genera and some 900 species worldwide. *Rhamnus* (European Buckthorn), p. 210; *Frangula* (native buckthorns), pp. 324–326; *Ceanothus* (ceanothus, including Blueblossom), p. 327.

Rhizophoraceae · Red Mangrove Family

Trees, shrubs, and vines, primarily of the tropics, often occurring along seashores and swamps, ecologically important for marine life and as sources of timber, fuel, and fruits. Leaves evergreen, opposite or whorled, simple, unlobed, leathery. Flowers usually in clusters, predominantly unisexual, with 3–16 petals. Fruit usually a berry, rarely a capsule. The family contains 15 genera and 120 species worldwide. *Rhizophora* (Red Mangrove), p. 196.

Rosaceae   Rose Family

Very large family of trees, shrubs, and herbaceous plants, widely distributed throughout temperate climates, esteemed for horticultural use and for edible fruits or seeds, which include apples, cherries, peaches, pears, almonds, and many more. The family contains the majority of North America's fruit trees and many of its flowering ornamental trees. Members provide important food and cover for wildlife. Leaves deciduous or evergreen, usually alternate (occasionally opposite), simple or pinnately or palmately compound. Flowers bisexual, usually with 4 or 5 petals or none, pollinated by insects (often flies) or wind. Fruit types include achenes, drupes, follicles, pomes (called "hips" in roses), and capsules. The family contains 95 genera and more than 2,800 species worldwide. For more on the family, see pp. 332–333. *Lyonothamnus* (Catalina Ironwood), p. 165; *Eriobotrya* (Loquat), p. 210; *Sorbus* (mountain-ashes), pp. 240–241; *Cercocarpus* (mountain-mahoganies), pp. 333–334; *Prunus* (cherries, plums, peach), pp. 335–346; *Pyrus* (pears), pp. 347–348; *Malus* (apples, crabapples), pp. 348–351; *Amelanchier* (serviceberries), pp. 352–353; *Crataegus* (hawthorns), pp. 354–355.

Rubiaceae   Madder Family

Trees, shrubs, and herbaceous plants, found predominantly in the tropics, important for quinine and coffee beans and as ornamentals. Members offer food and cover for birds and mammals. Leaves deciduous or evergreen, opposite or whorled, simple, often large, usually untoothed. Desert species often have scalelike or needlelike leaves. Flowers solitary or in clusters, bisexual; petals 4 or 5, fused, pollinated by insects. Fruit a berry, capsule, nutlet, or drupe. The family contains some 630 genera and 10,200 species worldwide. *Cephalanthus* (Buttonbush), p. 202; *Pinckneya* (Fevertree), p. 203.

Rutaceae   Rue Family

Nearly worldwide family of trees, shrubs, and a few herbaceous plants, often aromatic, best known for oranges, lemons, limes, and other citrus fruits. Leaves deciduous or evergreen, alternate, simple or pinnately or palmately compound. Flowers in clusters, conspicuous, usually fragrant, mostly bisexual; petals 3–5 (rarely 6) or none. Pollination by insects. Fruit a berry, drupe, capsule, follicle, or samara. The family contains some 156 genera and 1,800 species worldwide. *Poncirus* (Hardy Orange), p. 213; *Zanthoxylum* (pricklyashes, Hercules' clubs), pp. 214–215; *Ptelea* (hoptrees), p. 239; *Phellodendron* (Amur Corktree), p. 249; *Citrus* (oranges, grapefruits), p. 287.

Salicaceae   Willow Family

Trees and shrubs, primarily of the Northern Hemisphere, often growing in moist ground, important as ornamentals and sources of lumber, fuel, and medicinal extracts. Members planted to fight soil erosion and regenerate burned-out forests. Leaves mostly deciduous, simple, usually alternate. Flowers minute, without petals, in erect or pendulous catkins, unisexual, with sexes usually on separate plants. Pollination by insects or wind. Fruit a small, 2- to 4-valved capsule; seeds covered with white hairs. The family contains 2 genera and 435 species worldwide. *Salix* (willows), pp. 378–389; *Populus* (poplars, cottonwoods, aspens), pp. 390–398.

Sapindaceae   Soapberry Family

Trees, shrubs, and woody vines, widely dispersed in the tropics and subtropics, valued for ornamentals, lumber, oils, and edible fruits. Members are planted for shelterbelts and provide cover for wildlife. Leaves deciduous or evergreen, usually alternate, simple or pinnately compound. Flowers usually in clusters, small, unisexual, usually both sexes on same plant; petals 4 or 5 or none. Fruit varies widely in type and shape, from an inflated capsule to a berry. The family contains some 131 genera and 1,450 species worldwide. *Ungnadia* (Mexican-buckeye), p. 238; *Koelreuteria* (goldenrain trees), p. 238; *Exothea* (Inkwood), p. 248; *Sapindus* (soapberries), pp. 249–250.

Sapotaceae — Sapodilla Family

Trees and shrubs, primarily of tropical and subtropical regions, valued for lumber, extracts, and edible fruits. Twigs contain milky sap. Leaves evergreen, sometimes deciduous, usually alternate, simple, untoothed, leathery; lower surface sometimes densely hairy. Flowers solitary or clustered, bisexual, usually small; corolla 4- to 12-lobed. Fruit a fleshy berry. The family contains 53 genera and about 975 species worldwide. *Chrysophyllum* (Satinleaf), p. 303; *Sideroxylon* (bullies, Saffron-plum), pp. 304–305.

Scrophulariaceae — Figwort Family

Mostly herbaceous plants (but including some trees, shrubs, and woody vines), primarily of the Northern Hemisphere, many cultivated as ornamentals. Leaves mostly deciduous, simple, alternate or opposite. Flowers solitary or in clusters, often showy, bisexual, usually bilaterally symmetrical; corolla commonly tubular, 4- or 5-lobed, pollinated by insects. Fruit usually a capsule. The family contains about 269 genera and 5,100 species worldwide. *Paulownia* (Princesstree), p. 192.

Simaroubaceae — Quassia Family

Trees, shrubs, and herbaceous plants, mostly of the tropics and subtropics, important for ornament and medicinal extracts. Leaves deciduous or evergreen, alternate, usually pinnately compound, untoothed. Flowers in clusters, small, mostly unisexual; sexes on same or separate trees, petals 5; pollinated by insects. Fruit a samara or capsule, rarely a drupe. Plant parts often bitter. The family contains 13 genera and 110 species worldwide. *Simarouba* (Paradisetree), p. 248; *Ailanthus* (Tree of Heaven), p. 251.

Staphyleaceae — Bladdernut Family

Trees and shrubs, chiefly of the Northern Hemisphere and South America, cultivated for their often decorative displays of flowers and interesting fruits. Members sometimes planted for erosion control. Leaves deciduous, alternate or opposite, usually pinnately compound, often toothed. Flowers in branched, pendulous clusters, small, bisexual or unisexual, petals 5. Fruit a berry or an inflated, bladderlike capsule. The family contains 5 genera and 27 species worldwide. *Staphylea* (American Bladdernut), p. 164.

Sterculiaceae — Cacao Family

Trees, shrubs, and woody vines, mainly of tropical and subtropical regions of the world, best known as sources of chocolate and cola, also important for medicinal extracts, gums, and timber. Leaves deciduous, alternate, simple, often lobed, often with star-shaped hairs on 1 or both surfaces. Flowers solitary or in clusters, usually bisexual; petals 5 or none; pollinated by flies. Fruit a capsule, follicle, or samara, fleshy or woody. The family contains 67 genera and about 1,500 species worldwide. *Fremontodendron* (flannelbushes), p. 275; *Firmiana* (Chinese Parasoltree), p. 275.

Styracaceae — Storax Family

Resinous trees and shrubs, primarily of the tropics of the Americas and Asia, valued for fragrant extracts and often showy ornamental flowers. Leaves deciduous, alternate, simple, often with star-shaped hairs beneath. Flowers solitary or in clusters, conspicuous, bisexual; petals 2–7, fused. Fruit a capsule or samara, rarely a drupe. The family contains 11 genera and some 160 species worldwide. *Halesia* (silverbells), p. 317; *Styrax* (snowbells), p. 318.

Symplocaceae — Sweetleaf Family

Single-genus family of trees and shrubs, primarily of the tropical Americas and Asia, planted for ornamental merit. The leaves, often sweet-tasting, provide food for wildlife. Leaves deciduous to evergreen, alternate, simple. Flowers in clusters, usually bisexual; petals 5; pollinated by insects. Fruit usually a fleshy drupe, sometimes a berry. The family contains 1 genus and 250 species worldwide. *Symplocos* (Sweetleaf), p. 299.

Tamaricaceae — Tamarix Family

Trees, shrubs, and herbaceous plants, planted for ornament, as windbreaks, and for tolerance to drought and saline soils.

Tamarisks are considered noxious pests in some areas. Leaves mostly evergreen, simple, alternate, small and usually scalelike, commonly with salt glands. Flowers in dense clusters, small, bisexual; petals 4 or 5; pollinated by insects. Fruit a capsule with 3–5 valves. Each seed is tipped with a tuft of hairs. The family contains 4 genera and 78 species worldwide; there are no species native to North America. *Tamarix* (tamarisks), p. 152.

Taxaceae — Yew Family

Coniferous trees and shrubs, predominantly of the Northern Hemisphere, important as ornamentals. Leaves evergreen, needlelike, persisting several years. Reproductive structures unisexual, sexes usually on separate plants. Pollen cones solitary or clustered, shed annually. Pollination by wind. Seed enclosed in a fleshy, sometimes juicy, or leathery covering (aril), maturing in 1 or 2 seasons. The family contains 4 or 5 genera and 16–20 species worldwide. For more on the family, see p. 122. *Taxus* (yews), pp. 122–123; *Torreya* (torreyas), pp. 122–123.

Theaceae — Tea Family

Trees and shrubs, distributed in tropical and subtropical regions, valued for tea leaves and flowering ornamentals. Loblolly-bay is planted for riverbank ecosystem restoration. Leaves mostly evergreen, sometimes deciduous, simple, usually alternate, leathery, often glossy. Flowers usually solitary, mostly bisexual, often large and showy; petals usually 5. Fruit a 5-celled capsule, usually leathery or woody. The family contains 22 genera and some 610 species worldwide. *Gordonia* (Loblolly-bay), p. 328; *Stewartia* (camellias), p. 329; *Franklinia* (Franklin Tree), p. 329.

Tiliaceae — Linden Family

Trees, shrubs, and herbaceous plants, primarily of the tropics but extending to temperate regions, esteemed for fine lumber and ornamental merit. Leaves deciduous or evergreen, simple, usually alternate, often heart-shaped. Flowers solitary or in branched clusters, small, usually bisexual, often fragrant; petals usually 5. Pollination by bees. Fruit variable, dry or fleshy, in *Tilia* a nutlet attached to a leafy bract. The family contains 46 genera and about 680 species worldwide. *Tilia* (basswoods, lindens), pp. 375–377.

Ulmaceae — Elm Family

Trees and shrubs, mainly of the Northern Hemisphere, prized for ornamental beauty, good lumber, and edible fruits. The fruits and leaves provide food and cover for wildlife. Leaves deciduous or evergreen, simple, usually alternate, commonly asymmetrical at the base. Flowers solitary or in clusters, small, bisexual or unisexual, without petals, pollinated by wind. Fruit a small fleshy drupe, samara, or nut. The family contains 16–18 genera and 150–175 species worldwide. For more on the family, see p. 363. *Celtis* (hackberries, including Sugarberry), pp. 364–366; *Trema* (tremas), p. 366; *Planera* (Water-elm), p. 367; *Zelkova* (Japanese Zelkova), p. 367; *Ulmus* (elms), pp. 368–374.

Verbenaceae — Verbena Family

Trees, shrubs, vines, and herbaceous plants, primarily of the tropics and subtropics, important for flowering ornamentals, fragrant oils, and fine teak lumber. Plants are sometimes thorny. Leaves deciduous or evergreen, opposite or whorled, usually simple, aromatic. Flowers in branched or unbranched, showy clusters, usually bisexual; corolla often bilaterally symmetrical, usually with 4 or 5 lobes. Fruit a drupe or a 2- to 4-valved capsule. The family contains 41 genera and some 950 species worldwide. *Vitex* (Lilac Chastetree), p. 164; *Avicennia* (Black Mangrove), p. 195.

Zygophyllaceae — Creosote-bush Family

Trees, shrubs, and herbaceous plants, often resinous and aromatic, mostly from the tropics to warm-temperate areas. The family common name is shared by *Larrea tridentata*, a ubiquitous shrub in the hot deserts of North America. The family has ornamental merit and is an important source of timber. Leaves evergreen or deciduous, usually opposite, compound, occasionally spinelike. Flowers solitary or in clusters, bisexual; petals usually 5, pollinated by insects. Fruit often a capsule. The family contains 27 genera and about 285 species worldwide. *Guaiacum* (Texas Lignum-vitae), p. 165.

Tree Silhouettes

The form of a tree's trunk and the shape of its crown are influenced by the species' growth tendencies—for a short, thick trunk and long, horizontal branches, for example—as well as its environment. The same species will look very different if grown in a dense forest as opposed to an open field. Forest-grown trees tend to be narrow in outline, with few low branches and a high crown, whereas open-grown trees often produce low branches and spreading crowns. The shape silhouettes show open-grown specimens of representative species of the major North American genera. Be sure to read the description of a species' shape as you study the silhouette in order to get a more complete sense of its usual form.

Balsam Fir, p. 111
Abies balsamea

Subalpine Fir, p. 112
Abies lasiocarpa

Incense-cedar, p. 133
Calocedrus decurrens

Atlantic White-cedar, p. 137
Chamaecyparis thyoides

Sargent Cypress, p. 144
Cupressus sargentii

Utah Juniper, p. 150
Juniperus osteosperma

Eastern Redcedar, p. 147
Juniperus virginiana

Tamarack, p. 95
Larix laricina

Subalpine Larch, p. 97
Larix lyallii

Engelmann Spruce, p. 104
Picea engelmannii

White Spruce, p. 102
Picea glauca

Lodgepole Pine, p. 91
Pinus contorta

Pinyon, p. 92
Pinus edulis

Longleaf Pine, p. 75
Pinus palustris

Ponderosa Pine, p. 89
Pinus ponderosa

Red Pine, p. 66
Pinus resinosa

Pitch Pine, p. 76
Pinus rigida

Douglas-fir, p. 109
Pseudotsuga menziesii

Redwood, p. 125
Sequoia sempervirens

Giant Sequoia, p. 132
Sequoiadendron giganteum

Bald-cypress, p. 127
Taxodium distichum

Western Redcedar, p. 134
Thuja plicata

Eastern Hemlock, p. 119
Tsuga canadensis

Western Hemlock, p. 120
Tsuga heterophylla

Red Maple, p. 181
Acer rubrum

Ohio Buckeye, p. 159
Aesculus glabra

Pacific Madrone, p. 308
Arbutus menziesii

Gray Birch, p. 403
Betula populifolia

Bitternut Hickory, p. 233
Carya cordiformis

Pignut Hickory, p. 236
Carya glabra

Shagbark Hickory, p. 230
Carya ovata

Northern Catalpa, p. 193
Catalpa speciosa

Kentucky Yellowwood, p. 253
Cladrastis kentukea

Flowering Dogwood, p. 204
Cornus florida

Hawthorn, p. 354–355
Crataegus species

American Beech, p. 414
Fagus grandifolia

White Ash, p. 168
Fraxinus americana

Ginkgo, p. 154
Ginkgo biloba

Honeylocust, p. 217
Gleditsia triacanthos

Kentucky Coffeetree, p. 254
Gymnocladus dioicus

American Holly, p. 360
Ilex opaca

Butternut, p. 227
Juglans cinerea

Black Walnut, p. 226
Juglans nigra

Sweetgum, p. 270
Liquidambar styraciflua

Tuliptree, p. 277
Liriodendron tulipifera

Osage-orange, p. 288
Maclura pomifera

Cucumber-tree, p. 278
Magnolia acuminata

Black Tupelo, p. 296
Nyssa sylvatica

American Sycamore, p. 267
Platanus occidentalis

Eastern Cottonwood, p. 391
Populus deltoides

Quaking Aspen, p. 397
Populus tremuloides

Black Cherry, p. 335
Prunus serotina

Coast Live Oak, p. 456
Quercus agrifolia

White Oak, p. 443
Quercus alba

Burr Oak, p. 444
Quercus macrocarpa

Pin Oak, p. 435
Quercus palustris

Black Locust, p. 218
Robinia pseudoacacia

Pussy Willow, p. 385
Salix discolor

Black Willow, p. 386
Salix nigra

Sassafras, p. 274
Sassafras albidum

American Basswood, p. 375
Tilia americana

American Elm, p. 371
Ulmus americana

Cabbage Palm, p. 467
Sabal palmetto

California Fan Palm, p. 466
Washingtonia filifera

Mojave Yucca, p. 472
Yucca schidigera

Arboreta and Botanical Gardens

The following is a selected list of arboreta and botanical gardens in the United States (in alphabetical order by state) and Canada (by province).

United States

ALABAMA

Birmingham Botanical Gardens, Birmingham: http://www.bbgardens.org

Donald E. Davis Arboretum, Auburn: http://www.auburn.edu/arboretum

Huntsville Botanical Garden, Huntsville: http://www.hsvbg.org

University of Alabama Arboretum, Tuscaloosa: http://www.bama.ua.edu/~arboretum

ALASKA

Alaska Botanical Garden, Anchorage: http://www.alaskabg.org

ARIZONA

Arboretum at Arizona State University, Tempe: http://www.asu.edu/fm/arboretum.htm

Arboretum at Flagstaff, Flagstaff: http://www.thearb.org

Boyce Thompson Arboretum, Superior: http://ag.arizona.edu/BTA

Desert Botanical Garden, Phoenix: http://www.dbg.org

Tucson Botanical Gardens, Tucson: http://www.tucsonbotanical.org

CALIFORNIA

Fullerton Arboretum, Fullerton: http://arboretum.fullerton.edu

Los Angeles County Arboretum & Botanic Garden, Arcadia: http://www.arboretum.org

Mendocino Coast Botanical Gardens, Fort Bragg: http://www.gardenbythesea.org

Rancho Santa Ana Botanic Garden, Claremont: http://www.rsabg.org

San Francisco Botanical Garden at Strybing Arboretum, San Francisco: http://www.sfbotanicalgarden.org

Santa Barbara Botanic Garden, Santa Barbara: http://www.sbbg.org

UC Davis Arboretum, Davis: http://arboretum.ucdavis.edu

University of California Botanical Garden, Berkeley: http://botanicalgarden.berkeley.edu

University of California Santa Cruz Arboretum, Santa Cruz: http://www2.ucsc.edu/arboretum

COLORADO

Denver Botanic Gardens, Denver: http://www.botanicgardens.org

CONNECTICUT

Bartlett Arboretum & Gardens, Stamford: http://bartlett.arboretum.uconn.edu

Connecticut College Arboretum, New London: http://www.conncoll.edu/ccrec/greennet/arbo

DELAWARE

Ashland Nature Center, Hockessin: http://www.delawarenaturesociety.org/ashland/ashland.html

DISTRICT OF COLUMBIA

United States Botanic Gardens: http://www.usbg.gov

United States National Arboretum: http://www.usna.usda.gov

FLORIDA

Fairchild Tropical Botanic Garden, Coral Gables: http://www.ftg.org

Harry P. Leu Gardens, Orlando: http://www.leugardens.org

John C. Gifford Arboretum, Coral Gables: http://www.bio.miami.edu/arboretum

Key West Tropical Forest and Botanical Garden, Key West: http://www.keywestbotanicalgarden.org

GEORGIA

Atlanta Botanical Garden, Atlanta: http://www.atlantabotanicalgarden.org

Georgia Southern Botanical Garden, Statesboro: http://welcome.georgiasouthern.edu/garden

State Botanical Garden of Georgia, Athens: http://www.uga.edu/botgarden

IDAHO

Idaho Botanical Garden, Boise: http://www.idahobotanicalgarden.org

ILLINOIS

Chicago Botanic Garden, Glencoe: http://www.chicago-botanic.org

Klehm Arboretum & Botanic Garden, Rockford: http://www.klehm.org

Ladd Arboretum and Ecology Center, Evanston: http://www.laddarboretum.org

Morton Arboretum, Lisle:
http://www.mortonarb.org

IOWA

Des Moines Botanical Center, Des Moines:
http://www.botanicalcenter.com

Dubuque Arboretum & Botanical Gardens at
Marshall Park, Dubuque:
http://www.dubuquearboretum.com

KANSAS

Overland Park Arboretum and Botanical
Gardens, Overland Park:
http://www.opkansas.org/_Vis/Arboretum/
index.cfm

KENTUCKY

Bernheim Arboretum and Research Forest,
Clermont: http://www.bernheim.org

MASSACHUSETTS

Arnold Arboretum of Harvard
University, Boston:
http://www.arboretum.harvard.edu

Botanic Garden of Smith College,
Northampton: http://www.smith.edu/
garden

MICHIGAN

Matthaei Botanical Gardens and Nichols
Arboretum, Ann Arbor:
http://www.lsa.umich.edu/mbg

MINNESOTA

Minnesota Landscape Arboretum, Chaska:
http://www.arboretum.umn.edu

MISSISSIPPI

Crosby Arboretum, Picayune:
http://www.crosbyarboretum.msstate.edu

MISSOURI

Missouri Botanical Garden, St. Louis:
http://www.mobot.org

NEW JERSEY

Cora Hartshorn Arboretum, Short Hills:
http://www.hartshornarboretum.org

Reeves-Reed Arboretum, Summit:
http://www.reeves-reedarboretum.org

NEW MEXICO

Rio Grande Botanic Garden, Albuquerque:
http://www.cabq.gov/biopark/garden

NEW YORK

Brooklyn Botanic Garden, Brooklyn:
http://www.bbg.org

F. R. Newman Arboretum, Ithaca:
http://www.plantations.cornell.edu

New York Botanical Garden, Bronx:
http://www.nybg.org

Planting Fields Arboretum State Historic
Park, Oyster Bay: http://www.
plantingfields.org

Queens Botanical Garden, Flushing:
http://www.queensbotanical.org

NORTH CAROLINA

Daniel Stowe Botanical Garden, Belmont:
http://www.dsbg.org

J. C. Raulston Arboretum, Raleigh:
http://www.ncsu.edu/jcraulstonarboretum

North Carolina Arboretum, Asheville:
http://www.ncarboretum.org

North Carolina Botanical Garden,
Chapel Hill: http://www.ncbg.unc.edu

Sarah P. Duke Gardens, Durham:
http://www.hr.duke.edu/dukegardens

OHIO

Chadwick Arboretum & Learning Gardens,
Columbus: http://chadwickarboretum.
osu.edu

Cleveland Botanical Garden, Cleveland:
http://www.case.edu/buildings/cultural/
garden_center.html

Cox Arboretum & Gardens MetroPark,
Dayton: http://www.coxarboretum.org

Dawes Arboretum, Newark:
http://www.dawesarb.org

Holden Arboretum, Kirtland:
http://www.holdenarb.org

Toledo Botanical Garden, Toledo:
http://www.toledogarden.org

OREGON

Hoyt Arboretum, Portland:
http://www.hoytarboretum.org

Mount Pisgah Arboretum, Eugene:
http://www.efn.org/~mtpisgah

PENNSYLVANIA

Awbury Arboretum, Philadelphia:
http://awbury.org

Jenkins Arboretum, Devon:
http://www.jenkinsarboretum.org

Morris Arboretum of the University of
Pennsylvania, Philadelphia:
http://www.business-services.upenn.edu/
arboretum

Scott Arboretum of Swarthmore
College, Swarthmore:
http://www.scottarboretum.org

Tyler Arboretum, Media:
http://www.tylerarboretum.org

RHODE ISLAND
Blithewold Mansion, Gardens & Arboretum, Bristol: http://www.blithewold.org

SOUTH CAROLINA
South Carolina Botanical Garden, Clemson: http://www.clemson.edu/scbg

TENNESSEE
Knoxville Botanical Gardens and Arboretum, Knoxville: http://www.knoxarboretum.org
Memphis Botanic Garden, Memphis: http://www.memphisbotanicgarden.com

TEXAS
Dallas Arboretum, Dallas: http://www.dallasarboretum.org
East Texas Arboretum & Botanical Society, Athens: http://eastexasarboretum.org
Fort Worth Botanic Garden, Fort Worth: http://www.fwbg.org
Houston Botanic Garden, Houston: http://houstonbotanicgarden.org
Mercer Arboretum & Botanic Gardens, Humble: http://www.hcp4.net/mercer/general.htm
San Antonio Botanical Garden, San Antonio: http://www.sabot.org
SFA Mast Arboretum, Nacogdoches: http://arboretum.sfasu.edu
Valley Nature Center, Weslaco: http://www.valleynaturecenter.org

UTAH
Red Butte Garden, Salt Lake City: http://www.redbuttegarden.org

VIRGINIA
Lewis Ginter Botanical Garden, Richmond: http://www.lewisginter.org
State Arboretum of Virginia (Blandy Experimental Farm), Winchester: http://www.virginia.edu/blandy

WASHINGTON
Bellevue Botanical Garden, Bellevue: http://www.bellevuebotanical.org
Washington Park Arboretum, Seattle: http://depts.washington.edu/wpa

WISCONSIN
Green Bay Botanical Garden, Green Bay: http://www.gbbg.org
University of Wisconsin-Madison Arboretum, Madison: http://uwarboretum.org

WYOMING
Cheyenne Botanic Gardens, Cheyenne: http://www.botanic.org

Canada

ALBERTA
Devonian Botanic Garden, Edmonton: http://www.devonian.ualberta.ca

BRITISH COLUMBIA
Queen Elizabeth Park, Vancouver: http://www.city.vancouver.bc.ca/parks/parks/queenelizabeth/index.htm
UBC Botanical Garden and Centre for Plant Research, Vancouver: http://www.ubcbotanicalgarden.org

MANITOBA
Frank Skinner Arboretum, Roblin: http://www.skinnerarboretum.com

NEW BRUNSWICK
Odell Park and Odell Arboretum, Fredericton: http://www.fredericton.ca/en/recleisure/odellarboretum.asp

NEWFOUNDLAND
Memorial University of Newfoundland Botanical Garden, St. John's: http://www.mun.ca/botgarden/home.php

NOVA SCOTIA
Annapolis Royal Historic Gardens, Annapolis Royal: http://www.historicgardens.com/
Harriet Irving Botanical Gardens, Wolfville: http://www.acadiau.ca/botanicalgardens/

ONTARIO
Arboretum at the University of Guelph, Guelph: http://www.uoguelph.ca/arboretum/
Great Lakes Forestry Centre Arboretum, Sault Ste. Marie: http://cfs.nrcan.gc.ca/subsite/glfc-arboretum/home
Toronto Botanical Garden, Toronto: http://www.torontobotanicalgarden.ca

QUEBEC
Montreal Botanical Garden, Montreal: http://www2.ville.montreal.qc.ca/jardin/en/menu.htm
Morgan Arboretum, Ste.-Anne-de-Bellevue: http://www.morganarboretum.org

YUKON
Faro Arboretum, Faro: (867) 994–3121

Resources and References

Conservation Projects and Organizations

Alaska Boreal Forest Council.
  http://www.akborealforest.org
American Chestnut Foundation.
  http://www.acf.org
American Forests.
  http://www.americanforests.org
American Phytopathological Society.
  APSnet: Plant Pathology Online.
  http://www.apsnet.org
Arboretum, University of Guelph.
  Elm Recovery Project.
  http://www.uoguelph.ca/arboretum/
  SpProjects/Elm_Recover1.htm
California Oak Mortality Task Force.
  http://nature.berkeley.edu/comtf
Canadian Boreal Initiative.
  http://www.borealcanada.ca
Ecological Internet. Forest Conservation
  Portal. http://forests.org
Elm Research Institute.
  http://www.landscapeelms.com
Fauna and Flora International. Global Trees
  Campaign. http://www.globaltrees.org
Florida Native Plant Society.
  http://www.fnps.org
Forest & Shade Tree Pathology.
  http://www.forestpathology.org
ForestEthics.
  http://forestethics.org
Forest Gene Conservation Association and
  Butternut Recovery Team. http://www.
  fgca.net/conservation/sar/butternut_
  recovery_team.aspx
Friends of Trees.
  http://www.friendsoftrees.org
Georgia Botanical Society.
  http://www.gabotsoc.org
Invasive Species. http://www.invasive.org
Longleaf Alliance. http://www.auburn.edu/
  academic/forestry_wildlife/
  longleafalliance
National Forest Foundation.
  http://www.natlforests.org
The Nature Conservancy.
  http://www.nature.org
The Nature Conservancy. The Global
  Invasive Species Team.
  http://tncweeds.ucdavis.edu/index.html

Save Our Hemlocks.
  http://www.saveourhemlocks.org
Save-the-Redwoods League.
  http://www.savetheredwoods.org
Society of American Foresters.
  http://www.safnet.org
Tree Conservation Information Service.
  http://www.unep-wcmc.org/trees
U.S. Department of Agriculture. Forest
  Service. Forest Health Protection,
  Southern Region. Laurel Wilt.
  http://www.fs.fed.us/r8/foresthealth/
  laurelwilt/index.shtml
U.S. Department of Agriculture. Forest
  Service. Invasive Species Program.
  http://www.fs.fed.us/invasivespecies
U.S. Department of Agriculture. Natural
  Resources Conservation Service. Plant
  Materials Program.
  http://plant-materials.nrcs.usda.gov
Whitebark Pine Ecosystem Foundation.
  http://whitebarkfound.org
Yggdrasil, Earth Island Institute.
  PrimalNature.org.
  http://www.primalnature.org

General Reference Web Sites

American Public Gardens Association.
  http://www.publicgardens.org
Angiosperm Phylogeny Website.
  http://www.mobot.org/MOBOT/research/
  APweb/welcome.html
Botanical Society of America.
  http://www.botany.org
eFloras.org.
  http://www.efloras.org/
The Gymnosperm Database.
  http://www.conifers.org
Holly Society of America.
  http://www.hollysocam.org
International Oak Society.
  http://www.saintmarys.edu/
  ~rjensen/ios.html
International Society of Arboriculture.
  http://www.isa-arbor.com
International Union of Forest Research
  Organizations.
  http://www.iufro.org

Magnolia Society International.
  http://www.magnoliasociety.org

North Carolina Botanical Garden and
  University of North Carolina, Chapel Hill.
  The Biota of North America Program.
  http://www.bonap.org

North Carolina State University. Native Trees,
  Shrubs, and Woody Vines. http://www.ces.
  ncsu.edu/depts/hort/consumer/factsheets/
  native/index-native.html

North Carolina State University. Trees. http://
  www.ces.ncsu.edu/depts/hort/consumer/
  factsheets/trees-new/index.html

Southwest School of Botanical Medicine,
  Bisbee, Arizona. *Britton & Brown
  Illustrated Flora: An Illustrated Flora
  of the Northern United States and
  Canada.* 2nd ed. (1913). Medicinal
  plant excerpts.
  http://www.swsbm.com/Britton-Brown/
  Britton-Brown1.html

University of Florida. 680 Tree Fact Sheets.
  http://hort.ufl.edu/trees

U.S. Department of Agriculture.
  Cooperative State Research, Education,
  and Extension Service. Cooperative
  Extension System Offices.
  http://www.csrees.usda.gov/Extension/

U.S. Department of Agriculture. Forest
  Service. Fire Effects Information.
  http://www.fs.fed.us/database/feis/plants/

U.S. Department of Agriculture. Forest
  Service. Silvics of North America.
  http://www.na.fs.fed.us/spfo/pubs/silvics_
  manual/table_of_contents.htm

U.S. Department of Agriculture. Forest
  Service. Treesearch.
  http://www.treesearch.fs.fed.us

U.S. Department of Agriculture. Forest
  Service. Woody Plant Seed Manual.
  http://www.nsl.fs.fed.us/wpsm

U.S. Department of Agriculture.
  Natural Resources Conservation Service.
  The PLANTS Database.
  http://plants.usda.gov

U.S. Department of the Interior. U.S.
  Geological Survey. Digital Representations
  of Tree Species Range Maps from *Atlas of
  United States Trees,* by Elbert L. Little, Jr.
  (and other publications).
  http://esp.cr.usgs.gov/data/atlas/little

General Reference Books

Anderson, E. F. 2001. *The Cactus Family.*
  Portland, OR: Timber Press.

Bailey, L. H. 1975. *Manual of Cultivated Plants
  Most Commonly Grown in the Continental
  United States and Canada.* Rev. 1949 ed.
  New York: Macmillan.

Britton, N. L., and A. Brown. 1970. *An
  Illustrated Flora of the Northern United
  States and Canada.* 2nd ed. 3 vols. Mineola,
  NY: Dover Publications.

Collingwood, G. H., and W. D. Brush.
  1984. *Knowing Your Trees.* Rev. 1938 ed.
  Washington, D.C.: American Forestry
  Association.

Elias, T. S. 2000. *The Complete Trees of North
  America: Field Guide and Natural History.*
  Boca Raton, FL: Chapman & Hall.

Farrar, J. L. 1995. *Trees of the Northern United
  States and Canada.* Ames: Iowa State
  University Press.

Flora of North America Editorial Committee,
  eds. 1993+. *Flora of North America North
  of Mexico.* 12+ volumes. New York and
  Oxford: Oxford University Press.

Grimm, W. C., and J. T. Kartesz. 2002. *The
  Illustrated Book of Trees.* Mechanicsburg,
  PA: Stackpole Books.

Hardin, J. W., D. J. Leopold, and F. M White.
  2000. *Harlow & Harrar's Textbook of
  Dendrology.* 9th ed. New York: McGraw
  Hill Higher Education.

Heywood, V. H., et al. 2007. *Flowering Plant
  Families of the World.* Buffalo, NY: Firefly
  Books.

Isely, D. 1998. *Native and Naturalized
  Leguminosae (Fabaceae) of the United
  States: (Exclusive of Alaska and Hawaii).*
  Provo, UT: Brigham Young University
  Press.

Kartesz, J. T., and C. A. Meacham. 1999.
  Synthesis of the North American Flora.
  Windows Version 1.0. CD-ROM. Chapel
  Hill: University of North Carolina.

Little, E. L. 1971–1981. *Atlas of United States
  Trees.* 6 vols. Washington, D.C.: U.S.
  Department of Agriculture.

Mabberley, D. J. 2008. *Mabberley's Plant
  Book: A Portable Dictionary of Plants.*
  3rd ed. Cambridge: Cambridge University
  Press.

Miller, H. A., and S. H. Lamb. 1985. *Oaks of North America*. Happy Camp, CA: Naturegraph Publishers.

Peattie, D. C. 2007. *A Natural History of North American Trees*. New York: Houghton Mifflin.

Perry, D. A., R. Oren, and S. C. Hart. 2008. *Forest Ecosystems*. 2nd ed. Baltimore, MD: Johns Hopkins University Press.

Sargent, C. S. 1961. *Manual of the Trees of North America*. 2 vols. Mineola, NY: Dover Publications.

Simpson, M. G. 2006. *Plant Systematics*. Burlington, MA: Elsevier Academic Press.

Sternberg, G., and J. W. Wilson. 2004. *Native Trees for North American Landscapes: From the Atlantic to the Rockies*. Portland, OR: Timber Press.

Tudge, C. 2007. *The Tree: A Natural History of What Trees Are, How They Live, and Why They Matter*. New York: Three Rivers Press.

Young, J. A., and C. G. Young. 1992. *Seeds of Woody Plants in North America*. Rev. 1974 ed. Portland, OR: Dioscorides Press.

Regional Guides and Web Sites
EASTERN NORTH AMERICA

Alabama Forestry Commission. *100 Trees of Alabama*. http://www.forestry.state.al.us/publication/100_trees_of_alabama.htm

Allen, C. M., D. A. Newman, and H. H. Winters. 2002. *Trees, Shrubs, and Woody Vines of Louisiana*. Pitkin, LA: Allen's Native Ventures.

Barnard, E. S. 2002. *New York City Trees*. New York: Columbia University Press.

Bell, R. C., and A. H. Lindsey. 2007. *Fall Color and Woodland Harvests: A Guide to the More Colorful Fall Leaves and Fruits of the Eastern Forests*. Chapel Hill: University of North Carolina Press.

Brown, C. L., and L. K. Kirkman. 1990. *Trees of Georgia and Adjacent States*. Portland, OR: Timber Press.

Coalition for Excellence in Tropical Biology. *The Miami Tree Puzzle*. http://bio.fiu.edu/trees

Cook, Will. *Trees, Shrubs, and Woody Vines of North Carolina*. http://www.duke.edu/~cwcook/trees

Duncan, W. H., and M. B. Duncan. 1988. *Trees of the Southeastern United States*. Athens: University of Georgia Press.

Gleason, H. A., and A. Cronquist. 1991. *Manual of Vascular Plants of Northeastern United States and Adjacent Canada*. Bronx, NY: New York Botanical Garden.

Godfrey, R. K. 1989. *Trees, Shrubs, and Woody Vines of Northern Florida and Adjacent Alabama and Georgia*. Athens: University of Georgia Press.

Institute for Systematic Botany. *Atlas of Florida Vascular Plants*. http://www.plantatlas.usf.edu

Kirkman, L. K., C. L. Brown, and D. J. Leopold. 2007. *Native Trees of the Southeast*. Portland, OR: Timber Press.

Lance, R. 2004. *Woody Plants of the Southeastern United States: A Winter Guide*. Athens: University of Georgia Press.

Miller, J. H., and K. V. Miller. 2005. *Forest Plants of the Southeast and Their Wildlife Uses*. Athens: University of Georgia Press.

Mousseau, T. A. University of South Carolina, Columbia. *South Carolina Plant Atlas*. http://cricket.biol.sc.edu/herb

Native Trees of Texas. http://aggie-horticulture.tamu.edu/ornamentals/natives/indexcommon.htm

Nelson, G. 1994. *The Trees of Florida: A Reference and Field Guide*. Sarasota, FL: Pineapple Press.

Petrides, G. A. 1998. *A Field Guide to Eastern Trees*. Peterson Field Guides. New York: Houghton Mifflin.

Powell, M. A. 1988. *Trees and Shrubs of Trans-Pecos Texas*. Big Bend National Park, TX: Big Bend Natural History Association.

Swanson, R. E., and F. R. Swanson. 1994. *Field Guide to the Trees and Shrubs of the Southern Appalachians*. Baltimore, MD: Johns Hopkins University Press.

WESTERN NORTH AMERICA

Abrams, L. 1984. *An Illustrated Flora of the Pacific States*. Stanford, CA: Stanford University Press.

Arizona-Sonora Desert Museum. 1999. *A Natural History of the Sonoran Desert*. Berkeley: University of California Press.

Calflora. http://www.calflora.org

Cronquist, A., et al. 2005. *Intermountain Flora: Vascular Plants of the Intermountain West, U.S.A.* 6 vols. Bronx, NY: New York Botanical Garden.

Hickman, J. C. 1993. *The Jepson Manual: Higher Plants of California.* Berkeley: University of California Press.

Hitchcock, C. L. 1955–1969. *Vascular Plants of the Pacific Northwest.* 5 vols. Seattle: University of Washington Press.

Kearney, T. H., and R. H. Peebles. 1960. *Arizona Flora.* 2nd ed. Berkeley: University of California Press.

Mathews, D. 1999. *Cascade-Olympic Natural History.* 2nd ed. Portland, OR: Raven Editions.

———. 2003. *Rocky Mountain Natural History: Grand Teton to Jasper.* Portland, OR: Raven Editions.

Munz, P. A. 1968. *A California Flora.* Berkeley: University of California Press.

North Dakota State University. *North Dakota Tree Handbook.* http://www.ag.ndsu.edu/trees/handbook.htm

Petrides, G. A. 1998. *A Field Guide to Western Trees.* Peterson Field Guides. New York: Houghton Mifflin.

Shreve, F., and I. L. Wiggins. 1964. *Vegetation and Flora of the Sonoran Desert.* Stanford, CA: Stanford University Press.

University of California, Berkeley. *The Jepson Herbarium.* http://ucjeps.berkeley.edu/jepson_flora_project.html

Van Pelt, R. 2002. *Forest Giants of the Pacific Coast.* Seattle: University of Washington Press.

Vines, R. A. 2004. *Trees, Shrubs, and Woody Vines of the Southwest.* Caldwell, NJ: Blackburn Press.

Welsh, S. L., et al. 2003. *A Utah Flora.* 3rd ed. Provo, UT: Brigham Young University Press.

Photo Credits

The photographs for each page are credited either left to right and top to bottom (lr/tb) or clockwise (cw). Most species accounts are credited clockwise, starting with the top photograph in the right column (usually the leaf photo).

h Steven J. Baskauf, http://bioimages.vanderbilt.edu
49 Leaf Undersides (lr/tb): **a** David Cavagnaro; **b** Michael P. Gadomski/Photo Researchers, Inc.; **c** Steven Arcella; **d** Charles Webber/California Academy of Sciences; **e** Nigel Cattlin/Photo Researchers, Inc.; **f, g** Will Cook, http://www.carolinanature.com
50 Features of Twigs (lr/tb): **a** Bill Johnson; **b** David Liebman, Pink Guppy; **c** Dr. Jeremy Burgess/Photo Researchers, Inc.; **d** Wm. Harlow/Photo Researchers, Inc.; **e, f** David Liebman, Pink Guppy; **g** Stephen P. Parker/Photo Researchers, Inc.; **h** Ken Brate/Photo Researchers, Inc.
51 Buds (lr/tb): **a** Rod Planck/Photo Researchers, Inc.; **b** Bill Cook, Michigan State University/http://www.bugwood.org; **c** Jessie M. Harris; **d** Bill Johnson; **e** John R. Seiler, Virginia Tech Department of Forestry
53 Flowers (lr/tb): **a** Will Cook, http://www.carolinanature.com; **b** David Liebman, Pink Guppy; **c** Will Cook, http://www.carolinanature.com; **d** Keith A. Bradley; **e, f** Jessie M. Harris; **g** Adam Jones/Photo Researchers, Inc.; **h** Steven Arcella; **i** Robert Sivinski; **j** Gerald & Buff Corsi, Focus on Nature, Inc.
54 Flowers cont. (lr/tb): **a** Michael L. Charters, http://www.calflora.net; **b** Gerald & Buff Corsi, Focus on Nature, Inc.; **c** Michael L. Charters, http://www.calflora.net; **d** John R. Seiler, Virginia Tech Department of Forestry; **e** Elizabeth Chute, http://www.elizabethchute.com; **f** David Liebman, Pink Guppy; **g** Jessie M. Harris; **h** Ken Brate/Photo Researchers, Inc.; **i** Steven J. Baskauf, http://bioimages.vanderbilt.edu
55 Fruit (lr/tb): **a** Shirley Denton; **b, c** David Liebman, Pink Guppy; **d** Michael P. Gadomski/Photo Researchers, Inc.; **e** Kenneth M. Highfill/Photo Researchers, Inc.; **f** Gail Jankus/Photo Researchers, Inc.; **g** Elizabeth Chute, http://www.elizabethchute.com; **h** Gil Nelson
56 Fruit cont. (lr/tb): **a** R. J. Erwin/Photo Researchers, Inc.; **b** Paul H. Wray; **c** Steven J. Baskauf, http://bioimages.vanderbilt.edu; **d** Gregory K. Scott/Photo Researchers, Inc.; **e** Dr. Mark S. Brunell, Department of

Biological Sciences, University of the Pacific; **f** Steven J. Baskauf, http://bioimages.vanderbilt.edu; **g** Will Cook, http://www.carolinanature.com; **h** David Liebman, Pink Guppy; **i** John Bova/Photo Researchers, Inc.; **j** Karl H. Switak/Photo Researchers, Inc.; **k** Steven J. Baskauf, http://bioimages.vanderbilt.edu; **l** Alvin E. Staffan/Photo Researchers, Inc.
57 Fruit cont. (lr/tb): **a** David Liebman, Pink Guppy; **b** Gilbert S. Grant/Photo Researchers, Inc.; **c** Steven Arcella; **d** Charles Webber/California Academy of Sciences; **e** Richard Parker/Photo Researchers, Inc.; **f** Gilbert S. Grant/Photo Researchers, Inc.
58 Bark (lr/tb): **a** Tom & Pat Leeson/Photo Researchers, Inc.; **b** Steven Arcella; **c** David Cavagnaro; **d** John Serrao/Photo Researchers, Inc.; **e** Kent & Donna Dannen/Photo Researchers, Inc.; **f** Richard Parker/Photo Researchers, Inc.; **g** Michael P. Gadomski/Photo Researchers, Inc.; **h** Steven Arcella; **i** David Cavagnaro; **j** Steven J. Baskauf, http://bioimages.vanderbilt.edu; **k** Will Cook, http://www.carolinanature.com
59 Bark cont. (lr/tb): **a** C. K. Lorenz/Photo Researchers, Inc.; **b** Gil Nelson; **c** Dan Suzio/Photo Researchers, Inc.; **d** Rod Planck/Photo Researchers, Inc.; **e** Bill Cook, Michigan State University/http://www.bugwood.org; **f** Will Cook, http://www.carolinanature.com; **g** Alan & Linda Detrick/Photo Researchers, Inc.; **h** Daniel Mathews; **i** Steven Arcella; **j** Michael L. Charters, http://www.calflora.net; **k** Geoff Bryant/Photo Researchers, Inc.; **l** Alan & Linda Detrick/Photo Researchers, Inc.
60 Trees with Needlelike Leaves: Geoff Bryant/Photo Researchers, Inc.
61 The Conifer Tree Shape (lr/tb): **a** Gregory Bergman; **b** Tom McHugh/Photo Researchers, Inc.; **c** Susan C. McDougall; **d** Dave Powell, USDA Forest Service/http://www.bugwood.org; **e** Gerald & Buff Corsi, Focus on Nature, Inc.
62 Key to Trees with Needlelike Leaves (lr/tb): **a** Michael P. Gadomski/Photo Researchers, Inc.; **b** Stephen P. Parker/Photo Researchers, Inc.; **c** Robert

Finken/Photo Researchers, Inc.; **d** Tom & Patt Leeson/Photo Researchers, Inc.
63 Key cont. (lr/tb): **a** Gerald & Buff Corsi, Focus on Nature, Inc.; **b** Christopher Christie; **c** Daniel Mathews; **d** Gerald & Buff Corsi, Focus on Nature, Inc.; **e** David Cavagnaro; **f** Gilbert S. Grant/Photo Researchers, Inc.; **g** Douglas Faulkner/Photo Researchers, Inc.
64 Pines (lr/tb): **a** Gerald & Buff Corsi, Focus on Nature, Inc.; **b** Will Cook, http://www.carolinanature.com
66 Red Pine (cw): **a** Michael P. Gadomski/Photo Researchers, Inc.; **b** (needles) Steven Arcella; **c** (tree) Joseph O'Brien, USDA Forest Service/http://www.bugwood.org; **d** V. P. Weinland/Photo Researchers, Inc.; **e** Michael P. Gadomski/Photo Researchers, Inc.
67 Scots Pine (cw): **a** E. R. Degginger/Photo Researchers, Inc.; **b** David Cavagnaro; **c** Steven Arcella
67 Austrian Pine: David Liebman, Pink Guppy
68 Jack Pine (cw): **a** Steven Arcella; **b** Bill Cook, Michigan State University/http://www.bugwood.org; **c** John R. Seiler, Virginia Tech Department of Forestry; **d** Steven Arcella
69 Virginia Pine (cw): **a, b** Steven J. Baskauf, http://bioimages.vanderbilt.edu; **c** (needles) Steven Arcella; **d** (tree) Michael P. Gadomski/Photo Researchers, Inc.; **e, f** Steven Arcella
70 Spruce Pine: a, b, c Will Cook, http://www.carolinanature.com
70 Sand Pine (lr/tb): **a** David Liebman, Pink Guppy; **b** Steven Arcella
71 Table Mountain Pine (cw): **a** Will Cook, http://www.carolinanature.com; **b** (needles) Steven Arcella; **c** (trees) Michael P. Gadomski/Photo Researchers, Inc.; **d, e** Will Cook, http://www.carolinanature.com
72 Shortleaf Pine (cw): **a** Steven J. Baskauf, http://bioimages.vanderbilt.edu; **b** Steven Arcella; **c** Steven J. Baskauf, http://bioimages.vanderbilt.edu; **d** Michael P. Gadomski/Photo Researchers, Inc.; **e** Steven Arcella; **f** Will Cook, http://www.carolinanature.com
73 Loblolly Pine (cw): **a** Paul Bolstad, University of Minnesota /http://www.bugwood.org;

b Steven Arcella; c Michael P. Gadomski/Photo Researchers, Inc.; d John Serrao/Photo Researchers, Inc.

73 Pond Pine: Christopher Earle, Gymnosperm Database

74 Slash Pine (cw): a David Liebman, Pink Guppy; b Steven Arcella; c John Serrao/Photo Researchers, Inc.; d Gilbert S. Grant/Photo Researchers, Inc.; e Leroy Simon/David Liebman, Pink Guppy

75 Longleaf Pine (cw): a Vladimir Bridan; b Jessie M. Harris; c Christopher Earle, Gymnosperm Database; d Steven Arcella; e Gil Nelson; f Will Cook, http://www.carolinanature.com

76 Pitch Pine (cw): a Michael P. Gadomski/Photo Researchers, Inc.; b Steven Arcella; c, d Michael P. Gadomski/Photo Researchers, Inc.; e Steven Arcella

77 Eastern White Pine (cw): a, b, c Steven Arcella; d Michael P. Gadomski/Photo Researchers, Inc.; e Steven Arcella; f David Liebman, Pink Guppy

78 Western White Pine (cw): a David Cavagnaro; b (needles) Steven Arcella; c (trees) Christopher Christie; d Daniel Mathews; e Gerald & Buff Corsi, Focus on Nature, Inc.; f Steven Arcella

79 Sugar Pine (cw): a David Cavagnaro; b Steven Arcella; c Gerald & Buff Corsi, Focus on Nature, Inc.; d Daniel Mathews; e David Cavagnaro; f (cone) Daniel Mathews

80 Whitebark Pine (cw): a Gerald & Buff Corsi, Focus on Nature, Inc.; b Kenneth W. Fink/Photo Researchers, Inc.; c Daniel Mathews

81 Limber Pine (cw): a David Liebman, Pink Guppy; b Steven Arcella; c, d Gerald & Buff Corsi, Focus on Nature, Inc.; e David Liebman, Pink Guppy

82 Intermountain Bristlecone Pine (cw): a Stuart Wilson/Photo Researchers, Inc.; b Gerald & Buff Corsi, Focus on Nature, Inc.; c Daniel Mathews

83 Colorado Bristlecone Pine: Gerald & Buff Corsi, Focus on Nature, Inc.

83 Foxtail Pine: David Cavagnaro

83 Southwestern White Pine: a, b, c Steven Arcella

84 Monterey Pine (lr/tb): a David Cavagnaro; b Alfred Brousseau, FSC, Saint Mary's College of California

84 Torrey Pine: David Winkelman/David Liebman, Pink Guppy

85 Knobcone Pine (cw): a, b, c Steven Arcella; d Gregory Bergman; e Steven Arcella; f Michael L. Charters, http://www.calflora.net

86 Coulter Pine (cw): a David Cavagnaro; b Steven Arcella; c Michael L. Charters, http://www.calflora.net; d David Cavagnaro; e Stephen P. Parker/Photo Researchers, Inc.

87 Gray Pine (cw): a, b Steven Arcella; c Gerald & Buff Corsi, Focus on Nature, Inc.; d David Cavagnaro; e (cone) Daniel Mathews

88 Jeffrey Pine (cw): a Michael L. Charters, http://www.calflora.net; b Gerald & Buff Corsi, Focus on Nature, Inc.; c Emil Muench/Photo Researchers, Inc.; d Dennis Flaherty/Photo Researchers, Inc.

89 Ponderosa Pine (cw): a Chris Evans, River to River CWMA/http://www.bugwood.org; b Steven Arcella; c Daniel Mathews; d, e Tom & Patt Leeson/Photo Researchers, Inc.; f David Cavagnaro

90 Bishop Pine (cw): a Geoff Bryant/Photo Researchers, Inc.; b (cone) Steven Arcella

90 Chihuahua Pine (lr/tb): a Christopher Earle, Gymnosperm Database; b John R. Seiler, Virginia Tech Department of Forestry

91 Lodgepole Pine (cw): a (branch) Steven Arcella; b, c Gerald & Buff Corsi, Focus on Nature, Inc.; d Daniel Mathews; e Gerald & Buff Corsi, Focus on Nature, Inc.; f (needle) Steven Arcella

92 Pinyon (cw): a, b Steven Arcella; c David M. Schleser/Photo Researchers, Inc.; d Jim Zipp/Photo Researchers, Inc.; e, f Steven Arcella

93 Singleleaf Pinyon: Gerald & Buff Corsi, Focus on Nature, Inc.

93 Mexican Pinyon: a, b Steven Arcella

93 Parry Pinyon: a, b Steven Arcella

94 Larches and True Cedars: Stephen P. Parker/Photo Researchers, Inc.

94 European Larch: Steven Arcella

95 Tamarack (cw): a Michael P. Gadomski/Photo Researchers, Inc.; b, c Daniel Mathews; d Michael P. Gadomski/Photo Researchers, Inc.

96 Western Larch (cw): a Christopher Christie; b David Cavagnaro; c Daniel Mathews; d Christopher Christie

97 Subalpine Larch (cw): a, b Daniel Mathews; c Christopher Earle, Gymnosperm Database; d John R. Seiler, Virginia Tech Department of Forestry

98 True Cedars (lr/tb): a Steven Arcella; b Christian Grzimek/Photo Researchers, Inc.; c, d Steven Arcella; e Geoff Bryant/Photo Researchers, Inc.

99 True Cedars cont. (lr/tb): a (Deodar cone) Robert Finken/Photo Researchers, Inc.; b Daniel Mathews; c, d Steven Arcella; e David Cavagnaro

100 Spruces (lr/tb): a (tree) Christopher Earle, Gymnosperm Database; b Gerald & Buff Corsi, Focus on Nature, Inc.

101 Red Spruce (cw): a, b (open cone) Steven Arcella; c Gerald & Buff Corsi, Focus on Nature, Inc.; d Michael P. Gadomski/Photo Researchers, Inc.; e (closed cone) Steven Arcella

102 White Spruce (cw): a, b Steven Arcella; c Michael P. Gadomski/Photo Researchers, Inc.; d Steven Arcella; e Michael Giannechini/Photo Researchers, Inc.

103 Black Spruce (cw): a, b Steven Arcella; c Rod Planck/Photo Researchers, Inc.; d Steven Arcella

104 Engelmann Spruce (cw): a Steven Arcella; b Gerald & Buff Corsi, Focus on Nature, Inc.; c Michael P. Gadomski/Photo Researchers, Inc.; d Steven Arcella

105 Blue Spruce (cw): a, b (open cone) Steven Arcella; c Michael P. Gadomski/Photo Researchers, Inc.; d, e (closed cone) Steven Arcella

106 Sitka Spruce (cw): a, b Steven Arcella; c Tom & Patt Leeson/Photo Researchers, Inc.; d Christopher Christie; e David Cavagnaro

107 Brewer Spruce: Daniel Mathews

107 Norway Spruce (cw): a Steven Arcella; b (bark) Daniel Mathews

108 True Firs and Douglas-firs (lr/tb): a, b Michael P. Gadomski/Photo Researchers, Inc.; c Ray Coleman/Photo Researchers, Inc.

109 Douglas-fir (cw): a Calvin Larsen/Photo Researchers, Inc.; b Gerald & Buff Corsi, Focus on Nature, Inc.; c Geoff Bryant/Photo Researchers, Inc.; d Daniel Mathews

110 **Bigcone Douglas-fir** (lr/tb): **a** David Cavagnaro; **b** Steven Arcella

110 **Fraser Fir:** Michael P. Gadomski/Photo Researchers, Inc.

111 **Balsam Fir** (cw): **a** Steven Arcella; **b** Noble Proctor/Photo Researchers, Inc.; **c** David Cavagnaro; **d** Gerald & Buff Corsi, Focus on Nature, Inc.

112 **Subalpine Fir/Rocky Mountain Alpine Fir** (cw): **a** Steven Arcella; **b** Jim Steinberg/Photo Researchers, Inc.; **c** Verna Johnston/Photo Researchers, Inc.; **d** Will Cook, http://www.carolinanature.com

113 **White Fir/Sierra White Fir** (cw): **a** Steven Arcella; **b** Jerry L. Ferrara/Photo Researchers, Inc.; **c** John Serrao/Photo Researchers, Inc.; **d** Steven Arcella

114 **Grand Fir** (cw): **a** Steven Arcella; **b** Charles Webber/California Academy of Sciences; **c, d** Steven J. Baskauf, http://bioimages.vanderbilt.edu

115 **Pacific Silver Fir** (cw): **a** Steven Arcella; **b, c** Daniel Mathews; **d** Susan C. McDougall

116 **California Red Fir** (cw): **a, b** David Cavagnaro; **c** Gerald & Buff Corsi, Focus on Nature, Inc.; **d** Betty Randall White; **e** Charles Webber/California Academy of Sciences

117 **Noble Fir** (cw): **a** Steven Arcella; **b** (Bristlecone) Charles Webber/California Academy of Sciences; **c** (Noble Fir cone), **d** Christopher Christie; **e, f** Daniel Mathews

118 **Hemlocks:** Daniel Mathews

118 **Needles in Flat Sprays:** Michael P. Gadomski/Photo Researchers, Inc.

118 **Carolina Hemlock: a, b** Steven Arcella

119 **Eastern Hemlock** (cw): **a, b** Michael P. Gadomski/Photo Researchers, Inc.; **c** Steven J. Baskauf, http://bioimages.vanderbilt.edu; **d** Steven Arcella

120 **Western Hemlock** (cw): **a** Verna R. Johnston/Photo Researchers, Inc.; **b** Betty Randall White; **c** Christopher Christie; **d** Daniel Mathews

121 **Mountain Hemlock** (cw): **a** Noble Proctor/Photo Researchers, Inc.; **b** Gerald & Buff Corsi, Focus on Nature, Inc.; **c** David Cavagnaro

122 **Yews and Torreyas:** Steven Arcella

122 **Pacific Yew** (cw): **a** Gerald & Buff Corsi, Focus on Nature, Inc.; **b** Scott Schechtel, http://www.oregonvisions.com; **c** Daniel Mathews

123 **Florida Torreya:** Gil Nelson

123 **California Torreya** (cw): **a** David Cavagnaro; **b** Gregory Bergman; **c** David Cavagnaro

124 **Bald-cypresses, Redwoods, and Kin:** Adam Jones/Photo Researchers, Inc.

124 **Japanese-cedar: a, b** Steven Arcella

125 **Redwood** (cw): **a** F. Gohier/Photo Researchers, Inc.; **b** (cones) Gilbert S. Grant/Photo Researchers, Inc.; **c** Michael Giannechini/Photo Researchers, Inc.; **d** Michael L. Charters, http://www.calflora.net

126 **Dawn Redwood: a, b, c** Steven Arcella

126 **Pond-cypress:** **a** Gilbert S. Grant/Photo Researchers, Inc.; **b** (bark) David Liebman, Pink Guppy

127 **Bald-cypress: a** John Serrao/Photo Researchers, Inc.; **b** Douglas Faulkner/Photo Researchers, Inc.; **c** Adam Jones/Photo Researchers, Inc.; **d** Steven Arcella

128 **Norfolk Island–pine** (lr/tb): **a** David Winkelman/David Liebman, Pink Guppy; **b** Steven Arcella

128 **Monkeypuzzle Tree** (lr/tb): **a** Steven Arcella; **b** David Liebman, Pink Guppy

129 **Trees with Scalelike Leaves:** Paul Bolstad, University of Minnesota/http://www.bugwood.org

130 **Scalelike Leaves** cont. (lr/tb): **a** Daniel Mathews; **b** Jerry L. Ferrara/Photo Researchers, Inc.

131 **Key to Trees with Scalelike Leaves** (lr/tb): **a** Dan Suzio/Photo Researchers, Inc.; **b, c** David Cavagnaro; **d** Christopher Christie; **e** Will Cook, http://www.carolinanature.com; **f** Bob Gibbons/Photo Researchers, Inc.; **g** Christopher Christie

132 **Giant Sequoia** (cw): **a** Steven Arcella; **b** Dan Suzio/Photo Researchers, Inc.; **c** Bill Kjaer/http://www.naturepl.com; **d** Adam Jones/Photo Researchers, Inc.

133 **Incense-cedar** (cw): **a** David Cavagnaro; **b** Gregory Bergman; **c** Daniel Mathews

134 **Western Redcedar** (cw): **a** Steven Arcella; **b** David Cavagnaro; **c** William H. Mullins/Photo Researchers, Inc.;

d Scott Schechtel, http://www.oregonvisions.com

135 **Northern White-cedar** (cw): **a** Steven Arcella; **b** David Cavagnaro; **c** David Liebman, Pink Guppy; **d** David Cavagnaro

136 **Oriental Arborvitae: a, b** Steven Arcella

136 **Hiba False-arborvitae:** Steven Arcella

136 **Sawara False-cypress: a, b** Steven Arcella

137 **Atlantic White-cedar** (cw): **a** (large branch) Steven Arcella; **b** Will Cook, http://www.carolinanature.com; **c** David Liebman, Pink Guppy; **d** Will Cook, http://www.carolinanature.com; **e** (small branch/cones) Steven Arcella

138 **Alaska-cedar** (cw): **a, b** Steven Arcella; **c** Steven J. Baskauf, http://bioimages.vanderbilt.edu; **d** Daniel Mathews; **e** Christopher Christie

139 **Port-Orford-cedar** (cw): **a, b** Steven Arcella; **c** Gary A. Monroe; **d** Steven Arcella

140 **Trees and Fire:** Ken M. Johns/Photo Researchers, Inc.

142 **Cypresses** (lr/tb): **a** Bob Gibbons/Photo Researchers, Inc.; **b** David Liebman, Pink Guppy; **c** Dr. Mark S. Brunell, Department of Biological Sciences, University of the Pacific

143 **MacNab Cypress** (lr/tb): **a** Dr. Mark S. Brunell, Department of Biological Sciences, University of the Pacific; **b** Gregory Bergman

143 **Baker Cypress: a, b** Steven Arcella

144 **Sargent Cypress: a, b** Steven Arcella

144 **Gowen Cypress: a, b** Steven Arcella

145 **Monterey Cypress** (lr/tb): **a** David Liebman, Pink Guppy; **b** Stephen P. Parker/Photo Researchers, Inc.

145 **Arizona Cypress** (cw): **a** Steven Arcella; **b** Dr. Mark S. Brunell, Department of Biological Sciences, University of the Pacific; **c, d** Michael L. Charters, http://www.calflora.net

146 **Junipers:** Jessie M. Harris

147 **Eastern Redcedar** (cw): **a** David Cavagnaro; **b** Steven Arcella; **c** Gil Nelson; **d** Alan & Linda Detrick/Photo Researchers, Inc.

148 **Common Juniper** (lr/tb): **a** Ken Brate/Photo Researchers, Inc.; **b** Steven Arcella

148 **Junipers of Texas:** Cynthia J. Willson

149 **Rocky Mountain Juniper:** David Cavagnaro

149 **Oneseed Juniper** (lr/tb): **a** Gilbert S. Grant/Photo Researchers, Inc.; **b** Robert Sivinski

150 **Utah Juniper** (cw): **a** Jeff Lepore/Photo Researchers, Inc.; **b** Robert Sivinski; **c** Dan Suzio/ Photo Researchers, Inc.

150 **Alligator Juniper:** Kent & Donna Dannen/Photo Researchers, Inc.

151 **Western Juniper** (cw): **a** Christopher Christie; **b** Jessie M. Harris; **c** David Cavagnaro

151 **California Juniper:** Charles Webber/California Academy of Sciences

152 **Tamarisks** (lr/tb): **a** Dr. Mark S. Brunell, Department of Biological Sciences, University of the Pacific; **b** Steve Perkins

152 **Australian-pine** (lr/tb): **a, b** Steven Arcella; **c** Rick Dronsky/ David Liebman, Pink Guppy

153 **Broadleaf Trees:** Stephen J. Krasemann/Photo Researchers, Inc.

154 **Ginkgo** (cw): **a** Steven Arcella; **b** Gilbert S. Grant/Photo Researchers, Inc.; **c** Steven Arcella; **d** Steven J. Baskauf, http://bioimages.vanderbilt.edu; **e** Alan & Linda Detrick/Photo Researchers, Inc.; **f** (fruit) Steven Arcella

156 **Key to Trees with Opposite Leaves** (lr/tb): **a** Betty Randall White; **b** Stephen P. Parker/Photo Researchers, Inc.; **c** Chris Evans, River to River CWMA/http:// www.bugwood.org; **d** Will Cook, http://www.carolinanature. com; **e** David Liebman, Pink Guppy; **f** Will Cook, http://www. carolinanature.com

157 **Key** cont. (lr/tb): **a** Glenn and Martha Vargas/California Academy of Sciences; **b** Paul H. Wray; **c** David Liebman, Pink Guppy; **d** Paul H. Wray; **e** Gil Nelson; **f** Steven Arcella; **g** David Cavagnaro; **h** Scott Camazine/ Photo Researchers, Inc.

158 **Horse-chestnut** (cw): **a** Steven Arcella; **b** David Liebman, Pink Guppy; **c** Steven Arcella; **d** David Cavagnaro; **e** Steven Arcella

159 **Ohio Buckeye** (cw): **a** Steven Arcella; **b** Gregory K. Scott/ Photo Researchers, Inc.; **c** D. E. Herman/USDA-NRCS PLANTS Database; **d** Richard Parker/ Photo Researchers, Inc.; **e** Steven Arcella; **f** Alvin E. Staffan/Photo Researchers, Inc.

160 **Yellow Buckeye** (cw): **a, b** (2 capsules) Steven Arcella; **c** Geoff Bryant/Photo Researchers, Inc.; **d** V. P. Weinland/Photo Researchers, Inc.; **e** William M. Ciesla, Forest Health Management International/ http://www.bugwood.org

161 **Painted Buckeye** (cw): **a, b, c** Bill Johnson; **d** Will Cook, http://www.carolinanature.com; **e** Wendy VanDyk Evans/http:// www.bugwood.org

162 **Red Buckeye** (cw): **a** Steven Arcella; **b** David Liebman, Pink Guppy; **c** Kent & Donna Dannen/Photo Researchers, Inc.; **d** David Liebman, Pink Guppy; **e** John R. Seiler, Virginia Tech Department of Forestry

163 **California Buckeye** (cw): **a** Betty Randall White; **b** Stephen P. Parker/Photo Researchers, Inc.; **c** David Weintraub/Photo Researchers, Inc.; **d** David Cavagnaro; **e** Gerald & Buff Corsi, Focus on Nature, Inc.

164 **American Bladdernut: a, b, c** Steven Arcella

164 **Lilac Chastetree: a, b** Steven Arcella

165 **Texas Lignum-vitae: a, b** Steven Arcella

165 **Catalina Ironwood** (cw): **a** Steven Arcella; **b** Jessie M. Harris; **c** David Cavagnaro

166 **Elderberries** (lr/tb): **a** Steven J. Baskauf, http://bioimages. vanderbilt.edu; **b** J. E. and Bonnie McClellan/California Academy of Sciences; **c** R. J. Erwin/Photo Researchers, Inc.; **d** David Cavagnaro; **e, f** Daniel Mathews

167 **Ashes:** Steven J. Baskauf, http://bioimages.vanderbilt.edu

167 **Black Ash** (cw): **a, b** David Liebman, Pink Guppy; **c** Jenny Winkelman/David Liebman, Pink Guppy

168 **White Ash** (cw): **a** Shirley Denton; **b** Michael P. Gadomski/ Photo Researchers, Inc.; **c** E. R. Degginger/Photo Researchers, Inc.; **d** Bill Johnson; **e** Alvin E. Staffan/Photo Researchers, Inc.

169 **Green Ash** (cw): **a** David Liebman, Pink Guppy; **b, c** Steven Arcella

169 **Mexican Ash: a, b** Steven Arcella

170 **Blue Ash** (cw): **a** Steven J. Baskauf, http://bioimages. vanderbilt.edu; **b** V. P. Weinland/ Photo Researchers, Inc.; **c, d** Bill Johnson; **e** Steven J. Baskauf, http://bioimages.vanderbilt.edu

171 **Carolina Ash** (cw): **a** Chris Evans, River to River CWMA/ http://www.bugwood.org; **b** Will Cook, http://www.carolinanature. com; **c** Shirley Denton

171 **Pumpkin Ash:** Steven Arcella

172 **Velvet Ash** (cw): **a** David Cavagnaro; **b** Michael L. Charters, http://www.calflora. net; **c** Robert Sivinski; **d** Richard Parker/Photo Researchers, Inc.

173 **Oregon Ash** (cw): **a** David Cavagnaro; **b** Steven Arcella; **c** David Cavagnaro

173 **Texas Ash:** Steven Arcella

174 **California Ash** (cw): **a** Betty Randall White; **b** Michael L. Charters, http://www.calflora. net; **c** Charles Webber/California Academy of Sciences; **d** David Cavagnaro

174 **Fragrant Ash** (lr/tb): **a** Steven Arcella; **b** Robert Sivinski

175 **Singleleaf Ash** (lr/tb): **a** Robert Sivinski; **b** Al Schneider, http:// www.swcoloradowildflowers.com

175 **Gregg's Ash:** David Cavagnaro

176 **Trees with Maplelike Leaves** (lr/tb): **a** Michael P. Gadomski/ Photo Researchers, Inc.; **b** Bill Johnson; **c, d** Michael P. Gadomski /Photo Researchers, Inc.

177 **Boxelder** (cw): **a** Steven J. Baskauf, http://bioimages. vanderbilt.edu; **b** David Liebman, Pink Guppy; **c** D. E. Herman/ USDA-NRCS PLANTS Database; **d** David Liebman, Pink Guppy

178 **Sugar Maple** (cw): **a** Steven Arcella; **b** David Liebman, Pink Guppy; **c** Michael P. Gadomski/Photo Researchers, Inc.; **d** Stephen J. Krasemann/ Photo Researchers, Inc.; **e** A. H. Rider/Photo Researchers, Inc.; **f** Leonard Lee Rue III/Photo Researchers, Inc.

179 **Southern Sugar Maple** (lr/tb): **a** David J. Moorhead, University of Georgia/http://www.bugwood. org; **b** David Liebman, Pink Guppy

179 **Chalk Maple: a, b, c** Will Cook, http://www.carolinanature.com

180 **Black Maple** (cw): **a** Michael P. Gadomski/Photo Researchers, Inc.; **b** David Liebman, Pink Guppy; **c** Dr. Mark S. Brunell, Department of Biological Sciences, University of the Pacific; **d** David Liebman, Pink Guppy; **e** Bill Johnson

181 **Red Maple** (cw): **a, b, c** Steven Arcella; **d** Gregory G. Dimijian/ Photo Researchers, Inc.; **e** E. R. Degginger/Photo Researchers, Inc.; **f, g** Steven Arcella

182 Silver Maple (cw): **a, b, c, d** Steven Arcella; **e** (tree) David Cavagnaro; **f** Steven Arcella

183 Striped Maple (cw): **a** David Liebman, Pink Guppy; **b** (autumn leaf) Steven Arcella; **c, d** David Liebman, Pink Guppy; **e** Steven Arcella

184 Mountain Maple (cw): **a** Michael P. Gadomski/Photo Researchers, Inc.; **b** Will Cook, http://www.carolinanature.com; **c** Bill Cook, Michigan State University/http://www.bugwood. org; **d** Steven J. Baskauf, http:// bioimages.vanderbilt.edu; **e** Alvin E. Staffan/Photo Researchers, Inc.

185 Norway Maple (cw): **a, b** Steven Arcella; **c** (bark) Steven J. Baskauf, http://bioimages. vanderbilt.edu

185 Sycamore Maple: a, b, c Steven Arcella

186 Bigtooth Maple (cw): **a** Steven Arcella; **b** Michael Kuhns, Utah State University; **c** John R. Seiler, Virginia Tech Department of Forestry; **d** Gerald & Buff Corsi, Focus on Nature, Inc.; **e** Robert Sivinski

187 Bigleaf Maple (cw): **a, b** Steven Arcella; **c** Susan C. McDougall; **d** David Cavagnaro; **e** David Weintraub/Photo Researchers, Inc.; **f** Gerald & Buff Corsi, Focus on Nature, Inc.

188 Vine Maple (cw): **a, b** Steven Arcella; **c** Winton Patnode/Photo Researchers, Inc.; **d** Dennis Flaherty/Photo Researchers, Inc.; **e** Daniel Mathews

189 Rocky Mountain Maple (cw): **a, b** Will Cook, http://www. carolinanature.com; **c** Daniel Mathews; **d** David Cavagnaro

190 Japanese Maple (cw): **a, b, c** (leaf variations) Steven Arcella; **d** (tree) Alan & Linda Detrick/ Photo Researchers, Inc.; **e** Steven Arcella;

190 Amur Maple: a, b Steven Arcella

191 Hedge Maple: a, b, c Steven Arcella

191 Katsura Tree: a, b, c Steven Arcella

192 Princesstree: a, b, c, d Steven Arcella

192 Southern Catalpa (cw): **a, b** Steven Arcella; **c** Michael P. Gadomski/Photo Researchers, Inc.; **d** Steven Arcella

193 Northern Catalpa (cw): **a** Will Cook, http://www.carolinanature. com; **b** Michael P. Gadomski/ Photo Researchers, Inc.; **c** David Liebman, Pink Guppy; **d** Steven

Arcella; **e** David Liebman, Pink Guppy; **f** Steven Arcella

194 Desert-willow (cw): **a** Steven J. Baskauf, http://bioimages. vanderbilt.edu; **b** Gerald & Buff Corsi, Focus on Nature, Inc.; **c, d** Steven J. Baskauf, http:// bioimages.vanderbilt.edu; **e** Robert Sivinski

195 Black Mangrove (cw): **a** Steven Arcella; **b** Glenn & Martha Vargas/California Academy of Sciences; **c** Gil Nelson; **d** David Liebman, Pink Guppy

196 Red Mangrove (cw): **a** Steven Arcella; **b** Gil Nelson; **c** Mark W. Skinner; **d** Steven Arcella; **e** John J. Bangma/Photo Researchers, Inc.

197 White Mangrove: Gil Nelson

197 Florida Swampprivet (lr/tb): **a** Steven Arcella; **b, c** Shirley Denton

198 Eastern Swampprivet (lr/tb): **a** Steven Arcella; **b** Thomas Barnes, University of Kentucky; **c** Ron Lance

198 Desert-olive: Alfred Brousseau, FSC, Saint Mary's College of California

199 Ornamental Privets (lr/tb): **a** Michael P. Gadomski/Photo Researchers, Inc.; **b** Dr. Mark S. Brunell, Department of Biological Sciences, University of the Pacific; **c** James H. Miller, USDA Forest Service/http:// www.bugwood.org

199 Olive (cw): **a** Steven Arcella; **b, c** Nigel Cattlin/Photo Researchers, Inc.

200 Devilwood (cw): **a** Steven Arcella; **b** Chris Evans, River to River CWMA/http://www. bugwood.org; **c, d** Shirley Denton; **e** Chris Evans, River to River CWMA/http://www. bugwood.org

201 Fringetree (cw): **a, b** Steven Arcella; **c** Jessie M. Harris; **d** David Liebman, Pink Guppy; **e** Steven Arcella; **f** Will Cook, http://www.carolinanature.com

202 Japanese Tree Lilac (cw): **a, b** Steven Arcella; **c** Alan & Linda Detrick/Photo Researchers, Inc.

202 Buttonbush: a, b, c Steven Arcella

203 Fevertree (cw): **a, b** Steven Arcella; **c** Jessie M. Harris

203 Wavyleaf Silktassel (cw): **a, b** Steven Arcella; **c, d** Michael L. Charters, http://www.calflora.net

204 Flowering Dogwood (cw): **a, b** Steven Arcella; **c** Adam Jones/ Photo Researchers, Inc.; **d** Steven

Arcella; **e** Adam Jones/Photo Researchers, Inc.; **f** Steven Arcella

205 Roughleaf Dogwood (cw): **a** Steven Arcella; **b** Steven J. Baskauf, http://bioimages. vanderbilt.edu; **c** Alvin E. Staffan/ Photo Researchers, Inc.

205 Shrubby Dogwoods (lr/tb): **a, b** Paul H. Wray; **c** Michael P. Gadomski/Photo Researchers, Inc.

206 Pacific Dogwood (cw): **a** Daniel Mathews; **b** Charles Webber/California Academy of Sciences; **c** Steven J. Baskauf, http://bioimages.vanderbilt.edu; **d** David Cavagnaro; **e** Alfred Brousseau, FSC, Saint Mary's College of California; **f** Betty Derig/Photo Researchers, Inc.

207 Kousa Dogwood (cw): **a** Dr. Mark S. Brunell, Department of Biological Sciences, University of the Pacific; **b** David Liebman, Pink Guppy; **c** Noble Proctor/ Photo Researchers, Inc.; **d** David Liebman, Pink Guppy

207 Cornelian-cherry (lr/tb): **a, b** Steven Arcella; **c** John R. Seiler, Virginia Tech Department of Forestry

208 Viburnums (lr/tb): **a** Will Cook, http://www.carolinanature. com; **b** Jessie M. Harris; **c** David Liebman, Pink Guppy; **d** Steven Arcella

209 Viburnums cont. (lr/tb): **a** David Cavagnaro; **b** Scott Camazine/Photo Researchers, Inc.; **c** Ted Bodner, Southern Weed Science Society/http:// www.bugwood.org; **d** James H. Miller, USDA Forest Service/http://www.bugwood. org; **e** Steven J. Baskauf, http:// bioimages.vanderbilt.edu; **f** Bill Johnson; **g** David Cavagnaro

210 European Buckthorn (lr/tb): **a** Chris Evans, River to River CWMA/http://www.bugwood. org; **b** David Liebman, Pink Guppy

210 Loquat (cw): **a, b** Steven Arcella; **c** Kenneth W. Fink/Photo Researchers, Inc.; **d** Nigel Cattlin/ Photo Researchers, Inc.

212 Key to Trees with Alternate, Compound Leaves (lr/tb): **a** Steven J. Baskauf, http:// bioimages.vanderbilt.edu; **b** Alvin E. Staffan/Photo Researchers, Inc.; **c** Gail Jankus/ Photo Researchers, Inc.; **d** John Kaprielian/Photo Researchers, Inc.; **e** Keith A. Bradley; **f** Richard Parker/Photo Researchers, Inc.; **g** Steven Arcella; **h, i** Steven

J. Baskauf, http://bioimages.
vanderbilt.edu
213 Key cont. (lr/tb): a
Michael P. Gadomski/Photo
Researchers, Inc.; b Charles
Webber/California Academy
of Sciences; c Steven Arcella; d
Elizabeth Chute, http://www.
elizabethchute.com; e Steven
J. Baskauf, http://bioimages.
vanderbilt.edu
213 Hardy Orange (lr/tb): a, b Will
Cook, http://www.carolinanature.
com; c Steven Arcella
214 Common Pricklyash (cw):
a Steven Arcella; b Steven J.
Baskauf, http://bioimages.
vanderbilt.edu; c, d David
Cavagnaro; e Ken Brate/Photo
Researchers, Inc.
215 Hercules' Club (cw): a John R.
Seiler, Virginia Tech Department
of Forestry; b Ken Brate/Photo
Researchers, Inc.; c Will Cook,
http://www.carolinanature.com
215 Lime Pricklyash (lr/tb): a
Steven Arcella; b Gilbert S.
Grant/Photo Researchers, Inc.
216 Devil's Walkingstick (cw): a
Bill Johnson; b Gail Jankus/Photo
Researchers, Inc.; c Will Cook,
http://www.carolinanature.
com; d Gilbert S. Grant/Photo
Researchers, Inc.; e Gail Jankus/
Photo Researchers, Inc.
217 Honeylocust (cw): a David
Liebman, Pink Guppy; b Steven
Arcella; c Gil Nelson; d Steven
Arcella; e David Cavagnaro;
f Richard Parker/Photo
Researchers, Inc.
218 Black Locust (cw): a David
Cavagnaro; b Stephen P. Parker/
Photo Researchers, Inc.; c John
Serrao/Photo Researchers,
Inc.; d Alvin E. Staffan/Photo
Researchers, Inc.; e Steven
Arcella
219 Clammy Locust (cw): a Will
Cook, http://www.carolinanature.
com; b, c Steven Arcella
219 New Mexico Locust (lr/tb):
a, b Steven Arcella; c Robert
Sivinski
220 Desert Ironwood (cw): a Betty
Randall White; b Steven Arcella;
c David Cavagnaro
220 Jerusalem Thorn (cw) :
a Steven J. Baskauf, http://
bioimages.vanderbilt.edu; b
(flower) Steven Arcella
221 Blue Paloverde (cw): a Steven
J. Baskauf, http://bioimages.
vanderbilt.edu; b Dan Suzio/
Photo Researchers, Inc.; c
Michael L. Charters, http://www.
calflora.net

221 Yellow Paloverde: Charlie
Ott/Photo Researchers, Inc.
222 Acacias (lr/tb): a Gil Nelson; b
Michael L. Charters, http://www.
calflora.net; c Hans Reinhard/
Okapia/Photo Researchers, Inc.;
d Joyce Photographics/Photo
Researchers, Inc.
223 Acacias cont. (lr/tb): a,
b Steven J. Baskauf, http://
bioimages.vanderbilt.edu; c
Michael L. Charters, http://www.
calflora.net; d Steven J. Baskauf,
http://bioimages.vanderbilt.edu;
e Steven Arcella; f Bill Johnson
224 Honey Mesquite (cw): a
Jessie M. Harris; b Karl H.
Switak/Photo Researchers, Inc.;
c Gregory G. Dimijian/Photo
Researchers, Inc.; d Steven
Arcella
224 Screwbean Mesquite: Steven
Arcella
225 Walnuts and Hickories (lr/tb):
a John R. Seiler, Virginia Tech
Department of Forestry; b Adam
Jones/Photo Researchers, Inc.
226 Black Walnut (cw): a Steven
J. Baskauf, http://bioimages.
vanderbilt.edu; b Bill Johnson;
c Michael P. Gadomski/Photo
Researchers, Inc.; d Steven
Arcella
227 Butternut (cw): a Steven
J. Baskauf, http://bioimages.
vanderbilt.edu; b (autumn leaf)
Bill Johnson; c Paul H. Wray; d
Bill Johnson; e Will Cook, http://
www.carolinanature.com; f Wm.
Harlow/Photo Researchers, Inc.
228 Arizona Walnut (cw): a Betty
Randall White; b Steve Hurst/
USDA-NRCS PLANTS Database;
c Alan & Linda Detrick/Photo
Researchers, Inc
228 English Walnut (lr/tb): a Steven
Arcella; b R. J. Erwin/Photo
Researchers, Inc.
229 Southern California Walnut
(cw): a Steven Arcella; b Michael
L. Charters, http://www.calflora.
net; c David Cavagnaro
229 Northern California Walnut:
Steven Arcella
230 Shagbark Hickory (cw): a
David Cavagnaro; b Steven
J. Baskauf, http://bioimages.
vanderbilt.edu; c, d Michael P.
Gadomski/Photo Researchers,
Inc.; e David Cavagnaro; f
Michael P. Gadomski/Photo
Researchers, Inc.
231 Shellbark Hickory (cw): a,
b (open fruit) Steven Arcella;
c John R. Seiler, Virginia Tech
Department of Forestry; d Bill
Johnson; e Steven Arcella;

f (closed fruit) John R. Seiler,
Virginia Tech Department of
Forestry
232 Mockernut Hickory (cw): a
Steven Arcella; b Steve Hurst/
USDA-NRCS PLANTS Database;
c, d Steven Arcella; e John
Serrao/Photo Researchers, Inc.;
f Steven Arcella
233 Bitternut Hickory (cw): a
Michael P. Gadomski/Photo
Researchers, Inc.; b Rosemary
Kautzky; c David Cavagnaro;
d, e Steven Arcella; f Michael P.
Gadomski/Photo Researchers,
Inc.
234 Pecan (cw): a John R. Seiler,
Virginia Tech Department of
Forestry; b David Liebman, Pink
Guppy; c Bill Johnson; d John R.
Seiler, Virginia Tech Department
of Forestry; e Gil Nelson
235 Water Hickory (cw): a, b
Shirley Denton; c Steve Hurst/
USDA-NRCS PLANTS Database;
d Shirley Denton; e David
Liebman, Pink Guppy
235 Black Hickory: Ron Lance
236 Pignut Hickory (cw): a Steven
Arcella; b (2 nuts) Steve Hurst/
USDA-NRCS PLANTS
Database; c (fruit in husk),
d Steven Arcella
236 Scrub Hickory: a, b Shirley
Denton
237 Sand Hickory (cw): a, b Will
Cook, http://www.carolinanature.
com; c Steven J. Baskauf, http://
bioimages.vanderbilt.edu; d
John R. Seiler, Virginia Tech
Department of Forestry; e Steven
J. Baskauf, http://bioimages.
vanderbilt.edu; f John R. Seiler,
Virginia Tech Department of
Forestry
238 Mexican-buckeye: a, b, c
Steven Arcella
238 Goldenrain Tree (cw): a,
b Steven Arcella; c Steven J.
Baskauf, http://bioimages.
vanderbilt.edu
239 Common Hoptree: a, b
Steven Arcella; c V. P. Weinland/
Photo Researchers, Inc.; d Jenny
Winkelman/David Liebman,
Pink Guppy
239 California Hoptree: Charles
Webber/California Academy of
Sciences
240 American Mountain-ash
(lr/tb): a Adam Jones/Photo
Researchers, Inc.; b Michael P.
Gadomski/Photo Researchers,
Inc.
240 Showy Mountain-ash:
Elizabeth Chute, http://www.
elizabethchute.com

241 European Mountain-ash:
Geoff Bryant/Photo Researchers, Inc.

241 Sitka Mountain-ash: Michael P. Gadomski/Photo Researchers, Inc.

241 Greene's Mountain-ash:
Gerald & Buff Corsi, Focus on Nature, Inc.

242 Smooth Sumac (cw): **a** Steven Arcella; **b** Kenneth M. Highfill/Photo Researchers, Inc.; **c** David Liebman, Pink Guppy; **d** Steven Arcella; **e** James L. Amos/Photo Researchers, Inc.; **f** A. W. Ambler/Photo Researchers, Inc.

243 Staghorn Sumac (cw): **a** Steven Arcella; **b** L. West/Photo Researchers, Inc.; **c** John Kaprielian/Photo Researchers, Inc.; **d** Jeff Lepore/Photo Researchers, Inc.; **e** Steven J. Baskauf, http://bioimages.vanderbilt.edu

244 Winged Sumac (cw): **a, b, c** Steven Arcella; **d, e** David Liebman, Pink Guppy

244 Prairie Sumac: Steven Arcella

245 Peruvian Peppertree (cw): **a** Gregory Bergman; **b** Dr. Mark S. Brunell, Department of Biological Sciences, University of the Pacific; **c** Michael L. Charters, http://www.calflora.net

245 American Pistachio: David Liebman, Pink Guppy

246 Poison Sumac (cw): **a** John M. Burnley/Photo Researchers, Inc.; **b, c** Gil Nelson

246 Poison Ivy and Poison-oak:
Susan Leavines Harris/Photo Researchers, Inc.

247 Florida Poisontree (lr/tb): **a** Keith A. Bradley; **b** Gilbert S. Grant/Photo Researchers, Inc.

247 Gumbo Limbo: Gilbert S. Grant/Photo Researchers, Inc.

248 Paradisetree (cw): **a** Gil Nelson; **b** (fruits) Keith A. Bradley

248 Inkwood (cw): **a** Keith A. Bradley; **b** (leaf) Steven Arcella

249 Amur Corktree (cw): **a** Steven Arcella; **b** Patrick Breen, Oregon State University/http://www.bugwood.org; **c** Geoff Bryant/Photo Researchers, Inc.

249 Wingleaf Soapberry (cw): **a** Steven Arcella; **b** (unwinged leaf) John R. Seiler, Virginia Tech Department of Forestry

250 Western Soapberry
(cw): **a** Steven J. Baskauf, http://bioimages.vanderbilt.edu; **b** Richard Parker/Photo Researchers, Inc.; **c** Steven

J. Baskauf, http://bioimages.vanderbilt.edu

250 Elephant Tree (lr/tb): **a** V. P. Weinland/Photo Researchers, Inc.; **b** Gerald & Buff Corsi, Focus on Nature, Inc.

251 West Indian Mahogany (cw): **a** Shirley Denton; **b** Steven Arcella; **c** Shirley Denton

251 Tree of Heaven (lr/tb): **a, b** Steven J. Baskauf, http://bioimages.vanderbilt.edu; **c** R. J. Erwin/Photo Researchers, Inc.

252 Japanese Pagoda Tree: a, b, c, d Steven Arcella

252 Carob (lr/tb): **a** Dr. Mark S. Brunell, Department of Biological Sciences, University of the Pacific; **b** Kenneth W. Fink/Photo Researchers, Inc.

253 Kentucky Yellowwood (cw): **a** Steven Arcella; **b** Steven J. Baskauf, http://bioimages.vanderbilt.edu; **c** Dr. Mark S. Brunell, Department of Biological Sciences, University of the Pacific; **d, e** Steven Arcella

254 Kentucky Coffeetree
(cw): **a** Steven J. Baskauf, http://bioimages.vanderbilt.edu; **b** Richard Parker/Photo Researchers, Inc.; **c** Steven Arcella; **d** David Liebman, Pink Guppy; **e** Robert Finken/Photo Researchers, Inc.; **f** Bill Johnson

255 Silktree (cw): **a** Steven Arcella; **b** David Liebman, Pink Guppy; **c** R. J. Erwin/Photo Researchers, Inc.

255 Chinaberry: a, b, c Steven Arcella

257 Key to Trees with Alternate, Simple Leaves (lr/tb): **a, b** Steven Arcella; **c** R. J. Erwin/Photo Researchers, Inc.; **d** Gil Nelson; **e** Charles Webber/California Academy of Sciences; **f** Will Cook, http://www.carolinanature.com; **g** Shirley Denton; **h** Steven Arcella; **i** R. J. Erwin/Photo Researchers, Inc.; **j** Gil Nelson; **k** David Liebman, Pink Guppy; **l** Gilbert S. Grant/Photo Researchers, Inc.

258 Key cont. (lr/tb): **a** Steven Arcella; **b** Steven J. Baskauf, http://bioimages.vanderbilt.edu; **c, d** Steven Arcella; **e** (mountain-mahogany) Alfred Brousseau, FSC, Saint Mary's College of California; **f** David Liebman, Pink Guppy; **g** Michael L. Charters, http://www.calflora.net; **h** Steven Arcella; **i** Gil Nelson; **j** Will Cook, http://www.carolinanature.com; **k** Stephen P. Parker/Photo Researchers, Inc.

259 Key cont. (lr/tb): **a** Steven Arcella; **b, c** David Liebman, Pink Guppy; **d** (Black Tupelo) Richard Parker/Photo Researchers, Inc.; **e** John Kaprielian/Photo Researchers, Inc.; **f** Ray Coleman/Photo Researchers, Inc.; **g** Steven Arcella; **h** Steven J. Baskauf, http://bioimages.vanderbilt.edu; **i** Shirley Denton; **j** Gilbert S. Grant/Photo Researchers, Inc.; **k** Richard Parker/Photo Researchers, Inc.; **l** Will Cook, http://www.carolinanature.com

260 Key cont. (lr/tb): **a** Steven Arcella; **b** Betty Randall White; **c** David Liebman, Pink Guppy; **d, e, f, g, h** Steven Arcella

261 Key cont. (lr/tb): **a** Steven Arcella; **b** John Serrao/Photo Researchers, Inc.; **c** R. J. Erwin/Photo Researchers, Inc.; **d** David Liebman, Pink Guppy; **e** Steven Arcella; **f** Steven J. Baskauf, http://bioimages.vanderbilt.edu; **g** David Liebman, Pink Guppy; **h** Gerald & Buff Corsi, Focus on Nature, Inc.; **i** Michael P. Gadomski/Photo Researchers, Inc.

262 Key cont. (lr/tb): **a, b** Steven Arcella; **c** Steven J. Baskauf, http://bioimages.vanderbilt.edu; **d** Gerald & Buff Corsi, Focus on Nature, Inc.; **e** Robert Bornemann/Photo Researchers, Inc.; **f** Gil Nelson; **g** Steven J. Baskauf, http://bioimages.vanderbilt.edu; **h** Steven Arcella; **i** Ray Coleman/Photo Researchers, Inc.; **j** Stephen P. Parker/Photo Researchers, Inc.

263 Key cont. (lr/tb): **a** Steven Arcella; **b** James Henderson, Gulf South Research Corporation/http://www.bugwood.org; **c** Gilbert S. Grant/Photo Researchers, Inc.; **d** Will Cook, http://www.carolinanature.com; **e** Gerald & Buff Corsi, Focus on Nature, Inc.; **f** Steven J. Baskauf, http://bioimages.vanderbilt.edu; **g, h** Michael P. Gadomski/Photo Researchers, Inc.; **i** John Serrao/Photo Researchers, Inc.

264 Key cont. (lr/tb): **a** Steven Arcella; **b** Gilbert S. Grant/Photo Researchers, Inc.; **c** Alan & Linda Detrick/Photo Researchers, Inc.; **d** Gil Nelson; **e** Alvin E. Staffan/Photo Researchers, Inc.; **f** Biophoto Associates/Photo Researchers, Inc.; **g** Steven Arcella; **h** Michael P. Gadomski/Photo Researchers, Inc.; **i** David Liebman, Pink Guppy; **j** John Serrao/Photo Researchers, Inc.

265 Key cont. (lr/tb): **a** Alvin E. Staffan/Photo Researchers, Inc.; **b** Betty Derig/Photo Researchers, Inc.; **c** Michael P. Gadomski/Photo Researchers, Inc.; **d** Steven Arcella; **e** Gerald & Buff Corsi, Focus on Nature, Inc.; **f** Michael L. Charters, http://www.calflora.net; **g** Betty Derig/Photo Researchers, Inc.; **h** Elizabeth Chute, http://www.elizabethchute.com

266 Key cont. (lr/tb): **a** Steven Arcella; **b** Steven J. Baskauf, http://bioimages.vanderbilt.edu; **c** V. P. Weinland/Photo Researchers, Inc.; **d** R. J. Erwin/Photo Researchers, Inc.; **e** Alvin E. Staffan/Photo Researchers, Inc.; **f** Steven Arcella; **g** John Serrao/Photo Researchers, Inc.; **h** Alfred Brousseau, FSC, Saint Mary's College of California; **i** Steven Arcella; **j** Paul H. Wray

267 American Sycamore (cw): **a** Michael P. Gadomski/Photo Researchers, Inc.; **b** Ron Lance; **c** Christine M. Douglas/Photo Researchers, Inc.; **d** S. E. Cornelius/Photo Researchers, Inc.

268 California Sycamore: a, b David Cavagnaro

268 Arizona Sycamore (cw): **a** Betty Randall White; **b** G. C. Kelly/Photo Researchers, Inc.; **c** C. K. Lorenz/Photo Researchers, Inc.

269 London Planetree (cw): **a** David Liebman, Pink Guppy; **b** Jim Steinberg/Photo Researchers, Inc.; **c** Geoff Bryant/Photo Researchers, Inc.

269 Oriental Planetree: Mira Arnaudova

270 Sweetgum (cw): **a** Michael P. Gadomski/Photo Researchers, Inc.; **b** Steven J. Baskauf, http://bioimages.vanderbilt.edu; **c** John Serrao/Photo Researchers, Inc.; **d, e** Steven Arcella; **f** (green fruit) Steven J. Baskauf, http://bioimages.vanderbilt.edu

271 Red Mulberry (cw): **a, b, c** David Liebman, Pink Guppy; **d** Dr. Mark S. Brunell, Department of Biological Sciences, University of the Pacific; **e, f** David Liebman, Pink Guppy

272 Mountain Mulberry: a, b Steven Arcella

272 White Mulberry (cw): **a, b** Steven Arcella; **c** Gilbert S. Grant/Photo Researchers, Inc.; **d** V. P. Weinland/Photo Researchers, Inc.; **e** Ron Lance

273 Paper Mulberry (lr/tb): **a** Gilbert S. Grant/Photo Researchers, Inc.; **b** Will Cook, http://www.carolinanature.com

273 Common Fig (lr/tb): **a** Gregory G. Dimijian, M.D./Photo Researchers, Inc.; **b** Joyce Photographics/Photo Researchers, Inc.

274 Sassafras (cw): **a, b, c** Steven Arcella; **d** John Serrao/Photo Researchers, Inc.; **e** David T. Roberts/Photo Researchers, Inc.; **f, g** Steven Arcella

275 California Flannelbush (cw): **a** David Cavagnaro; **b** Steven Arcella; **c** Alfred Brousseau, FSC, Saint Mary's College of California; **d** Gerald & Buff Corsi, Focus on Nature, Inc.

275 Chinese Parasoltree (lr/tb): **a** Steven Arcella; **b** Will Cook, http://www.carolinanature.com

276 Magnolias and Tuliptree (lr/tb): **a** David Liebman, Pink Guppy; **b** Steven J. Baskauf, http://bioimages.vanderbilt.edu; **c** Steven Arcella; **d** John Bova/Photo Researchers, Inc.

277 Tuliptree (cw): **a** Michael P. Gadomski/Photo Researchers, Inc.; **b** David Liebman, Pink Guppy; **c** Steven Arcella; **d** Michael P. Gadomski/Photo Researchers, Inc.; **e** Steven Arcella

278 Cucumber-tree (cw): **a** Will Cook, http://www.carolinanature.com; **b** Steven J. Baskauf, http://bioimages.vanderbilt.edu; **c** Alvin E. Staffan/Photo Researchers, Inc.; **d** Steven J. Baskauf, http://bioimages.vanderbilt.edu; **e** Steven Arcella; **f** Chris Evans, River to River CWMA/http://www.bugwood.org

279 Umbrella Magnolia (cw): **a** Chris Evans, River to River CWMA/http://www.bugwood.org; **b** Steven Arcella; **c** Steven J. Baskauf, http://bioimages.vanderbilt.edu; **d** Will Cook, http://www.carolinanature.com; **e** Daniel Mathews; **f** Will Cook, http://www.carolinanature.com

280 Sweetbay (cw): **a** (leaf upper/underside) Steven Arcella; **b** D & L Klein/Photo Researchers, Inc.; **c** David Liebman, Pink Guppy; **d, e** Steven Arcella

281 Southern Magnolia (cw): **a** (leaf upper/underside), **b, c** Steven Arcella; **d** Steven J. Baskauf, http://bioimages.vanderbilt.edu; **e** Dr. Mark S. Brunell, Department of Biological Sciences, University of the Pacific

282 Bigleaf Magnolia (cw): **a, b** Steven J. Baskauf, http://bioimages.vanderbilt.edu; **c** Steven Arcella; **d, e** Steven J. Baskauf, http://bioimages.vanderbilt.edu

283 Mountain Magnolia (cw): **a** Chris Evans, River to River CWMA/http://www.bugwood.org; **b** Steven J. Baskauf, http://bioimages.vanderbilt.edu; **c** Steven Arcella; **d** Will Cook, http://www.carolinanature.com; William M. Ciesla, Forest Health Management International/http://www.bugwood.org

284 Chinese Magnolia (cw): **a, b** Steven Arcella; **c** David Liebman, Pink Guppy

284 Star Magnolia (lr/tb): **a** Daniel Mathews; **b** David Liebman, Pink Guppy

285 Pawpaw (cw): **a** Steven Arcella; **b** Richard Parker/Photo Researchers, Inc.; **c** Steven J. Baskauf, http://bioimages.vanderbilt.edu; **d, e** Steven Arcella

286 Pond-apple (cw): **a** Steven Arcella; **b** Shirley Denton; **c** Ray Coleman/Photo Researchers, Inc.; **d** Shirley Denton

287 Cultivated Citrus (cw): **a** Steven Arcella; **b, c** David Liebman, Pink Guppy; **d** Dr. Mark S. Brunell, Department of Biological Sciences, University of the Pacific; **e** Gilbert S. Grant/Photo Researchers, Inc.

288 Osage-orange (cw): **a, b, c** Steven Arcella; **d** G. Carleton Ray/Photo Researchers, Inc.; **e, f** Steven J. Baskauf, http://bioimages.vanderbilt.edu; **g** (thorn) Steven Arcella

289 Strangler Fig (cw): **a, b** David Liebman, Pink Guppy; **c** J. H. Robinson/Photo Researchers, Inc.

289 Weeping Fig: Steven Arcella

290 Coco-plum (lr/tb): **a** Gil Nelson; **b** Shirley Denton

290 Button-mangrove (lr/tb): **a** Gerald & Buff Corsi, Focus on Nature, Inc.; **b** Gil Nelson

291 Seagrape (lr/tb): **a** Steven Arcella; **b** David Liebman, Pink Guppy

291 Pigeon-plum: a, b Steven Arcella

292 Russian-olive (cw): **a** Paul H. Wray; **b** Dave Powell, USDA Forest Service/http://www.bugwood.org; **c** R. J. Erwin/Photo Researchers, Inc.; **d** Patrick Breen, USDA Forest Service/http://www.bugwood.org

292 Camphortree: Gil Nelson
293 Red Bay (cw): **a** Steven Arcella; **b, c** Will Cook, http://www.carolinanature.com; **d** David Liebman, Pink Guppy
294 California Bay (cw): **a** Steven Arcella; **b** Dr. Mark S. Brunell, Department of Biological Sciences, University of the Pacific; **c** Gregory Bergman; **d** Michael L. Charters, http://www.calflora.net; **e** Gerald & Buff Corsi, Focus on Nature, Inc.
295 Alternate-leaf Dogwood (cw): **a** Steven Arcella; **b** Paul H. Wray; **c** Geoff Bryant/Photo Researchers, Inc.; **d** Steven Arcella; **e** Paul H. Wray
296 Black Tupelo (cw): **a** Steven Arcella; **b** Steven J. Baskauf, http://bioimages.vanderbilt.edu; **c** Richard Parker/Photo Researchers, Inc.; **d** Steven J. Baskauf, http://bioimages.vanderbilt.edu; **e** Will Cook, http://www.carolinanature.com; **f** Steven Arcella; **g** Steven J. Baskauf, http://bioimages.vanderbilt.edu
297 Water Tupelo (cw): **a** Steven J. Baskauf, http://bioimages.vanderbilt.edu; **b, c** Will Cook, http://www.carolinanature.com
297 Ogeechee Tupelo (lr/tb): **a** Steven Arcella; **b** Gilbert S. Grant/Photo Researchers, Inc.
298 Swamp Titi (cw): **a** Steven Arcella; **b** Will Cook, http://www.carolinanature.com; **c** Steven Arcella; **d** Ted Bodner, Southern Weed Science Society/http://www.bugwood.org; **e** Will Cook, http://www.carolinanature.com
299 Sweetleaf (cw): **a** Steven Arcella; **b** Ted Bodner, Southern Weed Science Society/http://www.bugwood.org; **c** Chris Evans, River to River CWMA/http://www.bugwood.org; **d, e** David Liebman, Pink Guppy
300 Sugar Sumac (cw): **a** Steven Arcella; **b** Bill Johnson; **c** Michael L. Charters, http://www.calflora.net; **d** Steve Perkins; **e** Bill Johnson
301 Lemonade Sumac (lr/tb): **a** Steven Arcella; **b** Michael L. Charters, http://www.calflora.net
301 Laurel Sumac (lr/tb): **a** David Cavagnaro; **b** Michael L. Charters, http://www.calflora.net
302 American Smoketree (cw): **a** Steven Arcella; **b** Bill Johnson; **c** David Liebman, Pink Guppy; **d** Steven J. Baskauf, http://bioimages.vanderbilt.edu; **e** Jenny Winkelman/David Liebman, Pink Guppy

303 Mango (lr/tb): **a** Keith A. Bradley; **b** Bob Gibbons/Photo Researchers, Inc.; **c** Steven Arcella
303 Satinleaf (cw): **a, b, c** Steven Arcella; **d** (flower) Shirley Denton
304 Gum Bully (cw): **a** Gil Nelson; **b** Steven Arcella; **c** Gil Nelson
304 Tough Bully: Gil Nelson
305 Buckthorn Bully (cw): **a** Ron Lance; **b** Steven J. Baskauf, http://bioimages.vanderbilt.edu; **c** Gil Nelson
305 Saffron-plum (lr/tb): **a** Shirley Denton; **b** Steven Arcella
306 Common Persimmon (cw): **a** Steven Arcella; **b** John Kaprielian/Photo Researchers, Inc.; **c** Steven Arcella; **d** John M. Coffman/Photo Researchers, Inc.
306 Texas Persimmon: Ron Lance
307 Farkleberry (cw): **a, b** David Liebman, Pink Guppy; **c** Jessie M. Harris; **d** Will Cook, http://www.carolinanature.com
307 Texas Madrone: a, b Steven Arcella
308 Pacific Madrone (cw): **a** Steven Arcella; **b** Steven J. Baskauf, http://bioimages.vanderbilt.edu; **c** Betty Derig/Photo Researchers, Inc.; **d** J. H. Robinson/Photo Researchers, Inc.; **e** Dan Suzio/Photo Researchers, Inc.; **f** Gerald & Buff Corsi, Focus on Nature, Inc.
309 Bigberry Manzanita (cw): **a, b** Michael L. Charters, http://www.calflora.net; **c** Steve Perkins; **d** Michael L. Charters, http://www.calflora.net
310 Common Manzanita (cw): **a** Dennis Sheridan/David Liebman, Pink Guppy; **b** David Cavagnaro; **c** David Winkelman/David Liebman, Pink Guppy; **d** Gerald & Buff Corsi, Focus on Nature, Inc.
310 Rusty Staggerbush (lr/tb): **a** Gil Nelson; **b** Chris Evans, River to River CWMA/http://www.bugwood.org
311 Sourwood (cw): **a** Steven J. Baskauf, http://bioimages.vanderbilt.edu; **b** Steven Arcella; **c** Steven J. Baskauf, http://bioimages.vanderbilt.edu; **d** Gil Nelson; **e** Will Cook, http://www.carolinanature.com; **f** Steven Arcella; **g** David Liebman, Pink Guppy
312 Mountain-laurel (cw): **a, b** Steven Arcella; **c** Steven J. Baskauf, http://bioimages.vanderbilt.edu; **d** Steven Arcella

312 Pacific Rhododendron (lr/tb): **a** Steven J. Baskauf, http://bioimages.vanderbilt.edu; **b** Pat & Tom Leeson/Photo Researchers, Inc.
313 Rosebay Rhododendron (cw): **a** Steven Arcella; **b** Jessie M. Harris; **c** Steven Arcella; **d** Michael P. Gadomski/Photo Researchers, Inc.; **e** Steven Arcella
313 Catawba Rhododendron (lr/tb): **a, b** Steven Arcella
314 Crapemyrtle (cw): **a** Steven Arcella; **b** Dr. Mark S. Brunell, Department of Biological Sciences, University of the Pacific; **c** Chris Evans, River to River CWMA/http://www.bugwood.org; **d** Will Cook, http://www.carolinanature.com; **e** David Liebman, Pink Guppy
314 Red-ironbark Eucalyptus (lr/tb): **a** Dr. Mark S. Brunell, Department of Biological Sciences, University of the Pacific; **b** David Cavagnaro
315 Bluegum Eucalyptus (cw): **a** David Cavagnaro; **b** R. J. Erwin/Photo Researchers, Inc.; **c** Joyce Photographics/Photo Researchers, Inc.; **d** Bruce M. Herman/Photo Researchers, Inc.; **e** Dan Suzio/Photo Researchers, Inc.
316 Punktree (cw): **a** Gregory G. Dimijian/Photo Researchers, Inc.; **b** David Liebman, Pink Guppy; **c, d** J. P. Jackson/Photo Researchers, Inc.; **e** Shirley Denton
317 Little Silverbell: a, b, c Steven Arcella
317 Two-wing Silverbell (lr/tb): **a** Steven Arcella; **b** John R. Seiler, Virginia Tech Department of Forestry
318 Bigleaf Snowbell (lr/tb): **a** Will Cook, http://www.carolinanature.com; **b** David Liebman, Pink Guppy
318 American Snowbell (lr/tb): **a** Steven Arcella; **b** David Liebman, Pink Guppy
319 Eastern Redbud (cw): **a, b** Steven Arcella; **c** Kenneth Murray/Photo Researchers, Inc.; **d** Adam Jones/Photo Researchers, Inc.; **e** Steven Arcella; **f** Chris Evans, River to River CWMA/http://www.bugwood.org; **g** Steven Arcella
320 California Redbud: a, b, c Steven Arcella
320 Chinese Tallow (cw): **a** Will Cook, http://www.carolinanature.com; **b** James Henson/USDA-

NRCS PLANTS Database; **c** Will Cook, http://www.carolinanature.com

321 Manchineel (cw): **a** Gregory Dimijian, M.D./Photo Researchers, Inc.; **b** David Liebman, Pink Guppy; **c** Richard Green/Photo Researchers, Inc.; **d** Ron Lance

322 Southern Bayberry (cw): **a** Steven Arcella; **b** Gilbert S. Grant/Photo Researchers, Inc.; **c** Ted Bodner, Southern Weed Science Society/http://www.bugwood.org; **d** Steven Arcella; **e** Gilbert S. Grant/Photo Researchers, Inc.

323 Scentless Bayberry (lr/tb): **a, b** Gil Nelson

323 Pacific Bayberry (cw): **a** Steven Arcella; **b, c** Gregory Bergman

324 Carolina Buckthorn (cw): **a, b** Steven Arcella; **c** Will Cook, http://www.carolinanature.com; **d, e** David Liebman, Pink Guppy; **f** Steven J. Baskauf, http://bioimages.vanderbilt.edu

325 California Buckthorn (lr/tb): **a** Dr. Mark S. Brunell, Department of Biological Sciences, University of the Pacific; **b** Charles Webber/California Academy of Sciences

325 Glossy Buckthorn: Ron Lance

326 Cascara Buckthorn (cw): **a, b, c** Daniel Mathews; **d** Steven Arcella; **e** Daniel Mathews

327 Blueblossom (cw): **a** Steven Arcella; **b** Daniel Mathews; **c** Gerald & Buff Corsi, Focus on Nature, Inc.

327 Greenbark Ceanothus (cw): **a, b** Steven Arcella; **c** Michael L. Charters, http://www.calflora.net

328 Loblolly-bay (cw): **a** Steven Arcella; **b** John Bova/Photo Researchers, Inc.; **c** Will Cook, http://www.carolinanature.com; **d** John R. Seiler, Virginia Tech Department of Forestry

329 Silky Camellia (lr/tb): **a** James Henderson, Gulf South Research Corporation/http://www.bugwood.org; **b** David Liebman, Pink Guppy

329 Franklin Tree: Nature's Images/Photo Researchers, Inc.

330 Witch-hazel (cw): **a** Steven Arcella; **b** Jeff Lepore/Photo Researchers, Inc.; **c** Gilbert S. Grant/Photo Researchers, Inc.; **d** Ray Coleman/Photo Researchers, Inc.; **e** Will Cook, http://www.carolinanature.com; **f** Steven Arcella

331 What's in a Tree Name?: Amy K. Hughes

332 Rose Family (lr/tb): **a** Bill Cook, Michigan State University/

http://www.bugwood.org; **b** Steven Arcella

333 Rose Family cont.: Ted Bodner, Southern Weed Science Society/http://www.bugwood.org

333 Birchleaf Mountain-mahogany: Terry Spivey, USDA Forest Service/http://www.bugwood.org

334 Curl-leaf Mountain-mahogany (cw): **a** Daniel Mathews; **b, c** Michael L. Charters, http://www.calflora.net; **d** William H. Mullins/Photo Researchers, Inc.; **e** Charles Webber/California Academy of Sciences

335 Black Cherry (cw): **a** Michael P. Gadomski/Photo Researchers, Inc.; **b** David Liebman, Pink Guppy; **c** Robert Bornemann/Photo Researchers, Inc.; **d** Barbara Tokarska-Guzik, University of Silesia, Poland/http://www.bugwood.org; **e** Jessie M. Harris; **f** Steven Arcella

336 Chokecherry (cw): **a** Steven Arcella; **b** Gerald & Buff Corsi, Focus on Nature, Inc.; **c** R. J. Erwin/Photo Researchers, Inc.; **d** Steven J. Baskauf, http://bioimages.vanderbilt.edu; **e** Dave Powell, USDA Forest Service/http://www.bugwood.org

337 Pin Cherry (cw): **a** Ron Lance; **b** Gerald & Buff Corsi, Focus on Nature, Inc.; **c** Bill Cook, Michigan State University/http://www.bugwood.org

337 Mahaleb Cherry: Ron Lance

338 Carolina Laurelcherry (cw): **a** Steven Arcella; **b** Ken Brate/Photo Researchers, Inc.; **c** Gil Nelson; **d** Will Cook, http://www.carolinanature.com; **e** Chris Evans, River to River CWMA/http://www.bugwood.org

339 Bitter Cherry (cw): **a** David Cavagnaro; **b** Betty Derig/Photo Researchers, Inc.; **c** Terry Spivey, USDA Forest Service/http://www.bugwood.org; **d** Daniel Mathews

340 Hollyleaf Cherry (cw): **a** Steven Arcella; **b** Michael L. Charters, http://www.calflora.net; **c** Gerald & Buff Corsi, Focus on Nature, Inc.; **d** Michael L. Charters, http://www.calflora.net

340 Catalina Cherry: Michael L. Charters, http://www.calflora.net

341 Cultivated Cherries (lr/tb): **a** Nigel Cattlin/Photo Researchers, Inc.; **b** Ron Lance

341 Ornamental Asiatic Cherries: Michael P. Gadomski/Photo Researchers, Inc.

342 Thorny Plums (lr/tb): **a** Rod Planck/Photo Researchers, Inc.; **b** Paul H. Wray; **c** Steven Arcella

343 Thorny Plums cont. (lr/tb): **a** Ottmar Bierwagen, Spectrumphotofile; **b** Will Cook, http://www.carolinanature.com; **c** David Liebman, Pink Guppy; **d** Will Cook, http://www.carolinanature.com; **e** K. M. Highfill/Photo Researchers, Inc.; **f** David Cavagnaro

344 Thornless Plums (lr/tb): **a** Alan & Linda Detrick/Photo Researchers, Inc.; **b, c** Steven Arcella; **d, e** Ron Lance; **f** Ted Bodner, Southern Weed Science Society/http://www.bugwood.org

345 Thornless Plums cont. (lr/tb): **a, b** Steven J. Baskauf, http://bioimages.vanderbilt.edu; **c** Steven Arcella; **d** Peggy Greb, USDA Agricultural Research Service/http://www.bugwood.org

346 Peach (cw): **a** Steven Arcella; **b** Gerald & Buff Corsi, Focus on Nature, Inc.; **c** Bonnie Sue/Photo Researchers, Inc.; **d, e** Will Cook, http://www.carolinanature.com; **f** Steven Arcella

347 Common Pear (cw): **a** Steven J. Baskauf, http://bioimages.vanderbilt.edu; **b** Jessie M. Harris; **c** Porterfield-Chickering/Photo Researchers, Inc.; **d** Betty Derig/Photo Researchers, Inc.

348 Callery Pear: **a** (tree) Adam Jones/Photo Researchers, Inc.; **b, c** Steven Arcella

348 Ornamental Flowering Crabapples: **a, b** Jessie M. Harris

349 Common Apple (cw): **a** Steven Arcella; **b, c** Gerald & Buff Corsi, Focus on Nature, Inc.; **d** Steven J. Baskauf, http://bioimages.vanderbilt.edu; **e** Gerald & Buff Corsi, Focus on Nature, Inc.

350 American Crabapples (lr/tb): **a** Ron Lance; **b** Steven Arcella; **c** Will Cook, http://www.carolinanature.com; **d** Gil Nelson

351 American Crabapples cont. (lr/tb): **a, b** Ron Lance; **c, d, e** Steven Arcella; **f** Betty Derig/Photo Researchers, Inc.; **g** Alfred Brousseau, FSC, Saint Mary's College of California

352 Serviceberries (lr/tb): **a** Adam Jones/Photo Researchers, Inc.; **b** Steven J. Baskauf, http://bioimages.vanderbilt.edu; **c, d** Betty Derig/Photo Researchers, Inc.; **e** Richard Parker/Photo Researchers, Inc.

353 Serviceberries cont. (lr/tb): **a, b** Steven Arcella; **c** Michael P. Gadomski/Photo Researchers,

Inc.; **d** Steven Arcella; **e** Bill Johnson; **f** Steven Arcella

354 Hawthorns (lr/tb): **a, b, c, d** Steven Arcella; **e** R. J. Erwin/ Photo Researchers, Inc.; **f** David Liebman, Pink Guppy; **g** Steven Arcella

355 Hawthorns cont. (lr/tb): **a, b, c** Steven Arcella; **d** Biophoto Associates/Photo Researchers, Inc.; **e, f** Michael P. Gadomski/ Photo Researchers, Inc.; **g, h** Steven Arcella; **i** Tom Branch/ Photo Researchers, Inc.; **j, k, l** Steven Arcella

356 Hollies (lr/tb): **a** David Liebman, Pink Guppy; **b** Michael P. Gadomski/Photo Researchers, Inc.

356 Common Winterberry (lr/tb): **a** Steven Arcella; **b** Alan & Linda Detrick/Photo Researchers, Inc.

357 Mountain Winterberry (cw): **a** Steven Arcella; **b** Gail Jankus/Photo Researchers, Inc.; **c** Stephen P. Parker/Photo Researchers, Inc.; **d** Steven Arcella

358 Possumhaw (cw): **a** Steven Arcella; **b** Steven J. Baskauf, http://bioimages.vanderbilt. edu; **c, d** David Liebman, Pink Guppy; **e** Steven J. Baskauf, http://bioimages.vanderbilt.edu; **f** Steven Arcella; **g** Will Cook, http://www.carolinanature.com

359 Yaupon (cw): **a** Steven Arcella; **b** Will Cook, http://www. carolinanature.com; **c** Gilbert S. Grant/Photo Researchers, Inc.; **d** Will Cook, http://www. carolinanature.com

360 American Holly (cw): **a, b** Steven Arcella; **c** Michael P. Gadomski/Photo Researchers, Inc.; **d** David Liebman, Pink Guppy; **e** Gail Jankus/Photo Researchers, Inc.

361 English Holly: a, b, c Steven Arcella

361 Myrtle Dahoon: Steven Arcella

361 Tawnyberry Holly: Shirley Denton

362 Dahoon: Gil Nelson

362 Large Gallberry: Gil Nelson

363 Elms, Hackberries, and Kin (lr/tb): **a** Harry Rogers/Photo Researchers, Inc.; **b** Betty Randall White; **c** Alvin E. Staffan/Photo Researchers, Inc.

364 Northern Hackberry (cw): **a** Will Cook, http://www. carolinanature.com; **b** Bill Johnson; **c** David Liebman, Pink Guppy; **d** Chris Evans, River to River CWMA/http://www. bugwood.org; **e** Steven Arcella;

f Michael P. Gadomski/Photo Researchers, Inc.; **g** John Serrao/ Photo Researchers, Inc.

365 Netleaf Hackberry (cw): **a, b** Betty Randall White; **c** David Cavagnaro; **d** Alan & Linda Detrick/Photo Researchers, Inc.

366 Sugarberry (cw): **a** Chris Evans, River to River CWMA http://www.bugwood.org; **b, c** Steven J. Baskauf, http:// bioimages.vanderbilt.edu; **d** Will Cook, http://www.carolinanature. com

366 Florida Trema: Gil Nelson

367 Water-elm (cw): **a** Steven Arcella; **b** Steve Hurst/USDA-NRCS PLANTS Database; **c** John R. Seiler, Virginia Tech Department of Forestry

367 Japanese Zelkova (cw): **a** Steven Arcella; **b** Steve Hurst/ USDA-NRCS PLANTS Database; **c, d** Steven Arcella

368 Cedar Elm (lr/tb): **a** Steven Arcella; **b** Gregory Bergman

368 September Elm: a, b Steven J. Baskauf, http://bioimages. vanderbilt.edu

369 Winged Elm (cw): **a** Steven Arcella; **b** Steven J. Baskauf, http://bioimages.vanderbilt. edu; **c** David Liebman, Pink Guppy; **d** Gilbert S. Grant/Photo Researchers, Inc.

370 Rock Elm (cw): **a** Paul H. Wray; **b** Bill Johnson; **c** John R. Seiler, Virginia Tech Department of Forestry; **d** Bill Johnson; **e** Alvin E. Staffan/Photo Researchers, Inc.

371 American Elm (cw): **a** (leaf), **b** (autumn leaf) Steven Arcella; **c** David Liebman, Pink Guppy; **d** William Harlow/Photo Researchers, Inc.; **e** Steven Arcella; **f** Paul H. Wray

372 Slippery Elm (cw): **a** E. R. Degginger/Photo Researchers, Inc.; **b** Alvin E. Staffan/Photo Researchers, Inc.; **c** Richard Parker/Photo Researchers, Inc.; **d** Will Cook, http://www. carolinanature.com

373 English Elm: Ken Preston-Mafham, Premaphotos Wildlife

373 Chinese Elm (lr/tb): **a** Steven Arcella; **b** David Liebman, Pink Guppy

374 Siberian Elm (cw): **a, b** USDA NRCS Archive, USDA NRCS/ http://www.bugwood.org; **c** Bill Johnson; **d** Patrick Breen, Oregon State University/http://www. bugwood.org

375 American Basswood (cw): **a** Steven Arcella; **b** R. J. Erwin/

Photo Researchers, Inc.; **c** Ray Ellis/Photo Researchers, Inc.; **d** Jenny Winkelman/David Liebman, Pink Guppy; **e** John M. Coffman/Photo Researchers, Inc.

376 Littleleaf Linden (cw): **a, b** Steven Arcella; **c** Geoff Bryant/ Photo Researchers, Inc.; **d** Steven Arcella

376 European Linden: Steven Arcella

377 Largeleaf Linden (cw): **a** Steven Arcella; **b** Norbert Pelka/Okapia/Photo Researchers, Inc.; **c** Steven Arcella; **d** Elizabeth Chute, http://www. elizabethchute.com

378 Willows: E. R. Degginger/ Photo Researchers, Inc.

379 Scouler's Willow (cw): **a** Betty Randall White; **b** R. J. Erwin/ Photo Researchers, Inc.; **c** Dave Powell, USDA Forest Service/ http://www.bugwood.org; **d** Betty Randall White; **e** Beatrice F. Howitt/California Academy of Sciences

380 Pacific Willow (lr/tb): **a** Betty Randall White; **b** David Cavagnaro

380 Bonpland Willow: a, b Betty Randall White

381 Red Willow (cw): **a** Charles Webber/California Academy of Sciences; **b** (bark) Michael L. Charters, http://www.calflora.net

381 Arroyo Willow (lr/tb): **a** J. E. & Bonnie McClellan/California Academy of Sciences; **b** Steven Arcella

382 Sitka Willow (cw): **a** (leaves) Steven Arcella; **b, c** Alfred Brousseau, FSC, Saint Mary's College of California

382 Hooker Willow (cw): **a** David Cavagnaro; **b** (fruit) Susan C. McDougall

383 Northwest Willow: David Cavagnaro

383 Feltleaf Willow: V. P. Weinland/Photo Researchers, Inc.

384 Sandbar Willow (lr/tb): **a** David Liebman, Pink Guppy; **b** Steven Arcella

384 Peachleaf Willow (lr/tb): **a** Ron Lance; **b** Steven Arcella

385 Bebb Willow: John R. Seiler, Virginia Tech Department of Forestry

385 Pussy Willow (cw): **a** David Liebman, Pink Guppy; **b, c** Bill Johnson

386 Black Willow (cw): **a** Paul H. Wray; **b** Steven J. Baskauf, http://bioimages.vanderbilt. edu; **c, d** David Liebman, Pink

Guppy; **e** Richard Parker/Photo Researchers, Inc.

387 Coastal Plain Willow (lr/tb): **a** Gil Nelson; **b** Steven J. Baskauf, http://bioimages.vanderbilt.edu

387 Purple-osier Willow: Bill Johnson

388 Crack Willow: Steven Arcella

388 White Willow (cw): **a** Michael P. Gadomski/Photo Researchers, Inc.; **b** Bob Gibbons/FLPA/Photo Researchers, Inc.; **c** Bill Johnson

389 Weeping Willows (lr/tb): **a** Kenneth W. Fink/Photo Researchers, Inc.; **b** Miriam Reinhart/Photo Researchers, Inc.

389 Corkscrew Willow: David Liebman, Pink Guppy

390 Swamp Cottonwood (cw): **a, b** Steven Arcella; **c** David Liebman, Pink Guppy

391 Eastern Cottonwood (cw): **a** Paul H. Wray; **b** Ron Lance; **c, d** John M. Coffman/Photo Researchers, Inc.; **e** David Cavagnaro; **f** Richard Parker/ Photo Researchers, Inc.

392 Narrowleaf Cottonwood (cw): **a** Betty Randall White; **b** Dave Powell, USDA Forest Service/http://www.bugwood. org; **c** William H. Mullins/ Photo Researchers, Inc.; **d** V. P. Weinland/Photo Researchers, Inc.

393 Fremont Cottonwood (cw): **a** Michael L. Charters, http://www. calflora.net; **b** Gerald & Buff Corsi, Focus on Nature, Inc.; **c** R. J. Erwin/Photo Researchers, Inc.; **d** G. C. Kelley/Photo Researchers, Inc.; **e** Betty Randall White; **f** Gerald & Buff Corsi, Focus on Nature, Inc.

394 Balsam Poplar (cw): **a, b** Betty Randall White; **c** Geoff Bryant/ Photo Researchers, Inc.; **d** D. E. Herman/USDA-NRCS PLANTS Database; **e** Bill Cook, Michigan State University/http://www. bugwood.org

395 Black Cottonwood (cw): **a, b** Betty Randall White; **c** Charles Webber/California Academy of Sciences; **d** Michael L. Charters, http://www.calflora.net

396 White Poplar (cw): **a** David Cavagnaro; **b** (bark) Steven Arcella

396 Lombardy Poplar (lr/tb): **a** David Cavagnaro; **b** David Liebman, Pink Guppy

397 Quaking Aspen (cw): **a** Paul H. Wray; **b** Jim Steinberg/Photo Researchers, Inc.; **c** Gerald & Buff Corsi, Focus on Nature, Inc.; **d** Steven Arcella; **e** Michael P.

Gadomski/Photo Researchers, Inc.

398 Bigtooth Aspen (cw): **a** Steven Arcella; **b** David Cavagnaro; **c** Steven Arcella

399 Birches, Alders, and Kin (lr/ tb): **a** Steven J. Baskauf, http:// bioimages.vanderbilt.edu; **b** L & D Klein/Photo Researchers, Inc.; **c** Christopher Christie

400 American Hornbeam (cw): **a, b** Steven Arcella; **c** Steven J. Baskauf, http://bioimages. vanderbilt.edu; **d** Michael P. Gadomski/Photo Researchers, Inc.

400 European Hornbeam: a, b, c Steven Arcella

401 Eastern Hophornbeam (cw): **a** Steven Arcella; **b** Michael P. Gadomski/Photo Researchers, Inc.; **c** David Cavagnaro; **d, e** Gil Nelson

402 Paper Birch (cw): **a** Steven Arcella; **b** Michael P. Gadomski/ Photo Researchers, Inc.; **c** Bill Johnson; **d** David Cavagnaro; **e** Rod Planck/Photo Researchers, Inc.; **f** Jenny Winkelman/David Liebman, Pink Guppy

403 Gray Birch (cw): **a, b** Steven Arcella; **c** Bill Johnson; **d** Steven Arcella; **e** Michael P. Gadomski/ Photo Researchers, Inc.

404 European White Birch (cw): **a** Bill Johnson; **b** John R. Seiler, Virginia Tech Department of Forestry; **c** Steven Arcella

404 Virginia Roundleaf Birch: a, b Steven Arcella

405 River Birch (cw): **a** Steven Arcella; **b** Steven J. Baskauf, http://bioimages.vanderbilt. edu; **c** Bill Johnson; **d** Robert Finken/Photo Researchers, Inc.; **e** (mature bark) Michael P. Gadomski/Photo Researchers, Inc.; **f** (inner bark) David Liebman, Pink Guppy; **g** Steven J. Baskauf, http://bioimages. vanderbilt.edu

406 Sweet Birch (cw): **a, b** Bill Johnson; **c** Michael P. Gadomski/ Photo Researchers, Inc.; **d** Will Cook, http://www.carolinanature. com; **e** Steven J. Baskauf, http:// bioimages.vanderbilt.edu; **f** Will Cook, http://www.carolinanature. com; **g** Michael P. Gadomski/ Photo Researchers, Inc.

407 Yellow Birch (cw): **a** Steven J. Baskauf, http://bioimages. vanderbilt.edu; **b** Bill Johnson; **c** Bill Cook, Michigan State University/http://www.bugwood. org; **d** Bill Johnson; **e** Michael P. Gadomski/Photo Researchers,

Inc.; **f** Steven Arcella; **g** Steven J. Baskauf, http://bioimages. vanderbilt.edu

408 Water Birch (cw): **a** Verna R. Johnston/Photo Researchers, Inc.; **b** J. E. & Bonnie McClellan/ California Academy of Sciences; **c** Charles Webber/California Academy of Sciences; **d** Verna R. Johnston/Photo Researchers, Inc.

409 Red Alder (cw): **a** David Cavagnaro; **b** Steven J. Baskauf, http://bioimages.vanderbilt.edu; **c** Christopher Christie; **d** Daniel Mathews

410 White Alder (cw): **a** David Cavagnaro; **b** Geoff Bryant/Photo Researchers, Inc.; **c** Steven Arcella; **d** David Cavagnaro

411 Thinleaf Alder (lr/tb): **a** Daniel Mathews; **b** Steven Arcella

411 Sitka Alder: David Cavagnaro

412 Eastern Alders (lr/tb): **a** Michael P. Gadomski/Photo Researchers, Inc.; **b, c, d** Steven Arcella

413 Black Alder (cw): **a, b** Paul H. Wray; **c** Steven Arcella

413 Beech Family (lr/tb): **a** Michael P. Gadomski/Photo Researchers, Inc.; **b** Steven J. Baskauf, http:// bioimages.vanderbilt.edu

414 American Beech (cw): **a, b** Steven Arcella; **c** John Serrao/Photo Researchers, Inc.; **d, e** Steven Arcella; **f** Steven J. Baskauf, http://bioimages. vanderbilt.edu

415 European Beech (cw): **a** Steven Arcella; **b** Charles R. Belinky/ Photo Researchers, Inc.; **c** Kees van den Berg/Photo Researchers, Inc.; **d** Michael P. Gadomski/ Photo Researchers, Inc.; **e** Chris Evans, River to River CWMA/ http://www.bugwood.org

416 American Chestnut (cw): **a** Steven Arcella; **b, c** Ray Coleman/ Photo Researchers, Inc.; **d** David Liebman, Pink Guppy; **e** Will Cook, http://www.carolinanature. com; **f** John M. Coffman/Photo Researchers, Inc.

417 Chinkapin (cw): **a** Michael P. Gadomski/Photo Researchers, Inc.; **b** Steven Arcella; **c** Gilbert S. Grant/Photo Researchers, Inc.

417 Chinese Chestnut (lr/tb): **a, b** Michael P. Gadomski/Photo Researchers, Inc.; **c** Steven Arcella

418 Giant Golden Chinkapin (cw): **a, b** (2 leaves) Daniel Mathews; **c, d** Will Cook, http://www. carolinanature.com; **e** (bark) David Cavagnaro; **f** Will Cook, http://www.carolinanature.com

419 **Tanoak** (cw): **a** Steven J. Baskauf, http://bioimages. vanderbilt.edu; **b** Stephen P. Parker/Photo Researchers, Inc.; **c** Charles Webber/California Academy of Sciences; **d** David Cavagnaro; **e** Tom McHugh/ Photo Researchers, Inc.

420 **Oaks**: **a, b** Steven J. Baskauf, http://bioimages.vanderbilt.edu

422 **Sawtooth Oak** (lr/tb): **a** Steven Arcella; **b** Michael P. Gadomski, Photo Researchers, Inc.

422 **Dwarf Chinkapin Oak**: **a, b** Chris Evans, River to River CWMA/http://www.bugwood. org

423 **Chinkapin Oak** (cw): **a** Steven Arcella; **b** Alvin E. Staffan/Photo Researchers, Inc.; **c** Harry Rogers/Photo Researchers, Inc.; **d** Steven J. Baskauf, http:// bioimages.vanderbilt.edu

424 **Chestnut Oak** (cw): **a, b** Steven Arcella; **c, d** Chris Evans, River to River CWMA/http://www. bugwood.org; **e** Will Cook, http://www.carolinanature.com

425 **Swamp Chestnut Oak** (lr/tb): **a** Ron Lance; **b** Steven J. Baskauf, http://bioimages.vanderbilt.edu

425 **Water Oak** (lr/tb): **a** Chris Evans, River to River CWMA/ http://www.bugwood.org; **b** Steven Arcella

426 **Laurel Oak** (cw): **a** Chris Evans, River to River CWMA/ http://www.bugwood.org; **b** Shirley Denton; **c** Leroy Simon/ David Liebman, Pink Guppy; **d** Gil Nelson; **e** Chris Evans, River to River CWMA/http://www. bugwood.org

427 **Willow Oak** (lr/tb): **a** Steven Arcella; **b** Steven J. Baskauf, http://bioimages.vanderbilt.edu; **c** Kent & Donna Dannen/Photo Researchers, Inc.

427 **Bluejack Oak** (lr/tb): **a** (leaves) Steven Arcella; **b** Chris Evans, River to River CWMA/http:// www.bugwood.org

428 **Shingle Oak** (cw): **a** Steven Arcella; **b** Alvin E. Staffan/Photo Researchers, Inc.; **c** Bill Johnson; **d** Steven Arcella; **e** Steven J. Baskauf, http://bioimages. vanderbilt.edu

429 **Myrtle Oak** (cw): **a** Shirley Denton; **b** Gil Nelson; **c** Ken Brate/Photo Researchers, Inc.

429 **Chapman Oak:** Ron Lance

430 **Southern Live Oak** (cw): **a** Chris Evans, River to River CWMA/http://www.bugwood. org; **b** David Liebman, Pink Guppy; **c** Gilbert S. Grant/Photo Researchers, Inc.; **d** Jack Rosen/ Photo Researchers, Inc.; **e** Gregory Bergman

431 **Sand Live Oak** (cw): **a** Gil Nelson; **b** (acorns) David Liebman, Pink Guppy

431 **Oglethorpe Oak: a, b** Chris Evans, River to River CWMA/ http://www.bugwood.org

432 **Blackjack Oak** (cw): **a, b** Steven Arcella; **c** Richard Parker/Photo Researchers, Inc.

432 **Arkansas Oak:** Gil Nelson

433 **Northern Red Oak** (cw): **a, b** Steven Arcella; **c** Alvin E. Staffan/Photo Researchers, Inc.; **d** Gregory K. Scott/Photo Researchers, Inc.; **e** Steven Arcella

434 **Black Oak** (cw): **a** David Liebman, Pink Guppy; **b** Alvin E. Staffan/Photo Researchers, Inc.; **c** E. R. Degginger/Photo Researchers, Inc.; **d** Steven Arcella

435 **Pin Oak** (cw): **a, b** Steven Arcella; **c** Chris Evans, River to River CWMA/http://www. bugwood.org; **d** Steven Arcella; **e** Steven J. Baskauf, http:// bioimages.vanderbilt.edu

436 **Northern Pin Oak: a, b, c, d** Steven Arcella

436 **Texas Red Oak:** Ron Lance

437 **Scarlet Oak** (cw): **a** Steven Arcella; **b** Alvin E. Staffan/Photo Researchers, Inc.; **c** Steven J. Baskauf, http://bioimages. vanderbilt.edu; **d** Chris Evans, River to River CWMA/http:// www.bugwood.org; **e** Steven Arcella; **f** Steven J. Baskauf, http://bioimages.vanderbilt.edu

438 **Shumard Oak** (cw): **a** Will Cook, http://www.carolinanature. com; **b** Steven Arcella; **c** Richard Parker/Photo Researchers, Inc.

438 **Georgia Oak:** Chris Evans, River to River CWMA/http:// www.bugwood.org

439 **Southern Red Oak** (lr/tb): **a** David Liebman, Pink Guppy; **b, c** Steven Arcella

439 **Cherrybark Oak: a, b** Steven J. Baskauf, http://bioimages. vanderbilt.edu

440 **Turkey Oak:** David Liebman, Pink Guppy

440 **Bear Oak: a, b** Steven Arcella

441 **Overcup Oak: a, b, c** Steven Arcella

441 **Bastard Oak** (lr/tb): **a** Ron Lance; **b** Steven Arcella

442 **Swamp White Oak** (cw): **a, b** Paul H. Wray; **c** Kent & Donna Dannen/Photo Researchers, Inc.

442 **Bastard White Oak:** Ron Lance

443 **White Oak** (cw): **a** Steven Arcella; **b** Paul H. Wray; **c** E. R. Degginger/Photo Researchers, Inc.; **d** Gil Nelson

444 **Burr Oak** (cw): **a** Steven Arcella; **b** Alvin E. Staffan/Photo Researchers, Inc.; **c** Kent Foster/ Photo Researchers, Inc.; **d** Steven Arcella

445 **Post Oak** (cw): **a** Steven Arcella; **b** Paul H. Wray; **c** Steven J. Baskauf, http://bioimages. vanderbilt.edu; **d** Richard Parker/ Photo Researchers, Inc.

446 **Sand Post Oak:** Shirley Denton

446 **English Oak** (cw): **a** David Liebman, Pink Guppy; **b** Bill Johnson; **c** Joyce Photographics/ Photo Researchers, Inc.; **d** Steven Arcella

447 **Gambel Oak** (cw): **a** Gerald & Buff Corsi, Focus on Nature, Inc.; **b** Dave Powell, USDA Forest Service/http://www. bugwood.org; **c, d** USDA Forest Service–Rocky Mountain Region Archive, USDA Forest Service/ http://www.bugwood.org; **e** R. J. Erwin/Photo Researchers, Inc.

448 **Lacey Oak:** Steven Arcella

448 **Graves Oak** (lr/tb): **a** Steven Arcella; **b** Ron Lance

449 **Mohr Oak:** David Cavagnaro

449 **Mexican Blue Oak:** David Cavagnaro

450 **Arizona Oak** (cw): **a** Betty Randall White; **b** V. P. Weinland/ Photo Researchers, Inc.; **c** (bark), **d** (leaves) Betty Randall White

450 **Netleaf Oak:** Robert Sivinski

451 **Turbinella Oak: a, b** Steven Arcella

451 **Gray Oak:** Robert Sivinski

452 **Emory Oak** (cw): **a** Betty Randall White; **b** V. P. Weinland/ Photo Researchers, Inc.; **c** Betty Randall White

452 **Palmer Oak:** David Cavagnaro

453 **Silverleaf Oak** (cw): **a** Betty Randall White; **b, c** Robert Sivinski; **d** Betty Randall White; **e** Steven J. Baskauf, http:// bioimages.vanderbilt.edu

454 **Canyon Live Oak** (cw): **a** Betty Randall White; **b** Steven Arcella; **c** Gregory Bergman; **d** Betty Randall White; **e** David Cavagnaro

455 **Interior Live Oak** (cw): **a, b** Betty Randall White; **c** (leaf variations) Steven Arcella; **d** David Cavagnaro

455 **Engelmann Oak: a, b** Steven Arcella

456 **Coast Live Oak** (cw): **a, b** Steven Arcella; **c** Earl Scott/Photo

Researchers, Inc.; **d** David Cavagnaro

457 Channel Island Oak: a, b Steven Arcella

457 California Black Oak (cw): **a** Steven Arcella; **b, c** Betty Randall White

458 Valley Oak (cw): **a** Steven Arcella; **b** Beatrice F. Howitt/California Academy of Sciences; **c** Gerald & Buff Corsi, Focus on Nature, Inc.; **d** Richard Parker/Photo Researchers, Inc.

459 Oregon White Oak (cw): **a** Steven J. Baskauf, http://bioimages.vanderbilt.edu; **b** Michael P. Gadomski/Photo Researchers, Inc.; **c, d** Steven J. Baskauf, http://bioimages.vanderbilt.edu

460 Blue Oak (cw): **a, b** David Cavagnaro; **c** Dennis Flaherty/Photo Researchers, Inc.; **d** Betty Randall White

461 Palms (lr/tb): **a** Betty Randall White; **b** Jenny Winkelman/David Liebman, Pink Guppy

462 Coconut Palm (cw): **a** Verna R. Johnston/Photo Researchers, Inc.; **b** Glenn & Martha Vargas/California Academy of Sciences; **c** Stephen J. Krasemann/Photo Researchers, Inc.; **d** Scott Camazine/Photo Researchers, Inc.

463 Date Palm (cw): **a** Kenneth W. Fink/Photo Researchers, Inc.; **b** Ray Ellis/Photo Researchers, Inc.; **c** David Cavagnaro

464 Canary Island Date Palm (lr/tb): **a** Geoff Bryant/Photo Researchers, Inc.; **b** Jack Fields/Photo Researchers, Inc.; **c** Tom McHugh/Photo Researchers, Inc.

464 Cuban Royal Palm: Geoff Bryant/Photo Researchers, Inc.

465 Queen Palm: S. Dimmitt/Photo Researchers, Inc.

465 Saw Palmetto: Chris Evans, River to River CWMA/http://www.bugwood.org

466 California Fan Palm: Francois Gohier/Photo Researchers, Inc.

466 Mexican Fan Palm: a, b Keith Bradley

467 Cabbage Palm: Jeff Lepore/Photo Researchers, Inc.

467 Mexican Palmetto: Noble Proctor/Photo Researchers, Inc.

468 Florida Thatch Palm (cw): **a, b, c** Shirley Denton; **d** Keith Bradley

469 Fishtail Palm (cw): **a** Vladimir Bridan; **b** David Cavagnaro; **c** Bill Johnson

470 Yuccas: Dan Suzio/Photo Researchers, Inc.

470 Moundlily Yucca: David Cavagnaro

471 Aloe Yucca (lr/tb): **a** James H. Carmichael, Jr./Photo Researchers, Inc.; **b** David Cavagnaro

471 Soaptree Yucca (lr/tb): **a** Jim Steinberg/Photo Researchers, Inc.; **b** Steven Arcella; **c** Gilbert S. Grant/Photo Researchers, Inc.; **d** David Cavagnaro

472 Mojave Yucca (cw): **a** Mark Newman/Photo Researchers, Inc.; **b** (fruits) Dan Suzio/Photo Researchers, Inc.; **c** (flowers) Gerald & Buff Corsi, Focus on Nature, Inc.

472 Sierra Madre Yucca (cw): **a** Betty Randall White; **b** Gilbert S. Grant/Photo Researchers, Inc.; **c** Vladimir Bridan

473 Faxon Yucca: Gregory Bergman

473 Joshua Tree (cw): **a** Charlie Ott/Photo Researchers, Inc.; **b** Gerald & Buff Corsi, Focus on Nature, Inc.; **c** Nature's Images/Photo Researchers, Inc.

474 Cacti: C. K. Lorenz/Photo Researchers, Inc.

475 Chain-fruit Cholla (cw): **a** Vladimir Bridan; **b** Richard Spellenberg, Ph.D., New Mexico State University; **c** Gerald & Buff Corsi, Focus on Nature, Inc.

476 Saguaro (cw): **a** Gregory Ochocki/Photo Researchers, Inc.; **b** R. Van Nostrand/Photo Researchers, Inc.; **c** C. K. Lorenz/Photo Researchers, Inc.; **d** Steven J. Baskauf, http://bioimages.vanderbilt.edu

Front cover: Giant Sequoias, Yosemite National Park, California, Lester Lefkowitz/CORBIS

Spine: Vine Maple Craig Tuttle/CORBIS

Back cover: (lr/tb): **a** Canada Plum Ottmar Bierwagen, Spectrumphotofile; **b** Chalk Maple Will Cook, http://www.carolinanature.com; **c** Pitch Pine Michael P. Gadomski/Photo Researchers, Inc.; **d** Burr Oak Kent Foster/Photo Researchers, Inc.; **e** Red Maple Gregory G. Dimijian/Photo Researchers, Inc.; **f** Saguaro Gregory Ochocki/Photo Researchers, Inc.; **g** Bitter Cherry Terry Spivey, USDA Forest Service/http://www.bugwood.org

Front flap: About This Guide, Sugar Maple (cw): **a** Steven Arcella; **b** David Liebman, Pink Guppy; **c** Michael P. Gadomski/Photo Researchers, Inc.; **d** Stephen J. Krasemann/Photo Researchers, Inc.; **e** A. H. Rider/Photo Researchers, Inc.; **f** Leonard Lee Rue III/Photo Researchers, Inc.

Front endpaper: Keys (lr/tb): **a** Steven Arcella; **b** Gilbert S. Grant/Photo Researchers, Inc.; **c** Alan & Linda Detrick/Photo Researchers, Inc.; **d** Gil Nelson; **e** Alvin E. Staffan/Photo Researchers, Inc.; **f** Biophoto Associates/Photo Researchers, Inc.; **g** Steven Arcella; **h** Michael P. Gadomski/Photo Researchers, Inc.; **i** David Liebman, Pink Guppy; **j** John Serrao/Photo Researchers, Inc.

Title page (lr/tb): **a** Paper Birch Rod Planck/Photo Researchers, Inc.; **b** Pecan David Liebman, Pink Guppy; **c** Canada Plum Ottmar Bierwagen, Spectrumphotofile; **d** Flowering Dogwood Adam Jones/Photo Researchers, Inc.; **e** Giant Sequoias, Yosemite National Park, California, Lester Lefkowitz/CORBIS

Acknowledgments

This book was a true collaboration. The editors would like to thank all the botanists, naturalists, photographers, and artists who contributed to this guide, as well as all of those who came before to study, identify, dissect, draw, and write about the trees of North America. We are extremely grateful to the guide's principal consultants, Gil Nelson and Richard Spellenberg, who reviewed all the text and photographs, rewrote descriptions, wrote text to fill in gaps, and answered hundreds of questions with endless patience and constant good humor. Their many years of learning and expertise have added immeasurable value to the guide.

We thank the late Bruce Kershner, who wrote the first draft of most of the species accounts, for the energy and enthusiasm he funneled into this project. We appreciate the meticulous and thoughtful work that Daniel Mathews put into writing the guide's general introduction, "North American Forests," and other sections, and into reviewing various texts and photographs. We extend thanks to Terry Purinton, who wrote "Tree Families," as well as several dozen species accounts; and Gerry Moore, who wrote species accounts and reviewed text and photographs. We thank Steven Arcella for his diligence in photographing hundreds of botanical specimens for this guide, and Andrew Block, who was instrumental in assisting Steven Arcella in finding and identifying trees, in addition to serving as a text and photo consultant. Ned Barnard, Paul Cox, Dan Potter, and Ross Clark also pitched in as reviewers. The late John Thieret, the original consultant for this guide, provided invaluable expertise, support, and inspiration.

We thank Chanticleer's publisher Andrew Stewart, former associate publisher Alicia Mills, and Nathaniel Marunas, Betsy Beier, Andrea Rotondo, Michael Vagnetti, Mike Ferrari, and Sharon Bosley of Barnes & Noble. George Scott first proposed this series, and Charles Nix conceived the original series

design. We are grateful to art director Drew Stevens for a clean and flexible design that is both elegant to look at and useful in the field. We thank production manager Arthur Riscen and photo editor Sumi Sin. Many thanks to copy editor Patricia Fogarty and indexer Jennifer Dixon. Valerie Kenyon, Linda Eger, Chloe Hanna, Areta Buk, Lisa Mantoni, Mary Sutherland, Benito Santos Lorenzo, Cameron Brindisi, and Joice Passos provided additional support. Anita Duncan and the staff at Photo Researchers, Inc., Zan Carter, Ruth Jeyaveeran, and Laura Russo contributed to photo research and editing. Dolores Santoliquido executed the line drawings throughout the guide; Mauricio Rodriguez produced the range maps; and Gary Antonetti of Ortelius Design created the North American forests map and the endpaper map of North America.

Many thanks go to the staffs of the arboreta and botanical gardens who allowed us to take botanical samples and photographs as well as to those who collected samples and sent them to us. Our thanks go to the staffs of the following (the individuals mentioned were particularly helpful): New York Botanical Garden, Bronx, NY; Brooklyn Botanic Garden, Brooklyn, NY (Jackie Fazio); Queens Botanical Garden, Flushing, NY; Arnold Arboretum, Boston, MA (Ralph Ebener); Dawes Arboretum, Newark, OH (David Brandenburg); U.S. National Arboretum, Washington, DC (Mary Byrne); Davis Arboretum, Auburn, AL (Christy Hartsfield); Gifford Arboretum, Coral Gables, FL (Derek Artz); San Antonio Botanical Garden, San Antonio, TX (Paul Cox); Denver Botanic Gardens, Denver, CO; Desert Botanical Garden, Phoenix, AZ (Wendy Hodgson); Arboretum at Flagstaff, Flagstaff, AZ (Cheryl Casey); Rancho Santa Ana Botanic Garden, Claremont, CA; Santa Barbara Botanic Garden, Santa Barbara, CA; UC Davis Arboretum, Davis, CA (Mia Ingolia); Hoyt Arboretum, Portland, OR (Dan Moeller).

Amy K. Hughes and Flynne Wiley

Contributors

Bruce Kershner
Author of species accounts

Those lucky enough to hike with Bruce Kershner, an international authority on old-growth forests, will never again "see" a forest in quite the same way. The author or coauthor of 10 books, including the *Sierra Club Guide to the Ancient Forests of the Northeast,* forest ecologist Bruce Kershner discovered more than 250 old-growth forests. Named environmentalist of the year by a number of prominent organizations, he was a founder of several associations dedicated to surveying and preserving old-growth forests. Shortly before Bruce Kershner died on February 16, 2007, he learned that his dream of state protection for the majestic old-growth trees of the Zoar Valley in western New York had been fulfilled. During a distinguished career, he was a science teacher, conservation director for the Buffalo Audubon Society, senior environmentalist for Great Lakes United, and adjunct professor at the University at Buffalo. He held a master's degree in forest ecology from the University of Connecticut and a BS in botany from Binghamton University. Thanks go to James Battaglia for his assistance in research and reviewing the text. Additional thanks go to Jerry Horowitz and Brendan McMahon for data entry, and to Adam Rosen for computer support. This book would not have been possible without the loving support of Bruce Kershner's family: Helene, Libby, Joshua, Joel, and Pearl Kershner, Randy Kaplan, and Sheine Wizel. Additional thanks go to Diane Peters, Julie Makar, Michael Buckley, Barbara Sherman, Glen Gelinas, and Sallie Randolph. As Bruce would say: "May the forest be with you!"

Daniel Mathews
Consultant; author of Introduction, "North American Forests," "Threats to Trees and Forests," introductions to all groups in "Trees with Needlelike Leaves" and "Trees with Scalelike Leaves," and "Trees and Fire"

Daniel Mathews is a field-guide writer living in Portland, Oregon, with a wife, a son, a daughter, a dog, a cat, and a bachelor's degree in literature. Aside from writing about them, his involvements with trees have included building a split-shake cabin from old redcedar

logs on the cabin site; spotting fires from Desolation Lookout (formerly Jack Kerouac's post); five years in an off-the-grid cabin heated with wood; and teaching backpacking natural history seminars in the Cascade Range. He is coauthor of *America From the Air: A Guide to the Landscape Along Your Route;* author, photographer, and publisher of *Rocky Mountain Natural History* and *Cascade-Olympic Natural History;* and a contributing author to *National Audubon Society Field Guide to the Rocky Mountain States* and *National Audubon Society Field Guide to the Pacific Northwest.*

Gil Nelson
Principal Consultant; author of "How to Identify a Tree," "Visual Glossary," and species accounts

Dr. Gil Nelson, an author and photographer specializing in botany, gardening, ecology, nature recreation, and natural history, has written 10 books, mostly on the botany and natural history of the southeastern United States. He directs the Deep South Plant Specimen Imaging Project at the Robert K. Godfrey Herbarium at Florida State University and holds a fellowship in botany at the Tall Timbers Research Station and Land Conservancy. He regularly speaks and consults on a wide range of environmental science topics. He resides with his wife, Brenda, in the community of Beachton in southwestern Georgia. Thanks go to Brenda, Ron Lance, Dan Pittillo, Ed McDowell, Linda Chafin, Keith Bradley, and Wilson Baker.

Richard Spellenberg
Principal Consultant; author of species accounts

Dr. Richard Spellenberg received his PhD degree in botany in 1968 from the University of Washington, and took a position in teaching and research at New Mexico State University that year. There he taught botany, plant morphology, plant anatomy, and plant taxonomy, and studied the four o'clock family (Nyctaginaceae) in North America and the oaks of the Sierra Madre Occidental in Mexico, retiring from NMSU in 2000. He has published several technical articles on those families, and has authored the *National Audubon Society Field Guide to North American Wildflowers: Western Region,* produced by Chanticleer Press for Alfred A. Knopf, and *Sonoran Desert Wildflowers,* produced by Falcon Guides of Globe Pequot Press. He continues to study the native plants of southwestern North America as an associate of the biology department at NMSU.

Terry Purinton
Author of "Tree Families" and species accounts
Arthur T. (Terry) Purinton is a writer and naturalist. His articles and editorial contributions appear in books and magazines on science, education, and writing. He is currently researching how climate change affects local horticultural practices. Terry lives and works on a small estate full of specimen trees in Westchester County, New York.

Andrew Block
Consultant
Andrew Block is a freelance wildlife biologist and naturalist with a degree in wildlife management from SUNY Cobleskill. For 17 years he was employed as a horticultural consultant at the New York Botanical Garden in the Bronx. Other places he has worked are the Wildlife Conservation Society/ Bronx Zoo, Wallkill River National Wildlife Refuge, Queens Botanical Garden, Great Eastern Ecology, Inc., Audubon Greenwich, Metropolitan Conservation Alliance, and Montgomery Botanical Center. His main interests besides trees are birding around the world and observing animals anywhere he can. He currently lives in Bronxville, NY, with a menagerie of nine snakes.

Gerry Moore
Consultant; author of species accounts
Gerry Moore is the director of the department of science at Brooklyn Botanic Garden, where he has worked for the past eight years. He received his PhD degree from Vanderbilt University in 1997 and was a postdoctoral research fellow at Duke University.

Species Index

Boldface type indicates a main species entry.

Staff for This Guide

Prepared and produced by Chanticleer Press, Inc.

Founding Publisher: Paul Steiner
Publisher: Andrew Stewart

Series Editor:	Amy K. Hughes
Art Director:	Drew Stevens
Editor:	Flynne Wiley
Photo Editor:	Sumi Sin
Production:	Arthur Riscen
Copy Editor:	Patricia Fogarty
Editorial Assistants:	Valerie Kenyon, Chloe Hanna
Designer:	Areta Buk
Illustrations:	Dolores R. Santoliquido
Range Maps:	Mauricio Rodriguez
Other Maps:	Ortelius Design

Editorial inquiries may be sent to: NWF Field Guides
P.O. Box 479
Woodstock, VT 05091
editors@thefieldguideproject.com

Quick Index

See the Species Index on page 515 for a complete listing of all species by common and scientific name.